THE SIMON & SCHUSTER
GUIDE TO WRITING

Douglas Olson, *Detail, Door*
Reprinted by permission of Douglas Olson.

THE SIMON & SCHUSTER GUIDE TO WRITING

Second Edition

Jeanette G. Harris

University of Southern Mississippi

Donald H. Cunningham

Auburn University

PRENTICE HALL, Upper Saddle River, New Jersey 07458

Library of Congress Cataloging-in-Publication Data

Harris, Jeanette,
    The Simon & Schuster guide to writing / Jeanette G. Harris, Donald
H. Cunningham. — 2nd ed.
      p.   cm.
    Includes index.
    ISBN 0-13-456575-4
    1. English language—Rhetoric.   2. English language—Grammar.
3. College readers.   I. Cunningham, Donald H. II. Title.
PE1408.H3456   1996b
808′.042—dc20   96-30357
                                            CIP

Editor-in-Chief: Charlyce Jones Owen
Acquisitions Editor: Mary Jo Southern
Development Editor: Joyce Perkins
Director of Production and Manufacturing: Barbara Kittle
Senior Managing Editor: Bonnie Biller
Project Manager: Lois Lombardo
Manufacturing Manager: Nick Sklitsis
Prepress and Manufacturing Buyer: Lynn Pearlman
Creative Design Director: Leslie Osher
Interior and Cover Design: Amy Rosen
Photo Researcher: Rona Tuccillo
Electronic Art Creation: Lori Kane
Cover Photo: View to Molokai, Lanai, HI—David Muench Photography, Inc.

This book was set in 10.5/12.5 Garamond Light by V&M Graphics and was printed and bound by
RR Donnelley & Sons Company. The cover was printed by Phoenix Color.

Credits begin on p. 755, which constitutes a continuation of this copyright page.

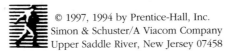

© 1997, 1994 by Prentice-Hall, Inc.
Simon & Schuster/A Viacom Company
Upper Saddle River, New Jersey 07458

Printed in the United States of America
10 9 8 7 6 5 4 3 2 1

ISBN   0-13-456575-4

Prentice-Hall International (UK) Limited, *London*
Prentice-Hall of Australia Pty. Limited, *Sydney*
Prentice-Hall Canada Inc., *Toronto*
Prentice-Hall Hispanoamericana, S.A., *Mexico*
Prentice-Hall of India Private Limited, *New Delhi*
Prentice-Hall of Japan, Inc., *Tokyo*
Simon & Schuster Asia Pte. Ltd., *Singapore*
Editora Prentice-Hall do Brasil, Ltda., *Rio de Janeiro*

In memory of Cowboy and B.B.

ABOUT THE AUTHORS

JEANETTE GREGORY HARRIS received her B.A., M.A., and Ed.D. from East Texas State University. She currently serves as Chair of the English Department and teaches composition at the University of Southern Mississippi.

Her past administrative duties include Director of Composition at the University of Southern Mississippi, Director of Composition and Director of the Writing Center at Texas Tech University, and Supervisor of the Writing Center and Coordinator of Reading Instruction at East Texas State University.

Author of *Expressive Discourse* (Southern Methodist University, 1990) and co-author of *Contexts: Writing and Reading,* Third Edition (Houghton Mifflin, 1993) and *Interactions,* Third Edition (Houghton Mifflin, 1997), Harris also has recently co-edited a collection of case studies entitled *Writing Centers in Context* (National Council of Teachers of English, 1994).

DONALD H. CUNNINGHAM received his B.A., M.A., and Ph.D. in English at the University of Missouri. Cunningham currently teaches composition at Auburn University, where he is also Director of Technical and Professional Writing. Cunningham's previous responsibilities have included Director of Technical Communication at Texas Tech University, Acting Chair of the Department of Languages and Literature and Coordinator of Writing Courses, Morehead State University, and Coordinator of Written and Oral Communications at Southern Illinois University–Carbondale.

Author of many books and articles, Cunningham edited *The Teaching of Technical Writing* (National Council of Teachers of English, 1975) and co-authored *How to Write for the World of Work,* Fifth Edition (Harcourt, Brace, 1994) and *Fundamentals of Good Writing* (Macmillan, 1988).

CONTENTS

PREFACE

For the Instructor

As with the first edition, we want this second edition of *The Simon & Schuster Guide to Writing* to provide students with a variety of reading and writing experiences—experiences that will prepare them for the reading and writing they will do throughout their lives, not just as college students but as professionals, citizens, community and family members, and literate human beings who use language to enrich and enhance both their personal and public lives.

Several basic convictions of the first edition guided us as we shaped this second edition:

- ❖ First, we believe it is important to integrate reading and writing instruction as fully as possible. Thus, each chapter includes reading instruction and assignments that reinforce the writing instruction and assignments. We also encourage and guide students in reading their own work in progress.

- ❖ Second, we believe students learn to read and write primarily by engaging in reading and writing. Thus, we provide students with a wide range of reading and writing assignments that are personal as well as public and pragmatic as well as aesthetic.

- ❖ Third, we believe that learning is incremental and requires reinforcement. Thus, instruction related to important concepts such as purpose and audience, modes of development, and thesis/support occurs in each chapter.

- ❖ Finally, we believe that a college-level writing book should reflect the diverse nature of the typical college classroom. Thus, in the readings we balance the number of female and male authors and include authors with diverse ethnic backgrounds. In addition, the assignments are designed to accommodate students of different ages and backgrounds.

New Features in the Second Edition

Although the basic features of this edition remain nearly identical to those in the first edition, we have made some significant revisions, added a number of new features, and expanded instruction in several important areas. The major ones are these:

* *Expanded treatment of research.* We have added to our coverage of research in several ways. We have created a new part, Part Three, *Strategies and Resources for Research*, that includes all the material in the first edition related to research. In addition, we have included in this new part a section on writing letters of inquiry and expanded information about electronic sources. We have also updated the documentation sections to conform to the current editions of the *MLA Handbook for Writers of Research Papers,* 4th ed. (1995) and the *Publication Manual of the American Psychological Association,* 4th ed. (1994). Part Three and Chapter 8, *Writing from Sources,* which now includes four student research papers, constitute the two parts of the book that focus primarily on the research process. We also have added to the major writing assignments in Chapters 2 through 8 a section on generating ideas through invention and research that helps integrate research into the writing process.

* *New reading selections.* There are fifteen new reading selections and thirteen selections by student writers. The reading selections in Chapter 8, *Writing from Sources,* now consist entirely of student research papers. We have revised the questions following each reading selection to emphasize both text-based and reader-based questions. Text-based questions focus students' attention on such matters as organization, language, tone, and rhetorical strategies. Reader-based questions encourage students to think about how their own life histories influence their reading of a particular text and how they react personally to what they read. Although the reader-based questions primarily encour-

age students to contribute to the making of meaning in a text, they also help students experience the richness and complexity of the text.

❖ *Expanded writing instruction.* We have increased the writing instruction throughout the textbook. For example, we have added to our coverage of audience analysis and invention in Chapters 2 through 8 and have added sections on thesis and patterns of development to Chapters 3 through 8. In Part Four, *Strategies for Writing and Reading*, we have added sections on introductions, conclusions, and summarizing.

❖ *New section, "Discovering Yourself as a Writer."* To conclude each chapter in Chapters 2 through 8, we have added a section that encourages students to think about their writing and to reflect on what they are learning about themselves as writers.

❖ *Revised writing assignments.* In addition to the general assignment suggested by the theme of each chapter, we have provided in this edition specific suggestions for writing topics. To increase our emphasis on revision and the important role that reading assumes in that process, we have added to each writing assignment a separate section, *Reading and Revising Your Text*. In addition, we have added a section, *Generating Ideas through Invention and Research*.

Scope and Organization of This Book

The organization of *The Simon & Schuster Guide to Writing* is simple, yet innovative. It is divided into five parts.

Part One, *Concepts* (Chapter 1), provides students with an overview of the important concepts of purpose and audience. Part One also describes the reading/writing process and includes a student text in various drafts to illustrate the progression from initial rough draft to completed product.

Part Two, *Purposes* (Chapters 2 through 8), is the main part of the book—the part students will use most often in class. Each chapter in this section focuses on a specific purpose and theme and guides students through a writing assignment that is based on that purpose and theme.

Each chapter in Part Two consists of the same six sections.

1. Introduction to the purpose.
2. Instruction in reading for this purpose.
3. Reading selections that reflect both the purpose and theme of the chapter.
4. Discussion of the rhetorical decisions and strategies involved in writing for the particular purpose.
5. A detailed writing assignment that guides students through the process of writing a text.
6. A section that encourages students to reflect on what they have learned about themselves as writers while doing the writing assignment for the chapter.

Part Three, *Strategies and Resources for Research,* explains to students in detail not only where and how to search for information but also how to use the resources and information they find. The section begins by explaining the major tools of library and field research and then provides students with instruction in how to evaluate, use, and document sources.

Part Four, *Strategies for Writing and Reading,* is designed primarily for students to use individually. It consists of approximately thirty entries that explain the terms and concepts we think a student in a writing course might need to know. The entries are arranged alphabetically so that both you and your students can easily locate a specific one. In addition, these entries are clearly cross-referenced in the main part of the text (Chapters 1–8). That is, when a particular concept or strategy (such as coherence or thesis statement) is discussed or even mentioned in the text, students are referred to the corresponding entry in the reference section. Thus if students encounter a term they do not understand or want to know more about, they can simply turn to this section and read about it.

These reference sections, Parts Three and Four, give both you and your students great flexibility. Their entries can be used in a number of different ways. You may assign particular entries to the class as a whole or to individual students. You may use some of the entries as the basis for classroom instruction and discussion or may simply allow students to use these sections on their own.

Part Five, the *Handbook,* consists of entries on diction, usage, punctuation, and mechanics. Like Parts Three and Four, it is intended primarily as a resource for students.

The Supplements

The second edition of *The Simon & Schuster Guide to Writing* is supported by the following supplements, among others:

❖ *The Instructor's Manual,* which consists of three sections. The first section of the manual includes general information and suggestions for teaching the book. The second part provides specific suggestions and strategies for teaching each chapter in Parts One and Two. The third section consists of articles by well-known composition theorists and teachers.

❖ *The New York Times: A Contemporary View* provides a newspaper-sized collection of time-sensitive articles from one of the world's most distinguished newspapers, *The New York Times.* These articles demonstrate the ongoing connection between what is learned in the classroom and the type of writing that occurs in the world around us. These collections are updated twice yearly.

❖ *On-Line Handbook* is a computerized reference system that is compatible with most word processing packages. By using this reference system, students can access information from the handbook section of *The Simon & Schuster Guide to Writing* as they compose on the word processor. The *On-Line Handbook* also includes information on MLA and APA documentation formats and is available in both IBM and Macintosh versions.

❖ *Blue Pencil* is an interactive editing program that allows students to practice writing-related skills by making revisions in paragraph-length passages on the computer screen. The program is organized around skill categories that students encounter most often in their writing. An on-screen counter keeps track of needed corrections, and the program gives feedback each time the user enters a response. Users can also request additional feedback. *Blue Pencil* is available in IBM and Macintosh versions.

❖ *Blue Pencil Authoring System* is a program that allows you to modify *Blue Pencil,* as well as to create new material for it. On-line directions and a manual are included with the authoring system.

For more information about these supplements, about many other available supplements, or to see any of them, please contact your Prentice Hall sales representative.

Acknowledgments

Like the first edition, this one has been a collaborative project that involved more than just our efforts. Scholars, researchers, and theorists in our discipline have helped shape our thinking while colleagues around the country have contributed counsel and advice. We would like to single out for special recognition the following:

❖ The colleagues who read parts of an early draft of this book and participated in a focus group during the 1992 Conference on College Composition and Communication—Lady Falls Brown, Texas Tech University; Christine Hult, Utah State University; Francis Hubbard, Marquette University; Jimmie Killingsworth, Texas A&M University; Elizabeth Metzger, University of South Florida; Duane Roen, Arizona State University; David Russel, Iowa State University; and Irwin Weiser, Purdue University.

❖ Those at Prentice Hall who helped produce this second edition, especially Joyce Perkins, who is not only a superb editor but also a wise and generous person. We would also like to thank Mary Jo Southern for her encouragement and Lois Lombardo for guiding us safely through the important production stage.

❖ Christi Rucker, who helped at almost every stage in the production of this edition.

❖ Jeannine Schneider, who assisted us in locating a number of the student essays that we include in this edition.

❖ John S. Harris, whose long-time friendship is cherished and whose knowledge of firearms informed the discussion of Ernest Hemingway's "The Short Happy Life of Francis Macomber" in Part Three.

❖ The reviewers who critiqued various drafts of this edition: Cathryn Amdahl, Harrisburg Area Community College; Betty L. Dillard, Sul Ross State University; William Dynes, University of Indianapolis; Kim D. Gainer, Radford University; Miriam F. Hart, Ohio University; Ronald J. Heckelman, University of Houston–Downtown; William B. Lalicker, Murray State University; Martha Ann Smith, Brookhaven College; Valorie Worthy, Ohio University.

Finally, as with the first edition, we are indebted to our students, past and present, for teaching us how to teach. We are especially indebted to those students who contributed their work to this edition: Tammy Adams, Gaylon Askew, Kristin Bailey, Yi-An Heidi Chen, Andy Clark, Frank Cedeño, Adrianne Eggers, Toni Gagnon, Morgan Hands, Rebecca Williams Skidmore, Warren Slay, Joan Marie Snider, Paige Snyder, Kerry Whittman, and Jim Whorton.

Once again, we dedicate this book to the memory of Albert F. McKee, Don's stepfather, and Bernice B. Gregory, Jeanette's father—two of the most influential persons in our lives.

Jeanette G. Harris
Donald H. Cunningham

PREFACE

For the Student

We wrote this book to help you become a stronger, more confident writer and a better, more critical reader. But a textbook is effective only if students understand how to use it. This one is fairly straightforward, but you may need to know a few things about how it is organized. Part One focuses on the basic concepts you need to understand if you are to become a better writer and reader. Part Two consists of a series of chapters, each of which explores a different purpose for writing. Each chapter includes reading selections and writing assignments as well as instruction on both writing and reading. These two sections, Parts One and Two, you will probably use most often in class.

In contrast, Parts Three and Four are designed for you to use on your own as well as in class. These two sections allow you to take responsibility for your own learning. They are our attempt to make this book as useful as possible for you as an individual student. Part Three, *Strategies and Resources for Research*, provides you with detailed information about how to research a subject and how to include the results of your research in your own writing. Anytime you want to research a subject about which you are writing, you can refer to this section.

Part Four, *Strategies for Writing and Reading*, explains a number of concepts and terms you may need to know. The entries in this section are arranged alphabetically and thus are easily accessible. Throughout the book, the terms included in this section appear in boldface type, and the page number for the entry is found in the margin. If you do not understand one of these key terms or simply want additional information, you can turn to Part Four and read about it.

Part Five, the *Handbook*, consists of guidelines for diction, usage, punctuation, and mechanics. This part of the book, like Parts Three and Four, is intended primarily as a resource for students.

Several other features of this edition deserve mention. First, you will find at least one student essay included in the reading selections for each chapter as well as a variety of professional essays. All of these reading selections focus on a single purpose and theme. Second, each writing assignment not only includes a variety of topic suggestions but also guides you step-by-step through the assignment. And, finally, following each writing assignment is a section entitled *Discovering Yourself as a Writer*, which encourages you to explore your own process and to evaluate the results of that process.

THE SIMON & SCHUSTER
GUIDE TO WRITING

PART ONE

CONCEPTS

Frederick Evans, *The Sea of Steps*, 1903.
The Royal Photographic Society, Bath.

1

▼

HOW WRITERS AND READERS CONSTRUCT TEXTS

*There is no royal path to good writing; and such paths as
exist . . . lead through . . . the jungles of the self, the
world, and of craft.*

JESSAMYN WEST

We wrote this textbook because we wanted to share what we
know about reading and writing. Of course, we have other reasons—
some of them less altruistic and certainly more practical than the one
we've given. As a student, you also write for a variety of reasons—to
fulfill an assignment, to communicate, to remember, to learn, to prove
that you know something, to share your feelings, to record your
thoughts, to organize your life, and, perhaps, to change the minds of
others. Obviously, people write (and read) for a great variety of reasons. However, some reasons for writing have become commonplace.
That is, large numbers of people write for these same reasons.

This textbook focuses on some common purposes for writing:
writing to explore, to reconstruct experience, to instruct and advise, to
inform, to persuade, and to solve problems. We chose these purposes
from the multitude of reasons why people read and write because they
represent the kind of writing that people routinely and typically do. This
book provides you with a variety of reading and writing experiences—
experiences that will prepare you for the reading and writing you will
do throughout your lives—not just as college students, but as professionals, citizens, members of a family and community, and literate
beings who use language to enrich both your personal and public lives.

▶ PURPOSE — WHY A TEXT IS CONSTRUCTED

We focus on reasons for writing rather than on types of writing
because *purpose* is the driving force behind all acts of reading and
writing. People always read and write for specific purposes, and these
purposes significantly shape the forms their texts take. To illustrate,

here are two accounts of an automobile accident: one a poem by Karl Shapiro, the other a police officer's report.

Auto Wreck
Karl Shapiro

Its quick soft silver bell beating, beating,
And down the dark one ruby flare
Pulsing out red light like an artery,
The ambulance at top speed floating down
Past beacons and illuminated clocks
Wings in a heavy curve, dips down,
And brakes speed, entering the crowd.
The doors leap open, emptying light;
Stretchers are laid out, the mangled lifted
And stowed into the little hospital.
Then the bell, breaking the hush, tolls once,
And the ambulance with its terrible cargo
Rocking, slightly rocking, moves away,
As the doors, an afterthought, are closed.

We are deranged, walking among the cops
Who sweep glass and are large and composed.
One is still making notes under the light.
One with a bucket douches ponds of blood
Into the street and gutter.
One hangs lanterns on the wrecks that cling,
Empty husks of locusts, to iron poles.

Our throats were tight as tourniquets,
Our feet were bound with splints, but now,
Like convalescents intimate and gauche,
We speak through sickly smiles and warn
With the stubborn saw of common sense,
The grim joke and the banal resolution.
The traffic moves around with care,
But we remain, touching a wound
That opens to our richest horror.
Already old, the question Who shall die?
Becomes unspoken Who is innocent?

For death in war is done by hands;
Suicide has cause and stillbirth, logic;

And cancer, simple as a flower, blooms.
But this invites the occult mind,
Cancels our physics with a sneer,
And spatters all we knew of denouement
Across the expedient and wicked stones.

Shapiro describes the auto wreck in subjective and emotional terms, focusing ultimately not on the accident but on death—especially death by accident—and its effect on those who witness it. If Shapiro's purpose had been to explain exactly what happened—as a journalist's, police officer's, or insurance adjuster's purpose would have been—he would have constructed a very different text. Since his purpose was to construct a poem—a text seldom read primarily for information—he was free to construct a subjective, selective account of the accident.

Notice how the following traffic accident report, written in an exact and factual manner by the investigating officer, differs from Shapiro's poem in content, organization, and **style and voice**.

STYLE AND VOICE, PAGE 656

On March 3, 1997, at approximately 10:05 p.m., my partner, Cpl. Alex Kolwalski, and I were dispatched to the intersection of West Main Street and Airport Road, where a two-vehicle accident had just occurred. We arrived at the scene at 10:07, and our back-up unit with Cpl. Kimberly Arnold and Sgt. Frank Sydow arrived at 10:09.

Upon our arrival a witness, Terry Lee, 2816 Forsythe Avenue (phone number 621-6059), said that at approximately 9:55 P.M. she had witnessed a two-vehicle accident. A 1995 green Chevrolet (Silverado) pickup truck had just passed her at a relatively high speed, northbound on Airport Road, when the driver tried to turn right onto West Main Street and overshot the center line on Main Street and struck a white 1992 Dodge Caravan owned and driven by Mary Powell, who was stopped westbound on Main Street.

The driver and owner of the pickup truck (PA 134-682), Elmer Houghton, 106 Red Gate Road (PA dl 821-76-9440), received a cut on his forehead and an apparent broken nose. The truck sustained extensive damage to the front bumper and left front fender and was undrivable.

The driver of the Caravan (NJ 288-496), Mary Powell (NJ dl 546-18-3826), 4480 Tyler Street, Elkhurst, New Jersey, was unconscious and bleeding from severe lacerations on her head and a compound fracture of the left leg just above the knee. A passenger in the Caravan, Gerald Thompson, 4482 Tyler Street, Elkhurst, New Jersey, who was sitting in the right front seat, received injuries to his left arm and leg and deep lacerations on his left cheek and ear, apparently from broken glass. My partner and I administered pressure bandages to Powell's cuts, and then I called an ambulance to the scene. Upon arrival at 10:21 P.M., the paramedics placed a temporary splint on Powell's left leg and took both Powell and Thompson to Northside Medical Center. Powell had regained consciousness and was able to communicate with the paramedics as they put her in the ambulance. Thompson stated that both he and Powell were wearing their seat belts when the accident occurred.

The Caravan sustained extensive damage to the driver's door and the mid-section of the left side. The driver's door was jammed and could not be opened.

Houghton was shaken, but he was able to answer my questions satisfactorily. He said that he was traveling at approximately 50 mph and slowed to approximately 25 mph as he began his right turn onto Main Street. He stated that he apparently misjudged the distance between his truck and the intersection. He stated that he applied his brakes but skidded into the left side of the Caravan. The witness, Terry Lee, corroborated Houghton's account of the accident. There were two skid marks measuring 12 feet, six inches behind Houghton's truck. There were no other witnesses.

After being examined by paramedic Wu Chang, Houghton refused treatment and said that he would see his private physician. There being no evidence that Houghton was intoxicated, I issued him a citation for negligent driving and causing an accident and released him on his own recognizance to report to the City Magistrate's office at 8:45 A.M., March 4, 1997.

I called for tow trucks to remove both vehicles from the scene. Cpl. Kolwalksi and I swept up the broken glass and retrieved a rearview mirror and short strip of metal that had been dislodged from the van. Cpl. Arnold and Sgt. Sydow directed traffic during our handling of the situation.

Note that the accident report is not only longer but also far less dramatic and much more factual than the poem. The report's style is direct and straightforward, its tone matter-of-fact, whereas the poem's style is metaphoric, imaginative, and indirect, its tone reflective. The report begins at the beginning, with the accident, and then relates each subsequent development in strict chronological order. The poem begins with the arrival of the ambulance and only suggests the accident, dwelling on the aftermath rather than the event itself. The report tells what happened to the people in the accident; the poem explores the feelings of those who witnessed the accident. The report depends primarily upon factual information; the poem focuses on sensory images. All these differences are directly related to the writers' purposes: the police officer's need to reconstruct the accident as accurately as possible and the poet's desire to evoke in readers the imminent sense of death at the scene of the accident.

A writer often has multiple and complex purposes. A novelist may write to share something with readers, to create a thing of beauty, to earn money, and to keep proving to himself and others that he can still write. A research scientist may write a grant proposal to gain funding for a project, to get a grant for her laboratory, to earn a promotion at her university, to establish her position in the scientific community, and to enjoy the power that a large grant confers.

Writers have purposes for writing that they do not think about but that help shape what is written. The novelist's desire to create something of beauty is tempered by his awareness of his publisher's deadline; the scientist's desire for funding is counterbalanced by her need to present herself in writing as a credible professional. Writing purposes, both conscious and unconscious, are the forces that nudge and stretch and squash a text into a certain shape.

When you have a writing assignment, you probably write primarily because the assignment is required, but you may also have other purposes—to communicate information, to express your ideas, to impress your teacher (and perhaps your classmates), to demonstrate knowledge, and to improve your skills as a writer. These multiple purposes inform your writing process and shape the resulting text. You may think you are solely motivated by your instructor's assignment, but once you begin to write, other motivating forces probably invade the process.

The rhetorical purposes we explore in this book are common and varied. You will write to explore, to reconstruct your own experiences, to instruct and advise, to inform, to persuade, and to solve problems. You will also have other reasons for writing each assignment, and they will influence the resulting text. Inevitably, the experience you gain with these rhetorical purposes and the awareness you develop about your own motivations will make you a better reader and writer.

A U D I E N C E — T O   W H O M
A   T E X T   I S   A D D R E S S E D   ◀

Like its purpose, a text's audience also influences the form it assumes. *Audience* consists of the people for whom a text is written—those the writer expects will read it. Experienced writers always consider their readers when they write. In fact, *consider* may be too weak a word. Good writers do more than acknowledge the existence of an audience. They write *for* their readers, analyzing their needs and purposes in order to produce an appropriate text. Think of the Shapiro poem: audience and purpose, much more than subject, determine the content and form of the text. The poet is writing for readers literate enough to appreciate the rich details, metaphoric language, rhythms, ambiguities, and nuances of meaning found in the poem and with enough leisure time to enjoy reading a poem.

In contrast, the police officer who describes a similar accident is writing primarily for readers who want to spend as little time as necessary with the text. The readers of accident reports—police officials, clerks, lawyers, judges, social workers, insurance people, litigants—want readily available, unambiguous information. The police officer's account includes accurate, specific information ("On March 3, 1997, at approximately 10:05 P.M., my partner, Cpl. Alex Kolwalski, and I were dispatched to the intersection of West Main Street and Airport Road, where a two-vehicle accident had just occurred."). It focuses on what happened and why ("A 1995 green Chevrolet [Silverado] pickup truck had just passed her traveling at a high rate of speed, northbound on Airport Road, when the driver tried to turn right onto West Main Street and overshot the center line and struck a white 1992 Dodge Caravan . . ."). The reader of a police report is interested not in how the ambulance looked and sounded as it approached, but rather in the fact that an ambulance was summoned and by whom. Compare Shapiro's "quick soft silver bell beating, beating,/ And down the dark one ruby flare/ Pulsing out red like an artery," with the police report's "I called an ambulance to the scene. Upon arrival at 10:21 P.M., . . ."

Thus, the purpose of the reader, as well as that of the writer, influences a text. Like writers, readers have different purposes. They may read to satisfy emotional or aesthetic needs, to acquire information, to get advice, to learn how to do something, or simply to amuse themselves. A reader who is reading to be amused does not read in the same way or have the same expectations as a reader who is reading for information. For this reason, experienced writers not only identify who the readers of a text may be, but also *analyze* the purposes, needs, expectations, tastes, limitations, and biases of those readers.

One of the ways writers analyze readers is to classify them in certain ways. One simple but useful strategy for analyzing readers is to classify them as *expert* or *inexpert*—that is, to determine how well informed readers are. In writing for inexpert readers, writers may need to provide definitions and general background information as well as new information. In contrast, readers who are experts require less general information and fewer definitions. They are more interested in new information. For example, a recipe for a beginning cook might include directions for peeling and chopping garlic, while the same recipe written for an experienced cook need only include the information that chopped garlic should be added.

Another way in which experienced writers analyze their audience is by classifying readers according to their attitudes toward the subject:

Favorable readers are receptive, interested, and disposed to accept a writer's views because these views coincide with their own attitudes toward the subject.

Neutral/undecided/apathetic readers may be skeptical or uninterested but are not resistant to a writer's views. However, they need to be convinced of the rightness of the writer's position and interested in the writer's subject before they can be informed, advised, or persuaded.

Hostile or biased readers are predisposed *not* to agree with the writer's views. They are the most resistant readers and require the writer's most persuasive efforts.

Writers who are writing for a hostile audience, as Martin Luther King, Jr., is in "Letter from Birmingham Jail" (see pp. 245–262), usually attempt to overcome their readers' hostility or bias before stating their own opinions. Even if readers are merely apprehensive about a subject, as some novice computer users are, writers must attempt to deal with this apprehension if readers are going to be receptive to the ideas and information being presented. Thus, a number of years ago those who wrote manuals for Macintosh Computer owners began to use familiar, humorous icons to make the manuals more "user friendly" and to use simple directions such as "Select printer" instead of complicated instructions such as "Activate the interface expansion mode."

Another strategy writers use to analyze their audience is to classify readers in terms of their relationship to the writer. Writing to someone you know well who shares your immediate environment is fairly simple because you can safely assume that such a reader already possesses much of the information needed to understand your text. More difficult is writing to someone at a distance whom you do not know. Most difficult is writing for a large, diverse, unknown audience that exists in a different environment. Thus, an owner of a small company may spend only a minute composing a memo to employees, but labor a little longer over a letter to a potential customer. And, if asked to write an article for a trade journal, this same writer might require weeks or even months to construct a final draft that provides readers with all the information they need.

Because concepts of audience and purpose are the foundation of effective rhetoric, we emphasize them repeatedly throughout this book.

PROCESS—HOW A TEXT IS CONSTRUCTED

Although every writer constructs a text in a particular way and every reader comprehends a text in a particular way, all texts are written and read using roughly the same general process. Here is a generalized version of how texts are constructed—how writers write and readers read.

Writing

Any piece of writing originates as an idea. The most informal note, like the most complex treatise, originates as an idea that both anticipates and shapes the completed text.

But writing is not as straightforward as this statement suggests. Writers do not simply come up with an idea and then transfer it directly onto paper or a computer screen. The written text that evolves from an idea is constructed by means of a *process*. In some instances, this process is brief and seemingly uncomplicated, as when you leave a note for a friend. In most instances, though, the process is more complicated, involving a series of forward and backward movements between the writer's ideas and the written text. This back and forth pattern characterizes the writing process. A freshman student, Kerry, went through the following process of planning, constructing, revising, and editing as he wrote an essay about a trip he had made to Saltillo, Mexico.

GENERATING IDEAS.   From several topics Kerry chose the following one because he had recently made a trip to Mexico:

> Write a travel narrative, describing what you learned (not what you saw or where you stayed) on a trip. Don't bore read-ers with a day-by-day itinerary of your travels; instead, provide a candid and thoughtful narrative of your mental adventures and explorations of different people, attitudes, and assump-tions. One point—you don't have to travel to an exotic locale to tell an intriguing story.
>
> —Adapted from Elizabeth Cowan Neeld, *Writing*, 3rd ed. (Glenview, IL: Scott Foresman/Little Brown, 1990), p. 112.

Kerry had just returned from Mexico and thought it would be easy to write an essay about the week he had spent there at a Catholic mission. He also chose this topic because the trip had been important to him. Of course, it had been exciting to travel to a foreign country, but the trip had also given him a glimpse of a kind of life very differ-ent from his. Kerry spent little time planning what he was going to write about, confident that he had plenty to say and that the words would come once he began to write.

DRAFTING THE TEXT.   The night before the first draft of his essay was due, Kerry sat down and quickly wrote six pages about his trip, describing the highlights of his visit to the Catholic mission. Here is the introductory paragraph of that early draft:

> During the summer of 1992 I joined a church group in a journey to a small mission in Saltillo, Mexico. This would be my second time to travel to Saltillo. Unfortunately I was much younger the last time, and most of the experiences once learned were now lost to time. I had planned to return every year after that first year, but I was forced to stay home because of pre-season football practice. With an opportunity to finally return I left with great expectation.

Kerry then provided his readers with an account of the highlights of his visit to the mission. He began with a description of the mission itself and the priest who was in charge of it, Father Quinn. Then came accounts of side trips that his group made during the week to rancheros and barrios in the area. He also wrote about Bean Day, a day when beans were given to people who came to the mission:

> The last day we spent was a shocker to all of us.
> We had Bean Day. Bean day is where we give beans to as
> many people that can get to the mission. People start
> filling the church the night before. We started at
> 6:00. Once the church was empty Father Quinn would take
> a bunch of guys to let the people outside of the church
> in. We made a human chain and extend outward letting
> the people between the two chains in. It was an amazing
> feeling to know that all these people were going to be
> helped by the little thing we did. Total I would guess
> we gave beans and flour to near 5,000 people.

Kerry ended his first draft with this paragraph:

> The trip to Saltillo does miraculous things. You
> leave with a bunch of strangers and return with friends
> you could never part with. It seems kind of humorous
> looking back on my trips to Mexico. While you are there
> you are hot, dirty, smelly, and wishing you were home.
> Spending all week praying to be home as soon as I walk
> in my door I wished I was back in Saltillo.

The next day Kerry read his essay aloud to a group of his class-mates and got their mildly positive response. "Yeah, sounds like a good trip," commented one of the students in his group; but another pointed out that the essay didn't seem to have a thesis—a main idea or main point. Still Kerry left class feeling relieved—his first essay written and his first peer response session over.

READING AND REVISING THE TEXT.   Before the writing class met again, Kerry was expected to revise his essay, so he wrote it out again, cor-recting some spelling and punctuation errors, adding and deleting a few words, changing a few phrases, and writing the essay more neatly;

but he didn't change the essay in any significant way. He turned the essay in and put it out of his mind.

When Kerry read his instructor's comments a few days later, he was disappointed because she did not tell him the essay was fine, just as it was, nor did she tell him exactly how to change it. She had written only, "Kerry, your essay has some wonderful bits and pieces but lacks a clear focus. Let's talk briefly after class." After class she suggested that he was attempting too much and should focus, as he revised, on the part of his trip that had been most meaningful to him.

That night Kerry read his essay again. Not having seen it for several days, he read it with a new perspective. He began to see what the student in the response group and his teacher had seen: The essay lacked a clear focus. He had included too much and had not really explained anything fully. Thinking back to the trip, Kerry tried to remember what had happened and how he had felt. Although the whole week had been exciting, and he had learned a great deal about Mexican culture, the experience of giving people food on Bean Day was his most vivid memory.

Turning on his computer and opening a new file, Kerry began a new draft of his essay. He decided to scrap the introductory paragraph because it was too general and not very clear. The new introduction focused on his Bean Day experience:

> To the average American citizen a scoop of beans means no more than a bad supper. However, I've learned not to take beans or any food, for that matter, for granted.

After writing a completely new introduction, Kerry decided to keep the next few paragraphs, which provided background information about the trip and the mission. Then he cut the paragraphs about the side trips to the neighboring rancheros and barrios. He hated to get rid of such a big chunk of his essay, but he realized now that this information didn't add anything; in fact, it detracted from what he really wanted to accomplish.

Rereading the original paragraph about Bean Day, Kerry realized how skimpy and unclear it was. He wrote a new description of that experience, a description that grew from a paragraph to almost five pages. When he was ready to end the essay, he didn't hesitate to cross out the old conclusion and write a new one that reflected his new focus. When Kerry read the new draft through, he realized that in this revision he had improved his essay about 100 percent.

PREPARING THE FINAL DRAFT OF THE TEXT.   When his teacher read the new draft, she agreed that he had written a much stronger essay. At this point, the essay went into Kerry's working portfolio. When the time came for Kerry to decide which essays he wanted to include in his final portfolio, he selected the Bean Day essay as one. Rereading the essay a couple of months after he had written it was a strange experience. He could see some minor errors he had not noticed before, but he still liked the essay and felt it communicated clearly something that had been important to him.

In order to edit the essay, he reread it carefully, correcting the errors he identified and marking anything he thought might be an error. He also changed a few phrases and rewrote a couple of sentences so they would be clearer or easier to read. Later he asked his instructor about the sentences that he suspected might include errors and asked a friend to read the essay over to see if he had missed anything. Then, confident that he had done what he could to ensure his essay was free of errors, he typed it in its final form and placed it in his portfolio. This is that essay:

Bean Day

To the average American citizen, a scoop of beans means no more than a bad supper. However, I have learned not to take beans, or any food, for granted.

During the summer of 1992, I joined a church group on a journey to a small mission in Saltillo, Mexico. The mission is supported by the Diocese of Biloxi, and is visited by their youth groups during the summer. These groups help Father Quinn, an older man with sun-beaten skin, silver hair, and a heart of gold. Father Quinn volunteered to run the mission for three years. Now, 30 years later, he is still in charge of the mission.

The mission is a large area around a church with a big courtyard. During the day, the children from the city came to the mission to play. When we came in from the ranchos and barrios, where we passed out food and clothing, we would have time to play in the courtyard with the children. We learned a lot about history and people playing with those kids. Many of the games they play are similar to ones played in the United States. I

believe that is what was so remarkable about our playing. We expected those kids to be different from us,
and they had thought we were different from them. It
turned out we are a lot alike, which showed in the way
we picked up each other's games quickly and in the way
they understood the games we taught them.

There were a lot of faces in the yard, no one face
really remembered. It was the time spent with the dirty
little faces that will always be special to me.

The last day we were at the mission was a surprise
to all of us. We were there during the week of "bean
day." Father Quinn has beans trucked into the mission
all during the month, and on one Friday of the month he
gives them out. We called this "bean day." People from
all over the city and surrounding towns came for those
beans that would feed their families for a couple of
weeks. They started showing up the afternoon before bean
day and sat in the church. When the church was filled,
Father closed the doors and people waited out by the
street. During the night the people held an all-night
vigil. As we slept in the dorms, we could hear the
rosary being prayed in the church.

By the time the side door to the church was opened
the next morning, people had begun to pass out from the
heat and the long wait. The calm crowd dashed madly to
the six stations we had set up. We shoveled beans into
anything the people had that would hold them. We could
only give them two scoops full of beans. After that, we
asked them to move on, but some of them just sat there
asking for more. It is hard to say "no" to a sad face
asking for more than just two scoops of beans. But, it
would have been even harder to say "We have no more" to
the last person in that line.

When the church was empty, Father Quinn asked the
adult men and some of the older boys to help him get
the people still outside into the church. If the doors
were just opened, the fight to get in would crush people into the doors. That is why Father Quinn needed us.

We made a human fence on each side of the door. Father
told us when he opened the door to walk out and hold
onto the gate and to let only the people inside the two
fences in.

When he opened the door, the number of people was
shocking. We walked out and people were pushing and
hitting to get in. The best comparison I can make is
this: If a rock concert were to have a fire, the fight
to get to the door would be much like this fight to get
food. When one part was cleared, we would open another
one. We worked for over an hour until everyone was in
the courtyard getting beans or waiting in the church.

This experience was an eye-opener for me, but the
one picture I will always remember is one of an old
lady. After all the beans were gone and the people had
cleared out of the courtyard, there the old lady was,
down on all fours, going from station to station looking for beans that had been dropped.

There were a lot of things that I took for granted
in my life. Sometimes, I still do take things for
granted. But now, when I find myself doing that, I
think about the pain I saw on this lady's face. A lady
scrounging for beans that would, most likely, feed her
children and her grandchildren, for a while longer.

You will probably discover, as Kerry did, that you cannot march
through the process in a neat, sequential fashion. Don't expect a writing (or reading) project to be orderly. Your mental image of what you
are writing will probably change as you write, and each time your
ideas change, you will have to change what you have written as well.

Even so, overall you will progress through several stages. You
usually begin a writing project by planning—thinking about what you
are going to write, discovering new ideas, making connections and
gaining new insights, researching for additional information, organizing your thoughts, and considering your purpose and audience. During this stage, you expand your initial idea of your text, and this
developing idea starts to grow into some kind of plan. You may also
want to spend some time *generating ideas through invention and
research* if you need additional information. **Invention** strategies may

INVENTION, PAGE 613

be as simple as freewriting or as complex as analyzing a subject from different perspectives. Research also takes many forms—everything from informal interviews to full-scale searches of electronic data bases. You will probably want to complete your preliminary research before you begin writing, but as you write you may think of other forms of research that will provide you with useful information. The important thing is to think of research broadly as the pursuit of information and then to be creative in discovering different sources of information.

When you have some idea of what you want to write, you are ready to begin *drafting your text.* Throughout this part of the writing process you must often move backward to go forward. You must think about what you want to write, write it, read it over to see if it corresponds to what you are thinking, and then change it or your mental image of your text so that they agree. In other words, you are going to change your mind frequently, rethinking what you want to write as you write it. This is a normal, productive part of the process. Ultimately, you will produce a piece of writing that satisfies you, or you will simply run out of time.

Once you have a completed draft, you should try to lay it aside for awhile and then begin the process of *reading and revising* what you have written. If you attempt to revise too soon, you will not be able to evaluate your text objectively. Revising your text involves rereading it carefully and critically. To do this, you must try to see your text through the eyes of your readers. You must also be willing to make major changes—to generate new material, to move information from one place to another, and even to delete large portions if necessary.

Next turn your attention to *preparing the final draft of your text—* to editing and proofreading and formatting what you have written so that it is as readable and correct as possible. By the time you begin this stage of constructing your text, you are primarily focusing on the accuracy and appearance of your text. This is the time to make sure that each sentence is well structured, that each word is correctly used, and that each mark of punctuation is appropriate. If you are using a computer, you make final decisions about format and run the spell check.

When we write about this progression of planning, drafting, reading and revising, and preparing the final draft of your text, the process seems to be sequential and linear, but your own writing experiences tell you otherwise. You may begin to write before you have finished planning, or you may revise even before you actually begin writing. And, after you have produced a written text, you may still be changing your plans, just as Kerry changed his essay from a general description of his entire trip to Mexico to an essay about one experience he had there. At any point in the process you may be planning, writing, revising, or editing—shuttling back and forth among these four activities.

Reading

Like writers, readers construct texts. A writer begins with a mental image of the text and constructs a written text; a reader begins with a written text and constructs a mental image of it. Readers are also like writers in that they move back and forth between the two forms of the text—the one on the page and the one in their head. Readers as well as writers also move backward—rereading, reconfirming, and rethinking—as well as forward—anticipating what is to come and connecting the new and different information with what they already know.

Reading always involves an interaction between what is in the reader's mind, what is in the writer's mind, and what appears in the written text. Thus, readers may, and often do, read a text for purposes that differ from those of the writer. For example, in 1863, as part of a dedication ceremony honoring those who had been killed at the Civil War battle at Gettysburg, Abraham Lincoln constructed the following text, which has come to be known as the "Gettysburg Address."

> Four score and seven years ago our fathers brought forth on this continent a new nation, conceived in liberty, and dedicated to the proposition that all men are created equal.
>
> Now we are engaged in a great civil war, testing whether that nation, or any nation so conceived and so dedicated, can long endure. We are met on a great battlefield of that war. We have come to dedicate a portion of that field as a final resting-place for those who here gave their lives that that nation might live. It is altogether fitting and proper that we should do this.
>
> But in a larger sense we cannot dedicate, we cannot consecrate, we cannot hallow this ground. The brave men, living and dead, who struggled here have consecrated it, far above our poor power to add or detract. The world will little note, nor long remember what we say here, but it can never forget what they did here. It is for us, the living, rather, to be dedicated here to the unfinished work which they who fought here have thus far so nobly advanced. It is rather for us to be here dedicated to the great task remaining before us, —that from these honored dead we take increased devotion to that cause for which they gave the last full measure of devotion; that we here highly resolve that these dead shall not have died in vain; that this nation, under God, shall have a new birth of freedom; and

that government of the people, by the people, and for the
people, shall not perish from the earth.

Lincoln probably had several purposes for writing this speech
other than his primary one of honoring those who had died at Gettysburg. He may have also wanted to impress his audience so they would
vote for him or to encourage Northerners to support the war effort or to
remind people what they were fighting for. But no matter what writers
intend, readers form their own images of the texts they read or hear.

For example, in the years since Lincoln wrote the "Gettysburg
Address," it has been read for a variety of reasons that he could not
have imagined. Over the years rhetoricians have read it to learn how
to write a persuasive text; historians have read it to gain knowledge of
the Civil War and to understand Lincoln; students have read it to learn
more about American history; and the general public has read it
because it is now considered not only an important historical text but
also a great piece of literature. These different purposes for reading
have influenced the various texts constructed in the minds of readers.
A history student who reads the "Gettysburg Address" in the 1990s
does not construct the same text in his or her mind as that constructed
by a person who was present in 1863 when Lincoln delivered it. A history professor who reads it does not construct the same text as a student who also reads it. A feminist reading the text today may focus on
Lincoln's use of sexist language, while a politician may focus on his
rhetorical strategies.

In spite of the different purposes with which readers approach a
text, the written text and the writer's initial purpose significantly shape
a reader's mental text. In presenting precise information—building
specifications or instructions for assembling a bookcase or operating a
computer, for example—writers work hard to minimize the difference
between their written texts and the mental images their readers construct. Poets and novelists, on the other hand, may actually encourage
readers to construct mental images that are only loosely based on the
written text.

Reading and writing are thus very similar processes. Some might
even argue that they are the same process. Both writers and readers
construct texts in their minds, and both interact with the written text.
Although, like writing, the process of reading varies from one person to
the next, we can still generalize about the overall process of reading and
can suggest some strategies that usually make the process, especially the
process of reading difficult texts, more productive. The following three
strategies, for example, can help you become a better reader:

❖ Reread difficult texts

❖ Annotate texts to record your responses and reactions

❖ Summarize texts

REREAD DIFFICULT TEXTS.   If the text you are reading is difficult for you to understand, rereading is essential. Even the most experienced readers must frequently reread, especially when they lack background information on the text they are reading. The more you know about a subject, the easier you find it to understand a difficult text on that subject. Rereading a text compensates to some extent for lack of background information because each reading after the first builds on a slowly growing foundation of information.

Rereading is also necessary because a reader's attention can easily drift. You may think you have read every word on a page but have no idea what you have read. Everyone has had this experience. Perhaps you are thinking about an idea from a previous page or just daydreaming. Whatever the reason, the answer is to reread.

Sometimes a text is so complex that even a reader who is paying attention must reread to sort out complicated relationships, figure out complex ideas, or just wade through the author's impenetrable prose. Rereading is not a sign of failure but an essential part of the process.

ANNOTATE TEXTS TO RECORD YOUR RESPONSES AND REACTIONS.   To annotate means to mark a text—to write on the pages so that, in effect, you create a text of your own that merges with the one you are reading. You may respond to a text in a variety of ways and for a variety of purposes. You may respond to express your emotional reactions, to explore ideas encountered in the text, to clarify your attitudes toward the text, or to construct a mental image of the text. You can think of your annotations as a conversation, or dialogue, with the text.

How you mark a text really doesn't matter. That's up to you. Your purpose for reading will influence the responses you make. For example, a student in a history course might annotate Lincoln's "Gettysburg Address" as follows:

1776   <u>Four score and seven years ago</u> our fathers brought forth on this continent a new nation, <u>conceived</u> in liberty, and dedicated to the proposition that all men are created equal.   *Reference to the Declaration of Independence*

1863   <u>Now</u> we are engaged in a great civil war, testing whether that nation, or any nation so <u>conceived</u> and so

Gettysburg

dedicated, can long endure. We are met on a great battlefield of that war. We have come to dedicate a portion of that field as a final resting-place for those who here gave their lives that that nation might live. It is altogether fitting and proper that we should do this.

But in a larger sense we cannot dedicate, we cannot consecrate, we cannot hallow this ground. The brave men, living and dead, who struggled here have consecrated it, far above our poor power to add or detract. The world will little note, nor long remember what we say here, but it can never forget what they did here. It is for us, the living, rather, to be dedicated here to the unfinished work which they who fought here have thus far so nobly advanced. It is rather for us to be here dedicated to the great task remaining before us, —that from these honored dead we take increased devotion to that cause for which they gave the last full measure of devotion; that we here highly resolve that these dead shall not have died in vain; that this nation, under God, shall have a new birth of freedom; and that government of the people, by the people, and for the people, shall not perish from the earth.

Repeated references to birth, life & death.

Note three-part structure—past, present & future

SUMMARIZE TEXTS.   Summarizing encourages you to formulate your own version of the writer's main idea and major supporting points. Summaries reduce, often drastically, the original text while keeping its gist. Thus, you will usually eliminate all specific details, examples, repetitions, anecdotes, and anything else that is not essential. But summaries vary, depending on your purpose as a reader. If you are reading for specific information, your summary may be merely a list. The important thing is to put into words your mental image of the text. For example, a summary of the "Gettysburg Address" might read as follows:

> In his "Gettysburg Address," Lincoln argues that the Civil War is a test of the Constitutional belief that "all men are created equal." He points out that Gettysburg, the battlefield they have met to dedicate, has already been consecrated by the men who have fought and lost their lives in the war. But he urges those who are there for the consecration of the battlefield to dedicate themselves to the war and its great cause of freedom so that those who have perished in the war will not have died in vain.

In this summary, the eloquence and poetry are lost, but the basic ideas of the text have been retained. In constructing this type of summary, you focus on the main ideas and thus gain a clear under-standing of the author's purpose and message. At the same time that a summary forces you to focus on the author's ideas, it forces you to construct the text in your own mind and words, thus enabling you to make the text part of your own general knowledge.

CONCLUSION

In both writing and reading, a text is constructed by a process that involves moving back and forth between a written and a mental text. Nothing is more important to both reading and writing than these mental, interior parts of the processes. The time you spend thinking about what you are going to write is never time wasted. Don't rush into actually putting words on paper or into the computer. Of course, you can't put off writing forever, but what goes on in your mind before you write and as you write is essential to the process. This means that you should allow time between drafts to let what is in your head shape your written text and to let your written text reshape what is in your head. Finally, it means that you do not stop thinking when you begin writing. Writing and thinking occur simultaneously, one stimulating the other in an ongoing process.

If you have clearly understood what is going on as you read and write, you will gradually gain control of these processes. Writing is not a special talent given to some people nor a mysterious process that you cannot possibly understand. Nor is it a simple one-two-three process, even though descriptions of the process often make it sound neat and consistent. Constructing a text, whether you are a reader or a writer, is an interactive, meaning-making process that involves both the written text and your mental image of that text. The interaction between your mind and the text *creates* meaning.

PART TWO

PURPOSES

Dean Dablow, *Young Trees in the Snow.*
Reprinted with permission of Dean Dablow.

2

WRITING
TO
EXPLORE

The reason I write is to find out what I mean.

LESLIE MARMON SILKO

Y ou are often asked to write in order to demonstrate what you know, as on a test or research paper. But you may be less familiar with writing to explore—writing to find out what you know rather than to prove you know something. In a sense, each time you write, you write to explore, because writing is always an act of discovery. Even when you think you know exactly what you are going to write, you may surprise yourself, writing something other than what you had planned. When you write to explore, you write to find out what you want to say and how you want to say it, to see how much you remember, and to discover where your words lead you and whether that is where you want to go.

One of the most important reasons for writing is to discover what you have to say on a subject. For some reason, the act of writing helps bring back information, sensations, impressions, and emotions—in other words, it retrieves from memory things you may have forgotten you even knew. But you can also write to explore in order to forge new connections or construct new information—to see the past in terms of the present or select from memories certain data and combine them with present information to create new knowledge. Writing helps you to recall individual bits of information and relate them to one another—to see them not just as bits but as parts of a new whole. For readers to see the relationships, connections, implications, and meanings in what you write, you must first be able to see them for yourself.

Exploratory writing may be impermanent—a fleeting image on a computer screen, a note written and then destroyed, a rough draft later revised, a brainstorming list produced by a group or an individual and used to generate ideas. But many people have kept their written explorations in some permanent form, something to be read later by others. Exploratory writing in the form of diaries, journals, notebooks, and commonplace books enriches the world of literature. In this chapter's reading selections, you will discover more about yourself as a writer as you read other writers who have explored their writing experiences.

READING WRITTEN
EXPLORATIONS

Because much exploratory writing is personal, if not private, when you read someone else's journal, you may feel like an accidental audience—someone who is reading something not intended for him or her. True, people often keep a diary or journal without a clear sense of who the reader will be. Diarists often claim they are writing only for themselves, but even if they are writing only for their future selves, people who write in a journal or diary always have a sense of audience. By its very nature, writing is a communicative act. Writing connects a writer and a reader, even if the reader is the writer.

In his book about diaries entitled *A Book of One's Own*, Thomas Mallon, a prolific diarist himself, analyzes his own sense of audience and argues that people who keep diaries are always writing for a "you" as well as themselves:

> Is that the only person I'm writing for—myself when older?
> Or is there someone else? Who is this "you" that's made its way
> more and more often into these pages in the last few years, this
> odd pronoun I sometimes find myself talking to like a person
> at the other end of a letter? Sometimes when I'm writing on the
> right-hand leaf of a notebook I catch sight of a spelling or
> grammatical mistake I made on the left one the night before,
> and I correct it. For "you"?
>
> I can say without a trace of coyness that I have no idea who
> "you" is. I don't know if "you" is male or female, met or unmet,
> born or unborn, tied to me by blood or accident. But I do know
> that "you" has come to stay. What's more, I now realize that he
> or she has been hovering around . . . from the beginning.
>
> (New York: Ticknor and Fields, 1984), p. xvi.

Mallon's argument gains support from the number of people who eventually publish their diaries or journals. The writer Anne Lindbergh, wife of the aviator who made the first solo nonstop transatlantic flight, published several collections of her diaries, and in the introduction to one, she explains why she thinks people publish journals and diaries:

> Why do people publish diaries and letters? If they have had
> interesting lives, they may feel they can add a tiny segment to

the history of their times or put a missing fragment of mosaic in the picture. In terms of the individual there is the wish to give testimony to a journey taken by one human being which might amuse, enlighten, or explain other individuals to themselves. In the case of an individual who has lived somewhat in the public eye, there is always the hope of clarifying a record that has been obscured by rumors and blurred by distorted images. And finally, perhaps, the writer seeks some kind of personal summation in order to discover for himself the true essence of a life.

Bring Me a Unicorn,
(New York: Harcourt, 1971), p. xv.

How should you read published diaries and journals? Much as you would any other piece of writing. However, a diary, whether it is published or unpublished, always seems to be an honest revelation of the writer's thoughts and actions. It may not occur to you as a reader of a diary to question the truth or accuracy of what has been written. Yet diarists and journalists are only recording their perception of what happened, and like most writers, they want to present themselves in a good light. Before publishing his diary, Evelyn Waugh, a famous English novelist of the early twentieth century, deleted entries that didn't reinforce the impression of wit and humor he cultivated. Anäis Nin, a Paris-born American writer whose six volumes of diaries describe her life among the wealthy and the literary in Paris in the 1920s and 1930s, embellished her already exotic and extravagant life to create the story she wanted to live.

Reading a journal or diary is, for the most part, like reading other kinds of text. Be aware of the writer behind the text and try to decide what his or her purposes may have been. Read critically, weighing evidence and argument. And finally, know your own purposes for reading. If that purpose is to understand the writer of the diary or journal, then you need to know that the person presented in the text (the persona) is not necessarily the person who wrote it, just as a character in a novel is not necessarily an accurate reflection of the novelist.

And what if you are reading your own diary or journal? People often keep diaries and journals so they can reread them at a later time. Does being a reader of your own writing change the way you read a diary or journal? Not as much as you might think. Again, the purpose for reading is the most important factor. If you are reading a journal you kept when you were a child, you want to understand who that child was just as you would if you were reading a diary or journal written by a child you did not know. Since you are no longer the child you once were, you are still trying to glimpse the figure behind the words on the page.

People also read their own journals to remember what happened, to check on some bit of information, to relive experiences that have faded with time, or to rekindle ideas or stimulate thinking. In the following reading selections, for example, imagine Lord Lugard later rereading his East Africa journals as an old man, or picture Virginia Woolf turning to her journals to refresh her memory about the writing plans she often described in them.

► **READING SELECTIONS**

This chapter's reading selections show writers exploring the subject of themselves as writers. As you read these selections, you will learn a great deal about how these writers construct a text and about their attitudes toward their own writing. But you will also find these reading selections helpful as you begin the process of discovering yourself as a writer.

ON WRITING

Jim Whorton

As a member of a composition class, Jim Whorton was asked to keep a journal in which he reflected on his own writing process. As a creative writing major, Whorton focused mainly on his experiences in writing short stories, using his journal to explore how he felt about writing and himself as a writer. As you read, notice the specific details included in his description of how he constructs a text and the delightful "side trips" that occur as one idea leads him to another.

September 9

1   My girlfriend Kathryn and I were just discussing writing. I mentioned the required typing of all assignments in some composition classes. She vehemently argued that [if she were a writing teacher] she would require all essays to be handwritten, and if they were illegible she'd fail them unhesitatingly. Her position is that writing is a dying skill and it should be maintained. People in college should be able to write by hand. My position is similar but different too. I honor the tradition of writing in script, of having a handwriting. I like the idea of each of us having a signature that identifies us, even though individual samples are not themselves identical. If a student likes to write by hand, and takes care to do it well, I say more power to the student. I am less militant than Kat, though—I would not fail illegible papers, but return them to be recopied or typed.

2   I'm left considering the physicality of writing. A member of USM's English faculty told me that composition must always be done LONG-hand, because the motion of hand over paper fuels the imagination. Of course in typing there is as much physical activity or more than in longhand. I have a computer I like to write on, but the everpresent

possibility of an electric surge or slip-up eradicating my work makes me nervous. That's why I got this Remington Noiseless, a relic from the Thirties, according to the man who sold me the ribbon. Design changed very little in the early decades of mass-produced typewriters. You can tell the pre-WWII models by their lack of color. They are black. It was just after WWI that typewriters were mass produced in the US. Factories that had produced guns for the war, such as Remington, Smith and Wesson, became Remington Typewriters and Smith-Corona respectively. I paid just ten dollars for this very heavy piece of equipment at a thrift store called Bargains and Blessings. It works well except for the bell, which dings not.

3   I am rambling, but this is how I often write, therefore judge whatever comes into my head self-evidently apropos. Since this is a journal whose concern is writing. . . .

October 22

4   Got a story due for the workshop on the 25th. I decided to go with the new one, which I just started but is more interesting to me right now. So I'm hoping I'll get a late rush of energy and do something worthwhile with this story. I don't put a whole lot of stock in the idea of inspiration—I try to resist the idea because it seems too mystifying. So it's not that I expect the last-minute pressure to inspire me with great thoughts. But it might provoke me to greater exertion.

October 31

5   What I was saying above seems unnecessarily vague. The kind of inspiration I value and use is really just a feeling of freshness, or strangeness, that lets you see things and talk about them in a fresh way. This fresh feeling can be achieved just by doing something a little unusual, like getting up two hours early one morning, or staying up extra late, or taking a walk at a different time of day, or eating in an unfamiliar restaurant. The strangeness heightens your sensitivity to the familiar too.

6   So what I did to finish the new story was stay up late. Burn incense (which always seems *flaky* to me, and always will, but that's partly why I like it). Drink one glass of wine, maybe, a small glass only. Coffee maybe. Get worked up. Put the dogs to bed and sit there in the quiet with your computer screen. My suspicion of everything mystical helps me out, because it heightens the artificiality of the mood I'm creating for myself to write in.

7   But, this doesn't always work. Sometimes this flops.

8   Certainly you can't rely on this method for consistent success. Though maybe it is important to always be doing things that make you

feel weird. That sounds fruity, but it works, and it's the best way to live even if you're not writing. I don't mean scaring people, knifing yourself, driving cross-country. I do mean going into junk stores and touching bugs, tasting banana peel, etc.

December 3

9   It's not a simple matter, writing. I could make a list of things I've learned but then I might make another list that contradicts the first but is also persuasive. . . .

10   Am I too touchy about words? Am I too meticulous? Are words too precious to me? Is there a danger of ineffectualness in my language? One of the true low points of my semester was when I listened to a recording of myself reading my own writing and I was bored by it. The care and precision did not pay off.

11   What a drag that was.

12   Maybe I'm not as precise as I'd like to be.

13   Maybe I'm overly stodgy. . . .

14   I worry some about grades but I don't understand how people can get through school doing work JUST to get good grades. How can they stand the boredom. I'm sounding pretty snooty along about now—maybe I should back up and clarify what I'm talking about.

15   1) I'm interested in the most tedious aspects of language

16   2) I'm worried that this is not a good thing to be interested in

17   3) I'm worried I'll bore others

18   4) I'm worried I'll look up one day and find myself totally boring, as has happened recently

19   5) I'm trying to justify the presence of all this stuff here in my composition journal. Perhaps this is the most pressing issue of all.

▶   QUESTIONS TO CONSIDER

1. Whorton is clearly concerned with the physical as well as the mental process of writing. Does the "physicality of writing"—the physical method a writer uses to create a text—influence what is written? For instance, have you noticed differences in your writing process when you use a computer rather than a typewriter or a pen and pencil?

2. Whorton is also concerned about boring his readers. Should writers worry about boring those who read them? Why or why not? How can you determine if what you have written is boring?

3. Whorton mentions several things he does to gain a fresh perspective when he writes. Can you think of other ways to force yourself to see things in new ways?

4. Do you find Whorton's digressions interesting or distracting? Why are digressions to be expected in journal writing?

WRITING ACTIVITIES

Individual: Explore your own writing process by freewriting about it in your journal. Describe in detail exactly what you do when you write. Do you observe any particular rituals? Do these rituals vary depending on what you are writing?

Collaborative: Working with a group of students, compare your writing processes. Discuss how your writing methods, habits, and rituals are the same and how they are different. Then, based on your analysis of your individual processes, decide if there is a basic process that all of you seem to go through when you write. If so, describe that process.

Computer: To test the effect of the "physicality of writing," write a paragraph about yourself as a writer using pen (or pencil) and paper. Then, using a computer, write another paragraph about the same subject. Compare these two writing experiences. Was one easier? More satisfying? Faster? Did one result in a stronger, more interesting piece of writing?

ONE WRITER'S BEGINNING

Eudora Welty

Eudora Welty has spent nearly all of her life in Jackson, Mississippi, and has written primarily about this area and its inhabitants. As a writer and photographer, Welty has focused narrowly on what she knows best, but by dwelling on the particular so acutely and thoughtfully, she has expressed what is universal. Now in her eighties, she continues to write and enjoys not only a national but also an international reputation as a fiction writer. Her memoir, One Writer's Beginning, *from which this selection is taken, began as a lecture series. In it she explores why she became a writer and what kind of writer she became.*

1   Writing a story or a novel is one way of discovering *sequence* in experience, of stumbling upon cause and effect in the happenings of a writer's own life. This has been the case with me. Connections slowly emerge. Like distant landmarks you are approaching, cause and effect begin to align themselves, draw closer together. Experiences too indefinite of outline in themselves to be recognized for themselves connect and are identified as a larger shape. And suddenly a light is thrown back, as when your train makes a curve, showing that there has been a mountain of meaning rising behind you on the way you've come, is rising there still, proven now through retrospect.

2   It seems to me, writing of my parents now in my seventies, that I see continuities in their lives that weren't visible to me when they were living. Even at the times that have left me my most vivid memories of them, there were connections between them that escaped me. Could it be because I can better see their lives—or any lives I know—today because I'm a fiction writer? See them not as fiction, certainly—see them, perhaps, as even greater mysteries than I knew. Writing fiction has developed in me an abiding respect for the unknown in a human lifetime and a sense of where to look for the threads, how to follow, how to connect, find in the thick of the tangle what clear line persists. The strands are all there: to the memory nothing is ever really lost.

. . .

3   What discoveries I've made in the course of writing stories all begin with the particular, never the general. They are mostly hindsight: arrows that I now find I myself have left behind me, which have shown me some right, or wrong, way I have come. What one story may have pointed out to me is of no avail in the writing of another. But "avail" is not what I want; freedom ahead is what each story promises—beginning anew. And all the while, as further hindsight has told me, certain patterns in my work repeat themselves without my realizing. There would be no way to know this, for during the writing of any single story, there is no other existing. Each writer must find out for himself, I imagine, on what strange basis he lives with his own stories.

4   I had been writing a number of stories, more or less one after the other, before it belatedly dawned on me that some of the characters in one story were, and had been all the time, the same characters who had appeared already in another story. Only I'd written about them originally under different names, at different periods in their lives, in situations not yet interlocking but ready for it. They touched on every side. These stories were all related (and the fact was buried in their inceptions) by the strongest ties—identities, kinships, relationships, or affinities already known or remembered or foreshadowed. From story to story, connections between the characters' lives, through their motives or actions,

sometimes their dreams, already existed: there to be found. Now the whole assembly—some of it still in the future—fell, by stages, into place in one location already evoked, which I saw now was a focusing point for all the stories. What had drawn the characters together there was one strong strand in them all: they lived one way or another in a dream or in romantic aspiration, or under an illusion of what their lives were coming to, about the meaning of their (now) related lives.

The stories were connected most provocatively of all to me, per-   5
haps, through the entry into my story-telling mind of another sort of tie—a shadowing of Greek mythological figures, gods and heroes that wander in various guises, at various times, in and out, emblems of the characters' heady dreams.

Writing these stories, which eventually appeared joined together   6
in the book called *The Golden Apples*, was an experience in a writer's own discovery of affinities. In writing, as in life, the connections of all sorts of relationships and kinds lie in wait of discovery, and give out their signals to the Geiger counter of the charged imagination, once it is drawn into the right field.

The characters who go to make up my stories and novels are not   7
portraits. Characters I invent along with the story that carries them. Attached to them are what I've borrowed, perhaps unconsciously, bit by bit, of persons I have seen or noticed or remembered in the flesh—a cast of countenance here, a manner of walking here, that jump to the visualizing mind when a story is underway. (Elizabeth Bowen said, "Physical detail cannot be invented." It can only be chosen.) I don't write by invasion into the life of a real person: my own sense of privacy is too strong for that; and I also know instinctively that living people to whom you are close—those known to you in ways too deep, too overflowing, ever to be plumbed outside love—do not yield to, could never fit into, the demands of a story. On the other hand, what I do make my stories out of is the *whole* fund of my feelings, my responses to the real experiences of my own life, to the relationships that formed and changed it, that I have given most of myself to, and so learned my way toward a dramatic counterpart. Characters take on life sometimes by luck, but I suspect it is when you can write most entirely out of yourself, inside the skin, heart, mind, and soul of a person who is not yourself, that a character becomes in his own right another human being on the page.

It was not my intention—it never was—to invent a character who   8
should speak for me, the author, in person. A character is in a story to fill a role there, and the character's life along with its expression of life is defined by that surrounding—indeed is created by his own story. Yet, it seems to me now, years after I wrote *The Golden Apples*, that I did bring forth a character with whom I came to feel oddly in touch.

This is Miss Eckhart, a woman who has come from away to give piano lessons to the young of Morgana. She is formidable and eccentric in the eyes of everyone, is scarcely accepted in the town. But she persisted with me, as she persisted in spite of herself with the other characters in the stories.

9   Where did the character of Miss Eckhart come from? There was my own real-life piano teacher, "eligible" to the extent that she swatted my hands at the keyboard with a fly-swatter if I made a mistake; and when she wrote: "Practice" on my page of sheet music she made her "P" as Miss Eckhart did—a cat's face with a long tail. She did indeed hold a recital of her pupils every June that was a fair model for Miss Eckhart's, and of many another as well, I suppose. But the character of Miss Eckhart was miles away from that of the teacher I knew as a child, or from that of anybody I did know. Nor was she like other teacher-characters I was responsible for: my stories and novels suddenly appear to me to be full of teachers, with Miss Eckhart different from them all.

10   What the story "June Recital" most acutely shows the reader lies in her inner life. I haven't the slightest idea what my real teacher's life was like inside. But I knew what Miss Eckhart's was, for it protruded itself well enough into the story.

11   As I looked longer and longer for the origins of this passionate and strange character, at last I realized that Miss Eckhart came from me. There wasn't any resemblance in her outward identity: I am not musical, not a teacher, nor foreign in birth; not humorless or ridiculed or missing out in love; nor have I yet let the world around me slip from my recognition. But none of that counts. What counts is only what lies at the solitary core. She derived from what I already knew for myself, even felt I had always known. What I have put into her is my passion for my own life work, my own art. Exposing yourself to risk is a truth Miss Eckhart and I had in common. What animates and possesses me is what drives Miss Eckhart, the love of her art and the love of giving it, the desire to give it until there is no more left. Even in the small and literal way, what I had done in assembling and connecting all the stories in *The Golden Apples*, and bringing them off as one, was not too unlike the June recital itself.

12   Not in Miss Eckhart as she stands solidly and almost opaquely in the surround of her story, but in the making of her character out of my most inward and most deeply feeling self, I would say I have found my voice in fiction.

13   Of course any writer is in part all of his characters. How otherwise would they be known to him, occur to him, become what they are? I was also part Cassie in that same story, the girl who hung back,

and indeed part of most of the main characters in the connected stories into whose minds I go. Except for Virgie, the heroine. She is right
outside me. She is powerfully like Miss Eckhart, her co-equal in stubborn and passionate feeling, while more expressive of it—but fully
apart from me. And as Miss Eckhart's powers shrink and fade away,
the young Virgie grows up more rampant, and struggles into some sort
of life independent from all the rest.

    If somewhere in its course your work seems to you to have come   14
into a life of its own, and you can stand back from it and leave it be,
you are looking then at your subject—so I feel. This is how I came to
regard the character of Virgie in *The Golden Apples*. She comes into her
own in the last of the stories, "The Wanderers." Passionate, recalcitrant,
stubbornly undefeated by failure or hurt or disgrace or bereavement,
all the while heedlessly wasting of her gifts, she knows to the last that
there is a world that remains out there, a world living and mysterious,
and that she is of it.

    Inasmuch as Miss Eckhart might have been said to come from   15
me, the author, Virgie, at her moments, might have always been my
subject.

    Through learning at my later date things I hadn't known, or had   16
escaped or possibly feared realizing, about my parents—and myself—I
glimpse our whole family life as if it were freed of that clock time
which spaces us apart so inhibitingly, divides young and old, keeps
our living through the same experiences at separate distances.

    It is our inward journey that leads us through time—forward or   17
back, seldom in a straight line, most often spiraling. Each of us is
moving, changing, with respect to others. As we discover, we
remember, remembering, we discover; and most intensely do we
experience this when our separate journeys converge. Our living
experience at those meeting points is one of the charged dramatic
fields of fiction.

    I'm prepared now to use the wonderful word *confluence*, which   18
of itself exists as a reality and a symbol in one. It is the only kind of
symbol that for me as a writer has any weight, testifying to the pattern,
one of the chief patterns, of human experience.

    Here I am leading to the last scenes of my novel, *The Optimist's*   19
Daughter:

> She had slept in the chair, like a passenger who had come on
> an emergency journey in a train. But she had rested deeply.
>   She had dreamed that she *was* a passenger, and riding with
> Phil. They had ridden together over a long bridge.
>   Awake, she recognized it: it was a dream of something that
> had really happened. When she and Phil were coming down

from Chicago to Mount Salus to be married in the Presbyterian Church, they came on the train. Laurel, when she travelled back and forth between Mount Salus and Chicago, had always taken the sleeper. She and Phil followed the route on the day train, and she saw it for the first time.

When they were climbing the long approach to a bridge after leaving Cairo, rising slowly higher until they rode above the tops of bare trees, she looked down and saw the pale light widening and the river bottoms opening out, and then the water appearing, reflecting the low, early sun. There were two rivers. Here was where they came together. This was the confluence of the waters, the Ohio and the Mississippi.

They were looking down from a great elevation and all they saw was at the point of coming together, the bare trees marching in from the horizon, the rivers moving into one, and as he touched her arm she looked up with him and saw the long, ragged, pencil-faint line of birds within the crystal of the zenith, flying in a V of their own, following the same course down. All they could see was sky, water, birds, light, and confluence. It was the whole morning world.

And they themselves were a part of the confluence. Their own joint act of faith had brought them here at the very moment and matched its occurrence, and proceeded as it proceeded. Direction itself was made beautiful, momentous. They were riding as one with it, right up front. It's our turn! she'd thought exultantly. And we're going to live forever.

Left bodiless and graveless of a death made of water and fire in a year long gone, Phil could still tell her of her life. For her life, any life, she had to believe, was nothing but the continuity of its love.

She believed it just as she believed that confluence of the waters was still happening at Cairo. It would be there the same as it ever was when she went flying over it today on her way back—out of sight, for her, this time, thousands of feet below, but with nothing in between except thin air.

20   Of course the greatest confluence of all is that which makes up the human memory—the individual human memory. My own is the treasure most dearly regarded by me, in my life and in my work as a writer. Here time, also, is subject to confluence. The memory is a living thing—it too is in transit. But during its moment, all that is remembered joins, and lives—the old and the young, the past and the present, the living and the dead.

As you have seen, I am a writer who came of a sheltered life. A   21
sheltered life can be a daring life as well. For all serious daring starts
from within.

QUESTIONS TO CONSIDER

1. Welty believes that "to the memory nothing is ever really lost" and
that writing is one way to remember and to give shape to distant
memories. Do you agree, or do you think that you have truly forgotten some things?

2. Welty also believes that she has made discoveries "in the course of
writing." How can writing help you remember the past and at the
same time help you discover new meaning?

3. Welty states that discoveries always "begin with the particular, never
the general." How can specific details (the particular) lead to more
general insights and applications?

4. According to Welty, her stories reflect her "responses to the real
experiences" of her own life. Miss Eckhart, a character in "The
Golden Apples," seems to be the one she identifies with most
strongly. Explore the connection Welty makes between herself as
author and her character, Miss Eckhart. How are the two alike and
how are they different? Do writers always write about their own
experiences? What other sources do writers use?

5. What does the word *confluence* mean? Why does Welty like it?
What image does she use to illustrate it? According to Welty, how
does the idea of confluence explain human memory?

6. Reread Welty's final sentence, which is also the last sentence of the
book from which this selection is taken. What do you think she
means by "serious daring," and why does it always start from
within?

WRITING ACTIVITIES

Individual: Select a sentence or phrase from this selection that interests or intrigues you in some way, and write a response to it in your
journal.

Collaborative: With a group of your classmates, think of three ways in which a student can use writing as a memory prompt.

Computer: Think of an incident that you barely remember, and begin to freewrite about it on your computer screen. Initially, darken the screen so that you cannot see what you are writing. After writing "in the dark" for five minutes or longer, turn the contrast up so that what you are writing will be visible on your screen, and write another five minutes. Did writing about the incident from your past help you to remember it? Did writing on the dark screen help or hinder this process?

A WRITER'S DIARY

Virginia Woolf

*The English novelist and essayist Virginia Woolf pro-
duced volumes of diaries during her lifetime. She
filled her diaries not only with glimpses of her daily
life, but also with musings and observations about
herself as a writer—how she wrote, what she had
already written, what she planned to write. Clearly,
Woolf used her diaries to explore as well as record
ideas. In one entry, written on March 9, 1920, she
imagined herself reading her own diaries years later:*

*In spite of some tremors I think I shall go on with this diary for
the present. . . . I fancy old Virginia, putting on her spectacles to
read of March 1920, will decidedly wish me to continue.*

*The excerpts here from Woolf's diary were written over a period of two
years, from 1928 to 1930, during which time she thought about and
then wrote a novel that she initially called* The Moths *but later changed
to* The Waves. *As you read, notice how the novel takes shape in her
mind and then gradually becomes a written text.*

Saturday, August 12th, 1928

1   Shall I now continue this soliloquy, or shall I imagine an audience,
which will make me describe? This sentence is due to the book on
fiction which I am now writing—once more, O once more. It is a
hand to mouth book. I scribble down whatever I can think of about
Romance, Dickens etc. must hastily gorge on Jane Austen tonight and

dish up something tomorrow. All this criticism however may well be dislodged by the desire to write a story. *The Moths* hovers somewhere at the back of my brain. But Clive yesterday at Charleston said that there were no class distinctions. We had tea from bright blue cups under the pink light of the giant hollyhock. We were all a little drugged with the country; a little bucolic I thought. It was lovely enough—made me envious of its country peace; the trees all standing securely—why did my eye catch the trees? The look of things has a great power over me. Even now, I have to watch the rooks beating up against the wind, which is high, and still I say to myself instinctively "What's the phrase for that?" and try to make more and more vivid the roughness of the air current and the tremor of the rook's wing slicing as if the air were full of ridges and ripples and roughnesses. They rise and sink, up and down, as if the exercise rubbed and braced them like swimmer's in rough water. But what a little I can get down into my pen of what is so vivid to my eyes, and not only to my eyes; also to some nervous fibre, or fanlike membrane in my species.

Wednesday, November 28th, 1928

As for my next book, I am going to hold myself from writing till I have   2 it impending in me: grown heavy in my mind like a ripe pear; pendant, gravid, asking to be cut or it will fall. *The Moths* still haunts me, coming, as they always do, unbidden, between tea and dinner, while L. plays the gramophone. I shape a page or two; and make myself stop. Indeed I am up against some difficulties. Fame to begin with. *Orlando* has done very well. Now I could go on writing like that—the tug and suck are at me to do it. People say this was so spontaneous, so natural. And I would like to keep those qualities if I could without losing the others. But those qualities were largely the result of ignoring the others. They came of writing exteriorly; and if I dig, must I not lose them? And what is my own position towards the inner and the outer? I think a kind of ease and dash are good—yes: I think even externality is good; some combination of them ought to be possible. The idea has come to me that what I want now to do is to saturate every atom. I mean to eliminate all waste, deadness, superfluity: to give the moment whole; whatever it includes. Say that the moment is a combination of thought; sensation; the voice of the sea. Waste, deadness, come from the inclusion of things that don't belong to the moment; this appalling narrative business of the realist: getting on from lunch to dinner: it is false, unreal, merely conventional. Why admit anything to literature that is not poetry—by which I mean saturated?

Is that not my grudge against novelists? that they select nothing? The poets succeeding by simplifying: practically everything is left out. I want to put practically everything in: yet to saturate. That is what I want to do in *The Moths.*

Thursday, March 28th, 1929

3   Perhaps I ought not to go on repeating what I have always said about the spring. One ought perhaps to be forever finding new things to say, since life draws on. One ought to invent a fine narrative style. Certainly there are many new ideas always forming in my head. For one, that I am going to enter a nunnery these next months; and let myself down into my mind; Bloomsbury being done with. I am going to face certain things. It is going to be a time of adventure and attack, rather lonely and painful I think. But solitude will be good for a new book. Of course, I shall make friends. I shall be external outwardly. I shall buy some good clothes and go out into new houses. All the time I shall attack this angular shape in my mind. I think *The Moths* (if that is what I shall call it) will be very sharply cornered. I am not satisfied though with the frame. There is this sudden fertility which may be mere fluency. In old days books were so many sentences absolutely struck with an axe out of crystal: and now my mind is so impatient, so quick, in some ways so desperate.

Tuesday, May 28th, 1929

4   Now about this book, *The Moths.* How am I to begin it? And what is it to be? I feel no great impulse; no fever; only a great pressure of difficulty. Why write it then? Why write at all? Every morning I write a little sketch, to amuse myself. I am not saying, I might say, that these sketches have any relevance. I am not trying to tell a story. Yet perhaps it might be done in that way. A mind thinking. They might be islands of light—islands in the stream that I am trying to convey; life itself going on. The current of the moths flying strongly this way. A lamp and a flower pot in the centre. The flower can always be changing. But there must be more unity between each scene than I can find at present. Autobiography it might be called. How am I to make one lap, or act, between the coming of the moths, more intense than another; if there are only scenes? One must get the sense that this is the beginning; this the middle; that the climax—when she opens the window and the moth comes in. I shall have the two different currents—the moths flying along; the flower upright in the centre; a perpetual crumbling and renewing of the plant. In its leaves she might see things happen. But who is she? I am very anxious that she should have

no name. I don't want a Lavinia or a Penelope; I want "she." But that becomes arty, Liberty greenery yallery somehow: symbolic in loose robes. Of course I can make her think backwards and forwards; I can tell stories. But that's not it. Also I shall do away with exact place and time. Anything may be out of the window—a ship—a desert—London.

Sunday, June 23rd, 1929

However, I now begin to see *The Moths* rather too clearly, or at least 5 strenuously, for my comfort. I think it will begin like this: dawn; the shells on a beach; I don't know—voices of cock and nightingale; and then all the children at a long table—lessons. The beginning. Well, all sorts of characters are to be there. Then the person who is at the table can call out anyone of them at any moment; and build up by that person the mood, tell a story; for instance about dogs or nurses; or some adventure of a child's kind; all to be very Arabian Nights; and so on: this shall be childhood; but it must not be *my* childhood; and boats on the pond; the sense of children, unreality; things oddly proportioned. Then another person or figure must be selected. The unreal world must be round all this—the phantom waves. The Moth must come in; the beautiful single moth. Could one not get the waves to be heard all through? Or the farmyard noises? Some odd irrelevant noises. She might have a book—one book to read—another to write in—old letters. Early morning light—but this need not be insisted on; because there must be great freedom from "reality." Yet everything must have relevance.

Wednesday, September 25th, 1929

Yesterday morning I made another start on *The Moths*, but that won't 6 be its title; and several problems cry out at once to be solved. Who thinks it? And am I outside the thinker? One wants some device which is not a trick.

Friday, October 11th, 1929

And I snatch at the idea of writing here in order not to write *Waves* or 7 *Moths* or whatever it is to be called. One thinks one has learnt to write quickly; and one hasn't. And what is odd, I'm not writing with gusto or pleasure: because of the concentration. I am not reeling it off; but sticking it down. Also, never, in my life, did I attack such a vague yet elaborate design; whenever I make a mark I have to think of its relation to a dozen others. And though I could go on ahead easily enough, I am always stopping to consider the whole effect. In particular is there some radical fault in my scheme? I am not quite satisfied with this method of picking out things in the room and being reminded by them of other things. Yet I can't at the moment divine anything which keeps so close to the original design and admits of movement. Hence, perhaps, these October days are to me a little strained and surrounded with silence.

Saturday, November 30th, 1929

8   I fill in this page, nefariously; at the end of a morning's work. I have begun the second part of *Waves*—I don't know. I don't know. I feel that I am only accumulating notes for a book—whether I shall ever face the labour of writing it, God knows. From some higher station I may be able to pull it together—at Rodmell, in my new room. Reading the *Lighthouse* does not make it easier to write . . .

Sunday, January 12th, 1930

9   Sunday it is. And I have just exclaimed: "And now I can think of nothing else." Thanks to my pertinacity and industry, I can now hardly stop making up *The Waves*. The sense of this came acutely about a week ago on beginning to write the *Phantom Party*: now I feel that I can rush on, after 6 months' hacking, and finish: but without the least certainty how it's to achieve any form. Much will have to be discarded: what is essential is to write fast and not break the mood—no holiday, no interval if possible, till it is done. Then rest. Then re-write.

Wednesday, April 23rd, 1930

10   This is a very important morning in the history of *The Waves*, because I think I have turned the corner and see the last lap straight ahead. I think I have got Bernard into the final stride. He will go straight on now, and then stand at the door: and then there will be a last picture of the waves. We are at Rodmell and I daresay I shall stay on a day or two (if I dare) so as not to break the current and finish it. O Lord and then a rest; and then an article; and then back again to this hideous shaping and moulding. There may be some joys in it all the same.

Tuesday, April 29th, 1930

11   And I have just finished, with this very nib-ful of ink, the last sentence of *The Waves*. I think I should record this for my own information. Yes, it was the greatest stretch of mind I ever knew; certainly the last pages; I don't think they flop as much as usual. And I think I have kept starkly and ascetically to the plan. So much I will say in self-congratulation.

But I have never written a book so full of holes and patches; that will need re-building, yes, not only re-modelling. I suspect the structure is wrong. Never mind. I might have done something easy and fluent; and this is a reach after that vision I had, the unhappy summer—or three weeks—at Rodmell, after finishing the *Lighthouse.*

P.M.   And I think to myself as I walk down Southampton Row, "And I have given you a new book."

QUESTIONS TO CONSIDER ◀

1. In the first entry, Woolf mentions that a new novel (*The Moths*) "hovers somewhere in the back of [her] brain." How many months does Woolf spend thinking about the novel before she actually begins to write? How does her construction of her mental text prepare her for the construction of the written text?

2. Woolf seems to construct her text by focusing first on different images rather than characters and plot. What are the dominant images that shape her mental text?

3. What role does Woolf's diary seem to assume in the construction of this novel?

4. Woolf was in her late forties and an experienced writer when she wrote these entries in her diary. How does Woolf's journal reflect her maturity and experience as a writer?

WRITING ACTIVITIES ◀

Individual: Select an idea from Woolf's diary that surprises you or contradicts your impression of how novelists write. In a journal entry, identify the idea you selected, and explain why the idea surprises you.

Collaborative: Outline a schedule that reflects the construction of Woolf's novel (i.e., When did she begin it? How much time did she spend thinking about it, writing it, and rewriting it?).

Computer: Freewrite on screen about how you think using a computer would have changed Woolf's writing process.

ON KEEPING A NOTEBOOK

Joan Didion

Joan Didion, a well-known novelist and screenwriter, is best known for her nonfiction writing. Her introspective, subjective essays about herself as well as her more objective, informative accounts of current events and modern life are thoughtful, perceptive, and above all detailed. In this frequently anthologized selection, Didion explains why she keeps a notebook, or journal, and the role it plays in her life as a writer. As you read, compare her reasons for keeping a journal with those revealed by the other journal writers included in this chapter.

1   " 'That woman Estelle,' " the note reads, " 'is partly the reason why George Sharp and I are separated today.' *Dirty crepe-de-Chine wrapper, hotel bar, Wilmington RR, 9:45 a.m. August Monday Morning.*"

2   Since the note is in my notebook, it presumably has some meaning to me. I study it for a long while. At first I have only the most general notion of what I was doing on an August Monday morning in the bar of the hotel across from the Pennsylvania Railroad station in Wilmington, Delaware (waiting for a train? missing one? 1960? 1961? why Wilmington?), but I do remember being there. The woman in the dirty crepe-de-Chine wrapper had come down from her room for a beer, and the bartender had heard before the reason why George Sharp and she were separated today. "Sure," he said, and went on mopping the floor. "You told me." At the other end of the bar is a girl. She is talking, pointedly, not to the man beside her but to a cat lying in the triangle of sunlight cast through the open door. She is wearing a plaid silk dress from Peck & Peck, and the hem is coming down.

3   Here is what it is: The girl has been on the Eastern Shore, and now she is going back to the city, leaving the man beside her, and all she can see ahead are the viscous summer sidewalks and the 3 A.M. long-distance calls that will make her lie awake and then sleep drugged through all the steaming mornings left in August (1960? 1961?). Because she must go directly from the train to lunch in New York, she wished that she had a safety pin for the hem of the plaid silk dress, and she also wishes that she could forget about the hem and the lunch and stay in the cool bar that smells of disinfectant and malt and

make friends with the woman in the crepe-de-Chine wrapper. She is afflicted by a little self-pity, and she wants to compare Estelles. That is what that was all about.

Why did I write it down? In order to remember, of course, but exactly what was it I wanted to remember? How much of it actually happened? Did any of it? Why do I keep a notebook at all? It is easy to deceive oneself on all those scores. The impulse to write things down is a peculiarly compulsive one, inexplicable to those who do not share it, useful only accidentally, only secondarily, in the way that any compulsion tries to justify itself. I suppose that it begins or does not begin in the cradle. Although I have felt compelled to write things down since I was five years old, I doubt that my daughter ever will, for she is a singularly blessed and accepting child, delighted with life exactly as life presents itself to her, unafraid to go to sleep and unafraid to wake up. Keepers of private notebooks are a different breed altogether, lonely and resistant rearrangers of things, anxious malcontents, children afflicted apparently at birth with some presentiment of loss.

My first notebook was a Big Five tablet, given to me by my mother with the sensible suggestion that I stop whining and learn to amuse myself by writing down my thoughts. She returned the tablet to me a few years ago; the first entry is an account of a woman who believed herself to be freezing to death in the Arctic night, only to find, when day broke, that she had stumbled onto the Sahara Desert, where she would die of the heat before lunch. I have no idea what turn of a five-year-old's mind could have prompted so insistently "ironic" and exotic a story, but it does reveal a certain predilection for the extreme which has dogged me into adult life; perhaps if I were analytically inclined I would find it a truer story than any I might have told about Donald Johnson's birthday party or the day my cousin Brenda put Kitty Litter in the aquarium.

So the point of my keeping a notebook has never been, nor is it now, to have an accurate factual record of what I have been doing or thinking. That would be a different impulse entirely, an instinct for reality which I sometimes envy but do not possess. At no point have I ever been able successfully to keep a diary; my approach to daily life ranges from the grossly negligent to the merely absent, and on those few occasions when I have tried dutifully to record a day's events, boredom has so overcome me that the results are mysterious at best. What is this business about "shopping, typing piece, dinner with E, depressed"? Shopping for what? Typing what piece? Who is E? Was this "E" depressed, or was I depressed? Who cares?

4

5

6

7   In fact I have abandoned altogether that kind of pointless entry; instead I tell what some would call lies. "That's simply not true," the members of my family frequently tell me when they come up against my memory of a shared event. "The party was *not* for you, the spider was *not* a black widow, *it wasn't that way at all.*" Very likely they are right, for not only have I always had trouble distinguishing between what happened and what merely might have happened, but I remain unconvinced that the distinction, for my purposes, matters. The cracked crab that I recall having for lunch the day my father came home from Detroit in 1945 must certainly be embroidery, worked into the day's pattern to lend verisimilitude; I was ten years old and would not now remember the cracked crab. The day's events did not turn on cracked crab. And yet it is precisely that fictitious crab that makes me see the afternoon all over again, a home movie run all too often, the father bearing gifts, the child weeping, an exercise in family love and guilt. Or that is what it was to me. Similarly, perhaps it never did snow that August in Vermont; perhaps there never were flurries in the night wind, and maybe no one else felt the ground hardening and summer already dead even as we pretended to bask in it; but that was how it felt to me, and it might as well have snowed, could have snowed, did snow.

8   *How it felt to me:* that is getting closer to the truth about a notebook. I sometimes delude myself about why I keep a notebook, imagine that some thrifty virtue derives from preserving everything observed. See enough and write it down, I tell myself, and then some morning when the world seems drained of wonder, some day when I am only going through the motions of doing what I am supposed to do, which is write—on that bankrupt morning I will simply open my notebook and there it will all be, a forgotten account with accumulated interest, paid passage back to the world out there: dialogue overheard in hotels and elevators and at the hatcheck counter in Pavillon (one middle-aged man shows his hat check to another and says, "That's my old football number"); impressions of Bettina Aptheker and Benjamin Sonnenberg and Teddy ("Mr. Acapulco") Stauffer; careful *aperçus* about tennis bums and failed fashion models and Greek shipping heiresses, one of whom taught me a significant lesson (a lesson I could have learned from F. Scott Fitzgerald, but perhaps we all must meet the very rich for ourselves) by asking, when I arrived to interview her in her orchid-filled sitting room on the second day of a paralyzing New York blizzard, whether it was snowing outside.

9   I imagine, in other words, that the notebook is about other people. But of course it is not. I have no real business with what one

stranger said to another at the hatcheck counter in Pavillon; in fact I suspect that the line "That's my old football number" touched not my own imagination at all, but merely some memory of something once read, probably "The Eighty-Yard Run." Nor is my concern with a woman in a dirty crepe-de-Chine wrapper in a Wilmington bar. My stake is always, of course, in the unmentioned girl in the plaid silk dress. *Remember what it was to be me:* that is always the point.

It is a difficult point to admit. We are brought up in the ethic 10 that others, any others, are by definition more interesting than ourselves; taught to be diffident, just this side of self-effacing. ("You're the least important person in the room and don't forget it," Jessica Mitford's governess would hiss in her ear on the advent of any social occasion; I copied that into my notebook because it is only recently that I have been able to enter a room without hearing some such phrase in my inner ear.) Only the very young and the very old may recount their dreams at breakfast, dwell upon self, interrupt with memories of beach picnics and favorite Liberty lawn dresses and the rainbow trout in a creek near Colorado Springs. The rest of us are expected, rightly, to affect absorption in other people's favorite dresses, other people's trout.

And so we do. But our notebooks give us away, for however 11 dutifully we record what we see around us, the common denominator of all we see is always, transparently, shamelessly, the implacable "I." We are not talking here about the kind of notebook that is patently for public consumption, a structural conceit for binding together a series of graceful *pensées*; we are talking about something private, about bits of the mind's string too short to use, an indiscriminate and erratic assemblage with meaning only for its maker.

And sometimes even the maker has difficulty with the meaning. 12 There does not seem to be, for example, any point in my knowing for the rest of my life that, during 1964, 720 tons of soot fell on every square mile of New York City, yet there it is in my notebook, labeled "FACT." Nor do I really need to remember that Ambrose Bierce liked to spell Leland Stanford's name "£eland $tanford" or that "smart women almost always wear black in Cuba," a fashion hint without much potential for practical application. And does not the relevance of these notes seem marginal at best?:

In the basement museum of the Inyo County Courthouse in Independence, California, sign pinned to a mandarin coat: "This MANDARIN COAT was often worn by Mrs. Minnie S. Brooks when giving lectures on her TEAPOT COLLECTION."

Redhead getting out of car in front of Beverly Wilshire Hotel, chinchilla stole, Vuitton bags with tags reading:

MRS LOU FOX

HOTEL SAHARA

VEGAS

13   Well, perhaps not entirely marginal. As a matter of fact, Mrs. Minnie S. Brooks and her MANDARIN COAT pull me back into my own childhood, for although I never knew Mrs. Brooks and did not visit Inyo County until I was thirty, I grew up in just such a world, in houses cluttered with Indian relics and bits of gold ore and ambergris and the souvenirs my Aunt Mercy Farnsworth brought back from the Orient. It is a long way from that world to Mrs. Lou Fox's world, where we all live now, and is it not just as well to remember that? Might not Mrs. Minnie S. Brooks help me to remember what I am? Might not Mrs. Lou Fox help me to remember what I am not?

14   But sometimes the point is harder to discern. What exactly did I have in mind when I noted down that it cost the father of someone I know $650 a month to light the place on the Hudson in which he lived before the Crash? What use was I planning to make of this line by Jimmy Hoffa: "I may have my faults, but being wrong ain't one of them"? And although I think it interesting to know where the girls who travel with the Syndicate have their hair done when they find themselves on the West coast, will I ever make suitable use of it? Might I not be better off just passing it on to John O'Hara? What is a recipe for sauerkraut doing in my notebook? What kind of magpie keeps this notebook? *He was born the night the Titanic went down.* That seems a nice enough line, and I even recall who said it, but is it not really a better line in life than it could ever be in fiction?

15   But of course that is exactly it: not that I should ever use the line, but that I should remember that woman who said it and the afternoon I heard it. We were on her terrace by the sea, and we were finishing the wine left from lunch, trying to get what sun there was, a California winter sun. The woman whose husband was born the night the *Titanic* went down wanted to rent her house, wanted to go back to her children in Paris. I remember wishing that I could afford the house, which cost $1,000 a month. "Someday you will," she said lazily, "Someday it all comes." There in the sun on her terrace it seemed easy to believe in someday, but later I had a low-grade afternoon hangover and ran over a black snake on the way to the supermarket and was flooded with inexplicable fear when I heard the checkout clerk

explaining to the man ahead of me why she was finally divorcing her husband. "He left me with no choice," she said over and over as she punched the register. "He has a little seven-month-old baby by her, he left me no choice." I would like to believe that my dread then was for the human condition, but of course it was for me, because I wanted a baby and did not then have one and because I wanted to own the house that cost $1,000 a month to rent and because I had a hangover.

It all comes back. Perhaps it is difficult to see the value in having 16
one's self back in that kind of mood, but I do see it; I think we are well advised to keep on nodding terms with the people we used to be whether we find them attractive company or not. Otherwise they turn up unannounced and surprise us, come hammering on the mind's door at 4 A.M. of a bad night and demand to know who deserted them, who betrayed them, who is going to make amends. We forget all too soon the things we thought we could never forget. We forget the loves and the betrayals alike, forget what we whispered and what we screamed, forget who we were. I have already lost touch with a couple of people I used to be; one of them, a seventeen-year-old, presents little threat, although it would be of some interest to me to know again what it feels like to sit on a river levee drinking vodka-and-orange-juice and listening to Les Paul and Mary Ford and their echoes sing "How High the Moon" on the car radio. (You see I still have the scenes, but I no longer perceive myself among those present, no longer could even improvise the dialogue.) The other one, a twenty-three-year-old, bothers me more. She was always a good deal of trouble, and I suspect she will reappear when I least want to see her, skirts too long, shy to the point of aggravation, always the injured party, full of recriminations and little hurts and stories I do not want to hear again, at once saddening me and angering me with her vulnerability and ignorance, an apparition all the more insistent for being so long banished.

It is a good idea, then, to keep in touch, and I suppose that 17
keeping in touch is what notebooks are all about. And we are all on our own when it comes to keeping those lines open to ourselves: your notebook will never help me, nor mine you. *"So what's new in the whiskey business?"* What could that possibly mean to you? To me it means a blonde in a Pucci bathing suit sitting with a couple of fat men by the pool at the Beverly Hills Hotel. Another man approaches, and they all regard one another in silence for a while. "So what's new in the whiskey business?" one of the fat men finally says by way of welcome, and the blonde stands up, arches one foot and dips it in the pool, looking all the while at the cabaña where Baby Pignatari is talking on the telephone. That is all there is to that, except that several years later I saw the blonde coming out of Saks Fifth Avenue in New

York with her California complexion and a voluminous mink coat. In the harsh wind that day she looked old and irrevocably tired to me, and even the skins in the mink coat were not worked the way they were doing them that year, not the way she would have wanted them done, and there is the point of the story. For a while after that I did not like to look in the mirror, and my eyes would skim the newspapers and pick out only the deaths, the cancer victims, the premature coronaries, the suicides, and I stopped riding the Lexington Avenue IRT because I noticed for the first time that all the strangers I had seen for years—the man with the seeing-eye dog, the spinster who read the classified pages every day, the fat girl who always got off with me at Grand Central—looked older than they once had.

18   It all comes back. Even that recipe for sauerkraut: even that brings it back. I was on Fire Island when I first made that sauerkraut, and it was raining, and we drank a lot of bourbon and ate the sauerkraut and went to bed at ten, and I listened to the rain and the Atlantic and felt safe. I made the sauerkraut again last night and it did not make me feel any safer, but that is, as they say, another story.

1966

▶   QUESTIONS TO CONSIDER

1. Didion sets out in this essay to tell why she keeps a notebook (or, actually, a series of notebooks). But she does not begin her essay with a clear statement of the purpose of her notebooks; rather she explores her subject as she progresses, approaching it indirectly from several different angles as if she were discovering for herself just why she keeps a notebook and what she records in it. The result is an essay that illustrates what it means to explore a subject in writing. Unlike a well-organized essay that progresses logically from a stated thesis to supporting arguments, this essay seems to reflect the author's process of discovery. As a reader, how did you react to this exploratory essay? Was it difficult to read or understand? Or did you share the author's sense of discovery, gradually grasping her meaning as she struggled to find it herself?

2. Didion refers to her journal as a notebook and clearly distinguishes it from a diary. According to Didion, what is the main difference between the kind of notebook, or journal, she keeps and a diary? Would Didion classify the selections by Jim Whorton and Virginia Woolf as diaries or notebooks?

3. Didion begins her essay with a particular journal entry. From this initial consideration of a specific entry, she then continues until she has defined to her satisfaction why she keeps a notebook. Compare Didion's use of the particular in this essay to Eudora Welty's statement that discoveries always "begin with the particular, never the general."

4. Didion describes in vivid detail what she wrote in her journal on several different occasions and how she later used this material. From these specific examples, what do you learn about her writing process? How is her writing process like that of Woolf and Welty? How is it different?

5. Didion claims that her notebook entries were not intended for an audience other than herself, yet she has included them in an essay clearly intended for other readers. How do the notebook entries themselves differ from the essay? Would the entries make sense to a reader if they were not in the context of the essay?

WRITING ACTIVITIES ◀

Individual: Write a journal entry in which you respond to Didion's statement that her notebooks consist of "what some would call lies." Is it possible for anyone to be totally objective? Should a writer be concerned with facts or details?

Collaborative: Didion concludes that her notebooks are not an "accurate factual record" or even "how it felt to be me" but rather "what it was to be me." Discuss with a group of your classmates the differences between these definitions. Then experiment with a group journal entry that tries to capture "what it was to be you" on this particular day in class.

Collaborative: Compare the **style and voice** of Whorton, Welty, Woolf, and Didion. Then, working as a group, write an imaginary conversation that might have taken place among them on the subject of writing. Try to make each character's voice distinctive. When you have finished writing your conversation, assign the role of each character to a different member of your group, and read your conversation aloud to the other members of your class.

STYLE AND VOICE, PAGE 656

Computer: Compose a brief argument for or against the idea that in keeping a journal details are more important than facts. Then post your argument to your classroom network, or print a copy to share with classmates.

THE DIARIES OF LORD LUGARD

Frederick Lugard

From November 1889 to December 1890, Lord Lugard, an English adventurer, explorer, and big-game hunter, was employed by the Imperial British East Africa Company to command an expedition to Uganda. Lugard led a caravan that explored the routes in this region and established a series of stations. One of his responsibilities was to submit to the company regular reports and maps of the region he was exploring. Lord Lugard also kept detailed accounts of his experiences in East Africa in a series of diaries, which were published after his death. In the following excerpts from one of these diaries, he describes the adverse circumstances he endured as he was writing one of his routine reports. As you read, notice the pleasure that Lugard seems to take in his writing task, even though he is plagued by absolutely dreadful working conditions. If anyone ever had a good excuse for not writing, it was Lord Lugard.

1   . . . my left arm is now in a *very* bad state, a large purple lump has formed (*above* the wound strangely) and throbs and smarts dreadfully. It will burst if not lanced for it appears to be separate from the open channel thro' which a small amount of matter is daily discharged since I left England. The doctor wants to cut it open and extract dead bone. I declined, with thanks. I prefer nature to take her course to be[ing] experimented upon by young doctors, and the fact of the abscess being *above* the wound makes me think it *possible* that it arises from an inflammation of the sinews only, due to over-use, and exertion, and bad living, but I *think* there is dead bone. I have to wear it in a sling and it is of course quite useless, and very painful. So I should not be able to do much in the swimming line in case of an upset!

2   Now, however, I hope to sit tight here and work hard at the map and report. I have got into a spare room in a wooden house, but the situation is so exposed that it rocks with the constant hurricane, and I can rarely open door or window or everything is blown away, and the rain drives in. Consequently the ventilation is very bad, and the doctor says I am poisoning myself with Carbonic Acid gas!—which accounts for chippiness and headache.

3   I paid off the men who brought in my things. That scoundrel Matari, who up to the day we got here was so keen to redeem himself,

and whom I brought down partly on that account, finding his master
had gone into the interior declined to pay the ransom and claimed his
full pay. After all I have done for him, and understanding as he does
the whole question, it is 'base ingratitude.' However I did not feel justified in withholding the money, tho' it was only due to the fact that I
told his master he had agreed to pay the ransom that he was not
seized when down at the coast before. So he has more than stultified
me, and made me appear a liar to the Arabs. I almost regret now I did
not withhold the money, but I told him not to let me see his face again
unless he wanted me to go for him &c.!

My little cat gets on wonderfully, it is as savage as a tiger at feed-   4
ing time, and can't be touched. But at other times it is very affectionate
and licks my hand and knows me, . . . I 'correct' it pretty severely
(with my hand or a slipper) continually for it must learn obedience,
and *must fear* me. As it is, a guttural sound of disapproval from me
causes it to drop any mischief and scamper away, or prepare itself for
a fight if it will not part with its object. Then, after a good licking, it is
conquered and retires and a minute or two afterwards has clean forgotten all about it—quite unlike the dog tribe in this respect. No
amount of licking will cow it, and it will fight with teeth and claws a
long time before giving in, and forget immediately! I am very fond of
it indeed.

My skins are full of insects, and much spoilt. It is impossible to   5
get them thoroughly dried in this pouring rain, and I am afraid they
will not be worth anything by the time they get to England after all my
trouble. I gave Mackenzie a good slab of the rhino hide for a little
table. The big tortoise shell is a failure. All the pieces of 'tortoise' are
coming off in sections, and the shell is merely of bone. The horns and
heads are being macerated in water.

Hard at work at the map and report. Have completed the latter,   6
and sent it to be copied. The map is made under great difficulties. The
ink is thick, the light so bad I can hardly see, the house rocks with the
wind, and I am interrupted every moment—so much so that nearly all
of it has been done by lamp light at night. I have, however, a huge
drawing board, and a piece of tracing paper which takes in the whole
thing, and am making a nice bit of work of it, spite of difficulties. The
Sabaki and route run diagonally from one corner to the other. In the
large space left empty at the top right hand side, I have put three
square spaces about 12 inches by 14 inches each, for the three plans
of forts which I have made. That of Machakos I have put in, the other
two, one of Makongeni and one of the intermediate forts, I have not
time for nor have I the accurate measurements. Below there were
tables of notes on the country around the stockades, reasons for

selecting these points, structure of stockades &c. In the left bottom corner was the scale &c. and a long table of the bearings. I completed both the map (to this point) and the report by the return of the steamer on the [blank in diary].

▶ QUESTIONS TO CONSIDER

1. What are the conditions under which Lord Lugard is writing his report? Which of these conditions seem to you the most distracting?

2. What does Lugard's attitude toward these adverse conditions seem to be? How do they affect his writing task? What is his attitude toward the report and map that he is constructing? Does Lugard view this writing task as a chore, or does he seem to enjoy this work?

3. Who is the audience for Lugard's report? Do you think he imagines an audience for his diary? Support your answer with evidence from the entries.

4. How does Lugard's journal differ in purpose, content, and tone from those written by Whorton and Woolf?

▶ WRITING ACTIVITIES

Individual: Describe in a journal entry a time when you were distracted or discouraged from writing, and tell how you overcame this problem.

Collaborative: Discuss Lugard's attitude toward writing and how it differs from those of the other writers included in this chapter. Whorton and Woolf mention some distractions or difficulties that interfere with their writing. Make a list of these distractions, and identify those that seem to be legitimate reasons for procrastination as opposed to excuses.

Computer: Using your word-processing program, enter into a computer file a random list of things that distract you when you write. Then, using the block-and-move (or cut-and-paste) feature, create a brief outline in which you identify several categories (e.g., real reasons for not writing, legitimate distractions, fanciful distractions, mere excuses). Next, expand your outline into a brief essay on writing procrastination.

W RITING   TO   E XPLORE

Exploratory writing can be private—stuff you really don't want anyone else to read, at least not right now, but that you want to write down. Or it can be preliminary—writing that leads to other writing. For example, some people freewrite (that is, write quickly and freely) on a subject before they actually begin to compose what they want to say. Peter Elbow, a well-known writing teacher and theorist, believes that freewriting, or "free exploratory writing," as he calls it, is a powerful strategy for overcoming the fear of writing or inability to write that afflicts everyone at times. Elbow describes the process of freewriting in this way:

> Just write and keep writing. (Probably best to write on only one side of the paper in case you should want to cut parts out with scissors—but you probably won't.) Just write and keep writing. It will probably come in waves. After a flurry, stop and take a brief rest. But don't stop too long. Don't think about what you are writing or what you have written or else you will overload the circuit again. Keep writing as though you are drugged or drunk. Keep doing this till you feel you have a lot of material that might be useful; or, if necessary, till you can't stand it any more—even if you doubt that there's anything useful there.
>
> —*Embracing Contraries* (New York: Oxford, 1986), pp. 49–50.

Keeping a Journal

Although writing to explore can be completely spontaneous and unstructured, many people find that keeping a journal encourages them to write to explore in a more systematic, productive way. James Moffett, a well-known educator and writer, identifies five functions of a journal:

1. Notation (Taking down)

2. Recollection (Looking back)

3. Investigation (Looking into)

4. Imagination (Thinking up)

5. Cogitation (Thinking over and thinking through)

> —*Active Voices IV* (Upper Montclair, N.J.:Boynton/Cook, 1986), Table of Contents.

Thus, you can use a journal to freewrite, to explore new topics, to practice your writing, to reflect on your reading, to record your thoughts and feelings, to analyze your own writing behavior, or to take notes for reading and writing assignments. In Moffett's words, keeping a journal encourages you to take down, look back, look into, think up, or think over. If you collect your journal entries in a separate notebook or computer file, you will be able to keep up with what you write. A journal provides you with a record of your writing and reading experiences, becoming a text you may later enjoy reading for other purposes—to remember what it was like to be a student, to look up something that you have forgotten, to compare the writer you become to the one you used to be.

Because writing to explore is an important part of becoming an experienced writer and reader, we suggest that you keep two journals. In one journal, write about yourself as a writer; in the other, respond to the reading selections you read.

YOUR WRITING JOURNAL.   The primary purpose of this journal is to help you discover yourself as a writer. Entries will consist primarily of descriptions of your own writing process, analyses of your attitude toward writing and your perception of yourself as a writer, and notes for your writing assignments. You may also want to use this journal to experiment—to freewrite on different topics, to try out new styles, or to put into words half-formed thoughts and feelings. You may want to include in your journal your answers to the questions in the final section of each chapter (Discovering Yourself as a Writer). Your instructor may suggest other ways to use this journal and may want to read it from time to time.

YOUR READING JOURNAL.   The primary purpose of this journal is to help you become a more thoughtful reader, but it will serve other purposes as well. By encouraging you to review what you have read and to articulate your intellectual and emotional responses, this journal will help you become a stronger writer as well as a more effective reader. This journal will consist primarily of your responses to the individual writing activities that accompany each of the reading selections in this book. Sometimes you will be asked to react specifically to what you have read. At other times you will be directed to explore a related issue or to write about the topic of the reading selection from your own perspective. Your instructor may suggest other ways to use this journal and may want to read it, as well as your writing journal, from time to time.

You may often find yourself rereading the journals you keep in this course, especially if you use them to explore ideas and take notes on your reading and writing assignments.

Guidelines for Writing to Explore

When you write to explore, there are no rules. In fact, one of the cardinal guidelines of writing to explore is that anything goes. You don't have to worry about making errors or even making sense. You are writing to see what happens—what you know, remember, or think about a subject. Written explorations are musings, uncharted journeys, experiments and, as such, should not be structured or constrained. Your purpose is to write as freely as you can in order to discover as much as possible.

Don't be intimidated by the idea of writing without rules. Written explorations, like freewriting exercises, are not supposed to be perfect, as you can see from this chapter's reading selections. Three suggestions can help you write to explore more productively:

- Take risks.

- Be specific.

- More is better.

TAKE RISKS.   When you write to explore, don't play it safe. Forget the rules; experiment, surprise yourself. What is risk taking in writing to explore?

- Take the side of an argument with which you would normally disagree.

- Try out a new writing voice.

- Write about something you usually avoid thinking about.

- Assume multiple perspectives.

- Experiment with different sentence patterns and marks of punctuation.

- Write poetry instead of prose.

The whole idea of writing to explore is to see what happens. If you try to be careful and constrained, not much will happen. If you let yourself be adventurous and free, you may make some exciting discoveries about your subject or yourself as a writer.

BE SPECIFIC.   The most valuable part of what you write in a journal is not the big generalization ("My last essay was terrible!") but the small details ("My essay consisted of about fifteen different ideas stuck together in two impossibly long paragraphs."). Details feed readers' imaginations, allowing them to form images and reconstruct experiences. Details will also make you relive what you write about when you reread it years later. Collectively, details often lead you to discover a generalization that can evolve into a sound argument. On her first visit to Mexico, overcome by a new, exotic land, Anne Lindbergh wrote this in her diary:

> The best I can do is to piece together painstakingly the small superficial details, all—everything I can remember, everything no matter how little—and blindly hope that a miracle will happen, that this conglomerate, patched collection of fragments may ignite somehow—at least for me—and that some glimmering of the indescribable feeling may be relit in me.
>
> —*Bring Me a Unicorn*, p. 88.

If you write vaguely, leaving out the specific details, the entries may not make a lot of sense to you or anyone else when they are read later. At the time you are writing, you may know exactly what you mean when you say that something is great or dreadful, but later you will need the details. You won't be able to make much use of vague generalizations in the future. Settling for the general rather than the specific will not improve your present writing skills. Using specific details, on the other hand, will serve you well as both present writer and future reader. Whatever your subject, be as detailed as possible when you write to explore.

MORE IS BETTER.   Force yourself to go beyond your usual length limits, to write more than you initially think you can or normally do. First attempts at writing to explore can be obvious and trite, little more than conventional responses. When you force yourself to keep writing, however, you begin to produce ideas that go beyond the simple and superficial. So probe deeply into your subject by continuing to write even after you think you have emptied your mind of everything you have to say on the subject. The more you write and the more often you write, the more likely you are to learn about yourself, your subject, and your world.

W R I T I N G   A S S I G N M E N T

Journals are useful for writers on at least two different levels—for private explorations and as sources for public writing. Your writing assignment for this chapter focuses on the second of these. For this assignment, you are to use one or more of the entries you have written in your writing journal as the source of an essay. After reviewing the entries in your writing journal, you may discover a topic on your own. If not, the following suggestions may help you find a topic you want to explore.

1. Describe your best or worst experience with writing. This experience may have occurred in school or out, may pertain to something you were required to write or something you wrote because you wanted to, or may concern something you wrote recently or a long time ago.

2. Identify your goals as a writer. What level of literacy do you want to reach? What kinds of writing would you like to do? How do you plan to reach your writing goals?

3. Describe your attitude toward yourself as a writer, and analyze why you feel as you do.

4. Describe the person or experience that has influenced you most as a writer.

5. Analyze your own writing process by identifying the different stages or steps you normally go through in constructing a text. Which steps do you repeat? Which are productive and essential to your process? Which are counterproductive?

Generating Ideas through Invention and Research

If ideas for this assignment do not come readily to mind, try one or both of these suggestions.

INVENTION.   Quickly list as many different writing experiences as you can remember, beginning with the earliest (a Mother's Day card you labored over when you were six) and working toward the present (a senior term paper in your last high school English course or a letter of application for a job). Then review this list, thinking about which of these experiences were good and which were bad, how they shaped you as a writer, how they determined your writing goals, and so on.

RESEARCH.   To collect information about your early writing experiences, you may want to do some basic research. You could talk with someone (parent or grandparent, teacher, friend, etc.) who knew you as a child and remembers when you learned to read and write. Or you could reread something you wrote in the past—a poem, story, letter, or report that you constructed several years ago or when you were quite young. Your goal in this research project is to piece together your history as a writer—how you learned to write, who taught you to write, what sort of texts you constructed, and so on. Collect as much information as possible, and study it carefully before you begin to write.

Drafting Your Text

Once you have selected an experience or topic you want to write about, write as much as you can on the subject. Write quickly and steadily, not worrying about anything other than how much you can recall. Write until you have squeezed your memory dry on this subject. Even though you are now writing for an audience, you are still exploring your subject and may well make new discoveries as you continue to write.

Because you are still writing to explore, you will probably not have a definite thesis in mind initially. However, as you continue to write, you may discover a thesis, or at least a focus, for your essay.

Reading and Revising Your Text

After you have completed a draft of your essay, read what you have written, adding additional details as they occur to you. If you have written about a writing experience, try to picture in your mind the experience as it occurred. Have you captured the feelings that this experience evoked in you at the time that it occurred? How do you now feel about this experience? Has it in some way affected your attitude toward yourself as a writer? If you have identified your writing goals or analyzed your writing process, evaluate what you have written on the basis of its accuracy and completeness. Have you omitted something important?

Then reread your essay, this time looking for an idea that will serve as a thesis, or focus, for your essay. Exploratory essays often do not include explicit thesis statements but should have a clear focus. Revising a piece of private writing so that it communicates clearly to a public audience often involves this process of identifying a focus and reshaping the text so that the focus becomes clear to readers. Once you have identified the focus of your essay, you will need to reread it again, this time deleting irrelevant material. Although details are essential to good writing, you do not want to include details that are not clearly relevant to the focus you are now nurturing into existence.

Preparing the Final Draft of Your Text

Because this essay is based on journal entries, you may need to edit it carefully. When you are writing to explore, especially in your journal, you are not primarily concerned with usage and mechanics. However, in an essay, even an informal, exploratory essay, you must keep in mind your reader's reaction to what you have written. If your text includes obvious errors, your reader will be distracted.

Because this essay is based on writing that was initially private and personal, you may have difficulty viewing it objectively. Thus, you may want to ask someone else to read it at this stage, identifying for you errors you have failed to see.

DISCOVERING YOURSELF ◀
AS A WRITER

After you have completed this assignment, take a few minutes to reflect on this writing experience by answering the following questions:

1. What did you learn about yourself as a writer as you worked on this assignment? In what way did this writing experience change your perception of yourself as a writer, your process of writing, or your attitude toward writing?

2. What forms of research did you use for this assignment? What did you learn about research that will help you in other writing assignments?

3. Was the final draft of your text better or worse than you had expected? What would you do differently if you had the opportunity to do this assignment again?

4. How did writing this assignment make you a better reader?

5. What did you enjoy most about this writing assignment? What did you like least?

Front porch of the home of author Flannery O'Connor.
Glynne Robinson Betts/Photo Researchers.

3

▼

WRITING TO RECONSTRUCT EXPERIENCE

67

One writes out of one thing only—one's own experience.

JAMES BALDWIN

One of the oldest and most compelling reasons for writing is to reconstruct experiences in words. Long before they could write, people reconstructed their experiences in gestures and oral language, narrating stories about what they had done and describing what they had seen or how they felt.

NARRATION, PAGE 618

DESCRIPTION, PAGE 565

Although occasionally writers use one and not the other, **narration** and **description** nearly always occur in combination. Writers narrating stories often describe scenes or sounds or emotions. They may occasionally use description by itself—for example, in a poem or in an explanation of a mechanism—but it occurs most often with other types of discourse, especially narration.

You automatically use narration and description to weave the stories you tell, probably without conscious awareness of what you are doing rhetorically or linguistically. Telling stories is as natural as talking. That is, you don't think, "I'm going to tell a story now." You just tell it. Like any other familiar routine, you have internalized the patterns and conventions associated with storytelling.

Almost all discourse, both written and oral, is based to some extent on reconstructions of experience. From birth, you have been immersed in the stories family and friends tell, the stories you see on television and film, and the stories you read in books and magazines. In this chapter, you will read selections by writers who have reconstructed their experiences with celebrations, rituals, and rites of passage.

Why are stories so important to tell and listen to? To write and read? One reason is that stories—both those you create and those you read and hear—help you to understand your own experiences. Because stories, or narratives, are reconstructions of experience, they enable you to reflect upon your own experiences and thus to make some meaning of your life.

Reconstructions of experience take many different forms and serve both aesthetic and pragmatic purposes. Memoirs, personal experience essays, and autobiographies serve primarily aesthetic purposes; that is, they exist for their own sake much as a piece of sculpture or a musical composition does. Even more clearly aesthetic are novels, plays, short stories, and poems—many of which are also, at least indirectly, based on personal experience. In contrast, reconstructions of experience such as travelogues and diaries have pragmatic purposes. A travelogue provides readers with information; a diary provides a record of the writer's experiences.

You may not recognize some recollections of experience as narratives. The scientist's account of how a seed evolves into a plant is a story. So are the historian's reconstruction of a historical event, the psychologist's case study of a client, the manager's report of what happened to sales, and the engineer's analysis of a mechanical process. Other reconstructions of experience take forms that may not even *look* like stories. For example, résumés reconstruct a person's professional experiences, and many poems and song lyrics reconstruct human experience.

Because life is filled with stories, you probably feel quite comfortable with them. A technical report or a textbook or a set of instructions or a poem may be intimidating, but even if a story doesn't begin with the words "Once upon a time," you usually recognize it almost immediately and know intuitively how to read it. You know, for example, that it will be told in chronological order, moving through time and relating events in a more or less accurate reflection of the experiences it seeks to reconstruct.

READING RECONSTRUCTIONS OF EXPERIENCE

In reading texts that reconstruct a writer's experiences, you may have various purposes. Sometimes you want to share vicariously in the writer's experiences, especially if they seem exciting or amusing or if they remind you of experiences you have had yourself. At other times, you want to learn from the writer's experiences, to gain information or insights that the writer articulates or that you can infer. At still other times, you may read about a writer's experiences because they are familiar and, therefore, comforting. For example, certain types of experience have special meanings that go beyond the actual plot. Success stories and love stories tend to make us feel hopeful; war stories often inspire feelings of patriotism and pride; and stories about families remind us of those who created and cared for us.

Your purpose in reading about a writer's experiences will, therefore, determine to some extent how you read a text. Reading for pleasure usually means that you read in a more casual and less focused way than you do if you are reading for information. However, whatever your purpose or purposes, when you read to reconstruct experiences, you are always viewing these experiences from the writer's perspective. The writer, however objective he or she may strive to be, has constructed a personal, subjective version of what happened. As a reader, therefore, you must read to understand not only what has happened but also how the writer has interpreted the real event and shaped it into a narrative. That is, the writer always stands between you and the reality of the subject; the narrative you read can never be an absolutely accurate representation of the events that occurred.

Objective and Subjective Points of View

Your awareness of the writer's role as interpreter is an important factor in how effectively you read. Some writers reconstruct their experiences subjectively. What they write is filtered through their own experiences and unabashedly viewed from their own perspective. In this chapter's reading selections, Jesse Stuart and Warren Slay make no attempt to be objective. One of their purposes here is to reveal their personal views about the experiences they are relating. In effect, they are the main characters in the stories they tell. Because they want you to understand their points of view, they make no attempt to minimize their subjectivity. In contrast, Langston Hughes, Audre Lorde, and Maya Angelou appear to be objective as they begin their accounts but become increasingly subjective as they continue their narratives. And Ernesto Galarza is consistently objective as he tells of the fight that occurred at the Sixteenth of September celebration.

One question that you should ask yourself when you read a narrative based on the writers' experiences is just how important objectivity is. Do you think a narrative account is less valuable if it focuses primarily on the writers' own reactions rather than on the event itself? Again, the issue here is mainly one of purpose. For example, Angelou's purpose in describing the African celebration is not just to provide readers with details about the celebration—so different from our own Thanksgiving rituals—but to tell of her response to it, of how she was caught up in the event and became a participant rather than merely an observer. Although she doesn't articulate a **thesis** or main idea, her story suggests that she identifies with these Africans and their unfamiliar rituals, perhaps even more than she does with the familiar

THESIS, PAGE 663

but in many ways more alien rituals of the white-dominated North American society. Angelou serves her purposes by moving from a rather detached, objective stance initially to an obviously subjective response as she relates her own emotional reactions to the celebration.

Should, then, writers be objective or subjective in telling their stories? That depends on their purpose. A problem exists only if writers *pretend* to be objective and readers do not detect the pretense—do not understand this relationship between a writer's presence in a text and his or her purpose. If you believe a writer is objective but that writer is only pretending to be objective, you may not read a text accurately. Such a misreading is most likely if the writer uses as narrator an objective persona (character) who seems to represent the writer. In such cases, readers may attribute the persona's objectivity to the writer.

Likewise, as a reader, you need to realize that total objectivity is a myth, that all writers are subjective because they can view experience only from their own perspectives even if they are writing something as seemingly objective as a scientific report. Writers may eliminate all references to themselves and report the experience as if they are relating only the facts, but reconstructions of experience are essentially subjective however the writer presents them. When you read a writer's version of what happened, be aware of the writer and his or her purposes as a significant presence in the narrative. Often, the writer's presence is your main reason for reading such a narrative. You are not primarily interested in the events being described so much as you are interested in the writer—what he or she felt or thought or did. For example, most of the authors included in this chapter are well-known writers—celebrities of a sort—and provoke interest for that very reason. On the other hand, student writer Warren Slay, who wrote about his family's Thanksgiving, is not yet famous; therefore, his story provokes interest largely because many readers can identify in some way with the experience he reconstructs. Not incidentally, Slay's story is interesting primarily because he is very much a presence in it—not as a famous person but as a person whose voice is real and believable.

Recognizing Narration as Argument

In reading reconstructions of experience, be aware that writers usually have a purpose beyond simply telling a good story. Although they may not state a **thesis** explicitly, a controlling idea usually shapes their story THESIS, PAGE 663 and how they tell it. They are, in a sense, trying to convince readers of something they believe is important. Among the authors included in this chapter, Stuart believes it is important for a family to have continuity and a sense of the past. And Galarza, Angelou, and Lorde believe it is important for people to understand and respect cultures other than their own. If you read reconstructions of experience merely as stories, you may be amused or entertained or even enlightened, but you may also miss the larger point. Storytellers often have more than a single purpose, and the less obvious purposes may be the most important.

▶ READING SELECTIONS ◀

The following reading selections are all based on the writers' personal experiences with celebrations, rituals, and rites of passage. Although we usually think of occasions such as these as happy affairs—times when families get together and when people all feel good about themselves and their lives—they can also be difficult times. Many people dread holidays and celebrations or even ignore them because they are so painful. Other people look forward to them only to be disappointed when the reality does not meet their expectations. Thus the following reading selections are not all stories of families happily celebrating joyous occasions together, nor are they all accounts of traditional American holidays. Rather they tell of the complex emotions that people often have in response to these events.

DECEMBER: FROM *THE YEAR OF MY REBIRTH*

Jesse Stuart

Jesse Stuart was a schoolteacher, administrator, and writer. Known as a regional writer, he wrote primarily of the people who live in the mountains of eastern Kentucky, capturing in his fiction and poetry not only the struggles and hardships of their lives but also their humor and humanity. During his period of recuperation following a heart attack, Stuart wrote a memoir entitled The Year of My Rebirth. *In the following excerpt, he writes of a quiet Christmas he spent with his wife Naomi and daughter Jane that year. Notice as you read how Stuart's narration focuses on his fireplace—using it as both a symbol of his family's endurance and a unifying feature of his text.*

I have just closed the kitchen door so Jane and Naomi Deane won't   1
hear the noise of my typewriter. I am afraid if they hear me writing
into the night they will not be able to sleep. Then there is another
thing I would like to do by closing this door. I can't, but I like to
pretend. I'd like to close this door to preserve in this kitchen our
happiness, our love, the words that we have spoken tonight. I'd like
to keep it all in this kitchen fastened up forever. I wish there could be
another time when all this would unfold to other ears like voices from
a record. In some future day and time I'd like others to hear the

words spoken, the Christmas carols sung, the laughter, friendship, and family love that lived before our little fireplace in the corner of our kitchen tonight.

2   I know that I cannot reproduce these sounds, this love, with cold symbols on a printed page. But I am going to sit here and write down what I can. Actually nothing extraordinary happened at all. Our family of three lived for one evening in our kitchen.

3   First, about our kitchen. We have a fireplace in the corner. We don't have to have a fireplace now. We could close it, for we don't need it for either cooking or heat. We have hot-water heat which comes through convectors around our kitchen wall and produces an efficient even heat all over our house. Our four fireplaces could never do this. We know this is true, for in winters here, before the heater was installed, we had all four fireplaces going, and parts of this house were still cold.

4   But we will never close up any of the fireplaces, even the one in the kitchen. We like to sit before an open fire to watch the flames leap up from the wood, to warm our feet on the fender. We like to pull the red-hot coals from the grate and cook cornbread in a skillet, covered with a lid to hold the steam inside to give the cornbread flavor. We like to roast sweet potatoes, which we grow in our small creek bottoms, in the ashes. We like to hold an old-fashioned popcorn popper over the flame and watch the little grains jump up in the pan to pop open like big white flakes of falling snow. We like to boil sorghum with butter and pour it over the popcorn, which makes the best molasses popcorn balls in the world. Once we used to reboil our sorghum into a thick syrup, then put butter on our hands and pull it while it was still warm into long sticks of brown sorghum candy. We shaped it into brown twists similar to those of tobacco.

5   Sometimes we roast apples, which come from our trees, by putting them in a pan and putting the lid down tight under hot ashes. We like to sit a comfortable distance back from the fire holding long willow wands with marshmallows on their tips over the blaze until they start turning brown. We laugh and talk as we watch them swell with heat. When they catch fire, we jerk our long wands back in a hurry and blow the flames out.

6   Now, how can one do this sort of thing with furnace heat, or with coal in a grate? This is the reason why we have not closed any of our four fireplaces. They will not be closed as long as Naomi and I continue to live here. If Jane lives on here after we go, since she has grown up in the tradition of the family around the open fireplace in the evening, I believe she will always have some wood to burn and a

little fire, even if she is living in the year 2000 and is warmed by atomic heat.

On this very spot where I am using this typewriter, my mother and father used to sit around a table in their kitchen. Four of their seven children, for two were dead and one was born later, sat with them. Here we planned and talked and laughed. Only we didn't have an open fireplace. We had a big cookstove we called a wood range. It burned wood like a fireplace, and heat danced above its flat top like sunlight over a tin roof on a midsummer afternoon. Dad used to cut the stovewood for this range, and I carried armfuls inside the kitchen and put them inside the woodbox. In the mornings while Mom got breakfast, I used to go to the kitchen long before daylight and sit on the woodbox close to the stove while the kitchen got warm. But after the stove got really hot, we couldn't stay in this kitchen, no matter if it was twenty below outside, unless we raised a window to let the heat out.   7

Naomi and I rebuilt the fireplace and chimney in the old living room after we began housekeeping here. We figured that where this hearth stands is a great tradition of family life around the open fire. At least twenty families have lived here in the century and a half this house has stood. I can remember eight of these families myself. We estimated that six or seven thousand people, young and old, have sat before a blazing winter fire here and laughed, talked, joked, ate, and lived life joyously and fully in the years that have passed.   8

Before we tore down the old stone chimney, made by Eric Brickey, a stonemason of another century, the elements had eroded many of these large stones until they were so thin there was danger of the chimney's falling. Heat escaping from this chimney melted the snow for a radius of twenty feet around. This frightened us, so we tore it down and replaced it with one made of bricks. But this was not breaking any old tradition, for the stone chimney had replaced an even earlier one made of sticks and mud. And the bricklayer who made our chimney, Sam Brickey, was a grandson of Old Eric, who had built the stone chimney and fireplace almost a hundred years ago.   9

I wish the doors had been shut for each family in the century and a half past, and we could open them to look in on evenings of long ago when a man with buckskin moccasins on his feet and a coonskin cap on his head stood before the wood fire in a fireplace built of clay and sticks. I wish we could see his wife and their young children, the long rifle hanging to a joist and a powder horn on the wall. Captain George Naylor Davis (1781–1847) belonged to that time. He trained a company of men near here and took them by boat down the Ohio and Mississippi to help Andrew Jackson in the Battle of New Orleans. Later   10 he served on Andrew Jackson's staff, for the General took a fancy to him. Now Captain George Naylor Davis lies buried in Brick Union's rural churchyard, which is six miles from here. There were no roads then, no schools, no work but hunting, fishing, clearing of land, building, and trading furs with Indians.

11   Then, like turning the pages of a book, I would like to see each family that shared this fireplace up until the present. I myself can remember back to 1915.

12   Eric Brickey made the big chimney and fireplace so large it took a mule to pull a backstick for it. It took several men to roll one over the floor to get it in behind the andirons. Sam Brickey told us that his grandfather, Eric Brickey, called his stone chimneys, so many of which he built in this area, his "living monuments." Sam, in turn, called our new brick chimney one of his "living monuments." His living monument, too, would pass away when another age developed new chimney materials. But the tradition of the open fire would not pass away if we could do anything to keep it alive.

13   If we could close the kitchen doors to perpetuate what took place before our fireplace tonight, here is what we would pass along to some future inhabitants of this house.

14   It was after dinner, and we were drying the dishes. Naomi had already brought extra wood for the fire and filled the brass kettle that stands in the corner. I stopped drying long enough to put an extra stick of wood on the grate.

15   Naomi joined Jane in a Christmas carol, and while we finished the dishes and the flames leaped up through the wood in our kitchen fireplace, we sang "Silent Night." Christmas was a week or two off, but its spirit always precedes it. I remembered that this same song was sung before this same fireplace in the years from 1915 to 1918. And I am sure others sang it here long before then.

16   We sang "God Rest Ye Merry, Gentlemen" as we sat before the fire. Naomi got up to find a nutcracker, and I went to the woodshed to fetch a peck of hickory nuts and the two bricks which we keep for this purpose. I laid them on the hearth. Naomi was going to bake a hickory-nut cake, and we had to have the kernels. Jane used one of the bricks while I used the other to crack the hickory nuts. We put them in Naomi's lap, and she took the kernels from the nuts. We then threw the nuts, clean of their kernels, into the blazing fire.

17   We worked slowly cracking our thin-shelled hickory nuts. Naomi, Jane, and I had gathered them in October from a tall hickory tree that grows about a hundred yards up the valley at the edge of the pine grove. We had gathered ourselves plenty for the long winter but had

left enough for our squirrels. Now, by the time we had filled the crock
with hickory-nut kernels, we had cracked a peck. We had sung all the
Christmas carols we knew, including some we didn't know too well. Jane
had recited "The Night before Christmas" without a halt. We had each
recited a poem. Then Jane popped corn for herself and her mother, and
we finished with an evening cup of tea and a piece of angel-food cake.

That was all, except for the talk and the gaiety and the love that   18
I will not try to put down here.

Now Jane and Naomi are fast asleep. I have been sitting here   19
thinking about life in front of this fireplace over the century and a half.
The fire in the fireplace is now a bed of embers.

QUESTIONS TO CONSIDER ◀

1. As Stuart begins this account, he is quite explicit about his intention
to recreate what went on in his kitchen on this particular evening a
few days before Christmas. And he follows through on this intention, reconstructing in great detail the activities of the evening. But
he also achieves a larger purpose, one that he does not state explicitly. As he tells of how his "family of three lived for one evening" in
their kitchen, he also reveals much about the history of his family
and its values. What values does Stuart emphasize most in his account of his family, past and present?

2. Notice Stuart's skillful use of both **narration** and **description**.   NARRATION, PAGE 618
Reread the first few pages to identify which sentences or paragraphs   DESCRIPTION, PAGE 565
are descriptive and which are narrative. Then reread these pages
once more, this time reading just the narrative portions. How effective is the narration without the description? What does the description add?

3. Do you think Stuart's purpose in reconstructing his experiences in
this memoir is primarily aesthetic or pragmatic? That is, does this
story help the reader accomplish anything, or is it rather an aesthetic artifact—something a reader appreciates or enjoys reading?
What was your reaction to it?

4. How does Stuart's use of specific details and concrete language
contribute to his narrative? For example, in the fourth paragraph
he describes in detail some of the foods the family cooks in its
fireplace. What effect would it have on this narrative if Stuart merely
stated that they used the fireplace for cooking?

Individual: Write a journal entry in which you reconstruct in careful detail one particular holiday you remember well. Focus on a single detail, as Stuart focuses on the fireplace, making this detail the central image in your narrative.

Collaborative: Working with a group of your peers, discuss and list the multiple purposes that Stuart may have had in writing this story as part of his memoir. Then explain in a brief paragraph what you think his main purpose is, illustrating your explanation with evidence from the story. Compare your explanation with those of the other groups.

Computer: Using a computer, make two outlines. First, on the left side of the screen, outline the story that Stuart tells of the evening he spent in the kitchen with his family. Next, on the right side of your screen, outline the history of the fireplaces. Most word-processing programs allow you to create columns, which will make this process much easier. Or, if your word-processing program has a split-screen feature, you can use it to set up your two outlines. Then, viewing the two outlines simultaneously, determine how Stuart combines the two stories by making one outline of the two. Why do you think Stuart intertwined the two stories in the way he did? Do you see other possibilities?

SALVATION

Langston Hughes

Langston Hughes lived from 1902 to 1967, and during the last forty-five years of his life, he was considered by many to be America's foremost African-American literary figure. Working in every major fictional and nonfictional form, Hughes was known for his experimentation and innovations as a writer. From his beginning as a poet in Harlem to his later success as a playwright and his final reknown as a major literary figure, Hughes depended on his personal experiences and the racial and cultural history of African Americans as his primary sources. The reading selection below, which is taken from his autobiography The Big Sea, *tells of a rite of passage he experienced at a revival as a young boy.*

I was saved from sin when I was going on thirteen. But not really   1
saved. It happened like this. There was a big revival at my Auntie
Reed's church. Every night for weeks there had been much preaching,
singing, praying, and shouting, and some very hardened sinners had
been brought to Christ, and the membership of the church had grown
by leaps and bounds. Then just before the revival ended, they held a
special meeting for children, "to bring the young lambs to the fold."
My aunt spoke of it for days ahead. That night I was escorted to the
front row and placed on the mourners' bench with all the other young
sinners, who had not yet been brought to Jesus.

My aunt told me that when you were saved you saw a light, and   2
something happened to you inside! And Jesus came into your life! And
God was with you from then on! She said you could see and hear and
feel Jesus in your soul. I believed her. I had heard a great many old
people say the same thing and it seemed to me they ought to know.
So I sat there calmly in the hot, crowded church, waiting for Jesus to
come to me.

The preacher preached a wonderful rhythmical sermon, all   3
moans and shouts and lonely cries and dire pictures of hell, and then
he sang a song about the ninety and nine safe in the fold, but one
little lamb was left out in the cold. Then he said: "Won't you come?
Won't you come to Jesus? Young lambs, won't you come?" And he
held out his arms to all us young sinners there on the mourners'
bench. And the little girls cried. And some of them jumped up and
went to Jesus right away. But most of us just sat there.

A great many old people came and knelt around us and prayed,   4
old women with jet-black faces and braided hair, old men with work-
gnarled hands. And the church sang a song about the lower lights are
burning, some poor sinners to be saved. And the whole building
rocked with prayer and song.

Still I kept waiting to *see* Jesus.   5

Finally all the young people had gone to the altar and were   6
saved, but one boy and me. He was a rounder's son named Westley.
Westley and I were surrounded by sisters and deacons praying. It was
very hot in the church, and getting late now. Finally Westley said to
me in a whisper: "God damn! I'm tired o' sitting here. Let's get up and
be saved." So he got up and was saved.

Then I was left all alone on the mourners' bench. My aunt came   7
and knelt at my knees and cried, while prayers and songs swirled all
around me in the little church. The whole congregation prayed for
me alone, in a mighty wail of moans and voices. And I kept waiting
serenely for Jesus, waiting, waiting—but he didn't come. I wanted to

see him, but nothing happened to me. Nothing! I wanted something to happen to me, but nothing happened.

8   I heard the songs and the minister saying: "Why don't you come? My dear child, why don't you come to Jesus? Jesus is waiting for you. He wants you. Why don't you come? Sister Reed, what is this child's name?"

9   "Langston", my aunt sobbed.

10   "Langston, why don't you come? Why don't you come and be saved? Oh, Lamb of God! Why don't you come?"

11   Now it was really getting late. I began to be ashamed of myself, holding everything up so long. I began to wonder what God thought about Westley, who certainly hadn't seen Jesus either, but who was now sitting proudly on the platform, swinging his knickerbockered legs and grinning down at me, surrounded by deacons and old women on their knees praying. God had not struck Westley dead for taking his name in vain or for lying in the temple. So I decided that maybe to save further trouble, I'd better lie, too, and say that Jesus had come, and get up and be saved.

12   So I got up.

13   Suddenly the whole room broke into a sea of shouting, as they saw me rise. Waves of rejoicing swept the place. Women leaped in the air. My aunt threw her arms around me. The minister took me by the hand and led me to the platform.

14   When things quieted down, in a hushed silence, punctuated by a few ecstatic "Amens," all the new young lambs were blessed in the name of God. Then joyous singing filled the room.

15   That night, for the last time in my life but one—for I was a big boy twelve years old—I cried. I cried, in bed alone, and couldn't stop. I buried my head under the quilts, but my aunt heard me. She woke up and told my uncle I was crying because the Holy Ghost had come into my life, and because I had seen Jesus. But I was really crying because I couldn't bear to tell her that I had lied, that I had deceived everybody in the church, that I hadn't seen Jesus, and that now I didn't believe there was a Jesus any more, since he didn't come to help me.

▶   QUESTIONS TO CONSIDER

1. Hughes appears objective and detached in his first sentence, creating the illusion that what follows will be an accurate, unbiased account of what happened. However, he becomes increasingly subjective and emotional as the narrative continues. What effect does this progression from an objective to a subjective point of view create?

2. This narrative can be viewed as a straightforward account of a personal experience. If this view is accepted, the first sentence, in which Hughes states, "I was saved from sin when I was going on thirteen," serves as a **thesis statement**. However, the narrative can also be viewed as a rite of passage in which the young man actually becomes acquainted with sin rather than being saved from sin. Which of these interpretations corresponds most closely to your reading of this text? Are other interpretations possible?   THESIS, PAGE 663

3. Hughes seems to be viewing the revival initially as a child, but his perspective becomes less childlike and more adult as the story progresses. In what way does his prose style reflect what happened to him?

4. Hughes uses a number of direct quotations in his narrative. How does his reproduction of various people's comments strengthen his narrative? Notice how he punctuates these direct quotations.

5. Can the event Hughes describes be considered a celebration and/or a ritual as well as a rite of passage? Define each of these concepts, focusing especially on how they are alike and how they are different.

WRITING ACTIVITIES

Individual: In your journal write an objective account of some event that marked a rite of passage for you, giving only the facts—the setting, what happened, who was there, what they did and said, and so on.

Collaborative: Working in your assigned group, compare your objective descriptions. Then, generalizing from the information you have each included, write one sentence that seems to be true of all rites of passage. Compare your sentence with those composed by the other groups.

Computer: Enter the sentence about rites of passage generated by your group into your computer. Then, using this statement as a **topic sentence** write a paragraph in which you support it.   TOPIC SENTENCE, PAGE 672

GRANDPA'S OLD ROCKER

Warren Slay

The student who wrote this essay grew up in a small town. His narrative of the last Thanksgiving he spent with his grandfather not only tells what happened on that particular day, but it also suggests why his grandfather was special to him. As you read this story, notice how Slay uses dialogue and specific details to reconstruct this occasion—to help his readers experience the occasion as he experienced it and to evoke the setting in which the story occurred.

1   The old house was packed with people. All three of my mother's sisters and their families were there. It was Thanksgiving at Grandma and Grandpa's. All of the women were out in the kitchen. They were putting the food on Granny's old Masonite-topped table and laughing about who knows what. Most of the men, and us boys, were out on the old wooden front porch talking about hunting and how to make more money. Most of us on the porch were clad in camouflage overalls, coveralls, orange caps, and rubber boots because we had just got back from hunting. Going hunting on Thanksgiving morning was a time-honored tradition among us.

2   Grandpa was sitting there in the old rocking chair he had made years ago. He was doing what he said was the only thing he was expert at, grinning and rocking. His old overalls were faded and a little too short, and his leather work boots looked like they had just about walked their last mile. It's not that he didn't have better clothes; he just didn't wear them. When Granny would get on him about it, he'd just say, "Annie Lee, I'm an old man. I can wear old clothes if I want to." He wasn't able to go hunting any more, but he sat there and listened to our stories and told some pretty good ones himself.

3   Finally Granny shuffled to the door and said, "Coy, ya'll come eat." Then, we all got up and went to the kitchen. After someone said the blessing, we "men" fixed our plates and returned to the porch to eat and let Uncle Wayne finish his story, so we'd all quit wondering if he got unlost or not. After we finished, we gave all the scraps to Little Mike, my dog. Then the older men went into the small living room to watch football on the tiny black and white T.V. while all us little ones stayed outside in the yard to play.

That was the Thanksgiving of 1979. I was only seven, but I can 4
still vaguely remember that Thanksgiving. A few of the missing parts
have been filled in by stories from family, but I remember sitting on
Grandpa's lap and talking to him after everyone else had left to go
home. It was in conversations such as these that I learned many of the
things a little boy should know—like how to catch gopher hole crick-
ets and whistle.

It wasn't but a few months after this Thanksgiving that things 5
changed. Grandpa got sick and just got worse until April 19th, when
he passed on. At my young age I was not really affected by this happening. I was sad, and I knew I would miss him and all, but it wasn't
until a few Thanksgivings later that I realized what I really had lost.

We all still gather at Grandma's as we have for years and years.
Now, there are more grandkids and greatgrandkids than before, but
we do the same things we have always done. The only difference is
that Grandpa is not there.

I can't really say that Thanksgiving is a sad day for me now 6
because all of the family is together and good old Grandma is still
here, but I do catch myself staring at that old rocking chair every now
and again. As I look back in my mind, there is a lot I have forgotten
about Grandpa Coy, but I still remember that Thanksgiving. So, when
Thanksgiving rolls around now, I have those memories to fill the
emptiness in Grandpa's old rocker.

QUESTIONS TO CONSIDER ◀

1. How does Slay's emphasis on his grandfather's rocking chair compare to Stuart's use of the fireplace as a symbol? How many references to the chair can you find in the story?

2. One of the strongest features of this story is the writer's authentic
   voice. How does he achieve this impression that he is speaking   STYLE AND VOICE, PAGE 656
   directly and honestly to his readers?

3. Do you find this story too sentimental? That is, does the writer too
   obviously appeal to your emotions? Or do you like this quality of
   the story? Which images and statements contribute to the sentimentality? Do you view sentimentality as a positive or negative feature?
   Compare the degree of sentimentality in this story to that in Stuart's
   narrative. Can you come to any conclusions about when sentiment
   is appropriate?

4. In the first part of the story, the narrator is a young boy; in the last part he is a young man. How does Slay indicate this shift in time and perspective?

5. In his story, Slay includes dialogue he remembers from that Thanksgiving Day. Whom does he quote? Do you think he remembered the exact words that were spoken? Is Slay able to suggest other people's voices when he quotes them? What does his use of dialogue add to his narrative?

▶   **W R I T I N G   A C T I V I T I E S**

Individual: Write a journal entry in which you evaluate the strengths and weaknesses of this selection.

Collaborative: As a group, discuss the strengths and weaknesses of this narrative. Do you find it more or less interesting than the selections by professional writers that are included in this chapter? Then compose a note to the author, Warren Slay, suggesting specific ways he might revise his essay.

Computer: Working with a partner, select a topic and conduct an on-line dialogue by exchanging disks or using a network program. Then incorporate your computer conversation into a brief narrative, carefully punctuating each response to indicate who said what.

A Thanksgiving Feast in Aburi

Maya Angelou

Maya Angelou, the African-American writer who wrote and delivered a poem for President Clinton's inauguration, describes in the following narrative a celebration that took place in Aburi, Africa, while she was visiting there. You can compare this holiday to Thanksgiving, but there are important differences. As you read, note the differences between the American version of Thanksgiving and the African feast.

1   The music of the Fanti language was becoming singable to me, and its vocabulary was moving orderly into my brain.

Efua took me to a durbar, a thanksgiving feast in Aburi, about 2
thirty miles from Accra. Thousands of gaily dressed celebrants had gathered, waving, singing and dancing. I stood on the edge of the crowd to
watch the exotic parade. Hunters, rifles across their shoulders, marched
in rhythm to their own drummers. Soldiers, with faces set in grim determination, paced down the widened roads behind their drummers while
young girls screamed approval. Farmers bearing scythes and fishermen
carrying nets were welcomed loudly by the throng.

The annual harvest ritual gave each segment in the society its 3
opportunity to thank God and to praise its workers and their yield.

I was swaying to the rhythm when the drums stopped, and the 4
crowd quieted. The restless air steadied. A sound, unlike the other
sounds of the day, commenced in the distance. It was the harsh tone
of hundreds of giant cicadas grinding their legs together. Their rasping
floated to us and the crowd remained quiet but edgy with anticipation.
When men appeared out of the dust scraping sticks against corrugated
dry gourds, the crowd recovered its tongue.

"Yee! Yee! Awae! Awae!" 5

The scrapers, like the paraders who preceded them, gave no 6
notice to the crowd or to the small children who ran unceremoniously
close to their serried ranks.

Rasp, Rasp. Scrape! Scrape, Scour, Scrunch, Scrump. Rasp, Rasp! 7
Scree! The raspers faded into a dim distance.

The deep throb of royal drums was suddenly heard in the dis- 8
tance and again the din of celebration stopped. The people, although
quiet again, continued to move, sidle, exchange places and wipe their
brows. Women adjusted the clothes which held babies securely to
their backs. Rambunctious children played tag, men and women
waved at each other, smiled, but kept looking toward the sound of
the drums.

Efua touched my shoulder and offered me a large white hand- 9
kerchief.

I said, "Thank you, but I'm all right." She kept her hand 10
extended. I took the handkerchief.

Men emerged out of the dim dust. One set had giant drums 11
hefted onto their shoulders, and others followed in splendid cloth,
beating the drums with crooked sticks. The powerful rhythms rattled
my bones, and I could feel the vibrations along the edges of my teeth.

People began clapping, moving their feet, their hands, hips and 12
heads. They shouted clamorously, "Yee! Yee! Aboma!" And there was
still a sense of anticipation in the turbulence. They were waiting for
a climax.

13   When the first palanquin hove into view, I thought of a Chinese junk on the Yangtze (which I had never seen), and a ten ton truck on a California freeway (which I knew well). Long poled hammocks, sturdy as Conestogas, were carried by four men. In the center of each conveyance sat a chief, gloriously robed in rich hand-woven Kente cloth. At his side (only a few chiefs were female) sat a young boy, called the Kra, who, during an earlier solemn ceremony, had received the implanted soul of the chief. If the chief should die during the ritual, there would be no panic, for his people would know that his soul was safe in the young boy's body and, with the proper ritual, could be placed into the body of the chief's successor.

14   The drums beckoned, the kings appeared, and the air nearly collapsed under the weight of dust and thudding drums and shouting jubilation.

15   Each chief was prouder than the one preceding him. Each dressed in more gold and richer colors. Each black beyond ebony and shining with oil and sweat. They arrived in single file to be met by the adoring shouts of their subjects. "Na-na. Na-na." "Yo, Yo, Nana." The shouting united with the thumping of the drums and the explosion of color. Women and men bounced up and down like children's toys, and children not tall enough to see over the crowd were lifted by the nearest adults to see their passing royalty.

16   A flutter of white billowed over that excited scene. Thousands of handkerchiefs waving from thousands of black hands tore away my last reserve. I started bouncing with the entranced Ghanaians, my handkerchief high above my head, I waved and jumped and screamed, "Na-na, na-na, na-na."

▶   QUESTIONS TO CONSIDER

1. Angelou's reaction to the celebration changes as it progresses. What is her initial reaction? Her final reaction? Would this final response have occurred had she been watching the celebration from a distance? At what point in her narrative does her role change from observer to participant? How does her narrative reflect this change?

2. Angelou is describing a celebration she does not understand well and is writing for an audience who is even less knowledgeable than she is about this country and its customs, so she explains what occurs during the celebration carefully. But her primary purpose is not merely to inform her readers about this strange celebration. What is her primary purpose?

3. Notice the descriptive details that Angelou includes in her narrative. Her account of the celebration consists of a series of vivid images. To what senses (sight, sound, etc.) do these images appeal? Which is the strongest image for you as a reader?

WRITING ACTIVITIES

Individual: Rather than focusing primarily on the sense of sight, as writers often do, write a journal entry in which you describe in detail sounds or odors you associate with a particular ritual or celebration.

Collaborative: Angelou does not include a stated **thesis** but her main idea can be inferred. With the members of your group, write a brief introduction for this story in which you state the thesis. Do you think this introduction makes the narrative more or less effective? Why or why not?

THESIS, PAGE 663

Computer: Describe an event to which you responded strongly. For example, you might describe a graduation, a marriage (or divorce) ceremony, a parade, a sporting event, or a church service. In your first account of this event, begin with a thesis that states exactly what your response was. Next, copy your text to a new file and revise it so that the thesis statement appears at the end. Finally, copy the original text again (to a third file) and revise it once more, omitting the thesis statement entirely but including images and details that clearly suggest your main idea. Print all three versions of the text and determine which you prefer.

THE SIXTEENTH OF SEPTEMBER

Ernesto Galarza

In Mexico, the Sixteenth of September is celebrated as Independence Day—the day when Mexico gained its independence from Spain in 1821. Often people from Mexico who migrate to the United States continue to celebrate this holiday. In his account of growing up in a Los Angeles barrio, Ernesto Galarza includes the following story about a party that was held to celebrate this holiday. As you read, compare the customs Galarza describes with those we observe when we celebrate the Fourth of July.

1   In the family parties, the funerals, the baptisms, the weddings and the birthdays, our private lives continued to be Mexican. And there was a public affair that once a year brought the *colonia* together, the celebration of the Sixteenth of September.

2   The year José was chosen a member of the committee to arrange the program for the Sixteenth, I was drafted to assist as interpreter in obtaining from the American authorities permits of one kind or another. As José's aide-de-camp I also helped decorate the hall with streamers of green, white, and red crepe paper and the colored portrait of Don Miguel Hidalgo hung under a large Mexican flag.

3   The program went along smoothly. The hall was crowded, family style with whole clans in attendance from babies to grandparents. There was a short speech by the president of the Comisión Honorifica; the crowning of the queen, elected with votes paid for by her admirers; the singing of the national anthem; a poetic reading; and one hour before midnight *El Grito*, the call to arms in remembrance of the cry of the Illustrious Father of the Nation, the rebel Catholic priest, Don Miguel Hidalgo y Costilla.

4   For those between fifteen and thirty the real business of the Sixteenth was the dance. After *El Grito*, the floor was cleared, the mothers and elders sitting on chairs and benches along the walls, a stolid line of chaperons, the girls in a double row in front of them. Across from them the young men stood, like runners at the starting line of a hundred-yard dash. On the first downbeat of the band leader, they rushed across the floor, each man headed for his favorite girl who, according to the rules, accepted her partner on a first come first served basis.

5   During the early rounds of the dancing the rushes created no problems. I watched them from a back corner of the bandstand, my duty post as assistant to the floor manager. There were intermissions for soft drinks and beer.

6   But it wasn't the coca-cola or the brew that gradually enlivened the festival. It was the trips to the men's toilet for short nips from flasks of tequila and other fiery stuff.

7   By one o'clock in the morning a good deal of tequila had been consumed. Everybody knew, of course, that a Mexican's honor became more sensitive the more nips he had. In the presence of the choicest girls of the *colonia*, there are some things a man cannot tolerate. And in one of the rushes one of these things happened. Two young men collided within reach of the girl they both wanted for the dance. Like perfect gentlemen they picked themselves up from the floor paying no heed to the giggles of the girls and the owlish grins

of the old folks. I saw them rush out of the ballroom, my uncle at their heels. When I caught up with him in the toilet it was too late. The two bantams were in a corner, squared off and slugging it out, my uncle taking cuffs from both as he tried to separate them.

Instantly, word of the fight reached the dance floor and the men rushed to see it, first as spectators and then as partisans of the fighters. With Mexican honor now running hot through their veins, they insulted one another until the free-for-all began in earnest. I watched the *chicanos* pair off, pushing each other against the walls and swinging wildly. Two of them were on the floor kicking and rolling, half hidden under the swinging door of a toilet. A beer bottle crashed through a window.   8

José slugged his way through the melee to my corner, yanked me by the arm, and we headed for the ballroom. A policeman was already at the door of the toilet looking in bewilderment for a way to take hold of a roomful of rioting Mexicans.   9

The ballroom was emptying fast. Mothers were herding their daughters through the hall and out into the street. The elders gathered on the sidewalk waiting to group their families and hasten away. My uncle ordered the band to play on, "to restore the calm," as he said. But it was the police and not the music that restored the calm. Someone with more experience than José had yelled in the hall, "La Julia," and before the paddy wagon appeared in the street and a pair of cops walked in, the hall was deserted, except for ourselves and the musicians.   10

It was nearly dawn before we finished taking down the decorations, mopping up the spilled beer, scrubbing the blood on the toilet floor, sweeping up broken glass, and heaping the cigarette butts in a pail. The colored portrait of Don Miguel was the last thing we took down.   11

QUESTIONS TO CONSIDER   ◀

1. Who is Galarza's intended audience? Is he writing for other Mexican Americans—people who know something about the history of Mexico and life in a barrio—or for people who know nothing of these things? What specific clues do you find in his narrative that help you identify his audience? How does his choice of an audience shape his narrative? Does Galarza idealize the celebration in order to impress his audience, or does he give an objective account? Can an author, especially one who is writing about his own people and culture, really be objective?

2. How does this celebration compare to Fourth of July celebrations? Do Fourth of July celebrations sometimes get out of hand also? If so, how and why?

3. According to Galarza, Hidalgo was a "rebel Catholic priest" who helped the Mexican people win their independence from Spain. What effect does Galarza's mentioning the picture of Hidalgo at both the first and last of his account have on you as a reader? Is it more or less effective than Stuart's similar use of the fireplace in his story? How might Galarza have used this image more effectively?

▶   W R I T I N G   A C T I V I T I E S

Individual: Write a journal entry in which you tell of an exuberant celebration that included potentially dangerous activities. Include as many specific details as you can remember.

Collaborative: With the members of your group, discuss your individual responses to Galarza's narrative, focusing on whether your response was primarily positive or negative. Then, discuss whether you think your responses conform to Galarza's intention. That is, what response do you think he wanted you to have? Finally, identify and make a list of the features of the narrative that influenced your group's responses most strongly. Compare your list with those produced by the other groups.

Computer: Enter into a computer file your journal entry about your experience with an exuberant celebration. (If your journal is already in a computer file, simply move this entry into a new file.) Then conduct an on-line discussion about such events and their potential dangers, sharing your account with your classmates by exchanging disks or by using a network program.

THE FOURTH OF JULY

Audre Lorde

 *Poet and essayist Audre Lorde was born in New York City in 1934 to immigrant Caribbean parents. In 1991 she was named poet laureate of New York. Before her death in 1992, Lorde had published more than fifteen collections of poetry and essays. Her essay collection* A Burst of Light *won the American Book Award in 1989. The following selection is taken from her autobiography,* Zami: A New Spelling of My Name *(1982). In it, Lorde tells of a trip her family* took to Washington, D.C., just after World War II as a graduation present for her sister and her.

The first time I went to Washington, D.C., was on the edge of the summer when I was supposed to stop being a child. At least that's what they said to us all at graduation from the eighth grade. My sister Phyllis graduated at the same time from high school. I don't know what she was supposed to stop being. But as graduation presents for us both, the whole family took a Fourth of July trip to Washington, D.C., the fabled and famous capital of our country. 1

It was the first time I'd ever been on a railroad train during the day. When I was little, and we used to go to the Connecticut shore, we always went at night on the milk train, because it was cheaper. 2

Preparations were in the air around our house before school was even over. We packed for a week. There were two very large suitcases that my father carried, and a box filled with food. In fact, my first trip to Washington was a mobile feast. I started eating as soon as we were comfortably ensconced in our seats, and did not stop until somewhere after Philadelphia. I remember it was Philadelphia because I was disappointed not to have passed by the Liberty Bell. 3

My mother had roasted two chickens and cut them up into dainty bite-size pieces. She packed slices of brown bread and butter and green pepper and carrot sticks. There were little violently yellow iced cakes with scalloped edges called "marigolds," that came from Cushman's Bakery. There was a spice bun and rock-cakes from Newton's, the West Indian bakery across Lenox Avenue from St. Mark's School, and iced tea in a wrapped mayonnaise jar. There were sweet pickles for us and dill pickles for my father, and peaches with the fuzz 4 still on them, individually wrapped to keep them from bruising. And, for neatness, there were piles of napkins and a little tin box with a washcloth dampened with rose water and glycerine for wiping sticky mouths.

5   I wanted to eat in the dining car because I had read all about them, but my mother reminded me for the umpteenth time that dining car food always cost too much money and besides, you never could tell whose hands had been playing all over that food, nor where those same hands had been just before. My mother never mentioned that Black people were not allowed into railroad dining cars headed south in 1947. As usual, whatever my mother did not like and could not change, she ignored. Perhaps it would go away, deprived of her attention.

6   I learned later that Phyllis's high school senior class trip had been to Washington, but the nuns had given her back her deposit in private, explaining to her that the class, all of whom were white, except Phyllis, would be staying in a hotel where Phyllis "would not be happy," meaning, Daddy explained to her, also in private, that they did not rent rooms to Negros. "We will take you to Washington, ourselves," my father had avowed, "and not just for an overnight in some measly fleabag hotel."

7   American racism was a new and crushing reality that my parents had to deal with every day of their lives once they came to this country. They handled it as a private woe. My mother and father believed that they could best protect their children from the realities of race in america and the fact of american racism by never giving them name, much less discussing their nature. We were told we must never trust white people, but *why* was never explained, nor the nature of their ill will. Like so many other vital pieces of information in my childhood, I was supposed to know without being told. It always seemed like a very strange injunction coming from my mother, who looked so much like one of those people we were never supposed to trust. But something always warned me not to ask my mother why she wasn't white, and why Auntie Lillah and Auntie Etta weren't, even though they were all that same problematic color so different from my father and me, even from my sisters, who were somewhere in-between.

8   In Washington, D.C., we had one large room with two double beds and an extra cot for me. It was a back-street hotel that belonged to a friend of my father's who was in real estate, and I spent the whole next day after Mass squinting up at the Lincoln Memorial were Marian Anderson had sung after the D.A.R. refused to allow her to sing in their auditorium because she was Black. Or because she was "Colored," my father said as he told us the story. Except that what he

probably said was "Negro," because for his times, my father was quite progressive.

I was squinting because I was in that silent agony that character-   9
ized all of my childhood summers, from the time school let out in June to the end of July, brought about by my dilated and vulnerable eyes exposed to the summer brightness.

I viewed Julys through an agonizing corolla of dazzling whiteness   10
and I always hated the Fourth of July, even before I came to realize the travesty such a celebration was for Black people in this country.

My parents did not approve of sunglasses, nor of their expense.   11

I spent the afternoon squinting up at monuments to freedom and   12
past presidencies and democracy, and wondering why the light and heat were both so much stronger in Washington, D.C., than back home in New York City. Even the pavement on the streets was a shade lighter in color than back home.

Late that Washington afternoon my family and I walked back   13
down Pennsylvania Avenue. We were a proper caravan, mother bright and father brown, and three of us girls step-standards in-between. Moved by our historical surroundings and the heat of the early evening, my father decreed yet another treat. He had a great sense of history, a flair for the quietly dramatic and the sense of specialness of an occasion and a trip.

"Shall we stop and have a little something to cool off, Lin?"   14

Two bocks away from our hotel, the family stopped for a dish of   15
vanilla ice cream at a Breyer's ice cream and soda fountain. Indoors, the soda fountain was dim and fan-cooled, deliciously relieving to my scorched eyes.

Corded and crisp and pinafored, the five of us seated ourselves   16
one by one at the counter. There was I between my mother and father, and my two sisters on the other side of my mother. We settled our-selves along the white mottled marble counter, and when the waitress spoke at first no one understood what she was saying, and so the five of us just sat there.

The waitress moved along the line of us closer to my father and   17
spoke again. "I said I kin give you take out, but you can't eat here. Sorry." Then she dropped her eyes looking very embarrassed, and suddenly we heard what it was she was saying all at the same time, loud and clear.

Straight-backed and indignant, one by one, my family and I got   18
down from the counter stools and turned around and marched out of the store, quiet and outraged, as if we had never been Black before. No one would answer my emphatic questions with anything other than a guilty

silence. "But we hadn't done anything!" This wasn't right or fair! Hadn't I written poems about Bataan and freedom and democracy for all?

19   My parents wouldn't speak of this injustice, not because they had contributed to it, but because they felt they should have anticipated it and avoided it. This made me even angrier. My fury was not going to be acknowledged by a like fury. Even my two sisters copied my parents' pretense that nothing unusual and anti-american had occurred. I was left to write my angry letter to the president of the united states all by myself, although my father did promise I could type it out on the office typewriter next week, after I showed it to him in my copybook diary.

20   The waitress was white, the counter was white, and the ice cream I never ate in Washington, D.C., that summer I left childhood was white, and the white heat and the white pavement and the white stone monuments of my first Washington summer made me sick to my stomach for the whole rest of that trip and it wasn't much of a graduation present after all.

▶   QUESTIONS TO CONSIDER

THESIS, PAGE 663   **1.** Lorde does not state her **thesis** initially but ends her narrative with a long summary sentence that seems to function as a thesis statement. Reread this sentence, noticing especially her repetition of the word *white*. Would the sentence reflect accurately what occurs in the narrative if it did not include this color imagery?

2. What does Lorde's use of lowercase letters for words such as *united states*, *american*, and *president* suggest?

3. Lorde, like Langston Hughes, is recounting an experience that was a turning point for her as a child. As in the story by Hughes, it is not the experience itself—in this case, the trip—that is most significant, but rather what Lorde learns from the experience. For this reason, the experiences they describe can be viewed as rites of passage—times when a person leaves one stage of life and enters another. Do rites of passage always involve a transition from innocence to knowledge? What other transitions or lessons do you associate with rites of passage?

4. Did being excluded from mainstream American society as a child make Lorde more objective or just more cynical? Do you view objectivity and cynicism as positive or negative emotions? Explain your answer.

WRITING ACTIVITIES

Individual: Describe in your journal a time when you realized something was not as it appeared to be or when you gained some knowledge that involved a loss of innocence.

Collaborative: Discuss with your group Lorde's use of narration as argument. First establish what her argument is, and then determine how her story persuades readers to her point of view.

Computer: Write a response to Lorde's argument, and post it to your computer network.

Writing to Reconstruct Experience

When your purpose is to reconstruct an experience, you use your own experiences as the raw material for your text. Your purpose may simply be to communicate something that happened so that a reader can understand and empathize with that experience. Often, however, your purpose is not just to reconstruct the experience itself, but also to communicate its significance or your reaction to the experience. Thus, at some point in the process of reconstructing your experience, you should think about what you want your readers to understand about it.

Making the Experience Real

To make your experiences vivid and real for your readers, you need more than just the basic facts of who did what when. Three strategies can help you make your experience seem real to a reader:

- ❖ Use specific details.

- ❖ Use concrete language.

- ❖ Use analogies.

USE SPECIFIC DETAILS. Make your narrative vivid and interesting by using specific details in telling your story. For example, describing a car as red is better than just saying "a car," but calling the car a "bright red 1958 Dodge sedan with tail fins and a white roof" is even better. Telling your readers that an experience was exciting doesn't convey what you really felt, but providing a detailed account of an experience such as scaling the jagged stone face of a 15,000-foot mountain during a blinding snowstorm will probably convey to them something of the thrill you experienced.

USE CONCRETE LANGUAGE. Convincing narratives require more than specific details. They also require the use of concrete language—words that create a specific image in the mind of your reader. For example, *ambling, strolling, sauntering, strutting, slouching, hurrying, tip-toeing, wobbling,* and *weaving* are all more precise choices than *walking.* And describing someone as red-faced and trembling with indignation gives a more vivid picture than merely saying the person was angry.

Anger is an abstraction, a sterile concept that provides a reader with intellectual understanding. In contrast, concrete language creates an image of the way in which a person experiences anger, allowing the reader to visualize the reality of the anger.

The instruction to use specific details and concrete language doesn't mean merely slapping more adjectives into your sentences. You cannot convince a reader just by intensifying general statements. To tell readers that climbing the mountain was "very exciting" accomplishes no more than using "exciting" alone (and "exciting" doesn't evoke much!). Read the following two versions of the same experience, and determine which is more convincing:

First Version

My mother's decision to divorce my father ruined Christmas for me that year. When she told me she planned to leave us and move into an apartment, I was devastated. I will never feel the same about Christmas.

Second Version

"I am going to divorce your father," my mother said. "I am moving to another apartment next month." For several seconds her words hung in the air like frozen water drops, ready to fall down to the floor and break into thousands of pieces. I was standing in front of her in the Christmas-decorated living room, feeling the stable ground beneath my feet starting to tremble. With two simple sentences my mother had just torn apart the only place of safety I knew in this world—my home.

In the second version, specific details and images convince; they create a context that makes the writer's assertions believable. Without these vivid details and images, a reader may understand the writer's point—may even agree or sympathize with that point—but will not be able to reconstruct the experience. Good writing of any kind—whether a story or not—includes a wealth of specific details. And the more specific the better.

USE ANALOGIES.   Analogies—comparisons of one thing to something else—also increase specificity and evoke images. For example, stating that your steak was overcooked is not as convincing as saying that it tasted like a well-seasoned rubber tire. But stale, overused analogies only deaden your prose. Comparing something that is hard to a rock or a hammer doesn't accomplish anything. Comparing the same hard object to the heart of a Wall Street broker or a ten-carat diamond would

ANALOGIES, PAGE 517

be much more effective. For example, in the preceding paragraph the student writer says her mother's words "hung in the air like frozen water drops, ready to fall down to the floor and break into thousands of pieces." This analogy is not only original but also poignantly echoes the writer's feelings.

Developing a Personal Writing Voice

Abundant specific details and evocative language help to make narrative accounts real to a reader, and a personal writing voice can convince a reader that what is being said is not only real, but significant. The voice you adopt in a narrative depends on your purpose, on the kind of narrative you are writing, and on your attitude toward your subject. If, like Jesse Stuart or Warren Slay, you idealize or sentimentalize your subject, then your writing voice will reflect these sentiments. You will include details that are affirming, even flattering, and you will use words that reinforce these sentiments.

On the other hand, if you feel ambivalent toward your subject, as Maya Angelou does toward the African celebration in the first part of her essay and as Ernesto Galarza seems to toward the Sixteenth of September celebration, your voice will also reflect this ambivalence. An ambivalent voice differs from an objective stance in that it involves both positive *and* negative feelings, while an objective stance involves neither.

Finally, you may have a negative attitude toward your subject, as Audre Lorde has in her description of her family's experience in Washington, D.C. If so, your writing voice may range from detached to critical to hostile.

The degree of formality you adopt toward your subject also determines your writing voice. In general, a less formal approach sounds more intimate and personal, whereas a more formal treatment results in a more distant, impersonal voice. An informal writing voice evokes the sense of someone talking; it is conversational—identified with a specific person and often with a particular situation or context. In contrast, a formal writing voice seems to exist apart from any particular person, place, and time—outside of a personal context. Your writing's level of formality usually depends on such features as word choice (diction), person (use of *I* or *we* versus *you* versus *he*, *she*, *it*, or *they*), and sentence structure. Content—what you say about your subject—also affects formality. For example, the intimate details that Stuart, Hughes, and Slay include make their narratives seem informal.

You do not usually think consciously about the voice you plan to use when you write. Rather, the subject about which you are writing, your attitude toward that subject, the audience for whom you are writing, and your purpose in writing usually determine the voice you adopt. As you gain experience as a writer, you will develop a fairly consistent voice. However, because you may not yet have found your writing voice, you may need to give this issue deliberate thought when you write (see **style and voice**).

STYLE AND VOICE, PAGE 656

The Role of a Thesis in Writing to Reconstruct Experience

Essays that are based on personal experience often do not include an explicit statement of the writer's thesis; that is, the main idea is implied rather than stated. But, as a writer, *you* need to be aware of the point you want to make. Your thesis may change, in both substantive and incidental ways, as you construct your text (in fact, it probably should change), but you should at least give the matter some thought. You can decide later whether you want to include a thesis statement in the introduction or conclusion of your essay, but be sure that your essay has a main idea—that it makes a point beyond the mere telling of the story.

Notice that most of the readings included in this chapter do not have traditional introductions in which the writer tells the reader what to expect. If you feel the need to sum up your story in some way, making explicit its thesis, you may find that your conclusion is the appropriate place for this direct commentary (see **thesis statement**).

THESIS STATEMENT, PAGE 663

Patterns of Development in Writing to Reconstruct Experience

When you write to reconstruct an experience, you usually structure what you write as a narrative; that is, you tell a story. The plot of the story thus becomes the structure of your text; your narrative is structured in the same chronological order as the events occurred. This chronological sequence of events serves to connect the details you include and make them coherent to a reader. Although telling a story is usually a simple, straightforward process, you should keep in mind at least two guidelines:

* Maintain a single, unified focus.

* Put yourself in your reader's place.

MAINTAIN A SINGLE, UNIFIED FOCUS.   In telling a story, you are always selective since you cannot tell everything that happened. Be sure that what you have chosen to include reinforces the point you want to make. If you have included information or details that do not contribute to your main idea, indicate on your text that this material may later need to be deleted (but do not delete anything hastily—especially if you are working on a computer).

PUT YOURSELF IN YOUR READER'S PLACE.   In reconstructing your own experiences, you depend on your memory to provide you with the basic structure of your narrative. This structure must be clear so that readers can reconstruct the experience in their own minds. If the story you are telling is clear, a reader who was not present should be able to understand what happened. Do you include enough information about who did what where and when? Do you provide background information if it is needed? Do you identify characters and places adequately? Again, it is not easy to make these decisions because you know so much about your subject. Here you must really attempt to view your text through your reader's eyes. Try to distance yourself as much as possible from your text at this point, reading it as though you were seeing it for the first time and knew nothing about the experience.

You might consider rearranging the events in the story so that they do not follow the exact chronological order in which they occurred. Deviating from strict chronological order can be an effective way to focus a reader's attention on a particular part of the narrative or to suggest a strong cause-and-effect relationship. For example, you could begin with the ending, tell what happened or how you felt at the end, and then go back and tell what led to this outcome. You can, in fact, begin at any point in your narrative so long as you do not confuse your readers (see **narration**).

NARRATION, PAGE 618

Another pattern of development that is essential to reconstructions of experience is description. Just as narration creates the structure of your story, description makes your story seem real and interesting. Description involves the senses. It evokes a reader's memory of what it is like to feel, see, hear, smell, or taste something. Too often, inexperienced writers rely exclusively on evoking the sense of sight, telling what something looked like but omitting the other senses. For example, a writer may say that a lemon is oval and yellow but omit the pebbly texture of its skin or its tart taste, or how it feels to be squirted in the eye with an overly juicy slice of lemon. Sensory details focus not only on how things look, but also on how they feel and taste and sound and smell.

No matter how exciting its plot, a story will not interest a reader unless that reader can experience it. The main way to help readers experience your story is to include specific, concrete details that allow them, in so far as possible, to see and hear and feel and smell and taste what you experienced. Don't include meaningless details, and don't overwrite by using a string of adjectives or adverbs to modify every noun and verb you use. But do include pertinent, vivid, specific details to make your story come alive for your readers (see **description**).

DESCRIPTION, PAGE 565

W R I T I N G   A S S I G N M E N T

For this assignment, you are to write about a particular celebration, ritual, or rite of passage you have experienced. You should explain not only what happened, but *how* you felt and *why*. That is, you are going to record what happened and then interpret these events for a reader who does not know you or what happened to you on this occasion. The following suggestions may help you choose a topic:

1. Write about a particular celebration that you looked forward to but that disappointed you in some way.

2. Describe the rite of passage that in your mind marked your becoming an adult. Instead of describing a formal ritual or ceremony that typically functions as a rite of passage, write about an experience that was not intended to serve in this way but that assumed this purpose in your life (for example, when you first drove a car, when a younger sibling was born, when you moved away from home for the first time, and so on).

3. Write about a rite of passage in which your reaction was different from the one you expected. The event you describe may be one that is generally recognized as a rite of passage (for example, a graduation, a religious ceremony, a wedding, the birth of a child, the death of a parent), or it may be an ordinary event that functioned in your life as a rite of passage.

4. Describe a familiar celebration or ritual so that a person of another culture can understand its significance to you.

5. If you moved to this country from another one, do you enjoy the celebrations of holidays in this country as much as you did those in your native country? Write about a celebration that you enjoyed in another place and time but no longer celebrate.

6. Write a narrative that has a persuasive purpose. For example, you might write about your experience with a certain holiday celebration to argue against the commercial nature of the event.

Generating Ideas through Invention and Research

The suggestions that follow will help you generate ideas for this assignment.

INVENTION.   To stimulate your memory about the event you have chosen, freewrite about your experience. In freewriting, you simply write whatever comes to your mind on a subject. Do not attempt to be organized or even coherent; just "free associate" on paper or on your computer screen, writing anything and everything that occurs to you. For example, if you are writing about the most recent Fourth of July, try to remember everything that happened to you on this occasion and how you felt about what was happening. At this point, do not be concerned about correctness—how to spell a word or where to put punctuation marks. Just write to get information and ideas on paper. Freewriting is not a draft of an essay; it is just a way to generate ideas by recalling information that has been stored in your long-term memory. So write as rapidly and as freely as you can.

RESEARCH.   If you have a diary or journal that includes accounts of the experience you plan to reconstruct, reread the pertinent entries. If you do not have this type of personal record of the experience, you can research your subject by looking at family documents such as photographs, newspaper clippings, and letters. Or you can talk with someone who was also a participant in the experience—a family member, a friend, or even an objective outsider who happened to be present.

Drafting Your Text

Now it is time to start drafting your essay. Your freewriting should have warmed you up for this task. Some people sit down and write their entire text in a single session. As one student put it, "Usually, I sort of spit up words and get done with it." Other writers prefer to write one or two paragraphs, then rewrite what they have written before moving on to the next part. You will have to discover your own drafting pattern. If you need to be satisfied with your first paragraph before writing anything else, fine, do that. If you prefer to get the whole thing down before revising, that is also fine. There is no single right or even best way to draft a text. The important thing is to get something on paper or your computer screen so that you can react to it—can rethink and resee the text in your head, reshaping it so that you can then more effectively revise your written text.

Reading and Revising Your Text

Reading your own text objectively is the key to good writing, but it is also one of the most difficult parts of the process. Because you have written the text, you will have difficulty reading it objectively. Instead, you will see what you think is there. Your mental text will obscure your perception of your written text, giving you a sense of accomplishment that often is not warranted. If you want to learn to revise your texts so that they become better and better with each successive draft, you must learn to read each draft perceptively.

The first step to becoming an effective reader of your own writing is to slow down the process. If you read your text as soon as you have finished writing it, you have little chance of seeing what is really there. Wait until the mental text has faded somewhat before trying to read your written text. The longer the better, but at least wait a few hours (an entire day is much better). Then read your text as if you are a "dumb reader"—as if you know nothing about the subject other than what is on the paper (or screen) before you. In reading narratives, this is especially difficult. Since you were, of course, actually present to experience what you are writing about, it is not easy to pretend you are ignorant of what happened. But try.

Additional readings might focus on whether you used concrete language, fresh analogies, and realistic dialogue in telling your story. Or whether your writing voice is natural, direct, and real (as opposed to stilted, vague, and contrived—a voice that doesn't sound like you or anyone else the reader might want to know). As you become a more experienced writer and a more skilled reader of your own text, you can focus on all, or at least many, of these elements at the same time.

How many times should you read and reread your written text as you revise? That depends on how skilled you are as a reader of your own writing. Initially, you may have to reread many times, focusing on something different each time. Later, after you have gained more experience as a writer (and as a reader of your own writing), you may be able to accomplish several purposes in a single reading. In general, read your written text as many times as possible and on as many different occasions as possible. Multiple readings will probably always be necessary unless you are writing a text that is very brief (a few sentences) or very informal (a note to a friend). Don't rush through this essential part of the process.

As you read and reread your story, your mental version of it will inevitably change. You may have surprised yourself by writing something other than what you had planned to write, or you may have written exactly what you had planned to write only to discover that it is dull and trite. After reading your written text, you can reevaluate your original idea of your text. Was it too ambitious, too vague, too obvious? Are there problems you didn't anticipate, weaknesses you failed to predict? Don't be afraid to abandon your initial version if it now seems unrealistic or unworkable. Readjust your thinking to conform to the reality that confronts you in the form of the written text you have produced.

On the other hand, you may want to cling to your earlier idea if you are reassured that it is taking shape but just needs more work or if you are convinced that it is a good idea in spite of the failure of this written draft. You must be the judge about what needs "fixing" as you try to function as both writer and reader. Don't be afraid to take risks and experiment; it's not too late to try something new. Let the two forms of your text—what is in your mind and what is on the paper or computer screen in front of you—shape each other.

Preparing the Final Draft of Your Text

Editing is not the same as revising. When you revise, you are concerned with meaning and content, whereas in editing you are concerned with style, readability, and correctness. Therefore, you do not want to turn your full attention to editing until you are fairly confident that you have finished revising. There is no point in worrying about the punctuation of a sentence that is in a paragraph you may delete. However, once you have a written text with which you are satisfied, it is time to turn your attention to matters of style, readability, and correctness.

CREDIBILITY, PAGE 552

Editing is a courtesy to your reader, whether that reader is your teacher or a peer, an employer or a colleague, an individual or an audience of thousands. More importantly, a well-edited manuscript, one that is easy and pleasant to read, establishes your **credibility** as a writer. No matter how informed, exciting, or significant your content, your credibility as a writer also depends on whether you construct a text that readers can easily read—a text that is not wordy, confusing, awkward, or incorrect.

The problem is, of course, that inexperienced writers do not know how to edit a text—do not even recognize the editing problems that exist much less know how to correct them. No one deliberately writes badly or makes errors on purpose. One of the purposes of this book is to help you become a better editor. Each chapter will focus on different editing concerns and suggest ways for you to improve your editing skills. However, since you must take responsibility for the readability and correctness of your text from the first of the course, we offer these general suggestions:

(1) **TRUST YOUR INSTINCTS.** Writers can usually identify problems with style, readability, and correctness even if they do not know what the problem is, what to call it, or how to fix it. If you think, or even sense, that a problem exists, it probably does. For example, if you stumble over a sentence as you read your text aloud or have to reread a sentence if you are reading silently, that sentence probably needs some editing.

(2) **TRUST YOUR PEERS.** Let several classmates read what you have written. Ask them to point out sentences that are unclear or difficult to read, words that are misspelled or inappropriate, punctuation that is incorrect. Discuss with them how you might edit these sentences so that they are easier to read.

(3) **TRUST YOUR INSTRUCTOR.**   When teachers tell you they want you to come by and talk to them about your writing, they really mean it. Sure they're busy, but they respect students who are concerned enough to come by for a conference. A brief conference with your instructor can not only clear up a great many editing problems in a given text, but it can also provide you with the information you need to avoid the same problems in the future.

(4) **DON'T TRUST YOURSELF TO PROOFREAD EFFECTIVELY IMMEDIATELY AFTER YOU HAVE FINISHED WRITING YOUR TEXT.**   Reading aloud or pointing to each word as you read it may help alter your normal reading process and thus allow you to see what is really on the page (as opposed to what is in your head), but waiting until your text is "cold" is the best strategy. Even then, don't confuse reading and proofreading. When you read something, even something you have not written, you do not read every word, only those that are necessary to predict meaning. To proofread (or "goofread") effectively, you must alter your normal reading process so that you force yourself to see exactly what is there. This takes time and perseverance, and even then it is not easy. But a good writer is nearly always a good proofreader.

D I S C O V E R I N G   Y O U R S E L F
A S   A   W R I T E R

After you have completed this assignment, take a few minutes to reflect on this writing experience by answering the following questions:

1. What did you learn about yourself as a writer as you worked on this assignment? In what way did this writing experience change your perception of yourself as a writer, your process of writing, or your attitude toward writing?

2. What forms of research did you use for this assignment? What did you learn about research that will help you in other writing assignments?

3. Was the final draft of your text better or worse than you had expected? What would you do differently if you had the opportunity to do this assignment again?

4. How did writing this assignment make you a better reader?

5. What did you enjoy most about this writing assignment? What did you like least?

Jeff Etheridge, Samford Hall, Auburn University.

4

WRITING TO INSTRUCT AND ADVISE

The reasonable thing is to learn from those who can teach.

SOPHOCLES

In every society the experienced older members teach inexperienced younger members how to live—how to conduct themselves, relate to one another, survive in a particular environment. These instructions take many forms; the most basic are transmitted through observation. Children watch their elders and imitate what they see. More explicit are oral instructions, such as, "Don't touch," which is one of the earliest instructions that most children in our society hear. Oral instructions continue to be important sources of learning throughout a person's life. For example, you have probably received plenty of informal oral advice from friends, fellow students, parents, and teachers about how to be a successful college student. But in highly literate societies, written instructions also abound. The selections in this chapter provide you with written instructions and advice about survival and success as a college student.

In this chapter you will also learn how to write to advise and instruct others. So far, your experience with instructions has probably been more that of reader than writer. You have read instructions in your textbooks that tell you how to write an essay, solve an equation, or conduct an experiment. You have probably also read articles dispensing advice on everything from how to pass a college entrance exam to how to find a mate. But now you are going to learn how to write to instruct and advise others.

NARRATION, PAGE 618 Like narratives, instructions are often arranged chronologically (see **narration**). Instructions always involve a process, and a process is, in effect, a narrative—a story of what happens or what to do next. Whether a simple series of steps (how to withdraw money from an automatic teller machine), a complicated procedure (how to install a car radio), or a serious lesson in life (how to be a success), a process is usually presented in chronological order.

Some instructions actually are narratives—stories that teach a lesson. Much of what we have all learned in our lives has come from instructive stories, usually called parables or fables, which offer instruction in its most palatable, seductive form. These lessons clothed in narrative fabric—like the stories of the Prodigal Son, the tortoise and the hare, and the little boy who cried "Wolf"—instruct indirectly, slipping the lesson into a narrative framework that is easy to listen to, easy to understand, and easy to remember.

Thus, in writing and reading instructions, you will use many of the same patterns you use in writing to reconstruct experience. The difference is not in the structure, but in the purpose and the format. In writing to instruct, you often draw on what you have learned from your own experiences, but your primary purpose is to teach your readers how to do something or to advise them about something.

READING TEXTS THAT INSTRUCT AND ADVISE

Good written instructions are easy to read, easy to follow, and easy to remember. Unfortunately, they are also rare. Everyone has had the frustrating experience of trying to follow badly written instructions that are open to different interpretations, leave out important information, assume too much knowledge on the part of the reader, or do not explain what needs to be done in a straightforward manner. When people read instructions, they must often compensate for what the writer of the instructions did not do well.

Two basic types of instructions exist: (1) specific instructions, which explain the steps in a process that the reader follows immediately, and (2) general instructions and advice, which offer suggestions for the readers' consideration but do not assume immediate action on their part. In this chapter, we focus on general instructions and advice.

When you read instructions or advice, your primary purpose is nearly always to accomplish something—to improve your vocabulary, dress more stylishly, save money, find a job, lose or gain weight, and so on. Thus, reading instructions is usually a means to an end, a way of accomplishing some goal. Few other types of reading are so focused and specific in purpose.

The authors of the reading selections in this chapter are advising their readers about broad, ongoing action to be undertaken in the future rather than instructing them specifically how to perform an exact task. For example, Nikki Giovanni is offering advice to African-American students who may be planning to attend a predominantly white school, and Joshua Halberstam is telling students who want to be successful how to conduct themselves in class. These articles, like most of the many how-to books on the market, provide readers with advice and general guidelines to be acted upon later rather than with explicit instructions to be performed as they read.

You should read such articles and essays thoughtfully and critically, much as you would any general article or essay. For example, you will want to evaluate the expertise and experience of the author. Is the author a known authority on this subject? If not, does he or she explain convincingly why the advice that is given should be followed? Among the authors of the reading selections in this chapter, Nikki Giovanni and Joshua Halberstam are both college professors, so you may assume they know what college students should do to succeed. Stacey Colino, in contrast, is not a known authority on her subject—campus crime—but she establishes her credibility by citing other sources and including statistics that support her theories.

In addition, you will need to evaluate the usefulness of the instructions or advice. Good advice is realistic, pertinent, and ethical. That is, it should be something you can do, will benefit from doing, and will not feel guilty about doing. Evaluating instructions is, therefore, a rather subjective process. For example, what is realistic for one person may be impossible for another. If you are not an appropriate audience for the advice you are reading, it has no value for you. Advice is only good if it is appropriate for the person who is reading it.

READING SELECTIONS ◀

As a college student, you often seek the advice of others—teachers, administrators, counselors, and more experienced students. You may also occasionally seek written instructions from your college bulletin or schedule of classes. In addition, if you are applying for a loan, using the on-line catalog at the library, or taking advantage of a computer lab for preparing written assignments, you may need to follow specific written instructions. This chapter's reading selections offer you general instructions and advice about coping with some of the problems you are likely to encounter as a college student.

Campus Racism 101

Nikki Giovanni

Nikki Giovanni is a well-known African-American poet as well as a college professor. In this article, first published in Essence, *a magazine directed primarily at African-American readers, she is giving advice to African-American students who attend, or who are thinking about attending, predominantly white universities. Notice as you read how Giovanni convinces her readers that she is qualified to give advice on this subject.*

There is a bumper sticker that reads: "Too bad ignorance isn't painful." I like that. But ignorance is. We just seldom attribute the pain to it or even recognize it when we see it. Like the postcard on my corkboard. It shows a young man in a very hip jacket smoking a cigarette. In the background is a high school with the American flag waving. The caption says: "Too cool for school. Yet too stupid for the real world." Out of the mouth of the young man is a bubble enclosing the words "Maybe I'll start a band." There could be a postcard showing a jock in a uniform saying "I don't need school. I'm going to the NFL or NBA." Or one showing a young man or woman studying and a group of young people saying "So you want to be white." Or something equally demeaning. We need to quit it.

I am a professor of English at Virginia Tech. I've been here for four years, though for only two years with academic rank. I am tenured, which means I have a teaching position for life, a rarity on a predominantly white campus. Whether from malice or ignorance, people who think I should be at a predominantly Black institution will say, "Why are you at Tech?" Because it's here. And so are Black students. But even if Black students weren't here, it's painfully obvious that this nation and this world cannot allow white students to go through higher education without interacting with Blacks in authoritative positions. It is equally clear that predominantly Black colleges cannot accommodate the numbers of Black students who want and need an education.

3   Is it difficult to attend a predominantly white college? Compared with what? Being passed over for promotion because you lack credentials? Being turned down for jobs because you are not college-educated? Joining the armed forces or going to jail because you cannot find an alternative to the streets? Let's have a little perspective here. Where can you go and what can you do that frees you from interacting with the white American mentality? You're going to interact; the only question is, Will you be in some control of yourself and your actions, or will you be controlled by others? I'm going to recommend control.

4   What's the difference between prison and college? They both proscribe your behavior for a given period of time. They both allow you to read books and develop your writing. They both give you time alone to think and time with your peers to talk about issues. But four years of prison doesn't give you a passport to greater opportunities. Most likely that time only gives you greater knowledge of how to get back in. Four years of college gives you an opportunity not only to lift yourself but to serve your people effectively. What's the difference when you are called a nigger in college from when you are called a nigger in prison? In college you can, though I admit with effort, follow procedures to have those students who called you nigger kicked out or suspended. You can bring issues to public attention without risk of your life. But mostly college is and always has been the future. We, neither less nor more than other people, need knowledge. There are discomforts attached to attending predominantly white colleges, though no more so than living in a racist world. Here are some rules to follow that may help:

5   **Go to class.** No matter how you feel. No matter how you think the professor feels about you. It's important to have a consistent presence in the classroom. If nothing else, the professor will know you care enough and are serious enough to be there.

6   **Meet your professors**. Extend your hand (give a firm handshake) and tell them your name. *Ask them what you need to do to make an A.* You may never make an *A* but you have put them on notice that you are serious about getting good grades.

Do assignments on time. Typed or computer-generated. You have   7
the syllabus. Follow it. And turn those papers in. If for some reason
you can't complete an assignment on time, let your professor know
before it is due and work out a new due date—then meet it.

Go back to see your professor. Tell him or her your name again. If   8
an assignment received less than an *A*, ask why, and find out what
you need to do to improve the next assignment.

   Yes, your professor is busy. So are you. So are your parents who
are working to pay or help with your tuition. Ask *early* what you need
to do if you feel you are starting to get into academic trouble. Do not
wait until you are failing.

Understand that there will be professors who do not like you;   9
there may even be professors who are racist or sexist or both. You
must discriminate among your professors to see who will give you the
help you need. You may not simply say "They are all against me."
They aren't. They mostly don't care. Since you are the one who wants
to be educated, find the people who want to help.

Don't defeat yourself. Cultivate your friends. Know your enemies.   10
You cannot undo hundreds of years of prejudicial thinking. Think for
yourself and speak up. Raise your hand in class. Say what you believe
no matter how awkward you may think it sounds. You will improve in
your articulation and confidence.

Participate in some campus activity. Join the newspaper staff. Run   11
for office. Join a dorm council. Do *something* that involves you on
campus. You are going to be there for four years, so let your presence
be known, if not felt.

   You will inevitably run into some white classmates who are troubling because they often say stupid things, ask stupid questions—and
expect an answer. Here are some comebacks to some of the most common inquiries and comments:

Q   *What's it like to grow up in a ghetto?*
    A   I don't know.   12
    13
Q   *From the teacher: Can you give us the Black perspective on*
    Toni Morrison, Huck Finn, slavery, Martin Luther King, Jr.,   14
    and others?
    A   I can give you *my* perspective. [Do not take the burden   15
    of 22 million people on your shoulders. Remind everyone that
    you are an individual, and don't speak for the race or any
    other individual within it.]

Q   *Why do all the Black people sit together in the dining hall?*   16
    A   Why do the white students sit together?   17

18 **Q** *Why should there be an African-American–studies course?*

19 **A Because white Americans have not adequately studied the contributions of Africans and African-Americans. Both Black and white students need to know our total common history.**

20 **Q** *Why are there so many scholarships for "minority" students?*

21 **A Because they wouldn't give my great-grandparents their 40 acres and the mule.**

22 **Q** *How can whites understand Black history, culture, literature and so forth?*

23 **A The same way we understand white history, culture, literature and so forth. That is why we're in school: to learn.**

24 **Q** *Should whites take African-American–studies courses?*

25 **A Of course. We take white-studies courses, though the universities don't call them that.**

26 **Comment:** When I see groups of Black people on campus, it's really intimidating.

27 **Comeback: I understand what you mean. I'm frightened when I see white students congregating.**

28 **Comment:** It's not fair. It's easier for you guys to get into college than for other people.

29 **Comeback: If it's so easy, why aren't there more of us?**

30 **Comment:** It's not our fault that America is the way it is.

31 **Comeback: It's not our fault, either, but both of us have a responsibility to make changes.**

32   It's really very simple. Educational progress is a national concern; education is a private one. Your job is not to educate white people; it is to obtain an education. If you take the racial world on your shoulders, you will not get the job done. Deal with yourself as an individual worthy of respect, and make everyone else deal with you the same way. College is a little like playing grown-up. Practice what you want to be. You have been telling your parents you are grown. Now is your chance to act like it.

QUESTIONS TO CONSIDER

1. The first part of this article (paragraphs 1 through 4) establishes Giovanni's credibility and authority. How does she convince readers that she is qualified to write on this topic?

2. The second part of the article (paragraphs 5 through 11) gives specific suggestions for African-American students to follow in order to succeed on a predominantly white campus. Would these same steps be equally appropriate for all students?

3. The third part of the article (paragraphs 12 through 32) focuses on the questions that African-American students are sometimes asked and gives suggested responses for these inquiries. Do you think these responses are appropriate? What other responses might be given to the same questions?

4. This article is persuasive as well as instructive. What do you think Giovanni is trying to persuade her readers to do? How effective do you think she is? Can you offer some ways in which Giovanni might be more persuasive?

WRITING ACTIVITIES

Individual: Write a journal entry in which you tell of an experience you have had as a minority. For example, perhaps you are the only female or male in a class you are taking, or the only one from a rural background in your sorority or fraternity, or the only one in your carpool who smokes. How do you feel in these situations? Are your feelings the result of what the other people (the majority) actually say and do or what you imagine they think about you?

Collaborative: Working in a group, write at least one other possible answer for each of the questions that Giovanni poses and answers. Compare your answers with those written by other groups.

Computer: Notice the **format** of Giovanni's article—the use of indention, spacing, boldface type, and so on. Using your computer, design a format that makes the instructions given in the last part of the article even clearer and easier to read.

FORMAT, PAGE 582

CLASS IN THE CLASSROOM

Joshua Halberstam

Joshua Halberstam, who teaches ethics at New York University, has written a book entitled Acing College, *in which he gives students a professor's eye view of how to succeed in college. The subtitle of the book is* A Professor Tells Students How to Beat the System. *In this selection from that book, Halberstam advises students about classroom behavior. Notice, as you read, his slightly cynical tone and direct, no-nonsense advice; note, as well, your reaction to this approach.*

1   Kid knocks on my office door. He looks vaguely familiar. "My name is Scott," he says. "I'm in your logic class." Yes, that's why I recognize him; he's the fellow who showed up a couple of times at the beginning of the semester. Sat in the back, I think.

2   "So where have you been all term?" I ask with genuine curiosity. "Well," the student fumbles, "I'm taking this tough course in organic chemistry, and well, uh, like I got this lazy attitude, I admit. Anyway, I'd like an extension on my term paper deadline. And would you reconsider my midterm grade?"

3   I listen, but I don't listen sympathetically. I'm certainly not inclined to reward this student for his lack of interest in my class. It's not a matter of an official policy—I don't take attendance. But I don't have to do favors either, and I rarely do for students who don't show up to class.

4   "The most important thing in life is showing up," says Woody Allen. That's true, too, with regard to your classes.

5   In this chapter we'll discuss how to make the most of your time when you're in class. But these guidelines are useful only if you're there to use them.

SHOWING UP

6   On any given school day, you could probably think of seven thousand more fun things to do than go to class. One compelling alternative is to just stay in bed. In fact, staying in bed will loom as one of the greatest temptations of college life.

I take it for granted that if you aren't thoroughly dull or irrecoverably compulsive, you will miss class on occasion. What does it take for you to decide "forget it, I'll skip class?" A blah, rainy day? A gorgeous, sunny day? Students' cutting patterns get fixed pretty early in their college career. The question is not whether you will miss class, but how often.   7

Some professors include attendance as part of their course requirements. These professors usually carry out their threat. The more stringent ones will even fail the A student who has accrued too many absences. Unfair? I agree. In fact, I find this outrageous. With few exceptions (labs, for example), I favor abolishing all attendance requirements. College students are adults and should decide for themselves whether or not they want to come to class. If you never show up, you risk flunking your tests—but that's *your* problem. On the other hand, if you never show up and get A's on your exams, you should receive an A for the course.   8

Why do professors require attendance? Many will tell you it's because students need to attend their lectures to understand the material. And they quickly emphasize the need for an "attendance requirement" for those students who lack sufficient discipline to show up regularly without this externally imposed threat.   9

Hogwash. Professors require attendance, in most cases, because they are insecure. They're afraid that if they don't take attendance, no one will show up—and they're usually right. Not surprisingly, it's most often the dull teachers who force their students to suffer through their dreary lectures.   10

What can you do about these attendance requirements? Nothing. Maybe you can do something later when you become the college president, but until then, if you have an attendance requirement, show up. You have no choice.   11

But even if you don't have an attendance requirement, it's important to show up regularly.   12

If you want to ace your classes, cut out cutting. You might think your case is different. But I can only assure you of what all my colleagues and I see: A students show up to class regularly, and F students don't. Here's why.   13

Objectively

You'll learn more. Nothing beats being there. When you study without having been to class, you're learning the material for the first time. When you study after you've been to class, you're reviewing. What a difference!   14

15   **You learn what the professor considers essential.** Professors test you on what they consider important. What did the professor put on the blackboard? What did he emphasize? What did he repeat?

16   You can't get this information from another student's notes, or even a tape recording. You need to observe firsthand your professor's delivery: you need to know not only what was said but how it was said.

Subjectively

17   **In the subjective realm of grading, attendance always counts.** Professors respond positively toward students who come to class regularly. Repeated absences will lose you the benefit of the doubt when it comes to grading—and you might very well need that benefit.

18   College teachers are as sensitive as anyone else. Most people like to believe they are good at what they do, and college teachers like to think of themselves as good teachers. Your consistent cutting tells your teacher that you consider him a failure: he isn't sufficiently interesting to get you to come to class. And your teacher—at least on some level—will take it personally. He might take it out on you personally.

19   **Attendance is especially important in seminars, language, math, and science classes.** The smaller the class, the more your absences are noticed, so if you have to play hooky, cut a large lecture class. The worst classes to skip are seminars where student participation is expected. Cutting seminars undermines the whole class.

20   It's also essential to show up regularly to math, science, and language classes. If you are facile with words and know the tricks of extemporaneous writing, you might get by with absences in some of your humanities and social science classes. Math, science, and language classes are different: here, learning is cumulative, with each class building on the previous class. If you fall behind, it becomes increasingly difficult to catch up.

If You Do Cut

21   Don't make a big deal about it. Professors who require attendance might require a doctor's note or some other justification for your absence. Professors who don't take attendance don't care why you were out.

22   I never could understand why students bother bringing me notes explaining why they missed a class. I don't read them and I suspect

few professors do. (It's another matter if you miss an exam.) Nor do I understand why students bother to tell me they will miss the next class. Why call attention to an absence?

DO THE READINGS

Prepare for Class

I know this sounds like more obvious professor talk but believe me, preparation is far from common.   23

All students are "rah rah" the first week of class. They do the assigned readings and come to class rearing to go. Then the slack-off begins. By the end of the first month a sizable contingent have stopped coming to class prepared. By the end of the second month, you can count on one hand the number of students who read the material before coming to class. By the middle of the third month, forget it; the student who still prepares is now a rarity.   24

Read the assignments all through the semester and consider yourself an extraordinary phenomenon. College homework is a term-long affair. In high school you did your homework only when it was assigned and when you expected it to get checked. In college, you have to rely on your own schedule and discipline.   25

Figure it this way: you have to read the material eventually anyway, so you may as well read it before class. It's much more effective that way: even boring classes are improved, and you can contribute to the class.   26

The big hurdle is reading those stupefying assignments that seem to have been written as prescriptions for sleeping pills. To get these assignments done, you've got to make class preparation part of your daily routine.   27

But if You Don't Prepare

You won't always come to class prepared. Perhaps you have a test in another class. Or a heavy date the night before. Or a heavy date coming up. What then?   28

Try not to walk into class totally oblivious of the assignment. Cultivate the art of intelligent skimming; when you get good at it—and like everything else it's a matter of practice—you can pick up lots of information very quickly.   29

Okay, it was a *very* heavy date. Not only weren't you able to scan the assigned material, you can now barely keep your eyes open. In this situation, it isn't your eyes that matter, it's your mouth. Keep it shut.   30

31   Few displays of student behavior are as annoying to teachers as students spouting about subjects they know nothing about—but should, had they done the assigned reading. Don't fool yourself and make a fool of yourself in the process. If you haven't read the article, you don't know it. And if you don't know the assignment, don't advertise that you don't.

WHERE TO SIT

32   In some large lectures, your seating arrangement is alphabetically determined, so this isn't an issue. But in most classes you have a choice. Where should you sit? Which seat is most conducive to getting the A?

33   **Sit where the action is.**

34   Writers on power often talk about "power centers" in a room. Every class has its corresponding power center. It's the section that carries the weight of the class.

35   Watch your teacher's movements. (If your teacher is any good, you won't find her sitting behind her desk.) Speakers respond to the section of the audience that responds to them. If one side of the class reacts more vocally to the teacher than the other side, before long, the teacher will be addressing that part of the room more often. Move to that side.

36   Front or back? You can get an A or an F from the front or the back of the room, but in general, front or toward the front is better.*

37   Sitting up toward the front has two main advantages:

*   **Your professor notices you.** Bad enough that you're a nameless name in the crowd; why be a faceless face in the crowd? Also, teachers tend to think—justifiably or not—that students who sit up front are more conscientious.

*   **You insure your participation.** Sitting in the professor's eyeline forces you to behave. Your absences are noticed, so you'll make sure to show up in class. You are also less likely to read, talk, or sleep during even the most boring class. If the class is especially important or particularly dreary, sit up front. You'll need all the help you can get, and this helps.

---

*Students inform me that some of their professors look out above the first row into the class beyond, so a row or two up might be best of all.

The worst seat? It's the back corner seat near the door. You seem   40
uninvolved. **If you are stuck in the back, make sure to speak up
in class.**

A FEW NOTES ON TAKING NOTES

Unless you have a photographic memory, you need to take some   41
notes. You certainly can't expect to remember during final exam week
in May what your professor said back in March.

But don't confuse taking notes with stenography. A good lecture   42
gets you to *reflect* during class. You can't listen, think, and respond if
you're busy playing secretary.

Write down key phrases and ideas that will get you to remember   43
what was discussed (in some classes that will mean a lot of writing, in
others very little writing).

Many study guides offer instruction on how to take notes effec-   44
tively. These guides are a waste of time. You take notes to help *you* review when preparing for exams; what helps you might not help others.

A few of the more compulsive of these study guides recommend   45
that students rewrite their notes after each class. They also suggest that
you write a summary at the end of each class, restating the essential
points of the lecture. Sure, and I recommend that you do a triathlon
every morning and read one play by Shakespeare with dinner every
evening. Who are we kidding?

The Old Blackboard Reflex

When I feel mischievous in the middle of a lecture, I sometimes   46
turn and write on the board a word such as "ineluctable," or the
phrase "the cat's meow," or whatever comes to mind. I look up at the
class and, invariably, I see dozens of students earnestly copying my
words into their notebooks. The assumption: if it's on the blackboard,
it's important.

Agreed, instructors do use the blackboard to highlight important   47
points. But not everything on the board merits special attention; professors will use the board gratuitously, as the whim strikes them.
Sometimes they use it just to show the correct spelling of some
obscure word.

Remember, too, that much that isn't on the board appears on the   48
test. Use your judgment, not your reflexes.

Other People's Notes

49   If you missed class, it's a good idea to borrow someone's notes, especially in cumulative classes, the kind where each class builds on the previous one.

50   **Make sure, though, to borrow the notes immediately after the missed class.** If you wait until exam time, two things will happen. First, the notes lose their context, and you'll have an awful time trying to make sense of them. Second, getting the notes will be a battle. Your new friends won't eagerly part with them the night before the final.

51   Remember, too, not to trust completely in your classmate's notes. She may have gotten it down wrong. She might have been lost in a sweet fantasy just when the important stuff was discussed. She might have that photographic memory and not bother with careful notes.

Private Ruminations

52   In a later chapter, I encourage you to keep a journal of your personal thoughts, a sort of intellectual diary. You should also save a section in the back of your notebook for class-related meditations. Something your professor or a classmate said might trigger an interesting idea. Jot it down. These notes can become extremely helpful when you review for an exam.

LEAVE A MESSAGE
AND WE'LL GET BACK TO YOU

53   When tape recorders first started showing up on my students' desks, I had this terrifying image of lecturing to a classroom empty of people but dotted with little tape recorders on every desk. At the end of this imaginary lecture, my students would come to pick up their tape recorders. After a while, I figured that since no one was responding during class, I might as well just tape my lectures. So I'd bring in my tape recorder, set it up on the lectern, hit "play," and leave; all the other tape recorders would dutifully record my words of wisdom.

54   An old-fashioned nightmare. Soon, I suppose, video cameras will appear on desks to record lectures. Professors will have to take acting lessons, which, come to think of it, isn't such a bad idea.

55   Why tape record the class? I suppose that students use tape recorders as a security blanket. They're afraid they might miss some-

thing important and feel reassured knowing that the vital information is trapped in that little box, caught forever on a magnetic strip.

Beware: not even narcissistic professors like having their classes 56 taped. Having your lecture recorded is like having your classes audited by your boss. It kills spontaneity: you're always afraid you might say something incriminating or dumb.

For those who insist on bringing a tape recorder to class, here are 57 a few rules:

* Get your teacher's permission first. It's rude to record anyone 58 without telling him, and rudeness toward the person who grades you isn't clever.

* Don't use a tape recorder if it inhibits you from participating in 59 class. Some students who would otherwise speak up will shut down when they're being recorded.

* Don't rely on the recording. Gestures convey crucial information. 60 Your tape recorder can't capture the body language.

Since you have to listen to the class anyway, why not just pay 61 attention the first time?

CLASS PARTICIPATION

Want to get an A? Participate. 62

As I've said, showing up to class is essential, and not showing up 63 will hurt your grade. But coming to class isn't enough. According to a recent survey, only 20 percent of the average class asks questions, and you should join this minority if you want to secure the A.

Professors seek, need, and appreciate student involvement in 64 their class. We need applause, and the applause of the classroom is animated discussion. Even the most thick-skinned professor knows when he's not setting his class on fire. Students who make professors feel successful are rewarded with better grades.

Too Shy?

Are you uncomfortable speaking up in a group? What are you 65 going to do about it? Resign yourself to spending four years in silence, masquerading as part of the classroom furniture?

66   Perhaps you are reluctant to speak up because you don't want to sound like those annoying classmates who blabber inanities in class. You fear that you don't have anything of substance to add to the proceedings.

67   I know it's difficult, but try not to worry about what your classmates think of you. They won't judge you: they're too busy thinking about their own brilliant comments. Some people are too self-conscious to dance on a crowded floor in a discotheque. There too, no one notices.

68   A tinge of nervousness before speaking in a group is perfectly normal. Just bear in mind that making a comment in class is no major undertaking—your contribution counts as much as any of your classmate's. And rest assured, it gets easier with practice.

69   You will need to speak in public when you are out in the world. The college classroom affords a wonderful opportunity to become good at it.

Don't Lecture

70   About that blabbering classmate: every class has one. He thinks his classmates are paying money to hear him, not the professor, lecture. He has opinions about everything and makes sure everyone knows them. He considers himself provocative—but the only thing he provokes is a conspiracy to lynch.

71   Typically, this student loves to argue; he argues for the sake of arguing. He's not about the courage of his conviction; he's about contrariness: tell him it's raining and he'll say it's snowing, tell him it's snowing and he'll call it a beach day.

72   He believes belligerence is endearing, but everyone finds him immature, boring, and self-defeating.

73   If you genuinely disagree with your professor—and if you aren't catatonic, you'll disagree plenty of times—by all means, voice your objection. But challenging your professor's dominance for the sake of the challenge alone is a no-win strategy. The classroom is the professor's turf, his territorial imperative. **Attempts to undercut his authority bring you only one result: a lower grade.**

74   Another, milder class nerd is the student who insists on treating the class to private, boring anecdotes about his life. This clod isn't interested in asserting his brilliance; he just considers his personal life endlessly fascinating to everyone. So we have to listen to tales about how his mother tortured him as a child, how his uncle became a Bedouin in the Sahara, how he stopped a mugger on the subway, and

how his roommate ripped off the telephone company. Somebody should tell him that **nobody is interested.**

These students don't just irritate their classmates by using the classroom for their personal forum, they deflect the class discussion away from the direction the professor intended. Professors respond by lowering these students' grades.   75

Questions Are Better Than Comments

Teachers like comments that move the discussion along. They like questions even better, and among the best questions are requests for clarification.   76

"Could you explain that again?" is not an appropriate question if you didn't understand the discussion because you were busy doing the Sunday crossword puzzle. It is an excellent question if you paid attention and need to have a point repeated. This sort of question does your classmates a service. If you didn't follow what was said, the chances are that many of your classmates didn't either.   77

Requests for elucidation also help your grade. It shows you care about the material and want to understand the class discussion. But don't overdo it. You don't want to seem obstructive or slow.   78

Ask Questions about an Upcoming Exam

Has your professor told the class little or no information about the upcoming test? Ask. Wait till the end of class (some professors prefer questions at the end of the class period) and ask your professor what to expect: an essay or short-answer test, or a cumulative, open book exam? Sometimes your instructor doesn't tell the class because she simply forgets to, and your question is a welcome reminder.   79

Dress

I'd rather not believe that professors factor in a student's appearance in the determination of his or her grade, but studies indicate otherwise. Especially at the grade-school and high-school levels, good-looking students are graded more leniently than ugly students.   80

I think you are pretty safe dressing as you like in college, and I think you should dress as you like in any case. Don't be surprised,   81

however, if you run into that professor who takes you—and your work—
less seriously than you'd like because you wear outlandish clothing.

DEALING WITH BOREDOM

82   Fact one: You will have to sit through boring classes. Fact two: If
you are unlucky, you will sit through many boring classes.

83   This is the fourth class in which you've discussed the symbolic
role of birds in early Anglo-Saxon literature. Moreover, you're a computer science major with less than zero interest in birds, real or symbolic, and you're only taking this class to meet a humanities
requirement. You've been good. You've contributed your insights on
the relationships between bird chirps and microchips. And you're
bored out of your wits.

84   Don't read. Don't talk. Your professor can see your face, so look
alive. Bored or not, the grade counts.

85   It's time for creativity. Play mind games. Count how many times
your teacher uses the word *impact*. Decide who are the three best-
looking students in the class. Check out the other students' accents.
Picture your professor as a five-year-old . . . as an eighty-year-old.

86   If you're inventive, you can come up with dozens of mind games
that keep you entertained and, at the same time, keep your attention
focused on what's happening in class. This has the advantage of making it appear as if you're interested in the class; how could your professor know that when you are looking at him, you're imagining him
with a pacifier in his mouth?

THOU SHALT NOT

87   Here's a review of behavior you must avoid. Etiquette is not the
concern here (though that counts too). The concern is how to avoid a
lower grade than you deserve.

88   ❖ **Never badmouth the subject matter.** A quick and sure way to
get a lousy grade in a class: ridicule the subject you're studying.
You, a twenty-year-old undergraduate, have decided that economics is "bull," or that psychology is all smoke, or that Henry
James can't write for beans.

89   Your professor has devoted his life to the subject and will judge
you to be an ignorant, impudent brat. He will also welcome the
opportunity to grade your work as severely as he can.

❖ **Never study for an exam in another class.** This suggests to the 90
professor that you worry more about the other class than her
own. It's insulting.

❖ **Avoid coming late or leaving early.** In college, you are largely 91
anonymous. To get A's, you need to stand out. But that doesn't
include standing out like a sore thumb—arriving late and leaving
early are the wrong ways to call attention to yourself.

Don't stare at your watch, pack your books or put your coat on 92
five minutes before the end of the class. These maneuvers disrupt
the class and offend your professor. If you have to leave early,
tell your professor before class starts and sit near an exit.

❖ **Never read in class.** Textbooks from other classes are bad 93
enough, but magazines and newspapers are particularly offensive.

❖ **Don't sit at your desk without a notebook.** Bring paper and pen 94
even if all you do is doodle. Pretend you are a serious student.

❖ **Don't yack in class.** It's rude and makes you seem adolescent. 95

QUESTIONS TO CONSIDER

1. Did you find Halberstam's straightforward approach convincing?
Why or why not? Does his cynical tone and brusque style fit your
stereotype of a college professor? How many of your professors
actually conform to this stereotype?

2. What one piece of Halberstam's advice did you find most useful?
Why do you think this advice is valuable? Did you think following
Halberstam's advice would make you more successful in college?
That is, do his insider's tips actually provide you with valuable infor-
mation you would otherwise not know?

3. How does Halberstam's advice differ from the standard advice given
to students by parents and teachers? Did you learn anything from
this selection that you did not already know?

4. *Acing College*, the title of the book from which this chapter was
taken, suggests that the reason to read (and/or buy) the book is to
learn how to make good grades in college. In fact, above the title
on the cover of the book is written "Studying is not enough to guarantee A's." Should making A's be the most important goal of a college student? What other goals do you consider equally, or more,
important? Would Halberstam's advice help you attain these goals?

HEADINGS, PAGE 603

FORMAT, PAGE 582

5. Identify examples of the following formatting features that Halberstam uses: main headings, subheadings, bullets, boldface type, and italics (see **headings** and **format**). How do these features improve the readability of his text?

▶ # WRITING ACTIVITIES

Individual: In a journal entry, describe yourself as you usually appear and act in class. How do your appearance and actions differ from those recommended by Halberstam? Have you ever used any of Halberstam's suggestions successfully to get a better grade? Have you ever attempted one of Halberstam's suggestions and had it backfire on you? Analyze why these strategies did or did not work for you.

Collaborative: Compare your classroom behavior with that of a group of your classmates. Then decide on a set of instructions for ideal classroom behavior from a student's point of view. Make your instructions brief and specific.

AMPLIFICATION, PAGE 508

STYLE AND VOICE, PAGE 656

Computer: Choose one instruction from the list your group compiled, and revise it, amplifying (see **amplification**) it with personal experiences and examples, so that it becomes a piece of advice rather than an item from a set of instructions. Your **style and voice** should reflect the personal, informal way in which students communicate with one another.

CRIME ON CAMPUS

Stacey Colino
With Tina Oakland and Maryann Jacobi

This selection appeared first in Seventeen, *a magazine written primarily for a young female audience. Notice that the author begins by providing her readers with information. In fact, the first part of the essay, paragraphs 1 through 18, is both informative (this is what has been going on) and persuasive (something should be done about it). The next part of the article, paragraphs 19 through 42, consists of a series of questions and answers. The last part of the*

essay, paragraphs 43 through 48, is clearly instructive. As you read, decide how the first two parts of the essay contribute to the effectiveness of the final instructions.

Early on the morning of January 17, 1988—hours after the Winter Formal—University of Georgia sophomore Dana Getzinger woke up when a man tried to smother her in bed with a pillow. Wearing a ski mask and gloves, the intruder had broken into the off-campus apartment she shared with her roommates through a sliding glass door. As Getzinger fought him off, she felt what she thought was a punch in the stomach; as it turned out, she'd been stabbed. Several people who were staying in the apartment heard the intruder leaving and came to Getzinger's rescue.   1

After she recovered, Getzinger learned of four similar incidents that had occurred on campus. Each attack happened a month apart and within a one-mile radius of her apartment; all of the women had been raped. The man who committed at least two of the other crimes was caught, but Getzinger still doesn't know if he's the one who attacked her. What really angered her was that none of the crimes had been publicized to students. "We had no idea that this was going on," Getzinger says now. "We were living with such a false sense of security."   2

That's the way it's been for years at most colleges and universities across the country. In the past, these institutions haven't been required by law to report campus crimes to students, parents, employees, prospective students, or the government. And because they're competing for applicants, colleges and universities have little incentive to voluntarily report just how dangerous their campus might be. After all, a school would rather stand out in a prospective student's mind for its academic standing or its idyllic setting than for its crime rate.   3

"Colleges and universities are in a highly competitive market for students, for enrollment, for appropriations, and for gifts," says Michael Clay Smith, professor of criminal justice at the University of Southern Mississippi and author of *Coping With Crime on Campus* and *Wide Awake: A Guide to Safe Campus Living in the 90s.* "I don't accuse most college administrators of bad faith, but it is considered anathema to talk about negative aspects of campus life. An institution that says we don't have a campus crime problem, however, is either lying or ignorant. Students can only protect themselves if they comprehend the reality of the problem by seeing actual numbers at the schools."   4

"It's a really vulnerable time for students," says Dana Getzinger. "They've just stopped living with Mom and Dad, and they're on their own for the first time. So many people think that because they haven't   5 heard about crimes, they don't exist. People need to be told; otherwise they're even more vulnerable."

6   The news is that the situation is about to change. A federal law passed last fall will require colleges and universities to do what's in the best interest of their students: publish annual statistics on campus crime, publicize their campus safety policies, and submit an annual copy of campus crime figures to the Secretary of Education. (Similar laws in some states already require colleges and universities to provide this information upon request.) Under the federal law, schools will have to disclose how many incidents of murder, rape, robbery, aggravated assault, burglary, and motor vehicle theft occur on their campus every year. Called the "Student Right-to-Know and Campus Security Act," the measure will also require colleges and universities to publish the number of arrests for liquor law violations, drug violations, and possession of weapons.

7   Once the law takes effect on September 1, 1992, it will enable prospective students to size up a school more accurately. It will also serve to alert current students to what's going on at their own school and encourage them to take precautions. The hope is that forewarned will mean forearmed.

8   It took the determination of victims like Dana Getzinger and two devastated parents, Connie and Howard Clery, to finally bring national attention to the pressing problem of slack campus security. In one of the most widely publicized cases, freshman Jeanne Ann Clery was raped and murdered in her dorm room at Lehigh University, in Bethlehem, Pennsylvania, by a fellow student in 1986. The dormitory was protected by a series of heavy doors that locked automatically, but students had propped them open that night to allow people to come and go. Since then, Clery's parents have formed Security on Campus, Inc., and lobbied hard for state and federal legislation.

9   One obstacle has been that because colleges and universities haven't been required to report campus crimes, it's been difficult to gauge just how serious the problem is—or whether it's been getting worse. Right now, only 15 percent of colleges and universities report their crime rates to the FBI, and the ones that do are mostly state universities. Also, at many schools there are fraternity and sorority houses, as well as student houses and apartments, that are considered off-campus. Dana Getzinger's assault wasn't reported as a campus crime because she lived in an off-campus apartment—as do most University of Georgia upperclassmen. Then, too, there's the reluctance of schools to show themselves in a bad light.

10   Yet even the statistics that are reported are alarming. In 1989 there were 2 murders, 243 rapes, 552 robberies, 1,675 aggravated

assaults, and 105,994 property crimes reported on 360 of the nation's campuses. By some estimates, two to ten times as many crimes actually occur as are reported to police.

Contrary to popular belief, 80 percent of criminal activity on campuses is committed not by outsiders, but by students. Towson State University's Center for the Study and Prevention of Campus Violence found that of the 639 sexual assaults that were reported on campuses in 1988, 80 percent were perpetrated by an acquaintance. 11

College administrators say they often face an impossible task when it comes to protecting students. "Parents send children to colleges and universities and expect they'll be protected from everything around them," says Kathleen Curry Santora, vice president for operations of the National Association of Independent Colleges and Universities. "But now colleges are trying to achieve a balance between giving students the freedom they want and protecting them. People have very high expectations of colleges, and I don't see why we should be held to a higher standard than the rest of the country." 12

Indeed, crime on college and university campuses may simply be a reflection of society's ills, though there are experts who argue that schools are crime magnets. The real problem now is that students don't always understand that just because you're on campus doesn't mean you're safe. As nice as the quad looks, as friendly as fellow students seem, as much fun as it can be to run around at all hours and have no rules—campuses are potential crime areas, and students have to take precautions just like anyone anywhere. 13

While the federal legislation will help with the reporting of campus crimes, it won't stop the violence or theft. According to campus safety experts, colleges and universities need to do three things in order to fulfill their duty to students: alert them to the dangers around them, provide better security, and teach crime prevention. Most colleges and universities now offer a variety of safety programs, including escort services, after-dark shuttle buses, security systems in dormitories, and emergency call boxes strategically located on campus, in addition to roving security guards. 14

As a result of the Clery murder, Lehigh has introduced a security program in certain dormitories and sororities that includes electronic systems that signal when doors aren't properly secured. Plus, many schools now offer programs to boost student awareness of crimes like acquaintance rape. Trained student volunteers have been leading sessions on sexual victimization at the University of Florida since 1981, at the University of Michigan since 1986, and at the University of Colorado since 1987. 15

16   "It happens to a lot of people," says Judy Buck, coordinator of Colorado's Dare to Stop Rape program, "but they don't always know there's a name for it or recognize what it is. After we do a presentation, the phone calls to our counseling center vastly increase."

17   "Schools need to teach students more about crime prevention in such a way as to change the behavior of perpetrators as well as victims," says criminal justice professor Smith. "If we can do a better job of teaching what it means to live in a community with others, we *can* change behavior."

18   As many as one in six college women is a victim of rape or attempted rape each year. Some of these rapes are "stranger rapes," where an unknown man sneaks up on his victim, but more than half are acquaintance rapes, where the rapist and victim know each other. These statistics may seem overwhelming, but there are steps you can take to greatly increase your safety—on campus or off.

19   Each of the following questions describes a common situation that can easily lead to assault. Decide which option would be the safest in each situation.

20   **1.** The nice guy who sits next to you in calculus asks you out for next Saturday night. When you accept, he suggests going to a movie and then taking a drive. You
(a) agree with his plan, despite feeling uncomfortable about the drive.
(b) suggest going out with your roommate and her boyfriend.
(c) tell him the movie sounds great, but you'd like to save the drive for another time.
(d) agree, but plan to fake a headache and go home right after the movie.

Answer: *c*

21   If you agree to go for a drive with a guy you hardly know, you're placing yourself in a potentially dangerous situation. The majority of date rapes occur on a first or second date, on a weekend evening, in an isolated place like a car, a dorm room or apartment, the woods, or the beach. The single most important step you can take to protect yourself is to avoid being alone with a guy or guys you don't know well.

22   Option *c* offers a safe way to go out with a guy you like. To be safest, you may want to restrict your first few dates to public places like movie theaters or restaurants that you can get yourself to and from. That way you can avoid being alone in a car with him, and you can leave if he behaves badly.

If you choose *b* and arrange a double date, make sure you all 23
stay together. Option *d* is a bad idea, because it can make you seem
unsure of yourself or passive, and a lot of rapists know how to take
advantage of that. You need to communicate from the beginning what
your rules and limits are and that you're in charge of what you do.

2. You're at a fraternity party. After dancing with a guy you've met 24
there, you have a few glasses of punch to cool off. It tastes okay, but
you soon start to feel dizzy and nauseous. You
(a) ask a friend to take you home.
(b) ask the guy you've been dancing with to take you home.
(c) accept his offer to go into a nearby room and lie down until you
feel better.
(d) slip outside by yourself to get some fresh air and clear your head.

Answer: *a*

This is a very common date rape situation. Chances are your drink 25
was spiked (maybe even with grain alcohol, which is extremely potent
and very hard to detect). Many, perhaps most, date rapes occur when one
or both people have been drinking. When you've been drinking, your
natural good judgment and intuition are impaired, and you may take risks
you wouldn't otherwise take. You're also less able to defend yourself.

Your goal in this situation is to get help from a reliable person as 26
quickly as possible, so option *a* is your safest bet. It's unfortunate but
true that some guys will offer assistance with the hidden goal of luring
you into an isolated place, such as another room in the fraternity
house or a car or your dorm room. For this reason, avoid options *b*
and *c*. If you wait, you may become disoriented and even pass out, so
you probably shouldn't attempt to just slip out or go home alone.

3. You've been researching a term paper, and it's almost midnight 27
when you're ready to leave the library. The campus is practically
deserted. You
(a) walk quickly or jog back to your dorm or apartment.
(b) wait until a male student walks by and ask him for an escort.
(c) wait until a female student walks by and ask her for an escort.
(d) call the campus security service.

Answer: Probably *d*

Many colleges offer escort services to help students get around 28
campus safely after dark. If there's one available on your campus, consider using it.

29   Options *a, b,* and *c* are also reasonable responses. You have to select the one that feels right to you at the time, though you're safest asking another girl to walk with you. While it might feel safer to ask a guy, this can lead to trouble (see question 5). If you go home by yourself, jog or walk assertively to avoid looking like an easy target.

30   **4.** Shortly before your psychology midterm, a guy in your class you'd like to know better asks if you want to study together. You accept enthusiastically. "Great," he says. "Come by my apartment around seven tonight." He explains that the library is too crowded and the student union too noisy for studying. You
(a) accept without reservation—you prefer to study at home, too.
(b) tell him to come to your place instead.
(c) ask him if he has a roommate, and decline if he doesn't.
(d) tell him you don't want to go to his apartment and suggest another place you can study together.

Answer: *d*

31   Like most situations that can lead to date rape, this one is hard to read. He may be a serious student who does his best work at home or even just a guy who'd like to be alone with you, but would never hurt you. Nonetheless, going alone to his apartment—whether or not there's a roommate—can be dangerous. You probably wouldn't go to his apartment for your first date with him, so don't let a study session be any different. Turning the tables and inviting him to your place isn't necessarily any safer, unless your roommates promise to stick around. Your safest option is *d*. Chances are he'll be understanding—and would you really want a relationship with him if he weren't?

32   **5.** You're at a football game with a group of friends, and you've all had some beers. After the game, a guy you've just met offers to walk you back to your dorm, which is on the other side of campus. You
(a) accept with pleasure—it's a nice gesture.
(b) tell him you appreciate the offer, but decline politely.
(c) accept, but ask a friend or two to join you.
(d) accept, but tell him that you're in a hurry and really need to go straight home.

Answer: *b* or *c*

33   Chances are you've met a nice guy who wants to get to know you, but the combination of alcohol and isolation can lead to a bad situation. When you've been drinking, your problem-solving skills are

weaker than usual, so if problems develop, you may have a hard time dealing with them.

In this case, your safest options are *b* and *c*. By asking some friends to join you, you can get better acquainted with this guy without isolating yourself. Option *d* may *sound* good, but it really doesn't protect you, and it can make you sound unsure of yourself.

34

35

6. You've been having a great time at a party in an apartment complex next to campus. There were more guys than girls to begin with, so you've been dancing nonstop for hours. You could keep going, but you look around and notice there are only three girls and about nine or ten guys left. You
(a) leave immediately.
(b) ask another girl to let you know when she's leaving, so you can leave with her.
(c) keep an eye on the situation, but don't overreact—these are guys from your college, not strangers you met in a bar.
(d) ask both of the other girls to leave with you right away.

Answer: *d*

36

Girls who are the last to leave a party are at increased risk for rape, particularly gang rape, especially if everyone's been drinking. Some guys may assume that you want sex because you stayed behind after most others left. It's definitely time to leave this party, but try not to desert the other girls: Leave together if possible. For this reason, the best option is *d*. Option *b* may seem reasonable, but it has the disadvantage of prolonging your time in a risky situation. Option *a* is an okay choice, but it's probably best not to head out on your own.

7. Finally, this guy you've had a crush on has asked you out. You're thrilled and spend the whole afternoon getting ready. He shows up on time, looking great. But as you're headed out to dinner, he puts his arm around you, pulls you close, and runs his hand over your back in a way that makes you feel weird. You
(a) tell him angrily to get his hands off you.
(b) pull away, pretending to tie your shoelace or adjust your contact lens—he'll probably get the hint.
(c) tell him that you don't want him—or anyone you don't know well—to put his arm around you.
(d) decide not to do anything unless the situation escalates—he may not really mean anything by it.

37

Answer: *c*

38   It's possible your date is so pleased to see you that he's showing some spontaneous affection. On the other hand, he could be testing you to see how pliable you are. If you let him continue to touch you in a way that is suggestive and that makes you uncomfortable, you risk sending him subtle signals that you can be easily manipulated. Another kind of testing behavior is asking inappropriate questions, such as whether your roommates will be home after dinner or about your past sexual experiences.

39   All too often, women discount their discomfort in such situations to avoid "making a scene"; it may also seem better to quietly endure his advances than to risk insulting him or embarrassing yourself.

40   Most girls who were date rape victims, however, recall trying to ignore a variety of testing behaviors because they felt they were being "oversensitive." Direct, assertive, and firm refusals to allow a guy to touch you or speak to you in ways that are too familiar—option *c*—are more likely to prevent a date rape. If he persists or doesn't take you seriously, resort to option *a*.

41   **8.** You decide to start running—at least three times a week. The safest time for you to plan to go is
(a) early morning, varying your route.
(b) midday, varying your route.
(c) midday, following the same route.
(d) early evening, following the same route.

Answer: *None of the above*

42   Any time of day can be dangerous. Regardless of what time you want to run, map out some safe routes in advance that avoid isolated or wooded areas and stick to brightly lit, clear, and well-traveled pathways. Ideally, you should vary your route and the time you run to reduce the likelihood that someone could lie in wait for you. Best of all, jog with a friend: it's safer, and you're more likely to exercise regularly, too.

43   To stay safe, follow these guidelines:

44   **Trust your instincts.** If someone's making you uncomfortable or afraid, take immediate action. You are the best judge of what's appropriate in a given situation. It's better to overreact and risk embarrassment than to ignore your intuition and risk assault. Listen to your inner voice.

Watch where you're going. Don't end up alone or with a guy   45
you don't know well in an isolated place. If you're out of the sight of
others (even if they're only a dorm room away), your chances of being
raped or assaulted increase greatly.

Be assertive. Don't let a guy touch you or talk to you in a way   46
that makes you feel uncomfortable. Be firm about your objections.

Be careful about drinking. Remember that it will impair your   47
judgment and reactions. If you plan to drink, stay with your friends.

Whatever happens, don't blame yourself. If you are raped   48
or assaulted, what you need is counseling and medical attention, not
self-accusation. The student health service, women's center, dorm
adviser, campus security service, police, and dean of students should
all know what to do. You owe it to yourself to get help.

▶   QUESTIONS TO CONSIDER

1. Are you aware of crimes committed on your campus that have not
been reported? Why do you think many students are reluctant to
report campus crimes?

2. Colino begins with a narrative of a University of Georgia coed's
experience. What does this true story add to her article? Why do
you think the author continues to refer to this story throughout
her essay?

3. What purpose does the series of questions and answers near the
end of the article serve?

4. The article ends with five briefly stated instructions to help women
avoid sexual assault. Would these instructions be as effective if they
were just presented by themselves rather than in the context of the
essay? Why or why not?

▶   WRITING ACTIVITIES

Individual: Write a journal entry in which you describe an experience
you or a friend or acquaintance has had with campus crime.

Collaborative: Discuss with the members of your group the types of
crime that have occurred on your campus in recent years. List the
types of crime that seem to occur most often. Then write a set of

specific instructions telling students how to avoid one type of campus crime. Choose a **format** that is appropriate and easy to read.

FORMAT, PAGE 582

Computer: Enter into a new computer file the set of instructions your group wrote in the collaborative activity. Then, using your computer network or sharing disks, read and edit one another's instructions. Finally, combine and format all the instructions into a brief handbook on how new students can avoid being the victims of campus crime.

A STUDENT AT ANY AGE

Tammy Adams

Tammy Adams is married, has a child, and works full-time at a university. She is also a student. She wrote this essay in a freshman composition class in response to an assignment that directed the students to write to instruct. Because she was a returning student, one who had been out of school for a number of years, she decided to write an essay giving advice to other returning students. As you read, determine whether her advice might also apply to traditional students—those who enter college as soon as they graduate from high school.

1   For most students, entering college is exciting. It means leaving home for the first time and beginning a new life as an adult. However, for adult students who are returning to school, it is often a time of insecurity. These adult students have been in the "real world" for some time. Some are homemakers, some are mothers or fathers, and most are employees. Adults often enter school with feelings of fear and insecurity, questioning whether they can handle an already full load of adult responsibilities and at the same time compete with the younger traditional college students. As an adult student myself, I would like to give some words of advice to adult students who are planning to enter college.

2   First of all, turning in an application to the school should not be your first step. Your first step should be turning in an application at home. Adult students who succeed at completing their education usually have the cooperation of family members who help them reach the goal of completing their degree. Most of you who are returning to

school have either a spouse or children or a combination of both. Whatever your situation may be, your success as a student depends on the cooperation you receive from your family. For example, an adult student I know recently told me she was withdrawing from school for the semester because her husband had demanded that she withdraw. As an adult student myself, I know the advantage of having a supportive spouse. There are plenty of times that my husband takes over in the evenings to do supper and take care of our daughter so I can study. On weekends he frequently entertains the little one so I can write a report or prepare for exams.

Second, as an adult student, coming back to school after years of   3 not being a student, you should be prepared to ask a lot of questions. The adult student often tends to be reluctant to ask questions. After all, adults are supposed to know everything. Right? This reluctance generally stems from the age difference between the traditional young students and yourself. Although you may feel intimidated when it comes to asking questions, students, regardless of their age, should never hold back from asking questions. Assuming how something will be, rather than asking questions, generally results in your making a bad decision. For example, during my first semester I registered for a night class that was canceled due to the lack of students in the class. I assumed that since the course was canceled by the department, it was not my responsibility to drop the course from my schedule. However, not only did I not receive a refund for the course but on my grade report there was an "F" for the course. After making several phone calls, walking all over campus getting permission to drop after the deadline, and standing in a long line at the registrar's office, I had learned a very valuable lesson. Now I always call my department to verify procedure rules and regulations.

Finally, as an adult student, you need to take advantage of pro-   4 grams that are designed to help you. In the past decade universities and colleges have experienced a significant increase in the number of adult students. In the beginning nothing was done to try to help these particular students adjust to their new academic world. However, now there are many different programs to help the adult student adjust. One of the main programs available to you is the counseling center. Counseling centers usually offer counseling services, tests to help you determine a major, and lists of academic tutors available to help you during the semester.

Once you begin to feel in place, instead of out of place, you can   5 concentrate on academics rather than your fears and feelings of insecurity. The reason most adult students give for feeling that they are out of place is their age. However, with time you will begin to see that being older is not a disadvantage but rather an advantage. You will eventually realize that, while it is true that you have more difficulty finding study time because of work or family obligations, you have several advantages over the traditional student. Your life experiences will play a large part in your academic success. Because of your age, you will have more experiences to give in class discussions. The most interesting classes I have been in have been the classes in which there was a large variety of students, including older students. A friend of mine taking business management classes has found it easier to understand the course's content because most of what she is studying is similar to situations she deals with in her job. In a history class I took, those of us over 25 years had much more to contribute to class discussions, especially discussions on politics and world affairs.

6   There is no age limit on getting an education. If you have the desire and motivation, you can succeed as a student at any age. Once you overcome your fears and feelings of inadequacy, you may very well discover that you do extremely well in your new world of academics.

▶   QUESTIONS TO CONSIDER

1. According to Adams, what are the advantages and disadvantages of starting college after you have been out of high school for a number of years? Can you think of others?

2. Does Adams keep her audience (adult returning students) in focus throughout her essay? Identify instances in which it is clear that she is writing for this audience.

3. Is the essay interesting to all readers or just those to whom it is primarily addressed? Is the advice she gives adult students also useful to younger students? In what way?

4. Adams states that adult students have been in the "real world." How does the real world differ from the academic world? In what way is the academic world unreal? Is this a useful distinction for Adams to make in her introduction?

5. If you are a returning student, do you find Adams's advice useful? What other advice might she have included?

6. If you are a traditional student, just out of high school, which of Adams's suggestions do you find most helpful?

WRITING ACTIVITIES ◀

Individual: In a journal entry compare the advantages and disadvantages of being a returning adult student with those of being a traditional college student.

Collaborative: Discuss the advantages and disadvantages of being a returning adult student with a group of your classmates. Then each member of your group should interview an adult student and report his or her findings to the group. As a result of your discussion and interviews, determine what advice you would give adult students who are returning to college.

Computer: Still working as a group, enter into a computer file the advice your group decided to offer returning adult students. Then revise and format this text so that a reader would find it useful and easy to understand. Next, using your computer network (or by exchanging disks), compare the different formats each group used. Decide which **format**, or which features of each different format, you want to adopt; then compile the advice from all the groups into a single text using that format.

FORMAT, PAGE 582

VACATION TIPS

Ellen Goodman

Ellen Goodman, a Pulitzer Prize winner for journalism, is best known for her syndicated newspaper columns. Goodman writes primarily out of her own experiences and often gives advice based on what she has learned in her own life. In the following essay, she offers advice to college students who come home for the holidays. Although humorous in tone, the essay realistically points out several potential areas of disagreement between parents and college students and suggests some practical solutions. Notice, as you read, that Goodman's purpose is to instruct as well as amuse.

Lo, it is winter vacation and the fledglings have come home to roost. These are not just anybody's fledglings. They are ours, the very

1

same ones who emptied the nest, not to mention the nest egg, on their way to college last September.

2   How we felt their absence! How we now feel their presence!

3   Parents who had months of total access to their own cars (including the dial on the radio) are now struggling to readjust to the wonders of time-sharing. Parents who had control over the contents of their refrigerators are being led on a daily magical mystery tour of leftovers. Will the milk disappear? Will the cheese stand alone?

4   It is not that we don't deeply love our children and welcome them eagerly into the bosom of family. But in their months at college they have developed the life-style of a roommate rather than a family member.

5   Locked into the college youth ghetto, most have lost the knack of living with anyone over twenty-four. Their parents may regard their reappearance as the invasion of the life-style snatchers.

6   For this reason, to facilitate a smooth winter break, a family vacation that leaves no broken ties or limbs in its wake, I feel compelled to offer a vacation tipsheet. The following answers the age-old questions facing college students who come home for the holidays: What is the difference between a parent and a roommate?

7   1. Biorhythms. For reasons that are inexplicable, the biorhythm of a student undergoes a radical change upon entering college. The average college day begins at roughly 11 A.M. and runs until at least 2 A.M. This is not always understood by your parents, who may be misled by the appearance of a nine o'clock morning class on your registration card.

8   Parents, you should remember, stopped sleeping at the birth of their first child. By now, due to such mundane considerations as work and late-night anxiety attacks about your future, they have entirely lost the trick. They tend to go to bed at the shank of the evening, which is to say midnight.

9   Remember: Roommates can engage in deep conversations about the meaning of life at 1 A.M. Parents cannot. On the other hand, parents think you look sweet when you are sleeping. Unless it's noon.

10   2. Music. The high-rise dorm you left behind, Babel East, undoubtedly contained more sound equipment than people. Roommates appear to function best to stereophonic sound, their every conversation and action, even reading, comes with its own sound track. By now, quiet may make you nervous.

11   Parents, on the other hand, grew up somewhere between Chuck Berry and John Lennon, but decidedly before Sony. They regard music

as something to listen to. They actually turn off the radio when they
leave a room. They do not accept it as the permanent accompaniment.
Do not try to discuss your incomplete in physics or your desire to
spend the summer in Tibet to a hard rock beat.

3. Telephone usage. The telephone company has made its great-   12
est inroads with your generation. Roommates regard Alexander
Graham Bell as the one truly significant founding father, far surpassing
Thomas Jefferson. Roommates do not consider it unusual if you direct-
dial cross-country in order to get the telephone number of a friend
across the street.

Parents, on the other hand, tend to get nostalgic about letter-   13
writing, especially when they get telephone bills. One of the very first
genes lost in the aging process is the one that understands how urgent
it is to call the friends you just left at the airport in another area code.

4. Miscellaneous manners and matters: Roommates don't care if   14
you sit through a whole dinner. Roommates do not care if you come
home when you said you would. Roommates do not call the police
with your license number if you decide on the spur of the moment to
stay over at a friend's. Roommates do not assume that you are lying
on the side of the road. Parents do.

Finally, remember to be kind to your elders. After all, you are   15
going through a stage of life together. You are learning how to be a
part-time family.

P.S. There's one other difference between roommates and parents.   16
You can always get another roommate.

QUESTIONS TO CONSIDER ◀

1. Which of Goodman's purposes—to instruct or to amuse—does she
attain more successfully?

2. Are Goodman's specific suggestions useful, or is the essay mainly
valuable because Goodman points out convincingly that holidays
are difficult for both parents and students?

3. From whose point of view is Goodman writing? For whom is her
advice primarily intended? Does this shift affect the value or credibility of her advice?

4. Of the "tips" that Goodman includes, which do you find most useful? Why?

▶   WRITING ACTIVITIES

Individual: Write a journal entry in which you explore an issue about which college students and parents typically disagree. Begin with your own experiences, but generalize to other students. Propose a solution that would be useful in resolving the issue.

Collaborative: Compare the areas of disagreement that each of you described in your journal entries. Then write a set of instructions for parents suggesting how they might avoid problems with their children who are in college.

Computer: Enter the set of instructions that your group composed into a computer file, and format these instructions so that your intended audience can read them easily and refer to them readily.

Writing to Instruct and Advise

The purpose of instructions or advice is to explain to your readers how to do something or what they should do. If you are writing specific instructions, your readers will be performing the task in question even as, or immediately after, they read what you have written. If you are giving general instructions or advice, your readers may not be immediately engaged in the task or process, but they probably are interested in doing the thing you are writing about at some point in the future. In either case, your advice should be easy to read, adequately explained, and formatted in such a way that information is accessible to a reader who needs to go back and reread parts of the instructions.

Analyzing Your Audience

When you write to instruct or advise, you must know your audience well. You should know not only who your readers are, but also, if possible, what they are capable of understanding, their general intelligence and background experience with the subject, whether they are biased toward the subject in any way, how they feel about the task or goal you are addressing, and how much time they will likely be able to spend on the project. Although the audience for some instructions can be large and varied (readers of driver's license manuals, for example), most instructions are written with a smaller and less generic audience in mind.

The following questions will help you analyze your audience:

1. Who will my primary reader(s) be?

2. What is their specific knowledge of the subject?

3. What is their age, gender, education, and so on?

4. What possible biases may they have?

5. What is their purpose in reading my text?

The answers to these questions will not only provide you with valuable knowledge about the audience for whom you are writing, but they will also help you determine the purpose, scope, and organization of your text. For example, if you are giving advice about how to use a computerized data base to search for information, you need to know if your readers know how to access the data base. If they do, you can begin by simply explaining how to perform an author, title, or key-word search. If they do not, you will need to explain how to access the data base before telling them how to conduct the on-line search. It would also be helpful to know whether your readers are familiar and comfortable with computers. Otherwise, you may need to include some reassurance about how user-friendly computers have become in recent years.

The Role of a Thesis in Writing to Instruct and Advise

In writing to instruct and advise, your thesis is often a simple statement of purpose. That is, you begin by telling your readers the purpose of your essay in a straightforward, direct way. For example, Tammy Adams ends the first paragraph of her essay, "A Student at Any Age," by stating clearly, "As an adult student myself, I would like to give some words of advice to adult students who are planning to enter college." Her thesis statement leaves little doubt as to the purpose of her essay or the audience for whom it is intended. Likewise, Joshua Halberstam makes the following statement in the introduction to "Class in the Classroom": "In this chapter we'll discuss how to make the most of your time when you're in class."

If you do not want to begin with a stated thesis, there are other options. For example, the introduction to Stacey Colino's essay on campus crime does not include a thesis statement, but she concludes her essay with five guidelines, which are preceded by the statement, "To stay safe, follow these guidelines." Similarly, Nikki Giovanni waits until her concluding paragraph to state her thesis explicitly. In contrast, Ellen Goodman states her theses about midway through her essay in the form of a question: "What is the difference between a parent and a roommate?"

TITLES, PAGE 667 Do not make the mistake of assuming that your title takes the place of a thesis (see **titles**). A title may suggest or even state the purpose of your essay, but you should not let it serve as your thesis. Typically, a title merely announces a topic, whereas a thesis makes a statement about that topic. For example, your topic might be the stress that some college students experience during their first year, and to express this idea you could title your essay "Eliminating Stress from the Freshman Experience." But you would still need to make clear to your readers the purpose of your essay. So you might include in your introduction one of the following statements:

❖ If you do not learn to minimize stress when you are a freshman, you may never be an upperclassman.

❖ Learning to manage stress is more important than making the dean's list or joining the right clubs.

❖ One of the most valuable lessons you can learn as a freshman is how to eliminate unnecessary stress.

Of course, a stated thesis is not essential to a good essay. If you are sure that your main idea is communicated clearly, you can omit a thesis statement. But in most instances you will probably want to include a thesis statement, because writing to advise should always be direct and straightforward. If you decide to omit a thesis statement, you may want to include appropriate headings and/or forecasting statements to keep your readers informed (see **headings** and **forecasting statements**).

HEADINGS, PAGE 603

FORECASTING STATEMENTS, PAGE 580

Patterns of Development in Writing to Instruct and Advise

The most obvious way to develop an essay or article in which your purpose is to advise or instruct is to describe the process involved. If you are telling someone how to do something, you need to explain it step by step. Specific instructions are often structured as a list:

1. Do this,

2. Then do this,

3. Finally, do this.

If you are advising someone to do something that can be structured in this way, make your advice or instructions as simple and straightforward as possible. If your topic is more complex, you may need to create a context for your advice, provide background information on your topic, convince readers that your advice is sound, or even discuss alternative courses of action. But at some point, you may still want to include a step-by-step description of the process you are advocating. Clearly, this process description, like a narrative, needs to be presented in chronological order.

If a process is not involved but you still want to make certain definite suggestions, you should list or enumerate these points. For example, most of the reading selections in this chapter include such a list. A one-two-three list of the rules, suggestions, or steps that you want your reader to remember should be emphasized in some way, ideally near the end of your text.

Sometimes, however, a narrative is the best way to advise readers. For example, parables are nothing but simple narratives with or without an explicit moral or lesson stated in the conclusion. Or you can include a narrative as just one of several methods of development you use in writing to advise. Frequently, writers use a brief narrative or anecdote in their introduction. For example, in the reading selections in this chapter Joshua Halberstam and Stacey Colino begin with brief narratives that provide a context for the advice that follows and create interest in their topics. You can include narratives at any point in your text, but they are most often found at the beginning or end when the purpose is primarily to advise or instruct (see **narration**).

NARRATION, PAGE 618

Closely related to narration is cause and effect, another method that can be used effectively in writing to advise. Like narration, cause and effect involves chronological order and consequences. It is a natural way to develop a text when you are writing to advise, because you often want to caution your readers of the consequences if they do not do what you are suggesting or to assure them of the benefits if they follow your advice. It is, in fact, important that you explain *why* you are advising a certain course of action or advocating a specific way of doing something. Readers need to be persuaded that following your advice is in their best interest rather than simply being told to do what you say. Remember, effective advice focuses on *why* as well as *how* (see **cause and effect**).

CAUSE AND EFFECT, PAGE 522

A text is rarely, if ever, developed by only one method. Experienced writers use multiple methods to amplify and develop their topics. In addition to process description, narration, and cause and effect, you may also want to include exemplification, comparison/contrast, definition, classification, and analysis to make your advice clearer and more convincing (see **exemplification, comparison/contrast, definition,** and **classification**).

EXEMPLIFICATION, PAGE 574

COMPARISON/CONTRAST, PAGE 542

DEFINITION, PAGE 560

CLASSIFICATION, PAGE 527

Choosing an Effective Format

Whatever methods of development you use, you should take care to structure your instructions and advice so that the reader's task is as uncomplicated as possible. The structure, or format, you use depends to a great extent on whether you want to guide the reader through an immediate and specific task (such as operating a computer program or assembling a bookcase) or to give the reader advice about how to do something general in the future (how to choose a career, win an argument, improve a tennis serve, or dress for success). Specific instructions should be structured so that readers can easily recognize and locate the different steps and backtrack to reread important information. For example, if a reader needs to reread one step, that step should be easy to find—numbered, set off from the other steps, or perhaps in boldface type or capital letters (see **format**).

FORMAT, PAGE 582

One way of assuring that your instructions are clear is to provide your readers with good signals that help them perceive the basic structure, recognize the major steps or points, and anticipate what is to come. There are several ways to accomplish this goal:

1. Use numbers (as we are in this list) to designate major steps or points.

2. Use headings and subheadings (see **headings**) to indicate major and minor parts of your text.   HEADINGS, PAGE 603

3. Use clear signals (see **transitions**)— such as *first, second, third; next, then,* and *finally—etc.,* to help your reader recognize each new step or point.   TRANSITIONS, PAGE 676

4. Use paragraph structure to indicate clearly the different sections. Remember that in general you will discuss only one step or point in each paragraph.

Of course, careful writers often use a combination of these strategies. For example, appropriate paragraphing can be reinforced by clear transition signals, and numbered lists can be used in a section that is introduced by a heading. Remember that instructions usually require stronger formatting features than most texts because readers often need to reenter the text in order to reread a certain section or to locate just one particular bit of advice. You don't want a cluttered, overly formatted text, but you do want one that is formatted so that readers can read and follow your instructions or advice as easily as possible.

Establishing an Appropriate Voice

Specific instructions are usually written impersonally and objectively, and the writer's voice is usually that of an anonymous expert. Someone who is trying to install a smoke alarm doesn't need to know who wrote the instructions as long as they are clearly and accurately written. Exceptions exist, of course—especially when the person writing the instructions is a noted authority in the field. For example, Julia Child writing about cooking, Greg Norman writing about golf, and Colin Fletcher writing about backpacking and hiking all assume a definite persona in their texts. But most instructions of this type are limited to essential information presented clearly and anonymously.

In contrast, general instructions and advice are usually discursive. For example, authors who are advising their readers usually use an essay or narrative structure, embedding the advice into this familiar context rather than presenting it in isolation. In this type of essay, the author's persona and **credibility** are important factors. Readers do not   CREDIBILITY, PAGE 552 accept advice from just anyone. The writer must be perceived as knowledgeable, experienced, even wise, if the advice is to be accepted.

Try to communicate as directly as possible with your audience. If you are writing for other students like yourself but with less experience, your purpose is not to impress them but to assist them as they make the difficult transition to becoming a college student. Your writing voice should, therefore, be fairly informal and yet direct.

General Guidelines for Writing to Instruct and Advise

Six general guidelines can help you write effective instructions and advice:

- ❖ Clarity is essential.
- ❖ Amplify, amplify, amplify.
- ❖ Don't overload readers' minds.
- ❖ Use the imperative mood.
- ❖ Format for reading ease.
- ❖ Use graphics to reinforce words.

1. CLARITY IS ESSENTIAL. In most kinds of writing, clarity is desirable but not essential; in certain types of poetry and fiction, for example, ambiguity may even be a virtue. But unclear instructions are worthless and sometimes even dangerous. Remember, too, that clarity means more than being clear to you, the writer; your advice or instructions must also be clear to your readers. Reread your text repeatedly, and also ask other people to read it to be sure your instructions are clear and unambiguous.

2. AMPLIFY, AMPLIFY, AMPLIFY. Specific instructions should, of course, be brief and to the point. Readers who are primarily reading to accomplish something do not want to read words that are unnecessary. However, advice and general instructions can be *too* brief. Skimpy instructions lacking essential details and advice lacking effective examples are not very useful for readers. Writers often assume their readers know as much about the subject as they do, and thus they provide too little information. Be sure, if it is needed, that you amplify each step of the instructions so your reader knows exactly what you want him or AMPLIFICATION, PAGE 508 her to do and how to do it (see **amplification**).

3. DON'T OVERLOAD YOUR READERS' MINDS. Give readers a chance to respond to each command or suggestion before going on to the next one. In specific instructions this means giving readers only one command per sentence. If an instruction needs to be amplified, allot a single paragraph to it plus the amplification it requires. In more general instructions and advice, discuss only one step or suggestion per paragraph.

4. USE THE IMPERATIVE MOOD.   Composition teachers often caution their students against using the second person, *you*, when they write; but when you are writing to instruct or advise, *you* is appropriate and effective. Whether you are writing instructions or general advice, writing directly to your readers makes it easier for you to tell them what to do and for them to understand what to do. For example, "You turn the knob to the right" is much easier to understand than "The knob should be turned to the right," which can be a description of a preferred or desired condition (a knob that is pointing to the right) or an option (it *should* be turned to the right but doesn't necessarily have to be turned to the right) as well as an instruction. Often you can omit the pronoun *you* and just say "Turn the knob to the right." You are still using the imperative mood, but the pronoun is understood rather than stated.

Writers sometimes avoid the imperative because it sounds too direct or harsh. But readers who are trying to follow directions or instructions are not offended by direct commands. They will not perceive the writer who uses the imperative as bossy, but rather as authoritative and knowledgeable.

Even if you are writing general advice, it is better to use the second person. Trying to stay in the third person can become very awkward when you are telling someone how to do something, even if that person is not going to do anything immediately. However, if you are describing a process—*how* something is done—you may find the third person more appropriate.

Example

When *you* are making a decision about which college to attend, *you* must always consider cost.

When *students* begin the process of selecting a college, *they* usually consider cost an important factor.

5. FORMAT INSTRUCTIONS FOR READING EASE.   Especially if you are writing specific instructions, remember that the arrangement of your text on the page can make it more readable. The point of using lists, numbers, bullets, and different typefaces is not to decorate your text, but to make it easier for readers to understand and to locate specific information within your text. If you are working on a computer, try different formats to find one that is attractive and that helps readers access important information easily (see **format**). For example, simply arranging the steps of a process in a numbered list makes these steps easier for a reader to follow.

FORMAT, PAGE 582

6. USE GRAPHICS TO REINFORCE WORDS.   A picture may actually be worth more than a thousand words. Often you can illustrate a complex step with a simple diagram or illustration much better than you can by describing the process in words. Fortunately, you do not have to choose between words and pictures; use both. Thus, tell your reader to insert the computer disk into the mailer, and also provide a diagram illustrating this instruction. Keep graphics uncomplicated and label them clearly.

GRAPHICS, PAGE 596   Whether you are writing simple instructions or giving profound advice, your readers need to feel confidence in you and what you have written. When you write clear, complete, direct, and appropriately illustrated instructions and advice, you will gain your readers' confidence and gratitude (see **graphics**).

W RITING   A SSIGNMENT

As a college freshman, you have already had experiences that taught you how to survive as a student. At the very least, you have selected a college, enrolled in classes, and learned your way around campus. Perhaps you have also applied for financial aid, moved into a dorm, adjusted to a roommate, decided which organizations to join, and figured out how to manage your money, get along with a variety of people, and get your laundry done each week. In this writing assignment, you are to instruct or advise a new student about something you have learned. Try to avoid obvious and general advice that people can figure out for themselves. Instead, offer advice that is creative and specific to your experiences. The following suggestions are intended to guide you as you choose a topic for this assignment.

1. Advise new students about how to get by on a limited budget. Your advice can be humorous or serious.

2. Advise teachers about the most effective methods of instruction for students like yourself.

3. Write an article for your high school newspaper advising students how to prepare for college.

4. Write a parable that teaches a lesson about being a good or bad student.

5. Instruct new students about how to use the Internet, the on-line catalog at the library, or the computer labs on campus.

6. Advise students how to eat a healthy diet, get enough exercise (or sleep), or reduce the stress of being a student.

7. Write to a specific student audience—such as returning adult students, international students, students from small high schools,

students who commute, and so on—advising them how to adjust to student life.

8. Instruct students about how to set up a realistic daily and/or weekly schedule.

9. Advise students how to make a good first impression on their teachers or how to meet new people.

10. Advise students about how to survive the first semester of college.

Generating Ideas through Invention and Research

The suggestions below will help you generate ideas for this assignment:

INVENTION.   One of the best ways to begin this assignment is to spend some time thinking about your audience—their ages, expectations, attitudes, previous experiences, and, in general, what they do and do not know about college. As you come to understand your audience better, you will also begin to understand what type of instructions or advice you need to provide for them. To obtain a clear idea of your audience, generate a reader profile which includes not only major characteristics and attitudes, but also pertinent demographic data, such as age, gender, classification, marital status, and so on.

Remember that your readers will be entering freshmen who have not shared your experiences as a college freshman. Try to remember how you felt when you first arrived on campus as a new student who did not know how to read a college bulletin or schedule of classes, how to register for classes, how to drop or add a course, how to purchase a meal ticket or find the registrar's office, or what to wear or where to go. Your audience will probably be like you in significant ways, but at the same time they will not have had the recent experiences you have had. You are the expert on how to schedule classes so that you have enough time to prepare for each one, how to find time to work as well as go to school, how to figure out which professors to choose, or how to manage your money so that you don't run out by the middle of the month.

RESEARCH.   Although it is essential in writing to advise that you write about a topic with which you have first-hand experience, you may want to supplement that experience with other information. For example, talking to someone who works in the registrar's office would provide you not only with additional information about the registration process, but also with a different perspective on it. You might discover why the different steps in the process are necessary and how the current process evolved. If you consult other students, you might learn some shortcuts that you overlooked or some strategies that you have not yet discovered. A brief survey of selected students might also reveal such information as the average time required to register, the chances of getting the classes preferred, and the role of faculty advisement in the process.

Drafting Your Text

You may want to begin with a simple outline of the steps you plan to include or the points you want to make. Then you can expand upon each, amplifying it until it is fully developed. Or you can begin with an introduction in which you address your audience directly, explaining what your topic is (how to get enough exercise) and why it is important (to keep from gaining weight and to relieve stress) and establishing your own credibility as an expert on this topic (you've figured out how to incorporate exercise into a routine student schedule).

Be sure to tell your readers not only *what* to do but *why* they should do it as you suggest. Advice is more palatable if the rationale behind it is clear. For example, if you advise your readers to schedule a conference with each professor during the first few weeks of school, also tell them why they need to do this (to get to know the teacher, to make themselves known, to establish their seriousness as students, to obtain additional information about their courses, etc.).

Remember to include warnings and cautions if they are appropriate. For example, at most schools failure to pay fees by a certain date results in students being dropped from the class rolls and thus having to repeat the entire registration process at a time when most classes are full. Thus, instead of just telling students to be sure to pay their fees on time, warn them of the specific consequences of late payments.

Reading and Revising Your Text

As you read what you have written, focus on two things: clarity and completeness. If rereading your instructions convinces you that you need more information, you may need to do more research on your subject. For example, you may need to talk with some of your teachers to get their viewpoints or to ask more experienced students if they agree with what you have written.

Don't reread your text as soon as you have written it, or you will only see what you think is there rather than what is really there. When you read, pretend to be an uninformed reader so that you can anticipate how even the most confused and inexperienced new student may react to what you have written. It is also a good idea to ask several other people to read your instructions so that you get several reactions to them.

You will probably revise your text several times. The first time you revise you might focus on improving the clarity and completeness of your text. For example, you may add more information, explanations, and examples. Or if much of what you included was not really pertinent, you may need to delete the extraneous material and expand the remaining points so that they are more fully developed.

Remember to examine the sequence of the steps or points you have included. Even if your instructions are general rather than specific, sequence is often crucial. A step that is omitted or not in the correct order can cause readers serious problems.

After you are sure your text is clear and provides readers with the information they need to follow your instructions or advice, you can consider whether a graphic (e.g., map, picture, diagram, table, chart) would further help them. For example, a map of your campus might provide your readers with a useful point of reference if you are writing about the location of several different buildings. However, if you decide that a graphic is appropriate, be sure to make it as clear and effective as possible. A poorly drawn diagram, inaccurate map, or blurred illustration only confuses readers. Graphics help readers only if they are appropriate and clearly drawn or reproduced. Also, be sure to refer to the graphic appropriately in your text, referring readers to it at specific points rather than just tacking it on at the end (see **graphics**).

GRAPHICS, PAGE 596

Finally, at some point in revising, you need to consider whether to include specific cautions or warnings. You do not want to alarm your readers needlessly, but if you know of pitfalls they should avoid, it is your responsibility to alert them to these dangers, problems, or difficulties (selecting too many fat-rich foods at the cafeteria, waiting too late to register, being late to class, joining a fraternity when they can't afford it, etc.). In specific instructions, warnings are usually set off from the text in some way (indented; marked by a bullet, star, or asterisk; underlined; placed in a box; or highlighted) so that readers will not overlook them. In general instructions and advice, warnings should usually be explained in a separate paragraph rather than merely stuck on as the final sentence of a paragraph. It is always important to explain to your readers what will happen if they do not heed your warning—to give them reasons as well as telling them not to do something.

Preparing the Final Draft of Your Text

Errors and inconsistencies in your text may confuse your readers and will most certainly convince them that you are not a knowledgeable, credible writer whom they can trust. You should, therefore, be sure that your text is free of misspelled words and errors in punctuation and usage. In addition, edit your text carefully for the following:

❖ Parallel structure.

❖ Consistent point of view.

USE PARALLEL STRUCTURE.   Items in a series should be in parallel form. For example, if you include a numbered list of steps, structure all the steps the same way. Examine the steps listed here, which are not parallel:

a. Notes should be taken in class.

b. You should always write a summary of your notes.

c. Read your summary before attending the next class.

Now, read this revised list, noticing its more direct and readable parallel structure:

a. Take notes in class.

b. Write a summary of your notes.

c. Read your summary before attending the next class.

KEEP A CONSISTENT POINT OF VIEW.   Specific instructions are nearly always written in the second person. That is, the writer is speaking directly to the reader, often using the imperative mood, in which the pronoun *you* is understood but not stated. In writing general instructions or advice, writers often combine second-person with third-person point of view (writing *about* the situation, process, and so on, as well as *to* the reader). However, the following paragraph is marred by inconsistent shifts from first- to second- to third-person point of view:

> You cannot appreciate the difficulty of being a student while also working until you have experienced it. We have to juggle these two parts of our lives, changing roles constantly as we shift from work to school and back again. The roles we assume as students and employees are often quite different. In class students are expected to be subordinate to the teacher and to assume a rather passive role. But if you are employed in a competitive, aggressive environment, you must assume a very different role.

Consistency is generally important to good writing. In fact, publishers provide copy editors to help their authors achieve consistency. But consistency is especially important in writing to instruct. When you write instructions, act as your own copy editor, making sure you have not needlessly and illogically shifted from one point of view to another (see also **revising and editing**).

REVISING AND EDITING, PAGE 651

Notice the improvement in the paragraph above after the shifts in point of view have been corrected:

> You cannot appreciate the difficulty of being a student while also working until you have experienced it. You have to juggle these two parts of your life, changing roles constantly as you shift from work to school and back again. The roles you assume as a student and an employee are often quite different. In class you are expected to be subordinate to the teacher and to assume a rather passive role. But if you are employed in a competitive, aggressive environment, you must assume a very different role.

DISCOVERING YOURSELF AS A WRITER

After you have completed this assignment, take a few minutes to reflect on this writing experience by answering the following questions:

1. What did you learn about yourself as a writer as you worked on this assignment? In what way did this writing experience change your perception of yourself as a writer, your process of writing, or your attitude toward writing?

2. What forms of research did you use for this assignment? What did you learn about research that will help you in other writing assignments?

3. Was the final draft of your text better or worse than you had expected? What would you do differently if you had the opportunity to do this assignment again?

4. How did writing this assignment make you a better reader?

5. What did you enjoy most about this writing assignment? What did you like least?

Douglas Olson, *Cowhand Putting on Chaps.*
Reprinted by permission of Douglas Olson.

5

WRITING
TO
INFORM

159

*Information has become perhaps the world's fastest
growing and most important business.*

ALVIN TOFFLER

Another reason for writing, to share information with others, may
seem to you a less compelling purpose than writing to instruct or writing to reconstruct experience. Increasingly, however, the demand for
all kinds of information means that large numbers of people are
involved daily in writing to inform. Most of your experience in writing
to inform has probably come in academic writing—exercises, reports,
tests—assignments designed to prove that you *have* certain information. But writing to inform can also give you a chance to *share* information with an interested reader, as the writers in this chapter share
information about change. Although you may at times have voluntarily
written to explore or to reconstruct your own experiences, you may
have written to inform only when someone (usually a teacher) required you to do so.

But you live in a society that runs on information. People want to
know what is happening with the stock market and the weather, in
sports and education, in politics and entertainment. They want to
know the latest gossip about famous people—to learn about the scan-
dals and successes of the rich and powerful. They read histories and
biographies, cookbooks and travelogues, self-help books and reference books—everything from autobiographies to zoology texts. They
soak up televised information, which was writing to inform at some
stage, too. Libraries overflow with information; computer data bases
give users access to incomprehensible amounts of information; filing
cabinets in offices across the nation bulge with neatly and not-so-
neatly alphabetized information. Whether the field is business, education, medicine, law, engineering, finance, or government, staggering
amounts of information are being produced so rapidly that people
have problems storing and retrieving it.

Why do writers painstakingly gather bits and pieces of information
about some subject, interpret and analyze it, and then incorporate it into
their own writing in order to inform a reader? Similarly, why are readers
interested in information? Of course, humans are curious animals who
like to know how things work and what has happened. Information

allows its consumers to understand the world better. Beyond simple curiosity, however, lies another reason. Increasingly in this society, information is power. People in a society as complex as ours require enormous amounts of information in order to function. As a result, information is a valuable commodity in this world, and the ability to communicate information clearly and effectively is a valuable skill.

Plainly, now and later, you need to know how to write to inform—how to explain something to someone who wants or needs information you have. Although every discipline and profession has its own communication conventions—its own way of presenting information—you can use this chapter's general principles of good informative writing whatever your plans for the future.

R E A D I N G   T O   B E
I N F O R M E D

You are already an experienced reader of informative writing, since most textbooks fall into this category. You have probably also had some experience in reading magazines written primarily to inform, whether *People*, *Rolling Stone*, or *Science News*. You have also read newspapers, brochures, and miscellaneous nonfiction books that include vast amounts of information. In fact, you may have already encountered so much informative writing that you read it rather automatically, sifting through the information quickly and casually to find the author's main point or the specific piece of information you need.

However, you need to be aware that all information is not equal. That is, some information is better—more reliable, more accurate, more up-to-date, or from better sources—than other information. You cannot take information for granted. Just because an author includes facts, specific details, statistics, even charts and graphs, you cannot assume that information always equals truth.

How Information Is Used

Information is usually a means to an end rather than an end in itself. Authors rarely provide information without using it in some way—to illustrate a point, draw a conclusion, or support an argument. Exceptions exist, of course. For example, financial reports and weather bulletins in the daily paper (or on the radio or television) are usually pure information—just the facts. The daily television guide and the scores of athletic events also fall into this pure information category.

But most information exists in a larger context, and that context usually has some purpose beyond merely providing you with information. For example, in this chapter's reading selections, Beth Bailey's sociological study of courtship includes information to support her theories about why certain changes have occurred and the effect these changes have had on our society. Even information based on the writer's own experience should not be accepted without question.

Evaluating Information

Reading informative writing, therefore, involves not just understanding but also evaluating the information that is presented. Reading to be informed should always be a process of evaluating the accuracy and quality of the information included. Facts and figures can and do lie. Therefore, in reading to be informed, you need to question three aspects of the information included:

❖ What is its source?

❖ Is it relevant?

❖ Is it accurate?

WHAT IS ITS SOURCE?   First, you need to question the author's sources. Where does the information come from? Has the author presented information that comes from unreliable or biased sources? For example, can you really trust information about gun control if the only source is the American Rifle Association or information about the effects of smoking on health if the only source is the tobacco industry?

IS IT RELEVANT?   Second, you need to question whether the information pertains to the arguments it is intended to support. For example, does the author use national statistics to support an argument about a local problem? Or analyze the causes of drug addiction among teens with information that pertains to adults? Or cite migratory patterns of geese in Minnesota to explain the migration of egrets in Florida? Be sure the information included supports the assertions being made. Also be sure the information is current. Does the author use information about urban problems in the 1970s as if it were directly relevant to urban problems today? In general, dated information is suspect unless the author shows how it is appropriate.

IS IT ACCURATE?   Third, you need to question whether information is true to its source. Has the author been careless or dishonest in presenting the information? Such evaluations can be difficult to make. You cannot very well check all information you read by going back to the author's sources. But you can be aware that discrepancies can and do exist. You can become a skeptic—reading with a doubting, questioning attitude, refusing to accept information at face value just because it is in print. And, when your instincts tell you information is dubious, you can and should check the source to verify its accuracy.

Also evaluate the arguments and conclusions that writers derive from the information they present. Even if the information is accurate, the author's conclusions may be invalid. A clear and logical relationship should exist between the information presented and the conclusions drawn. As a reader, it is your responsibility to test the arguments you read, weighing the author's conclusions against the evidence (information) presented. Whether that information is derived from the writer's own experiences or from other sources, it should clearly and logically support the assumptions made, the arguments presented, and the conclusions drawn (see **credibility**).

CREDIBILITY, PAGE 552

▶ READING SELECTIONS

This chapter's reading selections, all written primarily to inform, focus on something that has changed. Because the idea of change is threatening to us, we seek explanations of how and why things change and the effects that result from the change. The authors of the reading selections in this chapter not only describe how something or someplace has changed, but also explore why the change occurred and what the results have been.

A BLESSING SENT FROM HEAVEN?

Morgan Hands

The author of the following essay, a student writer in a freshman composition course, views change as problematic. Describing the changes that occurred in his hometown of Eunice, Louisiana, after the oil bust in the late 1980s, Morgan Hands suggests that the affluence and progress of the boom period may have changed the town too quickly and too drastically. As you read, notice his comparison of the town before and after the decline in oil prices. Does this comparison help you understand how the town changed?

1   Eunice would tell a sad tale if it could speak. Like many of its neighboring cities, Eunice was once a thriving community—new buildings being built, new businesses opening, everyone working, and plenty of cash circulating. But one look at the city today and it is clear those days are gone forever.

2   Eunice, like many other cities in southern Louisiana, was almost entirely built around petroleum revenues. The petroleum revenues either directly or indirectly affected almost everything in Eunice. Obviously the petroleum revenues directly affected businesses such as gas stations, pipe companies, oil-field equipment specialists, and welders. But what is not so obvious is the fact that all the town's businesses, whether directly associated with the oil field or not, depend on petroleum-generated revenues. Take the average John Doe who earns a thousand dollars a week working for AWI workover-rigs. As a result of John's prosperity, he decides that he deserves a new watch or ring from the local jeweler. Maybe next month he can afford to buy that

new 27-inch, color stereo television from Perry's Home Electronics. And if John plays his cards right, he may even be able to afford that new pickup truck by the end of the year. It is not hard to see just what a dominant role petroleum revenues had on Eunice's economy.

Eunice was once a tiny farming community just southeast of Lafayette. Then the oil business came to town. Black-gold fever struck Eunice. Before the townspeople knew what was going on, they had all caught the fever. Most of the people around Eunice had been living off the land just as their ancestors had done centuries before them. A hard day's work only yielded a small return. But now the returns were much larger with oil at stake instead of rice or beans. Farmers began using their equipment to perform tasks for oil-related businesses. Some even sold their land and farm equipment to buy oil-field products and machinery. The petroleum era had begun. It was a blessing sent from heaven. Or was it?   3

Numerous new oil-related businesses started opening up around town and strengthening the other local businesses. They strengthened the economy so much, in fact, that the whole town began to rely almost entirely on these businesses for the revenues they generated. It was an excellent time for financial gain. The banks were giving loans to almost any and everyone. Small family-owned businesses began popping up all over town. Everyone was earning money as well as spending it. The city was literally flooded in cash and flourished with big department stores and expensive restaurants. Suddenly, yesterday's farmers were high rollers, cruisin' in Jaguars, Benzes, and Porsches. Everyone was living it up.   4

But an airplane can only fly so high before it starts on its crash-ing descent. The Middle East moved into the picture and began to dominate the petroleum industry. There wasn't much anyone could do about it. The federal government did what it could by placing additional taxes on imported oil. But it wasn't enough to stop the determined Middle Eastern countries. They had no trouble under-selling the United States' marketers. Within no time, they had driven the U.S. oil-field business into the ground. People had no choice but to file for bankruptcy and give up on the businesses to which they had given their lives. The Middle Eastern countries crushed the U.S. market and started a domino effect of bankruptcies that continues even today. Eunice had relied so greatly on the petroleum revenues that the crash affected not only oil-field-related businesses but every business. Because no matter what type of business it was, it relied on customers. And who employed most of these customers? The oil-related businesses.   5

6   One look at the main street in Eunice today and you'll see a strong-spirited community desperately trying to get back on its feet. You may even catch a glimpse of one of the big shots of yesterday. But don't bother looking for the Porsches or Jaguars; most of them have been repossessed. Now the big shots of yesterday drive the same cars they owned ten years ago, before black-gold fever struck. Those are the lucky ones. Some have seen the empires they created destroyed before their eyes and have never recovered from such a devastating blow.

7   Black gold created and destroyed a number of businesses and the men who built them. Black gold provided a roller coaster ride for the once boring town of Eunice, Louisiana. The ride was full of ups and downs, a definite thriller for those who were brave enough to ride.

▶   QUESTIONS TO CONSIDER

1. Is the title of this essay ironic? That is, does it say one thing but mean something else? What is Hands suggesting by his use of this title? Is the question mark essential to communicate his implication (see **titles**)?

TITLES, PAGE 667

2. Hands gives his readers three views of Eunice: He describes the town before it became prosperous from oil revenues, while it enjoyed that prosperity, and after it suffered the loss of those revenues. Which period of time does he describe most fully? Why does the writer emphasize this period in the town's history? Does the information he provides about the town in the other two periods give you a clear basis for comparison? That is, can you understand from the information Hands includes how drastically the town changed?

3. What is the primary source of information Hands includes in this essay? Is this information relevant?

▶   WRITING ACTIVITIES

Individual: Write a journal entry in which you describe some change that has occurred in your hometown or in some town you know well.

Collaborative: Working in groups, brainstorm about the economic changes that have occurred in the United States during the past decade. Then formulate a general statement about economic change in this country that reflects all of the changes you have listed.

Computer: Brainstorm a list of the major changes that have occurred during your lifetime in your hometown (or some community you know well). Use the block-and-move (or cut-and-paste) function of your word-processing program to group the changes according to some principle. Delete from the list those changes that are not related. You have now created an informal outline. If you want to develop this outline into a draft paper, move the cursor to one of the groups of related changes, and write a few sentences that express the nature of the changes—why they occurred or what their results were. Finally, formulate a general statement that might serve as a thesis, and place it at the beginning of the draft. You might also want to use your block-and-move (or cut-and-paste) function to position the thesis at the end of the draft to see which position seems to be more effective.

A CHANGED LIFE

Adrianne Eggers

This essay, written by Adrianne Eggers in a freshman English course, focuses not on the author's own experiences but on those of a fellow student. It is based on an interview the author had with a young woman she calls Tammy, whose life changed dramatically and irrevocably when she became pregnant while she was still in high school. As you read, notice that Eggers derives most of her information from the interview but also includes her own opinions and ideas.

"Okay, now we just wait a few moments for the sign; + is positive and – is negative. Dear God, please let it be negative. Okay, it's time to look. It is positive."   1

An unplanned pregnancy in a young female's life is one of the most dramatic possible changes in her life. It is a scary mess of emotions, moral questions, responsibilities, and difficulties. A woman can never be fully prepared for this first-time experience, but teenagers are even less prepared for it.   2

"Starting the second you find out you are pregnant, your life will never be the same again," relates Tammy while holding her ten-month-old son. Tammy went through many changes after finding out she was pregnant. She was scared and needed help, but could not look for support from the father of the child or her family.   3

4   Often an unplanned pregnancy leads to the break-up of the couple, and the mother is left to raise the child on her own. Sometimes this is the girl's choice, as in Tammy's case. She was involved in a very abusive relationship. Her boyfriend had come from a dysfunctional family, and he could not deal with problems in a constructive way. Instead, he would take his frustrations out on Tammy.

5   To make matters worse, many of Tammy's close friends also turned against her. They could not handle her situation and did not wish to be involved. This loss of friends was even more difficult for Tammy to deal with than dealing with her boyfriend. Only two close friends seemed to understand and to accept her as a friend who needed them. Everyone else seemed to think her a bad person because she was pregnant.

6   Tammy's family did support her though and helped her decide what to do about her situation. She ended her relationship with her boyfriend and enrolled in a different school so that she could participate in an Alternative Program for School-Aged Parents (APSAP). The school also had a day-care center just down the hall from the classroom where the pregnant teens did their school work. Even though Tammy still did not have close friends, her teacher and the school administrators were supportive.

7   Tammy's home environment was not always as positive as her school environment. She had to move into a small house with her sister, brother-in-law, brother, sister-in-law, and four-year-old nephew. The house they rented consisted of one bedroom which was large enough for only one bed and a tiny dresser, a cubby-hole sized kitchen, and a living room that looked like a hallway. The bathroom barely had enough room for a standing shower. Tammy had to get accustomed to living in close quarters with people whom she didn't always get along with. For example, she and her sister-in-law fought over many things while living together. But though there were conflicts and aggravations, it was important for Tammy to be with them. They gave her the physical and emotional support that helped her survive.

8   Emotional support was a lot easier to find than financial support for this pregnant teen and her family. A pregnancy is extremely expensive, about $2500 just to have the baby in a hospital, and not everyone at that age has enough insurance or cash to cover all of the expenses. In addition to the cost of medical care for the mother and baby, there is the cost of diapers, formula, clothing, bottles, crib, blankets, and much more for the baby after it is born. Tammy had to work twenty-five to thirty hours a week during the summer and ten to fifteen hours a week during the school year.

Although Tammy worked every chance that she had to support   9
herself and pay for the costs of the pregnancy and birth of the baby, it
was not enough. She had to turn to her father for help. This was difficult for Tammy because her parents had been divorced since she was
ten, and she had bitter feelings toward her father. Her father was not
very supportive of her, but he agreed to submit her medical bills to his
insurance. Tammy thought that this was great news, but nine months
after the baby's birth the bills were still not fully paid.

Fortunately, the state paid for all medical bills after the birth   10
because Tammy's son qualified as a child of a low-income, single parent. Since his birth, Tammy has had to take her son to the doctor's
office for an ear infection and regular check-ups but, as Tammy said,
"Nothing serious has happened to Timmy, but it is nice knowing that
the state will help if any problems arise."

However, there are some problems that the state cannot take   11
care of. Young women who become pregnant and their babies
are both at risk. They have to worry about miscarriages, sexually
transmitted diseases, premature births, and the general health of
both baby and mother. The changes that inevitably occur with
motherhood are more difficult for a young woman to adjust to.
This sometimes leads the mother into depression, failure in school,
drug and alcohol abuse, withdrawal from family and friends, and—
in the worst cases—suicide.

Although all of these changes seem negative, there were also   12
some positive changes Tammy experienced because of her pregnancy.
She started doing well in school and was motivated to graduate from
high school so that she could go to college. Her pregnancy also motivated her to make positive changes in her attitudes and relationships.
It strengthened her relationships with her family, especially her
mother. Tammy is no longer afraid to share her feelings and problems
with them.

Tammy now lives in a new home with just her sister and brother-   13
in-law. Next year she will live on her own with her son. She commutes
four days a week with her sister to a university, where she is studying
psychology. When she isn't at school, Tammy works or spends time
with her baby and her family.

Tammy believes her pregnancy has given her an opportunity to   14
enjoy children while she is still young. She also feels that having her
son has helped her grow up, and she realizes how important life is for
her now. She is no longer the wild, rebellious person she used to be.
Rather she is a responsible, motivated young woman who looks forward to taking care of and loving her son every day.

▶ QUESTIONS TO CONSIDER

1. Eggers begins her essay by talking about positive and negative test results; she concludes her essay by pointing out the positive and negative changes that resulted from Tammy's having a child. What effect does this framing device have on the essay? Are most changes both positive and negative, or are some clearly and exclusively one or the other?

2. Eggers focuses in this essay on Tammy's experiences rather than her own. Would the essay have been more effective had it been written from Tammy's point of view? What does Eggers contribute to the essay?

3. Eggers tries to distinguish clearly between her own ideas and opinions and those of Tammy. Is she consistently successful in doing this? Can you identify ideas, opinions, or information that is not clearly attributed to either?

4. What does Eggers do to make Tammy a sympathetic figure? Are there passages in which Tammy seems sentimentalized rather than sympathetic? What is the difference between a sympathetic character and one that is sentimentalized?

5. How does reading about Tammy make you feel about welfare reform? Is there an implicit argument in favor of welfare in this essay? If so, is it effective? Why, or why not?

▶ WRITING ACTIVITIES

Individual: Write a journal entry in which you argue for or against welfare reform.

Collaborative: With a group of your classmates, discuss the arguments for and against welfare for people like Tammy. Write a paragraph that summarizes both sides of this issue.

Computer: Write an argument for or against welfare reform, and post it to your computer network. Then respond to the arguments posted by your classmates. When you receive the responses to your own argument, defend or amend your initial position.

TWO CITIES

Stanley Kauffmann

This reading selection, which first appeared in
The New Republic, *focuses on the changes that have
occurred in New York City during the author's lifetime.
The author, Stanley Kauffmann, is a professional
writer, journalist, and editor. Since Kauffmann was
born, in the 1920s, he has witnessed many changes in
his hometown. As you read his essay, decide which
change he feels is most significant.*

A young friend asked me recently what it's like to live in the city   1
where I grew up. The question startled me. I never think of New York
that way. True, when I walk along certain streets, I remember things
that happened there, but the same city?

When I went to grammar school in the mid-1920s on 63rd Street   2
between Second and Third Avenues—now a chic residential neighborhood bristling with high apartment houses—I passed a blacksmith
shop on the way from the corner to the middle of the block. I can still
hear the hiss of the white-hot horseshoes being plunged into a bucket
of water, can still sniff the burny smell of the hoof to which a warm
shoe was fixed. I used to hitch rides to and from school on the back
step of horse-drawn ice wagons. I used to go shopping with my
mother in the pushcart market that lined both sides of Second Avenue
from 70th Street to 76th. Those pushcarts were under the Second
Avenue El. We lived on 68th Street near the corner of Second, and if
one of us was on the phone when an El train came along, we had to
halt the conversation until it passed. (Other boroughs still have Els, but
people under 50 can't imagine one in mid-Manhattan.)

In those 1920s, near the end of the great immigration wave, my   3
schoolmates were mostly Italian Catholic and Eastern European Jewish,
the children of foreign-born parents or foreign-born themselves. Both
of my parents had been born in New York, as had both of my grand-
mothers. My schoolmates called me, semi-derisively, "the Yankee."
Once a teacher asked me to carry a note to the principal. In his outer
office, an Italian woman, mother of one of the students, was waiting
to see him. While waiting, she was unembarrassedly nursing a baby.
I remember a blue vein in her very white breast.

4   Radio was still new in those days, wondrous. Many of my school-mates came from families too poor to own a set. I became something of a school celebrity because of radio and my father. He was a dentist, and in the professional society to which he belonged, he was in charge of a series of talks on dental hygiene that the society presented on the municipal radio station WNYC—fifteen minutes at midday once a week. Usually he invited other dentists to speak, but one week he did the talk himself. My mother wrote a note to my teacher asking that I be excused a half-hour before lunchtime that day, so that I could come home and hear my father. It was granted. I heard him, and I bragged. Some of my friends, especially the foreign-born ones, could hardly believe it. They actually knew someone whose father's voice had been broadcast all around New York City. One of them, probably quoting a parent, said, "Only in America."

5   Earlier, until I was 7 years old, we lived in Washington Heights, near the northern tip of Manhattan. A photographer used to come around with a pony on which children would sit to have their picture taken. I still have mine taken at 4. (My future wife, then unknown to me, had her picture taken on the same pony a few years later.) In the summer, a truck came around with a small carousel on the back. The driver turned the carousel by hand. There was a big iron wheel at the side, and he pumped up and down while six or eight children rode around. I loved it. (My wife, a few years later, loved it too.) A man occasionally wandered through the streets, garments draped over his shoulder, calling out, "I cash clo'. I cash clo'." He bought old clothes, usually men's, that people wanted to get rid of, and then sold them somewhere. Opposite our apartment house was a large vacant lot that had never been built on. It was surrounded by apartment houses, but the lot itself was untouched. I used to clamber over rocks and climb trees that Indians had known. This was true of Central Park, too, I knew, but that was for the city. This was for me and my friends, our own Indian territory.

6   I don't live in that city anymore.

7   Is New York worse now? Of course, and not just because many of my mementos are gone. We have an average of six murders a day, often including children. We have tens of thousands of homeless men and women, some of them mentally incompetent. We have a horrific drug problem. We share those miseries with other cities; one title we hold alone. New York streets are dirtier than those in any American city I've seen (let alone London or Paris).

8   But the greatest single change in New York in my lifetime is in the view of equality. Blacks are no longer required to "know their

place"—at any rate, not comparably with the rigors of the past. At least lip service is now paid to the idea of absolute equality. ("Assume a virtue, if you have it not," says Hamlet.) After World War II, Puerto Ricans flocked to New York. Soon came other Hispanics. Equality for them, too. The cash machine in my bank now asks, after I've inserted my card, whether I want my instructions in English or Spanish. New York has become, perhaps less willy than nilly, a gigantic testing ground for the idea that America has been mouthing for 200 years. This, too, is true of other American cities, but New York is the hugest crucible. Insofar as inherited hates and prejudices—in *all* of us—will permit, we are finding out whether equality can be more than a catch-word, whether equality is possible in race, religion, sexual preference, gender. (Female police officers, for example. Fully uniformed and packing pistols, they still avoid eye contact with a passing man, just like other women.) New York is at the head of the parade that is being asked to put its money where its Fourth-of-July mouth is.

The process is expensive. It costs everybody something. It abrades those who grew up in a stratified New York. It harries those, particularly black or Hispanic, who are on the frontier and must bear both the resentments in others and the frustrations in themselves. Surely crime rates and drug abuse are connected to the tauntings of unfulfilled equality. Surely the decline in civic pride is connected to those same frustrations.   9

"Superb-faced Manhattan!" sang Whitman. "Comrade Americanos! to us, then at last the Orient comes." Was he foreseeing sushi bars, Korean grocers and nail shops? Walt continued: 10

> To us, my city,   11
> Where our tall-topt marble and iron
>   beauties range on opposite sides, to walk
>   in the space between,
> To-day our Antipodes comes.

Will the vast experiment succeed? I'll never know; but the fact that it is happening helps to reconcile me to this dirty and dangerous city, this second New York of my life.   12

QUESTIONS TO CONSIDER ◀

1. How does Kauffmann use **comparison/contrast** and **description** in his article to support his argument that New York has changed?

COMPARISON AND CONTRAST, PAGE 542

DESCRIPTION, PAGE 565

2. Kauffmann, like Morgan Hands, uses his own experiences as a source of information. Especially in his description of the New York in which he grew up, he relies on his own story—the sights and sounds and odors that were part of his childhood experience. Are writers justified in using their own experiences to support their assertions? That is, are personal experiences a valid form of information?

3. Kauffmann's description of the New York of his childhood seems almost idyllic. But he begins his description of the city as it is now by asking "Is New York worse now?" He then answers his own question by replying, "Of course, . . ." But he concludes the article by pointing out one important change he views as positive: Racial equality is increasingly recognized in the city. Does Kauffmann imply that this one positive change somehow makes up for all of the negative changes that have occurred? Do you agree or disagree with this position?

ALLUSION, PAGE 507 **4.** Kauffmann includes in his essay several literary allusions (see **allusion**). In his final paragraph, for example, he refers to the nineteenth-century poet Walt Whitman, who often celebrated in his verses the worth of the individual and the kinship among humans. The quotation Kauffmann includes is from Whitman's poem "A Broadway Pageant." To understand this quotation, you need to know the word *antipodes* (an tip' po dez), which means "exact opposite" and is often used to refer to something that is on or from the opposite side of the earth. Reread the final paragraph of the article. Do you think Kauffmann's inclusion of this quotation strengthens his argument or makes his conclusion more effective? What does his reference to Walt Whitman suggest about the audience for whom he is writing?

5. What is the "vast experiment" that Kauffmann mentions in his final paragraph? Why will he never know whether it succeeds?

▶ **WRITING ACTIVITIES**

Individual: Write a journal entry in which you describe some way in which race relations have changed in your lifetime.

Collaborative: With a group of your classmates, discuss ways in which race relations have changed for the better in recent years and ways in which they have changed for the worse. Write a brief statement that expresses clearly your group's conclusions.

Computer: Revise your journal entry so that it is addressed to your classmates. If your journal entry doesn't have an explicit thesis statement, you can add one at this time. Using the block-and-move (or cut-and-paste) function, try different ways to organize your paragraphs (general to specific, cause and effect, effect and cause, etc.). If your computers are networked for text sharing, post your revised entry to the class. While your message is being read by your classmates, read those written by them and sent to you. If time permits, respond to any of your classmates' messages that interest you. Then, after you have read the responses sent to you, revise your own message so that it is an appropriate editorial for your school newspaper.

PROGRESS

John Sterling Harris

Most writing to inform is prose rather than poetry. However, poets also write to inform, including in their poetry factual information as well as imaginative descriptions and figurative language. Although the primary purpose of poetry is to create—to construct in language a work of art—poetry also communicates. The following poem by John Sterling Harris, a poet who is also a technical writer, describes how an old church was torn down and replaced by more modern, "progressive," structures. As you read, try to determine the poet's attitude toward the changing scene he describes.

The old church is down,
And where it stood
Lie scattered chunks of plaster
On dry rough-graded ground
Shielded from the rain a hundred years;   5
The dump trucks hauled away the scraps
Of age-darkened wood with
Many layers of white and ivory paint;
The bricks of the new addition,
Only half a century old,   10
Were carefully scraped of mortar
And stacked in cubical piles—
There is good demand for antique brick

To build the prosperous houses on the hill;
15   The huge old ceiling beams
And the rough-sawn red pine rafters,
Too big to use, too hard to cut,
Will make fence rails
And cattle shelters somewhere;
20   But the handmade adobe bricks
Of the chapel's yard-thick walls
Have no modern use;
The dozer knocks them down,
Not easily, but still too quickly
25   To return to the earth they came from.

It was always there,
And the schools and stores came later,
Because it was there;
Now the street is naked for its loss.

30   The officials point with pride
To the bright glass replacement up the street,
Praise the classrooms,
The long carpeted hallways
And the tall aluminum steeple
35   That has no bell;
They walk with relief over the old site
With its fearsome past all hauled away
And talk with the service station man
About his plans.

▶   QUESTIONS TO CONSIDER

1. The title of the poem, "Progress," is ironic. That is, the poet is saying one thing but means another. Although the word *regress* is the
literal opposite of *progress* when it is used as a verb, there is no
word that means the opposite of *progress* when it is used, as it is
here, as a noun (*regression* just doesn't mean the same thing as lack
of progress). Can you think of another word or phrase that would
more accurately reflect the poet's attitude toward the destruction of

the old church? Would a nonironic title be as effective as the ironic one the poet has chosen? Why or why not?

2. The poet states that the church "was always there." What effect does this overstatement create?

3. The poet suggests that the church was responsible for the creation of the town. Is this another instance of overstatement, or could it be an accurate reflection of the town's history?

4. To what new uses will the various parts of the demolished old church be put? What type of structure is going to replace the old church? Contrast these new uses and plans with the role the church played in the past.

WRITING ACTIVITIES

Individual: Change is often confused with progress. That is, we sometimes think that any type of change involves progress—that simply changing something makes it better. Describe some incidence of change that supposedly represented progress but that you found counterproductive, foolish, or sad.

Collaborative: Meeting in small groups, compare the incidents you described in the individual writing activity. Then formulate two definitions of the term *progress*: one that reflects popular thinking on the subject and one that represents the group's idea of what constitutes meaningful progress.

Computer (1): Choose one of the two definitions of *progress* that your group formulated, and enter it into the computer. Below the definition list examples that support it. Then revise the definition so that it can serve as the topic sentence of a paragraph. Expand several of the examples you have listed into sentences that support your topic sentence.

Computer (2): Using your word-processing system, write a prose summary of the poem "Progress." Try not to leave out any of the ideas included in the poem, but paraphrase them in your own words. Share your prose version with a peer, and discuss the differences between the poetic and prose versions.

THE TYRANNY OF CHOICE

Steven Waldman

Steven Waldman, a Washington correspondent for Newsweek, *argues in this article that consumers today are overwhelmed by the number of choices they face each time they make a simple purchase. The author identifies six drawbacks he believes result from the abundance of choices consumers face each day. His arguments are supported by a wealth of information about contemporary consumerism. Notice as you read that Waldman collected information for this article from his own experiences and observations as well as from written sources.*

1   Why did I nearly start crying the last time I went to buy socks? I'd stopped in a store called Sox Appeal, the perfect place, one might imagine, to spend a pleasant few minutes acquiring a pair of white athletic socks. After a brief visit to the men's dress sock department—dallying with more than 300 varieties, among them products embroidered with bikini-clad women, neckties, flowers, Rocky and Bullwinkle, and elegant logos such as "The Gold Bullion Collection: Imported" and "D'zin Pour Homme"—I finally made it into the athletics section. Here, the product-option high was even headier. Past the "Hypercolor" socks that change hue, combination "sport-and-dress" white socks, and "EarthCare" environmentally safe socks (which, unfortunately, boast of decomposing easily) were hosiery for every sport: racquetball, running, walking, cycling, hiking, basketball, and aerobics. I needed help.

2   "What if I play racquetball occasionally and run occasionally and walk sometimes, but don't want to get a different sock for each one?" I asked the saleswoman. She wrinkled her nose: "It's really a matter of personal preference." Did she have any standard-issue white tube socks? The nose-wrinkle again. "Well, yeah, you *could* get those, but . . ." I started reading the backs of the boxes, elaborately illustrated with architects' renderings of the stress points in the "Cushion-Engineered™ Zone Defense." After briefly contemplating the implications of the Cross-Training Sock—"Shock-Woven elastic arch brace contours to arch, providing additional support and normal articulation of the bones in the foot, while keeping sock migration minimal"—I spent another five minutes studying shapes (anklet, crew, or quarter) and

manufacturers, and grabbed a Cross Trainer, two walkers, and, in an environmental guilt-spasm, one pair of the EarthCare.

Since that day, the sock metaphor has crept constantly into my mind—and not just when I'm buying consumer products. At work I pick through dozens of options on my cafeteria insurance benefits plan. At the doctor's I'm offered several possible treatments for a neck problem and no real way to decide. At the video rental store I end up renting four movies even though I'll watch only one. Choices proliferate everywhere. My mental "tilt" light flashes continuously. I keep thinking that the more choices there are, the more wrong choices there are—and the higher the odds I'll make a mistake.

The topic of how much freedom freedom brings has fascinated philosophers throughout the ages. But when Sartre urged man to embrace and acknowledge his own power to choose, he did not have in mind figuring out the difference between hair conditioner, rejuvenator, reconstructor, and clarifier. So far, public debate on choice has been limited to just two realms: abortion and, more recently, public schools. But we're in the midst of a choice explosion that is much further reaching.

Think it over. A typical supermarket in 1976 had 9,000 products; today it has more than 30,000. The average produce section in 1975 carried sixty-five items; this summer it carried 285. (Kiwi has hit the top 20 list.) A Cosmetic Center outside Washington carries about 1,500 types and sizes of hair care products. The median household got six TV stations in 1975. Thanks to deregulation of the cable TV industry, that family now has more than thirty channels. The number of FM radio stations has doubled since 1970. A new religious denomination forms every week. (The 1980s brought us major additions such as the Evangelical Presbyterian Church and smaller groups such as the Semjase Silver Star Center, which follows the Twelve Bids from Patule that were given by extraterrestrial Space Brothers to Edmund "Billy" Meier.) In 1955 only 4 percent of the adult population had left the faith of their childhood. By 1985 one-third had. In 1980, 564 mutual funds existed. This year there are 3,347.

There has been a sharp rise in the number of people choosing new faces. More than twice as many cosmetic surgery operations were performed in the 1980s than in the 1970s, estimates the American Academy of Cosmetic Surgery. In the past decade a new periodical was born every day. Some have perished, but the survivors include: *Elvis International Forum, Smart Kids* (recent cover headline: "Should Babies Learn to Read?"), *American Handgunner, Triathlete, Harley Women, Log Home Living, Musclecar Classics,* and (my favorite) *Contemporary Urology.*

7   The growth of variety predates this recession, will continue after it, and, to a large extent, has persisted during it. *New Product News* reports that despite the depressed economy 21 percent more new products were introduced in supermarkets and drug stores in 1991 than the year before. Obvious benefits abound, of course, and not just for people with money. Telephone deregulation has made it cheaper to stay in touch with faraway friends; periodical proliferation meant I had *Fantasy Baseball* magazine to help me prepare for Rotisserie draft day; increased social tolerance has allowed more people (including me) to marry outside their faith or ethnic group; low sodium orange juice means people with high blood pressure can drink it (and it has increased juice sales); more cosmetics mean black women have shades that match their complexions. And so on. And in the words of Morris Cohen, a professor at the Wharton Business School: "If you're over-whelmed by the sock store, don't go there anymore." The beauty of the free market, he explains, is that each individual can select which options to exploit and which to ignore.

8   But Cohen's rational approach fails to account for how the mind actually processes all this variety. In fact, choice can be profoundly debilitating. It forces us to squander our time, weakens our connec-tions to people and places, and can even poison our sense of content-edness. What follows is a simple checklist—take your pick—of the drawbacks of our new way of choosing.

9   *Choice Erodes Commitment*. The same psychological dynamic that has led to a decline in brand loyalty can operate on more important decisions. The more options we have, the more tenuous our commit-ment becomes to each one. The compulsion to take inventory of one's wants and continually upgrade to a better deal can help explain every-thing from the rise of the pathological channel switcher who can never watch one TV show straight through to staggering divorce rates and employer-employee disloyalty. Baseball players have never had as many career options as they do now. As a result, sportswriter Thomas Boswell notes, the slightest sign of trouble leads the player or team to try some-place or someone better, producing many "insincere love affairs and very few committed marriages." Sound familiar? Yes, even the infamous male commitment problem results in part from the same thinking. I recently married a wonderful woman, but only after several years of embarrassingly tortured contemplation of what kind of "options" I might be foreclosing. There are, after all, 9,538,000 unmarried females aged 24–39, each with the potential to be more "perfect" than the one before.

10   *Choice Takes Too Much Time*. Taken individually, most choices are manageable and, for some sector of the population, a pleasure.

Stereo buffs love being able to select the finest woofers. But spend the optimal amount of time on each decision and pretty soon you run out of life. It's not surprising, then, that people feel more rushed than they used to. John P. Robinson, a professor of sociology at the University of Maryland who studied time diaries in 1965, 1975, and 1985, believes we feel harried partly because so much of our free time is absorbed by the process of deciding what to do with it. For all consumers, some time is simply wasted, not in figuring out which options suit them best but rather which distinctions matter. Before you can compare breakfast cereals' bran content you have to figure out if bran is really healthful. Should one care if a hair dryer has higher wattage? Are disposable diapers really worse for the environment than cloth? Being an educated consumer is a full-time job. You need to subscribe to several consumer magazines to do it properly. But which magazine to choose?

Choice Awakens Us to Our Failings. Choice-making lays claim to   11
an expanding portion of our mental energy because the perceived consequences of making the wrong selection keep growing. Under cafeteria insurance plans, if you choose to forgo the dismemberment benefits in favor of extra teeth cleanings, you have no one to blame after an accident but yourself. Each time I checked off a box on my benefit election form I flashed forward to some weepy scene when I had to explain to my wife why I had decided to consign us to poverty and despair. When the company dictated my dental plan I could at least curse the Bosses for their gross disregard of dental self-esteem and go about adapting to the situation. Arbitrariness had its comforts.

Similarly, before the mid-1970s, people had little choice about   12
how to invest their money. If inflation eroded their savings accounts, they were at least suffering, along with others, from the cruelty of an irresistible outside force. Today the availability of hundreds of possible investment "products" means everyone is fully capable of doing much worse than her neighbor. The wealthy try to solve that problem by spending still more money to hire financial advisers, only to confront a new set of worries about whether they have selected the best one. For the financially strapped, the anxiety can grow even more intense: the fewer dollars you have the more consequential each mistake becomes. Even when the stakes are small, we live in constant fear of being a Bad Consumer, which in a consumer-oriented society translates roughly into "sucker."

Choice Leads to Inept Consumption. The more choice available,   13
the more information a consumer must have to make a sensible selection. When overload occurs, many simply abandon the posture of rational Super-Consumer. Warning labels on products have become so

common that many shoppers simply ignore them all, including the important ones. Several friends have confessed that the selection of car models—591 and rising—has become so dizzying that they tossed aside *Consumer Reports* and relied entirely on the recommendation of a friend. Some become so paralyzed by the quest for the better deal that they postpone decisions indefinitely, while others become so preoccupied with absorbing the new features touted by a manufacturer that they forget to consider the basics. After all the fretting over the migration patterns of the socks, I took them home and found them to be quite fluffy and supportive, but the wrong size.

14   Consumers may be better informed than they were two decades ago, but salespeople have more tools with which to fight back. I spent three days studying up for a trip to Circuit City to buy a CD player. Despite having read several magazine and newspaper articles, I was, within minutes, putty in the salesman's hands. When I asked for a particular model, he rolled his eyes and laughed, "You must have gotten that from *Consumer Reports.*" With a simple well-timed chuckle he made me doubt my entire research regimen. He then battered me with a flurry of techno-terms and finally moved in for the kill by giving me an audio comparison test between two different systems that sounded exactly alike. My resistance was exhausted, so I bought the system he suggested, which, of course, cost more than I had intended to spend.

15   *Choice Causes Political Alienation.* Voters don't necessarily have more choices than they used to—an increase in primaries and referenda having been offset by the influence of incumbency and money— but the *way* voters choose has changed dramatically. As a result of the weakening of political parties, voting behavior now closely resembles the consumption of products. The biggest political group is not Democrats or Republicans, but "independents," shopper-equivalents who've dropped brand loyalty in favor of product-by-product analysis. Last century two-thirds of voters went straight party line; in 1980 two-thirds split tickets. In theory, this means voters carefully weigh the candidate's policies, character, and history. In reality, it's nearly impossible to sort through a candidate's "stands" on the "issues" from a blizzard of untrustworthy ads, a newspaper editorial, or a blip on the TV news. Was he the one who wants a revolving loan fund for worker retraining or the one who gives flag burners early parole? No wonder voters, like shoppers, act impulsively or vote according to the wisdom of their favorite interest group. Many who vote for ballot initiatives or lower offices simply follow the recommendation of the local newspaper, which is like buying a car on the word of the local auto columnist. When I was voting absentee in New York I selected judicial candidates

on the basis of gender and race since I knew little else about them. The ultimate political choice overload came in California in 1990, when voters received a 222-page ballot pamphlet to help them decide among twenty-eight initiatives.

Candidates have responded to the rise of the consumer-voter by turning to marketing professionals who've only made the voters' dilemma worse. In the 1950s political consultants were advertising men who selected a candidate attribute and then sold it, the way an automaker might remind consumers of a large car's natural advantages, like spaciousness and safety. Political consulting has evolved, though. Candidates now rely heavily on market researchers—i.e., the pollsters—trying less to determine what part of their essence they should highlight than what they should become to match voters' desires. Sometimes that means candidates become more responsive to public thinking, but more often it means politicians forget to consult (or have) their own core beliefs. Witness the breathtaking spectacle of pro-life pols who once assailed the supreme immorality of baby-killing quickly becoming pro-choice because of the supreme importance of polls. This "politics as consumption" (in the phrase of University of Rochester professor Robert Westbrook) seems to produce more gelatinous politicians—precisely the sort that voters have the hardest time judging. 16

Choice Erodes the Self. In theory, choice enables an individual to select the car, money market fund, or spouse that expresses herself most precisely. But if choice is self-definition, more choices mean more possible definitions. Kenneth Gergen, a professor of psychology at Swarthmore, argues in his new book, *The Saturated Self,* that the post modern personality becomes "populated" with growing numbers of "selves" as it's bombarded by an ever increasing number of potential relationships from TV, travel, telephones, faxes, computers, etc. From an insecure sense of self, you then spiral toward what Gergen calls "multiphrenia," in which the besieged, populated self frantically flails about trying to take advantage of the sea of choices. This condition may never merit its own telethon, but as choices increase so do the odds that multiphrenia will strike, leaving the scars of perpetual self-doubt. It's why the people who work hardest to improve their appearance never seem to feel much better than before they sampled the offerings of the Self-Perfection Industry (exercise videos, customized makeup, cosmetic surgery, health food). They become like politicians with their own private pollsters; the quest to re-create virtually supplants whatever person was once there. 17

Choice Reduces Social Bonding. The proliferation of choice helps cause, and results from, another trend—social fragmentation. Together 18 they ensure that Americans share fewer and fewer common experiences. A yuppie diet bears less and less resemblance to that of a lower-income family. I don't even know who's on the Wheaties box anymore because my cereal is located about ninety feet down the aisle. As marketers divide us into increasingly narrow segments, we inevitably see ourselves that way too. When there was one movie theater in a neighborhood, everyone sat under the same roof and watched the same film. Video rental stores enable you to be a movie junkie without ever having to sit next to another human being. Three decades ago, even when everyone was sitting in their own homes they were at least all watching "Gunsmoke." Today's viewing public scatters to its particular demographic niche on the cable dial.

19   Even the spiritual realm has evolved like a supermarket. "It has become a consumer-oriented, highly fragmented religious market-place," says David Roozen, director of the Hartford Seminary for Social and Religious Research. In a buyer's market, the individual can select the religious institution with which he or she is most comfortable. But as each generation discards the nasty (or difficult) parts of the faith, religious traditions decay. Moreover, instead of integrating people of different backgrounds under the same theological roof, denominations sprout to appeal to smaller groups of like-minded people. (If, for example, you decide the followers of the teachings of Billy Meier's Space Brothers aren't your kind of people, you can turn to the Universe Society Church, which observes the wisdom of Fahsz, an extraterrestrial contacted by someone named Hal Wilcox.) The comedian Emo Philips tells a joke about discovering similarities in religious backgrounds with someone he just met. "I said [are you] Protestant or Catholic? He said, 'Protestant.' I said, 'Me too! What franchise?' He says, 'Baptist.' I said, 'Me Too! Northern Baptist or Southern Baptist?' He says, 'Southern Baptist.' I said, 'Me Too!'" The two go back and forth in this vein. Finally, Emo asks, "'Northern conservative fundamentalist Baptist Great Lakes Region Council of 1879 or Northern conservative fundamentalist Baptist Great Lakes Region Council of 1912?' and he says 'Northern conservative fundamentalist Baptist Great Lakes Region Council of 1912.' And I said, 'Die Heretic!'"

20   How can we adapt to this world of choice? Some steps are being taken for us. The Food and Drug Administration recently announced rules to standardize product labels that should simplify our task in the supermarket. Some school districts have required uniforms in order to curb the clothing competition that has led to killings over sneakers. Regulatory agencies could further help by simply banning products

they consider unsafe, rather than slapping on warning labels that force us to perform quickie risk assessment studies. The market itself will develop some innovations to help us cope. "Price clubs" have sprouted up in which customers shop at huge warehouses stocked with just a few brands, but very low prices. Bicycle stores now offer "hybrids" for those who can't decide between mountain, city, touring, and racing. But the general trend remains overwhelmingly toward market fragmentation.

Dealing with an abundance of choices mostly requires a mental 21 reorientation. Choice overload helped me finally understand what was so offensive about the stereotypical yuppie obsession with "quality," of which I have often been guilty. It's not that some coffee beans aren't, in fact, more flavorful than others, it's that people who spend so much of their lives thinking about small differences become small people.

Imagine instead a world in which we used our choice brain lobes 22 for the most important decisions and acted more arbitrarily on the rest. Perhaps you might select a brand name and buy all its products for the next four years, scheduling Choice Day during non-presidential election years. Or you might embrace the liberating powers of TV commercials. As everyone knows, ads brainwash us into choosing products through insidious appeals to sex or other animal urges. But sometimes it feels good to let an ad take us by the hand. A few years ago I had an epiphany while deciding what to eat for dinner. I looked in the refrigerator, thought about nearby restaurants and markets, and grew puzzled. Just then an ad came on the TV for Burger King, featuring a luscious Whopper with fake charcoal stripes painted with perfect symmetry across the juicy meat. I put on my coat and immediately walked, zombielike, to the nearby Burger King and ordered a Whopper. I found it exhilarating, because I knew it wasn't the behavior of a rational economic player, and that it didn't matter.

As the Twelve Steppers say, we must acknowledge our powerless- 23 ness. We cannot knowledgeably make even a fraction of the appropriate choices available. Say it out loud. Today I will make several wrong choices. Now, whether you've selected an inferior vacuum cleaner, bought the large soda when the jumbo was a better deal, or accidentally prayed to the wrong god—forgive yourself. If we took some joy in being bad choosers, or at least placed less value on being stellar consumers of unimportant things, we would be training ourselves to accept a few extra drops of imperfection in our lives. Somehow, that would seem more like progress than having the choice between polypropylene arch brace contours and a solar-powered argyle.

▶   QUESTIONS TO CONSIDER

1. We usually think of choices as positive because they give us options. Does Waldman convince you that choices can also affect people negatively? Can you think of a recent experience when you were overwhelmed by having too many choices?

2. Waldman begins with a narrative about an experience he had when shopping for socks. This narrative serves not only as an illustration but also as a metaphor for the problem of having too many choices. In fact, he refers to it later in the article as the "sock metaphor." Is this humorous, personal experience an appropriate, effective introduction for the article? Why or why not?

NARRATION, PAGE 618

DESCRIPTION, PAGE 565

EXEMPLIFICATION, PAGE 574

COMPARISON/CONTRAST, PAGE 542

CAUSE AND EFFECT, PAGE 522

3. In addition to narration, Waldman uses description, exemplification, comparison/contrast, and cause and effect to develop his arguments. Find at least one example of each of these methods of development in his article (see **narration**, **description**, **exemplification**, **comparison/contrast** and **cause and effect**).

4. Waldman concludes his article by arguing that "dealing with an abundance of choices . . . requires a mental reorientation" on the part of consumers. What is the nature of the mental reorientation he advocates?

▶   WRITING ACTIVITIES

Individual: Describe in your journal a particularly difficult choice you have recently made as a consumer. How did you finally reach a decision? What did you learn from the experience that would help you make future decisions? Include as much specific information as possible in your description.

Collaborative: With a group of your classmates, brainstorm on a list of drawbacks that result when consumers do not have enough choices. Then compare your list with the drawbacks Waldman identifies as resulting from having too many choices. Which situation seems to result in the more serious drawbacks?

Computer: Write about one way in which your choices as a consumer have increased and one way in which your choices have become more limited during your lifetime. Post what you have written to your computer network, and read what others have written on this topic. Generalize from what you have written, and decide whether consumer choices in general have become greater or more limited. Then on the basis of this information, write a response to Waldman's article.

FROM FRONT PORCH TO BACK SEAT

Beth L. Bailey

This reading selection is the first chapter of a socio-logical study of changing patterns of courtship in twentieth-century America. The author, Beth Bailey, points out that courtship has literally moved from the front porch of the girl's home to the back seat of the boy's car, "from woman's sphere to man's sphere." In supporting her thesis, Bailey provides her readers with a wealth of information about dating, includ-ing how the word date *entered our vocabulary, why dating began, and what effects it has had on courtship in the United States. As you read, compare the dating practices Bailey describes with those you have experienced.*

One day, the 1920s story goes, a young man asked a city girl 1 if he might call on her. We know nothing else about the man or the girl—only that, when he arrived, she had her hat on. Not much of a story to us, but any American born before 1910 would have gotten the punch line. "She had her hat on": those five words were rich in mean-ing to early twentieth-century Americans. The hat signaled that she expected to leave the house. He came on a "call," expecting to be received in her family's parlor, to talk, to meet her mother, perhaps to have some refreshments or to listen to her play the piano. She expected a "date," to be taken "out" somewhere and entertained. He ended up spending four weeks' savings fulfilling her expectations.

In the early twentieth century this new style of courtship, dating, 2 had begun to supplant the old. Born primarily of the limits and oppor-tunities of urban life, dating had almost completely replaced the old system of calling by the mid-1920s—and, in so doing, had transformed American courtship. Dating moved courtship into the public world, relocating it from family parlors and community events to restaurants, theaters, and dance halls. At the same time, it removed couples from the implied supervision of the private sphere—from the watchful eyes of family and local community—to the anonymity of the public sphere.

Courtship among strangers offered couples new freedom. But access to the public world of the city required money. One had to buy entertainment, or even access to a place to sit and talk. Money—men's money—became the basis of the dating system and, thus, of courtship. This new dating system, as it shifted courtship from the private to the public sphere and increasingly centered around money, fundamentally altered the balance of power between men and women in courtship.

3   The transition from calling to dating was as complete as it was fundamental. By the 1950s and 1960s, social scientists who studied American courtship found it necessary to remind the American public that dating was a "recent American innovation and not a traditional or universal custom." Some of the many commentators who wrote about courtship believed dating was the best thing that had ever happened to relations between the sexes; others blamed the dating system for all the problems of American youth and American marriage. But virtually everyone portrayed the system dating replaced as infinitely simpler, sweeter, more innocent, and more graceful. Hardheaded social scientists waxed sentimental about the "horse-and-buggy days," when a young man's offer of a ride home from church was tantamount to a proposal and when young men came calling in the evenings and courtship took place safely within the warm bosom of the family. "The courtship which grew out of the sturdy social roots [of the nineteenth century]," one author wrote, "comes through to us for what it was—a gracious ritual, with clearly defined roles for man and woman, in which everyone knew the measured music and the steps."

4   Certainly a less idealized version of this model of courtship had existed in America, but it was not this model that dating was supplanting. Although only about 45 percent of Americans lived in urban areas by 1910, few of them were so untouched by the sweeping changes of the late nineteenth century that they could live that dream of rural simplicity. Conventions of courtship at that time were not set by simple yeoman farmers and their families but by the rising middle class, often in imitation of the ways of "society."

5   By the late nineteenth century a new and relatively coherent social group had come to play an important role in the nation's cultural life. This new middle class, born with and through the rise of national systems of economy, transportation, and communication, was actively creating, controlling, and consuming a national system of culture. National magazines with booming subscription rates promulgated middle-class standards to the white, literate population at large. Women's magazines were especially important in the role of cultural evangelist.

These magazines carried clearly didactic messages to their reader-   6
ship. Unlike general-interest (men's) magazines, which were more
likely to contain discussions of issues and events, women's magazines
were highly prescriptive, giving advice on both the spiritual and the
mundane. But while their advice on higher matters was usually
vaguely inspirational, advice on how to look and how to act was
extremely explicit.

The conventions of courtship, as set forth in these national maga-   7
zines and in popular books of etiquette, were an important part of the
middle-class code of manners. Conventional courtship centered on
"calling," a term that could describe a range of activities. The young
man from the neighboring farm who spent the evening sitting on the
front porch with the farmer's daughter was paying a call, and so was
the "society" man who could judge his prospects by whether or not
the card he presented at the front door found the lady of his choice "at
home." The middle-class arbiters of culture, however, aped and elabo-
rated the society version of the call. And, as it was promulgated by
magazines such as the *Ladies' Home Journal*, with a circulation over
one million by 1900, the modified society call was the model for an
increasing number of young Americans.

Outside of courtship, this sort of calling was primarily a woman's   8
activity, for women largely controlled social life. Women designated a
day or days "at home" to receive callers; on other days they paid or
returned calls. The caller would present her card to the maid (common
even in moderate-income homes until the World War I era) who
answered the door, and would be admitted or turned away with some
excuse. The caller who regularly was "not received" quickly learned
the limits of her family's social status, and the lady "at home" thus, in
some measure, protected herself and her family from the social confusion and pressures engendered by the mobility and expansiveness of
late nineteenth-century America. In this system, the husband, though
generally determining the family's status, was represented by his wife
and was thereby excused from this social-status ritual. Unmarried men,
however, were subject to this female-controlled system .

The calling system in courtship, though varying by region and the   9
status of the individuals involved, followed certain general outlines.
When a girl reached the proper age or had her first "season" (depending on her family's social level), she became eligible to receive male
callers. At first her mother or guardian invited young men to call; in
subsequent seasons the young lady had more autonomy and could
bestow an invitation to call upon any unmarried man to whom she

had been properly introduced at a private dance, dinner, or other "entertainment." Any unmarried man invited to an entertainment owed his hostess (and thus her daughter[s]) a duty call of thanks, but other young men not so honored could be brought to call by friends or relatives of the girl's family, subject to her prior permission. Undesired or undesirable callers, on the other hand, were simply given some excuse and turned away.

10   The call itself was a complicated event. A myriad of rules governed everything: the proper amount of time between invitation and visit (a fortnight or less); whether or not refreshments should be served (not if one belonged to a fashionable or semi-fashionable circle, but outside of "smart" groups in cities like New York and Boston, girls *might* serve iced drinks with little cakes or tiny cups of coffee or hot chocolate and sandwiches); chaperonage (the first call must be made on daughter and mother, but excessive chaperonage would indicate to the man that his attentions were unwelcome); appropriate topics of conversation (the man's interests, but never too personal); how leave should be taken (on no account should the woman "accompany [her caller] to the door nor stand talking while he struggles into his coat").

11   Each of these "measured steps," as the mid-twentieth-century author nostalgically called them, was a test of suitability, breeding and background. Advice columns and etiquette books emphasized that these were the manners of any "well-bred" person—and conversely implied that deviations revealed a lack of breeding. However, around the turn of the century, many people who did lack this narrow "breeding" aspired to politeness. Advice columns in women's magazines regularly printed questions from "Country Girl" and "Ignoramus" on the fine points of calling etiquette. Young men must have felt the pressure of girls' expectations, for they wrote to the same advisers with questions about calling. In 1907, *Harper's Bazaar* ran a major article titled "Etiquette for Men," explaining the ins and outs of the calling system. In the first decade of the twentieth century, this rigid system of calling was the convention not only of the "respectable" but also of those who aspired to respectability.

12   At the same time, however, the new system of dating was emerging. By the mid-1910s, the word *date* had entered the vocabulary of the middle-class public. In 1914, the *Ladies' Home Journal*, a bastion of middle-class respectability, used the term (safely enclosed in quotation marks but with no explanation of its meaning) several times. The word was always spoken by the exotica, the college sorority girl—a character marginal in her exoticness but nevertheless a solid product of the middle class. "One beautiful evening of the spring term," one such article

begins, "when I was a college girl of eighteen, the boy whom, because of his popularity in every phase of college life, I had been proud gradually to allow the monopoly of my 'dates,' took me unexpectedly into his arms. As he kissed me impetuously I was glad, from the bottom of my heart, for the training of that mother who had taught me to hold myself aloof from all personal familiarities of boys and men."

Sugarcoated with a tribute to motherhood and virtue, the dates— 13 and the kiss—were unmistakably presented for a middle-class audience. By 1924, ten years later, when the story of the unfortunate young man who went to call on the city girl was current, dating had essentially replaced calling in middle-class culture. The knowing smiles of the story's listeners had probably started with the word *call*—and not every hearer would have been sympathetic to the man's plight. By 1924, he really should have known better.

Dating, the great American middle-class institution, was not at all 14 a product of the middle class. Dating came to the middle class through the upper classes—and from the lower. The first recorded uses of the word *date* in its modern meaning are from lower-class slang. George Ade, the Chicago author who wrote a column titled "Stories of the Streets and of the Town" for the *Chicago Record* and published many slang-filled stories of working-class life, probably introduced the term to literature in 1896. Artie, Ade's street-smart protagonist, asks his unfaithful girlfriend, "I s'pose the other boy's fillin' all my dates?" And in 1899 Ade suggested the power of a girl's charms: "Her Date Book had to be kept on the Double Entry System." Other authors whose imaginations were captured by the city and the variety of its inhabitants—Frank Norris, Upton Sinclair, O. Henry—also were using the term by the first decade of the twentieth century.

The practice of dating was a response of the lower classes to the 15 pressures and opportunities of urban-industrial America, just as calling was a response of the upper stratas. The strict conventions of calling enabled the middling and upper classes to protect themselves from some of the intrusions of urban life, to screen out some of the effects of social and geographical mobility in late nineteenth-century America. Those without the money and security to protect themselves from the pressures of urban life or to control the overwhelming opportunities it offered adapted to the new conditions much more directly.

Dating, which to the privileged and protected would seem a sys- 16 tem of increased freedom and possibility, stemmed originally from the lack of opportunities. Calling, or even just visiting, was not a practicable system for young people whose families lived crowded into one or two rooms. For even the more established or independent working-class girls, the parlor and the piano often simply didn't exist. Some "factory girls" struggled to find a way to receive callers. The *Ladies' Home Journal* approvingly reported the case of six girls, workers in a box factory, who had formed a club and pooled part of their wages to pay the "janitress of a tenement house" to let them use her front room two evenings a week. It had a piano. One of the girls explained their system: "We ask the boys to come when they like and spend the evening. We haven't any place at home to see them, and I hate seeing them on the street."

17   Many other working girls, however, couldn't have done this even had they wanted to. They had no extra wages to pool, or they had no notions of middle-class respectability. Some, especially girls of ethnic families, were kept secluded—chaperoned according to the customs of the old country. But many others fled the squalor, drabness, and crowdedness of their homes to seek amusement and intimacy elsewhere. And a "good time" increasingly became identified with public places and commercial amusements, making young women whose wages would not even cover the necessities of life dependent on men's "treats." Still, many poor and working-class couples did not so much escape from the home as they were pushed from it.

18   These couples courted on the streets, sometimes at cheap dance halls or eventually at the movies. These were not respectable places, and women could enter them only so far as they, themselves, were not considered respectable. Respectable young women did, of course, enter the public world, but their excursions into the public were cushioned. Public courtship of middle-class and upper-class youth was at least *supposed* to be chaperoned; those with money and social position went to private dances with carefully controlled guest lists, to theater parties where they were a private group within the public. As rebels would soon complain, the supervision of society made the private parlor seem almost free by contrast. Women who were not respectable did have relative freedom of action—but the trade-off was not necessarily a happy one for them.

19   The negative factors were important, but dating rose equally from the possibilities offered by urban life. Privileged youth, as Lewis Erenberg shows in his study of New York nightlife, came to see the possibility of privacy in the anonymous public, in the excitement and freedom the city offered. They looked to lower-class models of freedom—to those beyond the constraints of respectability. As a society girl informed the readers of the *Ladies' Home Journal* in 1914: "Nowadays it is considered 'smart' to go to the low order of dance halls, and not only be a looker-on, but also to dance among all sorts

and conditions of men and women. . . . Nowadays when we enter a restaurant and dance place it is hard to know who is who." In 1907, the same magazine had warned unmarried women never to go alone to a "public restaurant" with any man, even a relative. There was no impropriety in the act, the adviser had conceded, but it still "lays [women] open to misunderstanding and to being classed with women of undesirable reputation by the strangers present." Rebellious and adventurous young people sought that confusion, and the gradual loosening of proprieties they engendered helped to change courtship. Young men and women went out into the world *together*, enjoying a new kind of companionship and the intimacy of a new kind of freedom from adult supervision.

The new freedom that led to dating came from other sources as well. Many more serious (and certainly respectable) young women were taking advantage of opportunities to enter the public world—going to college, taking jobs, entering and creating new urban professions. Women who belonged to the public world by day began to demand fuller access to the public world in general. City institutions gradually accommodated them. Though still considered risqué by some, dining out alone with a man or attending the theater with no chaperone did not threaten an unmarried woman's reputation by the start of the twentieth century. 20

There were still limits, of course, and they persisted for a long while. Between 1904 and 1907, *Ladies' Home Journal* advisers repeatedly insisted that a girl should not "go out" with a young man until he had called at her home. And in the early 1920s, Radcliffe girls were furnished with a list of approved restaurants in which they could dine with a young man. Some were acceptable only before 7:30 p.m.; others, clearly, still posed a threat to reputations. These limits and conditions, however, show that young men and women of courting age were *expected* to go out—the restrictions were not attempts to *stop* dating, only to control it. 21

Between 1890 and 1925, dating—in practice and in name— had gradually, almost imperceptibly, become a universal custom in America. By the 1930s it had transcended its origins: Middle America associated dating with neither upper-class rebellion nor the urban lower classes. The rise of dating was usually explained, quite simply, by the invention of the automobile. Cars had given youth mobility and privacy, and so had brought about the system. This explanation perhaps not consciously but definitely not coincidentally—revised history. The automobile certainly contributed to the rise of dating as a *national* practice, especially in rural and suburban areas, but it was 22 simply accelerating and extending a process already well under way. Once its origins were located firmly in Middle America, however, and not in the extremes of urban upper- and lower-class life, dating had become an American institution.

23   Dating not only transformed the outward modes and conventions of American courtship, it also changed the distribution of control and power in courtship. One change was generational: the dating system lessened parental control and gave young men and women more freedom. The dating system also shifted power from women to men. Calling, either as a simple visit or as the elaborate late nineteenth-century ritual, gave women a large portion of control. First of all, courtship took place within the girl's home—in women's "sphere," as it was called in the nineteenth century—or at entertainments largely devised and presided over by women. Dating moved courtship out of the home and into man's sphere—the world outside the home. Female controls and conventions lost much of their power outside women's sphere. And while many of the conventions of female propriety were restrictive and repressive, they had allowed women (young women and their mothers) a great deal of immediate control over courtship. The transfer of spheres thoroughly undercut that control.

24   Second, in the calling system, the woman took the initiative. Etiquette books and columns were adamant on that point: it was the "girl's privilege" to ask a young man to call. Furthermore, it was highly improper for the man to take the initiative. In 1909 a young man wrote to the *Ladies' Home Journal* adviser asking, "May I call upon a young woman whom I greatly admire, although she had not given me the permission? Would she be flattered at my eagerness, even to the setting aside of conventions, or would she think me impertinent?" Mrs. Kingsland replied: "I think that you would risk her just displeasure and frustrate your object of finding favor with her." Softening the prohibition, she then suggested an invitation might be secured through a mutual friend. She had been even stricter two years before, insisting that "a man must not go beyond a very evident pleasure in a woman's society, by way of suggestions." Another adviser, "The Lady from Philadelphia," put a more positive light on the situation, noting that "nothing forbids a man to show by his manner that her acquaintance is pleasing to him and thus perhaps suggest that the invitation [to call] would be welcome."

25   Contrast these strictures with advice on dating etiquette from the 1940s and 1950s: An advice book for men and women warns that "girls who [try] to usurp the right of boys to choose their own dates" will "ruin a good dating career. . . . Fair or not, it is the way of life.

From the Stone Age, when men chased and captured their women, comes the yen of a boy to do the pursuing. You will control your impatience, therefore, and respect the time-honored custom of boys to take the first step."

One teen advice book from the 1950s told girls never to take the initiative with a boy, even under some pretext such as asking about homework: "Boys are jealous of their masculine prerogative of taking the initiative." Another said simply: "*don't ask*," and still another recounted an anecdote about a girl who asked a boy for a date to the Saturday-night dance. He cut her off in mid-sentence and walked away.   26

Of course, some advisers stressed that women were not without resource. Though barred from taking the initiative, nothing forbade women from using tricks and stratagems, from showing by a friendly manner that they would welcome an invitation for a date.   27

This absolute reversal of roles almost necessarily accompanied courtship's move from woman's sphere to man's sphere. Although the convention-setters commended the custom of woman's initiative because it allowed greater exclusivity (it might be "difficult for a girl to refuse the permission to call, no matter how unwelcome or unsuitable an acquaintance the man might be"), the custom was based on a broader principle of etiquette. The host or hostess issued any invitation; the guest did not invite himself or herself. An invitation to call was an invitation to visit in a woman's home.   28

An invitation to go out on a date, on the other hand, was an invitation into man's world—not simply because dating took place in the public sphere (commonly defined as belonging to men), though that was part of it, but because dating moved courtship into the world of the economy. Money—men's money—was at the center of the dating system. Thus, on two counts, men became the hosts and assumed the control that came with that position.   29

There was some confusion caused by this reversal of initiative, especially during the twenty years or so when going out and calling coexisted as systems. (The unfortunate young man in the apocryphal story, for example, had asked the city girl if he might call on her, so perhaps she was conventionally correct to assume he meant to play the host.) Confusions generally were sorted out around the issue of money. One young woman, "Henrietta L.," wrote to the *Ladies' Home Journal* to inquire whether a girl might "suggest to a friend going to any entertainment or place of amusement where there will be any expense to the young man." The reply: "Never, under any circumstances." The adviser explained that the invitation to go out must "always" come from the man, for he was the one "responsible for the expense." This same   30 adviser insisted that the woman must "always" invite the man to call; clearly she realized that money was the central issue.

31   The centrality of money in dating had serious implications for courtship. Not only did money shift control and initiative to men by making them the "hosts," it led contemporaries to see dating as a system of exchange best understood through economic analogies or as an economic system pure and simple. Of course, people did recognize in marriage a similar economic dimension—the man undertakes to support his wife in exchange for her filling various roles important to him—but marriage was a permanent relationship. Dating was situational, with no long-term commitments implied, and when a man, in a highly visible ritual, spent money on a woman in public, it seemed much more clearly an economic act.

32   In fact, the term *date* was associated with the direct economic exchange of prostitution at an early time. A prostitute called "Maimie," in letters written to a middle-class benefactor friend in the late nineteenth century, described how men made "dates" with her. And a former waitress turned prostitute described the process to the Illinois Senate Committee on Vice this way: "You wait on a man and he smiles at you. You see a chance to get a tip and you smile back. Next day he returns and you try harder than ever to please him. Then right away he wants to make a date, and offer you money and presents if you'll be a good fellow and go out with him." These men, quite clearly, were buying sexual favors—but the occasion of the exchange was called a "date."

33   Courtship in America had always turned somewhat on money (or background). A poor clerk or stockyards worker would not have called upon the daughter of a well-off family, and men were expected to be economically secure before they married. But in the dating system money entered directly into the relationship between a man and a woman as the symbolic currency of exchange in even casual dating.

34   Dating, like prostitution, made access to women directly dependent on money. Quite a few men did not hesitate to complain about the going rate of exchange. In a 1925 *Collier's* article, "Why Men Won't Marry," a twenty-four-year-old university graduate exclaimed: "Get Married! Why, I can't even afford to go with any of the sort of girls with whom I would like to associate." He explained: "When I was in college, getting an allowance from home, I used to know lots of nice girls. . . . Now that I am on my own I can't even afford to see them. . . . If I took a girl to the theatre she would have to sit in the gallery, and if we went to supper afterward, it would be at a soda counter, and if we rode home it would have to be in the street cars." As he presents it,

the problem is solely financial. The same girls who were glad to "go with" him when he had money would not "see" him when he lacked their price. And "nice girls" cost a lot.

In dating, though, the exchange was less direct and less clear than in prostitution. One author, in 1924, made sense of it this way. In dating, he reasoned, a man is responsible for all expenses. The woman is responsible for nothing—she contributes only her company. Of course, the man contributes his company, too, but since he must "add money to balance the bargain" his company must be worth less than hers. Thus, according to this economic understanding, she is selling her company to him. In his eyes, dating didn't even involve an exchange; it was a direct purchase. The moral "subtleties" of a woman's position in dating, the author concluded, were complicated even further by the fact that young men, "discovering that she must be bought, [like] to buy her when [they happen] to have the money."

35

Yet another young man, the same year, publicly called a halt to such "promiscuous buying." Writing anonymously (for good reason) in *American Magazine*, the author declared a "one-man buyer's strike." This man estimated that, as a "buyer of feminine companionship" for the previous five years, he had "invested" about $20 a week—a grand total of over $5,000. Finally, he wrote, he had realized that "there is a point at which any commodity—even such a delightful commodity as feminine companionship—costs more than it is worth." The commodity he had bought with his $5,000 had been priced beyond its "real value" and he had had enough. This man said "enough" not out of principle, not because he rejected the implications of the economic model of courtship, but because he felt he wasn't receiving value for money.

36

In all three of these economic analyses, the men are complaining about the new dating system, lamenting the passing of the mythic good old days when "a man without a quarter in his pocket could call on a girl and not be embarrassed," the days before a woman had to be "bought." In recognizing so clearly the economic model on which dating operated, they also clearly saw that the model was a bad one—in purely economic terms. The exchange was not equitable; the commodity was overpriced. Men were operating at a loss.

37

Here, however, they didn't understand their model completely. True, the equation (male companionship plus money equals female companionship) was imbalanced. But what men were buying in the dating system was not just female companionship, not just entertainment—but power. Money purchased obligation; money purchased inequality; money purchased control.

38

39   The conventions that grew up to govern dating codified women's inequality and ratified men's power. Men asked women out; women were condemned as "aggressive" if they expressed interest in a man too directly. Men paid for everything, but often with the implication that women "owed" sexual favors in return. The dating system required men always to assume control, and women to act as men's dependents.

40   Yet women were not without power in the system, and they were willing to contest men with their "feminine" power. Much of the public discourse on courtship in twentieth-century America was concerned with this contestation. Thousands of sources chronicled the struggles of, and between, men and women—struggles mediated by the "experts" and arbiters of convention—to create a balance of power, to gain or retain control of the dating system. These struggles, played out most clearly in the fields of sex, science, and etiquette, made ever more explicit the complicated relations between men and women in a changing society.

▶   QUESTIONS TO CONSIDER

1. Bailey explores both the causes and effects of dating in this first chapter of her book. What are some of the factors Bailey claims led to the practice of a couple's dating as opposed to visiting in the girl's home? What effects has dating had on courtship in the United States?

2. A sociological phenomenon such as dating is open to interpretation. That is, no one knows exactly why it came into existence or how it has affected our society. In this chapter, Bailey is, in effect, arguing for her interpretation. Using factual information that she has gathered through a process of research, she pieces together her narrative about what has happened to courtship practices during this century. Bailey attempts to persuade her readers not by *insisting* on her view, but by *supporting* it with information. As a reader, do you find her evidence convincing and her arguments sound? Why or why not?

3. Bailey cites the increasing independence and freedom of females as one of the reasons that dating came into existence. Ironically, she also points out that dating changed the balance of power between males and females to give males the advantage. Why did dating give males an advantage? Do males still have an advantage in dating?

4. Bailey argues that dating is "clearly an economic act" and even compares it to prostitution. Is this comparison, or **analogy**, appropriate? Effective? Do you agree with her on this point?

ANALOGY, PAGE 517

5. In her conclusion, Bailey assumes a feminist stance, arguing that dating allows "men always to assume control" and forces "women to act as men's dependents." Do you find these final arguments appropriate? Convincing?

WRITING ACTIVITIES

Individual: Describe one way in which dating has changed in your lifetime.

Collaborative: Discuss with a group of your classmates the ways in which age, location, race, economic background, education, and technology seem to affect dating practices. List all the factors that affect dating, and identify the one you think is most significant.

Computer: Although Bailey presents an economic rather than a romantic view of dating, her arguments are predicated on the assumption of a very traditional model in which the male takes the female out and pays for all expenses. Write a paragraph in which you argue for or against this traditional model. Then, by posting your argument to your class network or by exchanging disks, share your argument with your classmates and respond to their arguments.

▶ W R I T I N G   T O   I N F O R M

When you write to reconstruct your own experiences, you focus primarily on yourself. Whether the result is fiction or nonfiction, your purpose is primarily to allow readers to know and understand you—to see the world and share certain experiences through your eyes. Conversely, when you write to inform, you focus primarily on your *subject*, piecing together various sources that may derive from research as well as your own experiences. Your purpose is to help readers understand not you but your subject. Although Stanley Kauffmann writes about being in grammar school and other personal experiences in his article on New York City, he is focusing not on himself but on changes in the city. Beth Bailey, on the other hand, has probably had numerous experiences with dating, but she does not mention her own experiences in her discussion of how dating replaced visiting as the primary form of courtship.

When you write to inform, if you want to include your own experiences, that's fine. Personal experiences and observations are valid forms of information and can be used effectively to support your ideas and opinions. But remember to keep the focus on your subject. When your purpose is to inform, subordinate yourself to your subject.

The Role of a Thesis in Writing to Inform

When you write to reconstruct your experience, often you do not need to include an explicit thesis statement, whereas when you write to inform, you nearly always do. If you are writing to inform, you want your readers to know your main point very soon after they begin reading. Stating your main idea clearly in the introduction ensures that the information you are providing is meaningful to your readers.

Specific items of information make sense only when they exist in a meaningful context, which a thesis helps to provide. For example, the fact that the cost of basic television cable service in a given area is $25 a month means very little by itself. But if you know that the basic cable rate in neighboring areas ranges from $12 to $20 or that the rate in the immediate past was $22 for the same service, the information begins to make sense. Even better, if you are informed at the beginning of the text that the writer thinks the cable rates in the area are too high or a recent increase is too great, then you can use the information that is presented to evaluate the writer's argument.

If you are communicating complicated information, you may also want to use a **forecasting statement** in the introduction to explicitly summarize the story's major events or stages before getting into the details. For example, Steven Waldman announces at the end of his eighth paragraph that "What follows is a simple checklist . . . of the drawbacks of our new way of choosing." He then proceeds to list and discuss six different drawbacks. The overview that a clear thesis and forecasting statement provide helps readers make sense of the information you include.

FORECASTING STATEMENT, PAGE 580

Thus, in writing to inform, one of your first concerns is to formulate at least a tentative thesis. A thesis differs from a topic in that it makes an assertion about the topic. For example, if your topic is electronic mail, your working thesis, or hypothesis, might be that electronic mail has changed the way people communicate. You might then want to narrow your focus still more, and your thesis might eventually be that people communicate less formally when they use electronic mail. In general, the process of formulating a strong thesis is one of narrowing a broad, general topic to a specific assertion you can support.

Remember that your initial thesis is not necessarily the one you will stay with until you complete your essay or report. Your initial thesis is always tentative—an hypothesis that you may modify slightly or drastically or even discard once you begin to write. In fact, some writers prefer to begin writing before they formulate even an hypothesis, knowing that their thesis will emerge as they write. However, most writers begin writing with at least a tentative idea of the point they plan to make (see **thesis statement**).

THESIS STATEMENT, PAGE 663

A clearly stated thesis at the beginning of your text may not be innovative or exciting and in some cases may not even be necessary. But in writing to inform, you want your readers to have an overview of your subject from the first.

Patterns of Development in Writing to Inform

When you wrote to reconstruct your own experiences, the narrative probably controlled the way you organized the story. Most likely, you used chronological order to relate the events you were narrating. You may decide to use narration again as you write to inform, or you may choose one or more different strategies. Here are the strategies you will find useful when you write to inform:

❖ Use narration.

❖ Use comparison/contrast.

❖ Use cause and effect.

❖ Use exemplification.

NARRATION, PAGE 618

EXEMPLIFICATION, PAGE 574

NARRATION. Because people like to hear and tell stories, it is natural to use **narration** when you communicate information. Narrative reconstructions of information, like stories, use chronological structure. Also like stories, they benefit from the use of specific details (see **exemplification**). Whether they are found in a novel or a report, narration and description are only as good as the specific details they include.

But there are differences between narrations used to reconstruct experience and those used to inform. A story you write about your first encounter with the registration process at your school differs from a report about that same process. In the story, you want to include your own subjective reaction to what you experienced, to give your readers some background information about yourself, and probably to exaggerate the length of the line in which you waited and the number of times you had to return to your advisor for a signature. In the report, you want to include other people's experiences with the process, to emphasize the process rather than yourself, and to be as accurate, factual, and objective as possible.

COMPARISON/CONTRAST, PAGE 542

ANALOGY, PAGE 517

COMPARISON/CONTRAST. In addition to narration and description, you will want to use other patterns of development in writing to inform. One of the most useful patterns for informative writing is **comparison/contrast**. Because the common theme of this chapter is the changing scene, each selection compares or contrasts something that existed in the past to what it became. That is, the authors compare what was to what is—most of them explicitly. Stanley Kauffmann describes the New York of his childhood and then compares it to the New York he lives in today. Morgan Hands compares Eunice, Louisiana, as it was during its prosperous days to the way it was after it had fallen on hard times. And Steven Waldman compares the choices we face today with those we faced in the past.

This comparison/contrast pattern can effectively develop and amplify your subject when you are writing to inform. If you are comparing something your readers know well to something they know less well, you can use their knowledge of the one to increase their understanding of the other (for a particular type of comparison, see **analogy**). A primary way people learn is by using existing knowledge to acquire new knowledge, old information to understand new information. If you are comparing two things that are equally known or unknown, the problem is rather more difficult. By comparing two things, however, you can help your readers form a clearer understanding of both.

When you use comparison/contrast, you usually choose one of two arrangement options. You may give all of the information about one subject and then shift to the other (topic by topic, as Kauffmann does in his article). Or you may intersperse the information about both subjects throughout your text (point by point, as Bailey does in her chapter). The "first one, and then the other" model (topic by topic) is easier to write but is not always the most effective. If you select the interspersed model (point by point), in which you go back and forth a number of times, you must be sure that your readers can follow your zigging and zagging from one point to the other. Point-by-point comparisons usually require clear **transitions** and careful organization so that your readers will not become confused.

TRANSITIONS, PAGE 676

For example, in the following paragraph, Joel Garreau compares new urban centers, which he calls Edge Cities, to more traditional urban centers. Notice that he provides his readers with clear signals so that they can follow his movement from one to the other.

> Our new city centers are tied together *not* by locomotives and subways, *but* by jetways, freeways, and rooftop satellite dishes thirty feet across. Their characteristic monument is *not* a horse-mounted hero, *but* the atria reaching for the sun and shielding trees perpetually in leaf at the cores of corporate headquarters, fitness centers, and shopping plazas. These new urban areas are marked *not* by the penthouses of the old urban rich or the tenements of the old urban poor. *Instead,* their landmark structure is the celebrated single-family detached dwelling, the suburban home with grass all around that made America the best-housed civilization the world has ever known. [italics added]
>
> —Joel Garreau, *Edge City: Life in the New Frontier* (New York: Doubleday, 1991), p. 4.

Be sure to signal your readers clearly each time you zig or zag from one topic to the other.

CAUSE AND EFFECT.   In a way, **cause and effect** is just a variation of narration. In explaining causes and effects, the writer tells a story: Because

CAUSE AND EFFECT, PAGE 522

this happened, then this and this and this happened (cause and effect), or this and this and this happened because this happened (effect and cause). All the writers in this chapter use this pattern to some extent: John Harris tells what happened when the old church was torn down; Morgan Hands tells what happened when Eunice went from boom to bust; Stanley Kauffmann tells what happened when New York changed from the place he knew as a child to the place in which he now lives; Beth Bailey tells what happened when "calling on" was replaced by dating; Steven Waldman describes the effects on consumers of having too many choices; and Adrianne Eggers relates the effect of an unplanned pregnancy on a young woman's life.

As with comparison/contrast, cause and effect provides you with choices. You must decide whether you want to begin with causes and then explain effects, or vice versa. You must decide whether to emphasize causes or effects or both. You must decide how much information your readers need about your subject in order to understand the causal relationship you are emphasizing.

EXEMPLIFICATION, PAGE 574

EXEMPLIFICATION. Like comparison/contrast and cause and effect, **exemplification** helps writers develop and amplify a subject. Using a specific example to explain a general statement is one of the best and most natural ways writers have to clarify difficult, abstract, vague concepts. Examples enable readers to understand information that would otherwise be incomprehensible. To say that it is hot in Phoenix, Arizona, in the summer is meaningless to someone who lives in Maine. But to provide readers with an example of the heat (you can't walk ten blocks without becoming shaky and light-headed, all without feeling a drop of instantly vaporizing sweat) gives them a basis for comparing their own experience of summer with that of someone in Phoenix and a concrete image that allows them to see and feel the heat.

If you have real examples to use, as Beth Bailey does in her study of courtship, then by all means use them. But if you cannot cite actual instances to illustrate the point you are making or to clarify the concept you are explaining, you can make one up. For example, Bailey also uses a hypothetical example, that of the 1920s gentleman caller, to illustrate her theory about the changes in courtship practices, and Morgan Hands cites the example of the fictitious John Doe as a representative example of the citizens of Eunice, Louisiana. However, if you use hypothetical examples, be sure they are based on valid information, and be sure your reader knows they are fictitious.

Should you use predominantly one pattern of development to structure and amplify your entire essay, or should you use more than one? Although you may want to emphasize one pattern, in general several patterns in combination produce a more complex, interesting, fully developed piece of writing. The authors of the reading selections in this chapter, for example, all use multiple patterns of development— narration, description, comparison/contrast, exemplification, and cause and effect.

Evaluating Information

In deciding what information to use, ask yourself the same questions you ask when you are reading to be informed:

❖ What is its source?

❖ Is it relevant?

❖ Is it accurate?

WHAT IS MY SOURCE?   Is the information from a reliable, unbiased source? Advertisements, for example, are usually not regarded as reliable sources of information. A magazine such as *Consumers' Guide*, a professional journal, or a government publication is generally a more reliable source. If you are interviewing someone, be sure that person is a credible source. Your best friend may not be the best source of information if your subject is recent changes in the design of automobiles unless he or she has owned a number of different cars or has collected model cars as a hobby. An automobile dealer, an automotive or safety engineer, or a mechanic would probably be a better source.

IS MY INFORMATION RELEVANT?   Information that is relevant pertains directly to your subject. For example, interviewing someone who knows how airplanes have changed in recent years would probably not provide you with relevant information if your subject is changes in automobile design. Likewise, talking to someone about changes in the design of European cars would not be useful if you are focusing on American cars.

Information may also be irrelevant if it is not current. If you are writing about recent changes in the design of American cars, you would not want to interview someone who has not bought a new car since

1982. Information derived from written sources is even more likely to be dated and, thus, irrelevant. If you are using written sources, focus primarily on periodicals, which are published at least every few months, rather than on books, which may require years to be published. Of course, if you are seeking general background information on a topic or researching a subject from the past—such as the first automobiles made in this country—you can rely on the information in books, even old books.

IS MY INFORMATION ACCURATE?   Information that is not accurate is worse than no information, because it destroys your credibility. If you are interviewing someone, ask permission to tape the interview. After you transcribe the taped interview into a written transcript, ask the person you interviewed to read it to verify its accuracy. If you cannot tape the interview, take careful notes, and verify each quotation with your source.

If you are using written sources, take careful notes, or obtain a photocopy of the material you plan to use, so you can later confirm that the information you included in your text conforms to the source material.

Also, be sure that the conclusions you draw are supported by the information you include. Do not go beyond the information you have cited to make claims that are illogical and unsupported.

Interviews as a Source of Information

One of the most effective ways of gaining information is by conducting interviews. An interview also provides you with someone else's perspective. Using another person's experiences as a source of information allows you to move beyond a totally subjective viewpoint to one that is more socially and politically aware. That is, you cease to see the world entirely from your own perspective and begin to view it from multiple perspectives.

However, you need to choose carefully the person you interview. Ideally, your interviewee will fit one or more of these criteria:

❖ Is knowledgeable about your subject

❖ Has first-hand experience with your subject

❖ Has a perspective different from your own

❖ Is easily accessible and willing to grant you an interview

The person you interview does not have to be famous or even an expert but should provide you with useful, pertinent information. For example, for an essay about the changes that have occurred in farming in recent years, you might interview someone who has farmed for a number of years. You might also want to interview your county extension agent, an agriculture professor at your school, and/or a local farming equipment dealer.

Sometimes writers simply transcribe an interview as it occurred and let the interviewee's words speak for themselves, but most often they shape the information from the interview into an essay, article, or report. In this case, you must decide what to include and what to omit and provide a context for the material you include. The best way to make these decisions is to determine what your thesis is and then select information that supports and develops it (see **thesis statement**).

THESIS STATEMENT, PAGE 663

An interview can merely be one of several sources you use, or you may want to focus on a single interview. In this case, your readers need to understand your interviewee's point of view, to get a sense of his or her personality, and perhaps even to be able to visualize this person. So you will include not only the interviewee's words and ideas, but also a physical description and information about the person's background and the context in which he or she exists. That is, you will want to make the person you have interviewed as real for your readers as he or she is for you. One of the best ways to achieve this goal is to include a wealth of specific details that reveal how the person looked and sounded. Direct quotations, which allow readers to hear the interviewee's own words, also bring him or her to life.

However you use your interview material, you should distinguish clearly between your own words and ideas and those of the person you interview. In "A Changed Life," Adrianne Eggers uses direct quotations from the young woman she interviewed but also summarizes some of the information she derived from the interview. She identifies the ideas and words of the person she interviewed (Tammy) in two ways: first, by using Tammy's name to introduce the material she contributed; second, by using quotation marks to identify Tammy's statements.

How do you decide when to quote an interviewee's words exactly and when to summarize what he or she said? In general, you want to quote your interviewee's words directly when the statement effectively makes a point you want to make or reveals something about your interviewee you want to dramatize. In addition, you may want to include some statements because the interviewee's language is forceful, imaginative, or distinctive. For a full discussion of how to conduct an interview and how to document the information you derive from an interview (see Conducting Interviews in Part Three).

▶ WRITING ASSIGNMENT

For this assignment you are to inform your readers about something that has changed. If you do not have an idea in mind, you may want to use one of these suggestions:

1. Write about a changing scene—how a particular scene, such as your campus, a shopping mall, your backyard, or a certain street, changes from one time to another. You may want to focus on time of day (how a busy street changes to a deserted one at night), season of the year (how your backyard looks in winter compared to summer or spring or autumn), or time of year (how your campus looks on the first day of classes compared to how it looks during Spring Break or the Christmas holidays).

2. Write about a place that has changed—a place such as your hometown, your grandparents' home, a familiar vacation spot, a room you particularly like, or a favorite hangout or place to eat. Even though you are familiar with this place, if possible you should conduct an on-site observation to refresh your memory and to collect specific, detailed information to include in your essay (see Conducting Observations in Part Three).

3. Write about a change in your own attitude or perception of something. Explain not only how this change occurred, but also why it happened and its effects. In this assignment, you may want to explore the relationship between reality and perception—how the perception of something affects the real thing. For example, how has your attitude toward your parents, education, work, immigration, sports, politics, or other races changed in recent years?

4. Write about how technology has changed society in the last decade. For example, how has a particular type of technology, such as computers or automation, changed your life? You may want to focus on either causes or effects or both.

5. Interview someone about a fashion, food, or social custom that has changed since this person was young. You could focus on clothing styles, types of restaurants, food fads, the roles men and women assume in marriage, or the relationship between males and females in the workplace. Then write an essay in which you compare the experiences

of the person you interview to your own (see Conducting Interviews in Part Three).

6. Write a memo to your employer describing a change that you would like to see made at work.

7. Write an editorial for your college paper arguing that a certain change should be made.

8. Interview someone who attended your school in the past or a teacher who has taught at your school for a long time. Then write an essay (or editorial) explaining one or more ways in which the school has changed, why it has changed, and whether the changes have resulted in positive or negative effects.

Generating Ideas through Invention and Research

If ideas for this assignment do not immediately come to you or if you need additional information, you can try one or both of these suggestions.

INVENTION.   To stimulate your thinking and to retrieve information from your memory, freewrite about the changes you have experienced in your lifetime or about the changes that you have observed in our society. Begin by writing on the general topic of change, and see what thoughts come to you. Keep writing for at least ten minutes, putting down anything that comes to mind without trying to structure what you are writing or even to make sense. From this freewriting, choose a single idea on which to focus and freewrite again. Repeat this process several times until you have narrowed your topic appropriately and generated enough information and ideas to begin your assignment.

RESEARCH.   Most informative writing involves some form of research. Students usually think immediately of the library when research is mentioned. And a library is an excellent resource for writers, providing abundant information on an amazing variety of topics. If you are writing about recent technological changes, you may want to consult library resources, especially periodicals but also books (histories, reference books, and so on) that can provide you with background information on this subject and corroborate your own experiences.

However, you should not think only of the library. Other forms of research may be more appropriate in this assignment. An on-site observation of a place you are writing about or an interview with someone who can give you information about your subject would be especially valuable. For example, suppose you are writing about how gas stations have changed from full-service "filling stations" with iceboxes full of soft drinks out front to pump-your-own-gas mini-shopping centers that sell a little of everything but provide no services. The library will probably not help you much on this one, but talking to the owner of a gas station who has experienced these changes would probably provide you with lots of good information.

Research, like writing, is an ongoing process. You will probably want to complete your preliminary research before you begin writing, but as you write you may think of other forms of research that will provide evidence to support your thesis. The important thing is to think of research as broadly as possible—as using any possible source of information. Don't limit your research to looking up your subject in the card catalog of the library. Think in terms of what will provide you with the information you need, and pursue that information in any way possible.

Drafting Your Text

You may want to begin your text by writing a discovery draft in which you merely sketch out the broad points you want to make. Let your essay take shape by allowing your writing to lead you where it will. A discovery draft is only a few steps removed from freewriting. You have a topic and a general idea of your thesis (an hypothesis), but you don't really know what you want to say. The important thing at this point is to get something on paper (or in a computer file).

Several drafts may be needed to shape your essay or report into the text you want it to be. In each successive draft, refine your thesis so that it becomes increasingly narrowed. Try to be more specific than just saying that something has changed. Define the change, analyze and evaluate it, or describe its result. For example, instead of merely stating that women's attitudes about housework have changed, you might say that women's attitudes about housework have become more casual or that women's changing attitudes about housework have resulted in messier homes but happier children.

As you write, you will want to develop your thesis in several different ways. Do you want to explain the changing scene you are writing about by telling a story, by comparing what was to what is, by providing examples that illustrate the change, or by explaining its causes and effects? These are important decisions and need to be made consciously if you do not discover them in the process of writing.

Reading and Revising Your Text

As you read what you have written, you will want to determine primarily two things:

1. Do you have a clear focus?

2. Do you support your thesis adequately with information?

DO YOU HAVE A CLEAR FOCUS?   First of all, you need to decide if you have a clear thesis—a main idea that controls the content of your essay or report. To be sure that what you have written clearly supports and develops your thesis, write a one-sentence summary of each paragraph (the topic sentence may serve as a summary of the paragraph). Now write your thesis and the sentence summaries after it. If you are using a computer, you can accomplish the same thing by making a copy of your text on a new file and then deleting everything but your thesis and the topic sentence of each paragraph. The idea is to construct an outline of what you have written so that you can determine if your essay or report is well focused. Keep this outline so that you can refer to it when you revise.

DO YOU SUPPORT YOUR THESIS ADEQUATELY WITH INFORMATION?   Once you are satisfied that your essay or report is unified and well focused, read it again, this time paying attention to the information you have included. Have you included the information that your readers will need? For example, if you are writing about the ways in which basketball has changed since you were a child, you will need to provide your readers with information about what the game was like then and what it is like now. You cannot assume that your audience will all know as much about the game as you do. Some of your class members may know very little about the game, but all of them will know certain things (such as what a basketball and goal look like and that the game involves five players trying to get the ball through the goal while another five players try to prevent them from doing this). Read your essay carefully to determine whether you have included too much or too little information. The amount of information you include, its appropriateness, and its clarity are essential when you are writing to inform. If you decide that you need more information and if that information is not already known to you, you may need to research your subject further—talk to a ball player, attend a ball game, or read an article about the sport or players.

After reading your essay or report several times, you will have some ideas about what you need to do as you revise. However, as you revise, you should continue reading and rereading what you have written. Possible revisions will keep occurring to you as you read and write, write and read, and read yet once more. You will find, in fact, that the more experienced you become as a writer, the more you will probably revise. Rather than learning to get it right the first time, you will discover that you are learning to revise until you get it right.

Now is a good time to go back and look at the outline of your text that we suggested above. Are there paragraphs that should be omitted? Is the order of your paragraphs logical? Use this outline as a revision guide. It will help you view your text more objectively.

Preparing the Final Draft of Your Text

If possible, you should ask someone to read your completed text and point out any minor errors or omissions that you have failed to notice. In the final analysis, however, you are responsible for what you write. Readers and editors can certainly help you improve your text, but you must individually assume final responsibility for what you write. Most important, of course, is whether what you have written is accurate, complete, and readable. But correctness and appearance play a significant role in how a text is perceived by others. Even if your information is useful and your text is clearly focused, it will not be well received by readers if it is carelessly written. Your text is a reflection of you and should present you at your best.

▶ DISCOVERING YOURSELF AS A WRITER

After you have completed this assignment, take a few minutes to reflect on this writing experience by answering the following questions:

1. What did you learn about yourself as a writer as you worked on this assignment? In what way did this writing experience change your perception of yourself as a writer, your process of writing, or your attitude toward writing?

2. What forms of research did you use for this assignment? What did you learn about research that will help you in other writing assignments?

3. Was the final draft of your text better or worse than you had expected? What would you do differently if you had the opportunity to do this assignment again?

4. How did writing this assignment make you a better reader?

5. What did you enjoy most about this writing assignment? What did you like least?

Douglas Olson, *Cats, Gibbonsville, Wisconsin.*
Reprinted by permission of Douglas Olson.

6

▼

WRITING
TO
PERSUADE

215

The art of writing has for its backbone some fierce
~~*attachment to an idea.*~~

VIRGINIA WOOLF

All writers write to persuade—to convince—regardless of what they are writing. The poet writes to persuade us that his love is like a red rose; the chef writes to persuade us that her recipe for clam chowder is the most succulent; and the technical writer writes to persuade us that installing a new memory board in a computer is easy. The writers of this chapter's reading selections want to persuade readers that what is generally accepted as true is not always what is true—that what seems to be reality may actually be a myth.

Why is almost every type of writing to some extent persuasive? One answer may be that persuasive writing is a socially acceptable version of humans' innate aggressiveness. Most people usually channel those aggressive instincts into civilized, productive forms of behavior, using words rather than weapons to persuade people to agree with them.

People also use persuasive writing to get things done. Social, political, and economic action depend on persuasive discourse. Whether a society is a democracy or a dictatorship, whether the goal is consensus or compliance, political leaders use language to govern, and the language they use is most often persuasive. The forms and methods of rhetorical persuasion may differ from one culture to another, but the persuasive purpose is the same.

In a market economy, many people use language to persuade. The U.S. economic system depends on persuading people to be consumers of products and services. As a result, everyone from General Electric to the child selling lemonade on a hot day tries to entice people to buy something or use something or do something. An entire industry—advertising—exists to persuade consumers. Consumers, in turn, must constantly make decisions about whom to believe, what to do, and when to act.

Underlying every attempt to persuade is at least one argument: If you use this shampoo, then you'll find romance; if you vote for me, then you will be more prosperous; if people don't demonstrate, then they never will gain their civil rights. Some arguments are forceful and direct; others are subtle and indirect. Some are objective and impersonal; others are subjective and highly personal. Some command; others cajole. In general, writers use anything that works to persuade their audience to believe and, in some cases, to act on their arguments.

As a reader, your responsibility is to recognize a writer's arguments and then evaluate them. Because the persuasive purpose is at least a secondary aim in almost all writing, you should be prepared to recognize and evaluate arguments whenever you read, whether a textbook, a comic strip, or a brochure. Otherwise you forfeit your right to defend yourself against the writer's arguments.

READING PERSUASIVE DISCOURSE

Much of what applies to reading texts that explore, reconstruct experience, instruct and advise, inform, and solve problems also applies to reading texts that persuade. For example, you must carefully evaluate the accuracy of any information in persuasive writing. You must be satisfied that the information is current, relevant, and accurate before you can accept any arguments based on it. If a writer cites inaccurate, dated, or irrelevant information, you will probably not be persuaded by his or her arguments (see Chapter 5, "Writing to Inform").

But reading persuasive texts intelligently requires more than just evaluating information. An argument is a complex form of discourse that operates on several levels at the same time. Aristotle, a Greek philosopher, scientist, and rhetorician, explained persuasive discourse by identifying three appeals—ways a writer tries to convince a reader:

- *Logos,* an appeal to logic
- *Pathos,* an appeal to the reader's emotion
- *Ethos,* an appeal based on the writer's credibility

When you evaluate a persuasive text, you should be aware of the author's use of these appeals. In addition, you should identify the author's unstated assumptions—those beliefs that are not explicit in the text but that are essential to understanding and evaluating the arguments that are stated.

Recognizing Appeals to Logic

An effective argument usually makes a strong appeal to the audience's powers of reasoning—to what is true, valid, or at least plausible. An illogical argument—that is, one that does not ring true to those who hear or read it—will probably be rejected. Thus, when writers write to persuade, they often base their arguments on logical premises—on statements that are generally accepted as true. For example, a writer arguing that the decline in traditional family structure in recent years is responsible for many of our social problems might build the following argument:

❖ If the family units that make up a society do not function well, then the society will not function well.

❖ Therefore, since our society is not functioning well, the problem must lie with the families that comprise it.

Now this argument may or may not be true. Someone could argue the other way around just as easily—that because society is not functioning well, the family is having trouble. Both statements are based on logical arguments. That is, each statement is based on another statement that is generally perceived to be true. In this case, both arguments are also based on the underlying assumption that a close **cause and effect** relationship exists between a society and the families in it.

CAUSE AND EFFECT, PAGE 522

It is important to realize that logical arguments are not necessarily true; they just conform to a particular pattern of reasoning and do not violate the audience's sense of logic—their sense of what *could be* true, what is possible or reasonable.

As a reader, you may be strongly influenced by an apparently valid logical appeal, but you need to analyze the argument to evaluate its worth. For example, a writer might argue that if the traditional family fails, then society will fail. This statement sounds logical. But whether a reader accepts this assertion depends on how he or she interprets what the writer means by words such as *family, traditional,* and *fail.* Family structure varies from age to age and from society to society. Many societies have endured without having the type of family structure that we consider traditional. And evaluating the success or failure of a family or a society may require different criteria for and definitions of failure (see **definition**).

DEFINITION, PAGE 560

Like the pattern of proving one assertion by citing another, the use of examples constitutes a common method of logical persuasion. For instance, it can be argued that because a certain number of non-traditional families exists, traditional family structure must no longer be the norm. Many careful scientific and statistical studies are based upon this type of research. Researchers examine a large number of individual phenomena and then generalize their findings to the society at large. For example, if a government survey indicates that more than half the families participating in the survey are nontraditional in structure, the researchers might legitimately conclude that the traditional family consisting of two parents (one male and one female) and several children is no longer the norm in our society.

However, this form of reasoning can be misused and misleading. If the number of specific phenomena examined is too small or not typical of the population at large, the results may not be accurate and should not become the basis of a generalization. For example, a writer who cites several apparently healthy, successful people from nontraditional families can legitimately argue that nontraditional families *sometimes* produce healthy, productive offspring. But, on the basis of these few examples, the writer should not claim that nontraditional families are as effective in this respect as traditional families or that *all* children reared in nontraditional families are healthy and successful. Anecdotal examples can support an argument but are seldom conclusive; you need to be skeptical when a writer or speaker makes sweeping generalizations on the basis of a few examples (see **exemplification**).

EXEMPLIFICATION, PAGE 574

As a reader, you should certainly value reasonable arguments, but you must analyze and evaluate logical appeals just as carefully as you would any appeal. Sometimes this analysis means examining closely the language of the argument. What terms does the writer use, and what do they mean in this particular context? If terms are not clearly defined, consensus is rarely possible. Even a seemingly simple term such as *family* can have different meanings. Is a couple a family? Can this couple be two males or two females and still be considered a family? Does a single parent plus children constitute a family?

Your responsibility as a reader, therefore, is not only to determine that arguments are logical or reasonable but also to evaluate the truth of the logic. Remember, a logical argument is not necessarily true. In the sense that *logical* is used here, it means only that a particular process of reasoning was used to reach the conclusion. This process can result in arguments that are inaccurate, misleading, or simply untrue. Thus, in reading any persuasive text, from a few lines of advertising to a book-length interpretation of ideas or events, you must evaluate the writer's logical appeals. On the basis of your evaluation, you can then accept or reject the writer's arguments.

The following questions can guide you in evaluating logical arguments:

1. Does the writer define key terms clearly?

2. Are the writer's assertions supported with sufficient, convincing evidence?

3. Does the writer use statistical evidence and examples responsibly by presenting them in context and by avoiding half-truths and incomplete information?

4. Does the writer oversimplify the issue by presenting it as an either/or situation?

5. Does the writer overgeneralize or jump to conclusions on the basis of too little evidence?

6. If the writer makes comparisons, do they emphasize relevant, significant similarities, or are they false analogies that focus on irrelevant or insignificant similarities?

7. If the writer establishes a cause-and-effect relationship, is it clearly causal as opposed to merely temporal (related in time of occurrence only)?

Recognizing Appeals to Emotion

In an ideal world perhaps all arguments would be based exclusively on logic; that is, arguments would appeal only to the sense of reason. In this ideal world, reasonable people would argue logically and rationally, and the most reasonable argument would triumph over less reasonable arguments. But in the real world, people are persuaded by emotion as well as by logic and reason.

You may find it hard to accept the idea of emotion as a valid appeal in persuasive discourse. You may consider emotional appeals as unworthy, if not downright unfair. Certainly, unscrupulous emotional appeals abound. Too many politicians appeal to people's greed, pride, and prejudices in order to gain power. Too many advertisers appeal to people's insecurity and desire to be attractive, successful, or comfortable.

One of the most terrifying examples of an unscrupulous emotional appeal was Hitler's appeal to the German people's pride and nationalism as he invoked claims of racial superiority in order to gain power in the 1920s and 1930s. Using emotional appeals, Hitler aroused feelings in some people that ended in heinous crimes against others. Rejecting emotional appeals entirely is easy if you think of Hitler's use of them as the standard.

But not all emotional appeals are illegitimate. People are, after all, emotional as well as rational creatures. The emotional appeal can be just as valid as the logical appeal, depending on how it is used and to what purpose. An editorial that arouses your sense of responsibility toward others to persuade you to support local charities is legitimate.

Likewise, a politician's appeal to your pride in democracy to convince you to vote is valid.

Interestingly, the same emotion can be used in both valid and invalid appeals. For example, those who are writing or speaking to persuade often use appeals to fear. Politicians evoke fear of higher taxes; evangelists evoke fear of divine punishment; doctors evoke fear of disease; and environmentalists evoke fear of ecological disaster. Appeals to fear are not in themselves invalid. In each case you must look at the writer's or speaker's purpose.

Even when you examine their purpose, you may find it hard to evaluate emotional appeals. A politician's main purpose may be to be elected, but he may also believe that higher taxes will harm the economy. An evangelist may preach about hell and damnation to increase donations but may also sincerely believe people need to hear this message. A doctor may want people to fear disease enough to take care of themselves (be inoculated, get regular checkups, eat right, etc.) but may also want more patients in order to become rich. And an environmentalist may engender fear of global warming in order to save the planet and/or to get a large grant from the government.

As you read a text, you should determine if emotional appeals are being used to manipulate you. Is the emotional appeal being used to evoke illogical fears or reprehensible emotions? Are your emotions being aroused about unprovable events or behaviors? Does an emotional appeal attempt to obscure the lack of valid arguments? If so, be wary of the arguments based on these appeals.

Emotional appeals are a powerful and valid persuasive strategy, and most effective arguments appeal to the emotions as well as to the intellect. Because emotional responses are a normal part of the reading process, it is important for you to be aware of what you are feeling as well as what you are thinking when you read. But you need to evaluate your emotional reactions and how the writer has evoked them as part of your assessment of the arguments you are reading.

The following questions can help you evaluate emotional appeals:

1. Does the writer use slanted language—terms that needlessly and irresponsibly evoke negative connotations?

2. Does the writer attack his or her opponent's character rather than focusing primarily on the issues?

3. Does the writer indulge in veiled threats by suggesting that one step will inevitably lead to another and ultimately result in some type of disaster, thus evoking the fear of the slippery slope or domino effect?

4. Does the writer polarize the issue by viewing it strictly as an either/or situation (the "America—love it or leave it" approach)?

5. Does the writer attempt to flatter you in order to win you over?

Recognizing Appeals to Credibility

CREDIBILITY, PAGE 522

Ethos is the appeal to the reader's belief in the writer's or speaker's **credibility**. One of the reasons you accept or reject an argument is your belief regarding the writer's or speaker's trustworthiness. If you perceive the writer or speaker as honest, intelligent, informed, and well-intentioned, then you probably will accept that person's arguments. If, in contrast, you perceive the writer or speaker as dishonest, stupid, uninformed, inexperienced, self-serving, or not having your best interests at heart, you are not likely to accept his or her arguments regardless of how brilliant, logical, or emotionally charged they may be. Ultimately, then, the reader's perception of the writer determines the effectiveness of an argument.

Some writers and speakers have established their credibility even before they write or speak; that is, their audience knows them, either personally or by reputation. When well-known actor Charlton Heston argues against gun control, readers react not only on the basis of what he says, but also on the basis of their perception of him as a strong, honest, trustworthy man. That this perception may be based solely on the roles Heston has played rather than on his own personality and character does not occur to many people. Compare the generally positive reaction most people have to Heston's arguments about gun ownership to the generally negative reaction generated by similar arguments made by a self-described separatist member of a militia.

Even people you do not really know anything about may seem trustworthy because they have certain credentials. They may teach at a prestigious university, have written thirteen books, have an impressive title or degree attached to their name, or have had experiences that lend them credibility. For example, Sir Edmund Hillary and Tenzing Norgay, the first people to scale Mt. Everest, had enormous credibility when they wrote about mountain climbing.

Writers also establish their credibility by citing familiar and respected sources. If a writer supports arguments with sources the reader knows and respects, the reader will often transfer the source's credibility to the writer. Politicians who are trying to appeal to African Americans, for example, will often cite Martin Luther King, Jr., and Jesse Jackson.

All writers, whether known to their readers or not, struggle to establish their credibility as they construct their texts. As a reader, you are a judge of that credibility. You need to be aware as you read texts intended to persuade that your perception of the writer influences your perception of the arguments you are reading. Remember, too, that in most instances you are dealing with just a perception. You may know the writer by reputation, but seldom do you really know the person who is writing. A skilled writer can create a very believable persona (the role a writer assumes in a text) to convince readers of the validity of his or her arguments. The persona may reflect the real author, but you shouldn't assume it to be the same as the author. It is your responsibility to evaluate the effect of this persona on your response to the writer's arguments.

The following questions can guide you in evaluating the credibility of a writer:

1. Does the writer use language responsibly?

2. Does the writer cite false authorities or fail to identify sources clearly?

3. Does the writer attempt to persuade by making false analogies or by establishing guilt by association?

4. Does the writer attack opponents personally rather than refuting their arguments?

5. Does the writer make hasty or sweeping generalizations on the basis of too little evidence or incomplete information and half-truths?

6. Does the writer argue for a result that will greatly benefit him or her?

Recognizing the Writer's Underlying Assumptions

Analyzing and evaluating the arguments in a persuasive text also means identifying the underlying assumptions upon which the arguments are based. What is the writer assuming that he or she does not necessarily state? For example, in the argument about the decline in traditional family structure, the writer is assuming that the biological father-mother-children families represent the best type of family structure. Often what is *not* stated is more important than what is stated. Implicit in almost every argument is one or more unstated assumptions on which the argument is based. The writer advances the argument as though you agree with him or her on the underlying assumptions, but she doesn't state them explicitly. For example, if a writer is arguing that traditional families are no longer the norm and that children are being neglected as a result, the assumptions are that families should take care of children and that traditional families perform this function best. If you share the writer's assumptions, you will probably accept the argument. If, in contrast, you believe that the government should share in the responsibility for children by providing adequate day-care facilities or that nontraditional families can also effectively nurture children, you may reject this writer's argument.

Stephen Toulmin, an English logician, has devised a system for analyzing arguments that identifies the unspoken assumptions connecting the evidence provided and the assertion (or claim) based on the evidence. These unspoken assumptions, or *warrants*, as Toulmin calls them, reveal (make explicit) the relationship between the evidence and the claim.

For example, examine the following diagram of an argument:

Evidence

The driver has consumed seven cans of beer in two hours.

⟶

Claim

His friends should not allow him to drive.

This argument involves the following unspoken assumptions:

1. Seven cans of beer in two hours will make a person incapable of operating an automobile safely.

2. Driving after consuming that amount of beer in that time span is dangerous, against the law, etc.

3. Friends should be responsible for one another.

To analyze the argument, a reader must evaluate not only the stated evidence and claim but also the unstated assumptions on which the argument is based. Most people would probably agree on the first two assumptions in the preceding example, even though some might point out that the alcoholic content of beers differs greatly and that different people's tolerance for alcohol also varies. Some readers might not readily accept the third assumption, that friends should be responsible for one another. They might argue that people are responsible only for themselves or that there are degrees of friendship.

You need to be aware that all arguments include unarticulated, implicit beliefs—whether they are called assumptions or warrants—on which the arguments depend. Often these unspoken assumptions involve value judgments that tell you more about the writer's basic orientation and beliefs than the arguments themselves. For example, if someone argues that protecting our timber industry is more important than protecting our forests, the underlying assumptions are that economic well-being is more important than the environment and that a choice must be made between the two. Whether or not you agree with these assumptions, you should realize that they are the foundation of the argument.

► READING SELECTIONS

This chapter's reading selections all deal with appearance versus reality. Each writer begins by explaining a myth or misapprehension, something generally accepted as true that is, at least in the writer's opinion, inaccurate or invalid. The writer then sets forth an argument in favor of his or her own version of reality—what is really true as opposed to what seems to be true. This convention of first presenting a myth or distortion and then correcting it is a common and effective strategy many writers use to initiate arguments.

Misadventures with a Ruler

Andy Clark

In this essay, student writer Andy Clark points out the difference between his perception and expectations of a product based on a television advertisement and the reality of that same product based on his actual experience with it. As you read, notice that Clark's account of his "misadventures" with the rolling ruler may make you smile but that the essay concludes with a serious point about false advertising claims.

1   Often on television advertisers make claims that are false. Infomercials have a good grip on this type of false advertising. It is impossible to count how many times Ron Popeil is on the tube with a new product. If it is not his food dehydrator that will literally save you thousands of dollars making beef jerky and dried soups, he is talking about his spaghetti maker, which even his annoying little grand-daughter can use. On one of these commercials I saw a product I thought I could not live without for "only $9.95 plus shipping and handling." It was The Rolling Ruler.

2   According to the commercial, The Rolling Ruler is more than just twelve inches of measuring fun—it is a super ruler. It has wheels on the back of it, which makes it more mobile than any other ruler in existence. It is made of rubber, which grips the paper to ensure a straight line every time. The wheels have marks on them, so you know exactly how far the ruler moves on the paper. Every half inch there is a hole where the pencil is supposed to go, guaranteeing that the pencil does not move around. According to the commercial, The Rolling

Ruler is not only a ruler; it is also a compass. If you use two pencils, you can draw circles. Just stick one pencil in the hole for an anchor and then use the other pencil to draw the circle. It also has a small protractor on it, so angles are a snap. With this ruler you can draw straight lines, graphs, circles, or pie charts. It can also make drawing blueprints for houses, bridges, and skyscrapers an easy task.

Once I saw this commercial, I was hooked. I had an acute need 3 to draw pie charts and blueprints of complex structures for no apparent reason at all. I watched endless hours of television just to see that commercial again so I could write down the address and order the ruler of my dreams. I not only had a pencil and paper ready but my VCR was also prepared to record the commercial just in case I got so excited that I did not remember it or was not quick enough to write it on paper. At last the commercial came on, and I quickly scribbled down the information that I needed. Within ten minutes I had the envelope ready to mail. In six to eight weeks I would be drawing charts and circles like never before.

The wait was intense. After two weeks I started meeting the mail- 4 man at the mailbox. After a few weeks of this, I began to meet the mailman four doors down. At first I guess the mailman thought it was amusing, but soon he started to greet me with profanities. I got the point after about a week and a half of being called names such as "You little scraunch" and "You dolt." After that I waited in my house. Finally, the day I was waiting for came. The Rolling Ruler was finally mine!

I ripped the package open as if it were a present on Christmas 5 morning. It wasn't quite what I had expected; on television they made it longer and shinier. And it didn't have rubber wheels as promised; they were made of plastic. But I did not care because it was finally here. What was I going to draw first? A circle? Or perhaps the Sears Tower?

I decided that my first project was going to be something easy. I 6 had to get used to my Rolling Ruler. I thought it would take me just a few minutes of practice to master my new toy. I figured a straight line would be a good start, so I stuck my pencil in the hole at the six-inch mark. As I began to move the pencil, the paper moved right along with it. Apparently the ruler was made for people with three hands— one to hold the ruler, one to hold the pencil, and one to hold the paper. I solved this problem by using tape to hold down the paper. The ruler was in position to draw again. I began and it moved all over the page. The plastic wheels were so slippery that they could not hold the ruler to a piece of fly paper.

After my first, failed experience with the ruler, I thought the com- 7 pass feature on it would be useful. I rummaged through my desk to retrieve another pencil. After getting one more sheet of paper taped down, I stuck one pencil in a hole as an anchor and the other in the other hole to draw with. However, circles were impossible to draw because both pencils would move. I figured that all I had to do was press on the anchor pencil harder, but I had to press so hard that each time the lead broke.

8   The protractor feature was equally useless. It was so small that the slightest mistake would change a thirty degree angle into a ninety degree angle. It was about as accurate as the President's budget estimates. The only angles I could measure with it were the corners of the paper.

9   I could not believe that I paid more than 99 cents for this piece of junk. The ruler was not only poorly made but also did not even come with all the standard features promised. To say I was disappointed is an understatement. What I thought was going to be the solution of all my drawing problems ended up being the worst investment I had ever made.

10   Commercials on television often make claims they cannot back up. The Rolling Ruler is only one of them. There are many other products that millions of people buy each day as a result of television ads that are just as worthless as The Rolling Ruler.

▶   QUESTIONS TO CONSIDER

1. Clark uses exaggeration to achieve a humorous effect in this essay. Can humor be an effective strategy in writing to persuade? Why, or why not? Is it effective in this essay?

2. Clark uses his own experience as evidence in this essay. How convincing is this form of evidence? What other types of evidence could he have used? How would they have changed his essay?

3. Throughout most of this essay, Clark uses an informal, slightly humorous, at times sarcastic tone. Identify the elements of the essay that contribute to this tone (see **style and voice**).

STYLE AND VOICE, PAGE 656

4. In the conclusion of this essay, the author shifts to a more serious tone. Would the conclusion be stronger if he had kept the humorous tone he used in the rest of the essay? Why, or why not?

5. Is Clark justified in concluding that "commercials on television make claims they cannot back up" and that "other products . . . are just as worthless as The Rolling Ruler," or is he overgeneralizing? If you agree with these conclusions, is it because Clark's experiences convinced you or because your own experiences confirm what he is saying?

WRITING ACTIVITIES ◀

Individual: Write a journal entry in which you describe a product you bought that did not meet your expectations.

Collaborative: Discuss with a group of your classmates the products you bought that did not meet your expectations. Focus on how your expectations were formed and why they were not met. Were you misled by advertising claims? Did the seller or advertisement use appeals based on emotion, logic, or credibility? Decide in each case what arguments were used to influence you to buy the product and what arguments you could use to convince the seller to take the product back or reimburse you for your expenses.

Computer: Use your journal entry and group discussion as the basis of a letter of complaint to the manufacturer or seller of the product that did not meet your expectations. You may want to begin by entering into a new computer file the information and arguments you plan to use in your letter. Then, using the block-and-move (or cut-and-paste) function of your computer, organize this material so that your reader will understand clearly how the product was represented to you as well as your own experience with it. Finally, format your letter appropriately.

BEAUTY AT ANY PRICE

Rebecca Williams

While a student in a freshman composition course, Rebecca Williams wrote the following essay about her experience as a beauty contestant. This experience changed her perception of beauty contests and her idea of what constitutes beauty. In her essay Williams argues that beauty contests are not the equitable and joyous competitions they seem to be. Ironically, Williams did not win the beauty contest, but her essay later won first place in an essay contest. As you read, notice how Williams uses her own experience as evidence for her assertions.

For many years, I dutifully watched the televised Miss U.S.A. and Miss Texas-U.S.A. pageants. I always saw the productions as exciting shows which quite naturally ran perfectly. I assumed that they were   1 produced by volunteers who were simply interested in honoring the best young woman in the country (or state). I pictured the contestants as sweet, intelligent young women who willingly gave up a year of their lives to represent their home towns and participate in those exciting live telecast pageants. Being a contestant-at-large in the 1987 Miss Texas-U.S.A. Pageant was an experience which changed my views about not only the pageants but also the contestants in them.

2   The overwhelming impression I formed while in San Antonio for the pageant is that pageants are a money-making business. In the case of Miss Texas-U.S.A., the system has been fully controlled by two men for thirteen years. Richard Guy and Rex Holt formed GuyRex Associates, Inc., which not only produces the pageant, but also markets expensive dresses for its contestants and manages its winner. GuyRex Associates, Inc. is getting rich, mainly because so many young women are willing to make a huge investment to compete for a major title. Each one of the 109 contestants in the 1987 pageant spent between $3,000 and $30,000 on evening gowns, other clothes, and professional training in preparation for the pageant. One thousand dollars of the total amount spent by each was mailed directly to GuyRex Associates for the contestant's entry fee. Since all pageant accommodations, food, prizes, and television time were provided by official sponsors, it isn't too difficult to guess who ended up keeping the $109,000.

3   Since the success of the pageant is largely dependent on television ratings, the producers willingly sacrifice realism and, in some cases, honesty in order to stage a spectacular pageant which will draw millions of viewers and thus bring in more "big bucks." A viewer of a televised pageant is often led to believe that the entire performance and competition are spontaneous and live. I found it very interesting to be backstage and see just how much time was spent memorizing cue cards, learning to lip-synch the words of professionally pre-recorded music, and pre-taping actual segments of the supposed live telecast itself. All orchestral music, singing, and applause were done by professionals and are taped long before the pageant week ever begins. Most pageants also televise the judges and official auditor hard at work on the night of the pageant. The image of these people working on the actual pageant night is almost totally false, since their work is already done. For example, in the 1987 Miss Texas-U.S.A. Pageant, the winner had known that she was to win shortly after preliminary judging, two days prior to the live telecast.

4   The producers weren't the only people trying to make a profit at the Miss Texas-U.S.A. Pageant. The winner was to receive over $100,000 in cash and prizes, so competition was fierce. No longer did I

see the contestants as friendly young women honored to represent their communities, but rather as professionals in the cut-throat business of beauty. I watched while many perfectly beautiful girls ruined their appearance by becoming engrossed with the desire to win, and by looking out for only themselves. These were not the sweet women I remembered seeing on television. They were indeed professionals, who invested not only thousands of dollars per year on pageant fees and evening gowns, but also years of their lives, all in order to compete for a title and the monetary rewards which go along with it.

After spending ten days behind the scenes of a pageant as one of the 109 contestants, I learned that what a viewer sees on television is only a show. Pageants are not the magical, suspense filled dreamshows that many young girls see them as being. They are the result of some entrepreneur's desire to become rich. Unfortunately, this wealth comes at the expense of the contestants who expend so much time, hope, and money, as well as the winner who, although she may enjoy it for a while, is often exploited by her new managers and sponsors. 5

Competing in the pageant also made me realize that the contestants and winner of the pageant were really no more beautiful than many other women in Texas. I've found that beauty is more than a perfect set of teeth or a 5′11″ frame carrying only 130 pounds. Beauty radiates from the inside of a person and is seen not in the way someone applies her make-up or in the clothes she wears but through her willingness to share her true beauty with everyone around her. 6

QUESTIONS TO CONSIDER ◀

1. How does Williams establish her credibility? Why is she qualified to write about beauty contests?

2. Williams begins her essay by describing her perception of beauty contests before she was a participant. She devotes only one paragraph to this description. Would more information about her earlier perceptions strengthen her essay? Why, or why not?

3. Williams's essay includes both logical and emotional appeals. Give examples of each, and analyze their effectiveness.

4. Does the fact that Williams's experience was limited to a single contest weaken her argument? Why, or why not?

5. Williams's main argument is that beauty contests are money-making businesses that are staged to impress television viewers. What other

objections could she have raised to beauty contests? Would these objections have been appropriate, given her purpose in this essay?

▶ WRITING ACTIVITIES

Individual: In a journal entry, write about your perception of or reaction to beauty contests.

Collaborative: With a group of your classmates, make a list of the pros and cons of beauty contests. Then write down one logical and one emotional appeal you could use to support each position. Compare your arguments with those of the other groups.

Computer: Choose one of the arguments from the pro/con list generated by your group in the collaborative activity. Enter this argument into a new computer file, and then develop it by adding supporting evidence. Share your argument with classmates through a network program or by exchanging disks. Respond to at least three of your classmates' arguments.

ON NATURAL DEATH

Lewis Thomas

Noted scientist and essayist Lewis Thomas argues in this essay that all deaths are natural. This essay is part of a collection of Thomas's essays entitled The Medusa and the Snail: More Notes of a Biology Watcher. *Like the other authors in this chapter, Thomas begins his essay by setting forth a common misperception—namely, that death is "an extraordinary, even an exotic experience" for humans. He then proceeds to argue against this view of death. As you read, notice the author's slightly humorous tone, especially in his introduction. Is this tone effective in presenting an argument about such a serious subject?*

1   There are so many new books about dying that there are now special shelves set aside for them in bookshops, along with the health-diet and home-repair paperbacks and the sex manuals. Some of them are so packed with detailed information and step-by-step instructions

for performing the function that you'd think this was a new sort of
skill which all of us are now required to learn. The strongest impression the casual reader gets, leafing through, is that proper dying has
become an extraordinary, even an exotic experience, something only
the specially trained get to do.

Also, you could be led to believe that we are the only creatures
capable of the awareness of death, that when all the rest of nature is
being cycled through dying, one generation after another, it is a different kind of process, done automatically and trivially, more "natural,"
as we say.

An elm in our backyard caught the blight this summer and
dropped stone dead, leafless, almost overnight. One weekend it was a
normal-looking elm, maybe a little bare in spots but nothing alarming,
and the next weekend it was gone, passed over, departed, taken.
Taken is right, for the tree surgeon came by yesterday with his crew of
young helpers and their cherry picker, and took it down branch by
branch and carted it off in the back of a red truck, everyone singing.

The dying of a field mouse, at the jaws of an amiable household
cat, is a spectacle I have beheld many times. It used to make me
wince. Early in life I gave up throwing sticks at the cat to make him
drop the mouse, because the dropped mouse regularly went ahead
and died anyway, but I also shouted unaffections at the cat to let him
know the sort of animal he had become. Nature, I thought, was an
abomination.

Recently I've done some thinking about that mouse, and I
wonder if his dying is necessarily all that different from the passing
of our elm. The main difference, if there is one, would be in the
matter of pain. I do not believe that an elm tree has pain receptors,
and even so, the blight seems to me a relatively painless way to go
even if there were nerve endings in a tree, which there are not.
But the mouse dangling tail-down from the teeth of a gray cat is
something else again, with pain beyond bearing, you'd think, all
over his small body.

There are now some plausible reasons for thinking it is not like
that at all, and you can make up an entirely different story about the
mouse and his dying if you like. At the instant of being trapped and
penetrated by teeth, peptide hormones are released by cells in the
hypothalamus and the pituitary gland; instantly these substances,
called endorphins, are attached to the surfaces of other cells responsible for pain perception; the hormones have the pharmacologic proper-
ties of opium; there is no pain. Thus it is that the mouse seems always
to dangle so languidly from the jaws, lies there so quietly when

dropped, dies of his injuries without a struggle. If a mouse could shrug, he'd shrug.

7   I do not know if this is true or not, nor do I know how to prove it if it is true. Maybe if you could get in there quickly enough and administer naloxone, a specific morphine antagonist, you could turn off the endorphins and observe the restoration of pain, but this is not something I would care to do or see. I think I will leave it there, as a good guess about the dying of a cat-chewed mouse, perhaps about dying in general.

8   Montaigne had a hunch about dying, based on his own close call in a riding accident. He was so badly injured as to be believed dead by his companions, and was carried home with lamentations, "all bloody, stained all over with the blood I had thrown up." He remembers the entire episode, despite having been "dead, for two full hours," with wonderment:

9   It seemed to me that my life was hanging only by the tip of my lips. I closed my eyes in order, it seemed to me, to help push it out, and took pleasure in growing languid and letting myself go. It was an idea that was only floating on the surface of my soul, as delicate and feeble as all the rest, but in truth not only free from distress but mingled with that sweet feeling that people have who have let themselves slide into sleep. I believe that this is the same state in which people find themselves whom we see fainting in the agony of death, and I maintain that we pity them without cause . . . In order to get used to the idea of death, I find there is nothing like coming close to it.

10   Later, in another essay, Montaigne returns to it:

        If you know not how to die, never trouble yourself;
        Nature will in a moment fully and sufficiently instruct you; she
        will exactly do that business for you; take you no care for it.

11   The worst accident I've ever seen was on Okinawa, in the early days of the invasion, when a jeep ran into a troop carrier and was crushed nearly flat. Inside were two young MPs, trapped in bent steel, both mortally hurt, with only their heads and shoulders visible. We had a conversation while people with the right tools were prying them free. Sorry about the accident, they said. No, they said, they felt fine. Is everyone else okay, one of them said. Well, the other one said, no hurry now. And then they died.

Pain is useful for avoidance, for getting away when there's time   12
to get away, but when it is end game, and no way back, pain is likely to
be turned off, and the mechanisms for this are wonderfully precise
and quick. If I had to design an ecosystem in which creatures had to
live off each other and in which dying was an indispensable part of
living, I could not think of a better way to manage.

QUESTIONS TO CONSIDER

1. Because Thomas is a well-known scientist as well as a writer, many
   readers recognize his name and thus know he is qualified to write on
   the subject of death. However, even readers who do not recognize
   Thomas's name usually find him believable. How does he establish
   his **credibility** in this essay?

CREDIBILITY, PAGE 552

2. Thomas supports his argument by citing his own personal experiences and observations. Is his evidence convincing? Is he justified in
   making the claim that all death is natural on the basis of the evidence he cites?

3. What appeals does Thomas use most effectively in this essay? What
   assumptions does he make?

4. This essay, as Thomas readily admits, is largely speculative. That is,
   he does not pretend to know for sure that what he is arguing is
   actually true. Is Thomas successful in convincing you of his arguments even though they are mainly speculative? Why, or why not?

5. What does Thomas mean by *natural* death? Define the term as he
   uses it.

6. Do you agree with Thomas that the death of a person is like the
   death of an animal or plant? Why, or why not?

WRITING ACTIVITIES

Individual: Write a journal entry in which you describe the death of a
person, animal, or plant that you have closely observed. On the
basis of your observations, come to some conclusion about death.

Collaborative: Discuss Thomas's argument that all death is natural.
Make a list of the evidence that Thomas uses to support his argument. Then analyze the evidence to decide if it is valid. Write a brief
conclusion, stating whether your group accepts or rejects Thomas's
argument and why.

Computer: Using the journal entry in which you described the death of a person, animal, or plant, freewrite at the computer, focusing on the feelings generated by this experience. Concentrate on emotions rather than logic as you write. Then read your freewriting, and identify one sentence that seems to express most accurately how you feel about this experience. Using the block-and-move (or cut-and-paste) function of your word-processing program, move this sentence to a new file, and use it as a topic sentence or thesis statement for a paragraph or brief essay.

THE DAY CARE DEMONS: MAKE YOUR OWN STATISTICS

Susan Faludi

This selection is part of a book by Susan Faludi entitled Backlash: The Undeclared War Against American Women. *Faludi's book is one of many feminist books to appear in recent years. Faludi argues in this piece that statistics about day care have been used irresponsibly by both politicians and the press. However, as you read, notice that Faludi's larger purpose is to argue that the misrepresentation of day-care studies and statistics has been used to discourage females from entering the workforce—to keep them in the home.*

1   The anti–day care headlines practically shrieked in the '80s: "MOMMY, DON'T LEAVE ME HERE!" THE DAY CARE PARENTS DON'T SEE. DAY CARE CAN BE DANGEROUS TO YOUR CHILD'S HEALTH. WHEN CHILD CARE BECOMES CHILD MOLESTING: IT HAPPENS MORE OFTEN THAN PARENTS LIKE TO THINK. CREEPING CHILD CARE . . . CREEPY.

2   The spokesmen of the New Right, of course, were most denunciatory, labeling day care "the Thalidomide of the '80s." Reagan's men didn't mince words either, like the top military official who proclaimed, "American mothers who work and send their children to faceless centers rather than stay home to take care of them are weakening the moral fiber of the Nation." But the press, more subtly but just as persistently, painted devil's horns both on mothers who use day care and day care workers themselves.

In 1984, a *Newsweek* feature warned of an "epidemic" of child   3
abuse in child care facilities, based on allegations against directors at a
few day care centers—the most celebrated of which were later found
innocent in the courts. Just in case the threat had slipped women's
minds, two weeks later *Newsweek* was busy once more, demanding
"What Price Day Care?" in a cover story. The cover picture featured a
frightened, saucer-eyed child sucking his thumb. By way of edifying
contrast, the eight-page treatment inside showcased a Good Mother—
under the title "At Home by Choice." The former bond seller had
dropped her career to be home with her baby and offer wifely assistance to her husband's career. "I had to admit I couldn't do [every-
thing]," the mother said, a view that clearly earned an approving nod
from *Newsweek.* Still later, in a special issue devoted to the family,
Newsweek ran another article on "the dark side of day care." That story
repeatedly alluded to "more and more evidence that child care may
be hazardous to a youngster's health," but never got around to providing it. This campaign was one the press managed to conduct all by
itself. Researchers were having a tough time linking day care with
deviance. So the press circulated some antiquated "research" and
ignored the rest.

At a press conference in the spring of 1988, the University of New   4
Hampshire's Family Research Laboratory released the largest and most
comprehensive study ever on sexual abuse in day care centers—a
three-year study examining the reported cases of sexual abuse at day
care facilities across the country. One would have assumed from the
swarm of front-page stories on this apparent threat that the researchers'
findings would rate as an important news event. But the *New York
Times* response was typical: it noted the study's release in a modest
article on the same page as the classifieds. (Ironically, it ran on the
same page as an even smaller story about a Wisconsin father beating
his four-year-old son so brutally that the child had to be institutional-
ized for the rest of his life for brain injuries.) Why such little interest?
The study concluded that there was no epidemic of child abuse at day
care centers. In fact, if there was an abuse crisis anywhere, the study
pointed out, it was at home—where the risk to children of molestation
is almost twice as high as in day care. In 1985, there were nearly
100,000 reported cases of children sexually abused by family members
(mostly fathers, stepfathers, or older brothers), compared with about
1,300 cases in day care. Children are far more likely to be beaten, too,
at the family hearth, the researchers found; and the physical abuse at
home tends to be of a longer duration, more severe and more traumatic
than any violence children faced in day care centers. In 1986, 1,500

children died from abuse at home. "Day care is not an inherently high-risk locale for children, despite frightening stories in the media," the Family Research Laboratory study's authors concluded. "The risk of abuse is not sufficient reason to avoid day care in general or to justify parents' withdrawing from the labor force."

5   Research over the last two decades has consistently found that if day care has any long-term effect on children, it seems to make children slightly more gregarious and independent. Day care children also appear to be more broad-minded about sex roles; girls interviewed in day care centers are more likely to believe that housework and child rearing should be shared by both parents. A National Academy of Sciences panel in 1982 concluded that children suffer no ill effects in academic, social, or emotional development when mothers work.

6   Yet the day care "statistics" that received the most press in the '80s were the ones based more on folklore than research. Illness, for example, was supposedly more pervasive in day care centers than in the home, according to media accounts. Yet, the actual studies on child care and illness indicate that while children in day care are initially prone to more illnesses, they soon build up immunities and actually get sick less often than kids at home. Day care's threat to bonding between mother and child was another popular myth. But the research offers scant evidence of diminished bonds between mother and child—and suggests that children profit from exposure to a wider range of grown-ups, anyway. (No one ever worries, it seems, about day care's threat to paternal bonding.)

7   With no compelling demographic evidence to support an attack on day care for toddlers, critics of day care turned their attention to infants. Three-year-old toddlers may survive day care, they argued, but newborns would surely suffer permanent damage. Their evidence, however, came from studies conducted on European children in wartime orphanages and war refugee camps—environments that were hardly the equivalent of contemporary day care centers, even the worst variety. One of the most commonly quoted studies in the press wasn't even conducted on human beings. Psychologist Harry Harlow found that "infants" in day care suffer severe emotional distress. His subjects, however, were baby monkeys. And his "day care workers" weren't even surrogate adult monkeys: the researchers used wire-mesh dummies.

8   Finally in 1986, it looked as if day care critics had some hard data they could use. Pennsylvania State University psychologist and social researcher Jay Belsky, a prominent supporter of day care, expressed some reservations about day care infants. Up until this point, Belsky had said that his reviews of the child development literature yielded

few if any significant differences between children raised at home and in day care. Then, in the September 1986 issue of the child care newsletter *Zero to Three*, Belsky proposed that placing children in day care for more than twenty hours a week in their first year of life may pose a "risk factor" that could lead to an "insecure" attachment to their mothers. The press and conservative politicians hurried to the scene. Soon Belsky found himself making the network rounds— "Today," "CBS Morning News," and "Donahue"—and fielding dozens of press calls a month. And, much to the liberal Belsky's discomfort, "conservatives embraced me." Right-wing scholars cited his findings. Conservative politicians sought out his Congressional testimony at child care hearings—and got furious when he failed to spout "what they wanted me to say."

Belsky peppered his report on infant day care with qualifications,   9
strongly cautioned against overreaction, and advised that he had only a "trickle," "not a flood," of evidence. He wrote that only a "relatively persuasive *circumstantial* [all italics are his] case can be made that early infant care *may* be associated with increased avoidance of mother, *possibly* to the point of greater insecurity in the attachment relationship." And he added, "I cannot state strongly enough that there is sufficient evidence to lead a judicious scientist to doubt this line of reasoning." Finally, in every press interview, as he recalls later, he stressed the many caveats and emphasized that his findings under-scored the need for better funding and standards for child care centers, not grounds for eliminating day care. "I was not saying we shouldn't have day care," he says. "I was saying that we need *good* day care. Quality matters." But his words "fell on deaf ears." And once the mis-representations of his work passed into the media, it seemed impossi-ble to root them out. "What amazed me was the journalists just plagiarized each other's newspaper stories. Very few of them actually read my article."

What also got less attention in the press was the actual evidence   10
Belsky used to support his tentative reassessment. He focused on four studies—any of which, as he himself conceded, "could be dismissed for a variety of scientific reasons." The first study was based on one center that mostly served poor welfare mothers with unplanned pregnancies— and so it was impossible to say whether the children were having trou-ble because they went to day care or because they had such grim and impecunious home lives. Belsky said he had evidence from more mid-dleclass populations, too, but the authors of the two key studies he used later maintained that he has misread their data. University of North Carolina psychologist Ron Haskins, author of one of the studies on the

effects of day care on aggression, flatly stated in a subsequent issue of *Zero to Three* that "my results will not support these conclusions." Belsky alluded to a final study to support his position that infants in day care might be "less compliant" when they get older. But he failed to mention the study's follow-up review, in which the authors rather drastically revised their assessment. Later behavioral problems, the researchers wrote, "were not predicted by whether the toddler had been in day care or at home" after all. In response, Belsky says that it all depends on how one chooses to read the data in that study. Like so many of the "findings" in this politically charged field of research, he says, "It is all a question of, is the glass half full or half empty?"

11   Social scientists *could* supply plenty of research to show that one member of the American family, at least, is happier and more well adjusted when mom stays home and minds the children. But that person is dad—a finding of limited use to backlash publicists. Anyway, by the end of the decade the press was no longer even demanding hard data to make its case. By then the public was so steeped in the lore of the backlash that its spokesmen rarely bothered to round up the usual statistics. Who needed proof? Everybody already believed that the myths about '80s women were true.

▶   QUESTIONS TO CONSIDER

1. Does Faludi convince you that statistics can be used irresponsibly and unscrupulously? Why, or why not? Do your own experiences with statistical evidence confirm or refute her argument?

2. Does she convince you that the irresponsible use of day care statistics has been motivated by the "backlash" against women? Why, or why not?

3. Faludi states that one study concluded "that there was no epidemic of child abuse at day care centers." What constitutes an epidemic of child abuse? What connotations does the word *epidemic* have? What other term or terms could she have used to express this concept more precisely and more neutrally?

4. Faludi identifies most of the studies and articles she cites only partially. In one case, for example, she merely refers to "actual studies on child care and illness" rather than telling her readers exactly which studies. Under what circumstances would a reader need more exact information about her sources? Would more exact information have been more convincing? More useful? Why, or why not?

5. Faludi is clearly arguing that existing studies of day care are seriously flawed and, even worse, misrepresented. She uses the word *evidence* frequently—criticizing those whose evidence is not valid or accurate. What evidence does Faludi include to support her own arguments?

WRITING ACTIVITIES

Individual: Write a journal entry in which you agree or disagree with Faludi's position.

Collaborative: Discuss your individual responses to this selection. Then, as a group, identify the major strengths and weaknesses of Faludi's arguments, and write a paragraph summarizing your conclusions.

Computer: Type into a new computer file the summary paragraph generated by your group for the collaborative activity. Expand your group's paragraph into your own individual critique of Faludi's arguments. Format the group paragraph by separating each sentence from the rest of the paragraph with several line spaces. Use each of these summary sentences as the topic sentence for a new paragraph that elaborates on the major strengths and weaknesses of Faludi's arguments.

UNPLUGGED:
THE MYTH OF COMPUTERS IN THE CLASSROOM

David Gelernter

With this article from The New Republic, *David Gelernter challenges the popular idea that computers improve the quality of education students receive. A professor of computer science at Yale University, Gelernter argues that in practice "computers make our worst educational nightmares come true." As you read, evaluate his arguments against the way computers are used in the schools as well as his suggestions for how they should be used.*

Over the last decade an estimated $2 billion has been spent on more than 2 million computers for America's classrooms. That's not   1 surprising. We constantly hear from Washington that the schools are in trouble and that computers are a godsend. Within the education establishment, in poor as well as rich schools, the machines are awaited with nearly religious awe. An inner-city principal bragged to a teacher friend of mine recently that his school "has a computer in every classroom . . . despite being in a bad neighborhood!"

2   Computers should be in the schools. They have the potential to accomplish great things. With the right software, they could help make science tangible or teach neglected topics like art and music. They could help students form a concrete idea of society by displaying on-screen a version of the city in which they live—a picture that tracks real life moment by moment.

3   In practice, however, computers make our worst educational nightmares come true. While we bemoan the decline of literacy, computers discount words in favor of pictures and pictures in favor of video. While we fret about the decreasing cogency of public debate, computers dismiss linear argument and promote fast, shallow romps across the information landscape. While we worry about basic skills, we allow into the classroom software that will do a student's arithmetic or correct his spelling.

4   Take multimedia. The idea of multimedia is to combine text, sound and pictures in a single package that you browse on screen. You don't just *read* Shakespeare; you watch actors performing, listen to songs, view Elizabethan buildings. What's wrong with that? By offering children candy-coated books, multimedia is guaranteed to sour them on unsweetened reading. It makes the printed page look even more boring that it used to look. Sure, books will be available in the classroom, too—but they'll have all the appeal of a dusty piano to a teen who has a Walkman handy.

5   So what if the little nippers don't read? If they're watching Olivier instead, what do they lose? The text, the written word along with all of its attendant pleasures. Besides, a book is more portable than a computer, has a higher-resolution display, can be written on and dog-eared and is comparatively dirt cheap.

6   Hypermedia, multimedia's comrade in the struggle for a brave new classroom, is just as troubling. It's a way of presenting documents on screen without imposing a linear start-to-finish order. Disembodied paragraphs are linked by theme; after reading one about the First World War, for example, you might be able to choose another about the technology of battleships, or the life of Woodrow Wilson, or hemlines in the '20s. This is another cute idea that is good in minor ways and terrible in major ones. Teaching children to understand the orderly

unfolding of a plot or a logical argument is a crucial part of education. Authors don't merely agglomerate paragraphs; they work hard to make the narrative read a certain way, prove a particular point. To turn a book or a document into hypertext is to invite readers to ignore exactly what counts—the story.

The real problem, again, is the accentuation of already bad habits. Dynamiting documents into disjointed paragraphs is one more expression of the sorry fact that sustained argument is not our style. If you're a newspaper or magazine editor and your readership is dwindling, what's the solution? Shorter pieces. If you're a politician and you want to get elected, what do you need? Tasty sound bites. Logical presentation be damned.   7

Another software species, "allow me" programs, is not much better. These programs correct spelling and, by applying canned grammatical and stylistic rules, fix prose. In terms of promoting basic skills, though, they have all the virtues of a pocket calculator.   8

In Kentucky, as *The Wall Street Journal* recently reported, students in grades K-3 are mixed together regardless of age in a relaxed environment. It works great, the *Journal* says. Yes, scores on computation tests have dropped 10 percent at one school, but not to worry: "Drilling addition and subtraction in an age of calculators is a waste of time," the principal reassures us. Meanwhile, a Japanese educator informs University of Wisconsin mathematician Richard Akey that in his country, "calculators are not used in elementary or junior high school because the primary emphasis is on helping students develop their mental abilities." No wonder Japanese kids blow the pants off American kids in math. Do we really think "drilling addition and subtraction in an age of calculators is a waste of time"? If we do, then "drilling reading in an age of multimedia is a waste of time" can't be far behind.   9

Prose-correcting programs are also a little ghoulish, like asking a computer for tips on improving your personality. On the other hand, I ran this article through a spell-checker, so how can I ban the use of such programs in schools? Because to misspell is human; to have no idea of correct spelling is to be semiliterate.   10

There's no denying that computers have the potential to perform inspiring feats in the classroom. If we are ever to see that potential realized, however, we ought to agree on three conditions. First, there should be a completely new crop of children's software. Most of today's offerings show no imagination. There are hundreds of similar reading and geography and arithmetic programs, but almost nothing on electricity or physics or architecture. Also, they abuse the technical capacities of new media to glitz up old forms instead of creating new   11 ones. Why not build a time-travel program that gives kids a feel for how history is structured by zooming you backward? A spectrum program that lets users twirl a frequency knob to see what happens?

12   Second, computers should be used only during recess or relaxation periods. Treat them as fillips, not as surrogate teachers. When I was in school in the '60s, we all loved educational films. When we saw a movie in class, everybody won: teachers didn't have to teach, and pupils didn't have to learn. I suspect that classroom computers are popular today for the same reasons.

13   Most important, educators should learn what parents and most teachers already know: you cannot teach a child anything unless you look him in the face. We should not forget what computers are. Like books—better in some ways, worse in others—they are devices that help children mobilize their own resources and learn for themselves. The computer's potential to do good is modestly greater than a book's in some areas. Its potential to do harm is vastly greater, across the board.

▶   QUESTIONS TO CONSIDER

1. The subtitle for this article is "The Myth of Computers in the Classroom." How widespread is the myth that computers improve the quality of education? Which of the following groups is most likely to believe that computers are useful in the classroom: students, teachers, parents, administrators, politicians, or computer experts?

2. In his final paragraph, Gelernter distinguishes between teachers and educators when he states that "educators should learn what parents and most teachers already know." What is the difference between a teacher and an educator? What is Gelernter implying by making this subtle distinction?

3. Evaluate Gelernter's three conditions for using computers in the classroom. Which of the three seems to you most sensible and useful?

4. When he writes in paragraph 10, "to misspell is human; to have no idea of correct spelling is to be semiliterate," Gelernter alludes to a famous line of poetry by Alexander Pope ("To err is human, to forgive divine."). What does he accomplish by including this allusion?

5. Can Gelernter's arguments against computers extend to technology in general? Can technology ever *surpass* teachers in helping students learn? Can it *assist* teachers in helping students learn? Are the problems with technology inherent in technology itself or with the way technology is used?

6. What type of evidence does Gelernter include to support his arguments?

7. Why do you think Gelernter, a professor of computer science at Yale, is not in favor of computers in the classroom?

▶ W R I T I N G   A C T I V I T I E S

Individual: Write a journal entry in which you tell about your experience with computers in the classroom.

Collaborative: Compare your own experiences with computers in the classroom with those of the other members of your group. Write a sentence in which you generalize about your collective experiences. Do your experiences confirm or contradict Gelernter's arguments?

Computer: Write a letter to Gelernter in which you agree or disagree with his arguments about computers in the classroom. Post your letter to your classroom's computer network, and then revise it after you have received responses from your classmates.

LETTER FROM BIRMINGHAM JAIL

Martin Luther King, Jr.

Martin Luther King, Jr., a clergyman and writer, is best known as the leader of the U.S. civil rights movement in the 1960s. He was awarded a Nobel Peace Prize in 1964 in recognition of his efforts to end segregation and to ensure the civil rights of African Americans in the United States. King was assassinated in 1968 in Memphis, Tennessee.

King's effectiveness as a leader was in no small part the result of his ability to speak and write persuasively. He wrote the following letter in response to a public statement issued by eight Alabama clergymen following a peaceful civil rights demonstration in Birmingham in which a number of the demonstrators, including King, were arrested. In the statement, the clergymen deplored the "unwise and untimely" demonstrations led by "outsiders" and encouraged African Americans to "withdraw support from these demonstrations, and to unite locally in working peacefully for a better Birmingham." As you read King's letter, notice that he explains patiently and persuasively his view of this situation—his vision of what had happened and why it had to happen as it did.

Public Statement
by Eight Alabama Clergymen

April 12, 1963

1   We the undersigned clergymen are among those who, in January, issued "An Appeal for Law and Order and Common Sense," in dealing with racial problems in Alabama. We expressed understanding that honest convictions in racial matters could properly be pursued in the courts, but urged that decisions of those courts should in the meantime be peacefully obeyed.

2   Since that time there had been some evidence of increased forbearance and a willingness to face facts. Responsible citizens have undertaken to work on various problems which cause racial friction and unrest. In Birmingham, recent public events have given indication that we all have opportunity for a new constructive and realistic approach to racial problems.

3   However, we are now confronted by a series of demonstrations by some of our Negro citizens, directed and led in part by outsiders. We recognize the natural impatience of people who feel that their hopes are slow in being realized. But we are convinced that these demonstrations are unwise and untimely.

4   We agree rather with certain local Negro leadership which has called for honest and open negotiation of racial issues in our area. And we believe this kind of facing of issues can best be accomplished by citizens of our own metropolitan area, white and Negro, meeting with their knowledge and experience of the local situation. All of us need to face that responsibility and find proper channels for its accomplishment.

5   Just as we formerly pointed out that "hatred and violence have no sanction in our religious and political traditions," we also point out that such actions as incite to hatred and violence, however technically peaceful those actions may be, have not contributed to the resolution of our local problems. We do not believe that these days of new hope are days when extreme measures are justified in Birmingham.

6   We commend the community as a whole, and the local news media and law enforcement officials in particular, on the calm manner in which these demonstrations have been handled. We urge the public to continue to show restraint should the demonstrations continue, and the law enforcement officials to remain calm and continue to protect our city from violence.

7   We further strongly urge our own Negro community to withdraw support from these demonstrations, and to unite locally in working

peacefully for a better Birmingham. When rights are consistently denied, a cause should be pressed in the courts and in negotiations among local leaders, and not in the streets. We appeal to both our white and Negro citizenry to observe the principles of law and order and common sense.

Signed by:

C. C. J. Carpenter, D.D., LL.D.,
Bishop of Alabama
Joseph A. Durick, D.D.,
Auxiliary Bishop, Diocese of Mobile, Birmingham
Rabbi Milton L. Grafman,
Temple Emanu-El, Birmingham, Alabama
Bishop Paul Hardin,
Bishop of the Alabama-West Florida Conference
of the Methodist Church
Bishop Nolan B. Harmon,
Bishop of the North Alabama Conference
of the Methodist Church
George M. Murray, D.D., LL.D.,
Bishop Coadjutor, Episcopal Diocese of Alabama
Edward V. Ramage,
Moderator, Synod of the Alabama Presbyterian Church
in the United States
Earl Stallings,
Pastor, First Baptist Church, Birmingham, Alabama

Letter from Birmingham Jail

April 16, 1963

My Dear Fellow Clergymen: [1]

While confined here in the Birmingham city jail, I came across your recent statement calling my present activities "unwise and untimely." Seldom do I pause to answer criticism of my work and ideas. If I sought to answer all the criticisms that cross my desk, my secretaries would have little time for anything other than such correspondence in the course of the day, and I would have no time for constructive work. But since I feel that you are men of genuine good will and that your criticisms are sincerely set forth, I want to try to answer your statement in what I hope will be patient and reasonable terms.

2   I think I should indicate why I am here in Birmingham, since you have been influenced by the view which argues against "outsiders coming in." I have the honor of serving as president of the Southern Christian Leadership Conference, an organization operating in every southern state, with headquarters in Atlanta, Georgia. We have some eighty-five affiliated organizations across the South, and one of them is the Alabama Christian Movement for Human Rights. Frequently we share staff, educational and financial resources with our affiliates. Several months ago the affiliate here in Birmingham asked us to be on call to engage in a nonviolent direct-action program if such were deemed necessary. We readily consented, and when the hour came we lived up to our promise. So I, along with several members of my staff, am here because I was invited here. I am here because I have organizational ties here.

3   But more basically, I am in Birmingham because injustice is here. Just as the prophets of the eighth century B.C. left their villages and carried their "thus saith the Lord" far beyond the boundaries of their home towns, and just as the Apostle Paul left his village of Tarsus and carried the gospel of Jesus Christ to the far corners of the Greco-Roman world, so am I compelled to carry the gospel of freedom beyond my own home town. Like Paul, I must constantly respond to the Macedonian call for aid.

4   Moreover, I am cognizant of the interrelatedness of all communities and states. I cannot sit idly by in Atlanta and not be concerned about what happens in Birmingham. Injustice anywhere is a threat to justice everywhere. We are caught in an inescapable network of mutuality, tied in a single garment of destiny. Whatever affects one directly, affects all indirectly. Never again can we afford to live with the narrow, provincial "outside agitator" idea. Anyone who lives inside the United States can never be considered an outsider anywhere within its bounds.

5   You deplore the demonstrations taking place in Birmingham. But your statement, I am sorry to say, fails to express a similar concern for the conditions that brought about the demonstrations. I am sure that none of you would want to rest content with the superficial kind of social analysis that deals merely with effects and does not grapple with underlying causes. It is unfortunate that demonstrations are taking place in Birmingham, but it is even more unfortunate that the city's white power structure left the Negro community with no alternative.

6   In any nonviolent campaign there are four basic steps: collection of the facts to determine whether injustices exist; negotiation; self-purification; and direct action. We have gone through all these steps in

Birmingham. There can be no gainsaying the fact that racial injustice engulfs this community. Birmingham is probably the most thoroughly segregated city in the United States. Its ugly record of brutality is widely known. Negroes have experienced grossly unjust treatment in the courts. There have been more unsolved bombings of Negro homes and churches in Birmingham than in any other city in the nation. These are the hard, brutal facts of the case. On the basis of these conditions, Negro leaders sought to negotiate with the city fathers. But the latter consistently refused to engage in good-faith negotiation.

Then, last September, came the opportunity to talk with leaders of Birmingham's economic community. In the course of the negotiations, certain promises were made by the merchants—for example, to remove the stores' humiliating racial signs. On the basis of these promises, the Reverend Fred Shuttlesworth and the leaders of the Alabama Christian Movement for Human Rights agreed to a moratorium on all demonstrations. As the weeks and months went by, we realized that we were the victims of a broken promise. A few signs, briefly removed, returned; the others remained.   7

As in so many past experiences, our hopes had been blasted, and the shadow of deep disappointment settled upon us. We had no alternative except to prepare for direct action, whereby we would present our very bodies as a means of laying our case before the conscience of the local and the national community. Mindful of the difficulties involved, we decided to undertake a process of self-purification. We began a series of workshops on nonviolence, and we repeatedly asked ourselves: "Are you able to accept blows without retaliating?" "Are you able to endure the ordeal of jail?" We decided to schedule our direct-action program for the Easter season, realizing that except for Christmas, this is the main shopping period of the year. Knowing that a strong economic-withdrawal program would be the by-product of direct action, we felt that this would be the best time to bring pressure to bear on the merchants for the needed change.   8

Then it occurred to us that Birmingham's mayoral election was coming up in March, and we speedily decided to postpone action until after election day. When we discovered that the Commissioner of Public Safety, Eugene "Bull" Connor, had piled up enough votes to be in the run-off, we decided again to postpone action until the day after the run-off so that the demonstrations could not be used to cloud the issues. Like many others, we waited to see Mr. Connor defeated, and to this end we endured postponement after postponement. Having aided in this community need, we felt that our direct action program could be delayed no longer.   9

10   You may well ask: "Why direct action? Why sit-ins, marches and so forth? Isn't negotiation a better path?" You are quite right in calling for negotiation. Indeed, this is the very purpose of a direct action. Nonviolent direct action seeks to create such a crisis and foster such a tension that a community which has constantly refused to negotiate is forced to confront the issue. It seeks so to dramatize the issue that it can no longer be ignored. My citing the creation of tension as part of the work of the nonviolent-resister may sound rather shocking. But I must confess that I am not afraid of the word "tension." I have earnestly opposed violent tension, but there is a type of constructive, nonviolent tension which is necessary for growth. Just as Socrates felt that it was necessary to create a tension in the mind so that individuals could rise from the bondage of myths and half-truths to the unfettered realm of creative analysis and objective appraisal, so must we see the need for nonviolent gadflies to create the kind of tension in society that will help men rise from the dark depths of prejudice and racism to the majestic heights of understanding and brotherhood.

11   The purpose of our direct-action program is to create a situation so crisis-packed that it will inevitably open the door to negotiation. I therefore concur with you in your call for negotiation. Too long has our beloved Southland been bogged down in a tragic effort to live in monologue rather than dialogue.

12   One of the basic points in your statement is that the action that I and my associates have taken in Birmingham is untimely. Some have asked: "Why didn't you give the new city administration time to act?" The only answer that I can give to this query is that the new Birmingham administration must be prodded about as much as the outgoing one, before it will act. We are sadly mistaken if we feel that the election of Albert Boutwell as mayor will bring the millennium to Birmingham. While Mr. Boutwell is a much more gentle person than Mr. Connor, they are both segregationists, dedicated to maintenance of the status quo. I have hope that Mr. Boutwell will be reasonable enough to see the futility of massive resistance to desegregation. But he will not see this without pressure from devotees of civil rights. My friends, I must say to you that we have not made a single gain in civil rights without determined legal and nonviolent pressure. Lamentably, it is an historical fact that privileged groups seldom give up their privileges voluntarily. Individuals may see the moral light and voluntarily give up their unjust posture; but, as Reinhold Niebuhr has reminded us, groups tend to be more immoral than individuals.

13   We know through painful experience that freedom is never voluntarily given by the oppressor; it must be demanded by the

oppressed. Frankly, I have yet to engage in a direct-action campaign that was "well-timed" in the view of those who have not suffered unduly from the disease of segregation. For years now I have heard the word "Wait!" It rings in the ear of every Negro with piercing familiarity. This "Wait" has almost always meant "Never." We must come to see, with one of our distinguished jurists, that "justice too long delayed is justice denied."

We have waited for more than 340 years for our constitutional   14
and God-given rights. The nations of Asia and Africa are moving with jetlike speed toward gaining political independence, but we still creep at horse-and-buggy pace toward gaining a cup of coffee at a lunch counter. Perhaps it is easy for those who have never felt the stinging darts of segregation to say, "Wait." But when you have seen vicious mobs lynch your mothers and fathers at will and drown your sisters and brothers at whim; when you have seen hate-filled policemen curse, kick and even kill your black brothers and sisters; when you see the vast majority of your twenty million Negro brothers smothering in an airtight cage of poverty in the midst of an affluent society; when you suddenly find your tongue twisted and your speech stammering as you seek to explain to your six-year-old daughter why she can't go to the public amusement park that has just been advertised on television, and see tears welling up in her eyes when she is told that Funtown is closed to colored children, and see ominous clouds of inferiority beginning to form in her little mental sky, and see her beginning to distort her personality by developing an unconscious bitterness toward white people; when you have to concoct an answer for a five-year-old son who is asking: "Daddy, why do white people treat colored people so mean?"; when you take a cross-country drive and find it necessary to sleep night after night in the uncomfortable corners of your automobile because no motel will accept you; when you are humiliated day in and day out by nagging signs reading "white" and "colored"; when your first name becomes "nigger," your middle name becomes "boy" (however old you are) and your last name becomes "John," and your wife and mother are never given the respected title "Mrs."; when you are harried by day and haunted by night by the fact that you are a Negro, living constantly at tiptoe stance, never quite knowing what to expect next, and are plagued with inner fears and outer resentments; when you are forever fighting a degenerating sense of "nobodiness"— then you will understand why we find it difficult to wait. There comes a time when the cup of endurance runs over, and men are no longer willing to be plunged into the abyss of despair. I hope, sirs, you can understand our legitimate and unavoidable impatience.

15   You express a great deal of anxiety over our willingness to break laws. This is certainly a legitimate concern. Since we so diligently urge people to obey the Supreme Court's decision of 1954 outlawing segregation in the public schools, at first glance it may seem rather paradoxical for us consciously to break laws. One may well ask: "How can you advocate breaking some laws and obeying others?" The answer lies in the fact that there are two types of laws: just and unjust. I would be the first to advocate obeying just laws. One has not only a legal but a moral responsibility to obey just laws. Conversely, one has a moral responsibility to disobey unjust laws. I would agree with St. Augustine that "an unjust law is no law at all."

16   Now, what is the difference between the two? How does one determine whether a law is just or unjust? A just law is a man-made code that squares with the moral law or the law of God. An unjust law is a code that is out of harmony with the moral law. To put it in the terms of St. Thomas Aquinas: An unjust law is a human law that is not rooted in eternal law and natural law. Any law that uplifts human personality is just. Any law that degrades human personality is unjust. All segregation statutes are unjust because segregation distorts the soul and damages the personality. It gives the segregator a false sense of superiority and the segregated a false sense of inferiority. Segregation, to use the terminology of the Jewish philosopher Martin Buber, substitutes an "I–it" relationship for an "I–thou" relationship and ends up relegating persons to the status of things. Hence segregation is not only politically, economically and sociologically unsound, it is morally wrong and sinful. Paul Tillich has said that sin is separation. Is not segregation an existential expression of man's tragic separation, his awful estrangement, his terrible sinfulness? Thus it is that I can urge men to obey the 1954 decision of the Supreme Court, for it is morally right; and I can urge them to disobey segregation ordinances, for they are morally wrong.

17   Let us consider a more concrete example of just and unjust laws. An unjust law is a code that a numerical or power majority group compels a minority group to obey but does not make binding on itself. This is *difference* made legal. By the same token, a just law is a code that a majority compels a minority to follow and that it is willing to follow itself. This is *sameness* made legal.

18   Let me give another explanation. A law is unjust if it is inflicted on a minority that, as a result of being denied the right to vote, had no part in enacting or devising the law. Who can say that the legislature of Alabama which set up that state's segregation laws was democratically elected? Throughout Alabama all sorts of devious methods are used to

prevent Negroes from becoming registered voters, and there are some counties in which, even though Negroes constitute a majority of the population, not a single Negro is registered. Can any law enacted under such circumstances be considered democratically structured?

Sometimes a law is just on its face and unjust in its application. For instance, I have been arrested on a charge of parading without a permit. Now, there is nothing wrong in having an ordinance which requires a permit for a parade. But such an ordinance becomes unjust when it is used to maintain segregation and to deny citizens the First-Amendment privilege of peaceful assembly and protest.   [19]

I hope you are able to see the distinction I am trying to point out. In no sense do I advocate evading or defying the law, as would the rabid segregationist. That would lead to anarchy. One who breaks an unjust law must do so openly, lovingly, and with a willingness to accept the penalty. I submit that an individual who breaks a law that conscience tells him is unjust, and who willingly accepts the penalty of imprisonment in order to arouse the conscience of the community over its injustice, is in reality expressing the highest respect for law.   [20]

Of course, there is nothing new about this kind of civil disobedience. It was evidenced sublimely in the refusal of Shadrach, Meshach and Abednego to obey the laws of Nebuchadnezzar, on the ground that a higher moral law was at stake. It was practiced superbly by the early Christians, who were willing to face hungry lions and the excruciating pain of chopping blocks rather than submit to certain unjust laws of the Roman Empire. To a degree, academic freedom is a reality today because Socrates practiced civil disobedience. In our own nation, the Boston Tea Party represented a massive act of civil disobedience.   [21]

We should never forget that everything Adolf Hitler did in Germany was "legal" and everything the Hungarian freedom fighters did in Hungary was "illegal." It was "illegal" to aid and comfort a Jew in Hitler's Germany. Even so, I am sure that, had I lived in Germany at the time, I would have aided and comforted my Jewish brothers. If today I lived in a Communist country where certain principles dear to the Christian faith are suppressed, I would openly advocate disobeying that country's antireligious laws.   [22]

I must make two honest confessions to you, my Christian and Jewish brothers. First, I must confess that over the past few years I have been gravely disappointed with the white moderate. I have almost reached the regrettable conclusion that the Negro's great stumbling block in his stride toward freedom is not the White Citizen's Counciler or the Ku Klux Klanner, but the white moderate, who is more devoted to "order" than to justice; who prefers a negative peace   [23] which is the absence of tension to a positive peace which is the presence of justice; who constantly says: "I agree with you in the goal you seek, but I cannot agree with your methods of direct action"; who paternalistically believes he can set the timetable for another man's freedom; who lives by a mythical concept of time and who constantly advises the Negro to wait for a "more convenient season." Shallow understanding from people of good will is more frustrating than absolute misunderstanding from people of ill will. Lukewarm acceptance is much more bewildering than outright rejection.

24   I had hoped that the white moderate would understand that law and order exist for the purpose of establishing justice and that when they fail in this purpose they become the dangerously structured dams that block the flow of social progress. I had hoped that the white moderate would understand that the present tension in the South is a necessary phase of the transition from an obnoxious negative peace, in which the Negro passively accepted his unjust plight, to a substantive and positive peace, in which all men will respect the dignity and worth of human personality. Actually, we who engage in nonviolent direct action are not the creators of tension. We merely bring to the surface the hidden tension that is already alive. We bring it out in the open, where it can be seen and dealt with. Like a boil that can never be cured so long as it is covered up but must be opened with all its ugliness to the natural medicines of air and light, injustice must be exposed, with all the tension its exposure creates, to the light of human conscience and the air of national opinion before it can be cured.

25   In your statement you assert that our actions, even though peaceful, must be condemned because they precipitate violence. But is this a logical assertion? Isn't this like condemning a robbed man because his possession of money precipitated the evil act of robbery? Isn't this like condemning Socrates because his unswerving commitment to truth and his philosophical inquiries precipitated the act by the misguided populace in which they made him drink hemlock? Isn't this like condemning Jesus because his unique God-consciousness and never-ceasing devotion to God's will precipitated the evil act of crucifixion? We must come to see that, as the federal courts have consistently affirmed, it is wrong to urge an individual to cease his efforts to gain his basic constitutional rights because the quest may precipitate violence. Society must protect the robbed and punish the robber.

26   I had also hoped that the white moderate would reject the myth concerning time in relation to the struggle for freedom. I have just received a letter from a white brother in Texas. He writes: "All Christians know that the colored people will receive equal rights eventually, but

it is possible that you are in too great a religious hurry. It has taken Christianity almost two thousand years to accomplish what it has. The teachings of Christ take time to come to earth." Such an attitude stems from a tragic misconception of time, from the strangely irrational notion that there is something in the very flow of time that will inevitably cure all ills. Actually, time itself is neutral; it can be used either destructively or constructively. More and more I feel that the people of ill will have used time much more effectively than have the people of good will. We will have to repent in this generation not merely for the hateful words and actions of the bad people but for the appalling silence of the good people. Human progress never rolls in on wheels of inevitability; it comes through the tireless efforts of men willing to be co-workers with God, and without this hard work, time itself becomes an ally of the forces of social stagnation. We must use time creatively, in the knowledge that time is always ripe to do right. Now is the time to make real the promise of democracy and transform our pending national elegy into a creative psalm of brotherhood. Now is the time to lift our national policy from the quicksand of racial injustice to the solid rock of human dignity.

You speak of our activity in Birmingham as extreme. At first I was   27
rather disappointed that fellow clergymen would see my nonviolent efforts as those of an extremist. I began thinking about the fact that I stand in the middle of two opposing forces in the Negro community. One is a force of complacency, made up in part of Negroes who, as a result of long years of oppression, are so drained of self-respect and a sense of "somebodiness" that they have adjusted to segregation; and in part of a few middle-class Negroes who, because of a degree of academic and economic security and because in some ways they profit by segregation, have become insensitive to the problems of the masses. The other force is one of bitterness and hatred, and it comes perilously close to advocating violence. It is expressed in the various black nationalist groups that are springing up across the nation, the largest and best-known being Elijah Muhammad's Muslim movement. Nourished by the Negro's frustration over the continued existence of racial discrimination, this movement is made up of people who have lost faith in America, who have absolutely repudiated Christianity, and who have concluded that the white man is an incorrigible "devil."

I have tried to stand between these two forces, saying that we   28
need to emulate neither the "do-nothingism" of the complacent nor the hatred and despair of the black nationalist. For there is the more excellent way of love and nonviolent protest. I am grateful to God that, through the influence of the Negro church, the way of nonviolence became an integral part of our struggle.

29   If this philosophy had not emerged, by now many streets of the South would, I am convinced, be flowing with blood. And I am further convinced that if our white brothers dismiss as "rabble-rousers" and "outside agitators" those of us who employ nonviolent direct action, and if they refuse to support our nonviolent efforts, millions of Negroes will, out of frustration and despair, seek solace and security in black-nationalist ideologies—a development that would inevitably lead to a frightening racial nightmare.

30   Oppressed people cannot remain oppressed forever. The yearning for freedom eventually manifests itself, and that is what has happened to the American Negro. Something within has reminded him of his birthright of freedom, and something without has reminded him that it can be gained. Consciously or unconsciously, he has been caught up by the *Zeitgeist*, and with his black brothers of Africa and his brown and yellow brothers of Asia, South America and the Caribbean, the United States Negro is moving with a sense of great urgency toward the promised land of racial justice. If one recognizes this vital urge that has engulfed the Negro community, one should readily understand why public demonstrations are taking place. The Negro has many pent-up resentments and latent frustrations, and he must release them. So let him march; let him make prayer pilgrimages to the city hall; let him go on freedom rides—and try to understand why he must do so. If his repressed emotions are not released in nonviolent ways, they will seek expression through violence; this is not a threat but a fact of history. So I have not said to my people: "Get rid of your discontent." Rather, I have tried to say that this normal and healthy discontent can be channeled into the creative outlet of nonviolent direct action. And now this approach is being termed extremist.

31   But though I was initially disappointed at being categorized as an extremist, as I continued to think about the matter I gradually gained a measure of satisfaction from the label. Was not Jesus an extremist for love: "Love your enemies, bless them that curse you, do good to them that hate you, and pray for them which despitefully use you, and persecute you." Was not Amos an extremist for justice: "Let justice roll down like waters and righteousness like an ever-flowing stream." Was not Paul an extremist for the Christian gospel: "I bear in my body the marks of the Lord Jesus." Was not Martin Luther an extremist: "Here I stand; I cannot do otherwise, so help me God." And John Bunyan: "I will stay in jail to the end of my days before I make a butchery of my conscience." And Abraham Lincoln: "This nation cannot survive half slave and half free." And Thomas Jefferson: "We hold these truths to be self-evident, that all men are created equal . . ." So the question is not

whether we will be extremists, but what kind of extremists we will be. Will we be extremists for hate or for love? Will we be extremists for the preservation of injustice or for the extension of justice? In that dramatic scene on Calvary's hill three men were crucified. We must never forget that all three were crucified for the same crime—the crime of extremism. Two were extremists for immorality, and thus fell below their environment. The other, Jesus Christ, was an extremist for love, truth and goodness, and thereby rose above his environment. Perhaps the South, the nation and the world are in dire need of creative extremists.

I had hoped that the white moderate would see this need. Perhaps I was too optimistic; perhaps I expected too much. I suppose I should have realized that few members of the oppressor race can understand the deep groans and passionate yearnings of the oppressed race, and still fewer have the vision to see that injustice must be rooted out by strong, persistent and determined action. I am thankful, however, that some of our white brothers in the South have grasped the meaning of this social revolution and committed themselves to it. They are still all too few in quantity, but they are big in quality. Some—such as Ralph McGill, Lillian Smith, Harry Golden, James McBride Dabbs, Ann Braden and Sarah Patton Boyle—have written about our struggle in eloquent and prophetic terms. Others have marched with us down nameless streets of the South. They have languished in filthy, roach-infested jails, suffering the abuse and brutality of policemen who view them as "dirty nigger-lovers." Unlike so many of their moderate brothers and sisters, they have recognized the urgency of the moment and sensed the need for powerful "action" antidotes to combat the disease of segregation. 32

Let me take note of my other major disappointment. I have been so greatly disappointed with the white church and its leadership. Of course, there are some notable exceptions. I am not unmindful of the fact that each of you has taken some significant stands on this issue. I commend you, Reverend Stallings, for your Christian stand on this past Sunday, in welcoming Negroes to your worship service on a nonsegregated basis. I commend the Catholic leaders of this state for integrating Spring Hill College several years ago. 33

But despite these notable exceptions, I must honestly reiterate that I have been disappointed with the church. I do not say this as one of those negative critics who can always find something wrong with the church. I say this as a minister of the gospel, who loves the church; who was nurtured in its bosom; who has been sustained by its spiritual blessings and who will remain true to it as long as the cord of life shall lengthen. 34

35   When I was suddenly catapulted into the leadership of the bus protest in Montgomery, Alabama, a few years ago, I felt we would be supported by the white church. I felt that the white ministers, priests and rabbis of the South would be among our strongest allies. Instead, some have been outright opponents, refusing to understand the freedom movement and misrepresenting its leaders; all too many others have been more cautious than courageous and have remained silent behind the anesthetizing security of stained-glass windows.

36   In spite of my shattered dreams, I came to Birmingham with the hope that the white religious leaders of this community would see the justice of our cause and, with deep moral concern, would serve as the channel through which our just grievances could reach the power structure. I had hoped that each of you would understand. But again I have been disappointed.

37   I have heard numerous southern religious leaders admonish their worshipers to comply with a desegregation decision because it is the law, but I have longed to hear white ministers declare: "Follow this decree because integration is morally right and because the Negro is your brother." In the midst of blatant injustices inflicted upon the Negro, I have watched white churchmen stand on the sideline and mouth pious irrelevancies and sanctimonious trivialities. In the midst of a mighty struggle to rid our nation of racial and economic injustice, I have heard many ministers say: "Those are social issues, with which the gospel has no real concern." And I have watched many churches commit themselves to a completely otherworldly religion which makes a strange, un-Biblical distinction between body and soul, between the sacred and the secular.

38   I have traveled the length and breadth of Alabama, Mississippi and all the other southern states. On sweltering summer days and crisp autumn mornings I have looked at the South's beautiful churches with their lofty spires pointing heavenward. I have beheld the impressive outlines of her massive religious-education buildings. Over and over I have found myself asking: "What kind of people worship here? Who is their God? Where were their voices when the lips of Governor Barnett dripped with words of interposition and nullification? Where were they when Governor Wallace gave a clarion call for defiance and hatred? Where were their voices of support when bruised and weary Negro men and women decided to rise from the dark dungeons of complacency to the bright hills of creative protest?"

39   Yes, these questions are still in my mind. In deep disappointment I have wept over the laxity of the church. But be assured that my tears have been tears of love. There can be no deep disappointment where

there is not deep love. Yes, I love the church. How could I do otherwise? I am in the rather unique position of being the son, the grandson
and the greatgrandson of preachers. Yes, I see the church as the body
of Christ. But, oh! How we have blemished and scarred that body
through social neglect and through fear of being nonconformists.

There was a time when the church was very powerful—in the   40
time when the early Christians rejoiced at being deemed worthy to suffer for what they believed. In those days the church was not merely a
thermometer that recorded the ideas and principles of popular opinion; it was a thermostat that transformed the mores of society. Whenever the early Christians entered a town, the people in power became
disturbed and immediately sought to convict the Christians for being
"disturbers of the peace" and "outside agitators." But the Christians
pressed on, in the conviction that they were a "colony of heaven,"
called to obey God rather than man. Small in number, they were big in
commitment. They were too God-intoxicated to be "astronomically
intimidated." By their effort and example they brought an end to such
ancient evils as infanticide and gladiatorial contests.

Things are different now. So often the contemporary church is a   41
weak, ineffectual voice with an uncertain sound. So often it is an arch-
defender of the status quo. Far from being disturbed by the presence
of the church, the power structure of the average community is con-
soled by the church's silent—and often even vocal—sanction of things
as they are.

But the judgment of God is upon the church as never before. If   42
today's church does not recapture the sacrificial spirit of the early
church, it will lose its authenticity, forfeit the loyalty of millions, and
be dismissed as an irrelevant social club with no meaning for the
twentieth century. Every day I meet young people whose disappointment with the church has turned into outright disgust.

Perhaps I have once again been too optimistic. Is organized religion   43
too inextricably bound to the status quo to save our nation and the
world? Perhaps I must turn my faith to the inner spiritual church,
the church within the church, as the true *ekklesia* and the hope of the
world. But again I am thankful to God that some noble souls from
the ranks of organized religion have broken loose from the paralyzing
chains of conformity and joined us as active partners in the struggle
for freedom. They have left their secure congregations and walked the
streets of Albany, Georgia, with us. They have gone down the highways
of the South on tortuous rides for freedom. Yes, they have gone to
jail with us. Some have been dismissed from their churches, have
lost the support of their bishops and fellow ministers. But they have

acted in the faith that right defeated is stronger than evil triumphant. Their witness has been the spiritual salt that has preserved the true meaning of the gospel in these troubled times. They have carved a tunnel of hope through the dark mountain of disappointment.

44   I hope the church as a whole will meet the challenge of this decisive hour. But even if the church does not come to the aid of justice, I have no despair about the future. I have no fear about the outcome of our struggle in Birmingham, even if our motives are at present misunderstood. We will reach the goal of freedom in Birmingham and all over the nation, because the goal of America is freedom. Abused and scorned though we may be, our destiny is tied up with America's destiny. Before the pilgrims landed at Plymouth, we were here. Before the pen of Jefferson etched the majestic words of the Declaration of Independence across the pages of history, we were here. For more than two centuries our forebears labored in this country without wages; they made cotton king; they built the homes of their masters while suffering gross injustice and shameful humiliation—and yet out of a bottomless vitality they continued to thrive and develop. If the inexpressible cruelties of slavery could not stop us, the opposition we now face will surely fail. We will win our freedom because the sacred heritage of our nation and the eternal will of God are embodied in our echoing demands.

45   Before closing I feel impelled to mention one other point in your statement that has troubled me profoundly. You warmly commended the Birmingham police force for keeping "order" and "preventing violence." I doubt that you would have so warmly commended the police force if you had seen its dogs sinking their teeth into unarmed, nonviolent Negroes. I doubt that you would so quickly commend the policemen if you were to observe their ugly and inhumane treatment of Negroes here in the city jail; if you were to watch them push and curse old Negro women and young Negro girls; if you were to see them slap and kick old Negro men and young boys; if you were to observe them, as they did on two occasions, refuse to give us food because we wanted to sing our grace together. I cannot join you in your praise of the Birmingham Police Department.

46   It is true that the police have exercised a degree of discipline in handling the demonstrators. In this sense they have conducted themselves rather "nonviolently" in public. But for what purpose? To preserve the evil system of segregation. Over the past few years I have consistently preached that nonviolence demands that the means we use must be as pure as the ends we seek. I have tried to make clear that it is wrong to use immoral means to attain moral ends. But now I must

affirm that it is just as wrong, or perhaps even more so, to use moral means to preserve immoral ends. Perhaps Mr. Connor and his policemen have been rather nonviolent in public, as was Chief Pritchett in Albany, Georgia, but they have used the moral means of nonviolence to maintain the immoral end of racial injustice. As T. S. Eliot has said: "The last temptation is the greatest treason: To do the right deed for the wrong reason."

I wish you had commended the Negro sit-inners and demon-   47
strators of Birmingham for their sublime courage, their willingness to suffer and their amazing discipline in the midst of great provocation. One day the South will recognize its real heroes. They will be the James Merediths, with the noble sense of purpose that enables them to face jeering and hostile mobs, and with the agonizing loneliness that characterizes the life of the pioneer. They will be old, oppressed, battered Negro women, symbolized in a seventy-two-year-old-woman in Montgomery, Alabama, who rose up with a sense of dignity and with her people decided not to ride segregated buses, and who responded with ungrammatical profundity to one who inquired about her weariness: "My feets is tired, but my soul is at rest." They will be the young high school and college students, the young ministers of the gospel and a host of their elders, courageously and nonviolently sitting in at lunch counters and willingly going to jail for conscience sake. One day the South will know that when these disinherited children of God sat down at lunch counters, they were in reality standing up for what is best in the American dream and for the most sacred values in our Judaeo-Christian heritage, thereby bringing our nation back to those great wells of democracy which were dug deep by the founding fathers in their formulation of the Constitution and the Declaration of Independence.

Never before have I written so long a letter. I'm afraid it is much   48
too long to take your precious time. I can assure you that it would have been much shorter if I had been writing from a comfortable desk, but what else can one do when he is alone in a narrow cell, other than write long letters, think long thoughts and pray long prayers?

If I have said anything in this letter that overstates the truth and   49
indicates an unreasonable impatience, I beg you to forgive me. If I have said anything that understates the truth and indicates my having a patience that allows me to settle for anything less than brotherhood, I beg God to forgive me.

I hope this letter finds you strong in the faith. I also hope that cir-   50
cumstances will soon make it possible for me to meet each of you, not as an integrationist or a civil-rights leader but as a fellow clergyman

and a Christian brother. Let us all hope that the dark clouds of racial prejudice will soon pass away and the deep fog of misunderstanding will be lifted from our fear-drenched communities, and in some not too distant tomorrow the radiant stars of love and brotherhood will shine over our great nation with all their scintillating beauty.

Yours for the cause of Peace and Brotherhood,
Martin Luther King, Jr.

▶ QUESTIONS TO CONSIDER

1. Although Martin Luther King, Jr., was well known to the clergymen he was writing, they did not perceive him as a reasonable man who was acting wisely. Thus, King attempts in this letter to convince his readers he is credible—that his actions were not "untimely and unwise" as they have charged. How does King accomplish this goal? Does the fact he is in jail argue for or against his credibility? Why, or why not?

2. King systematically refutes each of the clergymen's claims: (1) that he is an outsider who should not have been involved, (2) that the demonstrations were "untimely," and (3) that they were "unwise." What arguments does he use to refute each of these claims? How effective are his arguments?

CAUSE AND EFFECT, PAGE 522

CLASSIFICATION, PAGE 527

COMPARISON/CONTRAST, PAGE 542

DEFINITION, PAGE 560

DESCRIPTION, PAGE 565

EXEMPLIFICATION, PAGE 574

NARRATION, PAGE 618

3. King uses several different methods of development in his letter. Identify examples of the following methods: **cause and effect, classification, comparison/contrast, definition, description, exemplification,** and **narration**.

4. Although he is writing to people who disapprove of what he has done, King does not treat them as adversaries. Rather, he repeatedly attempts to identify with them and to point out areas of consensus. Identify several of these attempts.

5. Although King's tone is generally reasonable and even objective, there are times when he becomes impassioned. Reread paragraphs 14 and 29–30. In those passages, King makes strong emotional appeals. To what emotions is he appealing? How effective are these appeals? Would they be equally effective if they were not balanced by his appeals to reason and by his efforts to establish his own credibility?

6. How does King distinguish between just and unjust laws? Do you accept his distinction? Does this distinction help readers to recog-

nize and question the unspoken assumption that *all* laws are just? Is this strategy effective in supporting his primary assertion that the demonstrations were not untimely or unwise?

7. Which of King's appeals—to reason, emotion, or his own credibility—do you find most persuasive? Why?

WRITING ACTIVITIES

Individual: In a journal entry, answer King's question: "How does one determine whether a law is just or unjust?"

Collaborative: Make a list of the underlying assumptions upon which King bases his argument that the civil rights movement is the best way to avoid violent racial strife. Then decide which of these assumptions you accept and which you reject. Support your decisions.

Computer (1): Type King's last paragraph into a computer file. Rewrite the paragraph in an objective, matter-of-fact style, eliminating the colorful language and imagery of the original. Compare your rewrite with those of your peers and with the original, focusing especially on differences in style and tone.

Computer (2): Write a letter in which you address an audience you know is hostile to your position on some issue. Post the letter to your computer network to get feedback on your effort.

▶ W R I T I N G   T O   P E R S U A D E

When you write to persuade, you are attempting to convince your reader of something: that Reeboks are the best athletic shoes, that John F. Kennedy was or was not assassinated by Lee Harvey Oswald, that college entrance exams are unfair, that a local recycling program is needed. Whatever the issue, if you want to persuade your readers, you must do four things:

1. Construct logical arguments supported by evidence your reader will find convincing.

2. Use emotional appeals that predispose your reader to agree with your position.

3. Convince your reader that you are a credible person.

4. Refute opposing arguments.

Constructing Logical Arguments

Although all writing can be viewed as persuasive, writing that is primarily persuasive usually takes the form of an argument. That is, the writer makes an assertion (a statement that is possible or even probable but that is open to question or debate) and then supports it, presenting evidence to establish the validity of the assertion.

For example, you might assert that more women should be elected to Congress. You could support this assertion by arguing that

1. More than half of the population of the United States is female; therefore, at least half the congressional representatives should be female.

2. Men have not done a very good job in running the country, so women should be given a chance.

3. Women are more likely to compromise and negotiate than men and would be able, therefore, to reach consensus and pass legislation more often.

4. The women who have previously served in Congress have good records of achievement.

5. Women are less aggressive than men and thus would be less likely to get the country into a war.

6. Men have been in control long enough; it's time to give women their chance.

Although some of these reasons are clearly better than others, they all support the assertion that more women should be elected to Congress.

Notice that each of these supporting statements is another assertion that must in turn be supported. For example, you would need to provide evidence to support your assertion that previously elected female representatives have been effective. You could cite their good attendance records, the number of times they have been reelected, or the bills they have introduced that have become laws. To support your assertion that female representatives would be less likely to involve the nation in war, you could cite genetic studies indicating that males are typically more aggressive than females or law enforcement statistics showing that males commit more acts of physical aggression than females.

A good argument is erected by slowly and carefully supporting each assertion, one after another, until you have built a well-constructed, interlocking network of arguments. Thus, when you write to persuade, you make a single *primary* assertion, support it with secondary assertions, and in turn support them with examples and evidence. Each assertion must be supported by other assertions that must also be supported. In an effective argument, the secondary arguments ultimately convince your reader of the validity of your primary assertion.

Using Emotional Appeals

The arguments that you construct should be based primarily on logic—on reasonable conclusions a reader can draw on the basis of the evidence you have presented. But arguments can also be supported by emotional appeals. For example, in supporting the assertion that more females should be elected to Congress, you could appeal to your readers' sense of fairness, arguing that for women not to be equally represented is unfair, since they constitute more than half the population. You could also describe the position of women both today and historically as second-class citizens who have never been treated fairly. Or, becoming even more obviously emotional, you could characterize women as mother figures who want to nurture the nation as a whole but whose efforts have been rejected.

Emotional appeals work best not as your main supporting arguments, but rather as part of those arguments. If you use reasonable arguments to support your main assertion, you can then introduce an emotional appeal effectively as part of that argument. For example, Martin Luther King, Jr., uses increasingly more emotional appeals in his "Letter from Birmingham Jail." Beginning with comparatively dispassionate arguments about social justice and the nature of law, King progresses to this final restrained but impassioned statement: "Let us all hope that the dark clouds of racial prejudice will soon pass away and the deep fog of misunderstanding will be lifted from our fear-drenched communities, and in some not too distant tomorrow the radiant stars of love and brotherhood will shine over our great nation with all their scintillating beauty." Here King is appealing to his reader's best instincts rather than to logic.

A fine line separates an effective, legitimate emotional appeal from one that clearly tries to play on the reader's emotions. It is usually better to use subtle and restrained emotional appeals, merely suggesting an appropriate emotional response rather than crudely evoking it. Arguments won solely on the basis of inappropriate emotional appeals do little to help people work out satisfactory solutions to problems. Pictures of dead fetuses and accounts of women butchered by illegal abortionists have probably not advanced either side of the abortion debate, for example, and certainly have not lessened the ugly conflicts characterizing that volatile issue.

Establishing Your Credibility

You will also want to support your arguments by establishing your own credibility as a person whose words can be trusted. Three qualities can help establish this type of confidence:

❖ Be well informed.

❖ Be accurate.

❖ Be reasonable.

BE WELL INFORMED.   Accurate, pertinent, clear information is one of the most compelling forms of evidence you can use to support your assertions. The information must, of course, be directly related to the assertion you are making. You support your arguments by providing your readers with the appropriate information and then, if necessary, explaining the relationship between the information and your assertion. For example, in supporting the assertion that more females should be elected to Congress, you might provide your readers with statistical information about how many females now serve in Congress, what the total population of the United States is, and what percentage of that population is female. Then you could discuss the relationship among these statistical data, explaining how they support your assertion.

All of the writers included in this chapter depend on information to support their assertions. Rebecca Williams gives very specific information about a beauty pageant to prove that such contests are not what they appear to be. Susan Faludi cites statistical misinformation to prove her point that day care has been unjustly maligned. Lewis Thomas uses information derived from his own observations of nature and life to argue that the last stage of dying is probably painless and, thus, natural. You will probably research some of the information you use, but much of it will come from your own experiences and observations. In fact, most writers do not write about a subject unless they have some information of their own to contribute (see Part 3, Strategies and Resources for Research).

BE ACCURATE.   Whatever the source of your information, be sure it is accurate. Nothing destroys your credibility as completely as being wrong. If you are not sure of the information you are using, try to verify it. Then, if you are still not convinced of its accuracy, don't include it—or, at least, qualify it appropriately. Qualifiers such as *approximately, usually, in general, sometimes,* and *often* can help you make the point you want to make without running the risk of being inaccurate.

Another way of being accurate is to define any terms you use that are subject to various interpretations or that might be misunderstood. You and your reader should agree as completely as possible about what you mean when you use such terms as *day care, child abuse, equality,* or *natural death.* If readers do not understand your particular use of a term, even if they are familiar with its general definition, they may not know if they agree with you or not. Precise, accurate definitions are an important part of any argument (see **definition**).

DEFINITION, PAGE 560

BE REASONABLE.   Impassioned arguments, often dramatic, can be effective when the writer's passion is anchored in reason. However, they are seldom convincing when they become overly dramatic or when a writer becomes so impassioned that he or she becomes unreasonable or even aggressive. Just as listeners do not usually respond well to being yelled at, readers do not respond well to the written equivalent of yelling—to insistent, hysterical, unreasonable verbal aggression. Martin Luther King, Jr., is quietly impassioned in his "Letter from Birmingham Jail," but he is even more clearly reasonable and courteous in what he says and how he says it. A writer's credibility depends to a great extent on the reader's perception of him or her as a reasonable person, one who weighs evidence, takes a balanced view, and sees both sides.

One of the most effective ways to establish yourself as reasonable is to acknowledge opposing arguments, treating them with respect even as you refute them, as King does in his letter to the clergymen. Scorn, sarcasm, and harsh criticism usually alienate readers rather than convince them. Your goal in persuasive writing should be to prove your own point—not by convincing your readers that they are wrong, but by persuading them that your own argument is superior. One way to do this is related to an approach to therapy developed by a noted psychologist, Carl Rogers. Rogers encouraged therapists to create an environment favorable to successful therapy by acknowledging and accepting clients' feelings before trying to convince them to change those feelings. You can use the same strategy successfully when you are writing to persuade. By establishing common ground, accepting other views, compromising on key issues, and acknowledging the validity of other positions, you convince readers who would otherwise remain resistant and alienated. For example, when David Gelernter writes to persuade us that computers in the classroom may contribute to students' illiteracy rather than to their education, he first acknowledges that computers "have the potential to accomplish great things" in subjects like music or art, which focus on sound or image.

Remember, writing to persuade is not like a football game. You don't win by just beating your opponents. Rather, you work toward consensus—negotiating with your readers, sometimes refuting their arguments but also sometimes compromising with their position.

Refuting Opposing Arguments

It is not enough simply to make assertions, even if you do support them adequately. At times you must also acknowledge and refute opposing arguments. Especially if you are arguing against conventional wisdom—what most people accept as true—the burden of proof is on you. Thus, you need to acknowledge the prevailing viewpoint and in many cases to argue against it. For example, most people assume that diagnosing a disease early is an advantage in treating it, but the following argument acknowledges and refutes that assumption:

> . . . it's useful to look at a few common biases that complicate the issue of early detection.
> The first is lead-time bias—the assumption that catching a disease early in its existence will necessarily affect its rate of

progress. This is sometimes true and sometimes not. Let's assume you have a disease that usually kills you eight years after it starts. If we diagnose the disease in the fifth year, you'll live three years after the diagnosis. If we diagnose it in the third year, you'll live five years—and we gleefully proclaim that our early diagnosis has given you a longer survival span. Actually, it hasn't—it's just given you a longer time to know you've got the disease, which may or may not be a benefit. So just looking at years of survival after diagnosis isn't enough—we need to know how many people actually die of the disease with and without early detection.

> Susan M. Love, *Dr. Susan Love's Breast Book*,
> 2nd ed. (Reading, MA: Addison-Wesley, 1995),
> pp. 250–51.

If you fail to confront obvious opposing viewpoints, your own arguments will be suspect even if they are strong. But be sure you focus on opposing arguments rather than on the character of your opponents. Calling your opponents names or attacking them personally will only decrease your own credibility. In contrast, acknowledging that other viewpoints exist and refuting them with convincing counterarguments will strengthen your position and increase your credibility.

In acknowledging opposing viewpoints, however, you must be careful to focus clearly on your own. You will usually acknowledge other positions primarily by evaluating their strengths and weaknesses. Or you can point out the similarity between an opposing position and your own to create some common ground. In some instances, you may even want to devote more space to opposing positions, as Susan Faludi does; but be sure if you adopt this strategy that you are clearly refuting these arguments. Acknowledge other positions, establish common ground and points of consensus, even be generous, but keep the focus on your own arguments. Your readers should always know which side you are on.

If readers perceive you as a reasonable person, willing to see both sides of an issue but ready to defend your own position, you will probably have some effect on their convictions and possibly even their actions. But don't expect too much. Most arguments are neither won completely nor lost completely; small gains are what you can realistically expect.

The Role of a Thesis in Writing to Persuade

When you are writing to persuade, your primary assertion is, in effect, your thesis. Just as a thesis helps you to focus and organize your information when you write to inform or to solve problems, a thesis will help you produce a more unified, coherent text when you write to persuade. However, when your primary purpose is to persuade, your thesis must be more clearly argumentative. Thus, the thesis of a persuasive text is often referred to as an assertion.

Your primary assertion, or thesis, can simply be that whatever you are writing about is not what it is commonly supposed to be. However, a stronger argument can be built if you make a more specific statement about your topic. For example, Rebecca Williams does not just say that beauty contests are not what they appear to be; she also states clearly that beauty contests are primarily businesses that sacrifice honesty and the well-being of contestants to the profit motive. It is this idea of the beauty contest as a money-making proposition that gives her essay a clear focus.

An argumentative thesis usually presents its assertion as (1) controversial and/or (2) problematic:

❖ A controversial statement is one that not everyone is likely to agree with. David Gelernter's assertion that "computers make our worst educational nightmares come true" is a strong argumentative thesis because it creates a controversy: Most people assume that computers *are* an aid to learning.

❖ Experienced writers often emphasize the controversial nature of their argument by pointing out that it is contrary to popular belief or counterintuitive; in other words, it is problematic. The theme of this chapter, perception versus reality, is a convention experienced writers frequently use to frame an argument as problematic. They do this by contrasting their viewpoint to the myths, lies, illusions, misperceptions, legends, or conventional wisdom reflected in some other viewpoint.

Patterns of Development in Writing to Persuade

You can use several different methods of development in writing to persuade. In fact, experienced writers often use more than one method in supporting a single assertion. The web of arguments you weave—primary assertion supported by other assertions, which must in turn be supported and amplified by details and evidence—is largely composed of combinations of different methods of development.

COMPARISON/CONTRAST. For example, you could begin by comparing your perspective to a common perception or misperception. You might use other comparisons as you develop your arguments. For example, to argue that college athletes are abused, rather than privileged students, you might compare them to music majors (who are similarly over-scheduled) or contrast them with students who have a very light schedule. Or you might compare athletes to the gladiators of ancient Rome, who were exploited for the pleasure of those who watched them perform.

Comparing or contrasting your subject to something else allows you to establish connections in the mind of your reader—to control the associations that the reader will make. Showing points of comparison between today's and ancient Rome's gladiators, who were clearly abused for the entertainment of others strengthens your argument that college athletes are abused. This comparison may be doubly effective, because it can appeal to your readers' emotions as well as their sense of logic. Avoid comparisons, or analogies, that are false.

To be effective, a comparison must be appropriate and reasonable. You can justifiably compare college athletes to gladiators, even though there are significant differences between the two, because gladiators and college athletes are alike in that both participate in athletic contests. Comparing college athletes to slaves or women would not be as effective, even though it can be argued that, like athletes, they have often been abused or sacrificed for the pleasure of others. In other words, be sure there is a fundamental similarity between your subject and whatever you are comparing or contrasting it to. Also, consider carefully the connotations and associations that the comparison is likely to evoke in your reader. You want the comparison to work for, not against, your argument (see **comparison/contrast**).

COMPARISON/CONTRAST, PAGE 542

CAUSE AND EFFECT.   Cause and effect development can also be used effectively in writing to persuade. Arguing that something will have certain consequences (effects), either good or bad, can be very persuasive. For example, you could argue that continued abuse of college athletes will not only hurt individual athletes but also eventually hurt an athletic program. Then, of course, you would have to support this assertion also. One of the ways you could do this is to provide examples of athletic programs that have suffered because their athletes failed to pass and were ineligible to play, because they dropped out of school due to financial problems, or because they did not perform well as a result of pressure (see **cause and effect**).

CAUSE AND EFFECT, PAGE 522

Avoid suggesting cause-and-effect relationships where none exist. It is easy but simplistic and inaccurate to suggest that because one thing occurred before something else, there is a causal rather than simply temporal relationship between the two. For example, government spending for welfare programs has increased in recent years, and the condition of the underclass has worsened. Thus, you could argue that the condition of the underclass has worsened *because* government spending for welfare has increased, but this would be an invalid argument. There are simply too many other factors that must be considered. You might logically argue that increased government spending does not seem to have improved the condition of the underclass, but you should not argue that is has contributed to the problem. Just because two things occur together in a temporal sequence does not necessarily mean that a causal relationship exists between them.

NARRATION AND DESCRIPTION.   You could also support your assertion about the consequences of continued abuse of college athletes by using narration or description. You could, for example, describe in detail the effects that these abuses have on the athletes themselves or the program in general. Or you could tell a story, either true or hypothetical, about a single athlete or a single program (see **narration** and **description**).

NARRATION, PAGE 618

DESCRIPTION, PAGE 565

▶ W R I T I N G   A S S I G N M E N T

For this writing assignment, you are to persuade your readers that something is not as it appears to be. Like the authors of this chapter's reading selections, argue against a popular perception, a myth, or an accepted view of what seems to be. You might focus on the difference between television ads and real-life situations, between storybook romances and actual male-female relationships, or between political promises and what really happens when a politician is elected. Your purpose will be to persuade your readers that your viewpoint is more honest and accurate than some other viewpoint.

The following suggestions may help you discover a subject that interests you:

1. Argue that college is not what you were led to expect.

2. Argue that your generation is not as it is generally perceived.

3. Argue for or against an institution or policy that is under attack (welfare, public education, gun control, etc.).

4. Rewrite an essay you wrote for a previous assignment so that it becomes a persuasive text. For example, you might argue that a change you wrote about in Chapter 5 does not really represent a drastic departure from what existed before.

5. Argue against the idea that we have no modern heroes or that females are less often heroic figures than are males.

6. Argue that something generally perceived as good (technology, a college education, marriage, wealth, a long life, etc.) is really bad.

Generating Ideas through Invention and Research

To find something you can write about comfortably and competently, you may first need to spend some time gaining additional perspectives on the issue you are writing about or researching your subject.

INVENTION.   In every argument, there are at least two sides. Being able to look at a subject or issue from multiple perspectives is especially useful in writing to persuade. If you see an issue from only one perspective, you will find it difficult to persuade an audience composed of readers who have different perspectives. To gain additional perspectives on the subject you have chosen, examine it from the following perspectives:

1. *Time*—Examine your topic from different time frames: past, present, and future. For example, suppose you are an athlete and think you might want to write about why college athletes do not actually have the privileged positions they are thought to hold. Think about your perspective in the past, before you became a college athlete, your perspective now, and how your perspective is likely to change in the future.

2. *Point of view*—Think about your topic from other people's points of view. Suppose you are writing about welfare. How would a person on welfare view this issue as opposed to someone who has a secure living and pays a lot of taxes? How would a social worker or a person employed in a welfare office view this issue? Imagine your subject from as many different points of view as you can imagine.

3. *Distance*—Imagine your issue as it appears from a great distance, so that only the general outline is apparent. Then think of it as a close-up, in which you cannot see the general form or shape but can only focus on specific, discrete details. For example, if you are writing about your generation, try to imagine it as it might appear to a historian writing centuries later or to an alien from another planet. Then think about your generation in terms of the details or specific features that characterize it.

RESEARCH.   You should choose a topic you know something about rather than something about which you merely have a strong opinion. Otherwise, you risk producing a very general and superficial text.

Unless you have had some firsthand experience with guns or abortion, for example, your essay on gun control or banning abortions would probably be little more than an academic exercise.

In addition to having personal experience and/or basic information to begin with, you may want to research your subject by reading, questioning, observing, or interviewing. Experienced writers nearly always include some evidence derived from other sources—a quotation from an authority in the field, an interview with someone with firsthand experience, or a survey that confirms their findings. The library is always a good place to begin your research, but you may also want to write letters of inquiry, conduct interviews or observations, or gather data with questionnaires.

Drafting Your Text

Once you have a hypothesis, or tentative thesis, in mind for your argument, have identified several supporting arguments, and have collected information to use as evidence in your supporting arguments, you are ready to begin drafting. As you write your initial draft, try to include as much information as possible, for information is your most compelling evidence. Don't just mention a piece of information; give your readers details—lots of specific, concrete, abundant details. For example, don't just say that athletes are overscheduled; provide a full schedule of a day in the life of a typical college athlete—a blow-by-blow, minute-by-minute account of classes, practices, study halls, squad or team meetings, and visits to the trainer's room.

The arguments you present will be only as strong as the detailed information you include to support them. Merely asserting that college athletes are overstressed, overscheduled, and overrated is not enough. You must convince your readers that your assertions are valid, and abundant information is the best way to accomplish that goal.

Reading and Revising Your Text

Reading your own efforts to persuade is often like patting yourself on the back. Your arguments reflect your own convictions, so when you read them it is difficult not to find them convincing. They will make perfect sense to you, especially if you read them just after you have written them. However, if you let some time lapse before reading the draft you have constructed and read it with specific purposes in mind, you should be able to evaluate it more objectively.

1. Read it once to evaluate the balance of emotional and logical arguments you have used. Remember that logical arguments should

dominate but that subtle, indirect emotional arguments can also be effective.

2. Read it again focusing on the persona you have created in your text. Just how credible will a reader find you as a writer on this particular subject? Have you attempted to create a climate of consensus in your text by identifying points of agreement and acknowledging the validity of other views?

3. Read it once more to identify the implicit assumptions on which your assertions rest. One way to accomplish this is to make a list of each assertion included in your text and then write beside it the assumption(s) implied by the assertion. For example, if you argue that female athletes are not valued by your school, you are assuming that athletes should be valued and that females should be valued equally with males. Are you sure that your readers will share these assumptions? Weak arguments are often those that assume too much—that fail to articulate and support all of the assumptions made by the writer.

4. Finally, read it one last time with this question in mind: So what? If you are not making an assertion that matters, one way or the other, you are wasting not only your time but your readers' time.

You may have discovered in these successive readings a number of weak links in the chain of assertions and support you have constructed thus far. Now, as you begin to revise your essay, is the time to strengthen those weaknesses—to create a tightly constructed, well-balanced, and clearly focused argument.

We suggest that you begin the revision process by outlining your text. Your outline (an informal one) should reveal not only the organization of your text but also the basic links between assertions and support. Begin by writing your thesis—the primary assertion you are making—at the top of a sheet of paper or your computer screen. Beneath this primary assertion, list each supporting argument. Then beneath each supporting argument, indicate the evidence or support you have included. Whether the resulting outline looks like a simple list, a tree diagram, or a flow chart, it should indicate the order in which you present each argument and the evidence and/or secondary assertions you are using to construct each argument.

In addition, you can use the following questions to evaluate your arguments and guide your revision:

1. Do I define key terms clearly?

2. Do I base my conclusions on sufficient evidence and appropriately qualified generalizations?

3. Do I acknowledge the complexity of the issues and avoid over-simplifying the situation?

4. Do I establish legitimate cause-and-effect relationships and avoid assuming causal relationships where none exist?

5. Do I use statistics, examples, and anecdotal evidence responsibly and avoid half-truths or information that is not in context?

6. Do I use analogies that are appropriate and accurate and avoid false analogies?

7. Do I focus on issues rather than on the character of my opponents?

8. Do I effectively refute opposing viewpoints?

Preparing the Final Draft of Your Text

Because your credibility is so important when you write to persuade, you should edit your text carefully. Correctness in spelling, punctuation, and usage may seem irrelevant in persuading someone that your assertion is valid. However, observing the conventions of standard language usage can be important to establishing your credibility. Most readers will expect you to spell correctly, punctuate sentences correctly, use verbs correctly, and so on, and those who do will find you less convincing if you do not meet these expectations. It is much easier for a reader who is not in agreement with you to spot a misspelled word than to refute your argument. So don't sabotage your own arguments by discrediting yourself as a careful, knowledgeable writer.

The errors that are listed here are particularly damaging to reader confidence:

SPELLING ERRORS.   If you are using a computer, be sure to use a spell-check program. If not, verify the spelling of any word that you are not absolutely sure you have spelled correctly.

SENTENCE BOUNDARY ERRORS.   You can often detect fragments and run-on sentences if you read your text backward, sentence by sentence, so that you are examining the sentences out of their usual order.

A simple test that sometimes helps identify fragments is to add a tag question to each sentence.

> **Example:** College athletes often drop out of school after a single semester—don't they?

If the resulting construction (sentence plus tag question) makes sense, then the sentence is probably not a fragment. For example, try to add tag questions to the following fragments.

1. Dropping out of school after an initial semester characterized by frustration, exhaustion, and failure.

2. If athletes were told in advance what to expect—how much time, physical effort, and energy would be required of them.

3. An outstanding athlete, one who performs brilliantly time after time under incredible pressure and with very little financial reward.

Run-on, or fused, sentences can be more difficult to recognize, but it sometimes helps to identify all of the nominative case personal pronouns (*I, we, you, he, she, it, they*) you have used. Run-on sentences often occur when the second sentence begins with a personal pronoun.

Example: The student entered the class late *she* took a seat near the door.

You can correct this error in any of the following ways:

1. The student entered the class late. She took a seat near the door.

2. The student entered the class late; she took a seat near the door.

3. The student entered the class late and took a seat near the door.

4. The student entered the class late, and she took a seat near the door.

5. Because the student entered the class late, she took a seat near the door.

6. Entering the class late, the student took a seat near the door.

Another word to look for in identifying run-on sentences is *then*. This little word is often used to begin a new sentence, or independent clause, as in the example below.

Example: Athletes have to make all of the adjustments typical of college freshmen *then* they must also adjust to the very stressful world of college athletics.

Then is a conjunctive adverb (like *however, therefore,* and *consequently*) rather than a coordinating conjunction (like *and, but,* and *so*). When it is used to introduce an independent clause, it must either follow a semicolon or begin a new sentence.

> **Example:** Athletes have to make all of the adjustments typical of college freshmen; then they must also adjust to the very stressful world of college athletics.
>
> **Example:** Athletes have to make all of the adjustments typical of college freshmen. Then they must also adjust to the very stressful world of college athletics.

AGREEMENT ERRORS.   In the world of edited American English, subjects must agree with verbs and pronouns must agree with antecedents in both number and case. Number refers to singular and plural. Case refers to the function of a word—whether it is used as a subject or an object (*they* versus *them* and *who* versus *whom*). If you know you have not mastered these conventions, proofread your text carefully to identify the subject and verb of each independent clause in your text. If you are not sure about their agreement, ask your teacher or someone else whose mastery of these conventions you trust. You can then do the same with the pronouns in your text. Underline each pronoun, and identify its antecedent and its case function. You can then ask someone if any pronouns seem problematic.

LACK OF CONSISTENCY.   Unnecessary shifts in tense and point of view distract readers. Be sure that if you begin in the present tense, for example, you don't needlessly and illogically shift to the past tense. Similarly, if you begin with a third-person point of view (*he, she, it,* and *they*), don't suddenly shift to second person (*you, your, yours*). Change tense and point of view only if a change is justified and logical. To illustrate, if you include a narrative example in which something took place in the past, you will logically shift to the past tense. But avoid unnecessary, illogical shifts. Errors, especially those we have discussed, can distract a reader and damage your credibility. Learning to edit carefully can, therefore, make your arguments more persuasive. Here is valuable general advice about editing:

1. Be aware of the types of errors you are likely to make, and look especially for these when you edit.

2. Take the time to edit and proofread carefully (everyone makes errors, but careful writers take the time and care to look for errors and correct them).

3. Seek assistance when you need it.

The most effective way of improving your editing skills is to edit your own text carefully. Identifying your own errors and learning how to correct them will eventually result in your learning the correct conventions (see **revising and editing** and **proofreading**).

REVISING AND EDITING, PAGE 651

PROOFREADING, PAGE 643

DISCOVERING YOURSELF AS A WRITER

After you have completed this assignment, take a few minutes to reflect on this writing experience by answering the following questions:

1. What did you learn about yourself as a writer as you worked on this assignment? In what way did this writing experience change your perception of yourself as a writer, your process of writing, or your attitude toward writing?

2. What forms of research did you use for this assignment? What did you learn about research that will help you in other writing assignments?

3. Was the final draft of your text better or worse than you had expected? What would you do differently if you had the opportunity to do this assignment again?

4. How did writing this assignment make you a better reader?

5. What did you enjoy most about this writing assignment? What did you like least?

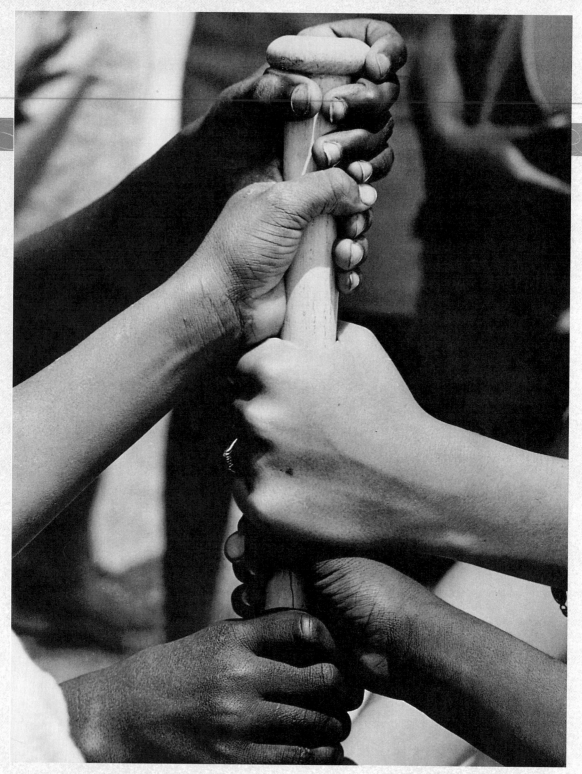

Bruce Roberts/Rapho/Photo Researchers.

7

WRITING TO SOLVE PROBLEMS AND PRESENT SOLUTIONS

A problem well put is half solved.

JOHN DEWEY

Writing to solve problems, like writing to explore, is a way of thinking on paper (or on the computer screen)—a way to find out what you already know, to organize your thoughts, to visualize a problem, and to make connections between what you know and what you need to know or do. The more complicated the problem, the greater the need to write. Writing helps you think, enables you to view a problem from different perspectives—to see relationships that you had previously overlooked—and ultimately allows you to discover solutions.

Once you have solved the problem, you usually need to convince someone that your solution will work. Writing to present a solution and convince readers of its value is more structured, more like writing to inform or instruct than writing to explore. Your purpose is no longer to solve the problem, but rather to persuade readers that a problem can or should be solved in a certain way. In this chapter, writers offer solutions to complex and compelling problems in human relations.

Writing to convince readers that a particular solution will work abounds, especially in business, government, and education. Reports in which an individual or a committee defines a problem, evaluates various solutions, and argues in favor of one are common forms of communication whether the problem is related to transportation, urban decay, deficit spending, or curriculum design.

Writing to solve problems takes other forms, too. Editors, columnists, politicians, researchers, and experts in every field from cosmetics to aeronautics often argue for a specific solution to a particular problem, whether the problem is how to conceal dark circles under the eyes or how to design a safer aircraft. Fiction, drama, and poetry frequently focus on solving problems, as well. Typically, the protagonist faces a problem and eventually solves it. Although the author may not overtly advocate a particular solution, he or she usually suggests a certain response or form of behavior as a type of solution.

When you propose a solution in the professional or business world, you usually write a rather formally structured memo or report. These reports, often called recommendation reports or proposals, typically consist of the following elements:

❖ Definition of the problem

❖ Evaluation of alternative solutions

❖ Arguments for proposed solution

Even informal reports usually include these elements. But almost endless variations are possible. If you are writing for a general audience rather than a professional audience, you may decide not to identify or evaluate alternative solutions. You may decide not to define the problem because you know your readers are familiar with it. Or you may decide that defining the problem is more important than a long discussion of the easily understood solution. In general, however, writing to solve problems and reading problem-solution writing involves consideration of these three elements.

READING PROBLEM-
SOLUTION TEXTS

When you read to find a solution to a problem, you probably already know something about the problem; otherwise, you wouldn't be reading about it. The information and experience you already have on the subject enable you to evaluate the proposed solution effectively. You must assume that the writer of a problem-solution text is biased in favor of the solution he or she is proposing, and so you must correct for this bias as you read. To do this, you should evaluate each of the three elements typically included in a problem-solution text.

Evaluating the Problem

First, decide whether the problem is really a problem. For example, is the depletion of the ozone layer of the earth's atmosphere really a problem? Scientists, environmentalists, politicians, and manufacturers of ozone-destroying products disagree not only about the seriousness of the problem, but about whether a problem actually exists. A report or article on this issue should probably include a discussion of the different points of view as well as convincing evidence that ozone depletion constitutes a problem that requires a solution.

Second, determine whether the writer has defined the problem accurately and clearly. What is his or her experience or knowledge of this problem? What sources are cited? What evidence is presented? A well-defined problem is one that you can understand clearly. You should have no questions about why the problem exists, what its consequences are, and who will be affected. You should also be able to determine from the author's discussion whether the problem is likely to become more serious and, if so, how soon. In other words, the author's definition of the problem should leave no doubt in your mind as to what caused the problem and what effects it will have.

Third, be alert to the possibility that the writer's view of the problem may be biased. Does it suit the writer's purpose to minimize or exaggerate the seriousness of the problem? Defining a problem is more often a matter of interpretation than a totally objective, scientific process. For example, a male may not view sexual harassment or gender-biased language as a significant problem, whereas a female may. In contrast, a female may not view affirmative action policies as a serious problem, whereas a male, especially a white male, may. In other words, as a reader, you often need to know not just what writers say but who they are, and then factor in their possible biases as you evaluate the problem. In some instances, you may recognize the writer's name, the organization he or she represents, or the position he or she holds. Often this information is provided for you, as in the biographical information on each of the writers in this book. In other instances, the book or journal in which the text appears may offer clues about who the writer is and what possible biases he or she may hold. For example, *The New Republic* is generally acknowledged to have a neoliberal political view, while *The Wall Street Journal* is considered a conservative publication. If you have no idea who the author is and what his or her biases may be, you may need to research the writer's background by asking somebody knowledgeable in the field or by looking in one or more biographical dictionaries or encyclopedias.

Evaluating Alternative Solutions

The most important consideration in evaluating the writer's discussion of alternative solutions is to determine if obvious solutions have been omitted and, if so, why. Most writers feel some obligation to acknowledge other solutions, at least briefly, before arguing in favor of their own solution. However, writers are not obliged to include (nor could they) a complete list of possible solutions. Expect selectivity. For example, David Blankenhorn points out in "Life without Father" that many people "urge us to accept the decline of fatherhood with equanimity. Be realistic they tell us. . . . Nothing can be done to reverse the trend itself." But he does not include other solutions that have been suggested, such as laws that force men to assume responsibility for the children they father or that make it more difficult for couples to divorce.

As a reader, you should decide whether the writer has included the most plausible alternative solutions and has presented them fairly and accurately. An author's failure to do so suggests that the proposed solution compares unfavorably to the omitted solutions.

If alternative solutions are included, you must decide whether they are fairly and accurately evaluated. Unless writers present alternative solutions objectively and fairly, they are not being responsible to their readers. Obviously, alternative solutions are not ones the writer favors, but he or she still has an obligation to discuss them as objectively as possible. If a writer dismisses alternative solutions cavalierly or discusses them only superficially, you should probably be suspicious that he or she is not fully informed about the alternative solutions or not willing to evaluate them fairly for fear that readers will prefer them to the proposed solution.

For example, suppose you are reading an article on the problem of providing adequate health care for people who live in the United States. You notice that the writer denigrates and then casually dismisses the Canadian health care model as a possible solution. Perhaps the writer claims that in the United States people would never tolerate the lack of choice inherent in the Canadian system and then doesn't discuss that solution further. What should you conclude? That the Canadian system is inadequate and does not deserve a more thorough evaluation? That the Canadian system is workable in Canada but not here? Or simply that the writer favors his or her proposal and doesn't want to discuss the pros and cons of alternative programs fully?

Evaluating the Proposed Solution

Finally, evaluate the proposed solution. The first question to ask is whether the proposed solution is presented clearly. If it is not, it is useless. If you cannot understand how the solution works, what it consists of, and what effects it will have, then you cannot evaluate it fairly.

The next question to ask is whether it will work. Even a brilliant solution is worthless if it is not workable. In effect, you must decide if the solution being proposed will solve the problem that has been defined. In addition, you must determine if it is practical, if it will cost too much, and if it is reasonable or even possible. For example, the U.S. health care problem could probably be solved fairly easily if cost were not a consideration. But a solution that bankrupts the nation is not acceptable. Similarly, the problem would be solved if physicians treated patients at cost but not for profit. However, such an idealistic solution is clearly unlikely.

You should also beware of solutions that solve only part of the problem. For example, if all employers, by law, had to offer health care insurance to their employees, the problem of universal health care would still not be solved, because many people are unemployed or cannot afford health insurance even if it is available.

Still another fallacy to be aware of is the either/or solution, in which the writer presents only two opposing solutions rather than presenting other, less polarized viewpoints. The best known either/or solution is the idea that people who don't "love" America (that is, anyone who criticizes anything American) should leave it. This simplistic approach leaves no room for subtleties or multifaceted viewpoints and encourages drastic action rather than compromise and negotiation.

The last question to ask is whether the proposed solution is ethical. A solution may be feasible and still not be ethical, and a writer who proposes a solution may be more interested in pragmatics than in ethics. For example, waste disposal problems are often solved at the expense of powerless people or at great cost to the environment. Dumping dangerous waste materials in a sparsely populated rural area may solve the problem of waste disposal but is hardly fair to the people, even if they are few, who live in the area. Similarly, dumping garbage in a river or harbor solves the disposal problem but damages the environment. People concerned about protecting the environment would not consider that solution ethical. So in the final analysis, a solution is acceptable only if it is considered ethical as well as workable.

Don't expect to find the three elements usually included in recommendation reports treated equally in every problem-solution text you read. For example, "The New Segregation" by Dinesh D'Souza, and "Bridging the Communication Gap" by Frank Cedeño, two of the readings included in this chapter, focus primarily on a discussion of the problem. The attention devoted to the problem as opposed to the solution depends on a number of factors, one of which is the writer's sense of who his or her readers will be. If readers do not need extensive information about the problem, writers do not provide it. If readers need extensive information about alternative solutions, writers include a full discussion of what else might be done before arguing for their own solution. In other words, a writer's sense of audience shapes the text he or she constructs. This is true of all writing, but especially true of problem-solution texts.

READING SELECTIONS ◀

This chapter's reading selections focus on human relations problems. Human relationships are fragile even under the best of circumstances. Even family members and friends sometimes have problems getting along together. Not surprisingly, then, human relations problems usually increase when the people involved differ in some way. Thus, problems exist between males and females, employers and employees, the educated and the uneducated, Democrats and Republicans, and even (or perhaps especially) children and parents. People of different ages, races, ethnic backgrounds, religions, and economic levels may have difficulty understanding one another. In fact, many of the most serious problems we face, as individuals and as a nation, result from these kinds of differences. Each author in this chapter focuses on one of these problems and proposes a solution.

LIFE WITHOUT FATHER

David Blankenhorn

In this article, taken from his book Fatherless America: Confronting Our Most Urgent Social Problem, *David Blankenhorn notes that fathers are increasingly absent in the lives of children and asks the simple but important question: "Does every child need a father?" Blankenhorn clearly believes that "disappearing Dads" are a major problem for our society as well as for individuals and proposes twelve specific solutions "to create a stronger national focus on the value of fatherhood." As you read, evaluate first the significance of the problem Blankenhorn describes and then the appropriateness of the solutions he proposes.*

The United States is becoming an increasingly fatherless society.   1
A generation ago, a child could reasonably expect to grow up with his or her father. Today, a child can reasonably expect not to. Fatherlessness is approaching a rough parity with fatherhood as a defining feature of childhood.

This astonishing fact is reflected in many statistics, but here are   2
the two most important: Tonight, about 40 percent of U.S. children will go to sleep in homes in which their fathers do not live (see table).

More than half of our children are likely to spend a significant portion of childhood living apart from their fathers. Never before in this country have so many children been voluntarily abandoned by their fathers. Never before have so many children grown up without knowing what it means to have a father.

3   Fatherlessness is the most harmful demographic trend of this generation. It is the leading cause of the decline in the well-being of children. It is also the engine driving our most urgent social problems, from crime to adolescent pregnancy to domestic violence. Yet, despite its scale and social consequences, fatherlessness is frequently ignored or denied. Especially within our elite discourse, it remains a problem with no name.

4   Surely a crisis of this scale merits a name—and a response. At a minimum, it requires a serious debate: Why is fatherhood declining? What can be done about it? Can our society find ways to invigorate effective fatherhood as a norm of male behavior? Yet, to date, our public discussion has been remarkably weak and defeatist. There is a prevailing belief that not much can or even should be done to reverse the trend.

5   As a society, we are changing our minds about men's role in family life. Our inherited understanding of fatherhood is under siege. Men are increasingly viewed as superfluous to family life: either expendable or part of the problem. Masculinity itself often is treated with suspicion, and even hostility, in our cultural discourse. Consequently, our society is unable to sustain fatherhood as a distinctive domain of male activity.

DISAPPEARING DADS

U.S. Kids Living with . . .	1960	1980	1990
Father and mother	80.6%	62.3%	57.7%
Mother only	7.7	18	21.6
Father only	1	1.7	3.1
Father and stepmother	0.8	1.1	0.9
Mother and stepfather	5.9	8.4	10.4
Neither parent	3.9	5.8	4.3

Sources: *America's Children* by Donald Hernandez; U.S. Census Bureau. Because the statistics are from separate sources, they don't total 100%.

The core question is simple: Does every child need a father?   6
Increasingly, our society's answer is "no." Few idea shifts in this century are as consequential as this one. At stake is nothing less than what
it means to be a man, who our children will be and what kind of society we will become.

My book is a criticism not simply of fatherlessness but of a *cul-*   7
ture of fatherlessness. For, in addition to fathers, we are losing something larger: our idea of fatherhood. Unlike earlier periods of father
absence in our history, such as wartime, we now face more than a
physical loss affecting some homes. The 1940s child could say: My
father had to leave for a while to do something important. The '90s
child must say: My father left me permanently because he wanted to.

This is a cultural criticism because fatherhood, much more than   8
motherhood, is a cultural invention. Its meaning is shaped less by biology than by a cultural script, a societal code that guides—and at time
pressures—a man into certain ways of acting and understanding himself.

Like motherhood, fatherhood is made up of both a biological and   9
a social dimension. Yet, across the world, mothers are far more successful than fathers at fusing these dimensions into a coherent identity.
Is the nursing mother playing a biological or a social role? Feeding or
bonding? We can hardly separate the two, so seamlessly are they
woven together. But fatherhood is a different matter. A father makes
his sole biological contribution at the moment of conception, nine
months before the infant enters the world. Because social paternity is
linked only indirectly to biological paternity, a connection cannot be
assumed. The phrase "to father a child" usually refers only to the act of
insemination, not the responsibility for raising the child. What fathers
contribute after conception is largely a matter of cultural devising.

Moreover, despite their other virtues, men are not ideally suited   10
to responsible fatherhood. Men are inclined to sexual promiscuity and
paternal waywardness. Anthropologically, fatherhood constitutes what
might be termed a necessary problem. It is necessary because child
well-being and societal success hinge largely on a high level of paternal investment: men's willingness to devote energy and resources to
the care of their offspring. It is a problem because men frequently are
unwilling or unable to make that vital investment.

Because fatherhood is universally problematic, cultures must mobi-   11
lize to enforce the father role, guiding men with legal and extralegal
pressures that require them to maintain a close alliance with their children's mother and invest in their children. Because men don't volunteer
for fatherhood as much as they are conscripted into it by the surrounding culture, only an authoritative cultural commitment to fatherhood
can fuse biological and social paternity into a coherent male identity.

For exactly this reason, anthropologist Margaret Mead and others have observed that the supreme test of any civilization is whether it can socialize men by teaching them to nurture their offspring.

12   The stakes could hardly be higher. Our society's conspicuous failure to sustain norms of fatherhood reveals a failure of collective memory and a collapse of moral imagination. It undermines families, neglects children, causes or aggravates our worst social problems and makes individual adult happiness, both female and male, harder to achieve.

13   Ultimately, this failure reflects nothing less than a culture gone awry, unable to establish the boundaries and erect the signposts that can harmonize individual happiness with collective well-being. In short, it reflects a culture that fails to "enculture" individual men and women, mothers and fathers.

14   In personal terms, the main result of this failure is the spread of a me-first egotism hostile to all except the most puerile understandings of personal happiness. In social terms, the results are a decline in children's well-being and a rise in male violence, especially against women. The most significant result is our society's steady fragmentation into atomized individuals, isolated from one another and estranged from the aspirations and realities of common membership in a family, a community, a nation, bound by mutual commitment and shared memory.

15   Many voices today, including many expert voices, urge us to accept the decline of fatherhood with equanimity. Be realistic, they tell us. Divorce and out-of-wedlock childbearing are here to stay. Growing numbers of children will not have fathers. Nothing can be done to reverse the trend itself. The only solution is to remedy some of its consequences: More help for poor children. More sympathy for single mothers. Better divorce. More child-support payments. More prisons. More programs aimed at substituting for fathers.

16   Yet what Abraham Lincoln called the better angels of our nature always have guided us in the opposite direction. Passivity in the face of crisis is inconsistent with the American tradition. Managing decline never has been the hallmark of American expertise. In the inevitable and valuable tension between conditions and aspirations—between the social "is" and the moral "ought"—our birthright as Americans always has been our confidence that we can change for the better.

17   Does every child need a father? Our current answer hovers between "not necessarily" and "no." But we need not make permanent the lowering of our standards. We can change our minds. We can change our minds without passing new laws, spending more tax dollars or empaneling more expert commissions. Once we change our philosophy, we

might well decide to pass laws, create programs or commission research. But the first and most important thing to change is not policies, but ideas.

Our essential goal must be the rediscovery of the fatherhood idea: For every child, a legally and morally responsible man.   18

If my goal could be distilled into one sentence, it would be this: A good society celebrates the ideal of the man who puts his family first. Because our society is lurching in the opposite direction, I see the Good Family Man as the principal casualty of today's weakening focus on fatherhood. Yet I cannot imagine a good society without him.   19

---

12 WAYS TO PUT FATHERS BACK IN THE PICTURE

25 Percent of U.S. babies born in 1993 were to unmarried mothers who ran their households alone, Blankenhorn estimates. To create a stronger national focus on the value of fatherhood, he recommends:

❖ A coalition of civic groups should ask every man to pledge that "every child deserves a father, marriage is the pathway to effective fatherhood, part of being a good man is being a good father, and America needs more good men."

❖ The president, acting through the White House Domestic Policy Council, should issue a brief annual report to the nation on the state of fatherhood.

❖ A few good men should create Fathers' Clubs in their communities.

❖ Congress should assist community organizers, clergy members and other local leaders who are serious about creating higher standards of male responsibility.

❖ Community organizers and veterans of the poor people's and civil rights movements should help build the infrastructure for a new grass-roots movement to empower families and strengthen community life.

❖ Policies should be changed to encourage a higher percentage of married couples in public housing.

❖ An interfaith council of religious leaders should speak up and act up on behalf of marriage.

❖ Congress should pass, and the president should support, a resolution stating that policymakers' first question about domestic legislation should be whether it will strengthen the institution of marriage.

❖ Local officials across the nation should follow the example of the Hennepin County (Minn.) Board of Commissioners by issuing a "vision statement" that urges citizens to move toward a community in which a "healthy family structure is nurtured."

❖ States should regulate sperm banks, prohibiting the sale of sperm to unmarried women and limiting artificial insemination to infertile married couples.

❖ Well-known pro athletes should organize a public service campaign on the importance of fatherhood.

❖ Prominent family scholars should write better high school textbooks about marriage and parenthood.

▶ QUESTIONS TO CONSIDER

1. The author begins this article by asserting that "The United States is becoming an increasingly fatherless society." What evidence does he include to support this assertion? Is this evidence convincing?

2. Blankenhorn also asserts that "Fatherlessness is the most harmful demographic trend of this generation." How does he support this assertion?

3. Blankenhorn states that "the core question is simple: Does every child need a father?" Do you think this is the core question to ask in addressing this problem? Are there other questions, perhaps more complex ones, that are equally essential to a satisfactory solution?

4. Blankenhorn speaks of the growing acceptance of fatherless households as an "idea shift" and argues that it is one of the most consequential in our history. What does he mean by an idea shift? What other idea shifts have occurred that are equally significant?

5. The author believes that "Fatherhood, much more than motherhood, is a cultural invention." Explain why he sees fatherhood as a cultural invention. What significant differences do you see between fatherhood and motherhood?

6. Why does Blankenhorn quote Margaret Mead? Does her comment lend credibility to Blankenhorn's argument? Why?

7. Is Blankenhorn guilty of the slippery slope fallacy when he argues that the problem of increasing fatherlessness will ultimately lead to

"a culture gone awry, unable to establish the boundaries and erect the signposts that can harmonize individual happiness with collective well-being?"

8. What is Blankenhorn's general solution to the problem of fatherlessness in our society? What specific strategies does he give to implement this solution? Evaluate his solution in terms of how realistic, effective, and fair it is.

WRITING ACTIVITIES ◀

Individual: Write a journal entry in which you evaluate the problem of fatherlessness in our society.

Collaborative: With a group of your peers, evaluate the alternative solutions that Blankenhorn presents.

Computer: Discuss on line your evaluation of Blankenhorn's general solution and the specific strategies he includes for solving the problem of fatherlessness.

BRIDGING THE COMMUNICATION GAP

Frank Cedeño

Frank Cedeño, the author of this problem-solution essay, spent a semester as a freshman composition student researching the differences between male and female communication styles. As a result of his research, Cedeño was able to define the problem that males and females often have in communicating with each other—the "gap" referred to in the title. As you read, notice that he devotes much less attention to the solution he proposes because it, in effect, depends on an understanding of the problem. Thus, in explaining the problem carefully, Cedeño is hoping to solve it. Does he succeed?

   Much research has been done on the different conversation styles   1
of men and women and the misunderstandings that result from these
differences. These misunderstandings about what is really being said
can cause serious problems in relationships between men and women.

Perhaps these differences can best be understood by examining the different rules that govern the conversation game men and women play.

2   Rule number one of the conversation game states that men seek status while women simply need support. Charles Derber, a sociologist at Boston College, has discovered that men will often shift conversations to their preferred topics (qtd. in Kohn, "Girl Talk" 65). Men grow up thinking of conversation as a contest. Their goal is to achieve the upper hand or at least avoid being pushed around. Women, however, typically use conversation to exchange confirmation and support. A woman is better able to respond supportively. Alfie Kohn states in *Psychology Today,* "The wife gives more active encouragement to her husband's talk about himself while the husband listens less well and is less likely to actively 'bring her out' about herself and her own topics" ("Girl Talk" 65).

3   Deborah Tannen, a linguistics professor at Georgetown University, cites an example of this difference in her article, "Can't We Talk?" A married couple had jobs in different cities. When friends commented that this arrangement must be difficult for them, the wife accepted their sympathy. The husband became irritated and would explain that the situation had advantages, which included long weekends and vacations together. Although his statement was true, it still puzzled his wife. To him, he explained, the comments implied: "Yours is not a real marriage. I am superior to you because my wife and I have avoided your misfortune" (20). The wife saw that her husband was viewing the world as a place where people tried to achieve and maintain status. She, on the other hand, saw the world as a network of connections in which people seek consensus.

4   Rule number two states that women struggle to preserve intimacy but men tend to focus on establishing independence. These differences in communication can cause serious conflicts in the way a situation is viewed. Consider the following scenario: Joe receives a phone call from an old friend saying he will be in town soon. Joe invites the friend to spend several days with him and his wife Linda. Later that evening he tells Linda, and she is upset. She wonders why Joe has not checked with her first. He angrily replies, "I can't say I have to ask my wife for permission!" Joe feels that checking with Linda would make him seem like a child or that he is not free to act on his own. Linda, however, feels that if the situation were reversed, checking with Joe would only show that her life is involved with her husband's (Tannen 21–22).

5   Rule number three states that men give advice whereas women only want understanding. For example, often women complain to men

about feeling physically unattractive. When this happens, men usually feel challenged to find a solution to this problem. But often women are only looking for emotional support. A compliment is needed more than a solution. If a woman tells a man that she is getting too fat, the last thing she wants to hear is that she ought to go on a diet! On the other hand, men avoid seeking help, advice, or consolation altogether. They resist the intimacy of discussing their feelings because it implies a need for advice (Adler 74). Their goal is to remain in control. Perhaps this is why so many men refuse to ask for directions when in a strange place. To ask for help is to put oneself in a position of inferiority (Adler 74).

According to rule number four, a woman's proposal is often interpreted by a man as an order. Most men resist being told what to do. When men react in this way, women are confused because they feel they are only making suggestions when they say, "Let's park closer to the store" or "Let's clean up before lunch." Their indirect style of talking is viewed by them as just a way of getting others to do what they want (Tannen 24).   6

Such proposals, suggestions, and questions are distinctively characteristic of women's conversation. Robin Lakoff, a linguist at the University of California, Berkeley, has pointed out several characteristics of this indirect style: 7

1. Women ask more questions (nearly three times as many as men)

2. Women make statements in a questioning tone

3. Women use more tag questions (statements such as "Don't you think?" or "Isn't it?")

4. Women lead off with questions that ensure a listener's attention ("Hey, y'know what?")

5. Women use more "hedges" or qualifiers and rely on intensifiers (such as "kinda" or "really")

Lakoff also notes that the use of intensifiers suggests women feel they are not persuasive, so they add intensifiers to make sure their listeners understand the importance of what they are saying (qtd. in Kohn, "Girl Talk" 66).

Rule number five ordains that men face conflict head on while women tend to compromise. Most women try to avoid confrontation even if it means going against their own beliefs. However, according to Tannen, "At times it's far more effective for a woman to assert her-   8 self, even at the risk of conflict" (24). Women find they are labeled as unfeminine by women as well as men if they speak assertively and directly. On the other hand, if they avoid conflict and adopt a more traditional role, they are not taken seriously and are considered unintelligent. Lakoff states it best, "A woman is damned if she does and damned if she doesn't" (qtd. in Kohn, "Girl Talk" 66).

9   Finally, and most importantly, rule number six states that men communicate primarily for information whereas women speak mainly to exchange feelings or emotions. Women become upset and are hurt when men don't talk to them. This is frustrating to men because they don't know why they have disappointed their partners. Tannen has found that women spend much of their time throughout their lives stating their feelings to friends and relatives. To them, this expression of emotion denotes involvement and caring. On the other hand, men keep their innermost thoughts to themselves to preserve an image of masculinity, communicating mainly to share information.

10   Barbara Langstern, in her article "Your Well-Being," sums up this communication conflict best. She feels the division between men and women frequently leads to extremes that are intolerable. She explains,

> The woman aches for emotional companionship and validation. She no longer wants to express all the feelings for the couple. But attacking the man's passivity usually causes him to retreat. He, uneasy expressing emotions, hardly will take his first step into an emotional tempest. (27)

11   Based on the communication differences discussed in this paper, one might conclude that it is useless for men and women to attempt to talk with each other. Mary Kay Blakely suggests in her article, "Why Can't Men and Women Speak the Same Language?" that the most effective solution may be to cease talking altogether (152). This solution, however, is not only impractical but unrealistic. Perhaps if men and women become conscious of their differences in conversation styles, less grief will occur. If they become aware that these gender differences in speech are simply reflections of the power struggle between men and women, better understanding can result (Kohn, "Kinder Sex" 34). Understanding how the other sex will probably react can prepare both men and women to avoid conflicts. Once they educate themselves by becoming aware of their different approaches to communication, they will have a better chance of preventing disagreements from spiraling out of control (Tannen 24). This awareness of basic

differences in conversation styles could provide the bridge across the communication gap that separates men and women.

LIST OF WORKS CITED

Adler, Jerry. "When Harry Called Sally . . ." *Newsweek* Oct. 1, 1990: 74.
Blakely, Mary Kay. "Why Can't Men and Women Speak the Same Language?" *Glamour* Nov. 1988: 151–52.
Gibson, Janice T. "Are Boys and Girls Really So Different?" *Reader's Digest* Oct. 1988: 15.
Kohn, Alfie. "The Kinder Sex." *Health* Sept. 1990: 32, 34.
———. "Girl Talk, Boy Talk." *Psychology Today* Feb. 1988: 65–66.
Langstern, Barbara. "Your Well-Being." *Vogue* Jan. 1988: 41.
Tannen, Deborah. "Can't We Talk?" *Reader's Digest* Dec. 1990: 19–24.

QUESTIONS TO CONSIDER ◀

1. Cedeño begins by describing the problem that males and females have in communicating. He explains that men and women both see conversation as a game with certain rules, but they play by different rules. Of the six rules he includes, which one accounts for the most serious communication problems between males and females?

2. Evaluate Cedeño's definition of the problem. Is it clear and convincing?

3. In this essay, Cedeño quotes a number of sources but does not include his own experience with this problem. Would the essay have been strengthened had he included a personal experience ?

4. What does Cedeño suggest is the best solution to this problem?

5. What other solutions might Cedeño have included? Would additional, more specific solutions have strengthened his essay, or do you agree with his general suggestion that awareness is the key to solving this problem?

6. Do you agree that male-female communication styles are different? If so, were you aware of these differences before reading this essay, or did Cedeño convince you that males and females follow different conversational rules? If he did, how?

▶ WRITING ACTIVITIES

Individual: In a journal entry, describe your own conversational style. How many of the rules that Cedeño includes accurately describe your conversational pattern? How difficult would it be to change your conversational style?

Collaborative: Discuss the six rules of conversation that Cedeño uses to structure his essay. Be sure you understand clearly the different *perceptions* that he claims males and females tend to have on each of these points. Then, to solve the problems created by these different perceptions, revise each rule so that it is a compromise—a rule for effective communication that both males and females could follow comfortably.

Computer: Conduct a network conversation on the topic of male-female communication styles. Do not identify yourself or your gender. Then, as a class, analyze the computer conversation to determine if the participants' gender can be identified by their conversation styles.

THE AGGRESSORS

Melvin Konner

Melvin Konner is an anthropologist, a physician, and a professor. In the following essay, which was published in the New York Times Magazine, *Konner describes the problem of male aggression and offers a solution based upon his belief that males are biologically programmed to be more aggressive than females. As you read his essay, think about whether you agree that the problem he describes is significant, and then carefully evaluate the rather drastic solution he proposes.*

1   Dr. Dan Olweus knows the bullies in Norway; at least those 8 to 16 years old in a population of 140,000 in 715 public schools. Olweus, a professor of psychology at the University of Bergen, was asked by the Norwegian Government to get a handle on the bullying problem. Concluding his recent study, he estimates that of the 568,000 Norwegian schoolchildren, 41,000, or 7 percent, bully others regularly. The bullies were far more likely to be male: more than 60 percent of the girls and

80 percent of the boys victimized in grades 5 to 7 were bullied by males. The tendency of girls to bully declined with age; in boys, it rose: a twofold difference in the second grade widens to fivefold in the ninth.

Many studies, even of remote, primitive societies, show that males predominate overwhelmingly in physical violence. Pick your behavior: grabbing and scratching in toddlers, wrestling and chasing in nursery-school children, contact sports among teen-agers, violent crime in adulthood, tank maneuvers in real, grown-up wars. In 1986, Alice H. Eagly and Valerie J. Steffen, then of Purdue University, published a survey of 63 psychological studies. They emphasized that no category existed in which women were more aggressive than men, and they said the tendency to produce pain or physical injury was far more pronounced in men. Joining a distinguished line of social and psychological researchers, Eagly and Steffen concluded that these differences "are learned as aspects of gender roles and other social roles." 2

That belief, a tenacious modern myth, becomes less justified with every passing year: sex difference in the tendency to do physical harm is intrinsic, fundamental, natural—in a word, biological. 3

Olweus, in a smaller study—one of scores contributing to this new conclusion—selected 58 boys aged 15 through 17, and compared blood levels of testosterone, the male sex hormone, to aggression. He found a strong effect of testosterone on intolerance for frustration and response to provocation. The puzzle of aggression is not yet solved, but it seems increasingly apparent that testosterone is a key. However, it is testosterone circulating not only post-pubertally, as has been commonly thought, but also during early development—specifically, during fetal life, at the stage when the brain is forming. The first clues to this process came from animal studies. In 1973, G. Raisman and P. M. Field reported a significant sex difference in a part of the rat's brain known as the preoptic area—a region that, in females, helps control the reproductive cycle; certain brain cell connections in this area were more numerous in females. Most interestingly, castration of males at birth, or early treatment of females with testosterone, abolished the adult brain difference. 4

This was the first of many similar studies showing that the differentiation not only of the brain but of behavior—especially sexual and aggressive behavior—depends in part on early testosterone exposure. This has proved to be true of rats, mice, hamsters, rabbits and monkeys, among other species. Clear anatomical differences have been found in the hypothalamus and amygdula regions of the brain as well as the preoptic area. 5

6   One ingenious study showed that the tendency to fight in adult mice, although greater by far in males, differs among females, depending on whether they spent their fetal life near males or other females in the womb. Females with males on each side in utero grew up to be fighters, but those with only one adjacent male were less pugnacious as adults. Those flanked by two other females in the womb became the least aggressive adults. Separate evidence indicated that the three groups of females also differed in their degree of exposure to intrauterine testosterone—which had evidently come from the blood of the nearby males.

7   No experimental evidence is available for humans, of course, but some clinical studies are suggestive. Sometimes human fetuses are exposed to hormones that have effects similar to those of testosterone—for example, synthetic progestions, used to maintain pregnancy. June M. Reinisch, now director of the Kinsey Institute, studied 25 girls and boys with a history of such exposure and found them more aggressive than their same-sex siblings, as indicated by a paper-and-pencil test. This finding was in line with studies of monkeys and other animals exposed to male sex hormones in utero. Females with such exposure engaged in more rough-and-tumble play during development than other females. As in the human study, the differences became apparent before puberty.

8   Some years ago, there was a bitter controversy over whether men with an extra male-determining Y chromosome—the XYY syndrome—were hypermasculine. One not-so-subtle humorist wrote in to *Science* that it was silly to get so excited over the extremely rare XYY syndrome, when 49 percent of the species was already afflicted with the XY syndrome—an uncontroversial disorder known to cause hyperactivity and learning disabilities in childhood, premature mortality in adulthood and an egregious tendency to irrational violence throughout life. "Testosterone poisoning," a colleague of mine calls it.

9   Is there no contribution of culture, then, to the consistent male excess in violence? Of course there is; but it acts on an organism already primed for the sex difference. Cultures can dampen it or exaggerate it. The role of modeling in encouraging aggression is well proved. Give a girl a steady diet of Wonder Woman and lady wrestlers while her brother gets Mr. Rogers, and you may well push them past each other on the continuum. But we now have a pretty good answer to Margaret Mead's famous question: What if an average boy and an average girl were raised in exactly similar environments? We don't know, she said. Now we do. The boy would hit, kick, wrestle, scratch, grab, shove and bite more than the girl and be more likely to commit a violent crime later in life.

Mead became famous for her elegant demonstrations of cultural   10
variation in sex roles. Among the Tchambuli, a New Guinea fishing
society, the women, "brisk, unadorned, managing and industrious, fish
and go to market; the men, decorative and adorned, carve and paint and
practice dance steps." Among the Mundugumor, river-dwelling cannibals,
also in New Guinea, "the women are as assertive and vigorous as the
men; they detest bearing and rearing children, and provide most of the
food. . . ." These quotations from her 1949 book "Male and Female"
helped provide the basis for the modern conception of the tremendous
flexibility of sex roles—as well they should have. But the Tchambuli
men, when they finished their dance steps, went headhunting. And
note that Mead's own words following her often-cited quote on the
Mundugumor are: "*leaving the men free to plot and fight.*" In every
known society, homicidal violence, whether spontaneous and out-
lawed or organized and sanctioned for military purposes, is committed
overwhelmingly by men.

The conclusion would seem to be that women should run the   11
world. If we can agree that the greatest threat to human survival over
the long haul is posed by human violence itself, then the facts of
human violence—the sex difference, and its biological basis—can lead
nowhere else. But what of Margaret Thatcher, Indira Gandhi, Golda
Meir; what of Catherine the Great and Elizabeth I, in earlier eras? They
are no use as test cases. All were women who clambered to the tops
of relentlessly male political and military hierarchies. They could
scarcely restrain the surges of all those millions of gallons of testosterone continually in flux under their scepters. And again: the categories overlap; the consistent differences are in averages. The gauntlets
those five women ran to get to the top and stay there can scarcely be
said to have been at the least-aggressive end of the female spectrum.
And women in a male world often find themselves outmachoing the
men—to gain credibility, to consolidate power, to survive.

Those negative examples notwithstanding, a steady, massive in-   12
fusion of women into positions of power, in a balanced way, throughout the world, should in fact reduce the risk that irrational factors—
"Come on, make my day" sorts of factors—will bring about an end to
life on earth. Political scientists and historians often argue as if there
were no resemblance between fistfights and war. Anthropologists and
biologists know better.

Interestingly, that same Norway that sent Dan Olweus off to   13
study—and try to diminish—bullying, appears to be in the vanguard.
Not only the Prime Minister, but 8 of the 18 members of the Cabinet, are

currently free of testosterone poisoning. In an almost all-male, consistently violent world of national governments, this little boat of the Norwegian Cabinet may run into some high seas. But it is a far cry from the Viking ships of yore, and I, for one, am keeping a hopeful eye on its prow.

▶ QUESTIONS TO CONSIDER

1. Do you agree that male aggression is an innate biological character-istic? If so, how is Konner's evidence persuasive? If not, what evi-dence could Konner provide that would be more persuasive? What factors other than biological ones influence male aggression?

2. Evaluate the author's proposed solution to the problem of male ag-gression on the basis of whether it is workable, practical, and ethical.

3. Konner includes no alternative solutions to the problem he defines. Can you think of alternative solutions?

4. This article appeared in the *New York Times Magazine*, which is read primarily by fairly well-educated, economically secure readers in the Northeast. How might the author have approached this same topic if he were writing for a medical journal, *Ladies Home Journal*, or *Esquire*?

5. Do you find the studies that Konner cites convincing evidence of his theory? What other forms of evidence might he have included?

6. In a single sentence, summarize the problem Konner is addressing and his proposed solution.

▶ WRITING ACTIVITIES

Individual: In a journal entry, write about the difference between male and female aggression. What problems can develop as a result of each?

Collaborative: Discuss the problems that can develop as a result of male or female aggression. Briefly define one of these problems, identify alternative solutions, and argue in favor of one solution.

Computer: Respond on your computer network to Konner's argument that "women should run the world." Your response should include a summary of Konner's argument, an evaluation of his argument, and your reaction to his solution.

AIDS ISSUES HAVEN'T GONE AWAY

Nancy L. Breuer

This article appeared in Personnel Journal, *a professional journal for personnel managers. The author, Nancy L. Breuer, is a Los Angeles-based writer and business consultant specializing in health and safety education. She describes a problem that did not exist a few years ago but that faces many employers now—how to deal with employees who are HIV positive. As you read, evaluate the solution that Breuer proposes.*

Driving into the parking lot one morning, the human resources director of a New York-based department store found employees milling around the back door, refusing to enter the building. She knew a longtime employee had called to say that he'd be returning to work that day after being hospitalized for *Pneumocystis carinii* pneumonia and wanted his co-workers to know his diagnosis. She put two and two together and reached a depressing conclusion: No one wanted to work with a colleague who had AIDS. 1

What happened next, however, surprised her. When the returning employee reached the parking lot, his co-workers wouldn't go inside until each person had offered him a hug, a card, flowers, or some balloons. Astonished and laden with tokens of his co-workers' goodwill and compassion, the AIDS-diagnosed employee began one of the best days of his working life. 2

Is this a fantasy or an event masterminded by management? No, it actually happened—spontaneously. Could it happen in your company? 3

Most people in American workplaces in the 1990s work beside people who have HIV infection or AIDS. The virus is found most often in people of working age; so far, its heaviest toll has been among people in their 20s, 30s and 40s. Because therapies constantly improve, HIV-infected people will be able to work longer and with greater productivity as the decade progresses. Even after bouts of serious illness, people who have HIV infection will return to work more often and for longer periods than has been true in the past. 4

Do most American workers have any reliable training to help them cope with this reality? The intensity and nature of the conversation following basketball star Magic Johnson's announcement that 5 he's HIV-positive suggest that they don't. Many employees remain ignorant and fearful. If the fear and ignorance aren't addressed, they're likely to worsen.

6   Thanks to the leadership of businesses that have provided workplace HIV education since the late 1980s, there are models that illustrate the value of making AIDS education ordinary.

7   The Prudential Insurance Company, Western Home Office, has been providing employee AIDS education seminars every six months since 1987, distributing a copy of the company's AIDS policy with employee orientation materials and handling reasonable accommodation matters and cases of AIDS-related discrimination quietly.

8   Dick Hunt, vice president for administration and a 39-year employee with the company, explains: "The longer you spend in human resources, the better nose you have for a bad situation and the better your batting average for avoiding them becomes. It was a matter of realizing that, if we did nothing, our first AIDS case would happen, and some people would panic out of ignorance." The Prudential made employee HIV training part of the regular human resources training menu; they made it ordinary.

9   Morrison & Foerster, an international law firm, took the same course and began employee HIV training in 1987. By now, says Personnel Manager Gene Bendel, when the firm announces an employee HIV training date, some employees ask, "Again? I thought I had that training last year." The company provides annual seminars so employees will be aware of new information about the epidemic. HIV training has become ordinary.

10   So far, the firm hasn't faced any HIV-related work disruptions or discrimination cases, even though the firm has faced employee HIV infection. "This is preventive education," Bendel reminds the firm. Even if there's no one with AIDS in the office today, "what about tomorrow?"

11   Dr. Ann Lewis, medical director for the Prudential at the Western Home Office, agrees. She points to the contrast between the company's first case and its most recent case as a dramatic example of the power of HIV education.

12   When the first case developed, Dr. Lewis had a stream of fearful employees in her office, afraid of contact and posing hypothetical questions. People didn't want to work in the same environment with a person rumored to have AIDS. Emotions ran high, productivity suffered and the myths about HIV transmission complicated efforts to communicate valid information.

13   Recently there was another case of symptomatic HIV infection in the same environment. Although co-workers are saddened by the wan-

ing energy of their colleague, no one is afraid to work beside the employee. No one questions the accommodation of installing a computer and printer in the affected employee's home to allow telecommunicating as a less fatiguing option to full, on-site work days. After several years of regular training, these employees know they aren't at risk and are simply concerned for their colleague.

Some companies resist training because of a fear that current medical information may be incomplete, that there may be ways of transmitting HIV that are yet unknown. Such fears, given free reign, aggravate the problem.   14

Although many individuals acknowledge that an HIV-infected person at work doesn't pose a risk to co-workers unless they're sharing needles or having sex, they're afraid the person becomes a threat when he or she becomes symptomatic. These people worry that the infected person's skin lesions, persistent cough and diarrhea might be passed along to their co-workers.   15

According to David Dassey, deputy medical director for AIDS programs in the Los Angeles County Department of Health Services, such fears are unfounded. Only people who have impaired immune systems fall ill with the specific infections that affect people who have HIV infection or AIDS. Each person carries many of the infections that make HIV-infected people ill. A healthy immune system suppresses such latent infections as herpes or mononucleosis and fights off such environmental infections as candidiasis (yeast infections). Other AIDS-related infections are caused by organisms common in the environment. A damaged immune system can't fight them off, and the person becomes ill.   16

The only exception is tuberculosis, an infection that afflicts many people, including some HIV-infected people. Any employee—HIV-infected or not—who has active tuberculosis shouldn't be at work during the days the TB is infectious. After a physician releases a tubercular patient to return to work after he or she has begun responding to treatment, the person poses no risk to co-workers.   17

In 1992, it's quite clear that someone who has AIDS poses no risk at work. There's no medical evidence to the contrary. But what about the argument that the workplace might be dangerous to an HIV-infected person because of all the germs to which he or she is exposed?   18

Employees sometimes worry that their colds or flu will make an HIV-infected co-worker sick. That isn't the case, Dassey explains. Those infections are handled easily by the part of the immune system that isn't seriously damaged by HIV, so controlling colds or flu is no more difficult for an HIV-infected person.   19

20   Even if HIV transmission or other infections isn't a workplace risk, there's a very real risk that employees will be paralyzed by their own panic. Often managers delay or avoid workplace HIV training to try to avoid provoking that fear. Is this a good idea? Not at all, says Bendel. He points out that strategic planning is used to anticipate business issues, and HIV *is* a business issue.

21   What would businesses that are providing HIV education say to those that aren't? Nissan Motor Corporation felt that the epidemic "had given rise to a number of critical human relations and legal issues" and decided it was "imperative to provide managers and supervisors some training on how to respond properly when confronted with the issues the crisis raises in the workplace," according to Ernest Stroman, manager of EEO and affirmative action programs at the U. S. headquarters office. "We found there's no need for any company to be apprehensive about providing this kind of training. Our managers and supervisors were extremely positive about it, and went so far as to recommend that the training be provided for all employees. Approximately 90% indicated their awareness of how the disease is transmitted was enhanced greatly and their apprehensions about contracting the disease were relieved substantially," Stroman says.

22   Bendel points out that many employers, often working with their health insurance providers, discuss drug addiction and alcoholism routinely in employee training programs, viewing it as a health issue that has a profound impact on the workplace. He encourages managers to fold HIV education into the same series of seminars.

23   Projections from the World Health Organization and the Centers for Disease Control in Atlanta tell us that we're only on the edge of this epidemic. Sadly, working effectively with HIV in the workplace is a necessary business skill for the '90s. Refusing to yield to fear is one way to reduce its impact and ease the pain—and to benefit from the courage of Magic Johnson and other HIV-infected people.

▶   QUESTIONS TO CONSIDER

1. If you have personally known someone who was HIV positive or actually suffering from AIDS, what was your reaction to this person? Was your reaction primarily rational or emotional?

2. The author introduces the problem she is addressing by telling a story. Is this narrative an effective way to introduce this rather sensitive subject? Why, or why not?

3. How well does Breuer define the problem of HIV-infected employees? From whose perspective does she primarily view this problem? The AIDS victim? Fellow employees? The employer(s)? What is the effect of using this perspective?

4. Breuer does not include alternative solutions in her article. Should she have? What alternative solutions can you suggest? Are these solutions feasible? Legal? Ethical?

5. How well does Breuer argue her case for educating all workers about AIDS as the solution to the problem of HIV-positive people in the workplace? Again, note the perspective she is taking. Whom does she cite? What evidence does she present? Whom is she trying to convince?

WRITING ACTIVITIES

Individual: In a journal entry, analyze your personal reaction to AIDS and the people who have it.

Collaborative: Discuss how Breuer's article would have differed had she been writing for a different audience. Make a list of changes you would make if you were revising this article for employees rather than employers.

Computer: Using the list of changes generated by your group in the preceding collaborative activity, revise the introduction (paragraphs 1–5) to this article so it is appropriate for an audience of employees rather than employers.

CULTURAL DIVERSITY 101

Joan Marie Snider

Joan Marie Snider is editor of La Mecha, *the student newspaper at New Mexico Highlands University. In this editorial, clearly written in response to some recent cultural conflicts on her campus, she argues that "it is possible to preserve one's own culture while acknowledging, and maybe even sharing, another's." As you read, notice how Snider explores her own cultural identity in an effort to establish common ground with readers from different cultural and ethnic backgrounds.*

1   I haven't figured out how to say this without sounding like some overprivileged whiny white bitch, or a sound-bite-infatuated Pollyanna, but: Can't we all get along?

2   But besides being trite and painfully naive, this is just a dumb question. No, we cannot all get along. People have been not getting along since before Time. Remember the Barbarian invasions? The Crusades? The Holocaust? The weight of history impresses on me that differences between people have always been more important than similarities.

3   But to be optimistic for a moment: We do seem to be discovering ways to overcome our differences. People now go to conflict resolution workshops where once they beat each other with clubs. This is a nice trend, I think. It means that we are beginning to see our world as something to share, not something to conquer.

4   Unfortunately, there are people who are stuck in the old conquering mode. There are people who would say, for example, that Highlands University should be the private domain of northern New Mexicans. This doesn't make any sense to me. It seems akin to huddling, each in our respective caves, afraid to come out or let anyone in lest they wield a club against us.

5   It just seems that with all the emphasis on what is "my" culture versus what is "your" culture, the fact that all of us here have more in common than not is lost. We see each other when we're buying our laundry detergent at Wal-Mart or renting videos at Furr's or standing in line for new IDs, but we don't realize that the fact that we're here, together, doing a lot of the same things, means that we have, at least to some extent, a shared culture.

6   But maybe it's just this, the specter of cultural amalgamation, which has prompted some to pick up the torch of cultural preservation. But—here's the whiny part—I'm not threatening anyone's cultural preservation when I wish someone Gesundheit and I'm not threatening it when I make tamales, Anglicized and mutilated though they may be. I'm not threatening it when I choose to be a part of a university which includes people from other backgrounds. It is possible to preserve one's own culture while acknowledging, and maybe even sharing, another's.

7   I have no doubt that my attitude toward culture is shaped in part by the fact that I'm very confused about what "my" culture is. The culture of my German ancestors was lost more than a century ago, as they respelled their names, gave up the German language and did everything they could to assimilate with the dominant culture of the Midwest. Growing up, "my" culture included Jell-o salads, Barbie dolls,

hymns by Henry Wadsworth Longfellow and the belief that anything pleasant is necessarily sinful. Not exactly the type of thing one might want to claim, let alone preserve. And I haven't even mentioned that it has been people of roughly my ethnic makeup who have been the oppressors in much of this planet's history. When I signed up for a German course in ninth grade, a friend, incredulous, asked me how I could study German after what Hitler had done. What could I say?

I'm glad that other people have more of a sense of their own 8 culture than I do of mine, but I still say it's time we started venturing out and realizing that we can visit neighboring cavedwellers without sacrificing the integrity of our own caves.

Maybe Conflict Resolution 101 should be on the core curriculum 9 and Playing Well With Others a section of the ACT. We could all learn from a friend who said she doesn't care if her professors are green or purple, as long as they are qualified to teach what she wants to learn. It might take a little adjustment, but different as we are, there's no reason we can't be part of the same university, to everyone's benefit. What a concept.

QUESTIONS TO CONSIDER ◀

1. Does Snider define the problem she is addressing clearly, or does she assume that her readers (students at her university) are familiar with the problem?

2. Analyze Snider's tone in this essay. Notice especially her vocabulary and her sentence structure. Is her informal, colloquial tone effective, given the seriousness of the problem she is trying to solve? Would a more formal, serious tone have been more persuasive? Why, or why not?

3. Do you agree with Snider that all of the students on a college campus have "to some extent, a shared culture"? Why, or why not? If you agree with this argument, do you agree with her reasoning that, because this is true, all students on a given campus should be able to get along with one another?

4. Does Snider's description of her own cultural background contribute to the effectiveness of her argument? Why, or why not?

5. Does her use of humor contribute to the effectiveness of her argument? Why, or why not?

6. Snider proposes that a course in Conflict Resolution should be required of students and that the ACT should test not only academic achievement but also how well students get along with others. Are these solutions meant to be taken literally? What other, more serious but unstated, solution is implied?

▶   W R I T I N G   A C T I V I T I E S

Individual: In a journal entry, explore your own cultural identity as Snider does in her editorial.

Collaborative: With a group of your classmates, identify a problem on your campus or in your community that is related to cultural diversity. Make a list of possible solutions; then, determine which of these solutions would be most effective.

Computer: Enter into a new computer file a description of the problem and the list of solutions your group identified. Then use this information (and, if you like, your journal entry about your own cultural identity) to write a problem-solution editorial for your own local newspaper. Circulate a draft of your editorial on your classroom network to get comments from your classmates, and then revise your editorial.

THE NEW SEGREGATION

Dinesh D'Souza

Dinesh D'Souza, a research fellow at the American Enterprise Institute, is the author of Illiberal Education: The Politics of Race and Sex on Campus. *In this article, which appeared in the Winter 1991 issue of* The American Scholar, *D'Souza argues that "America enters the last decade of the twentieth century with a strong and persistent residue of de facto segregation." He finds that college and university campuses are especially and increasingly segregated. As you read, evaluate his description of this problem, focusing specifically on the causes and effects of the problem that he identifies.*

1   Less than forty years ago, American society began a laborious and painful project to eliminate all vestiges of racial segregation from public life. On May 17, 1954, flanked by eight colleagues at a press conference,

Supreme Court Justice Earl Warren read from the momentous *Brown v. Board of Education* decision: "Does segregation . . . on the basis of race, even though the physical facilities and other tangible factors be equal, deprive the children of the minority group of equal education? We believe that it does." Programs to enforce public school desegregation were soon followed by ambitious efforts to integrate public transportation, hotels and restaurants, residential areas, in some cases even private clubs. By the mid-1960s, Martin Luther King, Jr.'s victory was virtually complete: it was socially disreputable and politically suicidal for public figures to advocate racial segregation, and despite pockets of bellicose resistance, the nation seemed united in its commitment to full integration of racial minorities into all facets of life.

2   Yet America enters the last decade of the twentieth century with a strong and persistent residue of de facto segregation. Indeed even without the support of law, social pressures appear actively to promote racial and ethnic isolation in many areas, threatening to reverse the trend of the past several decades, to thwart the national aspiration for integration, and to revive such concepts as "separate but equal," which had justified legal segregation since the late nineteenth century. Paradoxically, nowhere is the new segregation more evident than in that seemingly most progressive of institutions, the American university.

3   Universities were once thought a microcosm of society. But they are more than a reflection or mirror; they are a leading indicator. The campus environment is one where students live, eat, and study together, with the result that racial and cultural differences come together in the closest possible way. Of all American institutions, perhaps only the military brings people of such different backgrounds into more intimate contact. Moreover, university leaders are embarked on a conscious project to shape students into future leaders of an increasingly multicultural community. Consequently, the American campus becomes a very useful test case for institutional and social policies that draw racial groups together—or pry them apart; that promote integration—or separatism; that foster ethnic collegiality and harmony —or isolation and bitterness.

II

SEPARATE AND UNEQUAL

4   Anyone who is part of the American university culture, as well as informed outside observers, cannot fail to notice the proliferation of separatist minority organizations on virtually every college campus.

Universities that only a few years ago recognized an Afro-American Society and possibly an International Students Organization now sponsor a bewildering array of ethnic organizations.

. . .

5   On many campuses, separatism is not confined to membership in ethnically oriented extracurricular groups but extends to most aspects of campus life. Students at several universities have remarked on the widespread phenomenon of "black tables" at the university dining hall, where groups of African-American students insist on eating meals by themselves and regard white students who join them with undisguised antagonism. Surveying the University of California Berkeley campus, the *New York Times* reported what any observant visitor notices: "Blacks and whites root for the same team but sit in different sections . . . floors in the undergraduate library are in practice segregated by race . . . rarely does a single white or two comfortably join a dining room table occupied mostly by blacks."

6   Two recent graduates of Columbia have written that the university "is deeply divided along racial lines. Blacks gather in one area of the classroom, whites in another. Blacks and whites keep to different social circles. They don't participate in the same campus organizations, join the same fraternities, or hang out in the same bars. With infrequent exceptions, they are not friends. On this liberal, Ivy League campus where we expected to find racial harmony and friendship, there is rampant and growing mutual racism." These patterns are all too familiar at American universities across the country.

7   It is no exaggeration to say that many colleges are divided into sharply distinct ethnic subcultures—a black culture, a Hispanic culture, an Asian culture, and a (residual) white culture. Minority students often express contempt for what they describe as "white cultural norms," and they insist on adhering to manners and morals that they promote as authentically black, Hispanic, or Third World. Black students, for example, frequently identify with the protest culture of rap music and Malcolm X rhetoric. As one Howard University activist said, "Malcolm has replaced Martin as our leader." Responding to the new trend, a black student at Central Michigan University complained, in an article published in the *Chronicle of Higher Education*, "If I listen to a rock concert, people will say I am listening to white music. They will say I'm trying to act white. Certain activities are labeled 'white' and 'black.' If you don't participate in black activities, you are shunned."

. . .

III

INTEGRATION VS. PLURALISM

To justify these new developments, university leaders have developed a model of pluralism that they say replaces the antiquated concept of integration. While integration relied upon the concept of racial groups dissolving their distinctive cultural habits into a common American culture, pluralism affirms and accentuates ethnic differences. Malcolm Willis, vice-provost at Duke University, maintains that the paradigm of the "melting pot" has been replaced by that of the "salad bowl." In this view, far from asking racial and ethnic groups to jettison their particularities, universities help to preserve the varied cultural ingredients that produce a rich and savory "multiculturalism" or "diversity." 8

The only problem with this vision is that the campuses most dedicated to advancing pluralism of this sort are precisely the ones undergoing the greatest volume of racial tension and racial incidents. The national media has noted the rapid resurgence of bigotry on American campuses. The problem has been ascribed, by Reginald Wilson of the American Council on Education and the *Washington Post* editorial page, among others, to Reagan-era insensitivity and a failure to tutor young people in the lessons of the civil rights movement, thus allowing an upsurge of adolescent prejudice to express itself unembarrassed and unchecked. 9

But these explanations ignore the fact that the vast majority of racial incidents have been recorded at northern campuses with a progressive reputation. The South, ancestral home of socially sanctioned bigotry and segregation, seems to have accommodated minority students on its campuses relatively well. Administrators concede that ethnic hostility seems most acute at such places as Berkeley, Michigan, Oberlin, and the University of Massachusetts at Amherst, whose chancellor, Joseph Duffey, reacted to a racial brawl with the perplexed comment, "People here pride themselves on being liberals. They think things like this only happen in Forsyth, Georgia." An examination of a hundred racial incidents tabulated by the National Institute Against Prejudice and Violence indicates that the state with the most problems is Massachusetts, which is not exactly Reagan country. 10

. . .

Perhaps the most disturbing development in this separatist conflict is the recent establishment of white student unions on such campuses as Temple University and Florida State. Having financed a 11 battery of minority groups, including black student unions, university officials had no option but to recognize their white counterparts as official student organizations. Along the same lines, as a cultural alternative to Black History Month in 1989, white students at the University of Michigan put up posters announcing "White Pride Week," which was said to be a celebration of "yachts, sailboats, navy blazers, cool white presidents, all the kids we know are our own, polo stuff, L.L. Bean, Land's End, and plantations." Fred Sheehen of the South Carolina Commission on Higher Education expects this so-called white backlash to continue. When universities promote minority dormitories and groups, Sheehen predicts, soon fraternities may ask for segregated facilities on the grounds that "white males need a support group too." One college dean glumly speculated that, even as they mobilize against investments in South Africa, American universities are consolidating their own form of apartheid.

IV

MORE EQUAL THAN OTHERS

12   What is going on? How has the American university changed from an advocate of integration and racial harmony into an apparent sponsor of division and conflict? Why has the passion for eliminating racial classification, primary in the civil rights movement, given way to an equally strong drive to heighten and affirm racial distinction? The answer begins with admissions policies at American universities, which determine the composition of each freshman class.

13   The overwhelming majority of colleges are under constant pressure from state legislatures, civil rights groups, and faculty and student activists to increase minority representation. Administrators sometimes welcome this challenge, because many espouse a political philosophy in which racial groups on campus roughly approximate their proportion in the general population. "Proportional representation" is the new admissions buzzword—and it is official policy at such universities as Berkeley, where the university admits that only 50 percent of students each year are admitted according to the traditional criterion of academic merit. Many university leaders argue that since a college education provides many financial and social benefits in later life, equitable racial allocation of freshmen seats is the only just distribution of rewards in a democratic society.

14   The reason admissions policy must move beyond merit criteria, it is argued, is that, for various reasons, racial groups perform very differ-

ently on such academic indices as standardized test scores and grade point averages. Thus, the goal of proportional representation requires that colleges play down or ignore grades and test results and accept students from certain minority groups who are less well prepared than other students, who are consequently refused admission. In practice, this means that black, Hispanic, and American Indian students, who are considered members of under-represented groups, are given preference over better-qualified white and Asian students, who are considered over-represented. Regardless of its rhetorical aspirations, this is the contemporary reality of "affirmative action."

Unfortunately, the number of students from affirmative action minority groups who meet the demanding admissions standards of selective colleges is extremely small. In 1988, although nearly 100,000 black students took the Scholastic Aptitude Test (SAT), only 116 scored above 699 (out of 800) on the verbal section; only 342 scored that high on the math section. Fewer than 3,000 blacks scored above 599 on either part of the test. The average white-black differential in aggregate score was enormous: 198 points. The Asian-black differential was equally large: 192 points. Universities that seek 8 to 10 percent enrollments of black students are frequently forced to make substantial accommodations in academic criteria in order to meet their affirmative action targets.

Ernest Koenigsburg, a Berkeley business professor who has served on admissions committees, explained the way this works at his university. Imagine a student with a grade point average of 3.5 (out of 4.0) and an SAT score of 1,200 (out of 1,600). If such a student were black, Koenigsburg reports that his or her chances for admission are virtually 100 percent. If such a student were white or Asian, however, Koenigsburg calculates that the probability of admission would be less than 5 percent.

. . .

One reason these facts are not well known is that universities do everything they can to camouflage them—partly because their affirmative action policies are most defensible when stated at a high level of generality, partly because of a legitimate desire to protect the self-pride of minority students. Nevertheless, while it is possible to make admissions decisions in secret, it is impossible to conceal the consequences of affirmative action, because they will be walking around campus for the next several years.

. . .

Affirmative action students are usually astonished at their academic hardships, because for the year before college they have enjoyed the avid courtship of admissions officers, who have assured

15

16

17

18

them that they belong at the university, that standards have not been lowered to let them in—indeed that they have a distinct perspective that the university could not hope to gain from other students. The high expectations of these minority students are typically eroded by the end of the first semester, when the natural difficulties of adjustment to college life are compounded by academic pressures more severe than those faced by other undergraduates.

19   It is at this point, when minority freshmen find themselves in this predicament, that they begin to look for comfort and security among their peers in a similar situation. Many sign up for their campus Afro-American Society or Hispanic Student Association or ethnic theme house, where they attempt to share their hopes and frustrations in a receptive atmosphere. Now they begin to seek guidance from older classmates who have journeyed these unfamiliar and somewhat frightening paths.

V

THE GRIEVANCE INDUSTRY

20   While these separatist institutions provide a social enclave for affirmative action students, offering genuine camaraderie and support, they have no remedy for the students' academic problems. Virtually none provides programs in remedial reading, basic mathematics, or other skills related to course work. What they come up with instead is an attractive explanation—minority students suffer not because they are inadequately prepared for the work, but because of the pervasive bigotry that makes it impossible for them to advance. Although such racism may not be obvious at first, minority freshmen are informed that it operates in elusive forms, such as baleful looks, subtle insinuations, uncorrected mental stereotypes, and what educators Jeff Howard and Ray Hammond in a 1985 article in the *New Republic* termed "rumors of inferiority." Moreover, the university itself is said to have gone from "overt racism" to "institutional racism," evident in the disproportionately small number of minorities reflected in the faculty and among the deans.

. . .

21   While many universities sternly scrutinize the motives, behavior, and speech of alleged campus bigots, these suspicions do not usually extend to the minority activists themselves. A group of professors called Concerned Faculty at Michigan supplies the rationale for this double standard:

Behavior which constitutes racist oppression when engaged in
by whites does not have this character when undertaken by
people of color. For example, a white person may not proclaim
a lounge or campus organization only for whites. Yet there
is an important place on this campus for Black Student
Lounges, the Black Student Union, etc. Such associations do
not oppress whites, because people of color are not in a
position to deprive whites of the powers, opportunities and
recognition they need to advance their interests.

In the same vein, Gayatri Spivak, Andrew Mellon Professor of   22
English and Cultural Studies at the University of Pittsburgh, argues that
while it is essential to teach white students sensitivity to cultural diversity, such qualities as tolerance cannot reasonably be expected of
minorities. "Tolerance is a loaded virtue," said Spivak, "because you
have to have a base of power to practice it. You cannot ask a certain
people to 'tolerate' a culture that has historically ignored them at the
same time that their children are being indoctrinated into it."

However comprehensive the effort of universities to ameliorate   23
minority concerns, it seldom succeeds. Eventually minority discontent,
which was spawned in large part because of academic difficulties,
returns to the classroom. Minority students are now informed that even
as they agitate against widespread campus racism, the worst form of
bigotry stands right in front of them. In particular, as heard during
Stanford University's much-publicized "Hey hey, ho ho, Western culture's got to go" debate, most of the curriculum consists of works by
whites, collectively echoing a Eurocentric perspective. No wonder,
then, that students from different backgrounds have difficulty absorbing culturally alien texts. This realization leads quickly to demands for
a multicultural curriculum, including the establishment or expansion of
such distinctive programs as Afro-American Studies, which are said to
offer an authentic black perspective. Such perspectives can become
somewhat rarefied, as in Harvard law professor Derrick Bell's refusal
to teach for a year to pressure the university into granting tenure to a
black female, whose unique perspective Bell said neither white
women nor black men could hope to provide.

The extension of minority separatism to the classroom, specifi-   24
cally in such special programs as Afro-American studies and more
broadly through the invocation of distinct minority perspectives, creates in effect a color-coded system of scholarship, in which traditional
fields of inquiry are put down to the white way of thinking, which of
course needs to be balanced by equally important and valid minority

viewpoints. Far from resisting the establishment of separatist departments such as Afro-American Studies, college officials usually welcome it, because it provides an easy way to fulfill faculty affirmative action targets, thus keeping less-than-qualified minority teachers away from the mainstream curriculum. Moreover, such departments often become curricular equivalents for the social function served by minority organizations—they provide students with a refuge from the pressures of integrated campus life.

VI

THE NEW RACISM ON CAMPUS

25   Issues of race place most white students in a very uncomfortable position. Surveys have shown that today's generation of young people has remarkably tolerant views, including widespread acceptance of interracial dating. Even though many whites may not have lived or studied with blacks, Hispanics, or other minorities in the past, they seem generally committed to equal rights and open to building friendships and associations with people whom they know have been wronged through history.

26   Since they applied to college, many white and Asian American students know that other groups have enjoyed preferential treatment in admission. Even students who support affirmative action in principle have qualms when they see that it is now harder for them to gain acceptance to universities for which they have prepared. Even if they get in, many have friends in high school who they believe were denied admission to make room for minority students with weaker qualifications. For Asian students, many from disadvantaged backgrounds, such as the Cambodian boat people, it is impossible to justify such discrimination on the grounds of past crimes or present privilege—the cruel irony for this minority group is that quotas once intended as instruments of inclusion seem to have become instruments of exclusion.

27   Students are reminded of these concerns about equity when they see the obvious differences in preparation among various groups in class. Black and Hispanic difficulties become a confirmation of the suspicion that universities basically operate on a racial multiple-track admissions process. Yet it is obvious that this cannot be stated in public, partly because universities continue to deny that they lower requirements for select groups and partly because minorities would take serious offense at such "insensitivity." Consequently, most students discuss affirmative action only in private. But since students live

and study in close quarters, it is impossible to conceal common sentiments for long, and soon minority students suspect that people are
talking about them behind closed doors and about the issue most sensitive to them—namely, whether they belong at the university or not.
This strengthens minority sentiments about the existence of subtle and
elusive prejudices against them.

White students tend to have a mixed response to minority sepa-   28
ratism. For bigots among them, such self-segregation comes as a
tremendous relief, partly because it removes blacks and Hispanics
from the mainstream of campus life and partly because it reinforces
racist attitudes. Bigoted students confirm their prejudices in two ways:
first, by congratulating themselves on the validation of their suspicion
that minorities cannot succeed on their own and require special group
concessions; and second, by assuring themselves that it is perfectly
acceptable for them to prefer to associate only with whites, since
minorities clearly exercise a preference for their own. Mark Wright,
founder of a white student union at the University of Florida, told his
local newspaper, "When whites decide to stand up for issues that are
important to them, we are labeled racist. When blacks do so, they are
labeled civil rights activists."

While few students wish to join all-white institutions, many   29
observe that university policy toward racial groups employs a double
standard that apparently replicates the racial preferences of admissions
policy. Many students agree with the *Washington Post* columnist
William Raspberry, who has written that "you cannot claim both full
equality and special dispensation." Minority separatist institutions are
most irritating, not so much because they are separate, but because in
many cases they become institutional launching pads for systematic
attacks directed against whites. Many separatist groups are quick to
make accusations of bigotry, to the point where any disagreement with
the agenda of the Afro-American Society is automatically evidence of
racism. Here the doctrine of pluralism has become a framework for
racial browbeating and intimidation.

When they discover resentment among students over preferential   30
treatment and minority separatism, activists and university administrators typically conclude that they have discovered the latent bigotry for
which they have been searching. This resurgence of racism, they
claim, illustrates that "more needs to be done" in the form of redou-
bled minority recruitment, the establishment of ethnic studies requirements, recognition for a black sorority, a new Third World center
perhaps, and the inevitable establishment of a task force to make additional proposals. In short, university policies of preferentialism and
double standards create racial division and tension on campus, and

when this happens administrators call for an intensification and multiplication of such policies.

31   It is this balkanized environment that gives rise to racial jokes and racial incidents. These episodes are not spontaneous eruptions of old-style racism; they represent the uncorking of a tightly sealed bottle. When legitimate questions about equality and fairness are repressed by an atmosphere of accusation, intimidation, and censorship, they tend to ferment under the surface and finally erupt in perverse, rebellious, and outrageous expression. A close examination of the contemporary culture of racial humor on campus, as well as documented racial incidents, points to a large number that are directly related to the two-tier system of justice for racial groups, extending from admissions policy to life on campus, to the classroom. Needless to say, as universities redouble their current agenda for multiculturalism, pluralism, and diversity, these problems will continue to worsen and universities will experience more numerous, and more vicious, racial incidents.

▶   QUESTIONS TO CONSIDER

1. According to your experiences and knowledge, does D'Souza describe the problem of campus segregation accurately and fairly? For example, do you agree with his statement that "It is no exaggeration to say that many colleges are divided into sharply distinct ethnic subcultures?" Why, or why not?

2. What evidence does D'Souza include to support his assertions about the significance of this problem?

3. The author points out that "the vast majority of racial incidents have been recorded at northern campuses with a progressive reputation. The South, . . . seems to have accommodated minority students on its campuses relatively well." D'Souza attributes this phenomenon to the emphasis on multicultural programs and courses at the more progressive northern schools. Do you agree with his conclusion? Can you think of other reasons why southern schools seem to be less segregated than those in the north?

4. D'Souza blames this problem to a great extent on affirmative action policies and speaks of a "white backlash" that is occurring as a result of these policies. Do you agree that white students are rebelling against affirmative action policies that establish different admission standards for minority students in order to ensure that schools will be racially diverse? What would most college campuses, especially

those of prestigious, northern schools, be like without affirmative action? Is diversity an important element of an education?

5. D'Souza discusses the difference in scores on entrance exams earned by different racial and ethnic groups and concludes that "minority students from disadvantaged backgrounds have enormous difficulty simply keeping up during the first semester." Is it the fact that the students are from a minority group or that they are from a disadvantaged background that is responsible for their low test scores and academic problems? D'Souza also fails to discuss the possibility that the tests that are given to determine admission to college are thought by some to be racially biased. Does his decision not to address these types of issues weaken his argument, or is he justified in omitting them?

6. D'Souza gives no clear solutions to the problem of campus segregation, but readers can infer some possible solutions from his discussion of the problem. What types of solutions do you think he is suggesting?

7. Compare D'Souza's essay and Snider's editorial, both of which address the problem of cultural diversity. Which do you find more convincing? Why?

WRITING ACTIVITIES

Individual: Write in your journal a description of your campus in terms of racial and ethnic divisions. Be as objective and accurate as possible.

Collaborative: The author explores at some length both the causes and the effects of the problem of increasingly segregated college campuses. Working with a small group of your peers, identify both the causes and effects that D'Souza identifies.

Computer: If you have not already done so, enter your journal entry into a computer. Using your description of the racial and ethnic division that is found on your campus as the problem, discuss the causes and effects of this problem, and conclude by proposing a solution or solutions. Using the cut-and-paste or block-and-move function of your word-processing program, experiment by organizing your text in several different ways. For example, you could begin by presenting the solution(s) and then discussing the problem, or you might discuss the causes of the problem as a way of leading up to the problem (rather than discussing it first).

▶ Writing to Solve Problems and Present Solutions

Like writing to instruct, writing to present solutions falls into two general categories: writing for readers who plan to take immediate action and writing for readers who just want to think about the problem and consider the proposal as a possible long-range solution. Before writing to present a solution to a problem, you must decide which of these two purposes you are pursuing. If you are writing to propose a solution to be implemented now, you will probably write a letter, memo, or report. If you are writing to emphasize a problem or to suggest a possible solution for the reader's consideration (but not immediate action), you will more likely write an editorial, article, or essay.

Let's say the hard part is done; you have recognized a problem, figured out a solution, and determined the type of document to write. How do you write a memo, report, essay, or editorial that convinces readers to adopt or at least try your solution? Answering the following questions will help:

- ❖ Who is my audience?
- ❖ What should I include and emphasize?
- ❖ What organization plan should I use?

Determining Your Audience

First, you must decide who your readers will be, and then analyze their qualifications, needs, and expectations. You will be able to make many writing decisions based upon this analysis.

Be very specific about identifying your audience. "Anyone who is interested" or "someone who can solve the problem" will not do. You need to know, if not the exact person or persons, at least something about the type of person who will be your reader. For example, suppose you are writing about the problems you have experienced and observed working with other students on collaborative assignments. You might write a memo to a specific instructor who requires group work, to a department chair or dean who supervises faculty members who frequently include collaborative assignments in their courses, or to a professional education journal. Although you might know only the instructor personally, the other possible readers are also knowable. You know, for example, the approximate education and economic levels of chairs and deans as well as the fact that they tend to be busy administrators. The readers of a professional journal are less easily knowable, but you can generalize that such readers are probably teachers and are reading a journal because they want to improve their teaching or keep abreast of new developments in their profession.

Decisions about audience go beyond merely deciding who is interested in solving the problem. A more important consideration is, who has the power to solve the problem? For example, suppose you are a human resource specialist in a utilities company and have been asked by your supervisor, the personnel director, to recommend a plan to eliminate seventy-five employees. Your report will obviously be directed to your supervisor, but you should be aware that his or her managers will also read it, so you should consider them part of your audience, too. These secondary readers actually have the power to implement your solution. In addition, there may be a third set of readers—the employees who would be affected by the plan's implementation. Although you will write primarily for the personnel director, don't forget your other readers' needs and perspectives.

In contrast to being told to solve a problem, you may sometimes volunteer to solve a problem; that is, you may offer an unsolicited solution. The question of audience is even more complex in this situation. Suppose you want to suggest a way to improve the relationship between your community's police and the rest of its citizens. You could, of course, write a letter to the editor of your local newspaper or a guest editorial for the Sunday edition. Your proposed solution might have a wide readership if you presented it in the newspaper. However, unless an election or referendum related to this issue were about to take place, your solution might have little effect. Even though you might persuade the readers of the newspaper that your solution was workable, even brilliant, few of them would have the power to implement your solution. In such a situation, you would probably accomplish more if you wrote a letter to the chief of police or the local governing body. Not only are these people interested in the problem created by a bad relationship between the police force and the community, but they have the power to do something about it.

In contrast, if you merely want to point out such a problem, you might very well choose to write a letter to the editor of your local newspaper. In this case, you would be writing primarily to the people of the community, attempting to persuade them that a problem exists and that they need to be concerned about it. Such a letter might also get the attention of people who have the power to change the situation, because no one likes to be criticized, and these people might eventually attempt to solve the problem you identify.

You can see why decisions about audience affect later decisions—the type of document you write, your purpose in writing it, what you say, and the way in which you say it. Identifying your readers, the ones who will read what you have written and who have the power to solve the problem, is an essential first step.

The second step is to analyze your reader or readers. As experienced writers often do informally and almost automatically, you should learn to question yourself about your readers. For example, simple demographics are important. What is the age, gender, economic status, education level, and profession of the reader(s)? Beyond these basic facts, what are the interests, attitudes, and biases of those to whom you are writing? What do these people have to gain or lose by the solution you are proposing?

Answering the following questions will help you learn more about your audience:

- Who is my audience?
- Where do they live?
- What do they do?
- How much education do they have?
- How much information do they have about my problem?
- Do they have the power to solve my problem?
- Are they likely to be reading hurriedly or leisurely, carefully or superficially?
- Are they likely to be hostile or friendly readers?
- What do they have to gain or lose by my proposal?

Deciding What to Include and Emphasize

Once you know and understand the person(s) to whom you are writing, you should be able to answer the next question about what to include and emphasize. Think in terms of the three elements introduced at the start of this chapter:

1. Definition of the problem

2. Evaluation of alternative solutions

3. Argument for proposed solution

The attention you devote to each of these elements depends primarily on your audience and purpose. If you are writing a letter to the editor because you want to call attention to a problem (say the problem of police-community relations), you will probably want to emphasize the problem. You might mention that some of the police commissioner's efforts to solve this problem have been ineffectual or that a total reorganization of the police force is necessary, but your primary purpose is just to make people aware that a problem exists.

In contrast, if you are the personnel director who has been asked to devise a plan to reduce the number of employees in your company, you may say very little about the problem, which is probably all too well known by your employers. Instead, you will emphasize the solution you are proposing.

It is said that if there are no alternatives, there is no problem. In other words, if there is only one course of action, that is obviously the solution. However, in writing to present solutions, you must decide not only if alternative solutions exist but also whether to present them and, if so, how much attention to give them.

The decision about whether to include alternative solutions depends primarily on who your audience is. If your readers already know about other solutions, there is no need to discuss them extensively, although you may want to mention them briefly. For example, the utilities company management knows that one way to solve their problem is simply to fire the seventy-five employees. You don't need to remind them of this solution. But you might want to include and evaluate other solutions (early retirement, voluntary part-time employment, salary reductions, and so on) before arguing for your proposed solution of reorganization and reassignment.

The authors in this chapter's reading selections vary widely in what they emphasize and include. Some focus almost exclusively on the problem. For example, Frank Cedeño discusses the solution he proposes in just one paragraph, and he omits alternative solutions entirely. Likewise, Dinesh D'Souza writes extensively of the problem of campus segregation but offers no solutions. Others emphasize their solution and say very little about the problems. Breuer, for example, assumes that her audience understands the problem of AIDS victims in the workforce and is primarily concerned about a solution. Still others balance the two, devoting almost equal attention to problem and solution.

Developing a Plan of Organization

In writing to present a solution, you may want to follow the plan of organization suggested by the three key elements of a problem-solution document. That is, you may want to begin with a definition of the problem, move on to a discussion of alternative solutions, and then conclude with arguments that support your own solution. This plan has the virtue of meeting your readers' expectations, because it is the most common pattern for writing to present a solution. However, you shouldn't feel bound by this organization plan. Variations are possible and even desirable. For example, why not present your own solution before discussing alternative solutions? If you do this, you might want to discuss your solution again briefly in your conclusion in order to refocus your reader's attention to it.

Most of the writers of the reading selections in this chapter follow the traditional pattern of problem first and then solution (or solutions, if alternative solutions are considered). For example, Breuer, writing for a journal read primarily by personnel specialists, follows a straightforward, simple plan of organization. First, she briefly discusses the problem of HIV-infected employees in the workplace, and then she argues for her solution, providing her readers with numerous examples of companies that have successfully implemented this solution (i.e., educating all employees about the disease and its effects). If Breuer had organized her text as a personal narrative, telling about her own experiences with this problem, her readers might have become frustrated and impatient, for they need an immediate, workable solution to a problem that is only going to get worse in the near future. They are in a position to take action and need information to do so.

HEADINGS, PAGE 603 Often readers interested in solving a problem merely skim the first part of an article or report, focusing most of their attention on the solution. For such readers, you might want to include **headings** that identify the different sections of your memo, report, or article. Headings enable readers to read more quickly and efficiently. They are especially appropriate when you are writing to present a solution to someone who is going to make an immediate decision about your proposal. Also, when you write for such a reader, you should organize your text in the most direct, straightforward manner possible, including each element in the expected order. Also include strong transitions that indicate clearly each major section of your text. If you are writing for someone who is merely interested in the problem and wants to think about it, feel free to vary the usual pattern. As always, audience and purpose are the determining factors.

The Role of a Thesis in Writing to Solve Problems

In general, it is a good idea to inform your reader of your thesis at the beginning of your text. For example, many writers include their thesis at the end of their introduction. However, in writing to solve problems, writers often delay their thesis—sometimes until their conclusion, when they present their solution. Because the solution they are proposing is, in effect, their thesis, this placement makes sense. For example, Frank Cedeño states his thesis in the very last sentence of his essay. And David Blankenhorn places his thesis in the middle of his article, while Melvin Konner places his at the beginning of his conclusion. Nancy Breuer, in contrast, places her thesis at the end of her introduction, perhaps because her readers—business people who are responsible for personnel and management decisions—want information delivered as directly and clearly as possible.

Wherever you place your thesis, or even if you choose not to include an explicit thesis statement, be sure your readers know where you stand on the issue you are addressing. In writing to solve a problem, you do not want to leave your readers in doubt about the position you are taking.

Patterns of Development in Writing to Solve Problems

Several of the traditional methods of development can be used to develop your text. Let's see how each section of a problem-solution text might use various methods of development.

DEFINITION OF THE PROBLEM.   In defining the problem you are addressing, you may use almost any method of development. For example, Breuer begins her discussion of the problem of AIDS in the workplace with **narration**. More typically, however, you might use **description**, **exemplification**, **comparison/contrast**, or **cause and effect**. Cause and effect is perhaps the method of development most frequently used in defining a problem. Readers typically want to know what caused a

NARRATION, PAGE 618
DESCRIPTION, PAGE 565
EXEMPLIFICATION, PAGE 574
COMPARISON/CONTRAST,
PAGE 542
CAUSE AND EFFECT,
PAGE 522

certain problem and what its effects are likely to be. However, all of the methods of development mentioned here could be used appropriately. For example, suppose you are writing about the problem that some students have in relating to their instructors. You might want to describe a bad student-teacher relationship, compare it to a good student-teacher relationship, illustrate each, and then discuss the cause and/or effect of this problem in terms of student performance.

EVALUATION OF ALTERNATIVE SOLUTIONS.   If you include alternative solutions in your text, you may want to develop them (briefly) by using one or more of the same methods you used to define the problem: description, exemplification, comparison and contrast, or cause and effect, depending upon how much information your readers need to understand each one. In addition, you might also want to use **classification**. If, for example, you are identifying a number of different alternative solutions, help your reader by classifying the solutions in some way (e.g., those that are temporary and those that are permanent; those that involve reorganization and those that involve personnel; those that are favored by one group and those that are supported by another group).

CLASSIFICATION, PAGE 527

In evaluating different alternative solutions, you will, of course, use comparison and contrast, but you might also want to use classification and/or cause and effect.

ARGUMENT FOR PROPOSED SOLUTION.   You can use a variety of development methods in arguing for your own solution. In fact, it is difficult to think of one that could not be used. You will, of course, need to describe the solution you are proposing, perhaps providing your readers with examples (exemplification). And, just as you need to discuss cause and effect when you define a problem, you will probably also want to point out the effects you anticipate if your solution is implemented. You may also want to compare and contrast your solution with the alternative solutions you have included or even to classify it so your readers can see how it relates to other solutions. Finally, you may want to tell a story (narration) in order to make the problem seem more real and personal to your readers. Reconstructions of personal experiences can be compellingly persuasive. In deciding how extensively to develop each section of your text, remember to keep your purpose in mind. Your primary purpose is to present your own solution and argue for its implementation.

W R I T I N G   A S S I G N M E N T

For this writing assignment select a problem involving human rela-tions—how people do or, in this case, do not get along—and write an essay, editorial, memo, or report proposing a solution. The suggestions that follow may help you decide on a topic:

1. Write about the problem of working on collaborative assign-ments with other students.

2. Write about the problem of being a smoker in an office of nonsmokers.

3. Write about problems that often exist between older and younger generations, between native and nonnative students, or be-tween males and females.

4. Write about a human relations problem that exists in your work-place, church, or community.

5. Write about the problem of sexual harassment on campus.

6. Write about the problem that students and teachers have in communicating with one another.

7. Identify a problem related to cultural diversity on your cam-pus, and write an editorial or a letter to the editor of your campus newspaper about this problem and the solution you propose.

8. Interview several international students about the problem they faced in getting to know other students. Then write an article addressed to international students in which you discuss this problem and propose one or more solutions.

9. Write a report for an organization to which you belong in which you identify a problem among members of the organization or a problem between your organization and another on campus. Be sure to describe the problem objectively and propose a solution.

10. Write a letter or memo to an administrator in which you iden-tify and propose a solution to a problem that affects a particular group of students (e.g., disabled students, dorm students, students who eat in the cafeteria, and so on).

Whatever problem you choose to write about, focus on the prob-lem as it exists on your own campus (although you might want to include some statistics about the problem nationwide or mention that the problem is not limited to your school). In general, the more spe-cific you are, the better the results will be. However, if you choose to write about a topic such as parent-child or male-female relationships, you should probably not focus on yourself exclusively. Remember that

you are writing for an audience, not yourself. Write about your own
personal relationships only if you can meet the following standards:

1. You can discuss the problem objectively.

2. You can solve the problem.

3. Both the problem and solution are generalizable—that is, they can
appropriately be applied to other people and other situations.

In choosing a problem to write about, you must strike a delicate
balance. You will probably want to focus on a specific problem that
you know a great deal about and think you can actually solve. But you
don't want to be too personal—to write about a problem affecting just
you and not relevant to others.

Even so, remember these are guidelines, not ironclad rules that
must be followed regardless of your interests and inclinations. Some
people like to tackle big issues like race or parent-child or male-
female relations. Most of the reading selections included in this chapter do just that. If you want to write about such a topic, be sure you
know the problem well (perhaps even firsthand) and have a viable
solution to propose. Realize, however, that such a problem is more
challenging—more difficult to write about convincingly and more difficult to solve.

Whatever problem you choose to write about, be sure that you
have a serious proposal to present to your readers—something they can
consider as an eventual or possible solution. Ideally, your solution should
be as specific as your problem. Just telling your readers that the people
in question should get along better is a poignant hope but not a solution.

Generating Ideas through Invention and Research

In addition to selecting a problem and identifying your audience, you
may want to learn more about the problem before you begin to write.

INVENTION.   One way to begin thinking about this assignment, or any
writing project, is to brainstorm. Brainstorming can be oral or written. If you have a group of peers with whom you are working, you
may want to have an oral brainstorming session in which each member of the group volunteers ideas. The point here is to be as open-
minded as possible, giving every idea that is suggested an equal
opportunity, regardless of how extreme or innovative it may be. En-

courage everyone to volunteer his or her most creative ideas, and consider these ideas seriously.

If you are working alone, you can brainstorm in writing by simply making a list of ideas as they come to you. Do not omit any idea that occurs to you. Include it on your list, and evaluate it later. The idea is to generate a long list that will give you lots of ideas to evaluate and consider.

After you have run out of ideas to include on your list, you may want to cluster (or group) related ideas. You may want to start a new page on which you organize the related ideas into several categories; or you can simply draw lines and circles on the original list to indicate related ideas. The point is to produce a visual map of your brainstorming that makes clear the relationship among the different ideas you have included (see **invention**).

INVENTION, PAGE 613

RESEARCH. You may need to research the problem about which you are writing through both field and library research. For example, you could observe a situation in which the problem exists, taking careful notes so that you can reconstruct your observation experience when you begin to write. Or you might interview people who are familiar with the problem but have perspectives different from your own or who have had more experience than you have with this particular problem. You could also survey students and faculty members to ascertain how many of them view this problem as significant.

You may also want to obtain additional information from written documents (see Conducting Library Research in Part Three, pp. 407–444). For example, if you are writing about race relations on your campus, you may want to research the issue of race relations on other campuses. Or you may want to research the history of race relations on your own campus by reading old newspapers and archival material about your school. You could also use the reading selection in this chapter by Dinesh D'Souza, "The New Segregation," as a source.

Drafting Your Text

You can begin writing by constructing an outline based on the different elements usually included in a problem-solution text:

- ❖ Definition of the problem
- ❖ Evaluation of alternative solutions
- ❖ Argument for proposed solution

As you develop each of these elements into a major section of your text, you may well discover that you want to omit one or more or that one will be much longer than the others. That's fine. Just let your text take shape as it will, growing naturally as you expand and develop each section.

Reading and Revising Your Text

Allow some time to elapse after you finish a draft of your text before you read it. Of course, you will read your text, at least in bits and pieces, many times as you are drafting it. But when you have finished a draft, let it "rest" for a day or so (longer, if possible) before reading through it carefully. Then try to put yourself in your intended reader's place—try to imagine how a reader will respond to what you have written. This trick of pretending you are the intended reader takes practice. It is much easier to read from your own point of view. As the writer, you know all about the problem and understand perfectly how the solution is supposed to work. However, your reader will not have these advantages, so you must try to gain his or her perspective.

Because you identified your audience specifically in the planning stage, you should know exactly who your readers are. Imagining yourself as a specific reader should be much easier than imagining yourself as a vaguely defined, nebulous reader.

In this imagining-yourself-as-reader process, be sure to carefully consider the possible attitudes of your intended reader toward the problem you are discussing. Is this a friendly reader or an indifferent reader or a hostile reader? A busy, impatient reader or a leisurely reader? Is this person convinced a problem exists, or do you need to persuade him or her? Does this person want a solution? If so, is he or she biased in favor of another solution? Here are other questions to ask yourself as you read:

- Is my problem well defined?

- Have I represented other solutions fairly?

- Is my solution workable? Practical? Ethical?

- Is my text clear and easy to read?

As you read, write notes to yourself on the text so that you will remember what you need to do when you begin to revise. For example, suppose you discover that you need to reorganize your text. You can bracket or circle the material to be moved and draw an arrow indicating the position in the text where you want to insert it. If you decide that one section needs to be developed more fully, write a note to that effect. If some material needs to be deleted, scratch it out. In other words, don't rely on your memory. Annotate your text as you read it so you will know exactly what you want to do when you revise.

Also carefully evaluate the development of your text now. Have you assumed too much knowledge on the part of the reader and omitted necessary information? It is easy to assume your reader knows as much as you do about the problem and views the problem exactly as you do. But this may not be the case. You may also have assumed that your reader will be able to see the good sense of your proposed solution even though you have given him or her very few details. Especially if you are expecting your reader to implement your proposal at once, be sure that you have given that person enough information to make a decision. A decision to act is not easily made. If you do not give your reader sufficient information, it will not matter how persuasively you have written.

Preparing the Final Draft of Your Text

A text that persuades your readers that the problem you are addressing needs to be solved and that you have the best solution requires not only effective organization and adequate information, but also appropriate **style and voice**. A brusque, no-nonsense voice and formal style may be exactly what some readers want, whereas others prefer a personal, easygoing tone and informal style.

STYLE AND VOICE, PAGE 656

Editing for style and voice is not easy, because these qualities of a text seem so abstract and nebulous. Just what constitutes style and voice? How do you know if your style and voice are appropriate? Style and voice indicate your relationship with your reader. If you want that relationship to be familiar, even personal, you reveal yourself freely in your text, using first-person point of view, giving your opinions freely, even including information about yourself (as Joan Marie Snider does, for example). If you want that relationship to be impersonal and more formal, you reveal very little about yourself (as Nancy Breuer, Frank Cedeño, Melvin Konner, and Dinesh D'Souza do).

In making these decisions, you must once again consider your audience. Who are your readers? What would be an appropriate relationship for you to have with them? If you are writing to other students, for example, you can be rather personal and fairly informal. In contrast, if you are writing to an administrator, the readers of a newspaper, or your employer, you will want to maintain a certain level of formality and not intrude on your text.

Once you have determined the appropriate relationship, read your text to see if its style and voice reflect the relationship. The following questions may help you determine whether your style and voice are appropriate:

- ❖ Have you referred to yourself or your experiences?

- ❖ Have you used first-person point of view (I)?

- ❖ Have you addressed the reader(s) directly as *you?*

- ❖ Are your sentences short and fairly simple?

- ❖ Have you used colloquial or slang expressions?

- ❖ Have you used humor?

- ❖ Would you describe your text as chatty, friendly, or personal?

- ❖ Would your reader know you as a person better after reading your text?

If you answered "yes" to most or all of these questions, you have probably written in a very personal voice and informal style. If you answered "yes" to only a few of these questions, you have probably written in a somewhat personal voice and informal style. If such a voice and style do not reflect an appropriate relationship with your intended reader(s), you probably need to edit your text so it is more formal and less personal (see **revising and editing**).

REVISING AND EDITING,
PAGE 651

▶ D ISCOVERING Y OURSELF AS A W RITER

After you have completed this assignment, take a few minutes to reflect on this writing experience by answering the following questions:

1. What did you learn about yourself as a writer as you worked on this assignment? In what way did this writing experience change your perception of yourself as a writer, your process of writing, or your attitude toward writing?

2. What forms of research did you use for this assignment? What did you learn about research that will help you in other writing assignments?

3. Was the final draft of your text better or worse than you had expected? What would you do differently if you had the opportunity to do this assignment again?

4. How did writing this assignment make you a better reader?

5. What did you enjoy most about this writing assignment? What did you like least?

Douglas Olson, *Farm Buildings, Near Random Lake, Wisconsin.*
Reprinted with permission of Douglas Olson.

8

▼

WRITING

FROM

SOURCES

337

The writer . . . is careful of what he reads, for that is what he will write. He is careful of what he learns, for that is what he will know.

ANNIE DILLARD

Whatever your writing purpose, you may decide to research your subject and include the results of that investigation in your text. Researching a subject allows you to see the text you are constructing in a larger context. As you pursue your research, you also begin seeing the individual parts as whole, and your ideas expand and become part of an ongoing intellectual conversation. Research enables you to learn more about a subject, to test your own ideas and arguments against those of others, to provide readers with additional information and multiple viewpoints, and to gain credibility in the eyes of your readers. When you report on your research, you may want to focus primarily on the sources you have discovered, objectively reporting the results of your investigation. More often, however, you will use your sources to develop and support your own arguments, as the student writers in this chapter do.

Your first introduction to this type of writing was most likely a research paper—a common assignment that requires you to research a subject and report on it. But reporting on research is more than an academic exercise. Such reports are common in business, government, and science. Recommendation reports and grant proposals, for example, nearly always involve the results of the writer's investigation of his or her subject. And research is not limited to science, government, and business. Reviews of books, music, art, and film also use other sources. In fact, *most* experienced writers use a variety of sources, including their own experiences, when they construct texts. Such writers see research and investigation as an essential part of their writing process.

Using multiple sources makes special demands on both writer and reader because they have to construct a text that includes not one voice but several. Writers must present multiple voices distinctly and yet blend them into a whole that makes sense to a reader. Only if the voice of the writer is clear and strong will the text be unified and coherent. Likewise, readers of a text based on multiple sources hear many voices, not just one. They must evaluate diverse viewpoints—not only the ideas, information, arguments, analyses, and recommendations of the writer, but also those of his or her sources.

This chapter focuses on the research process. In it you will find the information you need to formulate a research question, plan a research project, locate and evaluate sources, and integrate sources appropriately and effectively into your own text. These topics and others related to research are also the focus of Part Three, Strategies and Resources for Research.

READING TEXTS THAT USE SOURCES

In one sense, all texts are based on research. All writers use not only their own experiences, but what they have learned from other sources—from other texts and from other people—when they construct a text. When readers confront such a text, they comprehend and react to it in different ways than they do when they read a text that does not include outside sources.

Understanding Why to Evaluate Sources

A writer's use of several sources provides a reader with different viewpoints and more information. But because skillful writers usually select and structure their sources to reinforce their own viewpoints, readers may accept these source-supported arguments without analyzing the role those sources assume in the argument. Even readers who are not swayed by the sheer number of sources may succumb to the authority of the sources the writer includes. For example, if an article on the enforcement of environmental laws includes supporting evidence from a Supreme Court justice, the attorney general of the United States, and several district judges, readers may accept the writer's arguments primarily because they are impressed with the cumulative authority of these sources.

It is also easy to be unduly impressed with arguments supported by research studies. If a writer argues that "research indicates that . . .," readers may uncritically accept this vague reference to research as proof rather than evaluate the evidence. However, research studies do not always yield accurate, correctly interpreted results. Even careful research—honestly and accurately designed, conducted, and evaluated—

may be flawed. Medical researchers who undertake extensive research, much of it well executed, frequently have to revise their research findings in the light of subsequent research. Remember the on-again, off-again benefits and dangers of alcohol, oat bran, caffeine, cholesterol, exercise, and aspirin?

Some readers also equate the results of polls with proof that an argument is sound. Yet each week, especially during election years, new polls appear that make previous ones obsolete. Polls are, after all, only collected opinions. Many are limited in scope and purpose yet reported as if they were a valid representation of national, if not global, reality.

Knowing How to Evaluate Sources

How, then, does a careful reader navigate these dangers of misinformation and misrepresentation when reading a source-based text? In general, you should use the same strategies in evaluating a source-based text as you would in evaluating any text. That is, you should evaluate the arguments that are advanced, the unstated assumptions that are made, the information and evidence that is presented, and the language that is used. However, in evaluating source-based texts, you may also find the following five guidelines useful:

❖ Consider context.

❖ Correct for bias.

❖ Question the accuracy and relevance of the sources.

❖ Scrutinize documentation of sources.

❖ Focus on the argument.

CONSIDER CONTEXT. Out of context, a person's words can easily be misrepresented. Responsible writers never deliberately take a person's words out of context in a way that changes their meaning; unscrupulous writers often do. For example, a politician may state in a speech that she believes "national health care would benefit every level of society but no one more than the average, working-class American." Parts of this statement, taken out of the full context, could read as follows:

> Senator Anne Hawkins argued that "national health care would benefit . . . no one . . . ."

So beware of snippets—a few words taken out of their original context and placed in the writer's own sentence—because they are incomplete and may be misleading.

CORRECT FOR BIAS.   When you are reading a text that includes multiple sources, you must be aware of not only the writer's possible bias, but also that of the sources. For example, if a report on environmental issues cites only sources known to be concerned that the Earth's ecology is being harmed (Audubon Society, Sierra Club, National Resource Defense Fund, and so on) and ignores opposing viewpoints of government, industry, and others, you can assume that the sources are probably biased. Likewise, if the sources for an article on animal rights consist only of reports of research funded by the cosmetic and fur industries, you can assume they are probably not objective.

QUESTION THE ACCURACY AND RELEVANCE OF THE SOURCES.   Don't accept any source without question. Research studies can be misleading, polls are seldom scientific, and even authorities can be misquoted, quoted out of context, or simply wrong. Just because someone with a long title after his or her name says that something is so, it is not necessarily so. Even though most sources can be trusted, don't assume all sources can be trusted. Examine all sources carefully, noting especially their relevance and timeliness. The writer may have quoted a physician as saying that moderate amounts of alcohol are not harmful to most adults, but this opinion is not relevant if the issue is whether females should consume alcohol during pregnancy. Similarly, this same statement in a journal article published twenty-five years ago— even in the most reputable scientific journal—would not be valid today, because only recently have medical researchers determined the effects of alcohol on the unborn fetus.

SCRUTINIZE DOCUMENTATION OF SOURCES.   It is increasingly common to find undocumented sources (that is, material from sources that are not appropriately acknowledged) in popular magazines and journals. Although scholarly and academic journals still require careful documentation, popular books, magazines, and newspapers frequently include references to unnamed sources ("a recent study indicates . . . ," "a high-ranking official confirmed . . . ," "an eye-witness reports . . . ," and so on). Even more common is the practice of citing a source by name but not providing full documentation—the details that permit a reader to find out where, when, and even why the statement was made.

The reason for omitting such information may be stylistic. That is, the writer may not want to include formal documentation because it would be intrusive or alter the tone of the text. In such cases, the writer should take responsibility for providing readers with basic information such as the name of the source and the title (and, if possible, the date) of the work from which it is taken or a description of the occasion on which it was spoken (personal interview, speech to Congress, and so on). ~~You should be skeptical of all sources that are not~~ documented at least informally.

FOCUS ON THE ARGUMENT.   All texts are at some level persuasive. The writer is attempting to persuade readers of something—a certain product is best, a particular method is superior, a recent movie or book is terrible, an issue should be resolved in this way or that way, something is wrong, something is right, everything is wrong, and so on. When writers research a subject and present their findings, sometimes they are merely sharing with you the results of their research as objectively, accurately, and fairly as possible; more often they are using their research to support their own arguments.

As a reader, you need to focus on the writer's arguments rather than on the sources. However, evaluating those sources—why they are there and how they are being used and what effect they are having on you—should be part of your analysis of the writer's argument. What role are the sources playing in the writer's argument? Is the argument valid in itself, or does it depend entirely on the authority of the sources used to support it? Examples of weak arguments supported by strong sources abound. Advertisements often use a beautiful woman's name in association with a cosmetic product to help convince readers that the product brings beauty to the user. Having a successful man endorse a car helps persuade readers that the car somehow ensures success.

Whatever you are reading, be aware that the writer is trying to persuade you of something and that one of his or her most powerful weapons is the use of sources. Although most writers try to be as accurate and responsible as possible in reporting the results of their research, some writers use sources irresponsibly, even unethically. Readers must make every effort to tell the difference between the two.

READING SELECTIONS ◀

The reading selections in this chapter are all written by students who conducted some type of research and included the results of their research in their own texts. The first essay is based on a single source; the second one is based on interviews; and the last two essays include multiple written sources. As you read, notice how these students use their sources to support and develop their own arguments, how they integrate their sources into their own writing so that the two are effectively blended, and how they acknowledge their sources.

A FAILED EDUCATION

Gaylon Askew

In this single-source essay, Gaylon Askew begins by quoting from "Lives on the Boundary" by Mike Rose—an essay from the book by the same name. In this essay, Rose describes his childhood as a member of America's educational underclass and explains how he was able to overcome this "failed education" to become a professor at a major university. Askew compares his own experiences with public education to those described by Rose. Although he includes only this one source, his entire essay is clearly a response to that source. As you read, notice that he refers to his source not only in his introduction but also at several other points as he relates his own experiences.

Mike Rose's essay "Lives on the Boundary" is very smooth. "A failed education is social more than intellectual in origin." I like that thought. Mike's stories show us how some people fall or get pushed out of the line of the American educational system. I also enjoyed reading accounts of his vivid childhood memories. My own personal foray into public school best identifies with one of Rose's ideas: "Education can be a desperate smothering embrace, an embrace that denies the needs of the other." We have all felt that "smothering embrace" at one time or another. It could be from education or life in general. The biggest failure of my life was elementary school. I'll try not to bore you.

In 1979 Jimmy Carter was president, there was a severe gas shortage, hostages in Iran, and I entered kindergarten. School. I didn't want to be there. I remember that much and a surrealistic vision of twenty mothers hugging twenty children in our big class room. I lived for recess. Amid the monkey bars and slides I could do anything I wanted. That's just how I liked it. The swings were my favorite. The motion and brief sense of weightlessness are very hypnotic. It was usually a high school kid who would yell at me to stop swinging. Only then would I tear my eyes away from the blue sky and see that we were the only two people on the play ground. He would smile and tell me how long recess had been over this time. Although I didn't realize it at the time, I was a day dreamer. No, I was borderline comatose.

3   Second grade wasn't much better. The teachers dazzled my parents with the new medical term "Attention Deficit Disorder." I was told "Gaylon, you're behind," and "you need to catch up." How exactly did one catch up? I imagined small light bulbs appearing above the other students' heads as they caught on. Then of course, I would wake up. Our teacher had been saying something about multiplication. We were handed a small times table and told to memorize it. I wore the paper out trying to memorize the answers imprinted on it. Test day finally came, and as usual the class was divided into two sides. Whichever side finished first received candy. I've never cared much for candy, but the other kids did, so it was very important to win. Once again it came down to me on one side and a small timid girl with mouse brown hair on the other. I did know the answers. I just wasn't very fast. It didn't help that my friends were threatening my life. My best friend was in on it even though he was a severe diabetic and I had no idea what he would do with the candy. The girl and I would just look at each other in mute sympathy.

4   At the end of my third grade year I received a 64. A D minus was passing but not satisfactory. There were classes where a student such as I could receive special attention, and luckily I would receive it in the third grade again. My principal used the words "held back." Maybe smothered would have been a better term. To me all this meant that I was officially stupid. There was no denying it. Needless to say my confidence was at an all time low. I missed my old friends and didn't see much of my new class mates. For my remedial classes I was sent to a white sterile building in an empty lot across the street. The single large room was filled with several rows of cubicle desks. In a library these desks are used to help one person concentrate. "One" is the key word. I felt alone with my laminated worksheet and wax pen. Unfortunately I was more interested in unlocking the secrets of the light bulb than the work in front of me. The only bright spot in the

room was in the form of a mildly retarded kid named Jerry Biggers who had a perpetual silly grin. I remember feeling embarrassed as other kids and even teachers made fun of Jerry. He received no encouragement, and it soon became apparent that the teachers had given up on him. I wondered what life would be like for Jerry Biggers.

I never did find that magical teacher, like the one that saved Mike   5
Rose's life. By myself I learned to do only what the school system required, and pursue other interests on my own time. The most important thing I ever learned would be self-confidence. Once you have confidence, then you can accomplish anything, and take pride in your work. That is a far greater reward than candy any day. Fifteen years later I found out what life had in store for Jerry Biggers. The summer after graduation I was doing time in the local plastic factory. While on break I noticed a three foot rod with duct tape and a leather loop on one end. Along its length was written "Jerry Biggers's Beat'em up Stick, Use in case Jerry does something stupid." For most of us embarrassment and humiliation are things we must occasionally overcome, but for others it's a way of life.

QUESTIONS TO CONSIDER ◀

1. In his introduction Askew includes several direct quotations from his source and establishes the fact that he identifies with Rose. The rest of the essay focuses primarily on Askew's own school experiences. What purpose does this introduction serve, and how effectively does it introduce readers to the essay?

2. At what other points in the essay does Askew mention his source? What purpose is served by the continuing references to the book by Mike Rose?

3. Askew does not provide his readers with a full account of his early education, but he includes lots of specific details and relates several brief narratives. Which of these descriptive details and anecdotal accounts give you the clearest impression of what his school life was like and the type of student he was?

4. Why does Askew include Jerry Biggers's story? Do you think he identifies with Biggers as well as Rose? Why, or why not?

5. What does Askew say is the most important thing he ever learned? Did he learn this lesson in school?

▶   WRITING ACTIVITIES

Individual: In your journal, analyze Askew's use of his source material.

Collaborative: With a group of your peers, discuss ways in which Askew could have used his source material differently.

Computer: Using your word-processing program, write a brief essay about your own education. Begin your essay by using one of the quotations from Rose included in Askew's essay. You may agree with the statement you quote, as Askew does, or you may disagree with it. In either case, your essay should explain not only how you feel about your education, but also the connection between your attitude and that of Rose. When you have completed your essay, distribute it on line to your classmates so that they can respond to it.

PARACHUTE KID—IS IT A SAFE LANDING?

Yi-An Heidi Chen

When Yi-An Heidi Chen, a freshman at Stanford University, was asked to write a research paper in a course entitled Writing and Critical Thinking, she chose as her topic "parachute kids"—Taiwanese children whose parents send them to the United States to be educated. Although she cared deeply about this topic, and as a parachute kid herself had a great deal of personal experience with it, she was initially discouraged because she could find no written sources on the subject in the library. However, Chen's teacher encouraged her to continue her research by using interviews as her primary sources. The result was the essay below, which was published in Notes in the Margins, *a publication of the writing program at Stanford. As you read the essay, notice how Chen uses her sources both to define her subject and to support her own arguments.*

1   When I first heard the term "parachute kid," I was a freshman at Stanford. Like most of my close friends who were also parachute kids, I did not know the name with which the press had branded us. As I began to question my experience and that of my friends, I came to understand the gravity of our situation.

My personal experience, however, did not help me to overcome two main obstacles in the research—the silence among the parachute kids' community and my underlying discontent with our situation. It was particularly difficult to find parents who were willing to share their experience with me. Furthermore, I had to learn to keep my emotions from interfering with the objectivity of the paper. Despite all of these challenges, I have learned not only to share my experience with other parachute kids, but more importantly, to discuss the issue with many parents including my own. After all, unlike many problems in the world, "parachute kid" is a phenomenon that stems from love, not irresponsibility, hatred, or negligence.

2

Wendy was my best and only friend in America. When I caught a glimpse of her walking down the aisle, I wanted to run away. Pity, pain, guilt, and helplessness overwhelmed me as I prepared myself to face her.

3

"What does this say?" Wendy asked in a trembling voice as she pointed at the Chinese newspaper in her hands. Wendy came to the US by herself when she was eight. She could not read any Chinese. The article was about the murder of her father three days ago in Taiwan.

4

"He is dead, huh . . . ? Isn't he? Why didn't you tell me about it?"

5

I could not bear to see the self-acclaimed "toughest girl in town" break down into tears. Our common experience as "Xiao Liu Xue Sheng," or "Parachute kids," bonded the "bad girl and the triple nerd" into a friendship of complete trust and reliance. Away from our families in a foreign land, we provided comfort for each other. Despite the strong bond we shared, I could not tell her about her father's death because Wendy's mother had wanted me to keep the knowledge from her. Wendy's visa would not allow her to return to the US if she ever left the country. Her mother was afraid that Wendy might jeopardize her future in America by flying back to Taiwan.

6

According to a 1990 UCLA master's thesis by Helena T. Hwang and Terri H. Watanabe, about 30,000 to 40,000 Taiwanese students, age 8–18, live as unaccompanied minors in the US, like Wendy and I (Fu, 1994). They are called the "parachute kids," because they are "literally dropped off in America to go to school, while their parents, often wealthy business owners, ply their trade in the Far East" (Fu, 1994). Each year, numerous unaccompanied minors from Taiwan are dropped off in American cities with a high Taiwanese population. Both the parents and the kids believe that they have entered into an arena of unlimited educational opportunities. Unfortunately, many of them later find the US to be a bleak, empty, and foreign land full of hostility

7

and disillusionment. Even if America's fabled technology and liberal education provide for a better learning environment, the forced separation of these children from their families often brings more detrimental effects on these kids' character growth than the limited academic success that their overseas studies might provide.

8   The primary reason that these families consent to undergo such a painful separation is the competitive educational system in Taiwan. Since the government only offers nine years of compulsory education, students must take high school and college entrance exams in order to continue education beyond junior high school. Unlike the standardized tests such as the SAT in America, these exams are only given once a year. Furthermore, Taiwanese society exemplifies the worst aspects of a meritocracy: individuals are judged primarily on their performance on the exams. Consequently, these exams predetermine every aspect of a student's life from his or her education to career. They even have a bearing on one's "value in the marriage market" (A. Chen, personal communication, April 22, 1995). As a result, students start preparing for these exams as early as elementary school. They often suffer tremendous stress from competition (S. Li, personal communication, May 5, 1995). I-Yun Lai, a student at Taiwan National University, recalls this "memory of her dreary youth":

> During my junior high and high school years, I functioned with five hours of sleep every day. I attended "cram school" at night until ten o'oclock, got up at six every day so I could make it to school at seven fifteen for quizzes. (personal communication, April 28, 1995)

9   For six years, I-Yun crammed for the exams like the rest of her peers, living with the fear that her hard work would not pay off. Under the intense competition, even hard work does not guarantee success. Since everyone aspires to receive a college education and the space is limited, fewer than 10% of all students, or about one-third of all applicants, gain admission into a four-year college (Fu, 1994). In the US, however, higher education is more accessible. Not only does the government provide eleven years of compulsory education, but college education is also available to all who can afford it. As a result, many parents send their children to the US. After all, their children "will definitely get a degree, even if it means attending a community college" (L. L. Lin, personal communication, May 3, 1995).

10   While most of the parachute kids come to the US to "escape educational persecution," other factors such as military drafts contribute to the problem (Y. T. Cheng, personal communication, April 29, 1995).

Since all males, unless they have physical disabilities, must serve in the Taiwanese army for a minimum of one year and ten months, parents often view military service as "a waste of their sons' prime time" (Cheng). Furthermore, the military life is infamous for "breaking the city boys into real men" (A. Ho, personal communication, May 4, 1995). Allen Ho, a parachute kid who is now a freshman at UC Berkeley, explains why his parents sent him abroad to avoid the "inhumane training": "I had a cousin who mysteriously died in a remote island while serving in the army. Ever since then, my mother has been very paranoid about sending me to the army."

Shao-Ming Ma, a graduate student at Stanford, confirms some of   11
the harsh conditions in the Army:

> I was sent to a remote island. I was completely separated from
> civilization. Things that you take for granted in life—tap water,
> electricity, and city life were not there. I even contracted some
> local disease that nearly put me to death because there wasn't
> any treatment around. (personal communication, May 6, 1995)

Allen's cousin and Shao-Ming's experience may be on the   12
extreme side. Yet, as the economy booms and the size of the family shrinks, Taiwanese parents often pamper their kids with luxuries. Many parents worry that their sons will not be able to endure the harsh military training, and thus send them abroad to dodge the draft.

But if military service and education were the only factors,   13
parachute kids would come from all over Asia, since countries like Japan, Singapore, and Korea also have similar educational and military requirements. The predominance of Taiwanese parachute kids in America reflects Taiwan's unique social and cultural environment. Taiwan's political situation, its admiration of Western culture, and the "Chinese Diaspora" tradition all contribute to the phenomenon. In terms of its political environment, corruption and insecurity cause many to leave their homeland. Not only do people loathe the low morals among the officials, but they also fear the possibility of China's take over of Taiwan. The "Chinese Diaspora" tradition further augments their insecurities. In Aihwa Ong's paper on "South China Diaspora," she asserts that the Chinese "place their faith in the family and personal relationship rather in the government" (1993, p. 755). For example, during a recent symposium discussing the parachute kid phenomenon, many concerned community leaders defended the practice by pointing out that "the Chinese have a long tradition of sending children to live with relatives or friends for economic and

social reasons" (Hamilton, 1993b, p. 3). Since they do not fully trust the authorities, the Taiwanese, like the Chinese, have a lesser sense of national identity, and thus immigrate more often than other ethnic groups. The Diaspora tradition also fosters admiration for Western culture. Taiwanese who have studied abroad are at least "gilded," if they fail to turn to gold (S. Li, personal communication, May 5, 1995). Once a person gets a degree abroad, his social status and annual salary rise immediately. These cultural characteristics explain why the parachute kid phenomenon is unique to the Taiwanese.

14   Not only do these social forces tear thousands of Taiwanese families apart, but they also push these families into a new world of grief and disillusionment. When the kids first arrive at their dream land, they must first learn to adjust to their new living arrangements. While some stay with relatives or family friends, a few live in random host families; others simply live on their own. Parents send their children abroad with an assumption that their relatives will look after their children. These parents fail to understand the challenge in assimilating into the lifestyle of another family. Pei-An Chao, who lived with a relative before attending college, tells of her experience:

> I am the youngest kid in the family. I was always pampered
> and protected by my parents. When I moved into my uncle's
> house, I felt I was forced to grow up in one night. You are an
> adult from the moment you are away from your family. People
> simply don't leave any room for you to make any mistake.
> (personal communication, April 29, 1995)

Not only does Pei-An have to learn to adjust to a new environment and learn a new language, but she also has to do all the cooking, laundering, cleaning, and billing. Yet, Pei-An believes that the harshest part of her experience is not the actual work but the psychological adjustment. "It is really hard to see that when I am not allowed to forget to do my laundry, my cousins who are about the same age as I am, are protected like porcelain dolls," she says, in a bitter tone. Like Pei-An, many parachute kids feel that their parents push them into the adult world before they are ready. They often wish that they can "just be a child" like their peers (A. Chen, personal communication, April 22, 1995).

15   While adjusting to relatives' lifestyle imposes challenges on these youngsters, living with a random host family leaves them vulnerable to potential exploitation. Nelson Fu reports that some families host up to ten kids in a house, and ration their food while demanding an

exorbitant fee from the parents (Fu, 1994). Amy Chen, a parachute kid in LA, recounts her experience in a host family with her younger sister:

> Our host family was pretty messed up. The husband and wife fought all the time. We had to hide in our room. In general, they fed us well compared to the other families. It was not until later when they interrogated me for complaining to my friends about life in there that really upsets me. How can they have the audacity to accuse me when they obtain the knowledge by reading my mail without my consent? (personal communication, April 22, 1995)

Amy moved out of her host family after the incident, because 16 both her parents and she believed that to live alone is "much easier than to live under someone else's roof."

As a result of the complications of living with another family, many 17 parents buy their own house and let their kids stay with hired adults or by themselves. In Amy's case, she has been taking care of her younger sister since she was fourteen. Not only does she manage to maintain a household, but she also has to handle other emergency situations like illness or car accidents. Of all the unexpected situations, Amy recalls the night of the LA riot to be the "longest night in her life," because she was alone with her little sister. Even an adult, under the same circumstances, would feel overburdened by the responsibilities. Yet, thousands of parachute kids deal with these challenges on an everyday basis.

Besides the living arrangements, parachute kids struggle with 18 other psychological adjustments. While the other new immigrants also encounter language and cultural barriers, parachute kids must face the barriers by themselves without support and guidance from their families. As a result of their solitude, parachute kids often experience loneliness. In some cases, extreme loneliness and emptiness lead to serious depression. Christina Lam, a student at UCLA, told reporters about her serious depression as a result of her parachute kid experience: "I went into this serious depression, where I just wanted to die. I had no idea what to do. I had no older person to talk to. I am very hesitant to get involved with people now, I think because I was left alone" (Fu, 1994). Even though not every parachute kid suffers a serious depression like Christina, most of the parachute kids experience the unbearable loneliness whenever they return to "their empty home after all the frustration in school" (S. Li, personal communication, May 5, 1995).

While some kids turn to complete isolation and depression, many, 19 like Wendy and I, find solace from other parachute kids. Unfortunately, these parachute kid "cliques" can often become an excellent source of gang membership. Gangs provide a sanctuary for these kids who crave for strong bonding experience. Tony, a gang member, explains his association with gangs:

> I am associated with the gangs but I don't think I am involved in it. I just make good friends with the big brothers. Besides, my gang doesn't really do really illegal stuffs. It is more like a male-bonding experience. We unite together so people respect us more. When you are constantly looked down on by people because you can't speak English well, gangs seem to be the place for you to find the strong bonding and respect you crave for. (personal communication, May 6, 1995)

Even though many parachute kids, like Tony, joined the gangs initially for the bonding experience, how likely is it for parachute kids to resist crimes once they are in a gang? Not only are they free from any parental restraint, frustration in school and emptiness in their family life often provoke parachute kids into petty fights and crimes. While Tony claims that many gangs in LA are more for "male bonding than crime-making," Christopher Kuk, a probation officer in San Gabriel area refutes the story. "You name it: extortion, murder, robberies; we're seeing more and more of these parachute kids involved," says Kuk (Fu, 1994). The most appalling fact is that more and more kids, like Tony, who do not conform to the stereotypical "gangster" image, join the gangs. Coming from a happy family, Tony is a shy and amicable junior in UCLA. Yet loneliness and frustration push parachute kids like him into gangs and crime.

20   Even if the kids are strong enough to resist gangs and crime, they still have to confront other complications such as their legal status. Many parachute kids come to the US with a tourist visa. Even if they change it to a student visa or F-1 upon their arrival, the visa does not guarantee them the right to return to the US if they leave the country. If they visit Taiwan, the American immigration officers will reevaluate their visa and often deny them reentrance into the US (Y. T. Cheng, personal communication, April 29, 1995). For fear of not being able to return to the US, kids do not visit their homeland until after they finish their degrees. It was because of this legal complication that Wendy could not attend her father's funeral. Furthermore, since the F1 visa requires that the students reside with their guardians, those parachute kids who live by themselves are technically illegal aliens (Hamilton, 1993a, p. 1). Because of their illegal status, many parachute kids

hesitate to request assistance when they encounter health, security, and psychological problems. They fear that authorities will find out about their illegal status and deport them back to Taiwan.

Not only does the American government impose many legal   21
restrictions, but the Taiwanese government also prevents male para-chute kids from returning home. Since the law prohibits males from leaving the country once they reach fourteen, most of the male para-chute kids cannot return to Taiwan (S. M. Ma, personal communica-tion, May 6, 1995). Ying-Ting, a parachute kid in LA, has not seen his brother in Taiwan for over five years because neither of them can legally leave their countries. Since his parents can only visit him once or twice a year, Yin-Ting admits that he feels an "invisible cultural gap" between his parents and him. Bombarded constantly by the American values, many kids thus find that their gradual Americanization makes communication with their parents difficult (A. Ho, personal communi-cation, May 4, 1995).

Besides their legal status, many kids also have to assume respon-   22
sibilities to parent their younger siblings. Even though many parents claim that they send their children abroad in their children's best inter-est, many female parachute kids are sent over as surrogate moms for their siblings. Stella Li, a computer science major at UC Berkeley, explains why she gave up her aspirations in order to accompany her brother to America:

> I was doing very well in high school. I was going to attend
> one of the best universities and become a lawyer. My parents
> forced me here because my brother was having problems in
> Taiwan. They wanted to separate him from bad influences. I
> came with him so I could take care of him and make sure that
> he studied hard. (personal communication, May 5, 1995)

Even though they are still teenagers themselves, these surrogate   23
moms assume tremendous responsibilities of parenthood. Not only must they sacrifice their dreams, but their precious youthful memory is also marred by the demanding parenting responsibilities. Is it fair for the parents to shift their responsibilities to their teenage daughters?

If both the American press and the Taiwanese press successfully   24
informed the public of the gravity of the issue, the tides of parachute kids would probably diminish. Yet, both the press and the parachute kid families fail to provide the public with a realistic account of the experience. The lack of media coverage indicates that the public is still unaware of the issue. Furthermore, even when the press occasionally

addresses the issue, it fails to discuss about kids who cannot adjust to the environment. The press creates a misleading parachute kid stereotype—a 4.0 G.P.A. class president who drives a BMW around and complains occasionally about loneliness. In Fu's essay, Nancy, Silvia, Judy, and Mickey all conform to the stereotype. Besides receiving good grades, they are either class presidents, homecoming princesses, or "self-acclaimed social butterflies," suggesting that they integrate well into the American life. In Hamilton's (1993a) article, all of the kids are either holding a position in the student government, getting straight A's, or studying in famous private schools. However, these examples do not represent the common parachute kid experience. Not all of the kids come from wealthy families. Even if they do, the majority of them never integrate into the American culture. The lack of representation of the hardships these kids face impairs the objectivity and depth of the press coverage.

25   The failure of the press to adequately present the issue shows their lack of understanding of the parachute kid culture. Since many parachute kids never obtain basic English proficiency, the American press cannot communicate with the ones who are having the hardest time adjusting. Even if they manage to indirectly communicate with them, these kids are suspicious of adults, "Lao-Mei" (Americans), and reporters. Their anti-American sentiment is strong, because native students and some of their own teachers often mistreat them. Parachute kids do not just slam the door against the Americans and the adults. Being a parachute kid myself, my adjustment to life here prevents my camaraderie with these kids. Grace Lo, the coordinator of the Stanford Parachute Kid Organization and a parachute kid herself, explains the hostility as a result of their "inferiority complex." Since their parents constantly compare them with the very few successful cases and are generally unaware of the hardship the majority experiences, kids often resent the "successful" ones (G. Lo, personal communication, April 23, 1995). Unlike the "successful ones" who are eager to share their experience in overcoming hardships, these kids respond to my interview with silence and evasion. As a result of these complications, the press fails to inform the public of the gravity of the issue. Without attention from the public, these kids cannot receive the proper attention they desperately need. Moreover, this worsens the situation, as more families that are unaware of the hardship continue to send their children abroad.

26   While many parents send their kids over to the US due to ignorance, some of the parents make the decision with knowledge of the hardship their kids will face. These parents feel that their kids' academic success and character growth justify the hardship. Mrs. Yang, a

mother of four parachute kids, was the only parent who responded to my request for an interview:

> I think I made the right decision. Now that I look at the maturity and independence in my daughters, I know that all the hardship has paid off. My husband and I work very hard to support them and we also suffer a lot from the separation. Sometimes I think it is easy to just blame the parents. Very few try to understand how hard it is for a mother to leave her children abroad. If we had a choice, we would never tear a happy family apart. When you know that there is no way for your children to get into any college or even a high school, you must plan their future for them. (C. H. Yang, personal communication, April 30, 1995)

Mrs. Yang's daughters, I-Pei, Caroline, Lisa, and Winnie adjusted   27
to the environment well. Not only do they receive good grades in school, but they also maintain a very close relationship with Mrs. Yang.

While one can cite the Yangs' experience as a success, an inter-   28
view with I-Pei reveals some of the hardship that even a successful parachute kid can suffer. Even though she probably would not have been able to get into a university in Taiwan, I-Pei is not sure whether her college education here can compensate for the separation and hardship she has experienced. I-Pei explains the discrepancy between her own evaluation of the parachute kid experience and that of her mother's. Like many of the kids I interviewed, she does not tell her parents of the difficulties she experiences:

> There is no way for me to go back [to Taiwan] anyway. I wouldn't be able to catch up with the curriculum. I know my parents work so hard to send me here. Since telling them the truth will not change the situation but only break their hearts, I simply don't tell them the hardship I face. Besides, they are on the other side of the Pacific, what can they do when Winnie has a fever over 100 degrees? (I. P. Yang, personal communication, May 5, 1995)

I-Pei's situation explains the lack of communication between   29
parents and kids. Since kids often feel that telling their parents the truth cannot help the situation, they often conceal their struggles from their parents.

There are also some kids who do not intend to conceal their feel-   30
ings from their parents. They simply have mixed feelings about their

experience. At first, many, like Yin-Ting, who are doing very successfully in school, reply that they "do not regret" coming here because they receive a "more well-rounded education" (Y. T. Cheng, personal communication, April 29, 1995). They agree that the education here is more "well-rounded" because it develops not only one's intellectual interests but also other social and leadership skills as well (S. Li, personal communication, May 5, 1995). Nevertheless, America is not the "zero-pressure youth paradise" they envisioned (L. L. Lin, personal communication, May 3, 1995). Not only do they face the challenges of being away from home, but "you must discipline yourself in order to receive the academic benefit fully" (Cheng). Even though these parachute kids could not give me a direct evaluation of their experience when I interviewed them, their immediate response to my question of whether they would ever send their own children here as parachute kids is interesting. All of the fifteen parachute kids I interviewed said no. Even though I cannot claim that the majority of the parachute kids feel this way, the result makes one wonder whether their parents are acting in the best interest of their children.

31   When I told Mrs. Yang about my observation, she repeated again that if the parents did not send their children here, the kids "will have no future" because they cannot receive a high school and college education in Taiwan (C. H. Yang, personal communication, April 30, 1995). Stella Li gives an insightful rebuttal:

> I know that my brother will get his college degree somewhere, but what does his degree mean anyway? I know that he won't get into a college in Taiwan. But at least, he would find a job, work productively, and hopefully mature from the experience. Maybe he would be mature enough to choose to come back to school. Even if not, at least he would have a purpose in life. Right now, he wanders aimlessly every day because he'll "get a degree" anyway. (Li, personal communication, May 5, 1995)

32   Stella's frustration with the society's obsession with "degrees" provides us with an answer. Parents and the society should reevaluate their value system. Does a child's academic success outweigh his character growth? How can parents claim that their kids are "successful" in terms of their grades when the kids identify their parents only as "ATM machines" (Hamilton, 1993a, p. 4)?

33   While some parents claim that their children's maturity and independence prove their successful character growth, we should note that the independence and maturity are often the results of a forced

response to a hostile environment. Even though parents think that they are making the best decision for their children, they should also realize that the child has a right to shape his future as well. The "successful" kids all agree that "self-initiative" is the secret to their success, both in academic and in character growth. Before "rescuing" their kids from the academic competition and military service, parents should understand the struggle that the family will face. If a kid should ever be sent abroad, it should only be under the condition that both the parents and the kid fully understand the hardships involved and consent to meet the challenges.

In concluding my paper, I would like to say that my intent has   34 not been to indict the parents for sending their kids here. "It is easy to simply blame the parents without realizing the hardship they suffer," as Mrs. Yang said. I know that my father works fourteen hours a day to support his children abroad; I know what it means when my parents call me at three A.M. their time because they cannot rest with the thoughts of their kids alone in America. Most of the parents have done so much for their children that no one really has the right to blame them. Yet when I think of Wendy's remark a few weeks after her father's death, I feel an obligation to inform the parents. Someone has to tell them so they can make the best decision for their children with full knowledge of the price the family must pay:

> It is strange that it doesn't hurt inside that Papa died. I cried because I guessed I should and because I felt betrayed by friends and family for not treating me like an adult. To be honest with you, I can hardly remember what Papa was like.

REFERENCES

Fu, N. (1994, April). Parachute kids and astronaut parents. [Online]. Available: Lexis Nexus. Library: News. File: Allnws.

Hamilton, D. (1993a, June 24). A house, cash—and no parents. *Los Angeles Times*, pp. A1, A16.

Hamilton, D. (1993b, July 29). Chinese-American readers call for action on "parachute kids." *Los Angeles Times*, Metro Section p. B3.

Home alone—up-market L.A. style. (1993, June 27). *Los Angeles Times*, p. M4.

Ong, A. (1993). On the edge of empires: flexible citizenship among Chinese in diaspora. *Position*, *1*, 745–778.

Romney, L. (1993, November 28). She's gained respect "just for being me." *Los Angeles Times*, San Gabriel Valley, Home Edition p. J1.

▶ QUESTIONS TO CONSIDER

1. What explanation does Chen give for the large number of parachute kids who come to the United States from Taiwan? What methods of development does she use in her explanation?

2. Chen begins with a rather abstract explanation of the problem—the social, political, and educational forces that encourage Taiwanese families to send their children to the United States. But she follows this explanation with several accounts of the difficult adjustments endured by the young people who have had this experience. As a reader, how do you respond to these different explanations? Which do you find more compelling?

3. Chen accuses the American press of distorting the image of parachute kids. How does the press depict these young people? How does Chen's portrayal differ from that image?

4. How does Chen present a balanced account of the parents' reasons for sending their children away from home as opposed to the children's experiences? If she did not present both viewpoints, would her essay be as persuasive as it is?

5. Although Chen states that she does not blame the parents, it is clear that she finds the situation of the parachute kids destructive in many ways. What are the main effects of this experience on the young people?

6. In her conclusion, Chen returns to her narrative about her friend Wendy and quotes her as saying that she "can hardly remember what Papa was like." This final argument is based on pathos, or emotion, rather than logic. Do you find it effective? Would it be equally effective if Chen had not also included in her essay a number of arguments that were clearly based on logos, or reason?

7. Unlike the other student writers in this chapter, Chen uses APA documentation. In APA documentation, an interview is noted as a "personal communication," at the point in the text where the source is used. Personal communications are not included in the list of references at the end of the paper because they are not "recoverable" by anyone but the writer of the papers. Chen's paper includes 12 telephone and personal interviews, information that would be included in an MLA Works Cited list. Compare APA documentation to the MLA style used by the other writers. Which do you find more useful and informative? Why?

▶ WRITING ACTIVITIES ◀

Individual: Summarize in your journal Chen's main arguments for and against the practice of sending children from Taiwan to America to be educated.

Collaborative: With a group of your classmates, analyze Chen's essay. Then assume the role of the parents of parachute kids and write a brief defense of your decision to send your children away for their education.

Computer (1): Interview one of your classmates on this issue, recording verbatim several statements that he or she makes. Ask the person you are interviewing to read the statements you have recorded (on screen) to verify their accuracy. When the interview is over, summarize it briefly, inserting the direct quotations appropriately.

Computer (2): Using Chen's essay as your source, write a brief article or editorial for your college newspaper in which you explain the phenomenon of parachute kids and summarize Chen's arguments.

THE NECESSITY FOR GREENPEACE

Paige Snyder

Paige Snyder was a college freshman when she wrote the following essay about the environmental organization Greenpeace, with which she had worked. In her essay Snyder defends the methods used by Greenpeace, in particular the method known as direct action. As you read this essay, notice that Snyder uses Martin Luther King, Jr.'s, "Letter from Birmingham Jail" as one of her sources (see Chapter 6). Like King, Snyder argues that nonviolent direct action is justified as a method of resistance because it is a means to a justifiable end—in this case the preservation of the planet. As you read, notice how Snyder uses her personal experiences as well as written sources to support her argument.

Greenpeace is an effective environmental group, for it raises the   1
public's awareness concerning environmental issues, in addition to
concerning itself with the awesome task of making our world clean

and safe for those who inherit it for the remainder of history. I know from personal experience the numerous chores we face, the sociological changes that must come about, the new kind of enculturation we must integrate into our world, to accomplish the goal of the earth being indefinitely self-supporting and conducive to good health and living. My work at Greenpeace has reinforced my knowledge that Greenpeace and organizations like it are an important piece in the puzzle of bringing about all these positive changes.

2   It is a simple task to set forth all the facts on environmental catastrophes. Numerous magazines like Greenpeace's (which is printed on recycled paper) and responsible television like the Public Broadcasting System are constantly informing the public on relevant issues. This is one reason why I do not feel the need to dedicate this paper to persuading people that the environment is in trouble. For while there are continuing debates among professionals as to the extent of some problems (such as the size of the hole in the ozone layer), there is agreement that a new awareness must come about soon, because we are destroying our home. Another topic I will not debate is whether or not action must be taken to prevent further ecological damage and repair past abuse. This is simple, because if environmental crises are common knowledge, then there can be no objections to taking care of the problems. Of course, this line of reasoning assumes that individuals are interested in propagating their species, as well as those of every other living organism. So excluding those who do not believe life should continue on earth, one must conclude that knowledge about our current condition would warrant education and change. Therefore, this paper will focus on the methods that Greenpeace employs, especially the method known as direct action. I will argue that, given the seriousness of our environmental plight, the end in this case justifies the means.

3   Greenpeace was founded in 1971 by a handful of people attempting to stop the testing of nuclear weapons. Since that time, it has grown into a group numbering over 3.5 million members worldwide and is represented by offices in over 30 countries. The issues that Greenpeace is involved in include ocean ecology (stopping the testing of nuclear weapons under water, preventing the extinction of sea creatures), atmosphere and energy (finding new, clean alternatives for energy, outlawing practices that destroy the ozone layer and actions that increase the greenhouse effect), the rain forest (stopping the raping of the forests by eliminating the market for products made from rainforest timber, helping the locals to retain their land and make money by practices which replenish the trees and undergrowth). These are several of Greenpeace's central campaigns. The philosophy

of Greenpeace is that no one owns this planet. We only borrow it from the generation before us and must pass it on to those who follow us. And like anything that is borrowed, we must take better care of it than if it were our very own, especially when survival depends on it. In order to achieve its goals, Greenpeace's first tool is negotiation and discussion with environmental abusers. But more often than not, these offenders are large corporations, or even the government, and a request for them to change a major part of their operations usually goes unconsidered. So Greenpeace uses a tactic known as non-violent direct action. This philosophy has been used successfully for many years by people like Gandhi and Martin Luther King, Jr. And much like the wrath that their actions drew, Greenpeace has found itself on the defensive many a time against those who feel it is unnecessary to be so disruptive. But as Dr. King found, when people refuse to admit there is a problem, let alone be willing to discuss it, direct action can be the only peaceable way to bring all sides to the table. And so, Greenpeace organizes rallies, boycotts, and bans. In addition, they often block activities at places such as illegal nuclear testing sites or illegal dumping grounds.

I have faced much criticism of Greenpeace in my job as a canvasser but always thrived off of it. It was usually intelligent thinking from insightful people, and it made me continually question things, which I found made my convictions even stronger and myself more informed. Ironically, it was usually the members who asked the most questions and even criticized selected actions. Greenpeace is an organization of people, and thus is fallible to an extent. Not all 3.5 million members will agree on every decision made. But this essay is addressed to those who feel there is no need for a group like Greenpeace, or worse yet, those who feel Greenpeace causes more harm than good and is not constructive in its means of education, mediation, and direct-action campaigns. The essay "Greenpeace Wages Redwar" begins with this statement: 4

> Because of the growing environmental fad of the last few   5
> years, much of the public has invested nearly blind faith in
> organizations claiming to play David to the Goliath of environ-
> mental exploitation. Among the leading beneficiaries of this
> public trust has been the international activist organization
> Greenpeace. (Ellison 7)

This statement gives very little credit to the millions of people   6
who donate their time and money to Greenpeace's efforts. I have

worked for Greenpeace at the grassroots level, going door to door
canvassing, enlisting new members, and visiting old members. More
than anyone else in the organization, the canvassers know who the
members are, where their heads are at, and how they view the organization they are investing in. I must first say that there are people who
join blindly, usually either to get me to leave their door, or because
they want to support the cause, but aren't interested in hearing about
what they are supporting. But out of thousands of members I met, this
"blind-faith" group constitutes only a handful. As I mentioned before,
it is the members, both prospective ones and those who have been
members for years, who ask most of the questions. They want to
know what we are currently involved in and what they can do to help
in other than financial ways.

7   My job at the grassroots level was not solely fundraising,
although that is one central objective. At any given time, we would
be running at least one letter campaign and a petition campaign. One
obstacle to the public's involvement in environmental legislation is
lack of knowledge concerning what bills are being proposed and
voted on. So Greenpeace finds out the calendar for Congressional
voting, and in the months and weeks ahead of votes, educates the
public on those bills by going door to door. For example, last summer
(1990) Congress had legislation pending on the banning of CFCs.
When I went door to door, I carried on my clipboard a description
of the bill and presented it to anyone who expressed interest. They in
turn could write a letter to their Congressmen and Congresswomen
expressing how they wished their representatives to vote. Over the
course of a week, Greenpeace canvassers across the country would
collect thousands of letters, which we would then send to Washington.
Far from preying on those with blind faith, Greenpeace needs and
wants more than financial support. It seeks to increase knowledge in
and involvement by the public. I found this job so rewarding because
people constantly thanked me for bringing them this information and
giving them the means to help change things.

8   But education, letter-writing, and petitions only accomplish so
much. Unfortunately, many companies do not respond to the public's
request to clean up their acts. And so we end up using the last resort,
which is direct action. In speaking of the necessity of using direct
action, I will be continually referring to Martin Luther King, Jr., most
specifically to his letter written while in Birmingham jail. Dr. King
speaks of the need for non-violent action where injustice exists and
when the opposition will not negotiate. In arriving at the decision to

take such action, he speaks of the phases one must go through. "In any non-violent campaign there are four basic steps: collection of the facts to determine whether injustices exist; negotiation; self-purification; and direct action" (King 85). By the time Greenpeace arrives at the conclusion that direct action is required, its members have gone through these steps.

I feel now is the time to give an illustration of one such time 9
when Greenpeace finally took a direct action, and what came as a result of that decision. Throughout the 1970s and early 1980s, the French government had been conducting illegal nuclear tests (atmospheric and underground) throughout the Pacific. These tests, conducted despite an international ban, resulted in widespread radiation leakage and protests from the citizens of Polynesia, where much of the testing was taking place. Despite these protests and the attempts of Greenpeace to make these tests known to the world, the international community did nothing. On July 7, 1985, Greenpeace sent its ship, the Rainbow Warrior, to New Zealand to prepare for a direct action against French nuclear testing in Mururoa. Greenpeace had been in the region previously, to attempt to draw attention to the illegal tests and to accumulate first-hand evidence, such as photographs (Danielsson 23–31). Chris Masters describes how the protest was to unfold and the risks that Greenpeace members were willing to take.

> The Rainbow Warrior and the other protest boats would launch 10
> Zodiac inflatable speedboats from just outside the twelve-mile
> limit and attempt to land on the atoll. About a dozen Zodiacs
> would carry Greenpeace members of many different national-
> ities. They knew from experience the French would be forced
> to arrest the protesters and then face the embarrassing prospect
> of having to deport each of them to their home countries.
> (Danielsson 29)

Before the planned protest, the Rainbow Warrior was blown up 11
by French agents, and a Greenpeace photographer was killed. Despite the tragedy, Greenpeace brought another environmental scandal to light. Masters writes, "The French media began to sense a Watergate and competed enthusiastically for new details of L'affaire Greenpeace" (Danielsson 29). The illegal testing stopped, and those responsible for exploding the boat were sentenced to ten years in prison.

While canvassing, I met resistance to direct action, much of 12
which stemmed from ignorance. The above-mentioned incident was

remembered by many to be a case of Greenpeace blowing up a
French boat as part of its direct action campaigns. If violence were a
part of Greenpeace's philosophy or behavior, I would not feel secure
supporting it, nor would most of its 3.5 million members. I would now
like to speak to those who feel that non-violent direct action serves no
constructive purpose. Let me again refer to King's letter.

13   Non-violent direct action seeks to create such a crisis and foster
        such a tension that a community which has constantly refused
        to negotiate is forced to confront the issue. It seeks so to dra-
        matize the issue that it can no longer be ignored. . . . The pur-
        pose of our direct-action program is to create a situation so
        crisis-packed that it will inevitably open the door to negotia-
        tion. (King 86–87)

14   I know from experience that the corporations and governments
        which are targets of these actions are usually those who believe the
        actions are unnecessary. This is true for obvious economic and political
        reasons, but also because it is the poor and minorities who face the
        most immediate effects of environmental problems. They are the ones
        who live next to the dumps and incinerators, who work in unsafe facto-
        ries making chemicals and hazardous products. King realized that those
        who do not directly see the injustice do not see the immediate need for
        change. "Frankly, I have yet to engage in a direct-action campaign that
        was 'well timed' in the view of those who have not suffered unduly. . . ."
        (King 87). Those who are removed from the immediate effects of the
        environmental crisis do not see it as a crisis. While canvassing in a nice
        rural neighborhood in Massachusetts last summer, I came across a
        woman who insisted that there was no problem where she lived and
        that somehow this town was cleaner and healthier than those surround-
        ing it. I asked her how this was possible, when she shared the air and
        drinking water with a neighboring town which had severe health prob-
        lems due to a toxic incinerator. To this she had no answer.

15   Then there are the people saying, "I agree with you in the goal
        you seek, but I cannot agree with your methods of direct action" (King
        91). My answer is the same as Dr. King's: "Shallow understanding from
        people of good will is more frustrating than absolute misunderstanding
        of people of ill will" (91). What I found most difficult to comprehend
        were those people who agreed with my every point, but felt I should
        wait and not press the issue. Once again I agree with King, who pro-
        poses that "such an attitude grows out of a tragic misconception of

time, from the strangely irrational notion that there is something in the very flow of time that will inevitably cure all ills" (92). But time did not magically alleviate racial injustice, and time will not mystically reverse all the damage humans have done and will continue to do to the environment. Fortunately, there are people who do see that only human perseverance will overcome human errors, and they do what they can do, like supporting such groups as Greenpeace, that take a stand and take action.

Greenpeace fills an essential role in educating the public and   16
making changes in corporate and governmental behavior toward the environment. And more and more, the effectiveness of their philosophy is being recognized. A writer in a Japanese magazine expresses a desire to increase environmental activism in Japan:

> The activities of the nongovernmental or citizen environmental   17
> organization that emerged in many nations over the past 20
> years have led to continuous reforms in governmental policies
> and corporate behavior. . . . Greenpeace International has
> around 3.5 million supporters worldwide and an annual budget
> of about 125 million dollars, making it the largest "environmen-
> tal pressure group." (Holliman 285)

Fortunately, more and more people in the United States and   18
around the world see the urgent need for changes in environmental policies, as *Fortune* magazine reported in 1990.

> The New York Times/CBS poll regularly asks the public if pro-   19
> tecting the environment is so important that requirements and
> standards cannot be too high, and continuing environmental
> improvements must be made regardless of cost. In September
> 1981, 45% agreed and 42% disagreed with that plainly intem-
> perate statement. Last June, 79% agreed and only 18% dis-
> agreed. For the first time, liberals and conservatives, Democrats
> and Republicans, profess concern for the environment in
> roughly equal numbers. (Kirkpatrick 46)

The same article also notes that "William Bishop, Proctor &   20
Gamble's top environmental scientist, was an organizer of Earth Day in 1970 and is a member of the Sierra Club. One of his chief deputies belongs to Greenpeace" (47).

So change is coming about, and more people are aware of envi-   21
ronmental problems and willing to take action on that knowledge.

But these changes in thought did not occur by waiting for the truth to sink in. The realization that something must be done to save our environment resulted from tireless campaigning and canvassing by Greenpeace and groups like it, who are bound and determined to make a difference, despite much indifference. And changes in policies that directly or indirectly affect our environment's well-being came about because of direct action campaigns, which forced the recognition of the problems and insisted on negotiation that would achieve positive change. While it is a good first step to acknowledge the environmental crisis this world is in, it is not enough. We must all be willing to do whatever is necessary to right our wrongs, including giving our time, money, and support for groups like Greenpeace, which persevere. They do what they must do, including taking direct action, and we must understand why, and be willing to do just as much. Let's continue the trend of awareness that is sweeping our world, and act on it.

WORKS CITED

Danielsson, Bengt. "Poisoned Pacific: The Legacy of French Nuclear Testing." *The Bulletin of the Atomic Scientists* 46.2 (1990): 23–31.

Ellison, Bryan J. "Greenpeace Wages Redwar." *The New American* 6.24 (1990): 7–12.

Holliman, Jonathan. "Environmentalism with a Global Scope." *Japan Quarterly* 37 (1990): 284–90.

King, Martin Luther, Jr. "Letter from Birmingham Jail." *I Have a Dream: Writings and Speeches That Changed the World.* Ed. James M. Washington. San Francisco: HarperCollins, 1992. 83–100.

Kirkpatrick, David. "Environmentalism: The New Crusade." *Fortune* 12 Feb. 1990: 44–55.

▶ QUESTIONS TO CONSIDER

1. Throughout the essay Snyder uses her personal experience as a canvasser for Greenpeace to support her arguments. Could her close association with the organization also be seen as a reason why she cannot effectively defend it? Why, or why not?

2. Snyder states that "while there are continuing debates among professionals as to the extent of some problems, . . . there is agreement

that . . . we are destroying our home." Can her assertion that there is agreement on this issue be challenged? How?

3. Snyder clearly states that one of the basic assumptions in her pro-environmental action argument is that "individuals are interested in propagating their species." Is her assumption valid? Why, or why not? Is Snyder's overt statement of this assumption an effective persuasive strategy?

4. Snyder bases her defense of nonviolent direct action on the arguments of Martin Luther King, Jr., as he articulated them in his "Letter from Birmingham Jail" (Chapter 6). As her main source, how does King strengthen Snyder's argument? Is he an effective source primarily because of what he says or who he is?

5. In addition to King, Snyder uses several other sources to support her arguments for Greenpeace's use of direct action. Which of these sources do you find most persuasive? Do you recognize the names of any of these sources? How important is it to use sources whom your readers know?

6. Snyder uses both examples from her own experiences and material from sources to support her argument. Do you find her own experiences or the source material more convincing? Is the combination of personal experience and source material effective? Why?

WRITING ACTIVITIES

Individual: Snyder argues that time alone will not take care of the problems Greenpeace and similar environmental groups address, and thus, direct action is needed. Write a journal entry in which you agree or disagree with this argument.

Collaborative: Snyder compares environmental issues with civil rights issues. Discuss whether you think this is a valid comparison. Make a list of ways in which the two issues are alike and ways in which they are different.

Computer: Interview a classmate about whether he or she is for or against direct action as a means of protecting the environment. Use your computer to record several exact responses of the person you interview. Then compose an account of the interview in which you include several of the quoted responses.

FAMILY SQUABBLE: THE BRITISH REACTION TO THE LOSS OF THE AMERICAN COLONIES

Kristin Bailey

Kristin Bailey describes, in this essay, how popular writers and artists in England used the analogy of a child rebelling against a parent to explain the American Revolution. Bailey relies extensively on multiple written sources, because she clearly has no personal experience with this subject. However, her own knowledge of British and American history obviously contributes significantly to this essay. As you read, notice especially Bailey's skill in integrating her source material effectively into her essay. Although she includes extensive source material, Bailey remains clearly in control of her essay.

1   Dating from at least the Renaissance, the English saw a direct connection between their monarchy and the family structure. The Great Chain of Being and the idea of plenitude contributed to the idea that the English form of government was natural, with the monarch serving in the position of the natural ruler or patriarch just as the family was a natural structure, with the father filling the dominant position. However, that system began to break down in the late-seventeenth and eighteenth centuries. According to Gordon J. Scochet, after reaching its height in the seventeenth century, the "self-conscious invocation of the family in political discourse" began to break down as philosophers such as Locke, Hobbes, and Hume began to raise questions about whether the family unit was a natural development or a social institution (324–25).

2   A similar transformation concerning the monarchy occurred at about the same time as a result of the regicide of Charles I and the Glorious Revolution of 1688. Once one king had been killed and a second displaced in favor of one whose religious beliefs the people preferred, it was impossible to maintain the pretence that the English monarchy was based on the divine right of kings. The monarchy, like the family, was now seen by many as a contractual arrangement of sorts set up to facilitate societal functions.

3   However, the symbolic relationship between family and monarchy reappeared briefly late in the century when Britain was undergoing a

period of considerable turmoil: the loss of the American colonies at the end of the Revolution—after Cornwallis's surrender in 1781 and after the loss was made official with the signing of the Treaty of Paris in 1783. As Linda Colley explains, the loss of their colonies was an almost incomprehensible blow to the British (143–45). As they grappled with the situation, trying to come to grips with the humiliating defeat they had just suffered, some Britons revived the old family/monarchy symbolic system but in a new form. Now the trait that had probably helped lead to its downfall a century earlier was part of the reason the system was revived. The monarchical relationship of Britain to her colonies and the patriarchal relationship of a husband and father to his family were both increasingly seen as contractual relationships, and contracts could be broken and violated. The way the traditional symbol was treated shifted in other ways as well. Now it seems to have been used to refer not to the monarch him or herself but to the state as a whole; people even began to refer to the whole country as to a member of a family. Specifically, Britain was often seen as the parent or husband to America. The familiar and concrete example of the family relationship seems to have helped some Britons to understand what had happened with the colonies.

Just as in America, factions in Britain felt differently about the revolution. While many Britons supported England in the attempt to hang on to the American colonies despite the difficulties of a war fought across an ocean, some saw Britain as a tyrannical ruler who had goaded the colonists into rebelling, while still others objected on the grounds that the British were now fighting fellow Protestants (Colley 137). The first signs of the re-emergence of the analogy between the state and the family were seen in the groups protesting the war.

Visual satirists among the protesters of the war sometimes chose to make their point by portraying America as the abused child of Britannia or wife of King George III. The earliest of these prints appeared in reaction to the allegedly unfair taxation acts passed by England. One of the earliest, a 1767 print, *The Colonies Reduced*, drawn in response to a trade conflict between England and America, depicts a dismembered America with her limbs/colonies strewn around her trunk. The companion to this print features a family squabble as Britannia tries to stab America, who flees into the protective arms of France. Even Britannia does not escape this melee unscathed, though; a figure representing Lord Bute stabs her and holds her skirt up for two other assailants who flog and stab her bare buttocks (Carretta 210–11). Later prints depict similar family fights. In *Bunkers Hill, or the Blessed Effect of Family Quarrels* (1775), Britannia and America fight, while Bute, North, and Mansfield look on from above and France and Spain jump into the fight on America's behalf (Carretta 216–18). *Poor Old England Endeavoring to Reclaim His Wicked American Children* (1777) portrays a crippled England holding a whip and attempting to pull the American colonists back across the Atlantic by strings attached to their noses (Carretta 179–80). Finally, in 1780, George III is accused of joining the "savages" and eating his own children in *The Allies*. In this rather gruesome engraving, a caption explains that even some of the Indians complained at the harsh treatment given to the women and children, and a dog, a traditional symbol of loyalty, vomits over the atrocious act (Carretta 190–92).

6   British loyalists did not let these attacks go unanswered. In 1776, they responded with *The Parricide: A Sketch of Modern Patriotism*, which shows an armed America attacking her mother Britannia, who is being restrained by a group of colonists while a leashed British lion struggles to free himself and come to her defense (Carretta 189–91). Although the blame was not universally assigned to any one party in these pictures, it is clear many people were beginning to see British and American tensions as a nasty family conflict.

7   The representation of this tension as a family fight between Britain and America was not restricted to the visual arts and was not always shown so violently. Journalists in popular magazines and newspapers of the 1780s also exploited this relationship. One author explicitly reclaims the family structure for the political rather than the private sphere, reversing the action Scochet observed by counting marriage "with every political institution" and crediting

8   The only reason [women] do not receive the same usage from men of the world, as from the savages of the forest, arises more . . . from political considerations than from any innate sentiments of gallantry peculiar to the masculine character. ("Women" 409–10)

At least temporarily during this time, there seems to have been an attempt to shift perceptions of the family back to a more political sphere and away from the privacy of the home.

9   Several authors wrote about the family relationship that they saw between America and Britain. For instance, in October, 1782, after the war was over and the peace talks at Versailles were underway, *The London Magazine* published "An Argument for Recovering the Friendship of the Americas." The author of this column reports, "It has often been said, but happily to very little purpose, that indulgence

spoils the very best disposed children." He or she continues by adding
that mothers, on the contrary, say that children should be spared harsh
punishment and by suggesting that Britain should deal with America as
if the former colonies were children to be cajoled into good behavior:

> Are they not willing . . . to yield up every thing generously but   10
> to part with nothing by force. You must not think of getting the
> better of their good sense by any kind of trick or chicanery, but
> they are effectually and forever yours, the moment you refer to
> the candour of their feelings, and the magnanimity of their
> natures. (457)

After comparing the relationship between Britain and America to a
parent/child relationship and saying that Britain should be the one to
behave like the adult and make the first conciliatory move toward the
former colonies, the author moves on to compare the countries to a married couple. And interestingly enough, Britain is the wife in this scheme:

> Let us, for once, take a lesson from the females. In this respect,   11
> their powers are instructive and irresistible. Has not their sover-
> eignty, in domestic life, at least, been felt and acknowledged in
> all ages? Mark how they aspire and rise to universal dominion
> and empire? They never struggle or contradict, but uniformly
> accomplish their designs by apparent submission. Their indul-
> gence of others is only to secure their own; and they possess
> the blessed art in perfection, of seemingly giving way, solely
> that they may the more effectively keep their ground. Trust me
> the Americans will be easier duped than conquered. (458)

The author calls on his readers to learn a lesson from women here and
to see a new way of possibly dealing with the Americans to try to end
the conflict. This author makes one final shift in defining the family
relationship he sees between Britain and America before leaving the
subject. This time, America is the child of a paternal rather than mater-
nal Britain. If they are not appeased, they—in the guise of the "dogs of
war"—will run wild, and "dare invade the inheritance of their fathers"
(458). Although this author does not show exactly how the two countries are related, there is no doubt that in his mind the connection
between America and Britain is best described in familial terms.

    Another author sees a similar connection between women's roles   12
in marriage and ministers' roles in government. When giving instructions on how to prepare young people for marriage, this Lord Kaim
[sic] observes that a woman "governs in the family as a minister does

in the state, procuring commands to be laid on her, for doing what she inclines to do" ("Instructions" 416). Another author discussing the marriage state refers to God, the creator of marriage as "the great Supreme Governour of the Universe," even using political terminology there ("On Connubial Happiness" 216). And yet another uses the decidedly timely, politically-loaded phrase "domestic tranquility" to refer to a happy marriage ("A Country Curate's Address" 27).

13   Even marital infidelity is treated analogously to matters of state. In explaining how infidelity can be caused by overreaching ambition, another author explains:

14   Misled by [ambition] we have seen the hero laying waste
        provinces, and sacrificing whole nations to his ambition! What
        wonder then if the philosopher has likewise yielded to its
        sway; and that, what has so often been subversive of the rights
        and liberties of mankind, should likewise be prejudicial to
        truth! The same passion though exerted on different objects,
        still produces similar effects ("An Inquiry" 30).

Even among all these comparisons between the family structure and the relationship between Britain and America, however, "A Country Curate's Address to Married Persons at the Altar" is striking. Here, the bride is described in the same kind of language that could be used to describe America:

15   For your sake she has left her friends, all her connections, and
        all the world, and should she meet with a tyrant instead of a
        lover, she may repent of this day while she lives. Never incense
        or insult her. Every woman has many ways of revenging her
        injuries; and as you wish to keep your own temper and quiet,
        ruffle not her's [sic]. (26)

Not only is the bridegroom here being told how to treat his new wife, but the belated advice would have been applicable to Britain's relationship with America. The idea that the Britain-America relationship was closely akin to a family seems to have become nearly pervasive in the years surrounding the end of the war.

16   The connection between marriage and the state also appeared in the more traditional literary genres of the period. Important issues throughout the century were discussed on the stage. This analogy was being brought to life on the stage at the same time these issues were being drawn and written about by journalists. In particular, I want to examine selected works by two of the more successful playwrights

who were publishing at this time: Hannah Cowley and Richard Cumberland. Both these writers are recognized for their patriotism, and they must have recognized the possibilities they had to help shape the reconstruction of the British character and to help re-establish who would rule Britain after the loss of the colonies.

Cowley was not generally a politically outspoken playwright, aside from her occasional fits of "flag-waving patriotism" (Gagen 104). However, her own attitude toward marriage, that it should be "a loving partnership rather than a union of a ruler and his subject" (Gagen 104), is perfectly in accord with the message behind the rebirth of the symbolic discourse between the family and the state. Surely she could not resist infusing the plays that were first performed during the period just as the war was ending with this message. *Which Is the Man?* (1782) has an overtly patriotic ending, praising the quality of the men who serve as soldiers in the British Army:

17

> Intrepid spirit, nice honour, generosity and understanding, all
> unite to form him.—It is these which will make a British soldier
> once again the first character in Europe.—It is such soldiers
> who must make England once again invincible, and her glitter-
> ing arms triumphant in every quarter of the globe . . .
> Animated by such passions [for love and country], our fore-
> fathers were invincible; and if we would preserve the freedom
> and independence they obtained for us, we must imitate their
> virtues. (Cowley 5.1. p. 53–54)

18

The play as a whole is an amusing look at some of the ridiculous habits in fashion among the upper classes, not at all as seriously patriotic throughout as the ending makes it sound; one does not hear the drums beating in the background throughout the entire play. However, Cowley slips in moments of flag-waving throughout, so the reader cannot forget the context of the play: "I feel, that whilst my country is struggling amidst surrounding foes, I ought not to devote a life to learned indolence, that might be gloriously hazarded in her defence" (1.1. p. 6). She also includes comments on the direction the English national character seems to be heading, having the moralizing old guardian Fitzherbert fret that:

> Our traveling philosophers have done more towards destroying
> the nerves of their country, than all the politics of France. Their
> chief aim seems to be, to establish infidelity, and to captivate
> us with delusive views of manners still more immoral and
> licentious than our own. (2.2. p. 15)

19

These other topics of concern for the reconstruction of Britain aside, Cowley also addresses the marriage question directly. Fitzherbert cautions Belville, the romantic hero and newly-wed husband, about how easily influenced a wife's character is. He warns that

20   You may make her what you will. Treat her with confidence, tenderness, and respect, and she'll be an angel; be morose, suspicious, and neglectful, and she'll be—a woman.—The Wife's character and conduct is a comment on that of the Husband. (2.2. p. 18)

This line of thought coincides directly with that being expressed in the magazine essays discussed earlier in which men and Britain were instructed how to treat women and America for the most positive results. Comments of this nature scattered throughout the play echo the concerns being expressed elsewhere in the culture and bring Cowley into dialogue with the other authors expressing their opinions.

21   Richard Cumberland is as patriotic as Hannah Cowley. In fact the Cumberland play I will examine here follows the same publication pattern that hers does; *The Walloons* (1782), the first play he wrote in this period—written just after he returned home from a trip abroad and found that his government bureaucracy job had been eliminated—is even more patriotic than Cowley's *Which Is the Man?* In this play, Cumberland addresses the kind of conflict Britons felt about the different sides of the American Revolution. Although the British in *The Walloons* are fighting the Spanish not the Americans, Cumberland gives us examples of characters with the same kinds of divided loyalties many English felt about the war with the colonies: traitors within households and even exiled Englishmen who joined the Spanish forces but who still cannot forget their homeland enough to plot against England. From the prologue on, this play is filled with patriotic speeches about loyalty to Britain. The action and speech, from Agnes's refusal to marry her lover because he has taken up arms against her beloved England to the joy felt by two exiled Englishmen who have fought for Spain at being able again to recognize that "my natural sovereign now is my liege lord, and legal master" (Cumberland 4.2. p. 135), emphasize the importance of loyalty to one's own country. Cumberland connects the ideals of loyalty to country and marriage throughout the play, not just in Agnes's plotline. One of the major characters in a related plot, Lady Dangle has two husbands, one in Spain and one in England. Because of her continental connections with a Spanish Catholic priest, she unknowingly harbors a traitor to

England in her husband's ancestral home. This shows even more explicitly than Agnes's refusal of her lover Montgomery that no good can come from these kinds of divided loyalties. Cumberland makes no attempt to disguise his purpose here, even mandating in the prologue: "Nor, Britons, you our moral scene despise,/Still from the Stage does true instruction rise" (lines 19–20). This play is unabashedly patriotic, and Cumberland instructs his audience to take some of that emotion away with them and apply it to the character and leadership reconstruction going on in Britain at this time.

In the difficult years during and immediately after the American   22
Revolution, the British found it difficult to understand what had gone wrong in the new world and why they might lose part of their empire. In order to help explain this conflict, many authors and artists recognized the value the traditional but out-dated monarchy/family analogy could have in explaining the situation. Because of parallel shifts in beliefs, both the British government and the family were now seen as largely contractual arrangements; the basic analogy that had become defunct in the seventeenth century was now viable again. By comparing the British government, or even England as a whole, to the family, artists and authors were able to explain to their audience how the colonies' rebellion was feasible; if the parent or spouse (England) treated the child or wife (America) badly, the abused subject had a right to rebel and to demand better treatment or freedom. This analogy with a familiar and concrete example was so commonly used during the period because it helped the British subjects understand how and why their empire was beginning to crumble.

WORKS CITED

"An Argument for Recovering the Friendship of the Americans." *The London Magazine* Oct. 1782: 457–58.

Carretta, Vincent. *George III and the Satirists from Hogarth to Byron*. Athens, GA: U Georgia P, 1990.

Colley, Linda. *Britons: Forging the Nation, 1707–1837*. New Haven: Yale UP, 1992.

"A Country Curate's Address to Married Persons at the Altar." *The London Magazine* Jan. 1783: 26–27.

Cowley, Hannah "Which Is the Man?" *The Plays of Hannah Cowley*. Ed. Frederick M. Link. Vol. 1. New York: Garland, 1979.

Cumberland, Richard. "The Walloons," *The Plays of Richard Cumberland*. Ed. Roberta F. S. Borkat. Vol 3. New York: Garland, 1982.

Gagen, Jean. "Hannah Cowley." *Dictionary of Literary Biography: Restoration and Eighteenth-Century Drama*. Ed. Paula Backscheider. Vol. 3. Detroit: Gale, 1989.

"An Inquiry into the Causes of Infidelity." *The London Magazine* Jan. 1783: 29–32.

"Instructions Preparatory to the Married State." *The London Magazine* Sept. 1781: 416–18.

Keenan, Joseph J., Jr. "Richard Cumberland." *The Dictionary of Literary Biography: Restoration and Eighteenth-Century Drama*. Ed. Paula Backscheider. Vol. 3. Detroit: Gale, 1989.

"On Connubial Happiness." *The London Magazine* Sept. 1783: 216.

Scochet, Gordon J. "Patriarchalism, Naturalism and the Rise of the Conventional State." *Materiali Per Una Storia Della Cultura Guiridica*. XIV (December 1984): 323–37.

"Women." *The London Magazine* Sept. 1782: 409–10.

▶ QUESTIONS TO CONSIDER

1. Because Bailey's topic is not one that readers can be expected to know much about, she provides in the first part of her essay considerable historical background information. In fact, throughout her essay, Bailey's purpose is to inform as well as to persuade. Does she achieve an effective balance between these two purposes? Why, or why not?

2. Bailey states her main argument, or thesis, at the end of the third paragraph of her essay. Can you identify this thesis? Could she have emphasized it more? In what way?

3. Bailey introduces most of her sources at the beginning of the source material in addition to including information about the source in the parenthetical citations at the end of the source material. Why is this a good practice? When does she not follow this practice?

4. Review Bailey's use of direct quotations as opposed to summaries in presenting her source material. Which does she use more often? Which is more effective?

5. Bailey's source material derives from the fields of history, art, journalism, and literature. As evidence to support her thesis, is this variety of sources convincing? Would her essay be more or less informative if she focused on one type of evidence? Would it be more or less persuasive if she relied on only one type of evidence?

6. Unlike the other essays in this chapter, this one does not include the author's personal experiences. We learn nothing about Bailey herself in this essay. What effect does the absence of the author's personal experiences have on this essay? Given her topic and purpose in this essay, could Bailey have included her own experiences or made her own voice clearer?

WRITING ACTIVITIES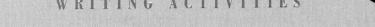

Individual: In a journal entry, compare this research essay to one or more of the other essays included in this chapter, focusing especially on voice, types of sources, use of sources, and strength of arguments.

Collaborative: Select five of the sources that Bailey uses, and analyze them. Consider, for example, how Bailey integrates the source into her essay, how well the source supports Bailey's arguments, and how credible the source is.

Computer: In a new computer file, copy Bailey's thesis (paragraph 3) and the topic sentences from her remaining paragraphs to create a summary of this essay. Then rewrite this summary, condensing it and putting it in your own words.

W R I T I N G   f r o m   S O U R C E S

Viewed most simply, research involves reading, listening, and observing. A literary scholar may spend years reading about a single author or work; a reporter may interview dozens of witnesses; and a scientist may observe the results of countless laboratory experiments. However sophisticated the results, the methods still involve reading, listening, and observing. In researching a topic, you will use these same basic methods (see Part Three, Strategies and Resources for Research).

Experienced writers use the results of their research in several ways. First, they use the information they have found to help their readers understand the subject they are reporting on. Experienced writers also use the results of their research as evidence to support their own assertions and ideas. That is, the source material reinforces and supports the writer's own arguments.

Overview of the Process

A successful research project requires careful planning and a significant amount of time. You cannot wait until the night before your project is due to begin your research. Although the way people conduct research and use the results of that research varies from one individual to another, you may find it useful to follow, at least generally, the following procedure:

Formulate a research question

Analyze research project

Conduct initial research: observations, library research, interviews

Evaluate and synthesize sources

Formulate a thesis/hypothesis

Write initial draft focusing on your own arguments

Integrate sources into your text

Conduct additional research if needed

Acknowledge and document sources

Prepare final draft of manuscript

Now that you have an idea of the entire process, we will explain each of the individual steps. You can also refer to Part Three, Strategies and Resources for Research, where you will find detailed discussions of these steps plus additional information on related topics.

Formulate a Research Question

Most research projects begin with a problem or question: Is it better to lease or rent a car? Do males and females have different ways of communicating? Which on-line service is best? How has rap music influenced our vocabulary? Initially, you may begin by thinking in terms of a topic or subject; however, you should begin your research by formulating a question—a question which interests you and which you can answer by means of some type of research.

Although you may begin with a very general question, your research will help you focus on a more specific one. Force yourself to think specifically about the question you want to answer. A viable research project involves more than merely collecting information on a topic. As soon as possible, you should formulate a research question that defines your purpose. Further research will help you answer your initial question and formulate your thesis. The more you learn about the issue you are researching, the more focused your research will become. (See Analyzing the Research Project in Part Three, pp. 401–407.)

Analyze Your Research Project

Research is time consuming and requires great patience. Don't expect to investigate an issue in a few hours or even a few days. Allow plenty of time for this stage of the process. The more you learn, the more you will be able to learn. Each new source of information you discover will lead you to other new sources, and the better you learn your way around the library, the more productive your research will become. Even after you have begun to construct your text, your research may continue; but don't rush this initial stage.

To ensure that you will complete your project on time, construct a schedule based on the overview of the process on page 378. Your schedule should be both realistic and definite. Allow adequate time not only for your initial research, but also for additional research you may need to do later in the process. Include plenty of time for constructing your text, as well. Writing a paper based on multiple sources is much more time consuming than writing an essay based solely on your own experiences and opinions. Also be sure to allow enough time for last-minute chores, such as returning to the library to check the accuracy of a source. Once you have completed your schedule, you may want to discuss it with your instructor.

As in all writing tasks, before beginning a research project, you need to be clear about the purpose of your research and who will read the results. As a student in a writing course, you have one obvious purpose: to complete an assignment your instructor will read. But you should go beyond the obvious to explore other reasons and other audiences. For example, do you want to discover whether the river where you fish or where your community gets its drinking water is being polluted or how the use of insecticides may affect the health of people in your community?

Similarly, decide in advance who your readers will be—college administrators; a city or county official; state or national legislators; or a certain group of readers such as sports enthusiasts, homemakers, business people, pro- or anti-environmentalists, and so on. Whether you are writing to an industrialist or an environmentalist makes a big difference not only in what you say, but in how you say it. It also makes a difference in the sources you use to support your point of view. Quoting a Sierra Club member will probably not impress the owners of timber companies, just as citing profit-and-loss statements will probably not impress a Sierra Club member. (See Analyzing the Research Project in Part Three, pp. 401–407.)

Conduct Your Initial Research

Although your immediate impulse may be to head for the library when you start a research project, be aware of other sources, too. The books, popular magazines, scholarly journals, newspapers, and government documents in a library obviously provide a researcher with valuable information (see Searching the Literature in Part Three, pp. 418–424). But you may also want to read materials not kept in libraries; letters, brochures, pamphlets, instructions, guidelines, family records, and city and county records provide useful information, as well.

You can also learn a great deal about a subject by talking to people. Interviewing someone with knowledge or experience related to your subject can provide especially valuable source material (see Conducting Interviews in Part Three, pp. 447–450). Careful, well-planned observation experiences can also yield a wealth of information about a subject (see Conducting Direct Observations in Part Three, pp. 444–447).

Most experienced researchers use more than one method of investigation. They often read about a subject to gain some background knowledge of it, talk with other people (both in interviews and in informal conversations) to gain additional viewpoints and to test their own ideas, and then, if possible, also observe the phenomenon they are investigating.

For example, if you are investigating the effectiveness and practicality of solar energy as a source of heat, you might begin by reading articles, reports of energy studies, government documents, and builders' brochures on the subject. Then you might talk with an industrial or civil engineer with experience in this field, with the owner of a solar-heated house, and with a building contractor who installs solar energy systems. Finally, you might actually visit a home or building that uses solar energy to observe for yourself how well it works.

LIBRARY RESEARCH.   If you are not thoroughly familiar with your school's library, plan to spend some time just learning your way around. Making the effort initially to acquire a basic orientation to your library will save you time and prevent frustration later. Most libraries provide tours or printed material that explain what resources they have and where these resources are located (see Exploring the Library in Part Three, pp. 408–418).

Once you know how your library is organized, you can begin your search. Although initially you may be pleased to find any information, focus especially on locating current and unbiased information. Don't overlook such possibilities as government documents and statutes of law. In looking for magazine and journal articles, use indexes such as the *Humanities Index* and *Social Sciences Index* as well as the *Readers' Guide.* For general background information, encyclopedias, especially specialized ones (e.g., *The Encyclopedia of Religion and Ethics, McGraw-Hill Encyclopedia of Science and Technology, The Encyclopedia of World Art,* etc.), can be useful, but don't rely on them for current information. Computerized bibliographic searches are increasingly available and very useful.

Don't hesitate to ask for assistance with your research. The librarians at the reference desk can tell you what research tools are available to you and direct you to those that are most likely to be productive (see Searching the Literature in Part Three, pp. 418–424).

Initially, you will not read your sources carefully but will merely **skim and scan** them—reading superficially just to get the gist of the source to determine if it is going to be useful to you. Don't take notes or photocopy a source until you are fairly sure it is pertinent. Then, if possible, **photocopy the source** so that you will have an accurate copy of your own. Duplicating an article or chapter is not a substitute for a careful summary, but well-annotated photocopies can be invaluable when the time comes to select quotations and to acknowledge sources. Be sure to make a copy not only of the text itself, but also of the pages that give you the publication information you will need if you later need to document the source. Some magazines and journals include this information on each page, but many do not.

Once you have a good photocopy, you should **read the source carefully**. As you read, **annotate** your photocopy of the source thoroughly. For example, highlight the main points; mark information you think you may want to use later; underline statements you disagree with; circle sentences that you may later want to quote; make comments in the margin; and so on (see Chapter 1, pp. 21–23, and Keeping a Record of Your Research in Part Three, pp. 424–435).

It is important to keep an accurate record of the information you find. Now is the time to take notes on what you have read. Whether you use notecards, a journal or notebook, or a computer, you need to **make a record** of your research. Here is an efficient and useful process:

1. Attach (stapling is best) a blank sheet of paper to the photocopied source.

2. If your copy of the source does not include the information you will need to document it, write this information at the top of the sheet.

3. Summarize the entire source briefly in your own words.

4. Paraphrase important ideas that you may want to use in developing your own arguments. Indicate page numbers of the original source covered by your paraphrasing.

5. At the bottom of each sheet, write a brief note to yourself indicating how you plan to use this source in developing and supporting your own arguments.

Throughout your research, keep careful records of all you read, hear, and observe (see Keeping a Record of Your Research in Part Three, pp. 424–435). In addition to the traditional forms for recording the results of research, most writers today also take advantage of computers in recording and reporting on their research. Keeping notes in a computer file can eliminate much recopying and rewriting because you can later work directly from the notes you have entered into the computer. Computers also enable you to expand outlines, experiment with different forms of organization, and insert quotations easily. Many software programs also have features that make it easy to document sources.

OBSERVATIONS AND INTERVIEWS.   Try to include interviews and observations as well as library research in your investigation. Even if you are researching a national or even international issue, such as the relationship between environmental legislation and industry, you may be able to find someone at your school or in your city who can provide you with valuable information. Perhaps your college or university has an economist who studies the relationship between the environment and the economy. Or it may have a department or program of environmental science. Perhaps your city has an environmental organization such as a chapter of the Sierra Club or the Audubon Society. Local farmers and gardeners, hunters and outdoor enthusiasts also often have valuable knowledge about the regional animal and plant life. Local business people may be able to give you a personal view of the impact of environmental regulation. Requesting information from national organizations and agencies is also a possibility. A postcard or telephone call is often all it takes; sometimes a small fee is charged.

If you interview someone, write down in advance the questions you plan to ask, but allow the person you are interviewing to digress from your questions. Digressions may, in fact, be more interesting or useful than the answers to your questions. When possible, and with the interviewee's permission, tape the interview. If this is not possible, carefully write down any statements you plan to quote. Ask the interviewee to read the statements as you have written them to verify their accuracy.

Finally, you can learn a lot about something by observing it. You will need to observe carefully and record in writing exactly what you see. For example, observing how your school disposes of its trash and waste products might provide useful information if you are researching the subject of waste management on your campus. (For more about non-library techniques for gathering information, see Conducting Direct Observations, pp. 444–447; Conducting Interviews, pp. 447–450; Designing Questionnaires, pp. 450–454; and Writing Letters of Inquiry, pp. 454–459, in Part Three.)

Evaluate and Synthesize Sources

Because research nearly always results in more information than can possibly be included in a single report or essay, one of the writer's tasks is to evaluate the information he or she has collected and to decide what information to include. The following guidelines can help you with this important task:

❖ Use only pertinent information.

❖ Use only current information.

❖ Use only reliable information.

USE ONLY PERTINENT INFORMATION.   Don't use everything you learn just to show how much research you have done. Regardless of how interesting the information is, if it doesn't directly support your thesis, leave it out. For example, in researching the potential of solar heating, you may discover a detailed explanation of how to construct and install your own solar energy heating system. But if your purpose is not to teach readers how to build a solar energy heating system, don't include that information in your report. You might choose to mention in your discussion of initial costs that a do-it-yourself system is possible, and you could refer readers to the source of your information

USE ONLY CURRENT INFORMATION.   Unless your purpose is to provide your readers with background information or to focus on a historical topic, use only current sources that report up-to-date information. For example, you might want to include in a report on solar heating systems some background information about how early humans used the energy of the sun to keep warm. In fact, this information could be the basis of an effective introduction. But for the main part of your report, you would not want to use sources from the 1960s, when there was great interest in solar energy but when much of the current solar technology had not yet been invented. If your information is not up to date, you could misinform your readers about what is possible now.

USE ONLY RELIABLE INFORMATION.   This guideline can be difficult to follow, for evaluating the reliability of sources can itself involve considerable research. However, by the time you have completed your research and are ready to report on it, you have become something of an expert on your topic. You probably know enough to become suspicious if certain information seems out of line. For example, if most of your sources indicate that the cost of purchasing and installing an effective solar energy heating system is approximately $10,000, but a brochure from your local electric power company gives the cost as considerably more, you are justified in suspecting that the electric power company's information may not be reliable. Similarly, if an article in an environmental magazine claims that the cost is $6,000, rather than the $10,000 estimate of most of your sources, you probably don't want to quote the lower figure. However, you might decide to give your readers the range of prices you have discovered, carefully explaining the source of each.

Don't ignore sources that do not support your own opinions and ideas. Instead, acknowledge them; refute their arguments if possible; and try to find a common ground with them. Few arguments outside a courtroom are won decisively by one side or the other. Changing someone's mind is extremely difficult, if not impossible. However, an effective argument can lead to a compromise or an agreement on certain aspects of an issue. If, for example, you find that your sources disagree on the general effectiveness of solar energy heating systems but agree that they have been most successful in the Southwest, you can argue that solar energy should be used in that region rather than trying to convince readers of its universal effectiveness (see Reading and Evaluating Sources in Part Three, pp. 435–444).

Formulate a Tentative Thesis or Hypothesis

Research can be directionless until the writer develops a hypothesis, or tentative thesis (see Analyzing the Research Project in Part Three, pp. 401–407). Although writers may begin research with only a general subject or question in mind, they usually formulate a hypothesis as soon as possible to guide their research into more specific channels. After completing their research, they can then formulate a more definite thesis. Remember that in most reports of research, writers are not merely reporting on the results of their research but are using the information they have collected to develop and support their own ideas. Without a single controlling idea, a report of research can become a meaningless exercise for the writer and a confusing, useless document for the reader. If you are not sure what your thesis is by the time you have completed your research, spend some time focusing on this important element of your report.

Writers formulate a thesis in different ways. Often the thesis exists before the research has even begun. For example, a writer investigating whether solar energy is an effective, practical source of heat knows the question from the first but learns the answer only after completing the research. That answer then becomes the writer's thesis: Although they are expensive to install, solar energy systems provide home owners in certain parts of the country with an effective source of heat.

Sometimes a thesis evolves out of the writer's convictions, which are at least partially shaped by doing the research. Many student writers begin a research project believing one thing but modify their beliefs as a result of their research. For example, a writer who initially believes that recycling is the answer to our waste disposal problem may discover that the problem is far larger than he or she thought. As a result, the thesis for the report may change from "Recycling is the answer" to "Recycling is an important step in solving an enormous problem."

Occasionally, however, writers will not have a thesis even after researching an issue or topic. In this case, they must formulate a thesis from studying their sources. The best way to do this is to compare sources. What do they agree on and what do they not agree on? Points of disagreement usually offer the best opportunity for formulating a thesis, because a strong thesis usually focuses on an issue on which people disagree. Consensus does not usually lead to a strong thesis. But if there is a difference of opinion, the writer can decide which position to take and base the thesis on that position. For example, if some sources claim that solar energy is expensive and some argue that it is cost-effective, the writer can try to discover who is right and take that position as a thesis. In some cases, a thesis may voice a compromise position: Solar energy is initially expensive but in the long run can save money (see **thesis**).

THESIS, PAGE 663

Write an Initial Draft Focusing on Your Own Arguments

One pitfall in writing a text based on research is to rely too heavily on your source material. It is easy to lose your own voice in your effort to make good use of your sources. For that reason, begin your text by writing a draft in which you **do not include any source material**. This initial draft can be rough and even fragmentary (you can fill in the blanks later), but it should establish your own voice and develop your own arguments. Later you can expand your arguments by including information and ideas from your sources, but let this first draft be all yours. You do not want your sources to dominate your text. Rather, you want your readers to hear your own distinct, persuasive voice.

USE AN APPROPRIATE TONE AND STYLE. In arguing from sources, you want to sound knowledgeable and well informed but not necessarily formal. In most research-based reports and essays, it is fine to use first person and even to use your own experiences if they support your arguments. Don't be reluctant to sound like you. Readers respond much better to a real person's voice than to a neutral-sounding, impersonal, anonymous voice. Although a few texts traditionally require the writer to "disappear," most disciplines and professions now encourage writers to speak as clearly and directly as possible (see **style and voice**).

STYLE AND VOICE, PAGE 656

USE AN OUTLINE. Because research-based reports and essays are complex texts, you may want to use a preliminary planning outline to organize your ideas. Planning outlines can be as formal or informal as you like. A simple list will do. However, a fairly complete outline, showing not only the main points you want to make and the order in which you want to make them, but also how you plan to support those points, will be even more useful. You can indicate on this outline which sources you plan to use in developing each point.

Using a computer to make your outline may be the most efficient method, because you can later revise and rearrange it, insert material into it (e.g., summaries, quotations, information), and expand it. In fact, if you have taken notes and then developed an outline on a computer, you can often build your report or essay by expanding the outline as you write. Treat each entry in your outline as a point to be expanded, developed, and supported.

USE DIFFERENT METHODS OF DEVELOPMENT.   Experienced writers use various methods of development to structure the evidence they use from their sources. All of the methods of development discussed throughout this book are appropriate for research-based arguments. You may compare and contrast (solar energy is safer and more economical than nuclear energy); show cause and effect (solar energy doesn't pollute the atmosphere or deplete resources); describe (solar energy is clean and inexpensive); classify (solar energy, like energy derived from wind and water, is a natural source of energy); exemplify (solar energy has been used successfully in Arizona and New Mexico); and narrate (this is the way solar energy works).

NARRATION, PAGE 618

DESCRIPTION, PAGE 565

EXEMPLIFICATION, PAGE 574

COMPARISON/CONTRAST, PAGE 542

CLASSIFICATION, PAGE 527

CAUSE AND EFFECT, PAGE 522

Although you may use one method of development primarily, remember that most texts are developed through a combination of methods (see **narration**, **description**, **exemplification**, **comparison/contrast**, **classification**, and **cause and effect**).

Integrate Sources into Your Text

Once you have produced a rough draft, you can write other drafts that include the source material you want to use. Be sure, however, that the sources you include directly support and develop your thesis. Basically, you must make the following decisions at this stage in the construction of your text:

- ❖ Decide what source material to include.

- ❖ Decide whether to quote or summarize source material.

- ❖ Decide where to place source material in your text.

DECIDE WHAT SOURCE MATERIAL TO INCLUDE.   You are not using source material merely to decorate your text, to fill up space, or to impress your reader. The sources that you include should serve clear and useful purposes. Usually your purpose should be one of the following:

- To support your own arguments
- To provide a different viewpoint
- To provide additional information for your readers

Questions to ask yourself in determining what source material to use include the following:

1. Is this source material current enough to be credible?

2. Is this source someone who will be respected, or at least recognized, by my readers?

3. Will this source material support my arguments?

4. If not, is it important that I include this source because it represents a viewpoint I must acknowledge and refute?

DECIDE WHETHER TO QUOTE OR SUMMARIZE SOURCE MATERIAL. In general, you should quote sources in the following cases:

- The source is a well-known authority or expert.
- The language used by the source is especially forceful, compelling, or memorable.

Otherwise, it is usually better to summarize the source material you are using, because it is easier to integrate summaries into your text, and they are less intrusive. Be sure, however, that you introduce and acknowledge summarized sources in the same way that you do quotations.

DECIDE WHERE TO PLACE SOURCE MATERIAL IN YOUR TEXT. Initially, this may seem simple enough. But you cannot just insert source material arbitrarily into your text. You must determine carefully just where the material will be most effective. It is especially important that you be careful not to destroy, or distort, the organization of your own arguments. Inserting source material that does not clearly pertain to the arguments you have articulated in your text will only annoy or confuse your readers.

In general, source material should **follow**, not precede, your own arguments. Do not introduce a new argument by quoting or summarizing a source. Your own argument should be clearly articulated before you introduce your supporting evidence—that is, your source material. Thus, you might begin a paragraph by stating that solar energy is especially effective in the Southwest. You could then follow this statement by summarizing a source that explains why the climate of that region makes it particularly suitable for solar energy or by quoting someone who has lived in a house in northern Arizona that was heated by solar energy.

The only time you might consider violating this general rule is in the introduction to your essay. As we point out in Chapter 6, Writing to Persuade, presenting an opposing viewpoint initially and then challenging it can be an effective strategy in writing to persuade. Thus, you might want to begin with a striking quotation or a brief summary that will engage your reader's attention and then state your own opposing viewpoint.

Once you have decided what sources you want to include, whether you want to summarize or quote your sources, and where you want to place this material in your text, you must integrate your sources carefully into the draft you have written. This process may require extensive revising of your draft, because you cannot simply drop source materials into an existing text. You will probably need to rewrite the sentences before, and perhaps after, the source material to create an appropriate context for it. And you will definitely need to introduce the source material appropriately so that your reader will know that it is not your own words or ideas.

Merely using quotation marks to identify quoted material is not enough. Whether you are quoting or summarizing your source, you should always introduce it clearly so that your reader knows exactly where the source material begins and ends. You can, of course, do this in a number of ways. For example, the following statements are frequently used to introduce source material:

❖ According to John Doe, "solar energy may not be the answer to all our energy problems, but it is certainly not a lost cause" (56).

❖ For example, John Doe believes that, while solar energy may not be the single solution to our energy problems, it should be part of the solution (56).

❖ As John Doe points out, "solar energy may not be the answer to all our energy problems, but it is certainly not a lost cause" (56).

❖ I agree with John Doe that "solar energy . . . is certainly not a lost cause" (56).

In all of these examples, a reader would know exactly where the source material begins and ends. Equally important, your reader would know **whom** you were quoting or summarizing before beginning to read the source material. Even though a parenthetical citation at the end of the source material provides your readers with this information, it is better for them to know it earlier so that they are clear at all times as to whose ideas they are reading.

VERIFY ACCURACY OF SOURCE MATERIAL.   As you insert quotations and specific information into your text, check them carefully against the original. Once something is copied into your text, you will tend to assume it was copied accurately. So carefully verify the accuracy of everything you include, especially if you are quoting someone.

You do not need to be concerned with complete documentation at this point, but it is a good idea to include the page numbers of the source material you use. You can, of course, wait until later to worry about these details, but it will be easier and more efficient to do it at this point than to do it later.

Conduct Additional Research if Necessary

It is rare to plan a research project so well that you do not need to do additional research at some point. You simply cannot know in advance every source you need to consult or what issues or questions will arise. Your initial research merely begins the process. As you continue to work with your sources, you will discover new leads you want or need to pursue. And, once you begin to construct your own text, you may well find that the direction of your research changes slightly or, in some cases, substantively. Thus, you may discover, even very late in the process, that you need to do further research. Rather than seeing this additional research as a problem, view it as an opportunity to follow up new leads and to test your thesis in new ways. Having done your initial research and constructed a text, you will find yourself a more experienced researcher at this point, and the results of your late research may well be rewarding (see Integrating Sources into Your Text in Part Three pp. 460–466).

Acknowledge and Document Sources

To acknowledge a source is simply to identify source material clearly and state explicitly in your text that this material is taken from a certain source. To document a source is to provide certain information about it. For a written source this information usually includes the following:

- Name of source
- Title of source
- Name of publisher plus place and date of publication

In a way, you always include other sources in your own writing, without being aware of doing so. What you know derives from long-forgotten sources that have become a part of your general knowledge base. Your opinions, beliefs, ideas, and attitudes, too, have been shaped by diverse sources you may no longer remember. But when you knowingly and deliberately use other sources, you are obligated to acknowledge those sources appropriately. Not to do so is to plagiarize.

Many instances of plagiarism are unintentional, the result of an inexperienced writer's not knowing when, why, or how to acknowledge and document sources appropriately. But plagiarism, whether it is intentional or unintentional, is considered at best a serious oversight and at worst an act of dishonesty. So it is important that you indicate clearly to your readers any and all material derived from external sources—all information, ideas, opinions, or words other than your own that cannot obviously be considered general knowledge.

Writers acknowledge and document their sources in order to provide important information for their readers. If your readers are not able to distinguish your source material from your own ideas and opinions, they will be confused and annoyed. Your credibility as a writer and researcher depends on your ability to introduce your source material clearly and appropriately and to provide readers with accurate information about your sources. You can do this in several ways:

1. Always introduce your sources by mentioning their names (or identifying them in some way) before you quote or summarize what they have said or written.

2. Use quotation marks to indicate quoted material.

3. Follow both summarized and quoted source material with the appropriate parenthetical documentation. Include all sources in a list of works cited.

(For a detailed discussion of documentation of sources, see Part Three, pp. 398–503.)

Prepare the Final Draft

In the final editing and proofreading of your text, focus especially on how well you have integrated quotations into your own writing. Try reading your text aloud, even if no one is listening but you, to determine if the quotations you have used fit smoothly with and into your sentences. If a sentence sounds awkward to you, it probably is.

This is also the time to check the punctuation of quotations, the form of all your parenthetical citations, and your list of works cited. Handled correctly, these details indicate that you are a careful researcher, a knowledgeable scholar, and a good writer. In other words, they can help convince readers of your credibility and persuade them to accept your arguments.

Finally, and most important, check the accuracy of your documentation. Be sure each page number you supply is correct, each author's name is spelled correctly, every title is exactly like the original, and each date of publication is accurate. Also confirm the accuracy of each quotation you have used. This task will be easy for sources you have photocopied. But if you must go back to the library or must call someone you interviewed, take the time and make the effort. Inaccurate research suggests not just carelessness, but dishonesty (see **revising and editing**).

REVISING AND EDITING,
PAGE 651

 # W R I T I N G   A S S I G N M E N T

For this writing assignment, there is no general theme and no list of suggested topics. Your assignment is simply to research and report on some arguable issue, ideally one with which you have some first-hand experience. Try to select an issue that you have had personal experience with. For example, if you are interested in environmental issues, you might investigate the types of insecticides your city or local farmers use, how your city or school disposes of waste, or whether any hazardous waste products are being disposed of in your area. If you are interested in popular culture, you might investigate a type of music or film that you know something about. Or if you are interested in business, you might investigate a local business or industry, focusing on its effects on the community, how it handles labor disputes, or what forms of written communication it depends upon and values.

Because you will spend a significant amount of time on this assignment, it is important that you think carefully about what you want to research and whether you have the time and resources for such a project. In general, small, well-focused projects are more successful than large, vaguely defined projects. Thus, after you have identified a topic in which you are interested, you should narrow that topic to a specific research question—one that you can realistically expect to research and write about in the time you have been allotted for this project.

Generating Ideas through Invention and Research

INVENTION.   If you are having difficulty finding a topic and formulating a research question, you may want to take inventory of your own interests and resources by answering the following questions:

1. What are my hobbies and interests?

2. What work experiences have I had?

3. What topics have I previously researched?

4. What major or career am I interested in pursuing?

5. What previous experiences have I had as a result of travel, family history, reading, schooling, and so on that might suggest a research topic or question?

6. What does the location or history of my hometown suggest as possible research topics and questions?

7. What educational, political, environmental, or gender issues excite or interest me?

8. What do the other courses I am taking suggest as possible research topics or questions?

9. What do issues relating to my own generation suggest as possible research topics or questions?

10. What films, books, television shows, and music do I like?

RESEARCH.   Once you begin your research, you will be able to formulate a more interesting, focused research question and eventually a thesis. An interview is an especially useful form of research because a dialogue is possible. Although before scheduling an interview, you should always do enough library research to be able to formulate sensible, pertinent questions, an interview with an informed person early in your research process can be very useful. You can ask specific questions about the issue you are researching, learn about written sources that may be available to you, and even receive advice about how to pursue your research.

Observations can also prove useful, giving you a real sense of your topic as well as different perspectives. Throughout your research project, even after you have begun to write your paper, different forms of research can stimulate your imagination, help you forge new connections, and test your own arguments and ideas. So don't restrict your research to the library or to the first part of the process. Explore your subject in a variety of ways, and continue your research as long as possible.

Drafting Your Text

It is important initially to write a draft of your text in which you omit all source material, focusing on your own arguments and how you want to present those arguments. If you do not begin by writing in your own voice, it will be very difficult to establish that voice later in the process. So begin by writing a draft in which you get your ideas down and organize them in a logical sequence.

In drafting your text initially, concentrate especially on the following specific features:

- ❖ Focus
- ❖ Development

In a research essay, which tends to be longer than an essay that does not include multiple sources, it is important to have a strong focus that enables readers to follow your arguments easily. A well-focused text is one in which the writer's main argument is clearly articulated and every part of the text supports that argument. In order to achieve this goal, your thesis and topic sentences should clearly forecast the content that follows (see **forecasting statements**). Thus, you will probably want to state your thesis in the introduction and to begin each new section with a strong topic sentence that will guide your readers through your text, explicitly indicating the direction each paragraph is taking.

FORECASTING STATEMENTS, PAGE 580

In general, your argument should be developed by a combination of your own ideas and ideas and information from your sources. If you discover that some of your arguments are not well supported, that you have not developed them adequately on your own or supplied adequate evidence from your sources, you may have to do further research. But remember that your arguments can also be supported with evidence from your own experiences and ideas.

In addition to using your own experiences and the results of your research, you may want to develop your ideas by using the traditional methods of development. For example, suppose one of your arguments is that Americans generate a tremendous amount of waste because they rely so extensively on fast foods. You could compare the waste involved in a meal consumed at home with one consumed at a fast-food restaurant; point out the effects of this type of waste, describe in detail all the paper that is wasted in a single fast-food meal, or give examples of the types of waste involved in fast-food merchandising.

Reading and Revising Your Text

As you read and revise your text, remember that none of your paragraphs should begin with source material, whether in the form of quotations or summaries. You should firmly establish the point you are making in each paragraph before introducing source material.

To be sure your essay is focused and well organized, you may want to copy your thesis and each topic sentence onto a separate sheet of paper so that you can see their relationship to one another more clearly. These sentences, read together, should constitute a summary of your text. If you are using a computer, you can copy your text to a new file and then delete everything but the thesis and topic sentences to expedite this process. Each time you read your text, you will probably revise it in some way. Some of these revisions may be substantive—rearranging sections of your text, deleting extraneous material, adding additional evidence; some may be minor—rewriting an awkward sentence, correcting an error in subject-verb agreement, changing a word. Be sure to give special attention to the following features of your text.

If necessary, revise to sharpen focus. If you lose your readers as they attempt to read your text—if they can't trace the thread of your argument or see the relationship of what they are reading to your thesis—you will not convince them of anything. Readers are usually not willing to struggle with an unfocused text that wanders all over the subject and never makes a point. If your reading of your text doesn't reveal a clear, strong thesis, you must correct this flaw before you can hope to construct a good argument. However, including a strong thesis in your introduction doesn't always mean that your text is well focused. If the arguments you include in the body of your text do not support your thesis, your text will still not be well focused. To be well focused a text must have a strong thesis *and* arguments that clearly and directly support it. If your essay is long, you may want to begin each major section with its own introduction (see **forecasting statements**).

FORECASTING STATEMENTS, PAGE 580

If necessary, revise for more effective organization. Readers like to anticipate where your arguments are leading. Surprise endings may be popular in mystery stories, but they are not effective in research essays. To keep your readers on track, happy because they are following your arguments and because these arguments are leading to a logical conclusion, do two things. First, arrange your arguments so readers recognize the logic in your organization. One main point should lead naturally and logically into the next so readers have a clear sense of progression as they read. For example, if you are comparing the arguments for and against preserving a certain wilderness area, you do not want to discuss one and then the other haphazardly. It is more effective to discuss all the arguments for preservation and then those against preservation—or to organize the arguments point by point, discussing first the effects on wildlife, then the aesthetic arguments, and finally the economic considerations. Your arrangement of these main points depends upon your point of view. If you are convinced that preserving the wilderness area is important and you think the aesthetic arguments are the strongest ones in support of this position, then conclude with this point. However, if you are against the preservation because you think the economic considerations—creation of new jobs, manufacturing development, and so on—override all others, then conclude with this point.

The second thing you can do to help your readers perceive the logic of your organization is to tell them what is going on at strategic intervals. If you are progressing to a new point of view, inform your readers by including a clear **transition** statement. Most often, writers make transitions as they begin new paragraphs. Clear **topic sentences** can not only announce the topic of the paragraph, but also can lead the reader from the last point to the next one. You can also use **headings** to help readers perceive the organization of your text. Headings, and even subheadings, are especially useful in texts of five or more pages.

TRANSITION, PAGE 676

TOPIC SENTENCE, PAGE 672

HEADINGS, PAGE 603

If necessary, revise for better development. Now is also the time to look at the development of each of your main arguments. If these arguments are weak and underdeveloped, you may have to do further research. However, be sure your sources do not already dominate your arguments. Perhaps what is needed is further discussion and explanation of the sources you have already included or the expansion of your own arguments.

Remember, your sources are not your arguments; they are merely the evidence for your arguments. Although you may arrive at your arguments as a result of the cumulative experience of the research you have done, they should be expressions of your own point of view articulated in your own words. If they are weak, sticking another source in may not be the solution. You may need to rethink the issue, do further reading, and talk to other people in order to strengthen and revise them.

Preparing the Final Draft of Your Text

In preparing the final draft of your text, one of the things you will be most concerned about is whether your source material has been smoothly and effectively integrated into your own writing. Examine each quotation to be sure it is identified and introduced effectively into your own arguments. Be persistent in proofreading. Don't jeopardize your hard work on this essay by having a text marred by misspellings, usage problems, and stylistic inconsistencies or by incomplete or inconsistent documentation.

DISCOVERING YOURSELF ◀
AS A WRITER

Being as specific and reflective as possible, answer the following questions about your experience with this writing assignment:

1. What did you learn about yourself as a writer as you worked on this assignment? In what way did this writing experience change your perception of yourself as a writer, your process of writing, or your attitude toward writing?

2. What forms of research did you use for this assignment? What did you learn about research that will help you in other writing assignments?

3. Was the final draft of your text better or worse than you had expected? What would you do differently if you had the opportunity to do this assignment again?

4. How did writing this assignment make you a better reader?

5. What did you enjoy most about this writing assignment? What did you like least?

PART THREE

STRATEGIES AND RESOURCES FOR RESEARCH

▶ I N T R O D U C T I O N

Research begins with the need to find answers to questions. If the answers are already widely known and accepted, the questions are not of much interest. If you already know the answer to a question, you will need to do little, if any, research except to verify some point or to refresh your memory about some fact. However, if the question is of significant interest to enough people and the answer is unknown or controversial, it may lead to a research project.

A good way to psych yourself up for a research project is to think about how the need to do research comes into our lives and about the purposes and consequences of doing the research. In Chapters 1 through 8, we discuss purposes for writing. Those purposes also apply to research. However, the most important reason to do research is that it helps provide answers that usually have practical applications for the group who is interested in them. For example, you and your classmates in a literature class might be trying to figure out whether Margaret Macomber shot her husband by accident or on purpose during the safari in Hemingway's "The Short Happy Life of Francis Macomber." Or you might be a student in a management or international business class writing on the feasibility of American corporations seeking ISO Standard 9000 certification. Or you might be a student or a professional health care worker trying to determine the best public policy concerning the use of thalidomide—which was not approved for use in this country by the Food and Drug Administration after it had been proven to cause birth defects in babies whose mothers took the drug when they were pregnant—to help fight tuberculosis or the HIV virus. Or you might be doing research for a history or military science class in which you try to ascertain whether General McClellan's failure to pursue General Lee's retreating army in 1862 after the Union victory at Antietem enabled the Confederate army to regroup and continue fighting until 1865.

The information, knowledge, and perhaps even the wisdom that are required to answer such questions do not come out of nothing. They come from personal experience, reflection, and research. It is research with which we are concerned in this section. Writers often need to research their topic so that they will have sufficient information and a good understanding of what they write about. Their research may involve library research so that they can discover what has already been written about their particular topic. Their research may also involve gathering information by interviews and questionnaires and by direct observation. The appropriate methods will depend on the nature of the writing assignment and the type of information desired.

Research can be intriguing and rewarding—a very satisfying activity. But it requires careful planning, dedicated work, and perseverance. There is no formula or recipe to ensure good results; considerable thought must go into doing research. In Part Three we provide you with our best advice on how to do research—specifically, how to do the following:

- ❖ How to analyze the research project. Here you learn the questions you need to ask about the feasibility of the research project.

- ❖ How to conduct library research. Here you learn about the library and how to conduct literature searches, evaluate and read sources, and take notes.

- ❖ How to conduct field research. Here you learn about such research methods as conducting direct observations and interviews, designing questionnaires, and writing letters of inquiry.

- ❖ How to document sources. Here you learn how to integrate sources into your text and to acknowledge sources using Modern Language Association (MLA) or American Psychological Association (APA) documentation.

A N A L Y Z I N G   T H E
R E S E A R C H   P R O J E C T

Your chances of succeeding in research depend on how well you understand your research project. With a clear and guiding idea about what you are seeking to learn, why you want to learn it, how you might learn it, and to whom you plan to communicate your findings, you will set yourself up to be successful before you begin the research. To proceed, you will need answers to the following questions about your research project.

Is This a Question That Needs Answering?

You cannot answer a question until you know what the question is. The more focused you are on the research question, the more likely you will discover what you want to know. But it is important to keep an open mind: You may need to refocus or reformulate the research question as you go along. There are some disadvantages to focusing too narrowly in the early stages of research: You may miss opportunities to consider related questions; you may be unable or unwilling to look at the information you are collecting from a different perspective; or you may not be alert to information that might lead to a more important question. Researchers who do not keep an open mind and become inflexible seldom notice a chance piece of information or detail that can lead to new discoveries. But being able to formulate a research question, even a tentative one, is an essential step in research, which throughout its process may seem to be concerned with gathering information but which is essentially a series of acts of discovery.

For example, suppose you are writing a short research paper for a literature course and are interested in pursuing a question that had generated considerable discussion when your class read Hemingway's "The Short Happy Life of Francis Macomber": Did Margaret Macomber kill her husband accidentally or on purpose? Whether she murdered her husband is ambiguous; there is evidence that will lead to more than one interpretation. But you are interested in seeing if you can discover information that will make less ambiguous the cause of Macomber's death, the changing relationship between Macomber and his wife, and the guilt or innocence of Margaret as a murderer—a tall order, but one that has your intellectual juices and curiosity going. If you are able to answer the question satisfactorily for you, your classmates, and your teacher, you will have added to a fuller understanding of Hemingway's story, perhaps even to other pieces of his fiction, and to an increasing awareness of the use of technology such as firearms in twentieth-century fiction.

Let's further suppose that you noticed with interest as you read the story that Macomber and his guide, Robert Wilson, converse about guns and hunting dangerous prey. You noted further that Margaret has listened to some of these conversations, may have had experience in or at least some knowledge about hunting dangerous game, and has some information about hunting rifles. Perhaps brainstorming these matters has led you to several questions, including these two: What did Hemingway know about guns and how did he use that knowledge in his fiction? and Did Margaret Macomber shoot her husband intentionally or accidentally?

The first question gets at an important aspect of Hemingway's writing, but it is far too general to direct your research since it is not related specifically to this story. How can you become more focused, more specific? You might think about why that initial question is important. As you reflect on the question and your reasons for asking it, you should be able to ask a more direct, pointed question: Did Margaret Macomber murder her husband? Whatever your answer, to be convincing you will have to explain how you arrived at it. What evidence do you have that supports the contention that she shot her husband intentionally? What evidence do you have that supports the belief that she intended to shoot the charging buffalo but shot her husband by accident? Although the question identifies the main issue, it is not specific enough to focus and direct your research.

But you have a beginning. You will have to ask more specific questions to get your research moving in a productive direction. What was Margaret's state of mind at the moment she fired the fatal shot? What was her motive in firing? Was she trying to kill the buffalo that was charging her husband, or did she intend to shoot Macomber? Did she know enough about guns and about big-game hunting to choose deliberately a gun that was powerful enough to kill her husband at the distance that separated them but that was not powerful enough to kill the charging buffalo? Another question might be: Did Hemingway know enough about particular guns (she used a 6.5 Mannlicher) to use them in authentic and symbolic ways in his fiction? More questions are likely to come up, and as you reflect on them you will be able to ask, with greater clarity, further questions that will help explore more extensively the question of whether Margaret murdered her husband.

Does the Question Merit Research?

To determine whether a question merits researching, you need to ascertain what research has already been done on it and whether there is general agreement on the answer or solution. If you find universal agreement either that Margaret shot her husband accidentally or that she shot him intentionally, chances are that the topic is not an interesting research question and you will need to find another topic. However, universal agreement does not necessarily mean that the question is no longer interesting, for there is a widespread belief these days that there is no single correct reading of a text. You may be able to argue convincingly that the consensus is wrong—an opportunity to make others sit up, blink hard a few times, and consider reversing a long-held opinion. Chances are greater, though, that your reading of other investigations into the matter will show that opinion is divided, with some believing that Margaret tried to save her husband but accidentally shot him while others believe that Margaret murdered him after she recognized that he, with his newly acquired manliness, would have the strength to leave her. Divided opinion over the answer signifies a topic that merits research.

Is This a Question You Can Answer?

A feasible research topic is one that involves a question that has not yet been answered definitively and that is not beyond your capabilities to answer.

To discover whether you can handle the research, you need to discover how familiar you are with the topic and whether you can handle the technical level of information required; whether sufficient sources of information are available; and whether you have the time to do the research in the time allotted.

CAN YOU HANDLE THE LEVEL OF INFORMATION REQUIRED?   If you are familiar with big-game hunting and with the guns used to kill large animals and are familiar with the story and other Hemingway stories that portray relationships between men and women and that portray the use of guns, you probably have enough information and knowledge to move quickly into considering whether Margaret had a motive for killing her husband and was aware that the gun she picked up was capable of killing him but not the charging buffalo.

If you feel you need to learn more about the gun Margaret used and whether she knew how to fire it effectively, you may need to spend more time reading the story more closely, consulting basic reference works on guns, and asking a gun expert about the capabilities and performance of the gun she used and those of Wilson and Macomber. If you are not familiar with research on Hemingway as a fiction writer, you might read a book-length study or review article as a useful starting point. But you also need to read articles that deal with your specific topic—whether Margaret shot her husband on purpose or was trying to save him.

ARE SUFFICIENT SOURCES OF INFORMATION AVAILABLE?   In the earliest stages of your research, you probably used several sources of information in formulating your research question. Once you have done this, you are ready to start choosing your major research methods and lining up the sources from which you will gather information. There are several factors to consider here, especially whether sufficient sources of information exist that are credible to those who are interested in the answer to your research question.

The typical kinds of research in which you will engage are these: observing phenomena directly, seeking information from others by interviews, questionnaires, or letters; and reading what others who have conducted research or are otherwise knowledgeable about the question have published. If you are a novice, you will need to read general sources such as encyclopedias, popular and commercial magazines, newspapers, and books that provide introductory overviews of your research topic. If you can handle more technical material, you will need more scholarly journals and books about guns or literary critics' views on whether Margaret shot her husband intentionally. You may also want to gather information by interviewing or writing letters of inquiry to experts or other persons who may possess useful knowledge that may help you answer your research question. You may even need to directly observe physical phenomena (such as actually firing a 6.5 Mannlicher at a similar distance). We discuss a variety of library and field research methods and information sources in the remaining major sections of Part Three.

DO YOU HAVE ENOUGH TIME TO COMPLETE THE RESEARCH PROJECT? You need to be realistic about the time you can allot to the research question you are proposing to answer. It is easy to underestimate the time needed for researching a complex question. Researching a limited question thoroughly is better than exploring a large, broad question superficially. Unless you have done considerable research on the topic earlier, you will not be able to complete in a quarter or semester term a research project on the uses of technology in literature, on the symbolism of guns in twentieth-century American fiction, or even on Hemingway's knowledge of guns and how he uses that knowledge in his fiction. However, you should have enough time in a college course to complete the research and a paper on whether Margaret Macomber murdered her husband.

You should approach your research project as you would plan any significant work project, preparing a tentative schedule for your research and trying to anticipate how much time each stage of the project will take. Start with the date that the project is due and any interim deadlines, as for required progress reports and drafts. Estimate how much time you will spend reading, keeping in mind that some sources may not be available when you need them. Also, if you are planning to conduct field research, try to figure out how much time you will need for direct observations (and how many times observations might need to be repeated); to design and administer questionnaires (including a pilot study first); to receive answers to inquiry letters; and to arrange and conduct interviews.

Planning will probably save a lot of time later in your research project, but be prepared for things that still might not go smoothly. An important publication might not be available when you need it; a questionnaire might need revising; an inquiry letter might not be answered promptly; an interview might need to be rescheduled or might be unproductive; an important note might be misplaced. Don't underestimate the amount of time your research will take and remember that mishaps can occur.

Can You Develop a Hypothesis?

At some point during your research, you will need to develop a hypothesis to help make sense of the information you have collected and to help serve as the basis for further research. More likely, you will develop many hypotheses at different points during your research.

There are two notions about a hypothesis that you need to keep in mind. First, a hypothesis is not a casual guess or stab in the dark. It is a conjecture or supposition about the answer or solution to a research question or problem, based upon the researcher's reasoned attempt to discover the significance or meaning of information developed to that point. For instance, based upon your analysis of "The Short Happy Life of Francis Macomber," you might create the hypothesis that Margaret murdered her husband. Certain aspects of the story have encouraged you to think about her possible motive (she has recognized that her husband may have finally developed the courage to leave her); the opportunity (she pretends to shoot at the charging buffalo when she is actually aiming at the back of her husband's head, and she is confident that the eyewitness, their guide, will corroborate her claim that the shooting was accidental); and her ability to perform the act (she may know that the 6.5 Mannlicher is powerful enough to kill a human at the distance her husband was from her, and she has been vindictive and cruel). Of course, the decisions about motive, opportunity, and ability are also based upon hypotheses.

Second, a hypothesis is not "proven" in the sense that you can establish it as an absolute and unassailable truth. A hypothesis may or may not be true. It serves as a working idea—an assertion to be tested. "Prove," in this instance, carries the meaning of testing or trying out, not establishing the truth of a statement. However, the more evidence that supports a hypothesis, the more likely the hypothesis is accurate. But you need to be cautious. With all significant research questions, there is information that will admit more than one conclusion. Don't become too enamored with a hypothesis, because even a great amount of supporting evidence cannot be totally convincing. A fact or two that cannot be reconciled with the rest of the evidence can bring into question the accuracy of a hypothesis. There are several questions that should be examined in trying to determine whether Margaret Macomber murdered her husband:

Is there evidence that she was shooting at the buffalo? How close was the charging buffalo to Macomber? Is it possible that Margaret's anxiety affected her shooting? Is there evidence that Macomber might have moved into the line of fire just as his wife pulled the trigger? Is there evidence that Margaret tried to save her husband because her love for him had been rekindled by his newly found bravery? How does Wilson's belief that she shot her husband intentionally relate to the hypothesis? You should be equally pleased whether your research and reasoning lead you to support or reject the hypothesis. Being scrupulously fair will prevent your trying so hard to support a hypothesis that you commit several errors that can discredit your argument.

Use these principles to test your hypothesis:

- State the hypothesis as a declarative statement, not a question, so you are forced to defend or refute it.

- Consider evidence that does not support the hypothesis as well as that which supports it.

- Try to develop arguments to refute the hypothesis as well as ones to support it.

- Be willing to modify or abandon the hypothesis if the evidence does not support it.

- Retain the hypothesis as long as the facts support it, but do not cling to it if it is inconsistent with the facts.

CONDUCTING LIBRARY RESEARCH

Writers base much of their work on personal experience and on field research methods such as observation and interviewing, surveying by questionnaires, and writing letters of inquiry to generate primary data. However, few writers know everything that needs to be known about their subjects. Writers also need to develop their thinking and their inner explorations in relation to those of others who have written on the subject. Knowing how to gather information and read for research purposes is important.

The next sections explain how to use libraries and to search for sources, to keep a record of your research, and to read and evaluate sources.

Exploring the Library

Technology is revolutionizing the way information is stored and accessed. You may have access in your dormitory to the Internet or the Online Computer Library Center (OCLC) that connects you with every university library in the world, or your school's library may use a card catalog and casebound subject indexes. Fortunately, whether libraries are relatively small community or college libraries or massive research libraries at national research institutes or large universities, they all have essentially the same kinds of *basic* holdings and are organized and cataloged similarly. These common characteristics of all libraries allow you to locate reference materials and track down specific items in the library's collection fairly quickly, regardless of its size. (If you use a technologically advanced library, you will need specialized instruction on how to use its specific information systems.)

The discussion of library research here focuses generally on libraries that operate conventionally but that are becoming increasingly computerized.

Visit the Circulation Desk

You can start exploring the library by stopping at the circulation desk (where items are checked out and returned). Many circulation desks provide free printed brochures and general guides to the library. Here are some of the kinds of information about your library that are available at the circulation desk.

THE HOURS THE LIBRARY IS OPEN. Some libraries are open twenty-four hours a day; others are open at different hours during the week and on weekends. Check also for special holiday and semester- or quarter-break hours.

THE NUMBER OF ITEMS THAT CAN BE CHECKED OUT AND HOW LONG THEY CAN BE KEPT. Usually you will be able to check out a limited number of items. Try to avoid fines for not returning overdue library materials. You may not be allowed to check out items if you have an unpaid library fine or an overdue book.

THE PROCEDURE FOR REQUESTING ASSISTANCE IN LOCATING MISSING ITEMS. Occasionally you will be unable to locate an item even though it is not checked out to another patron. It may be lost, misshelved, or otherwise unavailable. Check at the circulation desk to learn the procedure for initiating a search for an item that is included in the library's holdings but that you are unable to locate.

THE CLASSIFICATION SYSTEM USED TO ORGANIZE THE LIBRARY'S COLLECTION.
Libraries use either the Dewey Decimal Classification System or the Library of Congress Classification System. See Figure 3.1 for a general breakdown of the Dewey system and Figure 3.2 for the Library of Congress system. Each system breaks down further into numerous subclasses. You will need to know the general classification number of an item to locate the general area of the library where it is housed.

THE TYPE OF CATALOG. Until recently, nearly all libraries used a card catalog, consisting of rows of file cabinets with alphabetically arranged small drawers that contain cards on all the holdings. Every item in the library had at least three cards in the card catalog: one for the author, one for the title, and one or more for the subject. Figure 3.3 (page 411) shows examples of cards for Albert Gore's *Earth in the Balance*. In recent years, libraries have been increasingly using or are planning to convert to a computerized catalog that uses computer terminals to gain access to the library catalog, which is displayed on a computer screen. Computerized catalogs not only contain complete listings of a library's holdings and where the items are located, but they also specify whether the item is checked out by some other patron. See Figure 3.4 (page 412) for the kind of screen you might get on such a system. A few libraries use a COM Catalog (computer output microform), in which entries are displayed on microfilm or microfiche.

THE EXTENT OF THE LIBRARY'S COLLECTION. All libraries have books and periodicals (newspapers, magazines, and journals), and more and more

000 General works
100 Philosophy and related disciplines
200 Religion
300 Social sciences
400 Language
500 Pure science
600 Technology (Applied sciences)
700 The arts
800 Literature
900 General geography and history

Figure 3.1 Dewey Decimal Classification System

General Works ....A
Philosophy & Religion........................B
Auxiliary Sciences of History C
History: General & Old World...........D
History: America.........................E–F
Geography. Maps. Anthropology........G
Economics & Business ....H–HJ
Sociology ....HM–HX
Political Science ....J
Law (General)....................................K
Education L
Music...M
Fine Arts ....N
Language & Literature......................P
Science..Q
Medicine ....R
Agriculture ....S
Technology ....T
Military Science ....U
Naval Science V
Bibliography. Library Science ....Z

Figure 3.2 Library of Congress Classification System

libraries are expanding their electronic resources. You need to know the variety of materials in your library, so find out about such sources as data bases, journals, government documents, proceedings and transactions of professional meetings, and technical reports. You also need to know about such quick-reference sources as abstracts, almanacs, atlases, bibliographies, dictionaries, directories, encyclopedias, handbooks, indexes, and yearbooks. Your library may also have film, recordings, works of art, maps, computer disks, and compact disks that can be checked out.

THE DIFFERENT AREAS OF THE LIBRARY WHERE CERTAIN PARTS OF THE COLLECTION CAN BE FOUND.   Different areas in the library house books for different disciplines, a reference section, special collections, a reserve desk where items that professors designate for use in specific courses are kept, current newspaper collections, a reading room, a microform collection, government documents, and so on. Walk around the library until you have a general idea of where things are located. If the library is large, it is likely to consist of several floors. Check to see if there are maps or guides for each floor as well as a general overview of the entire library.

THE LOCATION OF PHOTOCOPIERS AND CHANGE MACHINES. Most libraries have photocopiers that enable you to make copies of library material (usually at 10 cents a page). Know where several of these machines are in case there are lines of patrons waiting to use them.

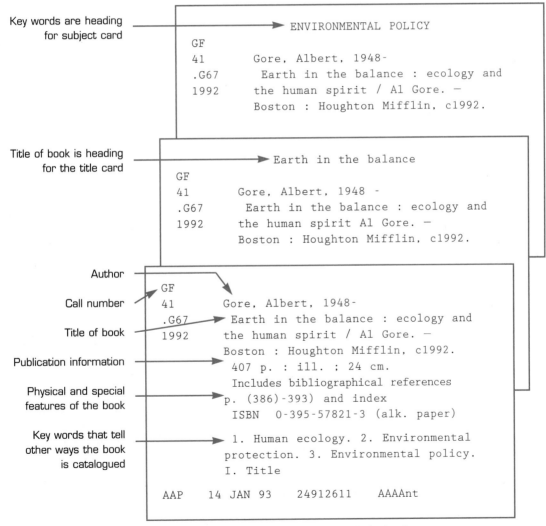

Figure 3.3 Author, title, and subject cards for book.

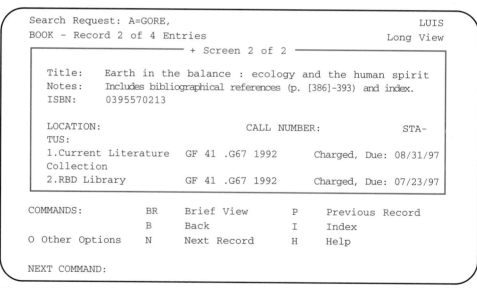

```
Search Request: A=GORE,                                    LUIS
BOOK - Record 2 of 4 Entries                          Long View
              ┌────────── + Screen 1 of 2 ──────────────┐
     Author:            Gore, Albert, 1948-
     Title:             Earth in the balance : ecology and the
                        human spirit
     Variant Titles:    Ecology and the human spirit.
     Publication Information: Boston : Houghton Mifflin, :1992
     Description:       407 p. : ill. ; 24 cm.
     Subjects:          Human ecology.
                        Environmental protection.
                        Environmental policy.
              └─────────────────────────Continued on next screen ┘

COMMANDS:          BR      Brief View      P      Previous Record
                   F       Forward         I      Index
O Other Options    N       Next Record     H      Help

NEXT COMMAND:
```

```
Search Request: A=GORE,                                    LUIS
BOOK - Record 2 of 4 Entries                          Long View
              ┌────────── + Screen 2 of 2 ──────────────┐
     Title:    Earth in the balance : ecology and the human spirit
     Notes:    Includes bibliographical references (p. [386]-393) and index.
     ISBN:     0395570213

     LOCATION:                      CALL NUMBER:            STA-
     TUS:
     1.Current Literature  GF 41 .G67 1992    Charged, Due: 08/31/97
     Collection
     2.RBD Library         GF 41 .G67 1992    Charged, Due: 07/23/97

COMMANDS:          BR      Brief View      P      Previous Record
                   B       Back            I      Index
O Other Options    N       Next Record     H      Help

NEXT COMMAND:
```

Figure 3.4 Computer screen of an on-line catalog showing entry for a book. The entry is from LUIS, the electronic library system of Auburn University. Copyright © 1993 by NOTIS Systems, Inc. All rights reserved.

Sign Up for Library Tours and Training Sessions

Once you have a sense of how the library is organized, check back at the circulation desk to see if the library staff provides tours or training sessions on how to use the library's electronic catalog and other computerized systems, such as computerized data bases. If your library subscribes to CD/ROM or on-line index and abstract services instead of to print versions, you will need to learn how to use them. Perhaps one of your instructors will arrange to have your class attend an orientation session for the library. If not, sign up on your own for a tour and training session, if they are available and if you feel the need to.

Visit the General Reference Section

There will be countless times when you will need to find such things as the winner of the Nobel Peace Prize for a particular year, the year and place of birth of a particular person, the location of Djibouti and its strategic importance in World War II, the literacy rate of people over ten years old in Vietnam, the atomic weight of a specific element, the date of the Galveston hurricane, the job prospects for college graduates in your major, and so on—answers to what librarians call "ready reference questions." These kinds of information are easily obtainable in publications that are kept in the general reference section—the most used part of any library. Reference works, such as almanacs, atlases, bibliographies, dictionaries, encyclopedias, handbooks, and yearbooks, are chock-full of factual information that is considered accurate and authoritative by virtually all readers. These sources, whether they are in print or electronic form, are excellent for acquiring basic facts that you may not know but that are essential to your research project.

You should spend some time learning the location of these kinds of reference works and their contents. Introduce yourself to the reference librarians on duty and ask about the scope of the reference section and the availability of brochures or booklets that might explain it. Librarians, who are usually available most of the hours that the library is open, can be very helpful in answering questions about such things as reference sources and electronic data bases. Check two or three atlases, encyclopedias, and handbooks, and review them to discover the variety of information available.

In addition to such basic ready reference works, you should also become familiar with periodical indexes and abstracting journals, which may be available in print, electronic, or microform versions.

CHECK PERIODICAL INDEXES FOR ARTICLES APPEARING IN MAGAZINES AND JOURNALS.   The most recent print information on a subject is usually found in periodicals. In fact, much of that information may never appear in books. Your library subscribes to several dozen, perhaps hundreds or even thousands, of periodicals, and the indexes are your guide to the articles published in them. General indexes, such as *Readers' Guide to Periodical Literature*, cover articles appearing in such commercial magazines as *Business Week, Scientific American,* and *Sports Illustrated.* More specialized indexes, such as the *Applied Science & Technology Index, Humanities Index,* and *Index to Government Periodicals,* will lead you to articles on more technical and advanced subjects. Figure 3.5 illustrates typical entries in the print version of the *Humanities Index.* Figure 3.6

Music festivals–*cont.*

Scotland

See also

Edinburgh Festival Fringe

Edinburgh International Festival

Music halls (Variety theaters, cabarets, etc.)

See also

Folies-Bergere

Striptease

Vaudeville

Conspiracies of meaning: music-hall and the knowingness of popular culture. P. Bailey. il *Past Present* no 144 p138-70 Ag '94

Music in advertising

Commercialization of the rap music youth subculture. M. E. Blair. bibl J *Pop Cult* v27 p.21-33 Wint '93

Effects of ambiguity and complexity on consumer response to music video commericals [with appendix] J. Hitchon and others. bibl *J Broadcast Electron Media* v38 p.289-306 Summ '94

Music in art

See also

Art and music

Dancing in art

Music in churches

See also

Church music

Psalmody

Music in drama *See* Music, Incidental

Music in education

Indian music in the Indian school in South Africa: the use of cultural forms as a political tool [with appendices] J. Pillay. bibl *Ethnomusicology* v38 p281-301 Spr/Summ '94

Music in literature

See also

Jazz in literature

Musical instruments in literature

Opera in literature

Singing in literature

Songs in literature

Lips together, teeth apart: another version of pastoral. B. Montgomery. *Mod Drama* v36 p547-55 D '93

Orpheus ascending: music, race, and gender in Adrienne Kennedy's She talks to Beethoven. P.C. Kolin. bible *Afr Am Rev* v28 p 293-304 Summ '94

Figure 3.5 Typical entries in the print version of the *Humanities Index,* April 1994–March 1995. (New York: Wilson, 1995), p. 793.

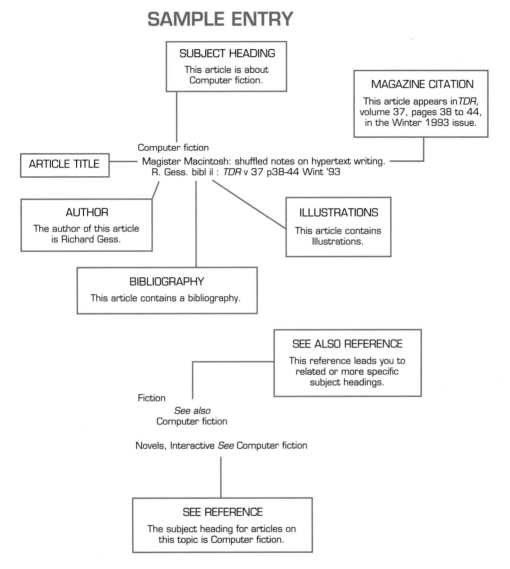

SAMPLE ENTRY

SUBJECT HEADING
This article is about Computer fiction.

MAGAZINE CITATION
This article appears in *TDR*, volume 37, pages 38 to 44, in the Winter 1993 issue.

Computer fiction
ARTICLE TITLE — Magister Macintosh: shuffled notes on hypertext writing.
R. Gess. bibl il : *TDR* v 37 p38-44 Wint '93

AUTHOR
The author of this article is Richard Gess.

ILLUSTRATIONS
This article contains Illustrations.

BIBLIOGRAPHY
This article contains a bibliography.

SEE ALSO REFERENCE
This reference leads you to related or more specific subject headings.

Fiction
See also
Computer fiction

Novels, Interactive *See* Computer fiction

SEE REFERENCE
The subject heading for articles on this topic is Computer fiction.

Figure 3.6 Explanation of index entry. *Humanities Index*, April 1994–March 1995 (New York: Wilson, 1995).

explains how to read an entry from the print version of the *Humanities Index*. Almost all other printed indexes are formatted and organized similarly. Figure 3.7 and and Figure 3.8 illustrate entries in the on-line version of the *Humanities Index*.

```
Search Request: A=MONTGOMERY B                Humanities and General
Search Results: 9 Entries Found                       Author Index

       MONTGOMERY BARBARA K
   1   INSTANCE OF RAPID CERAMIC CHANGE IN THE AMER <1990> (AR)
   2   INSTANCE OF RAPID CERAMIC CHANGE IN THE AMER <1990> (HU)

       MONTGOMERY BARBARA M
   3   BEHAVIORAL CHARACTERISTICS PREDICTING SELF A <1984> (HU)
   4   COMMENTARY ON INDVIK AND FITZPATRICKS STUDY <1986> (HU)
   5   COMMUNICATION IN INTIMATE RELATIONSHIPS A RE <1984> (HU)

       MONTGOMERY BENILDE
   6   LIPS TOGETHER TEETH APART ANOTHER VERSION OF <1993> (HU)
   7   WHITE CAPTIVES AFRICAN SLAVES A DRAMA OF ABO <1994> (HU)

       MONTGOMERY BRUCE
   8   HIGH FIELD SUPERCONDUCTIVITY <1996> (RG)
                              ————— CONTINUED on next page —————
STArt over         Type number to display record   <F8> FORward page
HELp               PRInt
OTHer options      MARk

NEXT COMMAND:
  ibm A
```

Figure 3.7 Author entry of journal articles in the on-line version of the *Humanities Index*.

```
    Search Request: A=MONTGOMERY B                Humanities and General
    DHUM RECORD -- 6 OF 9 Entries Found                     Brief View

     AUTHORS:       Montgomery, Benilde.

     ARTICLE TITLE: Lips together, teeth apart: another version of pastoral.

     JOURNAL:       Modern Drama 36:547-55 Dec'93




                                          ———— Page 1 of 1 ————
STArt over         HOLdings      PRInt        <F6> NEXt record
HELp               LONg view     MARk         <F5> PREvious record
OTHer options      INDex
Held by library--type HOL for holding information.
NEXT COMMAND:
  ibm A
                                                              03:29
```

Figure 3.8 Entry of journal article in the on-line version of the *Humanities Index*.

CHECK NEWSPAPER INDEXES FOR NEWS ARTICLES APPEARING IN MAJOR NEWS-PAPERS. *The New York Times Index* lists all the articles published in *The New York Times* since 1851. *The National Newspaper Index*, available only in microform or on a computer terminal, indexes articles from *The New York Times, Wall Street Journal, Christian Science Monitor*, and *Los Angeles Times. Business NewsBank Index*—available in CD-ROM format—goes beyond indexing and reproduces news articles from over 450 newspapers.

CHECK ABSTRACTING JOURNALS FOR ABSTRACTS (SHORT SUMMARIES) OF ARTICLES. Abstracting journals, which are available in both print and electronic forms, cover most disciplines. They are useful because they include an abstract (a short summary) of each article as well as its bibliographical citation. Their titles indicate their coverage: *Biological Abstracts, Chemical Abstracts, Forestry Abstracts, Pollution Abstracts, Psychology Abstracts* are a few of the many that are available. Figure 3.9 shows a typical entry from *Biological Abstracts*.

CHECK CD-ROMS AND OTHER ELECTRONIC DATA BASES FOR MATERIAL IN ELECTRONIC FORM. More and more information is available in electronic form, including most of the indexes and abstracting journals we have already mentioned. Since different libraries provide varying levels of electronic resources and support, check with one of the reference librarians to see what is available in your library. Often there is a fee for using a specific commercial data base, although some university and college libraries charge reduced fees or none to students

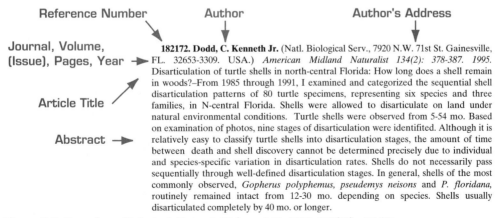

Figure 3.9 Entry from *Biological Abstracts*, Volume 100, 1995. 100(12): AB-381.

and faculty. And, of course, there are many on-line data bases and CD/ROM collections that are available at no charge because they have been produced by nonprofit organizations or federal or state governments or have been purchased by your library for your use. Instructions for using electronic information systems are usually posted near terminals. Most libraries offer workshops on how to use them or have persons who are trained in electronic searching who will help you.

Consult a Librarian

Your library has several professional librarians and library assistants. These persons are not just desk-bound clerks who arrange books and magazines or just book lovers who enjoy dusting the shelves. Most of them have degrees in library or information science, and many have become subject matter specialists who work as social science librarians or humanities librarians and who are quite knowledgeable about the resources in their assigned fields.

As a result of their education, training, and experience, they are experts in solving library research problems and can help you in searching for information in specific fields. They not only can suggest specific print and electronic resources, but they can also help in numerous other ways. They can explain the resources of the library that may not be obvious to you. They can inform you of workshops and seminars that the library sponsors on using the library or its computer-based resources. They can show you how to use on-line and CD-ROM information systems. They can even advise you on how to obtain resources from other libraries. In fact, they enjoy the challenges of helping locate hard-to-find sources and of finding that last piece of information that has eluded your best research efforts.

Searching the Literature

Once you have chosen your research project and have become familiar with the organization and layout of your library, you can begin to search for information about your subject.

To illustrate, let's say that you are enrolled in a course in which you are studying—among other things—the culture, social organization, and social and economic problems of rural communities in the United States, and that you have to do a research project as one of the major assignments. Because of your experiences during the past two summers working as an intern at a state government migrant health agency, you have become interested in migrant workers who have come to the United States to do agricultural work and who have expressed a desire to establish permanent residency in the community. You have become acquainted with one of the crew leaders and his family; they own a small piece of land just outside the town limits, and their two oldest children are enrolled in a local community college studying for careers outside farming. You have become especially interested in doing your required research project on the economic and social impacts that more permanent residency might have on small rural communities.

From your preliminary analysis of the research project and your interest in these migrant workers, you have decided to follow the suggestion of your instructor and pick a research topic that you already know a little about, have some interest in, and want to know more about. You see an opportunity to expand your knowledge and study the problems and opportunities of foreign migrant workers in a larger context—a good match between your interests and a major assignment in the course. You have also decided that the likely focus points of your research are (1) the problems faced by workers who attempt to curtail their nomadic life-style and seek a more stable and successful place in rural farm communities, and (2) the social and economic impact on the locale in which they choose to settle. Your main purpose is to inform the citizens of your community of the problems for and benefits to the community that are associated with the prolonged residency of these workers. It is your hope that your neighbors will support efforts to assist them in their settling into your community.

You have even created a tentative hypothesis: Migrant farm workers who establish permanent residency can positively affect the social and economic resources of the community in which they settle. Of course, you sense that your hypothesis will need to be thought out more thoroughly. Talking with more knowledgeable researchers and experts on the subject will help you sort out broad issues and direct you to more specific questions. But for now you feel that you need to search through material in the library to get a better idea of what information already exists and to see if that will help sharpen your hypothesis further.

What you need to realize as you start your search of the literature is that it will take time. You will need to locate far more sources than you will need, because some of the sources will not be available or will not work out for some reason. You need a plan to search a library for relevant literature. It should be one that will not be too detailed or rigid, but that will help you search systematically yet still be flexible enough for you to be able to follow promising leads.

The kinds of sources you will need depend upon how extensively you have analyzed your research project and how much you already know about your research subject. There are two general levels of material available to you: background material in mass communication publications and material in more specialized publications. Two or three hours looking into a few resources will help you get your bearings and build a list of potential readings (your working bibliography) quickly.

Sources for Background Information

If you need background information, the most obvious starting point in your search is sources that provide summaries of information, general overviews, and contemporary accounts of migrant working conditions. These sources enable you to get a handle on the size, scope, and complexity of your subject. Because news magazines, newspapers, and encyclopedias are familiar to you and are easy to use, you might begin by going to the library's reference section and using the *Readers' Guide to Periodical Literature*, and the *New York Times Index* (the *New York Times* is the most widely held newspaper in American libraries). You might also read about migrant workers in *Encyclopedia Americana*. If your library has *NewsBank* and its index, use it, too. *NewsBank* is a computerized data bank that contains articles from more than 450 American newspapers, and you can either print the articles you find or download them to your own disk.

Looking under headings such as "migrant laborers," "children of migrant workers," and "United Farm Workers of America," you will find a number of relevant articles listed in recent issues of *Readers' Guide*. Your examination of the *New York Times Index* and *NewsBank* indicates a steady stream of relevant articles appearing in newspapers. A five-page entry titled "Migrant Workers" in the current edition of *Encyclopedia Americana* provides you with an overview of the conditions of migrant workers in the United States and in other countries. In addition, there is a bibliography of nine books on the subject at the end of the entry.

Just looking in these four resources, you have identified several promising items. As you use the *Reader's Guide*, the *New York Times Index*, and *NewsBank*, you also notice three helpful features: First, most of the articles are relatively brief and written for nonspecialists; second, notations explain whether the item deals with immigrants or domestic migrant workers (you are seeking information about immigrants); and third, the resources are arranged in chronological order. The print sources consist of several volumes, each providing a guide to articles published in a given year; the computerized sources arrange all the entries into a multiyear chonological file. You make a mental note that you can check earlier years if you later decide to learn more about your subject over a long period of time. But right now you are interested in recent and current information, so you stay with the more recent volumes and dates. There appears to be plenty of material available for you to gain sufficient background on your research subject.

To find these articles and books that you have identified in the indexes and the encyclopedia bibliography, you have to record enough information to enable you to locate them. This is the beginning of your working bibliography (the list of publications that you plan to read). If you already know the documentation system you will use, use it. Doing so from the first will save you time in the long run. (See Using MLA Documentation to Acknowledge Sources and Using APA Documentation to Acknowledge Sources, pages 466–503.) For example, if, in your search for information on migrant farm laborers, you know you will be using the documentation style of the American Psychological Association, start changing the publication information from the highly abbreviated and unusual forms used by the *Readers' Guide*, *New York Times Index*, and *NewsBank* to APA style. A portion of your working bibliography might look like this:

Bardacke, F. (1993, Nov. 22). The Chavez legacy. The Nation, 257, 606+.

Brinkley, J. (1994, Oct. 15). California's woes on aliens appear largely self-inflicted. New York Times, 1+.

Cockcroft, J. D. (1986). Outlaws in the promised land: Mexican immigrant workers and American's future. New York: Grove.

Convention on migrant worker rights adopted. (1991, March 9). UN Chronicle, 28, 80-81.

Cutting bitter lives short. (1992, July 27). U.S. News & World Report, 113, 56-57.

Fewer migrant workers in corn belt this year. (1993, May/June). Successful Farming, 91, 20.

Protest in the chile fields. (1991, Feb.). The Progressive, 267, 80-84.

Stichter, S. (1985). Migrant workers. New York: Cambridge University Press.

Sources for More Specialized Information

If you think that you already possess sufficient background on migrant farm laborers and the opportunities and problems they face in shifting from a migratory to a more permanent residential life-style, and if you feel that you are able to handle material at a higher level than news magazines, newspapers, and encyclopedias, you need to locate more specialized resources. Ultimately, you will need to go beyond journalism and mass communication sources. To locate these more specialized sources, you must use indexes such as *The Social Sciences Index*, *PAIS* (Public Affairs Information Services, Inc.), and *Sociological Abstracts*. In a short time, looking under the same subject headings you used earlier, you will be able to add more items to your working bibliography on migratory farm laborers, including these:

```
        Henderson, Z. P. (1992, Fall). Migrant program
breaks down barriers. Human Ecology Forum, 20, 29-31.
        Martin, P. L. and D. A. Martin. (1994). The endless
quest: Helping American farm workers. Boulder, CO:
Westview.
        Perloff, J. M. (1991, May). Choice of housing and
wage compensation of hired agricultural workers. Land
Economics, 67, 203-12.
        Protecting the rights of migrant workers and their
families. (1991, May 23). Objective Justice, 34-66.
        Slesinger, D. P., B. A. Christenson, and E.
Cautley. (1986). Health and mortality of migrant farm
children. Social Science and Medicine, 23(1), 65-74.
        Stuart, P. (1992, Dec.). A better future for
migrant workers. Personnel Journal, 91, 67-74.
        What's our government doing for migrant workers?
(1992, Jan.). Personnel Journal, 91, 70.
```

While in the reference section, you should also check Eugene P. Sheehy's *Guide to Reference Books* (10th edition, 1986) and the supplement edited by Robert Balay (1992), for they identify all kinds of abstract journals, bibliographies, dictionaries, encyclopedias, and indexes that might have additional leads for you. Under the headings "Labor" and "Economics," you will find in Sheehy's, among other items, several publications that might prove useful, such as these:

Azevedo, R. E. (1978). <u>Labor economics: A guide to information sources.</u> Detroit: Gale.

Biegal, D. E. (1989). <u>Social support network: A bibliography.</u> New York: Greenwood.

Ghorayshi, P. (1990). <u>The sociology of work: A critical annotated bibliography.</u> New York: Garland.

In looking in Sheehy's you will probably notice that the U.S. Department of Labor, Bureau of Labor Statistics, publishes *U.S. Bureau of Labor Statistics*, which covers all the department's bulletins published since 1886 and all its reports since 1953. It also carries an extensive list of current government periodicals dealing with labor statistics in this country. In checking the *PAIS* index earlier, you might have become aware that several U.S. government agencies—from the departments of Agriculture to Education to Health and Human Services to Labor—have programs and publications that are important to migrant workers. A visit to your library's government documents section to use the U.S. Government Printing Office's *Monthly Catalog of United States Government Publications, Publication Reference File* (the latter in microfiche form only), or *Guide to Government Publications* will give you more items for your working bibliography:

- *Migrant Health Projects*, a quarterly publication published by the U.S. Department of Health and Human Services, Bureau of Health Care and Delivery and Assistance

- a quarterly newsletter for migrant and seasonal farm workers published by the Office of Economic Opportunity

- *Migratory Labor Notes*, a series of reports published by the U.S. Department of Labor, Bureau of Labor Statistics

- annual reports and general publications published by the U.S. Department of Justice, Bureau of Immigration and Naturalization Service.

You now sense that your search is going well. In just three or four hours you can develop a working bibliography that will give you plenty to read during the next three or four days. Your search is off to a strong start, but you are just beginning to uncover the proverbial tip of an iceberg. For now, you will probably be right in thinking that you deserve a break from the library. But keep in mind that you need to continue your search for more items as you also begin to read from your working bibliography. For your next visit to the library, you should plan to explore two other major sources:

- ❖ The library's catalog, to get call numbers of the publications on your working bibliography. You can also use the catalog as another subject index, for which you now know most of the subject headings to look under. If you cannot locate material under the subject headings you have been using, check the *Library of Congress Subject Headings* (which should be nearby) for key terms and related terms. If you are using an on-line catalog, use the Help menu.

- ❖ Guides to electronic material, such as the July 1993 issue of the two-volume set of *Gale Directory of Data Bases*. Volume 1 lists more than five thousand data bases; Volume 2 covers another three thousand or so CD-ROMs, diskettes, magnetic tape files, and batch access data base products. Make a note to stop by the library's information desk for the location of the on-line services office if you do not already know where it is. You will probably need to learn from a reference or on-line service librarian how the library has packaged various electronic sources for use. While your search strategy in using electronic sources will be similar to those you employ in using print sources, you should learn how to use the on-line sources to identify citations and to print or download them to your own disk.

You now have nearly twenty specific items to look up and read and leads to several additional sources that will help you locate more material. It is time to take that deserved break. But know when you are going to be back in the library to continue your search.

Keeping a Record of Your Research

The main way you keep a record of your research is by taking clear notes and organizing them so that the information is easily accessible to you later. Like searching for information (pages 418–424) and reading and evaluating sources (pages 435–444), note taking is an active process that requires large blocks of time. In fact, reading and recording the literature will probably take longer than the writing of your research paper or report.

Much of your note taking will consist of interpreting and making sense of what you are reading—not passively copying down "facts," but rather, noting things that you regard as significant to your own developing ideas and hypotheses. Taking notes prompts you to consider the importance of what you are reading to the topic you are researching; to evaluate the authority of the source; and to reflect on patterns of agreement and disagreement among others who have written on the topic. Note taking also helps you understand and remember what you read.

Your goals for taking notes should be to compile and maintain a working bibliography (the list of sources that you plan to read); to understand new material and analyze new ideas; to record appropriate quotations; and to develop a system that helps you find your notes and organize them the way you want them.

You might start out compiling your working bibliography and jotting a few notes in a notebook or notepad. However, partial bibliographical information and notes scribbled on notebook pages, old envelops, and other odd-sized scraps of paper are hard to keep track of and to organize. Take our word for it: You must develop a filing system for your notes, or you will spend a lot of time trying to find stray pieces of paper with important notes on them. To facilitate organizing you should use only one or two sizes of paper—perhaps note cards that are four-by-six inches in size or computer files that can be printed in that size if necessary. Cards this size are easy to sort and are small enough to fit easily in a jacket pocket, purse, backpack, or other kind of bag. If you wish to print notes that you have put on a computer, check the manual for your word processing program and printer to see how to print on different paper sizes and thicknesses. Tractor-fed note cards are available for letter quality and dot-matrix printers. You might also choose to photocopy articles or passages from books consistently on 8½″ × 11″ paper. Remember: If you use a lot of different sizes of cards or paper, sorting your notes will be difficult.

Other media for compiling a working bibliography are the new bibliographic software programs, such as Pro-Cite, WDCitation, or Scimate. Most of these programs, although not ultraexpensive, require a hard disk and a large amount of memory to operate efficiently. The chief advantages of using a bibliographic software program are that it enables you (1) to enter bibliographical information once to be formatted automatically in a specific documentation style[1] and (2) to perform search and sort functions on a large bibliographic data base. To learn more about how these programs work and what they cost, check with a local computer store.

---

[1] With one command, the program casts the information into the documentation style you select—American Psychological Association, Modern Language Association, Council of Biological Editors, and so on.

In the following pages, we assume that you will be using either note cards or a word processing program for recording your research. (Knowing the procedure discussed here will make it easier for you to use a bibliographic software program if you choose to.)

As you do your research, you will create two or three sets of files that will make up the bibliographic data base with which you will work throughout the project:

 ❖ your working bibliography, which contains bibliographic information to assist you in locating the sources that you plan to read or in documenting the sources that you use in your final paper or report

 ❖ informational notes (in the form of paraphrases, summaries, and accurately transcribed quotations) from your sources

 ❖ a third possible set includes photocopies of important articles and book passages that you are almost certain you will cite.

Compiling a Working Bibliography

As soon as you know you plan to read a source, create a bibliographic card or computer entry for it. Record the bibliographic information you will need to find the item again and to document it if you cite it in your paper. Failing to take down the information when you first see it or have the item in hand can lead to frustration and wasted time in repeated trips to an index or literature guide or in last-minute trips back to the library to check a date, a page number, the spelling of an author's name, or whatever. Having a complete set of bibliographic cards or computer entries to refer to is essential when you schedule your search for items or discuss your research with your instructor or fellow students. In addition, it will pay early dividends in case you need to compile a working bibliography as part of a research proposal or progress report.

Bibliographic cards or computer entries are illustrated in Figures 3.10 and 3.11—one for a book, one for an article. You do not have to record the information in exactly the form it will take in the documentation system of your final paper or report, but if you do, your final bibliography will be simple to assemble. Note that the book entry in Figure 3.10 includes the author's first and last name, date of publication, title of book (including edition number or volume number if appropriate), place of publication, publisher, and call number. The article entry in Figure 3.11 also includes the author's first and last name and, in this case, middle initial, plus the title of the article and periodical, volume number, issue number, and page numbers.

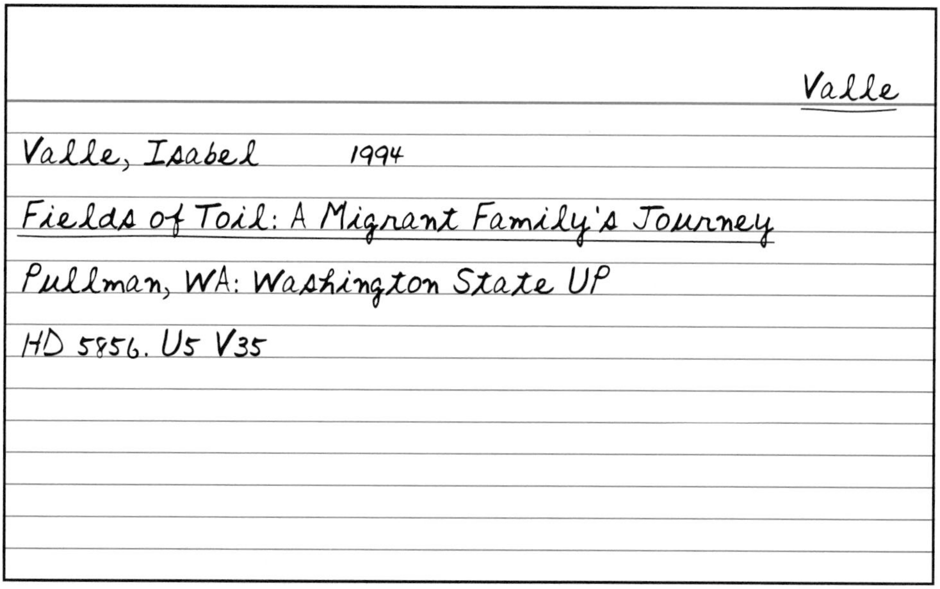

Valle

Valle, Isabel   1994

Fields of Toil: A Migrant Family's Journey

Pullman, WA: Washington State UP

HD 5856. U5 V35

Figure 3.10 Bibliography card: book

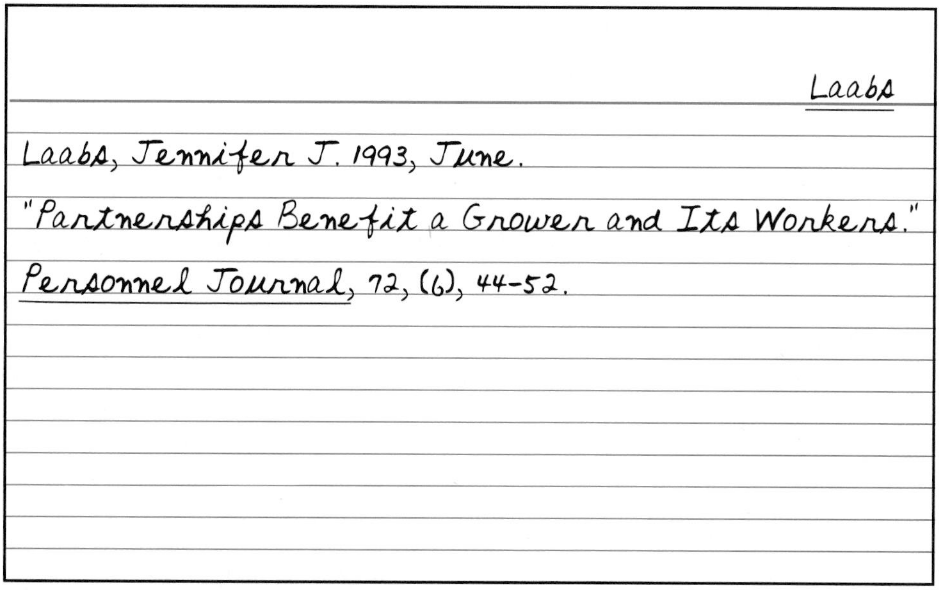

Laabs

Laabs, Jennifer J. 1993, June.

"Partnerships Benefit a Grower and Its Workers."

Personnel Journal, 72, (6), 44-52.

Figure 3.11 Bibliography card: article

As you continue your research, you may eliminate cards or entries that you think will not be used in order to keep the working bibliography to a manageable size. However, move cards and computer files to a separate "inactive" file instead of throwing them away or deleting them. As you reflect on your research at a later time, you may reevaluate sources that initially seemed unimportant or irrelevant.

Creating Informational Notes

It is virtually impossible to do library research, and then, at the end of the day, relying solely on memory, to write notes to reconstruct the important things that you have read. You must take notes as you read. Preferably, you should take notes on four-inch-by-six-inch cards. As an alternative, you can enter your notes into computer files and print them in card size if necessary.

Figures 3.12, 3.13, and 3.14 illustrate three kinds of note cards: quotation, paraphrase, and summary cards. Regardless of the type of note card, you will probably record three kinds of information: identifying headings, the note per se, and your comments and reactions to the note. See the annotations of note cards in these figures.

In the upper left corner of the note card (Figure 3.12), write a word or short phrase that identifies the topic to which the note relates. This topic identifier makes it easy for you to find the cards you have on a given topic; helps you begin thinking about the topics and subtopics of your paper or report; and makes it easy to stack your notes into different categories as you sort through your material. If you are writing your notes by hand, you might consider writing the topic identifier in pencil in case you need to change the wording as you revise your organization.

In the upper right corner of the note card, write a word or short phrase (sometimes the author's last name or the abbreviated title of the publication) to identify the source. This source identifier keys you to the bibliographic cards and saves you from having to write out the full publication information on each note card.

The main entry on the note card is a verbatim quotation, summary, or paraphrase. Make only one note per card, one card per note. More than one note per card or a note so long that it won't fit on one card lessens the ease of sorting cards. Also, it is easy to overlook a note that is written on the back of a card. Put quotation marks around a passage that is quoted verbatim so you will know in the future that the material is quoted.

Under the verbatim quotation, paraphrase, or summary, put the page number or numbers where the passage can be found in the source.

At the bottom of the card, write any comments you wish to make about the material, or record the ideas or insights that you have gained from reading the source material and thinking about it. Registering your own reaction is an important stage in incorporating the work of others into your own thinking. This is the place where you also comment on the ever-so-important rhetorical situation in which the original passage occurs in the original source so that you will not later "take a quote out of context" or otherwise distort the author's emphasis, purpose, or meaning (as best you can discern it). Distinguish your comments from the source material by drawing a long horizontal line to separate them; place slashes around your comments; or use one color ink to paraphrase, summarize, or quote the source material and a different color ink for your own comments.

NOTE CARD: VERBATIM QUOTE. You may wish to use verbatim quotes when the source has great credibility or makes a point so clearly and memorably that you see no reason to rephrase it. However, use quotations sparingly. Limit them to key points that are expressed in nicely turned phrases. Using too many quotations suggests that you have not synthesized your material and are merely stringing your source's words. A verbatim quotation note card is illustrated in Figure 3.12.

Topic identifier Source identifier Note

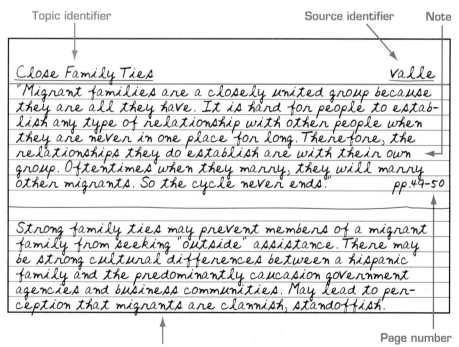

Researcher's comments

Page number

Figure 3.12 Note card: verbatim quotation

NOTE CARD: PARAPHRASE. In paraphrasing, you restate the material in your own words, taking care not to use the phrasing of the source. You may find it necessary to use key words from the original, but you must truly restate the material in your own words to avoid plagiarism. *If your paraphrase is too close to the original, you appear too indebted to the intellectual content and style of the original. If the similarity is extensive, you may appear to be passing off another person's writing as your own—even if you document the source.*

To help prevent your paraphrase from using too many words and repeating the structure and sequence of the original passage, read the original and then—in a highly selective and abbreviated way—jot down what you think are the key terms, or use your own words or phrases to represent the focal points. Avoid using complete sentences until you later reconstruct the material for your paper or report. This way, you are more likely to use your own language and not just substitute synonyms for a few of the words. Because your paraphrase is selective, contextualized, and from your viewpoint, you should make a note to yourself about the specific angle you have in paraphrasing. A paraphrase note card is illustrated in Figure 3.13.

NOTE CARD: SUMMARY. Brevity is the essence of a summary—variously referred to as an abstract, a digest, or a precis. In paraphrasing, you restate material in your own words, but you do not necessarily shorten the original source. In summarizing, you condense the information of the original source to the most important points that relate to a specific question or topic you are researching.

You may feel that the difference between a paraphrase and a summary is inconsequential. But it is a useful distinction to remember. Your summary will be a highly selective and abbreviated—but fair—digest. You exclude most details and supporting materials from the original source. You also should be careful not to add anything new to the material or change its emphasis. Since you will likely evaluate the ideas or viewpoints expressed in the original source, it is important that you understand the original passage. Later, when you incorporate the summary into your own paper or report, you must identify the source and contextualize the original source so that readers unfamiliar with the source can grasp its essential ideas and purpose. Not to summarize fairly invites criticism that you are distorting the ideas in the original source.

The length of a summary varies with the style and length of the original source and your purpose in summarizing. But generally your summary should probably not be longer than one-fourth of the original.

Hiring good crew leaders is an important way to provide for the needs of farm workers. When people speak of crew leaders, they think of someone who only recruits people to work the fields in various parts of the country. In Spanish they are referred to as "tronquistas" or "coyotes," the latter being a derogatory term. The literal translation of "tronquista" is "trucker," but migrant workers use the term to refer to someone who hires workers to harvest crops. The term "coyote" often indicates a swindler who charges people a fee to bring them to the northern states to work–but when they arrive, there is no work and people are left there with no way of returning home.

Some crew leaders are outstanding people in their communites who are looked up to and admired. "A crew leader is a real leader in the community," Guardado points out. "He has to have money in the bank because a lot of times he has to co-sign loans. And many times he serves as an adviser."

When migrant workers from Texas prepare for their long journey to the Pacific Northwest, they can be heard asking crew leaders such questions as "How's the temperature up there?"; "Are the roads cleared enough to travel them?"; "Do you know if there's going to be a big crop this year?"; and, "Will housing be prepared for us when we get there?" They also often ask favors of their crew leaders, the most common of which is arranging for financial loans.

← Source text

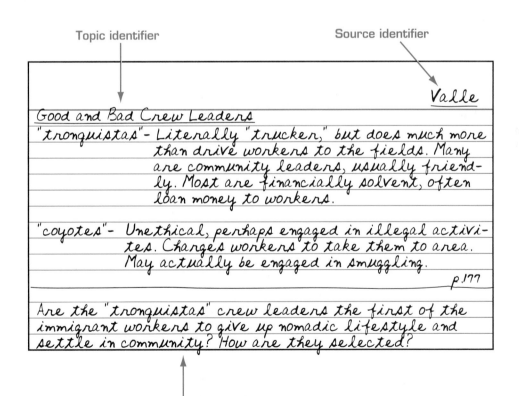

Topic identifier — Source identifier

Valle

Good and Bad Crew Leaders

"tronquistas"- Literally "trucker," but does much more than drive workers to the fields. Many are community leaders, usually friend-ly. Most are financially solvent, often loan money to workers.

"coyotes"- Unethical, perhaps engaged in illegal activi-tes. Charges workers to take them to area. May actually be engaged in smuggling.

p.177

Are the "tronquistas" crew leaders the first of the immigrant workers to give up nomadic lifestyle and settle in community? How are they selected?

Researcher's comments

Figure 3.13 Note card: source material and paraphrase

Summaries of long passages usually constitute a much lower percentage of the original source's length, as does the summary illustrated in Figure 3.14. The original source, a six-paragraph passage of well over three hundred words, is loaded with specific details—names, figures, examples, and so forth. The 22-word summary is about 6 percent of the length of the original.

As you summarize you should find the suggestions on reading and evaluating sources (pp. 435–444) helpful. Here we wish to re-emphasize these strategies.

- ❖ Since summarizing is a condensation of the major ideas in a source, you should look closely at the beginning of the passage and at the beginning of subsequent paragraphs, where the main ideas are usually expressed.

- ❖ Since you will want to attribute the major ideas to their originators, look not only for the name of the author of the original source, but also the names of persons being interviewed or cited by the author.

- ❖ Since you will want your summary to be comprehensive and fair, read the original source several times to check that you are not overemphasizing ideas that support your hypothesis or glossing over those that do not support your hypothesis.

- ❖ Since you may wish to record some of the significant supporting details in the source for further reference and review, place those details in the space on the note card devoted to your commentary to distinguish them from your summary.

- ❖ If there is a phrase or sentence that seems to represent what you want to use from the original, use it; but place it in quotation marks so that you will not inadvertently forget that you have quoted directly. You should also consider making a verbatim note card on the direct quotation.

Working with Photocopied Materials

Now that libraries have photocopy machines available for use by their patrons, we are tempted to make copies of materials instead of using them in the library or checking them out to read later. Working with photocopied material has several advantages. Carrying several photocopied pages in a folder or backpack is a lot easier than lugging around several books. Working with photocopies at home or a favorite coffee house is often more convenient and pleasant than working with the

"Over the past 25 years, the Duda family and the company's management team have pioneered many efforts to improve working conditions, housing, benefits and living standards for our migrant and seasonal farm workers," says Stuart Longworth, vice president of HR. "We're doing a lot of things that many other companies aren't doing in the agricultural industry."

One example of DUDA's commitment to worker's quality of life is the housing that it provides to migrant laborers at a nominal cost, a choice that the company has offered since 1960. In 1991, the organization spent more than $1 million for expansion of its housing facilities in LaBelle, Florida. The facility now houses 500 workers. DUDA built a 16-unit apartment complex in 1988 that houses as many as 96 workers during the citrus-harvesting season. This commitment to offering housing to its out-of-state migrant employees ensures a work force for DUDA's future labor needs.

. . .

Abuses of migrant workers often have resulted from the traditional crew-leaders system. At DUDA, however, such abuses aren't tolerated.

In addition, seasonal or migrant workers usually aren't eligible to receive benfits such as vacation pay, company-provided housing, pension plans and medical and life insurance. DUDA is one agricultural organization that has seen the paybacks of providing these benefits to its seasonal and migrant laborers. "We've tried to give our seasonal workers a better life," says Longworth.

Source text

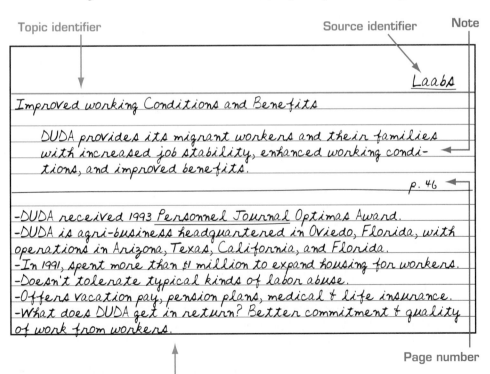

Topic identifier
Source identifier
Note

Laabs

Improved working Conditions and Benefits

DUDA provides its migrant workers and their families with increased job stability, enhanced working conditions, and improved benefits.

p. 46

-DUDA received 1993 Personnel Journal Optimas Award.
-DUDA is agri-business headquartered in Oviedo, Florida, with operations in Arizona, Texas, California, and Florida.
-In 1991, spent more than $1 million to expand housing for workers.
-Doesn't tolerate typical kinds of labor abuse.
-Offers vacation pay, pension plans, medical & life insurance.
-What does DUDA get in return? Better commitment & quality of work from workers.

Researcher's comments
Page number

Figure 3.14 Note card: source material and summary

original sources in the library. Having a whole source in front of you when you are quoting from it helps you make sure that any summary you write reflects the entire piece and enables you to check the appropriateness of quotations you use. Highlighting and marginal comments are quite helpful in understanding what is being read—acts that would deface or perhaps even destroy the value of library materials for other patrons.

However, the advantages of having photocopies of important documents do not eliminate the need to take notes and to use note cards; nor does it mean there are no problems in photocopying. Photocopying at a nickel or dime a page can become expensive, and waiting in line to use a photocopier is a drag. But two more substantial problems arise from photocopying.

First, extensive photocopying can discourage—or at least delay—reading entire articles or long passages from books and may eliminate careful reading and evaluation of sources. It can encourage collecting more material than you need or can possibly use, producing mounds of material that are in different formats and sizes and that contain a lot of material unrelated to your research—time-consuming and cumbersome clutter that can later lead to confusion and frustration as you search through photocopies to find what you have marked or flagged. It can discourage careful reading. Also, you may have to go over the same material twice, because it is difficult to start writing without some notes of your own that would have preserved your thinking as you worked with the sources. Making photocopies of material might even delude you into thinking that you are actually adding to your store of information, when, in effect, you are prolonging the relatively undefined and unfocused early stages of selecting material to read and record.

Second, extensive photocopying may be in violation of copyright laws. Publishers and writers who are owners of copyrighted material charge that the copying of substantial parts of published material or whole articles is not research, but is the building of an archive of material that should be purchased through normal means. Of course, you are most likely paying for the photocopying, but the owners of the copyright material are not receiving payment for their intellectual property. For now, it is a complicated legal question, and we encourage you to see if your library has guidelines on photocopying material.

Here are some suggestions on photocopying to minimize problems during your research.

❖ Be sure that the essential bibliographic information is on the material you photocopy. Increasingly, periodicals provide on each page (in the headers and footers) the titles of the journal and the article, the volume number and date of publication, along with the page number. However, this information will not tell you whether the periodical paginates continuously or separately with each issue. Book pages provide much less information, so you will have to get information from the title page. Write whatever information you need on the photocopy.

❖ Make a bibliography card on the source that you have photo-copied (see Figures 3.10 and 3.11).

❖ Make a summary card (see Figure 3.14), putting in your own words the gist of the original source, your notion of its purpose and audience, and the qualifications of its author. This important step helps you begin to digest the material so that it becomes part of your knowledge and reminds you of the significance of the source when you get around to reading it again.

❖ Read the photocopy the same way you would read the original source (see pages 435–444). Many readers develop their own system of annotations that might be incomprehensible to others. However, as long as it makes sense to you, use it. Those annotations will help preserve your reactions as you read and will jog your memory later as you revisit the piece.

Reading and Evaluating Sources

Getting information from published sources is essentially the same as getting information from interviewing someone. In both cases, you are acquiring another person's ideas, opinions, and perspective. But using published sources effectively depends on your abilities to read rather than listen and to select information that your readers will regard as up-to-date and authoritative.

Inexpert readers are likely to read all texts the same way and without any investigative method or direction. To them, reading is a simple task. But reading for research purposes is not merely a matter of running your eyes over a text and, through some kind of visual osmosis, passively absorbing its meaning. Nor is reading simply a process of extracting the fixed and identifiable meanings that reside exclusively in a text as if they were artifacts to be uncovered.

In reading to research, you must engage intellectually with a text, seeking to grasp the ideas the writer wishes to transmit and the basis for the writer's belief in those ideas; evaluating the writer's view of reality; relating the material to your own cultural, political, and emotional experiences and beliefs and to your own purposes; and integrating new information and insights with other texts you have read and with what you already know. In short, when you read for research purposes, you are an active creator of whatever meaning, pleasure, and value a text has. You are participating in a social process, carrying on a silent conversation with the writer about the text and integrating your views with those of others who have written on the topic you are researching.

Although it is impossible to predict the many kinds of responses to a text, there are remarkably similar strategies and conventions shared by writers and readers in constructing texts. Most accomplished writers take great care in using these conventions to help readers interact with their texts, which makes reading their texts comparatively easy. But whether a text is well written or not, the application of a few basic strategies can lead to successful reading. The strategies include

❖ exploring the text to discover its subject, scope, theme, and purpose and to evaluate its credibility. (For additional information about evaluating sources, see pages 340–342 and 383–385 in Chapter 8.)

❖ determining the overall organization of the text

❖ reading the text more intensively to synthesize it with your own thinking

Used flexibly, the strategies help you read and evaluate sources. Used rigidly, they can impede the development of critical reading skills. Not applied at all, your reading can go rough no matter how slowly or fast you read; how carefully you look at each word, phrase, and sentence; or how diligently you try to reread a passage.

Exploring the Text

Much of your reading is to acquire additional information and to understand viewpoints that you do not have or of which you are only vaguely aware. Thus, when you read as part of your research, you are a contextualized and purposeful reader with an interest in the subject or topic treated by the text. Exploring a text helps you learn what to expect in it, decide whether you want to read it more thoroughly, determine whether it is a credible source, and, if so, prepare to read it. When exploring a text of more than a few pages, set aside at least half an hour of uninterrupted time so you can really get into it. Of course, you have to read the entire text to understand everything that is going on, but during the first half hour or so you can become immersed enough in the text to understand and evaluate it.

In reading and evaluating a text, you should focus on the following questions.

WHAT IS THE OVERALL QUALITY OF THE PUBLICATION?   There is a wide range of sources available to researchers, but not all publications or publishers are equally credible or respectable. Material published in academic and scholarly journals, trade magazines, and respected popular magazines and newspapers is generally regarded as more credible, more balanced, and better researched than material published in tabloid journalism. Books published by academic, scholarly, and respected trade and commercial publishers is regarded as more credible, more balanced, and better researched than material appearing in books published by vanity or subsidy presses. As you become more experienced in research, you will become aware of the periodicals and publishers that have respected reputations in your field.

To help you analyze the quality of the sources you read, apply the following questions and those on page 388 in Chapter 8.

WHAT IS THE SIGNIFICANCE OF THE TITLE?   The **title** usually identifies the topic or basic points of the text and sometimes indicates the writer's general purpose or intentions. Thus, it can help you decide whether the text is relevant to your research.

TITLE, PAGE 667

WHAT DO YOU KNOW ABOUT THE WRITER?   Depending on the kind of research you are doing, there will be times when you need to be sure that you are using material from sources that your readers will acknowledge as authoritive. Sometimes material from popular magazines or presses might be acceptable. More often, though, more scholarly and professional accounts are required. In addition, some writers are so important in the area you are researching that their works must be read and cited. Knowing the writer's credentials often helps you determine the **credibility** of the text. It also enables you to characterize the source's authority in case you cite him or her in your own writing.

CREDIBILITY, PAGE 552

Knowing the identity of the writer is also important because you need to know from whose viewpoint the subject is being looked at. The writer may be a recognized authority on the subject, but there are also likely to be other aspects to consider. For instance, a head coach of an NCAA Division IA football team writing about the ethics of accepting additional income outside of a university salary in the form of personal contracts from manufacturers of athletic gear is likely to have a different viewpoint from a professor who serves on the school's athletics committee or the owner of a local sporting goods business who might also write on the issue. All three may be considered authorities on the matter, but each is likely to have a different perspective that influences the way he or she looks at the question and information concerning the issue.

The author of a book is identified on the title page. Sometimes the author's professional affiliation and title are also given on the title page. Frequently, the inside flap of a dust jacket or a paperback's back cover contains a brief note about the author's background and credentials. In magazines and collections of essays, the author's credentials are sometimes given in notes at the beginning or end of the essay or article.

WHAT IS THE DATE OF THE TEXT?   The contents may be correct, but could be out of date. Does the text contain up-to-date information? The publication date is important when you write about a subject that changes quickly. You want to avoid using material that more knowledgeable readers may consider old. There are, of course, instances when you may desire older sources, especially if you are investigating a problem or question in which contemporary accounts of a particular event are important. The date of a book or pamphlet is usually given on the title page, on the back of the title page, or on a separate copyright page. Essays and articles appear in magazines that carry the issue date on the front cover or on the table of contents page.

WHAT IS THE MAJOR THESIS, THEME, OR IDEA?   The title contains key words that suggest the important concepts that are treated in the text. In books and formal reports, the abstract, preface, introduction, and closing usually state the **thesis** and contain statements about the writer's reasons for writing the text, his or her objectives, the rationale or justification for the research reported or the topic treated, and sometimes about the importance or significance of his or her work. In essays and articles, the introduction and closing usually express these same things.

THESIS, PAGE 663

WHAT ARE THE IMPORTANT SOURCES OF INFORMATION?   As a researcher yourself, you probably will be more concerned about the writer's sources of information when reading for research than you would otherwise be. You will be analyzing how the writer develops and supports ideas and how information is derived: from field research? library research? personal experience? Does the writer use credible sources that you will need to look at? Are they dated? In addition, you might observe how the writer uses sources to make his or her case and see if you can learn some things to help you with your own thinking, research, and writing.

WHAT ARE THE WRITER'S PURPOSES OR OBJECTIVES?   Writers write primarily because something has motivated them to do so, and you will need to consider the purpose of the text so you can better analyze and evaluate the kinds of points the writer makes. Is the writer trying to provide general enlightenment on how government regulations affect businesses? Is the writer exploring a specific issue, such as the possible impact of proposed congressional legislation that would transfer a specific program from the federal government to the various states? Does the writer take a position on a proposed transfer and give reasons for supporting or opposing it? Is the writer providing instructions on how to administer a new state program? Is the writer offering advice on how a state agency can fund or implement a former federal program? Knowing the writer's purpose helps you understand the role of the writer and the role you are invited to take while reading the text. As our students occasionally remark, "Writers usually have designs on their readers, and it's best to know what they are."

Some writers state the purpose and objectives explicitly in the title of their text. "Why We Should Adopt Plan C" indicates that the writer is going to attempt to persuade you to adopt a specific course of action. Often the writer identifies his or her purpose in the opening of the text. Other writers do not state their purpose and objectives directly, leaving you to infer the purpose from your reading of the text.

HOW IS THE TEXT ORGANIZED?   Virtually all writers follow some organizational plan as they write their texts. Some texts are designed to be read linearly or serially, primarily from beginning to end. Others are designed so that readers can gain access to specific information directly by going straight to a particular block of information. Books, formal reports, and pamphlets provide a table of contents that lists the main sections, sometimes the subsections, and the page on which each section begins. The writers of books and reports usually explain the rationale for organizing their information and ideas in a preface or introduction. The writers of essays and articles may explain in their introduction the way their text is organized.

Most informative texts (for example, books, chapters of books, reports, articles, essays, and letters) are presented straightforwardly, which makes it fairly easy to get an overall view of the writer's purpose, thesis, and plan. Exploring literary texts (for example, poems, novels, short stories, plays) is different, because their purposes and formats are different. The best way to explore a literary text is to read it once just to experience it, to get a feel for it, to enjoy it. Just as when you watch a movie or a television program, you must be willing to become part of the world created by the author.

The purpose of exploring a text is to get an overview of the material. It may seem to be delaying unnecessarily the real event of reading, but we assure you that it is not. Exploring makes you concentrate on the text, provides you with a good sense of the writer's purpose and main points, and alerts you to the possibilities for meanings that the text may have for you.

Determining the Organizational Design of the Text

All texts are organized. That is, the writer does not simply throw together a random set of statements and call them a text. Rather, the writer selects and arranges the information related to her or his thesis or main point into a pattern that can be the design of an entire text or a piece of a text. Seldom will you come across a text that is a collection of isolated bits of information. The design is there, at least in the mind of the writer, even if some readers have difficulty recognizing the parts that make up the text or perceiving the plan by which the parts are organized.

Understanding how a text is organized prepares you for a closer, more careful reading of the text. You will be able to anticipate what is coming next and how it relates to what has gone before and to what is coming. You will have a mental map of the text that will enable you to find your way through it without having to read each sentence or paragraph as if it were an unfamiliar street of unknown origin, length, or destination. You will be able to use the writer's organizational plan to organize your own memory of the text.

THESIS, PAGE 663
The organization of informative texts is almost always hierarchical—that is, writers impose order on their information by organizing it into large ideas that are supported by subordinate ideas. In turn, the subordinate ideas are supported by still more subordinate ideas. The **thesis**, or main point, is usually stated explicitly at the beginning. The subsequent sections or paragraphs explain or support the thesis by providing specific facts and ideas. Each chapter or section contains its own thesis or central idea, which relates both to the larger thesis of the entire text and to the main ideas of its own stretch of text. Many paragraphs will have a **topic**

TOPIC SENTENCE, PAGE 672
sentence that presents a specific point related to the thesis. Often the topic sentence is the first sentence of the paragraph.

CLASSIFICATION, PAGE 527
COMPARISON/CONTRAST, PAGE 542
DESCRIPTION, PAGE 565
NARRATION, PAGE 618
CAUSE AND EFFECT, PAGE 522
Informative texts commonly include the following organizational patterns: **classification** by categories, **comparison** or **contrast** of subjects, **description** of a subject, explanation of a process, **narration** of an event, the relationship of **cause and effect**, statement of a problem and analysis of possible solutions, thesis and support, and so on. The table of contents, preface, and introduction are often packed with clues about what organizational patterns to expect. Sometimes the closing contains a summary of the main points, the order in which they were treated, and certain organizational clue words. Here are some suggestions on how to determine organization.

ANALYZE THE TITLE OF THE TEXT FOR CLUES ABOUT ORGANIZATION. Sometimes the title will contain explicit clue words, such as *classification, comparison, contrast, definition, description, process,* and similar words derived from them. A title containing a question often indicates a text that is organized primarily by question and answer. A title such as "Difficulties in Conforming to the Federal Disability Act" is likely to suggest a text that is organized around thesis and support, probably with attention to cause-and-effect relationships.

READ THE OPENING AND CLOSING FOR STATEMENTS ABOUT ORGANIZATION. If the text is divided into large sections, analyze their headings and read their openings (including their preface and abstract if they have them) and closings, too. These parts of a text often set contexts and frameworks or provide postviews of the discussion or analysis presented.

LOOK FOR HEADINGS THAT SIGNAL TOPICS, KEY IDEAS, OR ORGANIZATION. **Headings** are words or phrases that divide a text into sections and sometimes into subsections. Headings can help bring into focus the scope and the major ideas of the text.

HEADINGS, PAGE 603

READ THE FIRST SENTENCE OF EACH PARAGRAPH. An effective skimming technique is to read the first sentence of each paragraph, where the main idea of the paragraph and information on how it is organized can often be found.

USE YOUR FAMILIARITY WITH CONVENTIONS OF GENRE. The organization of texts such as novels, short stories, poems, songs, and plays can be classified into two major types. The first type consists of relatively stable conventional patterns and strictly defined subject matter and style that are associated with various genres, such as the sonnet, the ballad, the picaresque novel, the revenge tragedy, the epic, reggae, experimental lab reports, proposals, and manuals. Although there are many variations and much mixing of genres, our knowledge of genres—which becomes quite extensive from reading more and responding to texts—guides our expectations about how certain texts are organized. For example, prior knowledge about Greek tragedy or film Westerns enables a reader to anticipate likely events and their order. Familiarity with Petrarchan or Italian sonnets guides a reader's expectations about how the two major parts of the poem relate.

The second type of organizational plan consists of those unpredictable texts in which the writer has purposely chosen to go against some specific convention or to use a traditional technique in some new or unusual way, attempting to disrupt the normal reading processes to force readers into exploring new kinds of relationships between elements of a text. But even in these experimental texts, the content is usually arranged in some systematic—although original—way.

Regardless of the types of texts you read, being familiar with a wide variety of organizational patterns and generic conventions makes it easier to adjust your reading expectations to fit the expectations you have about how a specific text is organized. Once you determine the organizational design of a text, it will be easier for you to locate major ideas, follow the writer better through development of the topic, remember subordinate ideas and minor details, and understand how the sections of the text relate to one another. When you can do these things, your reading will be more purposeful and enjoyable.

Reading the Text Intensively

Once you possess an overview of the text provided by exploring it and by understanding its organizational design, you are anchored in its social circumstances and writing context, which gives you a good sense of what is being said to whom and for what purpose and how it is presented. You now have a framework that enables you to work intensively with the text—reading and, if necessary, rereading and further evaluating passages without getting lost among the details or losing the direction the text is taking.

Reading, underlining, rereading, and making notes help you work with a text—and in some ways rewrite it to make it your own. Anytime you circle an important word or underline a key phrase or statement, you change the emphasis of those elements. When you write a note in the margin in response to something you read, you add to the text. When you paraphrase a passage, you rewrite it. When you mark points with which you agree or disagree, you close the distance between the writer's text and your own developing mental text.

There are several strategies for marking and annotating text. Never use these strategies on texts from the library. Make any annotations of library texts on Post-Its or on photocopies.

NUMBERING THE ORDER OF IDEAS AND SUPPORTING POINTS.   Writers employ a variety of organizational patterns, and the awareness of these patterns helps readers understand more fully the writer's information. If the writer has not enumerated the major ideas, you can make your own numbered list.

MARKING IMPORTANT WORDS AND KEY TERMS AND PHRASES. Often writers themselves emphasize certain words and phrases by using different typefaces, underlining, and using all capital letters. You can do the same thing by underlining, bracketing, or in other ways highlighting what you consider to be important words and passages.

MARKING UNFAMILIAR WORDS AND PROVIDING SYNONYMS. If you are familiar with the terminology and jargon used by others who have written on your research topic, you will probably not have to look up definitions of many terms. However, if you do not understand the meaning of some words as they are used in context, you will need to mark them and look up their meanings in a dictionary, handbook, or encyclopedia. Looking up words in handbooks and encyclopedias can also introduce you to basic information that you might not possess as well as provide you with specialized definitions. To help you remember the meaning of a term, write a synonym in the margin.

MARKING STATEMENTS WITH WHICH YOU AGREE OR DISAGREE. This is a useful way to mark significant material for future reference or review. Your research invariably produces answers to questions, and these answers, in turn, are likely to create new questions. Your own knowledge and beliefs are often modified by this process, and you need a way to locate important points for consideration.

MARKING PASSAGES THAT YOU THINK YOU MIGHT QUOTE OR PARAPHRASE. It is important to let others speak for themselves, so be on the lookout for statements that are relevant for your purposes. Marking them makes it easier to find them again.

JOTTING OUTLINES AND WRITING PARAPHRASES. Marking and annotating a text in these ways will make reviewing it much easier, especially if you do not return to it for several days.

MAKING MARGINAL NOTES TO YOURSELF. The more difficult or complicated the text, the greater the need to annotate it. Annotations enable you to relate what you read to your own developing ideas. At times you will also want to make more elaborate notes that relate to parts of the texts you are reading. Anything you read that you might want to reflect on more can call for a note, particularly if it relates to your thinking about what makes an assertion true or false or what strategies the writer uses to connect with readers. You also might want to note the relationship of what you are reading to other information that you already have: A point or some data may relate or correspond to another writer's or your own idea or position; an idea may suggest some topic or subtopic to explore more thoroughly; or some piece of information may lead you to a breakthrough on answering some part of your research question.

▶ C O N D U C T I N G   F I E L D   R E S E A R C H

Writers often need to research a topic to gain sufficient information and a good understanding of what they plan to write about. These investigations may involve library research to discover or review what has already been written about the topic. Research may also involve gathering information firsthand, by direct observation or by interviews, questionnaires, and letters of inquiry. These kinds of field research are explained in the following four sections.

Conducting Direct Observations

While writers can get lots of information by library research and by interviews and questionnaires, much of what they write is based upon their experience and observation. In fact, much successful writing results from writers' abilities to observe accurately and in detail and from their exact memory and careful notes in dealing with the sensory experience. Henry David Thoreau's account of the ways of the ant, Annie Dillard's description of a mosquito sucking blood from a poisonous snake, Paul Theroux's depiction of a train arriving in a border town in Outer Mongolia, and a safety inspector's explanation of how a dust collector is malfunctioning illustrate a high degree of accuracy in observation and great precision in describing what the writers observed.

When conducting observations, keep a notebook to record interesting and unexpected observations and your responses to them. Don't regard anything as too trivial or insignificant to record.

CREDIBILITY, PAGE 552

Because firsthand reports carry so much **credibility**, part of researching your subject is to observe its tangible aspects. And because odds are overwhelmingly against your chances of writing with clarity and precision if you are not working from experience and observation, you should probably resist most temptations to write about something you have never observed—even if you have read the magazines and journals that cover your subject and have checked out every book your library has on the subject. If you are researching gender relationships among people, you must observe interactions between men and women, repeatedly and at length. Reading or hearing about the number of times that men or women make certain kinds of statements or gestures during conversations or group discussions does not replace the need to observe actual conversations and group discussions. Firsthand anecdotes and examples and details based on your observations help to keep your readers engaged with your writing.

Good writing is full of specific firsthand details. However, you cannot describe well what you have not seen and understood. Superficial observation usually reveals no more than the most obvious details. Inaccurate observation is worse—it leads to faulty information. To become a careful and accurate observer, you need to learn the valuable lessons that Samuel Scudder, an American entomologist, learned nearly 150 years ago when he studied under the naturalist Louis Agassiz at Harvard. In Agassiz's laboratory, Scudder learned to observe by having to look at a fish—the same fish—for days. We recommend that you read Scudder's account of his first days in Agassiz's laboratory, "In the Laboratory with Agassiz." It has been reprinted many times.

In addition to seeing, you also need to use your other senses—your senses of smell, taste, sound, and touch. Here are some suggestions for observing.

Observe Repeatedly and at Length

Several obstacles can make careful observation difficult. Frequently, several actions take place simultaneously; sometimes things happen too quickly or are too small to be seen by the naked eye; occasionally, things occur too slowly or are too large to observe in a single viewing; frequently, activities occur or parts exist that are invisible or inaudible or in other ways unobservable from a particular observation point. Quite often things do not occur or appear in the same way as they did previously or in other circumstances.

To overcome the barriers to observation you may have to do several things. You may have to resort to repeated observations and rely on technology (fast-speed, slow-motion, time-stop, or infrared photography; or enhanced computer imagery) or on more traditional things such as observation logs and sketch pads. You may have to observe the subject from several different angles and in several different contexts. You may also have to taste, touch, or smell the subject as well as look at and listen to it.

Actively Observe the Subject

You probably will not be able to observe a subject as well as a trained scientist can, but you should try to develop the observational skills learned from field studies and laboratory work.

Observation is not simply a matter of looking at external images and reproducing in our minds what exists outside. We see what we are trained to look for. A gently sloping meadow is seen differently by a farmer, a real estate developer, a military strategist, and an archeologist. But no matter what you are observing, you not only have to look at each detail, you have to look *for* each detail. Depending on the nature of your research, it might be appropriate for you to intervene in an event or to modify a feature to see what happens, or it might be desirable for you to remain an uninvolved, detached observer. But in either case, look and listen—and when appropriate, taste, touch, and smell the feature and record your observations about shape, size, sound, texture, aroma, and spatial and chronological relationships, and so on. Certainly not every detail you observe and record will go into your final draft, but you will not know what details are significant until you have made extensive and repeated observations and kept careful notes of your observations.

Develop a Hypothesis to Help Guide Further Observation

In the early stages of your research you should be as spontaneous, freely associative, and all-encompassing as you can be in your observations. Try not to have any preconceptions that would cause you to ignore, suppress, or exaggerate certain aspects of the subject. This kind of broad observation helps produce an enormous amount of data—so much information that you may feel as if you are in danger of sinking under its weight and of thinking that there is no way you can get a handle on all of it.

As when you conduct library research, at some point, usually after considerable observation, you will need to focus more narrowly on your subject and develop a hypothesis that will help you decide the kinds of information that are more interesting and significant for your purposes. The hypothesis should help explain the facts you have collected so far and also serve as a basis for further observation and analysis. For instance, in your observation of men and women in conversation, you may develop the impression that women ask more questions or nod in agreement more often and that, consequently, they are more supportive and accommodating than men. With this as your hypothesis, you are ready to focus on that particular aspect of your subject and are prepared to continue observing, deliberately looking for specific things that might be significant.

Further observation may encourage you to modify or abandon your hypothesis if data do not support it. However, further observation may support your hypothesis, and you may eventually regard it as your **thesis**, a proposition that you are prepared to defend.

THESIS, PAGE 663

Conducting Interviews

Interviewing involves asking somebody to give his or her thoughts about a particular topic. When you were deciding on your major area of study in college, you probably interviewed an academic advisor or a faculty member whose experience and knowledge added to your understanding of the major. If you ever had to select the site for an organization's banquet, you probably interviewed or surveyed group members to determine their preferences.

A face-to-face interview can be an effective way to gather authoritative information that is not readily available in published sources. Here are several suggestions on how to prepare for an interview, how to conduct an interview, and what to do following an interview.

Preparing for the Interview

Preparation for the interview involves gaining a basic understanding of the topic you are researching, developing the questions you will ask, and selecting one or more people to interview.

READ ENOUGH ABOUT YOUR RESEARCH TOPIC TO KNOW THE IMPORTANT QUESTIONS TO ASK. The more your interviewee thinks you know about the subject, the more interested he or she will likely be in the interview. Much basic information is available in encyclopedias, atlases, and almanacs, and you should do some preliminary reading so that you will be informed enough to ask intelligent questions about more technical and complex aspects of your topic. You do not want the person you are interviewing to think that you are asking him or her to do the basic homework for you.

DETERMINE THE OBJECTIVES OR GOALS OF THE INTERVIEW. It is important to know what kind of information you want from the interview. Your objectives will depend upon your stage of research. For example, you might be researching the occurrence of campus crime and already be knowledgeable about the basic and more general aspects of the topic but need to obtain specific information concerning the occurrence of date rape or burglaries on your own campus. Or you might be having difficulty finding published material on the development of computerized navigational aids for long-distance travel in automobiles. Asking a librarian who is knowledgeable about reference materials or a professor whose specialization is related to transportation, automotive technology, or computer applications will probably develop some useful leads to published material. Knowing what you want to learn from an interviewee will help you focus on the types of questions you need to ask.

PREPARE A THOROUGH LIST OF QUESTIONS.   Select the points or issues you wish to explore during the interview, and develop questions that will help you do that. Try to have at least a half dozen questions for a 20- to 30-minute interview. Also consider the kinds of follow-up questions you might ask in case the interviewee provides certain kinds of information that seem worth pursuing or responds too generally or vaguely to a question. For instance, questions such as "Why do you think this happened?" or "Can you explain a bit more about what you mean by . . . ?" or "What do you believe is the most important instance or example of this?" can help you gain additional information. This information will enable you to understand more thoroughly the interviewee's responses and may give you a useful authoritative statement to quote. Listen attentively to what the interviewee says, because the answer to a prepared question might suggest a new question that you had not previously thought of.

SELECT AN INTERVIEWEE WHO IS AN EXPERT ON THE TOPIC YOU ARE RESEARCHING.   Because interviews can provide you with valuable material and additional authority to support your ideas, you should select the most well-informed experts available. Special benefits can come from using expert testimony: Your readers will likely appreciate getting the expert information, and your own credibility will likely increase as a result.

ARRANGE A SPECIFIC PLACE AND TIME FOR THE INTERVIEW.   Experts are usually busy people, and you will probably need to schedule your interview well in advance. When you contact a person you do not know, introduce yourself, and explain the purpose of the interview, the kind of information you want, and why you want it. Even if you contact someone you have met before, be courteous, and explain your purpose. Be prepared to explain the nature and purpose of your research and to estimate the amount of time you think the interview will take. Also be prepared to meet at a time and place that is convenient for the interviewee. If you want to record the interview, be sure to ask permission beforehand.

Never assume that you may tape-record an interview without permission. It is unethical to conceal the taping of an interview. Most interviewees are cooperative and will agree to your taping the interview. However, if the interviewee does not agree to being taped, don't push it.

Conducting the Interview

Most interviews go quite well. Someone who agrees to be interviewed is taking your request and your research seriously and will be willing to help you. Just make sure that you do your part by showing up on time, having all the materials and equipment you need, and conducting the interview professionally.

ARRIVE ON TIME AND HAVE EVERYTHING YOU NEED. Arriving on time for an interview is not only courteous but also crucial in getting the cooperation of an expert who probably has a busy schedule. If you are unsure of the location of the interview, ask for directions, and start early enough to allow for extra time that might be needed to find a parking space and to locate the interviewee's office or work area. Make sure that you have your list of questions and whatever you need to take notes—pen, paper, tape recorder. If you use a tape recorder, check to see that it works and has fully charged batteries and sufficient tape. If you arrive a few minutes early, spend the time reviewing your key questions.

CONDUCT THE INTERVIEW PROFESSIONALLY. Your main responsibility during the interview is to keep it going by listening carefully to responses to your questions and asking the next question. Actually, once the interview is underway, it will probably resemble a conversation. But do not let the interview become chatty to the point that you begin stating your opinions—perhaps even arguing with the interviewee—and are not able to get answers to all your questions. Try to ask your key questions by the time the interview is about two-thirds over. Talk no more than necessary to keep the interview going. Let the interviewee do the talking. Allow the interviewee to respond freely to your questions, for what at first might appear to be a rambling response could result in a very important new perspective or statement. Remember, the purpose of the interview is to get the interviewee's opinions and ideas.

ASK FOLLOW-UP QUESTIONS WHEN NECESSARY. Be on the lookout for possible new developments of your topic. Follow-up questions such as "Could you explain that a bit more?" "Why do you suppose that is so?" and "Could you explain what you mean by 'integrated graphics applications'?" can elicit additional information. The additional information may help you understand an idea more fully or provide you with more details. Depending on the response to some of your later questions, you might want to ask for clarification of some earlier point that you believe might be an inconsistency or to correct some piece of information that you think you may not have remembered correctly.

TAKE MINIMAL NOTES.   As you listen to the interviewee, maintain as much eye contact as you can and still take notes. (Even if you tape the interview, be prepared to take some notes.) You won't be able to take voluminous notes, but try to write down key words or phrases that will help you recall the interviewee's full responses when you write up the results of the interview later. It is helpful to double-space your notes so that you can fill in details after the interview.

BE CONSIDERATE OF THE INTERVIEWEE'S TIME, AND END THE INTERVIEW WITHIN THE TIME ALLOTTED.   Watch the time. When the interview closes, thank the interviewee for his or her time and information, and ask if you can call if you have further questions. Also ask if the interviewee would like to see how you used the material from the interview. Offer to send the interviewee a copy of your completed paper.

Following the Interview

A good interview is likely to provide authoritative information that supports many of your own ideas. It might, perhaps, clarify your own thinking on certain points. It might even produce information that you never had thought about. Once you have completed the interview, go through your notes, fleshing them out with examples and illustrations that you can remember from the interview. Check your notes to be certain that the statements you attribute to the interviewee accurately reflect his or her ideas. If you taped the interview, you will want to listen to several parts of it carefully. If you find that you need more information on some point or want to be sure that you are quoting the interviewee correctly, call or visit the person to ask for additional information or to double-check your information. Be sure that your documentation of the interview includes the name of the interviewee (and his or her position or title if appropriate), and the place, date, and time of the interview.

Designing Questionnaires

A questionnaire is a formalized type of written interview in which the same wording and sequence of questions are used to gain information from a large number of people in exactly the same way. It is useful when you want to compile several comparable answers from several respondents. For instance, a questionnaire could help you learn how the students enrolled in a particular course prefer to schedule their lab sessions or could help you determine what juveniles in a specific community think of police officers. These groups, of course, could be interviewed individually, but using a questionnaire is a quick and easy way to get responses from a large number of a particular group of people.

Determine the objectives of the questionnaire, and select the group whose responses you want. You may give the questionnaire to respondents to fill out and return to you, or you may read the questions to each respondent and mark or record his or her answers on the form. However you administer the questionnaire, there are several points to consider.

Ask Closed Questions to Gather Factual and Quantitative Information

Closed questions limit possible responses to a specific answer from a list of allowable responses. The simplest kind of closed question requires the answer *yes* or *no*:

> **3.** Have you used the library's electronic catalog this term?
>
> Yes _____   No _____

Another type of closed question requires an answer from a list of possible responses:

> **4.** If your answer to Question 3 is "yes," about how often, on average, have you used the library's electronic catalog this term?
>
> _____ more than once a week
>
> _____ once a week
>
> _____ about once every two weeks
>
> _____ less often than once every two weeks

Sometimes the closed question is in the form of a rating scale, such as the five-point Likert scale, which requires respondents to choose the appropriate degree of agreement or disagreement with a statement.

> **5.** The library's electronic catalog is easy to use.
>
> (1) strongly agree   (2) agree   (3) uncertain
> (4) disagree   (5) strongly disagree

This type of scale is useful for measuring attitudes.

Ask Open-Ended Questions to Gather Opinions or Attitudes
Open-ended questions allow respondents more freedom in the answers
they give.

6. How has the library's electronic catalog affected your
research strategies?

_____

_____

_____

_____

_____

Answers to open-ended questions are difficult to quantify, but they can
be among the most interesting and helpful responses. Be sure to provide
adequate space so respondents can answer as fully as they desire.

Avoid Asking More Than One Question at a Time

7. Do you use the interlibrary loan service and the government
publications collection of the library?

Yes _____   No _____

How would someone who uses only the government publications collection answer this question? How would someone who uses only the
interlibrary loan service answer this question?

**Remember That the Way a Question Is Phrased
Can Influence Responses**
It is not possible to phrase questions in a totally neutral way, but be
aware of how phrasing can create biases. Consider, for example, a
question that Ross Perot asked readers of the March 1993 issue of *TV
Guide*. He posed the question this way:

Do you believe that for every dollar of tax increase there
should be two dollars in spending cuts with savings earmarked
for deficit and debt reduction?

Perot reported that 97 percent of nearly a million-and-a-half respondents favored bigger cuts in government spending.

A revised question read:

> Would you favor or oppose a proposal to cut spending by two
> dollars for every dollar in new taxes, with savings earmarked
> for deficit and debt reduction, even if that means cuts in
> domestic programs like medicine and education?

Only 33 percent responded "yes" when the question was posed this way.[2]

Design the Questionnaire So That It Is Easy to Use

The general layout of questionnaires varies a great deal, but these
three features are most helpful:

- Place instructions needed to fill out the questionnaire at the top
  of the first page of the questionnaire.
- Print the questionnaire in a typeface that is easy to read.
- Leave plenty of space for respondents to answer open-ended
  questions.

Take an Adequate Sample of the Group You Are Surveying

Since you will be drawing conclusions and perhaps making recommendations based upon statistical treatment of responses, be sure that you
have taken an adequate sample of the group you are surveying. Ideally,
you should strive to achieve universal sampling by canvassing all members of an identifiable group, but that is not always possible or feasible.
You may also do random sampling, in which every person in an identifiable group has a known chance to be selected. There are also other
types of sampling methods. The important things are to be sure that
you have an adequate sample before making generalizations about the
results and to be prepared to explain the criteria used for selecting
respondents and the procedure for administering the questionnaire.

Use the Exact Wording and the Same Sequence
of Questions in All Questionnaires

Personal interviews usually involve fairly free conversation between the
researcher and the interviewer. Questionnaires, on the other hand, consist of carefully worded questions or statements to which all respondents
are asked to respond. The primary purpose for using a questionnaire is
to ensure comparable answers, no matter who administers the question-

---

[2]Judith M. Taner, "The Trustworthiness of Survey Research," *The Chronicle of Higher
Education* 25: May 1994, p. B1.

naire or who answers the questions. Variation in the wording of questions can significantly influence respondents' answers and make the information useless to the researcher. Consider, for example, these three questions about beginning salaries offered to entry-level hotel and restaurant managers:

> "What is your gross income?"
> "What is your net income?"
> "How much is your salary?"

Clearly, it would be unwise to add or average the answers to these questions. The answer to the first question would be a gross salary figure; the answer to the second question would be a net salary figure; and the answer to the third question might be either a gross or a net salary figure.

Encourage Respondents to Answer All Questions and Return the Questionnaire to You

Whether the questionnaire is distributed personally or by mail, the instructions for completing the questionnaire must be clear so that respondents will answer every question that you want them to answer. Sometimes a questionnaire contains questions that are to be answered or not answered according to how a previous question or questions were answered. For example, the fourth question is to be answered only by respondents who answered *yes* to the third question, and the fifth question would be answered only by respondents who answered *no* to the third question. To make sure that respondents can follow the instructions and that the questions are unambiguous, you should test the questionnaire on a small group and revise questions or instructions if the test respondents have trouble.

If the questionnaire is mailed to respondents, you should make a special effort to secure a high return rate. Use a cover letter that explains the purpose of the research and how the respondent was selected; identify the sponsor of the research; and give assurance that the responses will be confidential. Enclose a stamped, addressed return envelop in the mailing to make it easy for respondents to return the questionnaire to you.

Writing Letters of Inquiry

Like interviews and questionnaires, letters of inquiry can elicit data, ideas, and opinions important to your research but unavailable in published documents.

Also like interviews and questionnaires, letters of inquiry are not trouble-free to use. Your inquiry may be insufficiently addressed and wind up on an e-mail list or in an in-box a long time before somebody decides where to route it or decides to discard it. Or your inquiry might be so vague that the respondent, if he or she makes the effort, must write back asking for clarification and thus begin an exchange of correspondence that could stretch out for several days or weeks. It's also possible that the persons or organizations you write to may not be receptive to your inquiry because you are asking for information that they normally do not provide to others.

Despite these potential difficulties, you may need to rely on letters of inquiry to obtain information that you can get no other way. Writing to sources that have specific expertise or authority on some aspect of your research question has many benefits. You might be able to elicit information from an expert who is not available for a face-to-face interview. You might be able to get up-to-date information about some obscure fact when there is nothing available in published documents. You might be able to go beyond the surface of statistics and other data by having an expert assist you in interpreting the data. You might be able to redirect a line of inquiry or be led to new resources by the answers an expert gives.

Once you decide to write a letter of inquiry—whether by e-mail, facsimile machine transmission, or postal service (commonly referred to as "snail mail")—review the general guidelines for designing questionnaires and conducting interviews. Then observe three additional rules of thumb:

❖ Select the right respondent.

❖ Be brief and clear.

❖ Know how to ask for what you want.

Select the Right Respondent

Identifying people or organizations that are likely to have the information you want is important, and it might take some research to find the right person to write to. Suppose, for example, that your research involves learning how often the plastic belt clips on portable radio/cassette players break, what causes them to break, whether manufacturers regard the breaks as a problem, and how they are responding to it. You want to write to the most authoritative source you can locate, so you might call the manufacturer's customer service, customer relations, or research department to begin your search. Most manufacturers have toll-free telephone numbers that you can find by calling toll-free operator assistance at (800) 555-1212. If the organization does not have a toll-free number, you can get a telephone number from directories in your library—*Ward's Business Directory, Moody's Manuals, Standard & Poor's Corporate Records, Million Dollar Directory.* To prevent being passed from office to office once you call an organization, identify specifically the subject you are researching, and ask to be connected with a person or office that might be able to answer your questions.

A telephone conversation might produce the information you want, but if you are seeking answers in more complex and coherent forms than are usually given in telephone conversations, get the name, position or title, and complete address of the person to whom you will be writing. Take a minute to verify the spelling of the person's name and the street, building, and city of the address or the e-mail address or FAX number.

Again, try to avoid sending an inquiry without having somebody's name.

Be Brief, Clear, Specific, and Organized

In writing the letter of inquiry, you need to apply those principles of purpose, audience, and persuasion that are discussed in many other parts of this textbook. You will not be writing to a multiple audience but to an individual who can give you authoritative answers and whose answers, by virtue of his or her professional responsibilities and knowledge, contain credible information and expert opinions.

Make your purpose clear by stating explicitly, but briefly, the research question you are working on, the reasons you have addressed the inquiry to this reader, the importance of the information you are seeking, and the use you plan to make of the information.

To assist the reader in responding to your inquiry, ask specific questions. Vague questions or nonquestions such as "I am seeking information about belt clips breaking. Can you help me?" or "Please send me what information you have relative to the problem of belt clips breaking" do not specify the information you want and are likely to alienate the reader because they imply that you expect the respondent to figure out what information is pertinent to your research question and then provide it.

Four or five questions are about the maximum number to ask. List them, numbering them for convenient reference when the respondent answers them. A good way to begin is to ask relatively general questions that help the respondent focus on your inquiry:

Does your company receive inquiries, requests, or complaints
from retailers and customers about the plastic belt clips on
your portable radio/cassette players breaking?

Ask your questions, one at a time, keeping them specific and brief:

1. Approximately how many requests for replacement clips have you received during the past year?
2. What is your company's policy on replacing broken clips? Are they covered under the product's warranty?
3. Is your company conducting research into the causes of belt clips breaking? If so, what do you believe are the major causes?
4. Is your company working on redesigning the clip to reduce breakage?

End your questions by asking if there is any additional information that the respondent thinks might be relevant to your research question and if there are additional persons or departments that you might contact for information that the respondent cannot provide.

Close your letter by stating your appreciation for the respondent taking the time to answer your questions. (But avoid the trite expression "Thanking you in advance.") Figure 3.15 is an example of a letter of inquiry.

Cushion an Imposing Inquiry

It is important that you have some sense of whether your inquiry will be difficult to answer. You can be reasonably sure that most of your inquiries will be answered either because (1) they are easy to answer or (2) answering them is often good public relations for the respondent or respondent's organization. However, you won't have the same assurance if your inquiries (1) are difficult to answer or (2) offer no immediate benefit to the respondent or the respondent's organization.

In the former situations, you need only be clear and courteous and not waste the respondent's time. In the latter situations, you have to be persuasive to get what you want. For instance, a researcher studying the practice of organizations monitoring employees' behavior by monitoring phone calls and e-mail messages and using hidden cameras, undercover agents, drug testing, and so on is seeking information that many organizations are not eager to share even though the law allows them to monitor employee behavior in certain instances. However, some of the employees and the representatives of such organizations as labor unions and the American Civil Liberties Union probably would be much more willing to cooperate with your inquiries.

There are several ways to make your respondents more receptive to your questions. You can, for instance, engage in a little honest flattery by explaining why you regard them as expert resources. Perhaps

Brandywine Apartments, C-5
2400 Wyeth Avenue
East Point, PA 16077

January 31, 1997

Director, Safety and Environmental Health
Woodward Manufacturing Company
160823 East Range Line Road
Cumberland Plateau, PA 17492-1503

Dear Director:

    I am a senior majoring in mechanical engineering
at Valley State University, and I am researching the
potential environmental concerns related to disposing
burned-out fluorescent light bulbs.

    My research indicates that many large organiza-
tions, such as banks and schools, regard the disposing
of fluorescent light bulbs as their primary environmental concern in disposing of waste. Hospitals report
that only the disposal of contaminated medical materials exceeds the disposal of fluorescent light bulbs as
their number one environmental concern.

    Would you please send me whatever information your
company provides wholesalers, distributors, and consumers
about the proper disposal of the fluorescent light bulbs
that your company manufactures. Specifically I am interested in receiving copies of or information on the following items:

- Instructions, procedures, or manuals and warning
  or caution labels on the storage, installation,
  removal, and disposal of fluorescent light bulbs.

- Seminars, workshops, or training sessions that
  your company conducts on the handling and disposal of fluorescent light bulbs.

    My research will culminate in a formal presentation
and written report in my ME 368 Advanced Projects I
class. The project is due March 20. Any information you
provide will be acknowledged in my presentation and
report.

Sincerely,

Jawanica R. Nelson

Jawanica R. Nelson

Figure 3.15 Sample letter of inquiry

they or their organizations are directly involved in an important issue that you are studying. Perhaps you have read publications by them, or someone has given you their names as experts to contact. However, flattery can easily be overdone, and potential respondents are sure to feel that you are attempting to be manipulative if they sense that your flattery is false.

A more effective approach is to personalize your inquiry and depend on the respondent's goodwill. To encourage goodwill, you should identify yourself as a student and be particularly polite in making your inquiry. Explain why you are researching the question; briefly review your research to date; and explain how it relates to the questions you are asking. Offer what you can to the respondent. You can state that you will share your research with others, thus drawing the respondent or the respondent's organization to the attention of your classmates who may someday be potential customers, employees, or supporters of the organization. You can also offer to send a copy of your research paper to the respondent. In addition, if you suspect that your respondent could well be apathetic and inclined to put off answering your inquiry, you should politely state the time when you must have an answer.

Remember, keep your letter brief; try for a page or two.

INTEGRATING AND ACKNOWLEDGING SOURCES

When you draw on sources other than your own observations and experiences for data, information, opinions, ideas, and ways of thinking, you must (1) integrate source material effectively into your text, (2) carefully credit those sources, and (3) let readers know where you got the information.

Integrating sources is the subject of the first section. Two widely used systems for acknowledging sources are covered in the next two sections:

- ❖ the "MLA style" of documentation, which is covered in detail in the *MLA Handbook for Writers of Research Papers*, 4th edition, by Joseph Gibaldi (New York: MLA, 1995), and

- ❖ the "APA style" of documentation, which is covered in detail in the *Publication Manual of the American Psychological Association*, 4th edition (Washington: APA, 1994).

Integrating Sources into Your Text

Effectively integrating source material into a text requires some effort and knowledge on your part. In quoting others, you are not just describing what you have read. You are offering the thinking of others as evidence in your own arguments. First, you must decide how to present the source material you want to include. Will you summarize it, paraphrase it, or quote it? Second, you need to introduce sources you are quoting rather than merely dumping quotations into your text. Third, you must punctuate quotations properly. Fourth, you must acknowledge your sources. Here are some general guidelines.

Summarizing, Paraphrasing, and Quoting Material

SUMMARIZE MATERIAL THAT IS PERTINENT BUT IS TOO LONG TO PARAPHRASE OR TOO UNINTERESTING TO QUOTE.   In a summary you include only the main idea and major supporting points of the source material, expressing them in your own words. For example, Rachel Carson, in *Silent Spring*[3] summarizes Justice William O. Douglas's book *My Wilderness: East to Katahdin*, providing her readers with a brief overview of some of the events in Douglas's book so that they can understand how they relate to and support her own arguments against indiscriminate spraying of chemicals:

> The second [adverse effect of chemical spraying] is of a kind that is always associated with the shotgun approach to nature: the spraying also eliminates a great many plants that were not its intended target. Justice William O. Douglas, in his recent book *My Wilderness: East to Katahdin*, has told of an appalling example of ecological destruction wrought by the United States Forest Service in the Bridger National Forest in Wyoming. Some 10,000 acres of sagelands were sprayed by the Service, yielding to pressure of cattlemen for more grasslands. The sage was killed, as intended. But so was the green, life-giving ribbon of willows that traced its way across these plains, following the meandering streams. Moose had lived in these willow thickets, for willow is to the moose what sage is to the antelope. Beaver had lived there, too, feeding on the willows, felling them and making a strong dam across the tiny stream . . . . Merely because of the presence of the willows and the beavers that depended on them, the region was an attractive recreational area with excellent fishing and hunting.

---

[3]Boston: Houghton Mifflin, 1962, pp. 67–68.

But with the "improvement" instituted by the Forest Service, the willows went the way of the sagebrush, killed by the same impartial spray. When Justice Douglas visited the area in 1959, the year of the spraying, he was shocked to see the shriveled and dying willows—the "vast, incredible damage." What would become of the moose? Of the beavers and the little world they had constructed? A year later he returned to read the answers in the devastated landscape. The moose were gone and so were the beaver. Their principal dam had gone out for want of attention by its skilled architects, and the lake had drained away. None of the large trout were left. None could live in the tiny creek that remained, threading its way through a bare, hot land where no shade remained. The living world was shattered.

You can see how Carson blends Douglas's writing into her own argument. Rather than a casual or brief allusion to Douglas's text, she summarizes Douglas's ideas and gives her readers an opportunity to see if she has dealt with her source fairly.

You may want to summarize articles or chapters from books for the same reason. You may also choose to summarize if the material in question is not particularly well written. But be careful not to make even subtle changes in meaning when transferring another person's words to your notes and your own words.

PARAPHRASE BRIEF PASSAGES THAT INCLUDE IMPORTANT INFORMATION BUT ARE NOT STATED IN LANGUAGE THAT IS UNUSUALLY FORCEFUL, INTERESTING, OR MEMORABLE. In a paraphrase you include all of the ideas and information in the original but put them in your own words. Thus, you do not want to paraphrase very long passages.

QUOTE MATERIAL IF IT IS (1) NOT TOO LONG, (2) FROM A SOURCE THAT HAS A GREAT DEAL OF CREDIBILITY, OR (3) IS STATED IN LANGUAGE THAT IS UNUSUALLY FORCEFUL, INTERESTING, OR MEMORABLE. In other words, you should quote material when it is important to retain the original language—language that is significant either because of who said it or how it is said. Direct quotations from authoritative sources add credibility to your arguments. But keep the quotations short.

Introducing Sources

Whether they are summarizing, paraphrasing, or quoting, careful writers introduce all source material by identifying the source. This may be done by citing the author's name, or if the name is not known or not significant, the title of the source, as in the following examples (MLA style).

> According to Alexander Harris, whose house includes
> a solar energy system, heating with solar energy is not
> always satisfactory (8). [summary]

> Sarah Wyatt, an industrial engineer, agreed that
> solar energy systems require constant supervision if
> they are to function properly. [paraphrase]

> Taylor Moore, Director of the Federal Bureau of
> Energy Research, stated: "Solar energy is not the solu-
> tion to all of our energy problems, but it is a viable
> alternative to the use of fossil fuels for heating
> homes and commercial buildings in the Southwestern
> regions of our country (52)." [quotation]

In each of the examples above, a reader knows exactly where the source material begins and knows the name of the person whose words are being summarized, paraphrased, or quoted. In the case of quotations, you may include the name at the end rather than the beginning because the initial quotation marks signal the beginning of the source material:

> "Solar energy is not the solution to all of our
> energy problems, but it is a viable alternative to the
> use of fossil fuels for heating homes and commercial
> buildings in the Southwestern regions of our country,"
> stated Taylor Moore, Director of the Federal Bureau of
> Energy Research (52). [quotation]

As these examples illustrate, you can also characterize a source's authority and credibility by identifying his or her position, profession, or status.

Punctuating Quotations

Summaries and paraphrases are not difficult to integrate into a text, because a writer is using his or her own words. However, quotations must not only be integrated carefully into the existing text, but they must also be punctuated correctly (that is, according to certain conventions of punctuation). The only general punctuation rule that applies to all quotations is to place double quotation marks around the quoted material. However, there are four types of quotations, each of which requires slightly different conventions of punctuation.

QUOTATIONS THAT ARE SEPARATED FROM THE SENTENCE IN WHICH THEY APPEAR.   Quotations may be punctuated as if they are separate sentences even though they appear as part of your own sentence. These quotations (1) are introduced, interrupted, or followed by a brief citation, (2) begin with a capital letter, and (3) are separated from the rest of the sentence by a comma or colon:

> According to Al Gore, "We cannot simply create larger and larger quantities of waste and dump it into the environment and pretend that it doesn't matter (159)."

> Gore states: "We cannot simply create larger and larger quantities of waste and dump it into the environment and pretend that it doesn't matter (159)."

> "We cannot simply create larger and larger quantities of waste and dump it into the environment," says Gore, "and pretend that it doesn't matter (159)."

> "We cannot simply create larger and larger quantities of waste and dump it into the environment and pretend that it doesn't matter," argues Gore (159).

QUOTATIONS PRECEDED BY *THAT* WHEN THEY ARE INTEGRATED INTO THE SENTENCE.   In making other quotations part of your own sentence, you may introduce them with phrases like ". . . says that," ". . . argues that," and so on. Do not begin these quotations with a capital letter, as in the following example, even if they begin with a capital letter in their original form:

> Gore argues that "we cannot simply create larger and larger quantities of waste and dump it into the environment and pretend that it doesn't matter" (159).

Occasionally, a quotation will not fit grammatically into the *that* structure. You may have to substitute words to create a smooth fit. Do not put the words you substitute inside the quotation marks. In the following example notice how "I have" in the quotation is modified to "he has," which becomes part of the writer's own sentence:

> Gore states: "I have found overwhelming public enthusiasm for the process."

> Gore states that he has "found overwhelming public enthusiasm for the process."

If this change is not made, the sentence becomes illogical:

> Gore states that "I have found overwhelming public enthusiasm for the process."

QUOTATIONS THAT ARE MORE THAN FOUR LINES LONG.   Separate long quotations (those that are more than four lines) from your own text by indenting each line in the quotation ten spaces from the left margin. These long, indented quotations are also often introduced by a colon, as in the following example:

> Recycling is often pointed to as the solution to waste management. However, as Al Gore points out, recycling is not always the answer:
>
>> In conducting workshops in Tennessee and hearings in Washington on recycling, I have found overwhelming public enthusiasm for the process. But I have also found tremendous disappointment among individuals and groups who have dutifully collected and sorted those elements of their municipal waste that they knew could be profitably recycled, only to find that it was impossible to find buyers for the material. (159)

Notice that quotation marks are not used when a long quote is indented and that the parenthetical citation is placed outside the displayed quotation.

There are three other minor rules of punctuation that you need to know in working with quotations:

USE ELLIPSES TO INDICATE OMISSION.   You may omit part of a quotation if you indicate the omission by the use of ellipses (three spaced periods):

```
          Gore argues that "we cannot simply create larger
     and larger quantities of waste and . . . pretend it
     doesn't matter" (159).
```

USE SQUARE BRACKETS TO INDICATE ADDITION.   You may add words to a quotation to make it clearer if you indicate the addition by the use of square brackets:

```
          Gore states that he has "found overwhelming public
     enthusiasm for the process [of recycling]."
```

```
          According to Gore, "These states [Washington and
     New Jersey] have achieved high rates of recycling."
```

USE SINGLE QUOTATION MARKS TO INDICATE A QUOTATION WITHIN A QUOTA-TION.   If the person you are quoting is quoting someone else or has used double quotation marks for any other reason, you indicate this double quotation by using single quotation marks to enclose the inside quotation.

```
          According to Rachel Carson, "When Justice Douglas
     visited the area in 1959, the year of the spraying, he
     was shocked to see the shriveled and dying willows--the
     'vast, incredible damage'" (68).
```

```
          Gore points out that "we have come to think of
     almost any natural resource as 'going to waste' if we
     have failed to develop it" (146).
```

Acknowledging Sources

Sources must not only be located, evaluated, integrated, and punctuated, but they must also be acknowledged. You must acknowledge any source that you use unless the information you obtained from the source is general knowledge that is available from multiple sources. For example, you might want to use a reference book to check the accuracy of the date you give for the dropping of the atomic bomb on Hiroshima. However, since information about the dropping of the atomic bomb on Hiroshima is generally known and could be found in a number of sources including encyclopedias, it is not necessary to acknowledge the source when you include that date in an essay or report of your own. However, if you summarize arguments in which the writer compares Hiroshima to the Gulf War or if you quote the source directly, you must, of course, acknowledge the source.

The conventions for acknowledging sources in writing are known as documentation. There are a number of different documentation styles, each of which involves slightly different conventions. Writers generally use the style used in the academic journals for their own profession or discipline. A commonly used style is MLA documentation. MLA documentation, like most styles used today, uses a two-part system to document sources: in-text, often parenthetical, citations to mark the place source material is used and a list of works cited. These two parts work together to provide readers with the information they need to identify, verify, or locate sources.

In the next two sections, pages 466–503, you learn how to use so-called MLA (for Modern Language Association) and APA (for American Psychological Association) systems of documentation, the two that you are most likely to use as an undergraduate student.

Using MLA Documentation to Acknowledge Sources

Used mostly by researchers in languages, literature, philosophy, art, and other subjects in the humanities, MLA (Modern Language Association) documentation has two parts. The first part, **in-text citations**, presents brief information about sources where they are referred to in the body of a paper or report. The second part, an alphabetical list of references called the **Works Cited** list, presents fuller information about each of the cited sources. For complete coverage of current MLA documentation, as well as of other scholarly, style, and format details that comprise "MLA style," see the *MLA Handbook for Writers of Research Papers*, 4th edition, by Joseph Gibaldi (New York: MLA, 1995).

MLA in-text citations identify sources—usually by author surname or, if no author is named, by title. The name or title that identifies the source may be placed in parentheses at the end of the cited material. In papers, writers often choose to include author names and titles of works as part of their discussions, keeping information in parentheses to a minimum. Page references are required for quotations, paraphrases, or summaries of material from print sources. These specific page numbers (and other "location numbers," such as line and volume numbers) are always put in parentheses at the end of the cited material, even when the author's name (or title) is part of the discussion.

```
      In recent decades, there has been strong interest
in examining issues related to gender and communica-
tion. And while Pearson has noted that "the cliches
about the language of women and men appear to be
```

```
stronger than the actual differences" (178), there is
some evidence that the communication styles of men and
women are often distinct. For example, some researchers
have found support for the fact that the "female" com-
munication style is more unsure, tentative and deferen-
tial than the "male" style. However, others argue that
these variations are due to the fact that males and
females have fundamentally different perceptions with
respect to the function of language. According to this
view, women are not more tentative in their styles, but
are more focused upon expressing concern for the lis-
tener. Thus, the function of "female" language is more
"socioemotional or affiliative" while "male" language
is more "instrumental or task-oriented" (Simkins-
Bullock and Wildman 151).
```

> Otnes, Cele, Kyungseung Kim, and Young Chan Kim. "Yes,
> Virginia, There *Is* a Gender Difference:
> Analyzing Children's Requests to Santa Claus."
> *Journal of Popular Culture* 28.1
> (Summer 1994): 17.

The Works Cited list (see Figure 3.16 on page 473) appears at the end of an essay or report, beginning on a new page sequenced with the pages in front of it. Here are Works Cited entries for the two sources cited in the passage on gender differences in language use:

```
Pearson, Judy C. Gender and Communication. Dubuque,
     IA: William C. Brown, 1978.
Simkins-Bullock, Jennifer A., and Beth G. Wildman. "An
     Investigation into the Relationships Between
     Gender and Language." Sex Roles 24 (Feb. 1991):
     149-60.
```

MLA In-Text Citations

Citations in your paper must refer to specific sources in your Works Cited list. Most of the following examples show parenthetical citations. (In practice, however, it often makes sense to include author names and titles of works, and even author credentials, in your first discussion of a particular source.) Place parenthetical citations at the end of the cited material. When you do not mention in your discussion the author name (or the title of a work for which no author is named), give it and, if needed, page numbers in parentheses. Use one space but no punctuation between a name and a page number in a parenthetical reference.

CITING AN ENTIRE WORK.   When you are citing an entire work (rather than referring to particular pages), you will probably mention its author and title in your own discussion. A first reference to an entire work might look like this:

> Gloria Anzaldua's novel <u>Borderlands/La Frontera</u>
> reflects her concern for both the physical and cultural
> borderland between the United States and Mexico.

CITING A WORK BY ONE AUTHOR.   Here is an example with the author's name and a page number in parentheses:

> One early study reports that "there are about six min-
> utes of commercials on the typical network news show,
> which means there are only twenty-four minutes avail-
> able for reportage of national and international
> events" (Berger 123).

When you use the author's name as part of your sentence, cite only the page number or numbers in parentheses:

> According to Arthur Asa Berger, professor of broadcast
> communication arts at San Francisco State University,
> "There are about six minutes of commercials on the typ-
> ical network news show, which means there are only
> twenty-four minutes available for reportage of national
> and international events" (123).

CITING A WORK BY TWO OR THREE AUTHORS.   Cite all names when there are two or three authors. List them in the order in which they appear on the title page of a book or in the byline of an article:

> Although Hemingway had married and divorced several
> times, he regarded himself as deeply Catholic (Herter
> and Herter 106-08).

> Mark Twain calls an autobiography "the truest of all
> books; for while it inevitably consists mainly of
> extinctions of the truth, with hardly an instance of
> plain straight truth, the remorseless truth is there,
> between the lines" (Anderson, Gibson, and Smith 374).

CITING A WORK BY MORE THAN THREE AUTHORS. There are two ways to cite a work by more than three authors. You can give the name of only the first author followed by "et al." (abbreviation for the Latin *et alia*, meaning "and others"; there is no period after *et*, but there is after the *al.*):

> In human beings only about 1 percent of DNA seems to be
> involved in coding genetic inheritance (Alberts et al.
> 62).

Note that in a parenthetical citation, there is no punctuation between the first author's surname and *et al.* However, in the Works Cited list, where the first author's name is given in full in inverted order, there is a comma between the author's name and *et al.*: Alberts, Joan C., et al. (see the examples on pages 475–476).

The other way is to give all the last names:

> According to managers of large technical documentation
> projects, looking for the right word processing program
> can be like searching the ocean to find a pearl
> (Bilbus, Hutchinson, Navarro, and Wu 189).

CITING A WORK BY A CORPORATE OR ORGANIZATIONAL AUTHOR. If, on a book's title page, no person is named as author or editor, but a corporation, a commission, a committee, or some other organization's name does appear, use the corporate name as "author." Use it for in-text citations, and make it the first element in the Works Cited entry (see the examples on page 476):

> Brainstorming is becoming increasingly important in
> solving management problems (Florida Power and Light
> Company 6).

> The Florida Power and Light Company, in a pamphlet that
> describes their management philosophy, points out that

```
brainstorming is becoming increasingly important in
solving management problems (6).
```

CITING A WORK WHEN NO AUTHOR IS NAMED. When no individuals or groups are named as author of a work, use the title for in-text citations and as the first element in the Works Cited entry (see page 476):

```
California had the highest number of adult/adolescent
and pediatric AIDS cases (7,648) reported from August
1990 through July 1991 (HIV/AIDS Surveillance 4).
```

CITING AUTHORS WITH THE SAME SURNAME. When you cite two or more sources whose authors have the same surname (Elizabeth Wright and Thomas Wright, for instance), include the author's initials or first name in all in-text citations:

```
Benjamin Franklin's printing firm won the first con-
tract to print money for the state of Pennsylvania
(Elizabeth Wright 148), but it was the Pennsylvania
Gazette and the Poor Richard's Almanac that made him a
wealthy man (Thomas Wright 17).
```

CITING TWO OR MORE WORKS WITHIN THE SAME PARENTHESES. When citing two or more works within the same parentheses, order the works alphabetically, and separate the works by semicolons:

```
Several proponents of nuclear power have pointed to
France's heavy reliance on nuclear energy (Donique;
Freed and Waters; Millicent).
```

CITING TWO OR MORE WORKS BY THE SAME AUTHOR OR AUTHORS. To cite the work of an author or authors who have other works cited in your paper, add the title of the work to the citation:

```
Crick has theorized about protein molecules which he
claims have several unusual properties ("Thinking About
the Brain").

Crick questions whether new computer algorithms for
neural networks can provide new understanding of the
```

```
computational properties of the brain ("The Recent
Excitement" 129).
```

CITING MULTIVOLUME WORKS.   When citing a volume number as well as a page number for a multivolume work, separate them by a colon and a space:

```
"Thought without speech is inconceivable," asserted the
philosopher Hannah Arendt (1: 32).
```

CITING INTERVIEWS, LETTERS, AND OTHER PERSONAL COMMUNICATIONS.   A personal interview is listed in the Works Cited list by the name of the interviewee; a personal letter is listed by the letter writer's name. So use those names in your in-text citations. If you are citing a published version of an interview or letter, follow the guidelines for the type of publication in which the cited source appears.

```
Al Kaline decided to retire from baseball when he could
no longer count the stitches on the baseball thrown by
the pitcher.

In a letter to Frank Meiers dated 2 January 1997 (Frank
Meiers Papers), Mary Powell wrote that "focus groups
can achieve excellent results in a very short period."
```

CITING AN INDIRECT SOURCE.   If possible, you should quote from original sources, not secondhand ones. However, sometimes only an indirect source is available—for example:

```
Macaulay's accuracy as an historian has been questioned
because of his apparent overconfidence on all matters
of historical judgment. Lord Melbourne is reported to
have said that he wished he could be "as cocksure about
anything as Macaulay is about everything" (qtd. in
Firth 54).
```

The citation leads the reader to this entry in the Works Cited list:

```
Firth, Charles H. A Commentary on Macaulay's History of
     England. London: Frank Cass, 1938.
```

MLA Works Cited List

Include in the Works Cited list at the end of your paper information about all the sources you refer to in your paper. Do not include in it any sources you have read but do not cite. Be *extremely* careful not to use ideas from a source without citing the source.

Format Guidelines.

Figure 3.16 illustrates the format for the Works Cited list.

- Start the list of works cited on a new page, continuing the pagination of the text.
- Center the heading *Works Cited* about 1 inch down from the top of the page.
- Double-space everything.
- Begin each entry flush with the left margin, but if the entry is more than one line long, indent any subsequent line(s) five spaces (or 1 computer tab—about ½ inch) from the left margin.

In addition, here are some other practices to observe:

- Use the author's or editor's full name as it appears on the title page or in the byline of the article. Omit titles, affiliations, and degrees:

  Powell, Colin
  not Powell, Gen. Colin

  Allups, Minerva
  not Allups, Minerva, Ph.D.

- List multiple authors in the order in which they appear on the title page or in the byline of the article.
- State the full title, including any subtitle, of works. Underline (or italicize) the title of a book, periodical, pamphlet, or report. Enclose in quotation marks the title of an article.

  The Night Country (if a book)
  "The Night Country" (if an article)

Works Cited

Bringa, Tone. <u>Being Muslim in the Bosnian Way: Identity and Community in a Central Bosnia Village</u>. Princeton: Princeton UP, 1995.

Brzezinski, Zbigniew. "After Srebrenica." <u>New Republic</u> 213 (7 Aug. 1995): 20-21.

"Congress and Bosnia." <u>Washington Post</u> 15 Dec. 1995: A24.

Donia, Robert J. <u>Bosnia and Hercegovina: A Tradition Betrayed</u>. New York: Columbia UP, 1994.

Glynn, Patrick. "The Age of Balkanization." <u>Commentary</u> 96 (July 1993): 21-24.

---. "America's Burden." <u>New Republic</u> 208 (25 Jan. 1993): 24+.

---. "Bosnia: Is It Too Late? Yes." <u>Commentary</u> 99 (April 1995): 31-34.

<u>Lessons from Bosnia</u>. Santa Monica: Rand, 1993.

Marshall, Tyler, and Kraft Scott. "Pact Shows Europe Still Looks to U.S." <u>Los Angeles Times</u> 15 Dec. 1995: A1.

Perlez, Jane. "Bosnian Serb Warriors Are Haunted in Peace." <u>New York Times</u> 15 Dec. 1995: A1.

Silber, Laura. <u>The Death of Bosnia</u>. New York: Penguin, 1995.

United States. Cong. Commission on Security and Cooperation in Europe. <u>Implementation of the Helsinki Accords: Hearing before the Commission on Security and Cooperation in Europe</u>. 103rd Cong. <u>War Crimes and the Humanitarian Crisis in the Former Yugoslavia</u>. Jan. 25, 1993. Washington: GPO, 1993.

Figure 3.16. Works cited list in MLA documentation style

❖ Include in each entry for a book the city of publication, the publisher's name (MLA calls for shortened forms), and the date of publication:

```
Upper Saddle River: Prentice, 1996.
```

—If the book is published outside the United States, add the name of the country. Also identify relatively unknown cities by state (not Detroit, but certainly Bear Run, MT). Use two-letter, capitalized postal abbreviations for states. If no place of publication is given, write "n.p." for "no place."

—Use shortened forms of publisher's names (e.g., "Erlbaum" instead of "Lawrence Erlbaum Associates, Publishers"). Books published by university presses have University and Press abbreviated (as in U of Texas P or Indiana UP).

—If no date of publication is given, write "n.d." for "no date."

❖ Arrange the entries alphabetically by the first element of each entry (usually an author's or editor's surname). A work that has a corporation or organization as its author is alphabetized by the first word of the corporation or organization (excluding *A, An, The*). A work with no identifiable author is alphabetized by its title (excluding *A, An, The*)—do not use *Anonymous* or *Anon*.

❖ If there is more than one work by the same author, arrange the entries in alphabetical order by title. After the first entry, instead of repeating the author's name, use three hyphens followed by a period:

```
Moustakas, Clark. Heuristic Research: Design,
     Methodology, and Application. Newbury Park: SAGE,
     1990.
---. Loneliness and Love. Upper Saddle River: Prentice,
     1972.
---. The Tower of Loneliness. Upper Saddle River:
     Prentice, 1975.
```

❖ For authors who have more than one work on the list, list single-author entries before any multiple-author entries. You may use hyphens for the single-author entries, but repeat the author's last name for the multiple-author entries.

```
Mandelbrot, Benoit. The Fractal Geometry of Nature. San
        Francisco: Freeman, 1982.
---. "An Interview." Omni 5 (February 1984): 721.
Mandelbrot, Benoit, Dann E. Passoja, and Alvin Paullay.
        "Fractal Character of Fracture Surfaces of
        Metals." Nature 308 (1984): 721.
```

Documenting Print Sources: Books

You can usually find most of the information you need to document a book on its title page and copyright page. The title page is commonly the work's first or second right hand page; it lists the title, the author(s) or editor(s), and the publisher. The copyright page is on the reverse side of the title page; it names the copyright holder and the year of publication, along with other information about the publication of the work.

BOOK BY ONE AUTHOR. When the book has a subtitle, as does the following one, separate the main title and subtitle with a colon.

```
Ikegami, Eiko. The Taming of the Samurai: Honorific
        Individualism and the Making of Modern Japan.
        Cambridge: Harvard UP, 1995.
```

BOOK BY TWO OR THREE AUTHORS. List the authors in the order they are listed on the title page of the book:

```
Ansolabehere, Stephen, and Shanto Iyengar. Going
        Negative: How Attack Ads Shrink and Polarize the
        Electorate. New York: Free, 1996.

Aronson, L. Jerrold, Rom Harre, and Eileen Cornell Way.
        Realism Reserved: How Scientific Progress Is
        Possible. Peru: Open Court, 1995.
```

BOOK BY MORE THAN THREE AUTHORS. Put a comma between the author's name and *et al.* in the Works Cited entry but not in the in-text parenthetical citation: (Dubois et al.):

```
DuBois, Ellen Carol, et al. Feminist Scholarship:
          Kindling in the Groves of Academe. Urbana: U of
          Illinois P, 1987.
```

BOOK BY A CORPORATE OR ORGANIZATIONAL AUTHOR. If a book's title page does not name a person as author or editor but does name a corporation, a commission, a committee, or some other organization, use the corporate name as "author." Give it as the first information in the Works Cited entry, and use it as the author name for in-text citations (for an example, see pages 469-470).

```
Florida Power and Light Company. FPL Quality
          Improvement Program: QI Story and Techniques.
          Miami: Florida Power and Light Company, 1987.

Lloyd's of London. Lloyd's Ports of the World.
          Colchester, England: Lloyd's, 1990.
```

BOOK WITH NO AUTHOR. If no individuals or organizations are named on a book's title page, make the title the first element in the Works Cited entry. (Do not use *Anonymous* or *Anon.*) Alphabetize such entries by the title, ignoring *A*, *An*, and *The* when alphabetizing. For example, alphabetize *An Encyclopedia of Minnesota Writers* by *Encyclopedia*, not by *An*.

```
Who's Who in Science and Engineering, 1992-1993.
          Wilmette: Marquis, 1992.
```

BOOK WITH AN EDITOR. When a book names an editor but no author on the title page, begin the Works Cited entry with the name of the editor, followed by the abbreviation *ed.* (for "editor"):

```
Gouma-Peterson, Thalia, ed. Breaking the Rules: Audrey
          Flack, A Retrospective 1950-1990. New York:
          Abrams, 1992.
```

If there is more than one editor listed, use the abbreviation *eds.*, which stands for "editors":

```
Canfield, J. Douglas, and Deborah C. Payne, eds.
          Cultural Readings of Restoration and Eighteenth-
          Century Theatre. Athens: U of Georgia P, 1995.
```

BOOK WITH A TRANSLATOR.   When a translator is named on the title page, after the author and title elements in the Works Cited entry, use the abbreviation *Trans.* (for "Translated by") followed by the translator's name:

> Esteva-Fabregat, Claudio. <u>Mestizaje in Ibero-America</u>.
> Trans. John Wheat. Tucson: U of Arizona P, 1995.

MULTIVOLUME BOOK.   If you use or are writing about a multivolume work, give the total number of volumes just before the city of publication:

> Hitchcock, H. Wiley, and Stanley Sadie, eds. <u>New Grove
> Dictionary of American Music</u>. 4 vols. New York:
> Grove, 1986.

Note the abbreviation *eds.* It stands for "editors" (use *ed.* for one editor) and starts with a lowercase letter.

If you are citing only one volume of a multivolume work, give its volume number before the publication information. In parenthetical references, give page numbers but not the volume number:

> Perkins, et al., eds. <u>The American Tradition of
> Literature</u>. Vol. 2. New York: McGraw, 1990.

If each volume in a multivolume work has its own title, you can list any volume you cite by its individual title. For example, here is such a Works Cited entry for Volume 1 of Hannah Arendt's two-volume work *The Life of the Mind:*

> Arendt, Hannah. <u>Thinking</u>. New York: Harcourt, 1978.

Or you can list the book by its individual title but include information about the total work:

> Arendt, Hannah. <u>Thinking</u>. New York: Harcourt, 1978.
> Vol. 1 of <u>The Life of the Mind</u>. 2 vols.

> Woodson, Thomas, Claude M. Simpson, and L. Neal Smith,
> eds. <u>Miscellaneous Prose and Verse</u>. Columbus: Ohio
> State UP, 1995. Vol. XXIII of <u>The Centenary
> Edition of the Works of Nathaniel Hawthorne</u>.

BOOK IN OTHER THAN FIRST EDITION. When documenting a book that notes on the title page that it is a second or subsequent edition or a special edition (*revised,* for example), give the edition information after the title:

> Law, Averill M., and W. D. Kelton. <u>Simulation Modeling and Analysis</u>. 2nd ed. New York: McGraw, 1991.

> Chevigny, Bell Gale. <u>The Woman and the Myth: Margaret Fuller's Life and Writings</u>. Rev. and expanded ed. Boston: Northeastern UP, 1994.

BOOK WITH MULTIPLE PUBLISHERS. If the title page lists more than one publisher, include them all, in the order given on the title page. Separate the information on each publisher by a semicolon:

> Kogen, Myra, ed. <u>Writing in the Business Professions</u>. Urbana, IL: National Council of Teachers of English; Urbana: Association for Business Communication, 1989.

PART OF A BOOK. In citing specific parts of a book, document as much information as necessary to pinpoint the reference, including the page numbers:

> Hardison, O. B., Jr. "Let's Play Architecture." <u>Disappearing Through the Skylight: Culture and Technology in the Twentieth Century</u>. New York: Viking, 1989. 107-20.

This entry describes a chapter from Hardison's book.

> Holmblad, L. P., and J. Ostergaard. "Control of a Cement Kiln." <u>Fuzzy Information and Decision Processes</u>. Ed. Madan M. Gupta and Elie Sanchez. New York: North-Holland, 1982. 389-99.

The entry describes an article by Holmblad and Ostergaard in a collection of articles edited by Gupta and Sanchez.

```
Miyamato, S., S. Yasurobu, and H. Ihara. "Predictive
     Fuzzy Control and Its Application to Automatic
     Train Operation Systems." Analysis of Fuzzy
     Information. Ed. James C. Bezdek. Vol. 2 of
     Artificial Intelligence and Decision Systems.
     N.p.: CRC Press, 1987. 59-72. 2 vols.
```

"N.p." stands for "no place." No place of publication is given in the book.

```
Oates, Mary. "Textile Industry." Encyclopedia of
     Southern Culture. Ed. Charles Reagan Wilson and
     William Ferris. Chapel Hill: U of North Carolina
     P, 1989. 57.
```

This example illustrates an entry in an encyclopedia that is not arranged primarily by alphabetical order. Thus, the page number is included. When entries in a reference work are arranged alphabetically, the page number(s) may be omitted.

```
Millay, Edna St. Vincent. "Oh, oh, you will be sorry
     for that word!" Collected Sonnets, Rev. and
     enlarged ed. New York: Harpers, 1988. 31.
```

The work documented is a poem from Millay's collection of poetry.

```
Suhor, Charles. Foreword. A Teacher's Introduction to
     Deconstruction. By Sharon Crowley. Urbana:
     National Council of Teachers of English, 1989.
     vii-viii.
```

The documented work is a foreword written by Charles Suhor in a book by Sharon Crowley. Note that a foreword, preface, introduction, or afterword is capitalized but is neither enclosed in quotation marks nor underlined.

ARTICLE IN A REFERENCE BOOK. Document an article in a reference book with the article title, the book title, publication information, and page numbers if the organization is not alphabetical. If the article's author is identified, give the author's name as the first element of information.

"Low-temperature Acoustics." <u>McGraw-Hill Encyclopedia</u>
<u>of Science and Technology</u>. 7th ed. 1992.

"Applications Software, Evaluation." <u>Encyclopedia of</u>
<u>Microcomputers</u>. Vol 1. New York: Dekker, 1988.
222-35.

"Kovacs, Bela A." <u>American Men and Women of Science</u>,
<u>1992-1993</u>. 18th ed. Vol. 4. New Providence, NJ:
Bowker, 1992. 483.

GOVERNMENT PUBLICATION. Document a government publication essentially the way you do a published book. If the document's author is identified, begin with his or her name. If you do not know the author, identify as author the government agency that issued the document. Underline the title. Then provide the usual publication information: place, publisher, and date of publication. Most federal publications are published by the Government Printing Office (abbreviated GPO). However, many documents issued by the federal government and most issued by state and local governments are not published by a central publishing office, so give the publication information that appears on the title page of the document.

U.S. General Services Administration. <u>Applying</u>
<u>Technology to Record Systems: A Media Guide</u>.
Washington: GPO, May 1993.

Alabama Department of Industrial Relations. <u>Alabama</u>
<u>Occupational Trends for 20005</u>. Montgomery: Research
and Statistics Division, Alabama Department of
Industrial Relations, January 1993.

UNPUBLISHED THESIS OR DISSERTATION. Enclose the title of an unpublished thesis or dissertation in quotation marks, and label it appropriately as a *Thesis* or *Diss.* Then provide the name of the degree-granting university and the year.

Guritno, P. "Moisture Sorption of Bagged Grain Stored
Under Tropical Conditions." M.S. Thesis. Kansas
State University, Manhattan, 1988.

```
Berthnal, N. "Motherhood Lost and Found: The Experience
     of Becoming an Adoptive Mother to a Foreign Born
     Child." Diss. Union Institute, Cincinnati, 1990.
```

Documenting Print Sources: Articles in Periodicals

Periodicals are publications that appear at fixed intervals—monthly, quarterly, etc. Entries for articles are similar to those for books; they include the author's name, the title, and publication information—which is the title of the periodical (underlined or italicized), the volume number (if the periodical is a scholarly journal), the date of publication, and the page numbers of the article. Most of this information can be taken from the periodical's cover or title page and table of contents. A few minor differences among article entries follow.

ARTICLE IN A JOURNAL WITH CONTINUOUS PAGINATION.   The pages of scholarly journals are usually numbered continuously through a single year. To assure that the reader gets the right issue, give the volume number, the year (the year in parentheses), and then the page numbers.

```
Knight, Virginia Curtin. "Zimbabwe: The Politics of
     Economic Reform." Current History 91 (1992): 219-23.

Vergano, P. J., R. F. Testin, and W. C. Newell. "Dis-
     tinguishing Among Bruises in Peaches Caused by
     Impact, Vibrations, and Compression." Journal of
     Food Quality 14 (1991): 285-98.
```

ARTICLE IN A JOURNAL THAT PAGES EACH ISSUE SEPARATELY.   For journals that begin each issue on page 1, add a period and the issue number after the volume number. The issue number is needed to assure that the reader will be able to get the right issue.

```
Guth, A. H., and P. J. Steinardt. "The Inflationary
     Universe." Scientific American 250.5 (1984):
     90-102.
```

If there is no separate issue number, provide the full date of publication:

```
Graham, Gordon. "The World on a Disk." Canadian
     Business 63 (May 1990): 72-75.
```

ARTICLE IN A POPULAR MAGAZINE.   Do not include volume and issue numbers even if they are given. Abbreviate all months except May, June, and July.

> Smolwe, Jill. "Enemies of the State." <u>Time</u> 8 May 1995:
>   58-68.

> "Hearty Baked Pasta." <u>Gourmet</u> Feb. 1994: 108+.

The "108+" indicates that the article is not printed on consecutive pages. In this entry the article appears on pages 108, 109, and 110 and then continues on pages 178 and 179.

ARTICLE IN A NEWSPAPER.   Document a newspaper title as it appears on the masthead, but omit any introductory article (*New York Times,* not *The New York Times*). Otherwise, the entry is similar to that of other periodicals.

> Blanton, Kimberly. "Study: NAFTA Hasn't Created Many
>   New Jobs." <u>Boston Globe</u> 4 Sep. 1995: 35-36.

REVIEW.   Document a review the way you would other articles, except include the phrase "Rev. of" (neither underlined nor enclosed in quotation marks), a comma, the word *by*, and the name of the author, editor, etc. (using the appropriate abbreviation if the work is by an editor or translator). Then give the title and publication information about the book being reviewed.

> McSherry, Bernadette. Rev. of <u>Restoration Justice on
>   Trial</u>, by Heinz Messmer and Hans-Uwe Otto. The
>   Netherlands: Kluwer, 1992. <u>Canadian Journal of
>   Criminology</u> 36.1 (Jan. 1994): 92-95.

Documenting Unpublished Papers or Speeches

In documenting an oral presentation, give the name of the speaker, the title of the presentation (in quotation marks), the meeting and sponsoring organization, the location, and the date. If the presentation has been published (perhaps as an article), give information about the published version.

> Poovey, Mary. "Speaking of the Body. A Discursive
>   Division of Labor in Mid-Victorian Britain."
>   Colloquium on Women, Science, and the Body:
>   Discourses and Representations. Society for the
>   Humanities, Cornell University, Ithaca. May 1987.

Documenting Interviews, Letters, and Other Personal Communication

Document letters and e-mail that you receive and personal interviews, telephone interviews, and unpublished letters as follows:

> Blair, Ray. Letter to the author. 15 Mar. 1996.
>
> Griffith, Jack. E-mail to the author. 4 Aug. 1996.
>
> Kaline, Al. Personal interview. 21 May 1993.
>
> Malone, Susan. Telephone interview. 25 July 1996.
>
> Meiers, Frank. Papers. Mary Powell Letter to Frank
>   Meiers. 2 Jan. 1997. Missouri State Historical
>   Society, Columbia.

If the interview or letter you are citing has been published, give information about the published version.

Documenting Electronic Sources

The newest and fastest growing sources of information in libraries today are electronic sources such as CD-ROMs and on-line data bases. If you cite material from an electronic source, your documentation in the Works Cited list will be similar to that used for printed sources.

However, an electronic version of an item that originally appeared in print may differ from the print version, and one version of an electronic source may differ from another. To help readers who want to use the same source that you have used, you need to identify as precisely as you can which electronic source you have used. Thus, in addition to the familiar information about authors, titles, publishers, and dates of publication of printed sources, you should also provide information about

❖ the medium of the source (CD-ROM, diskette, on-line, etc.)

❖ the vendor's name, if known (CompuServe, ERIC, Internet, Silver-Platter, UMI-Proquest, etc.)

❖ the date of electronic publication (for CD-ROMs and diskettes) or the date of access (for on-line sources)

Although each CD-ROM and on-line data base provides information that identifies its vendor's name and date of electronic publication, such information may be difficult to locate or unavailable in the version your library has provided. Some libraries make CD-ROMs available in their original format; others bundle several together into larger, more convenient data bases. Since local practice may vary from library to library, ask a librarian for the appropriate information if you are unable to find it in the source.

Here are ways to document major types of electronic sources.

PRINT SOURCE AVAILABLE IN ELECTRONIC FORM.   Many sources that appeared originally in print are now available in electronic form. If the electronic source you are using provides publication information for the printed source, begin your documentation with it, then provide the title of the electronic source (underlined), the publication medium (CD-ROM, diskette, on-line, etc.), and the electronic publication date.

> "Devil." <u>The Oxford English Dictionary</u>. 2nd ed. CD-ROM.
>   Oxford: Oxford UP, 1992.

> Kearney, Gretchen Warner, and Terrence J. Kearney.
>   "Transfer Student Expectations and Satisfaction:
>   Predictions for Academic Performance and
>   Persistence." Paper presented at the 19th Meeting
>   of the Association for the Study of Higher
>   Education. Tuscon: Nov. 10-13, 1994. <u>ERIC</u>. CD-ROM.
>   SilverPlatter. Mar. 1995.

> Montague, James. "TQM Reduces Problems and Stress."
>   <u>Business Credit</u> 97.2 (1995): 16. <u>ABI/INFO</u>. CD-ROM.
>   Feb. 1995.

```
U.S. Department of Commerce. Earnings by Occupation and
     Education: 1990 Census of Population and Housing.
     (Subject Summary Tape File SSTF 22A. United
     States--Albany-Schenectady-Troy NY MSA to
     Birmingham AL MSA). Washington: Bureau of Census,
     1990. CD-ROM. Oct. 1994.
```

DISKETTE. Document a diskette as you would a book. Just add the word *Diskette* after the title to indicate the medium of publication:

```
Lanham, Richard D. The Electronic Word: Democracy,
     Technology, and the Arts. Diskette. Chicago: U of
     Chicago P, 1993.

Thiesmeyer, Elaine C., and John E. Thiesmeyer. Editor:
     A System for Checking Usage, Mechanics,
     Vocabulary, and Structure. Vers. 5.0. Diskette.
     New York: Modern Language Association, 1994.
```

E-MAIL COMMUNICATION. Document personal e-mail as if it were a form of correspondence. Give the name of the writer, a description of the document, the name of its recipient, and the date of the document:

```
Burkette, Emily. E-mail to the author. 25 Jan. 1996.

Sansbury, Penny. "List of ITC Participants." E-mail to
     Les Pickett. 20 June 1996.
```

Using APA Documentation to Acknowledge Sources

Like MLA (Modern Language Assocation) documentation, APA (American Psychological Association) documentation uses in-text citations in the body of a paper or report that are linked to fuller information about the cited sources in an alphabetical list called References. APA documentation is used widely by researchers in the social and natural sciences. For complete coverage of current APA documentations as well as of the other scholarly, style, and format details that comprise "APA style," see the *Publication Manual of the American Psychological Association*, 4th edition (Washington: American Psychological Assocation, 1994).

APA in-text citations identify sources by a name and year. A reader sees a passage like the following and sees the name of the author or authors, the year of publication, and sometimes a page number or numbers:

```
          Louisiana farmers produce about 15 percent of the
U.S. rice crop (Johnson & Linscombe, 1988), and it is
important that the rice be kept dry in the high humid-
ity of the state. About a third of Louisiana's rice
growers use in-bin drying methods. However, Vermer and
Jacobsen point out that these drying methods must be
used carefully because rice is susceptible to damage
during handling and processing if it is dried in bins
at temperatures much above 38° C (1987, p. 80).
```

Author surnames may be in parentheses; the year of publication is usually in parentheses; page numbers are always in parentheses. A parenthetical citation falls inside the normal sentence punctuation. In parentheses, a comma separates the author name and the year. When page numbers are given, they are separated from the year by a comma.

The APA References list provides complete publication information so that readers can locate the works if they choose:

```
Johnson, L. E., & Linscombe,S. (1988). Outlook of
     Louisiana's Agriculture. Baton Rouge: Louisiana
     Cooperative Extension Service, Louisiana State
     University Agriculture Center.

Vermer, L. R., & Jacobsen, L. A. (1987). On-farm rice
     drying energy use. Applied Engineering in
     Agriculture, 3, 79-86.
```

APA In-Text Citations

The following examples illustrate the ways to use the APA's author-year method of citation in your essay or report. Place parenthetical citations at the end of the material taken from a specific source. If you do not mention the author's name in your discussion, give the author's surname, year of publication, and—if appropriate—the page number or numbers in parentheses.

CITING A WORK BY ONE AUTHOR.   When you refer to the work as a whole, place the author's surname and year of publication in parentheses:

```
Some students appear to be turned off by the expen-
sively produced admissions packages that they receive
from very exclusive schools (Desmond, 1996).
```

When you use the author's name as part of your sentence, cite only the year of publication and—when quoting directly, paraphrasing, or referring to a specific passage—the page number(s) in parentheses:

```
The reaction of William Desmond, a graduate of Loyola
High School in Baltimore, may be typical: "My euphoria
began to fade. I began to wonder about schools that
send out slick admission packages that cost $3 to mail"
(1996, p. 1).
```

CITING A WORK BY TWO AUTHORS.   Spell out *and* between the names of two authors in your sentence. In a parenthetical citation, use the ampersand (&) between the authors' names:

```
Briggs and Peat (1989) explain the new theories of
physics concerning synchronized chaos.
```

```
During the 1970s and 1980s, many scientists, mostly
physicists, developed theories of synchronized chaos
(Briggs & Peat, 1989).
```

CITING A WORK BY THREE, FOUR, OR FIVE AUTHORS.   Cite all the names the first time you refer to a work by three, four, or five authors. In subsequent references use the name of only the first author followed by "et al." (abbreviation for the Latin *et alia*, meaning "and others"; there is no period after "et," but there is after "al.").

<u>First Reference</u>

```
Crutchfield, Farmer, Packard, and Shaw (1985), four
pioneers in chaos theory, claim that finite precision
in measurements is inadequate.
```

<u>**Second Reference**</u>

```
Crutchfield et al. (1985) point out that it is impos-
sible to predict physical effects because of miniscule
gravitational forces.
```

CITING A WORK BY MORE THAN SIX AUTHORS. Use the name of the first author and "et al." for all citations. However, in the reference list provide the surnames and initials of each author (see the References list entry on pages 495–496).

```
Extensive surveys of students' opinions helped evaluate
the hypertext course (Beeman et al., 1987).
```

CITING A WORK BY A CORPORATE OR ORGANIZATIONAL AUTHOR. Cite the name of the corporation or organization as the author:

```
Brainstorming is becoming increasingly important in
solving managerial problems (Florida Power and Light
Company, 1989).
```

If the name is long and an abbreviated version is familiar or self-evident, you may use the abbreviation in subsequent citations. Otherwise, write it out each time. Since many readers would not recognize FP&LC as Florida Power and Light Company, it should be spelled out in subsequent citations. Use the corporate or organizational name as the first element in the References list entry (see the example on page 496).

CITING A WORK WHEN NO AUTHOR IS NAMED. When no individuals or groups are named as author of the work, use the title for in-text citations and as the first element in the References entry (see page 496).

```
California had the highest number of adult/adolescent and
pediatric AIDS cases (7,648) reported from August 1990
through July 1991 (HIV/AIDS surveillance, 1991, p. 4).
```

```
About 90 percent of the country's annual maize yield
(approximately 140,000 metric tons) is produced by
small scale farmers ("Guatemala agriculture," 1995).
```

CITING AUTHORS WITH THE SAME SURNAME.   When you cite works by two or more authors who have the same surname (Elizabeth Wright and Thomas Wright, for instance), use each author's first initial in all in-text citations to distinguish between the two:

> E. Wright has studied Franklin's many "firsts" in American business enterprises, including the first contract to print money for the state of Pennsylvania (1991, p. 148), but T. Wright says that by then Franklin was already wealthy from publishing the <u>Philadelphia Gazette</u> and the <u>Poor Richard's Almanacs</u> (1987, p. 17).

CITING TWO OR MORE AUTHORS WITHIN THE SAME PARENTHESES.   Cite several sources for the same idea or information by arranging them alphabetically by author names; separate the citations with semicolons:

> Several proponents of nuclear power have pointed to France's heavy reliance on nuclear energy (Donique, 1993; Freed & Watson, 1988; Millicent, 1992).

CITING TWO OR MORE WORKS BY THE SAME AUTHOR OR AUTHORS.   The work of an author or authors who have other works cited in the text is identified by the year:

> Francis Crick (1964) has theorized about protein molecules which he claims have several unusual properties.

If you want to cite two or more works by the same author in the same parenthetical citation, give the author's surname once, followed by the dates of publication arranged chronologically.

> Many prominent scholars and critics of jazz have written both on an individual artist and on the broader history of jazz (Brown, 1978, 1983; Giddens, 1981, 1985, 1988).

If you want to cite two or more of an author's works that have the same year of publication, use the alphabetical order of the titles to list the works in the References list, and then add *a* or *b* (and so on) after the year. In parenthetical references, use the year-letter combination:

> Bridgman (1955b) has emphasized that "science is what
> scientists do . . . there are as many scientific meth-
> ods as there are individual scientists" (p. 83).

CITING MULTIVOLUME WORKS.   Cite the author, year, and page num-bers(s). For multivolume works published in the same year, add *a* or *b* after the year to correspond to the reference list:

> "Thought without speech is inconceivable," asserted the
> philosopher Hannah Arendt (1978a, Vol. 1, p. 32).

CITING AN INDIRECT (SECONDARY) SOURCE.   If possible, you should quote from primary sources, not secondary ones. However, sometimes only a secondary source is available—for example:

> Macaulay's accuracy as an historian has been questioned
> because of his apparent overconfidence on all matters
> of historical judgment. Lord Melbourne is reported to
> have said that he wished he could be "as cocksure about
> anything as Macaulay is about everything" (as cited in
> Firth, 1938).

The citation leads the reader to the secondary source in the References list:

> Firth, C. R. (1938). <u>A commentary on Macaulay's History
> of England.</u> London: Frank Cass.

CITING INTERVIEWS, LETTERS, AND OTHER PERSONAL COMMUNICATIONS.   Since telephone conversations, interviews, and personal correspondence are not always included in the reference list, provide full information in the parenthetical citation:

> "Focus groups," according to Mary Powell, "can achieve
> excellent results in a very short period" (personal
> letter to F. Meiers, January 2, 1997).

APA References List

The References list at the end of the text includes every work cited, including all recoverable sources, such as interviews. Each work or source cited in your text must appear in the References list, and each entry in the References list must be cited in your text.

Figure 3.17 (page 492) illustrates the format for the References list.

Format Guidelines

❖ Start the reference list on a new page, continuing the pagination of the text.

❖ Center the heading *References* about 1 inch down from the top of the page.

❖ Double-space everything.

❖ For papers that will be typeset, begin each entry with a paragraph indent. For final manuscripts that will not be typeset, begin each entry flush with the left margin and indent any subsequent lines five to seven spaces from the left margin.

In addition, here are other practices to follow:

❖ Use the author's initials with his or her last name:

A. D. Santayana, not Andrew D. Santayana.

❖ List multiple authors in the order in which they appear on the title page of the book or in the byline of the article.

❖ Invert all authors' names:

Norwood, A. D., Sabino R. J., & Wallerstein, J.S.

❖ For edited books, place the editors' names in the author position, and enclose the abbreviation "Ed." or "Eds." in parentheses after the last editor.

❖ Capitalize only the first word and proper nouns of titles and subtitles:

Flashback: A brief history of film (for a book)

Communicating with Japan's leaders (for an article)

References

Bringa, T. (1995). Being Muslim in the Bosnian way: Identity and community in a central Bosnia village. Princeton: Princeton University Press.

Brzezinski, Z. (1995, August 7). After Srebrenica. New Republic, 213, 20-21.

Congress and Bosnia. (1995, December 15). The Washington Post, p. A24.

Donia, R. J. (1994). Bosnia and Hercegovina: A tradition betrayed. New York: Columbia University Press.

Glynn, P. (1993, April). Bosnia: Is it too late? Yes. Commentary, 99, 31-34.

Glynn, P. (1993, July). The age of Balkanization. Commentary, 96, 21-24.

Glynn, P. (1995, January 25). America's burden. New Republic, 208, 24+.

Lessons from Bosnia. (1993). Santa Monica, CA: Rand.

Marshall, T., & Scott, K. (1995, December 15). Pact shows Europe still looks to U.S. Los Angeles Times, p. A1.

Perlez, J. (1995, December 15). Bosnian Serb warriors are haunted in peace. New York Times, p. A1.

Silber, L. (1995). The death of Bosnia. New York: Penguin.

United States. Congress. Commission on Security and Cooperation in Europe. (1993). Implementation of the Helsinki accords: Hearing before the Commission on Security and Cooperation in Europe, One Hundred Third Congress, War Crimes and the Humanitarian Crisis in the Former Yugoslavia, January 25, 1992. Washington, DC: U.S. Government Printing Office.

Figure 3.17. References list in APA documentation style

(Note that unlike MLA style, APA style does not enclose titles of articles within quotation marks.)

- ❖ Capitalize the first word and other important words of titles of conference proceedings and of journals and magazines:

```
Japanese Journal of Experimental Social Psychology

Psychological Bulletin
```

- ❖ For books, include the city of publication, the publisher's name, and the date of publication:

```
Upper Saddle River, NJ: Prentice Hall, 1997.
```

—If the book is published outside the United States, add the name of the country. Also identify relatively unknown cities by state (not New York, NY, but certainly Bear Run, MT). Abbreviate states by their two-letter, capitalized abbreviations: AZ, CT, MN, TX, and so on.

—Give a shortened form of the publisher's name, ignoring *Co.*, *Inc.*, and the like, but spell out names of associations and *University* and *Press*: "Erlbaum" instead of "Lawrence Erlbaum Associates, Publishers"; "University of Texas Press" instead of the MLA-style "U of Texas P."

- ❖ Arrange the entries alphabetically by the surname of the author or editor. A work that has a corporation or organization as its author is alphabetized by the first word of the corporation or organization (excluding *A, An, The*).

- ❖ If there is more than one work by the same author, arrange them as follows:

—Single-author entries precede multiple-author entries:

```
Mandelbrot, B. (1982). The fractal geometry of
    nature. San Francisco: Freeman.
Mandelbrot, B. (1984). An interview. Omni, February
    5, 1984, 721.
```

Mandelbrot, B., Passoja, D., & Paullay, A. (1984). Fractal character of fracture surfaces of metals. Nature, 308, 721.

—References with the same first author and different second or third authors are arranged alphabetically by the last name of the second author, and so on.

Cleveland, W. S., Diaconis, P., & McGill, R. (1982). Variables on scatterplots look more highly correlated when the scales are increased. Science, 216, 1138-1141.

Cleveland, W. S., Harris, C. S., & McGill, R. (1982). Judgments of circle sizes on statistical maps. Journal of the American Statistical Association, 77, 541-547.

Cleveland, W. S. & McGill, R. (1986). An experiment in graphical perception. International Journal of Man-Machine Studies, 25, 491-500.

—References by the same author are arranged by year of publication, from the oldest to the most recent:

Smith, P. (1990). A joyful noise: A celebration of New Orleans music. Dallas: Taylor.

Smith, P. (1991). New Orleans Jazz Fest: A pictorial history. Gretna, LA: Pelican.

—References by the same author with the same publication date are arranged alphabetically by title (excluding *A, An, The*), and letters are added to the year to differentiate works for in-text citations:

Landow, G. P. (1987a). Context32: Using hypermedia to teach literature. In Proceedings of the 1987 IBM Academic Information Systems University AEP Conference. Milford, CT: IBM Academic Information Systems. 30-39.

Landow, G. P. (1987b). Relationally encoded links and the rhetoric of hypertext. Hypertext '87. Chapel Hill: University of North Carolina Press. 331-44.

Documenting Print Sources: Books

You can usually find most of the information you need to document a book on its title page and copyright page. The title page is commonly the work's first or second right-hand page; it lists the title, the author(s) or editor(s), and the publisher. The copyright page is on the reverse side of the title page; it names the copyright holder and the year of publication of the work.

BOOK BY ONE AUTHOR.   Provide the author's name, publication date, book title, and publication information (place and name of publisher). When the book has a subtitle, as does the following one, separate the main title and subtitle with a colon:

> Ikegami, E. (1995). <u>The taming of the samurai:
> Honorific individualism and the making of modern
> Japan.</u> Cambridge: Harvard University Press.

If the book has no apparent author, begin with its title:

> <u>ASAE standards</u> (35th ed.). (1988). St. Joseph, MI:
> American Society of Agricultural Engineers.

BOOK BY TWO TO SIX AUTHORS.   List the authors in the order in which they are listed on the title page:

> Ansolabehere, S., & Iyengar, S. (1996). <u>Going negative:
> How attack ads shrink and polarize the electorate.</u>
> New York: Free Press.

> Aronson, L. J., Harre, R., & Way, E. C. (1995). <u>Realism
> reserved: How scientific progress is possible.</u>
> Urbana: University of Illinois Press.

BOOK BY MORE THAN SIX AUTHORS.   List the authors in the order in which they are listed on the title page:

> Beeman, W. O., Anderson, K. T., Bader, G., Larkin,
> McClard, A. P., McQuillan, P., & Shields, M.
> (1987). <u>Intermedia: A case study of innovation in</u>

<u>higher education.</u> Providence, RI: Office of
Program Analysis, Institute for Research in
Information and Scholarship, Brown University.

BOOK OR ARTICLE BY CORPORATE OR ORGANIZATIONAL AUTHOR.   If a book's title page does not name a person as author or editor but does name a corporation, a commission, a committee, or some other organization, use the corporate or organizational name as "author." Give it as the first element in the References list entry, and use it as the author's name for in-text citations (for example, see page 488).

Florida Power and Light Company. (1987). <u>FPL quality
improvement program: QI story and techniques.</u>
Miami: Florida Power and Light Company.

Lloyd's of London. (1990). <u>Lloyd's ports of the world.</u>
Colchester, England: Lloyd's.

BOOK WHEN NO AUTHOR IS NAMED.   Move the title to the author position, before the publication date:

<u>Who's who in science and engineering, 1992-1993.</u>
(1992). Wilmette, IL: Marquis.

BOOK WITH EDITOR (ANTHOLOGY OR COMPILATION OF ESSAYS, ARTICLES, OR OTHER SHORT WORKS).   When a book names an editor but no author on the title page, place the editor's name in the author position, and enclose the abbreviation "Ed." or "Eds." in parentheses after the last editor's name.

Gouma-Peterson, T. (Ed.). (1992). <u>Breaking the rules:
Audrey Flack, a retrospective 1950-1990.</u> New York:
Abrams.

Canfield, J. D,, & Payne, D. C. (Eds.). (1995).
<u>Cultural readings of Restoration and Eighteenth-
Century theatre.</u> Athens: University of Georgia
Press.

BOOK WITH TRANSLATOR.   Place in parentheses the name of the translator between the book title and publication information, and use "trans." to indicate the person is the translator:

> Esteva-Fabregat, C. (1995). <u>Mestizaje in Ibero-America</u>
>   (J. Wheat, Trans.). Tucson: University of Arizona
>   Press.

MULTIVOLUME BOOK.   Indicate the volume number(s) in parentheses after the title of the work. If the title of the individual volume has a separate title, provide it, too:

> Arendt, H. (1978). <u>The life of the mind</u> (Vol. 1:
>   <u>Thinking</u>). New York: Harcourt.

BOOK IN OTHER THAN FIRST EDITION.   When documenting a book that notes on the title page that it is in a second or subsequent edition or a special edition (revised, for example), give the edition information in parentheses after the title of the book.

> Law, A. M., & Kelton, W. D. (1991). <u>Simulation modeling</u>
>   <u>and analysis</u> (2nd ed.). New York: McGraw-Hill.

> Chevigny, B. G. (1994). <u>The woman and the myth:</u>
>   <u>Margaret Fuller's life and writings</u> (rev. and
>   expanded ed.). Boston: Northeastern University
>   Press.

PART OF A BOOK.   In documenting specific parts of books, indicate as much information as necessary to pinpoint the reference:

> Hardison, O. B., Jr. (1989). Let's play architecture.
>   In <u>Disappearing through the skylight: Culture and</u>
>   <u>technology in the twentieth century</u> (pp. 107-20).
>   New York: Viking.

This entry describes a chapter from Hardison's book.

Holmblad, L. P., & Ostergaard, J. (1982). Control of a
cement kiln. In M. M. Gupta & E. Sanchez (Eds.),
<u>Fuzzy information and decision processes</u>
(pp. 389-99). New York: North-Holland.

This entry describes an article by Holmblad and Ostergaard in a collection of articles edited by Gupta and Sanchez.

Miyamato, S., Yasurobu, S. & Ihara, H. (1987). Predictive fuzzy control and its application to automatic train operation systems. In J. C. Bezdek
(Ed.), <u>Artificial intelligence and decision systems: Vol. 2. Analysis of fuzzy information</u> (pp.
59-72). N.p.: CRC Press. 59-72.

"N.p." stands for "no place." No place of publication is given in the book.

Oates, M. (1989). Textile Industry. In C. R. Wilson &
W. Ferris (Eds.), <u>Encyclopedia of southern culture</u>
(p. 57). Chapel Hill: University of North Carolina
Press.

This example illustrates an entry in an encyclopedia that is not arranged primarily by alphabetical order. Thus, the page number is included. When entries in a reference work are arranged alphabetically, the page number(s) may be omitted.

Millay, E. S. V. (1988). Oh, oh, you will be sorry for
that word! In <u>Collected sonnets</u> (rev. and enlarged
ed.) (p. 31). New York: Harpers.

The work documented is a poem from Edna St. Vincent Millay's collection of poetry.

Suhor, C. (1989). Foreword. In Crowley, S. <u>A teacher's</u>
<u>introduction to deconstruction</u> (pp. vii-viii).
Urbana: National Council of Teachers of English.

This entry describes a foreword written by Suhor in a book by Crowley.

ARTICLE IN A REFERENCE BOOK. Document an article in a reference book (such as an encyclopedia, dictionary, etc.) as you would a part of a book, as explained in the preceding items. Include the name of the author if the article is signed:

```
Kovacs, Bela A. (1992). In American men and women of
     science, 1992-1993 (18th ed.). (Vol. 4, p. 483).
     New Providence, NJ: Bowker.

Sheridan, T. P. (1993). Human-machine systems. In
     McGraw-Hill enclyclopedia of engineering (2nd ed.,
     pp. 546-50). New York: McGraw-Hill.
```

If the entry has no author, begin with the title of the article:

```
Applications software, evaluation. (1988). In
     Encyclopedia of microcomputers. (Vol. 1,
     pp. 222-35). New York: Dekker.
```

GOVERNMENT PUBLICATIONS. Document a government publication essentially the way you do a published book. If you can identify the document's author, begin with it. If you do not know the author, identify as the author the government agency that issued it. Give the publication date in parentheses. Underline the title. Then provide the place and name of the publisher. Federal publications available from the U.S. Government Printing Office should show it as the publisher.

```
U.S. General Services Administration. (1993, May).
     Applying technology to record systems: A media
     guide. Washington, DC: U.S. Government Printing
     Office.

Alabama Department of Industrial Relations. (1993,
     Jan.). Alabama occupational trends for 2005.
     Montgomery: Research and Statistics Division,
     Alabama Department of Industrial Relations.
```

UNPUBLISHED THESIS OR DISSERTATION. Document the author, date, and title of an unpublished thesis or dissertation as you would a book. Identify the work as an unpublished thesis or dissertation. Then give the names of the institution and the city. If the city may not be well known, also give the state.

> Guritino, P. (1988). <u>Moisture sorption of bagged grain stored under tropical conditions.</u> Unpublished master's thesis, Kansas State University, Manhattan.

> Berthnal, N. (1990). <u>Motherhood lost and found: The experience of becoming an adoptive mother to a foreign born child.</u> Unpublished doctoral dissertation, Union Institute, Cincinnati.

Documenting Print Sources: Articles in Periodicals

Periodicals are publications that appear regularly at fixed intervals—weekly, monthly, quarterly, and so on. Documentation is similar to that of books in that it includes the author's name, date of publication (in parentheses), title of the article (with only the first word of the title and of the subtitle and proper names capitalized), title of the periodical, and publication information such as volume number and page numbers. Note also that the title of the article is not underlined nor enclosed in quotation marks.

ARTICLE IN A JOURNAL WITH CONTINUOUS PAGINATION.   The pages of scholarly journals are usually numbered continuously through a single year. All you need to give to assure the reader gets the right issue is the volume number and the year (the year in parentheses immediately after the author's name).

> Knight, V. N. (1992). Zimbabwe: The politics of economic reform. <u>Current History, 91,</u> 219-23.

ARTICLE IN A JOURNAL THAT PAGES EACH ISSUE SEPARATELY.   For journals that begin each page on page 1, add the issue number (in parenthesis) after the volume number. The issue number is needed to asure that the reader will be able to get the right issue for a particular year.

> Guth, A. H., & Steinardt, P. J. (1984). The inflammatory universe. <u>Scientific American, 250</u>(5), 90-102.

Because this journal begins each issue on page 1, add the issue number in parentheses after the volume number: 250(5) stands for volume 250, issue 5.

ARTICLE IN A POPULAR MAGAZINE.   Give the date shown in the magazine: month for monthlies; month and day for weeklies. Give the volume number.

> Smolwe, J. (1995, May 8). Enemies of the state. <u>Time,</u>
>   <u>145,</u> 58-68.

If an article appears on discontinuous pages, give all page numbers, and separate the numbers with a comma.

> Hearty baked pasta. (1994, February). <u>Gourmet, 54,</u>
>   108-110, 178-79.

ARTICLE IN A NEWSPAPER.   Precede page numbers with *p.* or *pp.*:

> Blanton, K. (1995, September 4). Study: NAFTA hasn't
>   created many new jobs. <u>Boston Globe,</u> p. 35:2.

REVIEW.   If the review is untitled, make a statement in brackets that describes the item as a review, identifies the medium (a book, in this instance), and notes the title of the work reviewed:

> McSherry, B. (1994). [Review of the book <u>Restoration</u>
>   <u>justice on trial</u>]. <u>Canadian Journal of</u>
>   <u>Criminology, 36</u>(1), 92-95.

Documenting an Unpublished Paper or Speech

Give the month of the meeting if it is available.

> Poovey, M. (1987, May). Speaking of the body: A discur-
>   sive division of labor in mid-Vitorian Britain.
>   Paper presented at the Colloquium on Women,
>   Science, and the Body: Discourses and Represen-
>   tations, sponsored by the Society for the
>   Humanities, Cornell University, Ithaca.

Documenting Interviews, Letters, and Other Personal Communication

In APA style, because they do not provide recoverable data, personal communication such as letters and interviews are not included in the References list. Cite the source only in the text of your paper (for example, see page 490).

Documenting Electronic Sources

The newest and fastest growing sources of information in libraries today are electronic sources such as CD-ROMs and on-line data bases. If you cite material from an electronic source, your documentation in the References list will be similar to that used for printed sources. In fact, if the printed form and the electronic form of the material are the same, use the print form. However, if the print and electronic versions are not the same (or if you do not know), and you have used the electronic version, use the formats that follow.

PRINT SOURCE AVAILABLE IN ELECTRONIC FORM. Many sources that appeared originally in print are now available in electronic form. If the electronic source you are using provides publication for the printed source, begin your documentation with author and date of publication, then provide the title of the electronic source, the publication medium (CD-ROM, diskette, on-line, etc.), and the rest of the publication information.

Devil. (1992). <u>The Oxford English dictionary</u> (2nd ed.). [CD-ROM]. Oxford: Oxford University Press.

Kearney, G. W., & Kearney, T. J. (1995, March). Transfer student expectations and satisfaction: Predictions for academic performance and persistence. <u>ERIC</u> [CD-ROM]. Paper presented at the 19th meeting of the Association of Higher Education. Tuscon: November 10-13, 1994.

Montague, J. (1995, February). TQM reduces problems and stress. <u>Business Credit</u> [ABI/INFO] [CD-ROM], <u>97</u>(2), 16.

U.S. Department of Commerce. (1994). <u>Earnings by occupation and education: 1990 census of population</u>

```
and housing [CD-ROM]. Subject Summary Tape File
SSTF 22A. United States—Albany-Schednectady-Troy
NY MSA to Birmingham AL MSA. Wasington, DC:
Bureau of Census.
```

Diskette

Document a diskette as you would a book. Just add the word *Diskette* after the title to indicate the medium of publication:

```
Lanham, R. D. (1993). The electronic word: Democracy,
technology, and the arts [Diskette]. Chicago:
University of Chicago Press.
```

Computer Software

```
Thiesmeyer, E. C., & Thiesmeyer, J. E. (1990). Editor:
A system for checking usage, mechanics, vocabu-
lary, and structure (Version 4.0) [Computer soft-
ware]. New York: Modern Language Association.
```

E-Mail Communication

Electronic correspondence, such as e-mail messages, is cited as personal communication in the text (see page 490).

PART FOUR

STRATEGIES FOR WRITING AND READING

► INTRODUCTION

Arranged in alphabetical order for quick access, these entries range from allusion to transitions. Each entry is intended to stand alone as a short, self-sufficient unit providing information that will be useful to you in thinking about and discussing a specific aspect of writing or reading. In no sense do we assume that this section offers a complete survey of all the concepts and strategies that are important to becoming a good writer or reader. It would take a much larger book than this one to do that, for the number of helpful and interesting things to know about these matters is practically limitless. Here we have concentrated only on what we consider some of the most important. You can read these entries in any sequence that serves your purpose or interest.

► You might want to refer to a particular entry while you are reading other parts of this book. Whenever a term is used that is to be further discussed elsewhere, it appears in boldface type and is repeated in the margin, where you will also find a page reference for the more in-depth discussion. When you encounter an unfamiliar term or a term that you want explained further that is marked by boldface type, you will know that you can find additional information about it in this section.

► You might scan through this section until you locate an entry that discusses a principle or a strategy with which you are working. At times, as you write, you will be particularly aware of the need to refresh your memory or to learn more about a particular principle or strategy; you might need an overview of a concept, want information on some small detail, or wish to see some examples of the principle applied. The more you learn about a concept or strategy, the more intelligently you can use it to make the best choices among the available means for achieving an end.

► You might want to browse through this section until you discover an entry that deals with a concept about which you are interested in learning more. An entry can be selected at random and read leisurely as a mini-essay, not just used as a quick reference while you grapple with your writing.

Each entry will help you explore a specific rhetorical concept, but one that is related to several others. While every entry is useful in itself, its greater value lies in its potential to be related to several others. It is a starting point for further reading and thinking. The concepts and approaches in one entry can be useful in understanding others. The next entry that you read will probably depend on the associative trail that the first entry leads you to. In short, in using this section of the book, you can create your own pathway and move in any direction you want.

ALLUSION

▼

An allusion is a brief reference to a person, place, or event outside the text that adds richness and depth to a statement in the text. We have all noticed writers who have used allusions. T. S. Eliot's "The Love Song of J. Alfred Prufrock," for instance, is loaded with classical and Shakespearean allusions. At a pivotal moment in the poem, Prufrock reaches the decision not to assert himself, expressed in this line:

> No! I am not Prince Hamlet, nor was I meant to be.

Eliot uses the allusion to Shakespeare's Prince Hamlet to bring into the text the associations and knowledge of a much larger idea about the capacity or incapacity to act forcefully—perhaps even heroically. Prufrock is a man divided, like Hamlet, between melancholia, tenderness, and hesitation on the one hand and assertive, perhaps even violent, action on the other. Unlike Hamlet, Prufrock lacks "the strength to force the moment to its crisis" and will not "dare disturb the universe." In a brief statement, the allusion compresses the complexity of Hamlet's character with that of Prufrock's. The allusion refers directly to Hamlet and indirectly to Hamlet's initial procrastination and eventual violent action. It also helps create great irony: Prufrock, unable to assert himself in a social situation, is contrasted to Hamlet, who is finally able to avenge his father's murder.

When writers use allusions, they are revealing their own education and learning—the information and ideas that have influenced them and have informed their thinking and feelings. Allusions come from philosophy, science, art, music, literature, history, and they are specific to particular cultures. Native users of American English, like others whose backgrounds are informed by Judaism and Christianity, are influenced greatly by the Bible—perhaps more than by any other book or group of books. They frequently draw upon the Bible for stirring quotations, vivid images, anecdotes, and illustrative examples. References to Lot's wife, the Tower of Babel, and Armageddon, as well as state-ments such as "weighed in the balances and found wanting" and "handwriting on the wall," are only a few such allusions. Most writers are not classical scholars, but they have enough knowledge of myths, classical history, and classical literature to enable them to allude to Achilles' heel, the Trojan horse, Titans, Helen of Troy, nemesis, and the tasks of Hercules or Sisyphus. Is there an experienced writer who has not used, or at least thought of using, this statement: "The subject, like ancient Gaul, is divided into three parts" (an allusion to Julius Caesar's *Gallic War*)? Americans also have their own domestic reservoir of potential allusions in events such as Custer's last stand and Watergate; places such as Peoria, Mudville, and Valley Forge; and persons or char-acters such as Betsy Ross, Huck Finn, Babe Ruth, Huey Long, Dr. Strangelove, Oliver North, and Madonna.

New allusions are created all the time. We used to say that a political leader had met his or her Waterloo. We are now likely to say that he or she has met his or her Chappaquiddick or Watergate. Rambo has replaced Hercules; Marilyn Monroe has succeeded Aphrodite.

When writers use allusions, they expect their readers to under-stand the allusions without explanation. They assume a shared body of knowledge and values between themselves and their readers and expect their readers to fill in the necessary details. When an allusion works, it taps into associations that readers already have; conveys a lot in only a few words by connecting, associating, or comparing one thing with another; and creates the pleasure of recognition. An allusion to Machiavelli or to Machiavellian strategies requires readers to associ-ate what is being said with the manipulations of power explained in Niccolo Machiavelli's *The Prince*—a treatise on political power pub-lished in 1513. If the allusion is not recognized by readers, then their understanding of the text is limited. The desired effect will not only be lost, but readers may be baffled by the statement or even resentful that the writer is showing off his or her learning at their expense. So always ask yourself whether your readers will know enough about the allusion to get the associations you want to evoke.

AMPLIFICATION (DEVELOPMENT)

Almost all writing can be regarded as amplification, which is the addi-tion to or expansion of a point or an idea for clarification or proof. Writers are constantly involved in the painstaking, deliberate process of trying to anticipate when to leave a point or an idea undeveloped and when and how to develop it more fully.

Amplification strengthens writing three ways:

* It offers evidence to support assertions and arguments.

* It helps clarify any point that might not be immediately understood.

* It helps shape a thought, providing additional information that allows readers to adjust to an idea that might be unfamiliar or controversial.

Amplifying to Provide Support

Ideas, claims, statements, and assertions that are important require close examination and should not be made without some support. Probably 95 percent of the time, a point or an idea needs to be amplified. Although some readers grasp ideas quickly and easily, the writer cannot stay on a general, abstract level for very long. Otherwise, readers will be left with only a vague impression of what is meant. Even relatively simple ideas may be abstract or vague in readers' minds. Take a look at the following, very general, statement:

> The teeth of the rhinoceros are unlike the teeth of any other animal.

Unless this sentence is amplified, readers will be asking questions like these: What is so different about their teeth? Is it their size? Shape? Number? Location? Color? Durability? Use? Why is it important to know this? Amplification gives the details that translate the abstract and the general into the concrete and more accessible world of the senses.

Amplification helps us see. Here is the first line of John Keats's poem "The Eve of St. Agnes":

> St. Agnes' Eve—Ah, bitter chill it was!

The concrete language and the sensory details in the rest of the stanza build up a series of cold images and amplify the opening line to help readers see and feel the cold and to demonstrate the truth of the assertion that it was bitterly cold. (St. Agnes' Eve is January 20—according to folklore the coldest day of the year.)

St. Agnes' Eve—Ah, bitter chill it was!
The owl, for all his feathers, was a-cold;
The hare limp'd trembling through the frozen grass,
And silent was the flock in woolly fold:
Numb were the Beadsman's fingers, while he told
His rosary, and while his frosted breath,
Like pious incense from a censer old
Seemed taking flight for heaven, without a death,
Past the sweet Virgin's picture, while his prayer he saith.

Notice in the following passage by Carol Bly, an essayist and fiction writer living in the small town of Madison, Minnesota, how the second paragraph amplifies and extends the idea of the first paragraph. The descriptive details of the second paragraph call up specific images that define more sharply what would have remained only a general impression had Bly continued to stay on the relatively abstract level of the first paragraph:

> It is sometimes mistakenly thought by city people that grown-ups don't love snow. They think only children who haven't got to shovel it love snow, or only people like the von Furstenburgs and their friends who get to go skiing in exotic places and will never backslope a roadside in their lives: that is a mistake. The fact is that most country or small-town Minnesotans love snow. They relish snow in large inconvenient storms; they like the excesses of it, they like the threat of it, the endless work of it, the glamour of it.
>
> Before a storm, Madison is full of people excitedly laying in food stocks for the three-day blow. People lay in rather celebratory food, too. Organic-food parents get chocolate for the children; weight watchers lay in macaroni and Sara Lee cakes; recently-converted vegetarians backslide to T-bones. People hang around the large Super-Valu window and keep a tough squinty-eyed watch on the storm progress with a lot of gruff, sensible observations (just like Houston Control talking to the moon, very much on top of it all) like "Ja, we need this for spring moisture . . ." or "Ja, it doesn't look like letting up at all . . ." or "Ja, you can see where it's beginning to drift up behind the VFW." The plain pleasure of it is scarcely hidden.

> —"Great Snows," in *Letters from the Country*
> (New York: HarperCollins, 1981), pp. 40–41.

Even texts that seem to consist of only narrative or descriptive details turn out, on closer examination, to be passages that move back and forth between general and specific statements. Here is a very brief passage in which each statement amplifies the statements that precede it:

> I locked the door, kept the world out; I vegetated, hibernated, remained in stasis, idled. No telephones, no television, no radio. Alone with the presence in the room. Who? Me, my psyche, the Shadow-Beast.

> —Gloria Anzaldua, *Borderlands/La Frontera;*
> *The New Mestiza* (San Francisco: Spinsters/Aunt
> Lute, 1987), p. 44.

Almost any idea or assertion that a writer wishes to convey represents an invitation for amplification so that both the writer and the reader can think it through, examine it more closely, and come to know more fully what it is or means. Follow the development of the passage below, in which Louis L'Amour, widely known as a best-selling author of historical fiction of the American West, begins his reflections on the role of reading in learning.

> This is not the story of how I came to be in Singapore. That will be told elsewhere. This is a story of an adventure in education, pursued not under the best of conditions. The idea of education has been so tied to schools, universities, and professors that many assume there is no other way, but education is available to anyone within reach of a library, a post office, or even a newsstand.
>
> Today you can buy the *Dialogues* of Plato for less than you would spend on a fifth of whiskey, or Gibbon's *Decline and Fall of the Roman Empire* for the price of a cheap shirt. You can buy a fair beginning of an education in any bookstore with a good stock of paperback books for less than you would spend on a week's supply of gasoline.
>
> Often I hear people say they do not have time to read. That's absolute nonsense. In one year during which I kept that kind of record, I read twenty-five books while waiting for people. In offices, applying for jobs, waiting to see a dentist, waiting in a restaurant for friends, many such places. I read on buses, trains, and planes. If one really wants to learn, one has to decide what is important. Spending an evening on the town? Attending a ball game? Or learning something that can be with you your life long?
>
> Byron's *Don Juan* I read on an Arab dhow sailing north from Aden up the Red Sea to Port Tewfik on the Suez Canal.

Boswell's *Life of Johnson* I read while broke and on the beach in San Pedro. In Singapore, I came upon a copy of *The Annals and Antiquities of Rajahstan* by James Tod. It was in the library of a sort of YMCA for seamen, the name of which I've forgotten but which any British sailor of the time would remember, for the British had established them in many ports, for sailors ashore.

—*Education of a Wandering Man* (New York: Bantam, 1989), pp. 1–2.

The passage consists mostly of examples, details, facts and figures, qualifications, illustrations, and even questions that start bringing an idea to life and lead to a deeper and more extensive understanding of L'Amour's concept of education. Well before the end of the passage the reader knows that an education is available to anyone who chooses to read, that books are easily accessible, and that time is available for reading. The amplification also captures some of the notion that books bring excitement even when the reader is tired, lonely, and nearly broke.

As the Keats, Bly, Anzaldua, and L'Amour passages illustrate, amplification gets us deeper into a subject, primarily by providing details for clarifying and exploring ideas, for translating experience into richly specific feelings and images, for validating—even celebrating—the experience and knowledge embodied in ideas, and for arguing the truth claims of a proposition. Amplification can be almost anything and everything—facts, statistics, examples, anecdotes, comparisons, and restatements of those facts, statistics, examples, anecdotes, and comparisons. A text becomes meaningful primarily in terms of the details and repitition used to make it interesting and believable.

An underdeveloped passage that lacks the kind of amplification illustrated in the passages cited above reads like this:

Hardly a week goes by without some new example of attempts to enforce conformity on campus. At the California State University at Northridge, an offer by the Carl's Jr. fast-food chain to install a branch in the newly expanded bookstore was rejected last May. To Stephen Balch, Northridge's decision was outrageously intolerant.

How long would you keep reading something like this? Not long, we bet. The passage is boring and difficult to read. It is difficult to read because it is difficult to understand. It is difficult to understand because there is so little amplification. The lack of amplification makes the passage seem superficial, general, and disconnected. Readers yearn for the details that will make things clear and connected. They do not know why the fast-food chain's offer was rejected, why Balch believed the university's decision was objectionable, or even who Balch is. Too much information is missing for this passage to be interesting, clear, meaningful, or convincing.

A writer who does not amplify takes it for granted that readers will understand what has been written. But it is usually a mistake to assume that readers can fill in the details for themselves, for usually they are less familiar with the subject than the writer. The odds are overwhelmingly against readers understanding everything that is said, even when the writer thinks the text is absolutely clear and precise. All writers fail to amplify at times, particularly when they think that a meaning is as obvious to a reader as it is to them. But it is the writer's responsibility to provide the details that will give meaning to his or her ideas. To remain satisfied with broad generalizations is to run the risk of being or appearing to be a lazy thinker and an irresponsible writer.

Here's how the passage above on enforcing conformity on campus actually was written for *Time* magazine:

> Hardly a week goes by without some new example of attempts to enforce conformity on campus. At the California State University at Northridge, an offer by the Carl's Jr. fast-food chain to install a branch in the newly expanded bookstore was rejected last May. The reason was not the quality or price of the chow but student and faculty objections to the conservative views of the chain's owner, Carl Karcher, who financially supports antiabortion groups such as the National Right to Life Action League. To Stephen Balch, Northridge's decision was outrageously intolerant. "You're not talking about Karcher doing anything on campus," he says. "You're not even talking about anything the fast-food chain did as a corporation. You're talking about something its owner did, certainly something he has a right to do, and something that a public institution should certainly not penalize people for."
>
> —John Elson, "Busybodies: New Puritans,"
> *Time* (August 12, 1991): 20.

The differences between the two versions are obvious, but the significance of these differences is especially important. The third, fifth, sixth, and seventh sentences clarify what is not stated and what is not already understood by most readers of the first version. The specific issues and proof are now there—who rejected the offer and why, and why Balch denounced the rejection.

However, these sentences illustrate only one level of amplification. There is another level of amplification within the third sentence, in which the writer amplifies several points further by identifying the views as conservative, giving the owner's name, labeling the support as financial, and providing an example of the kind of antiabortion group. This extensive amplification makes almost everything immediately clear. Probably the only question that most readers have after reading this paragraph is the identity of Stephen Balch. Extending the context provides the answer, for earlier in the text Balch is identified as president "of the National Association of Scholars, based in Princeton, N.J., which is dedicated to fighting lockstep leftism in academia." So the version that was published in *Time* does include all the information necessary for readers to understand the text.

Amplifying to Clarify a Point

The most important function of amplification is to provide information that makes ideas concrete, clear, and believable. What may not be obvious, however, is how much to amplify. Certainly, writers must provide evidence to support their assertions. But how does the writer know when enough is enough, when readers understand? There are no simple answers. It is not easy to strike a balance between providing enough information but not too much.

Writers too often assume their readers know as much about the subject as they do. But when writers and readers do not share a common context, frame of reference, or basic assumptions, then more background information, more context building, and more explanation are required. Writers who are knowledgeable about their subjects legitimately fear being tedious and prolix. But for the most part, their fear is unfounded. Up to a point, readers do not object to receiving familiar and sometimes redundant information. Often they are not able to recall immediately the information they already possess, and amplification triggers their memory and brings prior knowledge to the conscious level, as the writers do in this passage:

> All computers, from the smallest to the largest, rely on a special class of mathematical logic developed in the 1850s by British mathematician George Boole. Named for its inventor, Boolean logic is a system for reducing a problem to a series of

true or false propositions, which can be represented by zeros and ones. A problem-solver can then work out a solution with what is called binary mathematics.

—Stephen Bennett, Robert Hirshon, and Porter G. Randall, "Computers," in *The Almanac of Science and Technology: What's New and What's Known*, ed. Richard Golob and Eric Brus (Boston: Harcourt Brace Jovanovich, 1990), p. 229.

There are several points to be made about amplification in this passage. First, the degree of redundancy is very high; there is a lot of information overlap that most readers are not even aware of. But this kind of redundancy can improve comprehension. Examples of redundancies that most readers are unaware of occur in the first sentence: the plurality of the subject is conveyed by the adjective *all*, the *-s* ending on *computers*, and the plural verb form *rely*. The phrase "from the smallest to the largest" is also redundant information added to "All computers." In case readers miss any of the plural markers, several other markers convey the same information. This kind of amplification makes information more readable for all readers.

Later in the passage the amplification is more noticeably redundant. For instance, readers are informed that Boolean logic is named for its inventor, George Boole. Much less obvious, but still redundant, are the identification of Boole as a British mathematician and the point that Boole developed the system in the 1850s. But most readers of the encyclopedia-like publication from which this passage is taken would not perceive this information as overly redundant and might even regard much of it as new and helpful. One reason they read these kinds of publications is to acquire such basic information as is contained in the details of the amplification. They are the readers for whom amplification pays off well. But even more knowledgeable readers will not find the redundancies objectionable. They will probably be pleased to have their knowledge confirmed and will appreciate what new information they glean from the passage. For example, many readers will know that naming something after its creator, inventor, or discoverer is a common practice, but they may not know that Boole was a British mathematician or when he developed the system.

What about fully informed persons who already know everything in the passage—all about Boolean logic, binary mathematics, and George Boole? They are not the intended readers of this text. The kind of information in a text tells a lot about whom the writer has in mind as his or her intended audience.

Amplifying to Allow Readers to Adjust to a New Idea

Amplification also helps readers link information (especially assertions and their support) and adjust to new ideas or ideas that they find controversial. Notice how Gilbert Highet accomplishes this in the following paragraph, in which he asserts that Winston Churchill's *The Second World War* is autobiography, not history:

> Sir Winston Churchill's six-volume *The Second World War* is really an autobiographical record. He himself says it is "the story as I knew and experienced it as Prime Minister of Defence of Great Britain." Therefore it cannot be called anything like a complete history of the war. For example, Churchill tells the story of one of the crucial events of this century—the reduction of Japan to impotence and surrender by intensive bombardment culminating in what he calls the "casting" of two atomic bombs—in only eight pages, while a greater amount of wordage is devoted to a reprint of a broadcast he made to British listeners on VE day.
>
> —*Talents and Geniuses* (New York: Oxford, 1957), pp. 256–57.

Highet, professor of classics at Columbia University and chief literary critic for *Harper's* during his lifetime, begins his amplification by quoting Churchill in the second sentence, then restates his claim in the third sentence before adding a specific example to illustrate his claim. The second and third sentences allow the reader to remain briefly on a relatively abstract level before moving to the particular detail that Highet hopes is convincing. Those middle two sentences give the reader a bit more time to consider the claim before receiving the most specific evidence. Thus, amplification is an important tactic for pacing information for readers.

Ultimately, the strength of a text depends upon its amplification. Amplification is not just making a text longer or larger, but making it clearer. Development is not just adding more words, but enlarging or elaborating on a point to make it easier to understand. Virtually every idea is made more concrete, precise, and accessible by adding specific details. No less an authority than Cicero, the great Roman rhetorician who flourished just before the time of Christ, gives an excellent rationale for amplification in Book III of his *De Oratore:*

Our orator will find great value in amplifying his statements, since audiences perceive this technique as an effort to clarify confusing matters.

> —quoted in Donovan J. Ochs, "Cicero's Classical Theory," in *A Synoptic History of Classical Rhetoric*, ed. James J. Murphy (Davis, CA: Hermagoras Press, 1983), p. 124.

Because no one strategy of amplification is sure to work, writers and speakers make their ideas accessible in a number of ways: **analogy**, **classification**, **comparison/contrast**, **description**, **exemplification**, and **narration**. These are only a few of the strategies for amplification, and they do not limit or determine the many possibilities of development and expansion.

ANALOGY

An analogy is a special kind of comparison that shows ways in which two essentially different things are similar in important respects. It is a comparison between fundamentally different objects or concepts for the purpose of explaining or clarifying the less familiar one.

Any new idea, and certainly any new way of thinking, develops in the context of existing habits of thought. For a new idea to be meaningful to readers, it must fit into what they already know. Thus, writers must be able to explain new information or obscure concepts in terms of what their readers already know. An analogy can be effective in constructing a bridge from existing knowledge to new knowledge, from the old to the new, from the familiar to the unfamiliar.

Using Analogies to Clarify Difficult or Unfamiliar Subject Matter

Analogies are a primary means of explanation and are especially useful in helping readers to visualize the function, size, or structure of unfamiliar objects and to understand complex processes and concepts. They accomplish this by showing their similarities to familiar objects, processes, and concepts. Visual analogies, especially those explaining concepts of shape, are commonly based on such things as Roman and

Greek alphabetic letters (C-clamp, I-beam, Delta wing), anatomical parts (saw tooth, bottle neck, elbow joint), or other well-known objects (butterfly nut, kangaroo rat, kidney bean). Bicycle enthusiasts talk about brake shoes, drivetrains, eyelets, saddle seats, front forks, fork blades, fork crowns, gear teeth, spoke nipples, lock rings, mushroom clamps, and so forth—all parts of a bicycle that are named according to what they look like or, as in the case of brake shoes, what they used to look like. Many well-known places are known by their shape—the Bermuda Triangle, the Round Table, the Oval Office, the Mekong Delta, the Oklahoma Panhandle. Most such analogies consist of only a word or two and are so common that writers are not necessarily aware that they use them. They write of "mining" the ocean for minerals, of "skimming" profits from gambling casinos, and of certain forms of life being "high on the food chain." It is almost second nature now to call certain computer program features "windows," "desktops," "menus," and "scrapbooks." So don't think of an analogy as an ornament of style used to make writing and speech colorful or as something that is added to content. It is a way of thinking, and even the most ordinary language is saturated with word analogies.

Sometimes an analogy consists of a sentence, which might illuminate a difficult or new concept, as in "The finish of the automotive paint is orange peel," or clarify a strange sight, as in this sentence by Dale Peterson and Jane Goodall:

> The roots of some tropical forest trees grow high and wide,
> becoming large triangles of wood at the base, looking like fins
> of a rocket or buttresses of a cathedral.
>
> —*Visions of Caliban: On Chimpanzees and
> People* (Boston: Houghton Mifflin, 1993), p. 7.

There are also longer analogies such as the following one by Victor Hugo in *Les Misérables*, which uses a familiar object, the capital letter *A*, to describe the battlefield at Waterloo. The analogy provides a general visual impression that makes it easier to relate the details.

> Those who wish to form a distinct idea of the battle of
> Waterloo need only imagine a capital A laid on the ground.
> The left leg of the A is the Nivelles road, the right one the
> Genappe road, while the string of the A is the broken way
> running from Ohain to Braine l'Alleud. The top of the A
> is Mont St. Jean, where Wellington is; the left lower point is

Hougomont, where Reille is with Jerome Bonaparte; the right lower point is la Belle Alliance, where Napoleon is. A little below the point where the string of the A meets and cuts the right leg, is La Haye Sainte; and in the center of this string is the exact spot where the battle was concluded. . . .

The triangle comprised at the top of the A, between the two legs and the string, is the plateau of Mont St. Jean; the dispute for this plateau was the whole battle.

—*Les Misérables*, vol. II, book I (New York: Heritage, 1938), pp. 12–13.

Hugo's comparison of the battlefield (the unfamiliar subject being discussed) to the shape of the capital letter *A* (the familiar object that it is being compared to) gives readers something to grasp by comparing the unfamiliar terrain with a shape they can easily imagine, helping them understand the movements of military units during the battle.

Effective analogies must fulfill three requirements.

▶ Analogies should explain a complex or unfamiliar concept in terms of one that is simpler or more familiar to the reader. It would not do to compare something to a colony of ants or to the flow of water through a pipe unless the reader or listener were familiar with the ways of ants or water pipes. It would be explaining the unknown in terms of yet another unknown. The very reason for using analogy is to make the unfamiliar more easily understood by comparing it to the familiar.

▶ Analogies should be developed by detailing the points of similarity. In what ways is a communal society (the concept to be explained) like an ant colony? Its function? Its organization? Its development? How is the flow of electricity through a wire (the concept to be explained) similar to the flow of water through a pipe? In its principle of operation? In the method of measuring the flow? The more characteristics an analogy can reveal, the better the analogy.

▶ Analogies must not mislead by suggesting inappropriate or irrelevant features. Comparing an object to a triangle (a two-dimensional object) is misleading and confusing if the object looks more like a pyramid (a three-dimensional object). For example, the earth is not just circular (two-dimensional feature). It is spherical (three-dimensional feature)— spherical with a slight depression at each of its poles. Good analogies make it easier to understand the features or aspects of the subject under discussion. Bad analogies mislead by ignoring important features or by implying features or aspects that the object of the analogy does not have.

Using Analogies in Argument

In argument, analogies are sometimes used to persuade readers that things not normally thought of as similar are, in fact, similar, and that inferences can be based on those similarities. Handled well, an analogy can link ideas together (sometimes in surprising and pleasing ways), can build parallels between concepts, and can appeal to the reader's common sense and emotions. David Elkind, an eminent psychologist, uses an analogy in the fourth sentence (italicized) of the following passage to achieve exactly these effects in summing up his argument and clarifying his thesis that the education of children should be designed to meet their special needs as children rather than to hurry them into maturity:

> All children have, vis-a-vis adults, special needs—intellectual, social, and emotional. Children do not learn, think, or feel in the same way as adults. To ignore these differences, to treat children as adults, is really not democratic or egalitarian. *If we ignore the needs of children, we are behaving just as if we denied Hispanic and Indian children bilingual programs, or denied the handicapped their ramps and guideposts.* In truth, the recognition of a group's special needs and accommodation to those needs are the only true ways to insure equality and true equal opportunity.
>
> —*The Hurried Child: Growing Up Too Soon*, rev. ed. (Reading, MA: Addison-Wesley, 1988), p. 22.

A more extended analogy is developed by Malcolm X, the African-American civil rights leader of the early 1960s, as he argues that blacks who attempt to identify with whites undergo a painful experience both physically and psychologically. In *The Autobiography of Malcolm X*, written with the help of Alex Haley, he explains how, as a teenager, he used chemicals to redden and straighten his hair in order to conform to white standards of beauty. It was not until later in life that he realized that the process of "conking" his hair was analogous to self-degradation.

> My first view in the mirror blotted out the hurting. I'd seen some pretty conks, but when it's the first time on

your *own* head, the transformation, after the lifetime of kinks, is staggering.

The mirror reflected Shorty behind me. We both were grinning and sweating. And on top of my head was this thick, smooth sheen of shining red hair—real red—as straight as any white man's.

How ridiculous I was! Stupid enough to stand there simply lost in admiration of my hair now looking "white," reflected in the mirror of Shorty's room. I vowed I'd never again be without a conk, and I never was for many years.

This was my first really big step toward self-degradation: when I endured all of that pain, literally burning my flesh to have it look like a white man's hair. I had joined that multitude of Negro men and women in America who are brainwashed into believing that black people are "inferior"—and white people "superior"—that they will even violate and mutilate their God-created bodies to try to look "pretty" by white standards.

> —*The Autobiography of Malcolm X*
> (New York: Grove, 1966), p. 54.

Handled poorly, argument by analogy can be risky because it involves an inference. When an analogy is not logically sound—that is, when it leads to false reasoning or is based on features that resemble each other only in slight or remote ways—the argument is open to easy attack. For example, an argument based on analogy might assert that what happened once is likely to happen again, as follows: The graduate we hired from Ajax College did well in our accounting department; therefore, we should hire another Ajax College graduate. Experience, of course, should be considered in making decisions; people with similar training or education are very likely to be able to perform similarly in similar situations. But, in general, analogical resemblances are not adequate proof in argument. A decision to hire another Ajax College graduate because an earlier one succeeded on the job is as faulty as a decision *not* to hire another Ajax College graduate because an earlier one did poorly on the job. Such an argument is based upon hasty generalization (one example of failure or success does not predict future failure or success) and non sequitur reasoning (it does not necessarily follow that because one Ajax College graduate succeeded, another will too, or vice versa). Here is another analogy by Malcolm X, which is a little less successful than the one illustrated earlier. In a speech in which he criticized the participation of whites in the march on Washington, D.C., in 1962 for black civil rights, Malcolm X claims that whites took over the leadership of the demonstration and installed more moderate leaders, consequently diluting its grassroots nature:

> It's like when you've got some coffee that's too black, which means it's too strong. What do you do? You integrate it with cream, you make it weak. But if you pour too much cream in it, you won't even know you ever had coffee.
>
> —"Message to the Grass Roots," in *Malcolm X Speaks*, ed. George Breitman (New York: Grove Weidenfeld, 1990), p. 16.

The cream-in-the-coffee image is striking and perhaps appropriately suggestive. But as argument, the analogy is neither apt or informative, because the items being compared are so different. The analogy by itself does not represent evidence that integration weakens a civil rights demonstration. If the context required a more logical argument, Malcolm X would have to offer more evidence that appointing a white millionaire as cosponsor of the march and inviting Walter Reuther, a white labor union leader, and several white clergymen to speak at the rally damaged the political movement. We grasp Malcolm X's point, but the analogy is not convincing logic.

Analogies can be useful in argument. But they can also be the weakest link in an argument, so be wary of overly pat analogies. If an opponent is able to demonstrate that an analogy is strained or forced, hanging together by the slimmest of threads, so to speak, or that the analogy leads to a hasty generalization, then the argument is likely to collapse like a house of cards.

CAUSE AND EFFECT

When writers write about cause-and-effect relationships, they link events, attempting to show that one thing leads to another. They attempt to explain why something is happening or has happened (why there has been an increase in the number of accidents in petrochemical plants in the United States, for instance), or to predict what is likely to happen (the federal government may develop regulations to establish safer plant procedures), or both.

Generally, cause-and-effect organization is straightforward. The writer looks back to determine why something is happening or has happened or looks into the future to what its likely consequences will be, or both. The writer may begin with the cause and then proceed to the effect or effects, or the writer may begin with the effect and work back to the cause or causes. The following three samples represent common cause-and-effect patterns.

Analyzing Causes

One pattern focuses on causes—on describing something that is taking place now, or has taken place, and explaining its probable causes. In *Forecast 2000*, George Gallup, Jr., president of the well-known Gallup Poll public opinion research firm, claims that the existence of the traditional American family is threatened and proceeds to identify several cultural trends that may be causing the change.

> Twenty years ago, the typical American family was depicted as a man and woman who were married to each other and who produced children (usually two) and lived happily ever after. This was the pattern that young people expected to follow in order to become "full" or "normal" members of society. Of course, some people have always chosen a different route— remaining single, taking many partners, or living with a member of their own sex. But they were always considered somewhat odd, and outside the social order of the traditional family.
>
> In the last two decades, this picture has changed dramatically. In addition to the proliferation of single people through divorce, we also have these developments:
>
> ❖ Gay men and women have petitioned the courts for the right to marry each other and to adopt children. . . .
>
> ❖ Many heterosexual single adults have been permitted to adopt children and set up single-parent families. . . .
>
> ❖ Some women have deliberately chosen to bear children out of wedlock and raise them alone. In the past, many of these children would have been given up for adoption, but no longer. . . .
>
> ❖ In a recent Gallup Youth Poll, 64 percent of the teenagers questioned said that they hoped their lives would be different from those of their parents. This included having more money, pursuing a different kind of profession, living in a different area, having more free time—and staying single longer.

Most surveys show increasing numbers of unmarried couples living together. Also, there are periodic reports of experiments in communal living, "open marriages," and other such arrangements. . . .

❖ Increasing numbers of married couples are choosing to remain childless. . . .

So clearly, a situation has arisen during the last twenty years in which traditional values are no longer as important. Also, a wide variety of alternatives to the traditional family have arisen. Individuals may feel that old-fashioned marriage is just one of the many options.

—George Gallup, Jr., with William Proctor,
"The Faltering Family," in *Forecast 2000*
(New York: Morrow, 1984), pp. 115–16.

Analyzing Effects

A second pattern of cause and effect focuses on probable effects, as Norman Cousins does in explaining the consequences of administering pain suppressants to professional athletes:

Professional athletes are sometimes severely disadvantaged by trainers whose job it is to keep them in action. The more famous the athlete, the greater the risk that he or she may be subjected to extreme medical measures when injury strikes. The star baseball pitcher whose arm is sore because of a torn muscle or tissue damage may need sustained rest more than anything else. But this team is battling for a place in the World Series; so the trainer or team doctor, called upon to work his magic, reaches for a strong dose of butazolidine or other powerful pain suppressants. Presto, the pain disappears! The pitcher takes his place on the mound and does superbly. That could be the last game, however, in which he is able to throw the ball with full strength. The drugs didn't repair the torn muscle or cause the damaged tissue to heal. What they did was to mask the pain, enabling the pitcher to throw hard, further damaging the torn muscle. Little wonder that so many star athletes are cut down in their prime, more the victims of overzealous treatment of their injuries than of the injuries themselves.

—*Anatomy of an Illness* (New York:
Bantam, 1981), pp. 92–93.

Analyzing Cause and Effect

A third pattern of cause and effect combines the first two. In the following passage, Joan Didion discusses the causes and effects of migraines:

> Almost anything can trigger a specific attack of migraine: stress, allergy, fatigue, an abrupt change in barometric pressure, a contretemps over a parking ticket. A flashing light. A fire drill. One inherits, of course, only the predisposition. In other words I spent yesterday in bed with a headache not merely because of my bad attitudes, unpleasant tempers and wrongthink, but because both my grandmothers had migraine, my father has migraine and my mother has migraine.
>
> No one knows precisely what it is that is inherited. The chemistry of migraine, however, seems to have some connection with the nerve hormone named serotonin, which is naturally present in the brain. The amount of serotonin in the blood falls sharply at the onset of migraine. . . .
>
> Once an attack is under way . . . no drug touches it. Migraine gives some people mild hallucinations, temporarily blinds others, shows up not only as a headache but as a gastrointestinal disturbance, a painful sensitivity to all sensory stimuli, an abrupt overpowering fatigue, a strokelike aphasia, and a crippling inability to make even the most routine connections. When I am in a migraine aura (for some people the aura lasts fifteen minutes, for others several hours), I will drive through red lights, lose the house keys, spill whatever I am holding, lose the ability to focus my eyes or frame coherent sentences, and generally give the appearance of being on drugs, or drunk. The actual headache, when it comes, brings with it chills, sweating, nausea, a debility that seems to stretch the very limits of endurance. That no one dies of migraine seems, to someone deep into an attack, an ambiguous blessing.

> —"In Bed," in *The White Album* (New York: Simon & Schuster, 1979), pp. 170–71.

Using Cause and Effect Effectively

Cause-and-effect relationships can be difficult to establish with certainty for several reasons, and you need to know what to do and what to watch out for when writing causal analysis. Here are two suggestions.

▶ Know the basic pattern on which you are focusing—cause or effect or both. When attempting to explain what caused something, you deal with a relatively known situation (the rate of accidents in petro-chemical plants in the United States) but must research, analyze, and interpret a less well-known past (the age of the equipment in these plants, the level of training of employees, the financial condition of the industry, the level of production goals, and so forth) to determine the probable cause or causes of the present situation. When attempting to explain what will likely happen in the future as a result of a present situation, you deal with a relatively known situation but speculate on an unknown future (Will the petrochemical industry, which at present is allowed to set acceptable toxicity levels and plant safety procedures, develop more stringent standards, or will the federal government establish tougher standards and shift the responsibility of monitoring compliance to the Occupational Safety and Health Administration?). Obviously, these two patterns can combine when you are attempting to explain both causes and effects.

▶ Avoid the faulty conclusion known as the post hoc fallacy. Even when you believe you have accounted for probable causes and effects, there is always the possibility that some other, yet undiscovered, cause or causes exist or that some other unpredicted effect or effects will occur. For example, perhaps flaws in the design of new processing equipment are contributing significantly to the increased number of accidents. Perhaps the rate of accidents is not increasing, but there is better and more thorough reporting of them. If the latter is the case, perhaps no immediate corrective action is called for.

Cause-and-efffect relationships are usually involved and complex, so avoid jumping to conclusions from just a few facts or slim evidence. The most common type of faulty conclusion involving cause-and-effect relationships is the one known as the post hoc fallacy, a mistake that many of us make from time to time. This is a conclusion based on the assumption that if one event follows another, the second event is caused by the first. (Did the Reagan administration's move in the early 1980s to get big government off the back of big business lead to the petrochemical industry, instead of OSHA, setting toxicity levels and safe plant procedures? Did the era of leveraged buyouts in the early 1980s cause companies to incur massive debts in an attempt to protect themselves from hostile takeovers? Did cost-cutting practices lead to using inadequately trained personnel, to using aging equip-ment that should have been replaced, and to making other poor man-agement decisions?)

Just because event B follows event A, that is not sufficient reason to conclude that A caused B. Proving a causal relationship requires evidence other than an association in time. However, despite the difficulties in analyzing causality, you constantly connect events in cause-and-effect relationships. Everybody assumes that events have causes and that events have consequences (effects).

CLASSIFICATION
▼

The ability to perceive resemblances that allow us to group similar things together is fundamental to our shaping a meaningful world. It is not surprising, then, that much writing uses classification—a systematic form of thinking in which the writer identifies a topic, arranges the information about the topic into distinct groups or classes for convenience and order, and then explains each group or class in detail. When it is necessary, these groups can be subdivided into smaller categories.

Classification helps specify and label groups and relate them to one another, as Dale Peterson and Jane Goodall do in this passage that distinguishes three kinds of hunters they have encountered:

> There seem to be three categories of hunter in West Africa. Almost every rural person, I have been told, is a casual hunter, using, for example, simple snares to catch rats and squirrels. And villages usually have their own specialist hunters, one or more people who are good hunters and provide for the village. Peter the Little Hunter belongs to this category. But there are also professional market hunters, who will supply meat for restaurants or for companies that truck bushmeat into the urban areas.
>
> —*Visions of Caliban: On Chimpanzees and People* (Boston: Houghton Mifflin, 1993), p. 64.

Classification can be rigorous, complete, and detailed, as shown in the following three-paragraph passage that describes three different systems for financing public education in the United States. Notice how the writers introduce the classification by mentioning that there are three types of systems and then devote a paragraph to each.

States use three types of school finance systems, the oldest and most prevalent being the foundation plan. States employing foundation plans establish a dollar level of per pupil expenditure that is guaranteed to all districts taxing a rate greater than or equal to some state-specified minimum rate. Districts wishing to spend above the minimal level may do so, although this places poor districts at a disadvantage. Some foundation plans have been criticized for setting the minimum funding level too low.

A second system of school finance is a district power-equalizing plan. Under such plans, states finance matching grants to ensure that poor districts may spend as much for education as if they had tax bases equivalent to those of wealthier districts. State-matching rates are tied directly to the fiscal capacity of school districts. Equivalent percentage tax rates will raise the same amount of revenue in both poor and wealthier districts, since the state supplements poor districts.

Some states, including Maine, Minnesota, Missouri, Montana, Texas, and Utah, have adopted a hybrid of the foundation and district power-equalizing plans. In these mixed systems, matching funds to locally raised revenues is applied by the state up to the foundation level of spending, but not beyond.

—Marcia Lynn Whicker and Raymond A.
Moore, *Making America Competitive: Policies for
a Global Future* (New York: Praeger, 1988), p. 71.

Some classifications are introduced by a direct statement that lists the different categories before each is discussed, as in this discussion of types of bicycle storage bags:

Bags carried directly on the bike are of three kinds: saddle bags, handlebar bags and frame bags. The saddle bag . . . is so universally used in Britain that one wonders why it has not found its way to the US in a comparable quality and variety. It is attached to the back of the saddle. That is no problem on a leather model with carrying eyelets, while other saddle types may require the installation of a special clamp. . . . It is also possible to install a handlebar bag, which is more widely available in the US, behind the seat post by means of a clamping bracket sold under the name Seat Post Thing.

Saddle bags exist in various sizes, ranging all the way from 10 liters, which is barely enough for the absolute essentials, to

30 liters (that's more than a cubic foot). The latter is big enough for a weekend trip if you don't go camping. A large saddle bag, especially if it is used on a bike with a relatively low saddle, should be supported by means of some kind of rack or bracket to keep it off the rear wheel and the rear brake. It should have side pockets for small items and straps on the top to carry your rain gear. Before buying such a bag, look at it very critically and ascertain that it is properly supported and will neither interfere with your movements nor drag on the rear wheel or the brake.

Handlebar bags are unreasonably popular in the US and France, though I would put them at the bottom of my list of suitable bags. All right for carrying small items to which you want frequent access along the way, especially if it is of such a design that it can be easily removed from the bike. The only satisfactory models are those that are supported at the top by a bracket that fits on the handlebars, while the bottom of the bag is held down with elastic cords, preferably to the front fork-ends. A few external pockets and a transparent map compartment are helpful. Preferably it should open towards the rider. When buying this kind of bag, make sure it does not interfere with steering, braking or lighting. A special version of the handlebar bag is available to carry a camera and photographic accessories.

The frame bag . . . is a rare bird indeed. World travellers, who have to carry as much as possible, may find a use for a bag like that, in addition to every other bag that can be mounted on the bike. Trapezoidally shaped and tied between the frame tubes, it must be packed compactly to avoid its swelling to a thickness that interferes with the movement of your legs.

—Rob Van der Plas, *The Bicycle Touring Manual*, rev. ed. (San Francisco: Bicycle Books, 1988), pp. 74–75.

The first sentence of the first paragraph sets up the classification by identifying the three types of bags. The rest of the first paragraph and the second paragraph deal with saddlebags. The third paragraph focuses on handlebar bags. The fourth considers frame bags. The classification is ordered from the most familiar and common kind of bag, the saddle bag, to the least familiar, the frame bag. As you can see, once writers lay out a classification, they can use it as a framework for a clear and well-organized presentation.

Using Classification Effectively

Keep in mind these three important principles when using classification to organize a presentation.

▶ Use only one basis of classification at a time. For example, the classification of saddle bags, handlebar bags, and frame bags is logical and consistent and lends itself readily as a basis for comparison. But the classification of saddle bags, handlebar bags, frame bags, synthetic-coated bags, and zipper bags is unworkable because the last two types are not parallel with the first three but may be subtypes of them.

▶ Base the classification on a single feature that produces groups that are significant, and explain similarities or differences that are worth thinking about. For instance, classifying automobiles by their value is important to prospective buyers and to tax assessors (the value of the automobile determines the license fee). Classifying automobiles by color would not be important to tax assessors, but it might be to car buyers and to the persons who have to purchase the paint for the automobile manufacturer.

▶ Make sure the classification is complete. That is, the number of types, kinds, or classes should equal the whole topic. The classification of bicycle bags that attach directly to the bicycle is complete. If any of these types of bags were omitted, the classification would be incomplete.

COHERENCE

▼

In a coherent text the ideas are linked together so that they follow logically one after another. Unless there is some reason for surprising the reader, every sentence should seem to grow naturally out of the preceding one and lead normally into the next one. Coherence is what makes it easy for readers to read sentence after sentence, paragraph after paragraph.

Coherence in a Text

There are several ways to create coherence in a text:

❖ Give prominence to the main topic or subject of the text,

- Organize the text into a pattern that is easy to follow,

- Use transitions that show the relationship of one part of the text to another and signal major logical shifts, and

- Relate new information to information you have presented earlier or that the reader already knows.

▶ Perhaps the most basic strategy for establishing coherence in a text is to give prominence to its topic or subject. The frequency with which a topic appears cues readers to its importance, which in turn suggests that all information in the passage is related to that topic. In the following passage by Susan Orlean, the Bucklin Opera House in Elkhart, Indiana, is the main topic. Since it is the most prominent item in the passage, it persists as the subject of most sentences. It or its synonyms are the subject of six of the seven sentences: sentence 1, *Bucklin*; sentence 2, *The Bucklin Opera House;* sentence 3, *the opera house;* sentence 4, *the Bucklin;* sentence 5, *the building;* and sentence 6, *it.* The repetition of this concept and its prominent subject position create a chain of subjects that keeps the focus on the old opera house, makes it easy to know what the passage is about, and helps predict how the information in subsequent sentences is likely to connect to the information already given in preceding sentences.

> Bucklin is the biggest lot downtown. The Bucklin Opera House, an imposing rococo stone structure built in 1884, used to stand on the site. In its day, the opera house was probably the swankiest recreational facility in town. After burlesque and vaudeville went out of fashion, the Bucklin showed movies, and then the movies moved to the mall. No other use of the building cropped up. Eventually, it fell into complete disrepair and everyone gave up on it, so it was torn down. Some people in Elkhart consider the incident a shame, but as you might expect in a town of avid drivers, many others consider the parking lot a fine thing to have acquired in the deal.
>
> — "Cruising: Elkhart, Indiana," *Saturday Night*
> (New York: Knopf, 1990), p. 8.

▶ Organizing text into a recognizable pattern is another basic strategy for establishing coherence. The particular pattern used is relatively unimportant, but it is important to use some sequence that will hold together the ideas and sentences of the passage and that will be recognized by your readers. Readers can absorb new information quickly if it comes to them in an easily recognizable pattern. One of the most useful patterns is to arrange information from general to specific. As illustrated in the following passage, using specific examples (**exemplification**) is one of the most convincing means of supporting a generalization or abstract statement. This pattern directly provides evidence to back up the writer's assertion in the opening sentence, which is the **topic sentence** of the paragraph.

EXEMPLIFICATION, PAGE 574

TOPIC SENTENCE, PAGE 672

> Perhaps the most dramatic type of instinctive learning is imprinting. Young birds such as chickens, goslings, and ducklings show an inherited pattern of following, and normally follow their mother. In his famous study on geese, Konrad Lorenz got broods of newly hatched goslings to treat him as a mother figure and to follow him. Indeed, young goslings can imprint on almost anything that moves, including objects such as balloons. After a period of imprinting of only fifteen to thirty minutes, the young birds recognize and approach the moving object when they are exposed to it as long as several hours later.
>
> —Rupert Sheldrake, "Animal Memory," in
> *The Presence of the Past: Morphic Resonance
> and the Habits of Nature* (New York:
> Vintage, 1988), p. 172.

Another useful pattern is chronology, used by Susan Orlean in the passage quoted earlier to give a brief history of the Bucklin Opera House in Elkhart, Indiana.

When there is no topic sentence or obvious organizational pattern, there is often a need to combine the pattern with a hierarchical order, giving an overall view of the whole before providing additional details. Orlean does this in the following description of the chapel of the Bowery Mission in lower Manhattan:

> We got up and moved together into the chapel, and took seats in the back with the rest of the program men. The Bowery Mission chapel is a long, narrow room faced with rough, beige stone. It has many rows of wooden pews, a high, arching ceiling, a simple altar, a piano, and an organ. It seems to be unconnected, in both architecture and ambience, to the harshly lit dining rooms and the rest of the building. The pews on the right side of the chapel were filled with men who had been waiting out on the sidewalk. One or two of them had

fallen asleep, apparently just seconds after sitting down. Two women were seated in the front pew; one of them was pregnant and was missing one of her front teeth. The pews on the left side of the chapel were being saved for the Mennonites, who walked in after a moment and filed silently into their seats.

—"Praying: Lower East Side, New York, New York," in *Saturday Night* (New York: Knopf, 1990), p. 168.

One strategy that helps this passage cohere is the hierarchical network that presents the description in such a way that it helps build an image in the reader's mind. The details are not presented in a helter-skelter manner but are arranged so that the movement is from large features to more particular ones. And Orlean is in control of the hierarchy. After establishing her physical point of view, she first provides an overview of the chapel (the shape of the room, the design of the walls and ceiling, the style of the altar) before focusing on the pews and the persons sitting in them. Finally, she adds details about some of the individuals (men already sleeping and a pregnant woman with a front tooth missing). The hierarchy enables readers to follow Orlean's description easily—understanding clearly and quickly what the chapel looks like, how the pews are arranged, and which persons are the most interesting to her. Hierarchical networks that link details, such as Orlean employs in her description of the chapel, are among the most valuable cohesive strategies.

▶ Seldom is arrangement of information enough to achieve coherence; explicit logical connectors are also necessary. **Transitions** are im-

TRANSITIONS, PAGE 676

portant to coherence because they signal explicitly the relationships among ideas and details. Readers are able to follow the history of the Bucklin Opera House easily because of the transitional phrases "in its day," "after burlesque and vaudeville went out of fashion," "and then the movies moved," and "Eventually." The passage, organized chronologically, proceeds in an even clearer and more obvious direction because these phrases tie the sentences together and highlight the sequence.

All details are important, but, as we have already seen in the description of the Bowery Mission chapel, usually the more general features or large concepts are explained first, then the more specific and smaller ones. The following passage begins with the main idea, then moves to a specific example, then proceeds to a detailed analysis of the example. The paragraph is structured to create the movement. The writer reveals this structure and movement by using transitions every time he moves from one idea to another. The transitions are in bold type.

> In **other** films, such as *The Left-Handed Gun, Bonnie and Clyde*, and *Little Big Man*, [Arthur] Penn created a version of the western or the gangster film in which traditional meanings were inverted, **but** the effect was tragic rather than humorous. In *Little Big Man,* **for example**, the conventional western opposition between Indian and pioneers serves as the basis for the plot, which embodies two of the most powerful western myths, the Indian captivity and the massacre. **However**, the conventional renderings of these myths pit the humanely civilizing thrust of the pioneers against the savage ferocity and eroticism of the Indians and thereby justify the conquest of the West. Penn reverses these implications. In his film it is the Indians who are humane and civilized, while the pioneers are violent, corrupt, sexually repressed, and madly ambitious. **By the end, when** Custer's cavalry rides forward to attack the Indian villages, our sympathies are all with the Indians. **From this perspective**, the conquest of the West is mythologized from the triumph of civilization into a historical tragedy of the destruction of a rich and vital human culture.
>
> —John G. Cawelti, "*Chinatown* and Generic Transformation in Recent American Films," in *Film Theory and Criticism,* 3rd ed., ed. Gerald Mast and Marshall Cohen (New York: Oxford, 1985), p. 515.

As the passage demonstrates, transitions help the reader understand how the ideas within the paragraph are related.

▶ Another means of tying sentences and ideas together is to apply what discourse analysts call the given-new contract. This principle presents new information by connecting it with information that the reader already knows, either from familiarity with the topic (due to experience or education) or from information given in preceding sentences or paragraphs. (We decided to go to sleep *early. By nine o'clock,* although it was not yet dark, all the lights were off, and we were in bed.) In turn, readers will be able to relate any new information to what they already know. Thus, there is always a familiar context or old information (the given) that makes the new information more easily accessible.

The given-new order always adds new information by tying it to information given in previous statements. The first sentence of a passage may contain all new information. Subsequent sentences will probably have a combination of given and new information. In a series of sentences, the information is arranged so that most sentences begin with information that is tied to previous statements and move toward newer, less familiar information at the end.

To see the given-new contract in action, look again at the Susan Orlean passages about the Bucklin Opera House and the Bowery Mission chapel. In discussing the Bucklin parking lot, Orlean establishes in the first sentence that the topic is the Bucklin parking lot. The topic of the second sentence, "The Bucklin Opera House," is given information tied to previous information—the subject of the first sentence, "Bucklin." The new information in the second sentence is that the opera house "used to stand on the site." In the third sentence the given information is "the opera house," a substitution for the subjects of the first two sentences; the new information is that the opera house was a swanky recreational facility. This, in turn, sets up the burlesque, vaudeville, and movies as the given information in the fourth sentence. In the fourth sentence the new information is that the movies have moved to the mall. In the fifth sentence the given information is the subject, "it," which refers to the vacant building; the new information is that the building remained vacant after the movies were no longer shown there. In the sixth sentence the new information is that the building was demolished. And so the sentences go in the passage, one growing out of the other, with the new information being accompanied by at least some of the old information already given in previous statements. Once mentioned, the new information becomes given information, and additional information can be linked to it. Every sentence in the passage begins where the preceding one leaves off.

Orlean's description of the Bowery Mission chapel is arranged in a similar given-new chain of sentences. Each sentence begins with a subject that repeats information from the previous sentences or has been anticipated by information in the previous sentences. Any new information is gradually added in the remainder of the sentence.

To summarize, here are the ways of achieving coherence within passages:

❖ state the topic explicitly—often in a topic sentence;

❖ organize text according to appropriate patterns;

❖ use transitions to signal the relationships among ideas and sentences;

❖ introduce new information in the context of familiar information (the given-new contract).

These are also important methods of establishing coherence in even longer passages of text.

Coherence Within Longer Passages

Just as the elements within a short span of text must be joined together effectively, so in a longer passage the major sections must be organized so that one section leads smoothly into another. Here we consider three strategies for achieving coherence within longer passages:

FORECASTING STATEMENTS,
PAGE 580

❖ arrange the sections in a logical sequence;

❖ use **forecasting statements** to present an overview of the main topics or ideas in a passage;

❖ use grammatical parallelism to emphasize the parallelism of thought in a passage.

▶ Arranging the sections in a logical sequence is one of the most natural ways to achieve coherence. As we have seen with shorter texts, passages that are organized in some recognizable pattern—whether by topic, chronology, or space—are easier to understand and to remember. Regardless of pattern, the first topic should lead to the second topic, the second to the third, and so forth. Writers often use explicit topic sentences and transitions to connect the sections and indicate different directions the topic takes. In the following passage, Maria L. Muniz, a naturalized American citizen, describes her increasing sense of personal and cultural loss as she grew up in the United States separated from her extended family and her native culture. Since the content is strongly related to time, Muniz puts the paragraphs in a time sequence.

> And as I listened to this man talk of the Cuban situation, I began to remember how as a little girl I would wake up crying because I had dreamed of my aunts and grandmothers and I missed them. I remembered my mother's trembling voice and the sad look on her face whenever she spoke to her mother over the phone. I thought of the many letters and photographs

that somehow were always lost in transit. And as the conversation continued, I began to remember how difficult it often was to grow up Latina in an American world.

It meant going to kindergarten knowing little English. I'd been in this country only a few months and although I understood a good deal of what was said to me, I could not express myself very well. On the first day of school I remember one little girl's saying to the teacher: "But how can we play with her? She's so stupid she can't even talk!" I felt so helpless because inside I was crying, "Don't you know I can understand everything you're saying?" But I did not have words for my thoughts and my inability to communicate terrified me.

As I grew a little older, Latina meant being automatically relegated to the slowest reading classes in school. By now my English was fluent, but the teachers would always assume I was somewhat illiterate or slow. I recall one teacher's amazement at discovering I could read and write just as well as her American pupils. Her incredulity astounded me. As a child, I began to realize that Latina would always mean proving I was as good as the others. As I grew older, it became a matter of pride to prove I was better than the others.

As an adult I have come to terms with these memories and they don't hurt as much. I don't look or sound very Cuban. I don't speak with an accent and my English is far better than my Spanish. I am beginning my career and look forward to the many possibilities ahead of me.

—"Back, But Not Home," *New York Times,*
13 July 1979, sec. A, p. 25.

Each paragraph begins with a topic sentence and with references to Muniz's age. Major shifts at the end of the first, third, and last paragraphs are marked by additional references to time. Although this logical sequence should be apparent to readers, Muniz emphasizes the sequence by using explicit transitions.

▶ As a writer, you can reinforce coherence by using **forecasting statements**. By the time you have revised a passage, you have probably decided to arrange your content in a specific sequence. By providing a forecasting statement at the beginning of the passage that identifies the topics or ideas and the order in which they are to be taken up in the passage, you focus tightly on the upcoming information and make it easier for readers to understand the passage. The chief characteristic of

FORECASTING STATEMENTS, PAGE 580

passages that contain forecasting statements is that they predict what is to follow. Thus, readers and listeners are able to anticipate how the passage is organized.

Sometimes the forecasting statement is scarcely noticeable as a preview of the coming topics until readers become aware of the ideas unfolding in the order established at the beginning. But as readers recognize the thread of continuity that has been provided, they begin to sense the wholeness of the passage. Elizabeth Gray Vining, the author of several novels and biographies, creates an effective brief overview of the details that will follow in this passage from her autobiography, *Being Seventy.*

> There are two basically different ways of approaching what is so mincingly called the Later Years: the stick-it-out-in-the-world policy, and the duck-into-safety policy. The first one sounds so much more gallant, the second slightly craven.
>
> If you have a family, sons and daughters or devoted nieces and nephews, to step in and take responsibility if you fall in the bathroom and break your hip, then you can afford to live dangerously. If you are, as I am, entirely alone, I think you at least examine the second alternative.
>
> I have gone so far as to sign up as a "Founder" of Kendal, the Quaker Retirement Community now being built in Chester County near Longwood Gardens. I have paid half of the entrance fee for a one-bedroom apartment. I can still withdraw in the year that remains before it will be finished.
>
> —*Being Seventy: The Measure of a Year* (New York: Viking, 1978), pp. 29–30.

In these three paragraphs, Vining identifies in broad terms two ways of approaching the challenges of old age, then devotes a paragraph to each way.

Vining is fairly subtle in cuing the reader to the progression of thought. At other times, writers use more explicit forecasting statements. Below is an excerpt from Colin Fletcher's classic guide to backpacking, *The Complete Walker III,* in which he clearly informs his readers that he is going to discuss four types of backpacks.

> Once you decide to stay out overnight or longer you'll find you must carry a genuine house on your back.
>
> A few years ago that house was virtually always a pack with a large and clearly visible tubular aluminum frame as its central feature: the kind of pack now called "external-frame." But soon after the last edition of this book appeared, so did successful

"internal-frame packs." They begat "travel packs." And now "ultralight packs" have arrived. So we need some definitions.

—*The Complete Walker III* (New York: Knopf, 1989), pp. 101–102.

As readers read the last sentence of this opening, they anticipate that in just a few seconds they will be provided more specific information about each backpack in the order given. It would be a major mistake to present the information in a sequence other than the one forecast. Fletcher knows better than to make such a mistake. Following is the rest of the passage. Notice that Fletcher reinforces the topical order by arranging the illustrations in the same sequence given in the prose sentence and uses italics to highlight the key words at the beginning of each section. These strategies clearly display the coherence of the passage.

External-frame packs evolved from the old wooden-frame Yukon packboards, and although aluminum tubing replaced the much heavier wood, their structure remained essentially unchanged: a roughly rectangular frame with a bag attached to one side and a harness to the other. Down the years variations have visited the frames (including a few departures from aluminum), the bags have matured (some to the brink of senility) and harnesses have grown far more sophisticated and efficient. But the E-frame's essential architecture endures.

Internal-frame packs evolved from long, soft, frameless, back-snuggling mountaineering packs that hampered a climber's free movement and delicate balance as little as the load permitted and had no protuberances to be damaged by

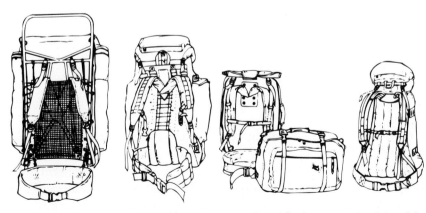

External-frame   Internal-frame   Travel Pack   Ultralightweight

or to interfere with the pack's being dragged up rockfaces—but which rode imperfectly and were abominably hot on the back. Then somebody inserted a rudimentary frame inside the pack bag to hold its forward surface just clear of the wearer's back yet still follow the back's contours. Today the frames remain rudimentary. Mostly, they consist of two flattened but curving aluminum stays arranged either in X form or running parallel up and down the back. Either arrangement radically improves the pack's ride and also holds it clear of your back so that cooling air can circulate—while retaining at least some of a mountaineering pack's clean-lined, nonsnagging qualities. Suspension systems on the best current I-frame packs are even more sophisticated and efficient than on equivalent E-frames.

Travel bags evolved from I-frames in response to the growing popularity of "adventure travel." The travelers' needs range wide. People planning backpack treks in distant places want something that will do the job on the trail but can without suffering or causing damage be slung hard and often into cab or bus and will even withstand the ravages of the human and mechanical gorillas who handle airplane baggage. At the other extreme are those "adventurers" who stride out for exotic, mildly roughing-it trips all over the world: their prime concern is luggage they can load without tears on dhow or camel or spaceship and can conveniently hump on their backs around airports or even along short trails. Intermediate demands abound. So we now face a continuous spectrum of devices ranging from near-expedition I-frame packs to modified suitcases.

Ultralightweight packs germinated with the New Wave. All therefore pare ounces to the practical limit, or beyond. Most are enlarged but gossamer day packs, with simple suspension systems and some back-contouring stiffener, such as a foam pad. But an emerging variation is a standard I-frame model shorn and abraded toward ethereality. At a guess, another wide spectrum of choices is about to materialize. Lightweight fanny packs form a subgenre.

—*The Complete Walker III*, pp. 102–103.

▶ Another method of creating coherence—and giving the coherence greater visibility—is to keep equivalent statements parallel. Parallel construction means putting statements with similar or identical functions into similar or identical forms. For instance, Muniz gives similar grammatical structure to most of the sentences in the passage quoted on pages 536–537 in order to underscore the parallel thoughts.

You can also use parallelism to strengthen longer passages by linking paragraphs together with obvious repetition of structure and words in the topic sentences. In the following series of paragraphs, Marie Winn, who writes frequently on the subject of children and family life, uses several facts and examples to support her contention that childhood in America has in recent years undergone some disturbing changes. Her use of parallelism in the opening sentence of each paragraph not only makes apparent that the paragraphs are dealing with the same topic (childhood) but also makes even more emphatic her views on various aspects of the topic (the joys of childhood, the limits of childhood, the image of childhood).

Something has happened to the joys of childhood. The child of a generation ago, observes the satirical magazine *National Lampoon,* spent his typical Sunday afternoon "climbing around a construction site, jumping off a garage roof, and onto an old sofa, having a crabapple war, mowing the lawn." The agenda for today's child, however, reads: "Sleep late, watch TV, tennis lesson, go to shopping mall and buy albums and new screen for bong, play electronic WW II, watch TV, get high." The bulging pockets of the child of the past are itemized: "knife, compass, 36¢, marble, rabbit's foot." The contemporary tot's pocket, on the other hand, contains "hash pipe, Pop Rocks, condom, $20.00, 'ludes, Merits."

Something has happened to the limits of childhood. An advertisement for a new line of books called "Young Adult Books" defines a young adult as "a person facing the problems of adulthood." The books, however, which deal with subjects such as prostitution, divorce, and rape, are aimed at readers between the ages of ten and thirteen, "persons" who were formerly known as children.

Something has happened to the image of childhood. A full-page advertisement in a theatrical newspaper showing a sultry female wearing dark lipstick, excessive eye-shadow, a mink coat, and possibly nothing else bears the legend: "Would you believe that I am only ten?" We believe it. For beyond the extravagances of show business lies the evidence of a population of normal, regular children, once clearly distinguishable as little boys and little girls, who now look and act like little grown-ups.

Something has happened to blur the formerly distinct boundaries between childhood and adulthood, to weaken the protective membrane that once served to shelter children from

precocious experience and sorrowful knowledge of the adult
world. . . .

—*Children Without Childhood* (New York:
Pantheon, 1983), pp. 1–2.

Each paragraph begins with the phrase "Something has happened
to . . ." Then the new point is mentioned. This repetition helps readers
remember the main points.

COMPARISON/CONTRAST
▼

Comparison plays a substantial part in enabling us to understand or explain almost any topic. It does so by exploring or describing the similarities and differences among things. Most of the time, when we compare
(see how things are alike), we also contrast (see how things are different). Thus, when we compare one insurance plan to another, one school
to another, one philosopher's views of values to another's, or one president's foreign policies to another's, we also contrast them. At times,
though, we want to emphasize either the similarities or the differences.

Comparison

Comparison brings together subjects that are usually regarded as different to show how they are similar. In the conclusion of a famous article that contrasts the characters of Ulysses S. Grant and Robert E. Lee as
individuals and as symbols of their respective northern and southern
heritages, Bruce Catton—an authority on the American Civil War—shows
how the two generals were also alike. The first paragraph summarizes
the major differences between Grant and Lee; the second provides the
transition to the discussion of their similarities, which are arranged from
the least important to the most important (climactic order).

> So Grant and Lee were in complete contrast, representing
> two diametrically opposed elements in American life. Grant
> was the modern man emerging; beyond him, ready to come
> on the stage, was the great age of steel and machinery, of
> crowded cities and a restless, burgeoning vitality. Lee might
> have ridden down from the old age of chivalry, lance in
> hand, silken banner fluttering over his head. Each man was

the perfect champion of his cause, drawing both his strengths and his weaknesses from the people he led.

Yet it was not all contrast, after all. Different as they were— in background, in personality, in underlying aspiration—these two great soldiers had much in common. Under everything else, they were marvelous fighters. Furthermore, their fighting qualities were really very much alike.

Each man had, to begin with, the great virtue of utter tenacity and fidelity. Grant fought his way down the Mississippi Valley in spite of acute personal discouragement and profound military handicaps. Lee hung on in the trenches at Petersburg after hope itself had died. In each man there was an indomitable quality . . . the born fighter's refusal to give up as long as he can still remain on his feet and lift his two fists.

Daring and resourcefulness they had, too; the ability to think faster and move faster than the enemy. These were the qualities which gave Lee the dazzling campaigns of Second Manassas and Chancellorsville and won Vicksburg for Grant.

Lastly, and perhaps greatest of all, there was the ability, at the end, to turn quickly from war to peace once the fighting was over. Out of the way these two men behaved at Appomattox came the possibility of a peace of reconciliation. It was a possibility not wholly realized, in the years to come, but which did, in the end, help the two sections to become one nation again . . . after a war whose bitterness might have seemed to make such a reunion wholly impossible. No part of either man's life became him more than the part he played in their brief meeting in the McLean house at Appomattox. Their behavior there put all succeeding generations of Americans in their debt. Two great Americans—Grant and Lee—very different, yet under everything very much alike. Their encounter at Appomattox was one of the great moments of American history.

> —"Grant and Lee: A Study in Contrasts," in
> *The American Story*, ed. Earl Schenck Miers
> (Great Neck, NY: Channel Press, 1956),
> pp. 204–205.

Contrast

Contrast examines subjects that are usually regarded as similar to show how they are different in significant ways. The following passage from a journal that has become an American classic, written by Richard Henry

Dana, Jr., describes little-known aspects of early nineteenth-century navy life by contrasting a sailor's life in steerage with one in the forecastle.

In the midst of this state of things, my messmate S— and myself petitioned the captain for leave to shift our berths from the steerage where we had previously lived, into the forecastle. This, to our delight, was granted, and we turned in to *bunk* and mess with the crew forward.

We now began to feel like sailors, which we never fully did when we were in the steerage. While there, however useful and active you may be, you are but a mongrel—a sort of afterguard and "ship's cousin." You are immediately under the eye of the officers, cannot dance, sing, play, smoke, make a noise, or *growl* (i.e. complain), or take any other sailor's pleasure: and you live with the steward, who is usually a go-between; and the crew never feel as though you were *one of them.*

But if you live in the forecastle, you are "as independent as a wood-sawyer's clerk" (nautice), and are a *sailor.* You hear sailor's talk, learn their ways, their peculiarities of feeling as well as speaking and acting; and moreover pick up a great deal of curious and useful information in seamanship, ship's customs, foreign countries, etc., from the long yarns and equally long disputes.

No man can be a sailor, or know what sailors are, unless he has lived in the forecastle with them—turned in and out with them, eaten of their dish and drunk of their cup. After I had been a week there, nothing would have tempted me to go back to my old berth, and never afterward, even in the worst of weather, when in a close and leaking forecastle off Cape Horn, did I for a moment wish myself in the steerage.

—*Two Years Before the Mast* (Edinburgh: Adam & C. Black, 1869), pp. 48–49.

Using Comparison and Contrast Effectively

Two suggestions will be helpful when you use comparison and contrast.

▶ Compare and contrast only subjects that belong to the same general category and share some important characteristics. Otherwise, the analysis will resemble the proverbial comparison of apples and oranges. Robert E. Lee and Ulysses S. Grant were senior generals of their respective armies, but they differed in several distinctive ways. Thus, they can be contrasted. But they also shared a number of significant characteristics. Thus, they can be compared. Likewise, the forecastle and steerage are both working and living spaces on ships, but the life-style in each is significantly different. Thus, daily experiences in the forecastle and in steerage can be contrasted.

▶ Use comparison or contrast to make a point beyond the mechanical listing of similarities and differences. For instance, Pierre Boulle's novel *Bridge over the River Kwai* and the Oscar-winning movie based on it differ in a number of ways. Perhaps the most notable difference is their endings. In the novel, the allied commando team fails in its mission to destroy the bridge. The movie ends with the commandos succeeding in blowing up the bridge. Merely pointing out that the endings are different would not be very significant. However, the contrast could be used to illustrate Hollywood's romantic image, which pretty much dictates that the allied commandos will succeed in their mission. Use comparison and contrast not as ends in themselves, but as strategies for making a point or clarifying an idea. See also **analogy**.

ANALOGY, PAGE 517

CONCISENESS
▼

Concise writing uses no more words than are necessary for clarity and good style. However, unless we are sending a telegram or having to state why we like Brand C "in twenty-five words or less," we usually are not concerned about how many words we use. We should be concerned, however, for unnecessary words take up space and the reader's time and do not provide new information, as the following examples illustrate.

wordy: She picked up the receiver, *put it to her ear*, and said "hello." (Where else would she put it? To her chin? Her elbow? Generally, placing the receiver to the ear precedes speaking into it. Any reasonable reader would understand that at once, so the phrase *put it to her ear* is unnecessary.)

concise: She picked up the receiver and said "hello." (Thirteen words reduced to eight.)

wordy: The Planaria were *few in number* but reproduced *in a rapid manner.* (*Few* always refers to quantity, so *in number* is unnecessary, since it merely repeats the idea expressed in *few*. The adverb *rapidly* easily replaces *in a rapid manner* with no loss of meaning.)

concise: The Planaria were *few* but reproduced *rapidly*. (Twelve words reduced to seven.)

wordy: *There was a total of* nine students in the class when the class was canceled. (*There was* is an expletive—like *it is, there are, here is,* and so on—that adds words to a sentence without adding or clarifying meaning. *Nine* already conveys the sense of *a total of.* The second *the class* unnecessarily repeats the first.)

concise: Nine students *were* in the class when it was canceled. (Fifteen words reduced to ten.)

No meaning or stylistic dignity is lost by cutting these words. But even if the more concise version is better, is cutting four or five words in each sentence worth the effort? A few words removed from one sentence may not appear to be much of an improvement. But if wordiness is a characteristic of your writing, then almost every sentence will pack a few unnecessary words. Cutting those unnecessary words could result in as much as a 15 to 40 percent lightening of the text. Over several pages that can be noticeable. And if you learn to delete unnecessary words, you will probably soon avoid them as you write.

Four principles will help you write concisely.

▶ **Never use two or more words when one will do.** This principle is especially relevant to verb forms, for a lot of clutter exists around verbs. Verb phrases that begin with *be* (and its forms of *is, are, was, were*), *give, have,* and *make* and end with a noun ending with *-ion, -ment, -ity,* or *-al* are usually wordy.

wordy: Supervisors and workers *are in agreement* on the proposed work schedule.

concise: Supervisors and workers *agree* on the proposed work schedule.

wordy: Your advisor *is to give approval of* your course schedule before you register for classes.

concise: Your advisor *must approve* your course schedule before you register for classes.

Likewise, change *have a need for* to *need*; *take into consideration* to *consider*; *make a change* to *change*; *take action* to *act*.

Many unnecessary words—especially prepositions—follow verbs. Some phrasal verbs (verbs followed by prepositions that have idiomatic meanings), such as *hold on* and *give in*, are acceptable, but most verbs are clear without a preposition:

> *wordy:* We plan to *meet up with* John at the mall.
> *concise:* We plan to *meet* John at the mall.

> *wordy:* The new accounting program automatically *figures up* the costs.
> *concise:* The new accounting program automatically *figures* the costs.

> *wordy:* The game *was over with* at five o'clock.
> *concise:* The game *was over* at five o'clock (or The game *ended* at five o'clock).

Many adjectives and adverbs are also overused.

> *wordy:* *The lot on the corner* was landscaped *in an appropriate manner.*
> *concise:* The corner lot was landscaped *appropriately.*

> *wordy:* The approach to the problem *which they used* was *carried out in an efficient way.*
> *concise:* *Their approach* to the problem was *efficient* (or *They approached* the problem *efficiently*).

▶ Delete qualifiers and intensifiers that mean little. Many statements contain words that unnecessarily repeat a meaning that is already clear. For example, when the words *about* or *approximately* precede what is clearly stated as an estimate or approximation, they should be omitted.

> *wordy:* The registrar estimated enrollment *at about* 20,000 students.
> *concise:* The registrar estimated enrollment *at* 20,000 students.

> *wordy:* The teacher assigned *about* 200 to 300 pages each week.
> *concise:* The teacher assigned 200 to 300 pages each week.

Many inexperienced writers mistakenly believe that strong and emphatic writing depends on the use of intensifiers like *absolutely, definitely, extremely, greatly, really,* and *very*. In the following examples, the attempts to intensify *splendid, necessary,* and *interested* are defeated by the unnecessary qualifiers. Such thoughts are expressed more forcefully without an intensifier.

> *wordy:* The party was *absolutely splendid.*
> *concise:* The party was *splendid.*

> *wordy:* It is *absolutely necessary* that we attend the committee meeting.
> *concise:* It is *necessary* that we attend the committee meeting (or We *must* attend the committee meeting).

> *wordy:* She was so *greatly interested* in the book that she could not *possibly lay* it down.
> *concise:* She was so *interested* in the book that she could not *lay* it down.

Here are several other expressions that contain unnecessary qualifiers (the unnecessary word is italicized): *absolutely* essential, repeat *again,* resume *again, most* unique, cooperate *together, old* adage, small *in size,* many *in number, somewhat* tired, *totally* exhausted, *really* big, divide *in two, completely* unanimous. Because the meaning of the italicized words is included in the meaning of the other words, the italicized words are not needed.

▶ Avoid overusing expletives ("there is," "there are," etc.) and *which* and *that* clauses. Usually the expletive is unnecessary and adds nothing to the statement.

> *wordy:* *There are* many folk dancers *who* make their own costumes.
> *concise:* *Many folk dancers* make their own costumes.

> *wordy:* Beside the hotel *there is* a parking garage.
> *concise:* Beside the hotel *is* a parking garage.

Many *who, which,* and *that* constructions can be revised to more concise structures with no loss of meaning or force.

> *wordy:* *Windows that are double-insulated* conserve energy.
> *concise:* *Double-insulated windows* conserve energy.

> *wordy:* We wrote five *papers that consisted of about* 1,000 words each.
> *concise:* We wrote five *papers of about* 1,000 words each.

Deleting *that consisted* and *that are* take away nothing important.

▶ When you are drafting a text, do not worry about **conciseness**. If you try too hard to be concise in writing your first draft, you may develop writer's block. But as you read over your draft, look for unnecessary words and expressions that inevitably crop up. If you are unsure about a word or expression, read the sentence without it. If your meaning is not affected, delete the word or expression.

CONCLUSIONS
▼

The conclusion of an essay, like the conclusion of a short story, movie, song, or speech, has two major functions: to convey a sense of completion and to get the audience's focus right where the writer wants it.

The kind of conclusion, of course, depends largely on the type of text. Not every piece of writing needs a formal conclusion. In a very short piece—say one of only a page or two—it may be enough to just stop after the last point is made, especially if previous points converge into it and if it is easily recognized as the last of a finite number of points. For example, if you are explaining the major types of migrations and you have made it clear to readers that there are five generally recognized types, you might end with the explanation of the fifth type.

To end with the last major point, it is essential that you present readers with a clear sense of the underlying structure of your text. For example, if, in explaining the general process of mitosis (cell division), you had established in the **introduction**, that there are four major phases of mitosis, you could end after describing the fourth phase, as the writer does in this example:

INTRODUCTIONS, PAGE 607

> During the final stage, telephase, the spindle that formed in the metaphase disappears, and each set of chromosomes is enveloped by new nuclear membrane and becomes diffuse and invisible. In addition, the cell constricts near its center between the two nuclei and divides. The two new cells are formed, each containing the same number of chromosomes as the original cell.

Explicit cues, such as "the final stage," the reference to an earlier stage ("the metaphase"), and the absence of text following the paragraph assist the reader in realizing that the text is ending. More writing would probably add nothing of value, unless you wanted to add some information about duration of the process or relate mitosis to other kinds of reproduction. However, to add a perfunctory sentence such as "These, then, are the four stages of mitosis" adds nothing, and readers would likely think that you are overdoing it.

THESIS, PAGE 663

Longer, more complicated pieces of writing need to pull things together at the end. Even when you have created a clear **thesis** at the beginning and have guided the reader along a carefully developed path of reasoning, readers may have lost the sharp impression of your thesis in going through the mass of details, supporting examples, and data. There are limits to readers' abilities to comprehend and remember what they read. In closing your text, you may need to let the multitude of details and facts of your analysis recede and to reassert your thesis as the final thought that you want readers to linger on. Such a conclusion does not need to be ringing or thunderous. Nor should it be a simple relisting of points that you have already made. However, it does need to reemphasize the thesis so that it sticks with readers. For example, the following paragraph would effectively conclude a paper on discipline problems in Chicago inner city high schools:

> Recently, I visited my parents in Chicago and drove past my old high school. Now a warehouse for the school district's surplus furniture and equipment, the building looks abandoned and dilapidated. Crude, obscene messages remain scrawled on the walls, and many of the windows are broken or missing. Evidently, the discipline problems finally defeated the valiant but discouraged teachers. I am glad the school is closed, for learning had become impossible in that environment.

This paragraph rounds off the text by restating the main idea that the writer wants to leave in the minds of readers. And that is what you want your conclusion to do—leave readers thinking about what you have said.

In addition to reemphasizing the thesis, conclusions can wrap up an argumentative text by presenting a summary of the argument. Such a wrap-up locks in place the main points of your argument as you presented it and serves as a strong ending. Here is an example:

> That Herbert Hoover had no particular sympathy for Hitler, that he believed that the American political tradition was irreconcilable with that of the Third Reich is evident from many sources, including the documentary record of his visit to Berlin.

But he believed, too, that Hitler's Germany posed no real threat to the West and that it was very wrong for the United States to take sides against it. Whether Hoover ever thought that there was at least a potential conflict between these two sets of beliefs we cannot tell.

—John Lukacs, "Herbert Hoover Meets Adolf Hitler," *The American Scholar* (Spring 1993): 238.

In writing a conclusion, you face the same challenges as in writing an introduction. The best conclusions are straightforward and appropriate and pack a bit of a punch, but they do not strain for an effect they cannot achieve (such as humor, cleverness, or brilliance). If you have not written a good text, your conclusion cannot save it. However, a poor conclusion can damage a good piece of writing by leaving a dreary feeling as the last impression the reader takes away from the paper. A good conclusion confirms the reader's perception that your text is well written. Thus, you should take care in writing your conclusion. Following are some suggestions that will be helpful.

▶ Refer to your introduction, or, at least, reemphasize in some way the **thesis** stated in your introduction. We are sure that occasionally a writer starts with what he or she sees as the final sentence of a paper and then attempts to write everything to build up to it. However, since the conclusion usually refers to the introduction or, at least in some way, the thesis, it is naturally among the last parts to be written. The concluding idea you want to leave with readers is already stated in your thesis. That's what you want to tap into in your conclusion—the main idea that is already there in your readers' minds. So as you prepare to write your conclusion, look back over the way you opened the paper. You will want the conclusion to echo the general impression you created in the introduction.

THESIS, PAGE 663

▶ If you cannot produce a conclusion quickly, don't just sit there sweating. Relax, and if you have time, get away from writing for a day or so and let your subconscious mind work on the conclusion. There are beneficial effects in getting away from your text for awhile. Of course, you will have to write far enough in advance of your deadline to give yourself time to do this. On coming back to the text later, you are likely to find that you have forgotten some of your reasoning and that you will have to reread your text to reacquaint yourself with your thinking. Seeing your text in a fresh light may help you discover the concluding statements you want.

▶ When you have gone as far as you can and still have not made much headway on your conclusion, discuss possible conclusions with some of your friends or classmates. They may be able to contribute useful suggestions and may be quite helpful in checking your enthusiasm for what you think is a clever conclusion or in helping you see the potential in a certain kind of conclusion. Even if the discussion does not lead to an immediate conclusion, the exchange of views is usually refreshing and can stimulate you to continue writing and revising.

CREDIBILITY
▼

Readers do not merely respond to a text; they respond to a text that is written by *someone*. Consequently, a text's impact depends greatly on how its audience responds to the writer's personality as it is projected in the text. A reader who believes in the writer's credibility and trustworthiness will not only be willing to read the text, but will also be inclined to believe and accept the writer's viewpoint. Readers who do not hold these beliefs will have so little confidence in the writer that their interaction with the text will be affected.

The bias toward one's own viewpoint is natural. You have credibility in your own eyes, for you have probably worked out your ideas and opinions fully in your own mind. But credibility is a matter of opinion and subjective judgment, and the reader's perception is the key to whether you connect with your audience. You possess high credibility if your readers perceive you as someone in whom they can have confidence; as someone who is intelligent, fair-minded, honest, and sincere; and as someone who is well-disposed toward them (in effect, as someone who possesses the same qualities that they attribute to themselves). Perceiving these qualities of character, intelligence, and goodwill, readers will accept you as a reliable source of information. On the other hand, you possess low credibility if readers perceive you as someone who is uninformed, prejudiced, manipulative, or self-serving. Perceiving these qualities, readers will probably not consider your text worth reading.

Several factors can make your credibility rise or fall in the minds of your reader. Some of the factors help establish initial credibility; others help create derived credibility. Initial credibility refers to the reader's image of you just before she or he begins to read your text. Derived credibility refers to the reader's image of you as he or she responds to your text. (For a more complete discussion of initial and derived credibility, see James C. McCroskey, *An Introduction to Rhetorical Communication*, 3rd ed. [Upper Saddle River, NJ: Prentice Hall, 1978], pp. 67–85. McCroskey uses the Greek term *ethos* in place of the more common term *credibility*.)

Initial credibility is based on your readers' prior knowledge of or prior experience with you even before they begin to read your text. The adage that your reputation precedes you is relevant here. Your initial credibility will be high if your readers regard you as trustworthy, educated, and well informed on the subject; open-minded and honest; or holding values similar to their own. Your initial credibility will be low if your readers perceive you as unreliable or dishonest, as close-minded and prejudiced, or as having suspect motives. Other factors also influence initial credibility. Things as simple as using good-quality paper, typing or handwriting neatly, and using an appropriate format can increase your credibility. Evidence of unconcern—such as getting your text to the reader later than the established deadline or using cheap or otherwise inappropriate paper (such as odd-sized or strange-colored paper)—can lower it.

High initial credibility will assure that your ideas will be received, at least initially, by readers who are favorably disposed toward you (either because they know in advance that they agree with your ideas or position on issues or because they know of your reputation for being honest). But initial credibility, though important, is not the most important factor on which your effectiveness as a writer depends. Usually you will be relatively unknown to your readers; therefore, you will have to build credibility with your text. And even if you are known by your readers, once they start responding to your text, what they read or hear will influence their perceptions even further. It is at this point that derived credibility becomes important, because it can either confirm or raise questions about initial credibility.

Here are four things you can do to enhance your derived credibility.

▶ Know what you are writing about. Don't pretend to know more than you actually do. Confine yourself to what you know is true and up to date, and know your subject inside and out before you try to tell somebody else about it. Misinformation and outdated information reduce your credibility considerably. Readers expect you to write with authority, not to guess at facts or use old information. If you are unsure about some fact or statistic—such as which American city has the largest population of Asian Americans, how many nuclear reactors are licensed for operation in Europe, or whether the headlights of jeeps during World War II were recessed into the grill—then check or double-check your sources for accuracy. If you are arguing the need to protect waterfowl from lead poisoning and are proposing that lead shot in shotgun shells should be illegal, make sure that such a law is not already in effect. The most basic procedures of credible research are to use up-to-date data and credible sources of information.

Since it is crucial that your readers have confidence in you as a source of valid information, you should attempt to establish your knowledge on the subject. Even persons who are likely to possess high initial credibility recognize that they must make their audience aware of their competence. C. Everette Koop, the Surgeon General of the United States during the Reagan administration, attempted to make his audience aware of his competence to deal with the effects of violence on children by citing his years of experience as a pediatrician:

> . . . I believe the pediatrician has a unique relationship with children and with parents. You gain certain insights about individuals and families that other physicians may not have the chance to see.
>
> I base that opinion, by the way, on the reflections of my own career of 35 years in pediatric surgery. Dealing with the young children who were my patients I saw firsthand the stresses of childhood and was aware of both the strengths and weaknesses of children trying to cope. I also had to understand the families of those children. I had to gain their confidence and win them as allies in the battle to help their children.
>
> In the process, I think I began to understand a great deal about the contemporary family.
>
> —"Violence and Public Health," *Representative American Speeches, 1982–1983*, ed. Owen Peterson (New York: Wilson, 1983), pp. 210–11.

Most of us are not recognized experts in the sense that Dr. Koop is, but we do have first-hand experiences sometimes referred to as the "Hell, I was *there!*" claim to credibility. First-hand reports have credibility, but don't overplay your hand. It is highly unlikely that you have personally experienced everything there is to know about a subject.

You will be credible when readers come to believe that you really know what you are writing about, that you take painstaking care to be accurate, and that your knowledge is up to date.

▶ Use the information you possess to support your ideas and proposi- tions. This doesn't mean that every single fact you dig up will go into the final version of your text. Nor does it mean that every statement you make has to have evidence to back it up. But until you have a genuine working knowledge of your subject, you will not know what evidence to use in support of propositions that need it.

Most of the time when you write, you are dealing with opinions, not absolute truths, and since you are attempting to persuade an audi- ence to accept your claims, you have an obligation to try to prove to them that you are right. There are fewer indisputable matters of fact than most of us realize. Even if what you state is true, the truth is not automatically apparent. You must give readers reasons to believe you.

There are, of course, times when you can rely almost solely on your credibility to persuade readers to believe you. When you are already held in high regard by them or when they are already in agree- ment with a point you wish to make, you can state that something is true without having to prove it.

Unless your readers already agree with a point you want to make or are willing to take your statement at face value, you will need to pro- vide support. Here is how Joyce Carol Oates, a professor of humanities at Princeton University and a prolific writer, backs up her statement that professional boxing is the most lucrative sport for its top athletes:

> There is something particularly American in the fact that,
> while boxing is our most controversial sport, it is also the sport
> that pays its top athletes the most money. In spite of the con-
> troversy, boxing has never been healthier financially. The three
> highest paid athletes in the world in both 1983 and 1984 were
> boxers: a boxer with a long career like heavyweight champion
> Larry Holmes—48 fights in 13 years as a professional—can
> expect to earn somewhere beyond $50 million. (Holmes said
> that after retirement what he would miss most about boxing
> is his million-dollar checks.) Dempsey, who said that a man
> fights for one thing only—money—made somewhere beyond
> $3,500,000 in the ring in his long and varied career. Now
> $1.5 million is a fairly common figure for a single fight. Thomas
> Hearns made at least $7 million in his fight with Hagler
> while Hagler made at least $7.5 million. For the first of his
> highly publicized matches with Roberto Duran in 1980—which
> he lost on a decision—the popular black welterweight champion
> Sugar Ray Leonard received a staggering $10 million to Duran's
> $1.3 million. And none of these figures takes into account vari-
> ous subsidiary earnings (from television commercials, for

instance) which in Leonard's case are probably as high as his
income was from boxing.

—"On Boxing," *New York Times Magazine*
(June 16, 1985): 37–38.

Oates has done two of the most important things that a writer can do
to increase credibility. She has quoted two experts (boxers themselves)
on the importance of money to boxers. And she has given several examples that illustrate her claim. Rather than just stating that the sport pays
its top athletes more than any other sport does, Oates gives the reader
several reasons to believe the claim.

Including evidence to support your assertions is effective in two
ways: 1) it avoids depending so much on your initial credibility, and 2) it
can even increase your credibility, especially if the evidence is new to
your audience and comes from a source that they regard as authoritative.

▶ Refer to the opinions of others as evidence in support of your own
points when you are expressing a view that contradicts something
your reader believes. But not just any experts will do. Your credibility
will rise or fall depending upon whether your readers recognize the
expert as a person or an organization that holds a credible opinion on
the subject. In the following passage from an article that discusses
women and drug addiction, the author uses two experts: a physician
whose credentials as an authority are identified, and a 29-year-old
drug abuser.

For women in the work place, alcohol and drug abuse is a
multifaceted problem. "Many working women feel underpaid,
undervalued, overworked, and overstressed; they're trying to
juggle too many roles with too little reward. Some become
frustrated and turn to alcohol or tranquilizers," says Reed
Moskowitz, M.D., director of the Stress-Disorders Medical
Services at New York University Medical Center. "Some women
may also feel they lack the aggressiveness to compete in a
male-dominated work place, and mistakenly think that drugs
such as cocaine will give them that aggressive edge. Other
women use drugs or alcohol to be one of the boys at business
functions or while entertaining clients. The insecurities that make
women feel they won't be accepted on their own terms also
contribute to their addiction." And in such professions as entertainment and finance, where the energy level is frenetic and
the stakes are high, the use of stimulants is even more common.

"Cocaine was everywhere when I started out on Wall Street," admits Carol, twenty-nine. "Here I was, black, a brand new M.B.A., and the youngest woman at my level. Everyone had high expectations for me. My family had struggled to send me to college, then I got this fellowship to a top grad school. I was carrying some heavy baggage."

Then an acquaintance turned Carol on to cocaine.

"This business can be a pressure cooker," says Carol. "Cocaine seemed to keep me on track, help my concentration. But after a while, I would get wired—really tense—and to come down, I needed to take a drink or a Valium. Finally, I was taking so many drugs, I couldn't handle the job."

—Rita Baron-Faust, "The Anatomy of Addiction," *Cosmopolitan*, (June 1990): 220.

Baron-Faust increases her credibility by presenting more than her own opinion. She quotes an expert on drug treatment and uses the testimony of a former addict to give a specific, real example of the drug problem instead of merely describing a hypothetical situation.

Look for unexpected opinions or viewpoints that will support your thesis. A writer who is arguing in favor of legalizing drugs can strengthen his or her case by quoting such persons as conservative columnist William F. Buckley, Jr., well-known economist Milton Friedman, and former Secretary of State George Schultz, who have all argued at one time or another that the U.S. government's war on drugs is futile and misguided. The opinions of these persons are especially effective, because most readers would expect that these political and social conservatives would be hostile to the writer's or speaker's argument.

On the other hand, someone who contends that the Holocaust never happened would damage his or her position by quoting information distributed by The Institute for Historical Review—an organization that has many neo-Nazi members—or by quoting the late George Lincoln Rockwell, the former leader of the American Nazi Party, while ignoring information from the archives of the Nuremburg War Crimes Trials. Someone who is trying to ban the teaching of the scientific theory of evolution in public schools must use sources other than the old, largely discredited creationists' propaganda tracts. Even if you have admirable goals, it is a mistake to use dubious arguments for attaining them. Since most readers would challenge the credibility of these sources on the grounds that they are biased, you should inform yourself of the background and political leanings of sources you come across in your research.

▶ **Regard your readers as people who are as intelligent, sophisticated, and well-meaning as you are.** Maintaining this attitude can be difficult when you are in the heat of an argument. But you can be confident in your position without being didactic, condescending, or close-minded. In fact, there is little chance that you can change the minds of people who disagree with you by showering ridicule and scorn on their position. Instead of looking at readers as opponents, look at them as co-seekers of the truth.

When we argue a position we acknowledge that other positions exist, although we have a natural tendency to regard our own arguments highly and to undervalue those of our opponents. However, readers are more likely to believe you if you go beyond merely presenting your own viewpoint and the opinions of others who support your viewpoint. If readers suspect that you are unwilling to consider opposing viewpoints or are ignoring certain sources of information, they will believe you are slanting your argument unfairly. To be credible, you should also acknowledge opposing positions and, if possible, refute them.

Refutation involves anticipating or identifying the opinions of opponents and attempting to undermine the arguments that support them, either by rejecting the premises upon which they are based, objecting to the conclusions reached, or both. Refutation can involve some heavy hitting. Be careful not to dismiss an opposing idea by citing only a single poor illustration of it or by misquoting or distorting an opponent's statement. Certainly, never refute an idea that your opponents never claimed. If readers get the impression that you are attributing opinions to your opponents that they do not hold, your credibility will suffer.

A common method of refutation is to present arguments in support of your own beliefs first, then refute opposing views. Louis Nizer, one of America's best-known lawyers, in contending that legalizing drugs would reduce most of the problems associated with illegal drug use, makes his proposal, then acknowledges objections to it and directly refutes them point by point.

> There are several objections that might be raised against such a salutary solution.
>
> First, it could be argued that by providing free drugs to the addict we would consign him to permanent addiction. The answer is that medical and psychiatric help at the source would be more effective in controlling the addict's descent than the extremely limited remedies available to the victim today. I am not arguing that this new strategy will cure everything. But I

do not see many addicts being freed from their bonds under the present system. . . .

Another possible objection is that addicts will cheat the system by obtaining more than the allowable free shot. Without discounting the resourcefulness of the bedeviled addict, it should be possible to have Government cards issued that would be punched so as to limit the free supply in accord with medical authorities.

—"How About Low-Cost Drugs for Adults?"
New York Times, 8 June 1986, sec. 4, p. 28.

Nizer's credibility comes in part from the fact that he is open-minded enough to consider with respect other viewpoints and to attempt to answer them. Don't be so steadfastly loyal to your own ideas that you fail to acknowledge and analyze the viewpoints of others.

However, while well-rounded arguments usually include some acknowledgment of opposing ideas, there are instances when refutation alone might be sufficient. For example, when opposing arguments are strong and well known, it might be a good strategy to meet the opposing arguments head on, focusing your argument on refuting the opposing viewpoints. In an article that appeared in *The New Republic*, Edward I. Koch, the former mayor of New York City and a strong advocate of the death penalty, presented his opinions by refuting, point by point, the major positions held by those with whom he disagrees: that the death penalty is barbaric punishment, that no other major democracy uses the death penalty, that an innocent person might be executed by mistake, that capital punishment is applied in a discriminatory manner, that the death penalty violates the biblical commandment "Thou shalt not Kill," and that the death penalty is state-sanctioned murder ("Death and Justice," *The New Republic* [April 15, 1985]: 12–15). In defending the death penalty, Koch attempts to show that these six beliefs are false, either because the evidence that supports them is incorrect or because the reasoning that leads to them is unsound. If Koch can convince his audience that those who oppose the death penalty have failed to make their case, he may convince his readers to adopt his point of view.

Above all else, your credibility depends upon your not putting down those who disagree with you. Too often, we tend to regard an argument as a war in which it is acceptable to undercut and attack our opponents any way we can. But ranting and raving and showing disrespect for your audience, even when you may feel a sense of moral outrage, creates a negative image of yourself. Perhaps there is no more exemplary instance of a writer maintaining respect for those who hold opposing views than the opening of Martin Luther King, Jr.'s *Letter from Birmingham Jail.*

Disappointed at the lack of support from white and more socially conservative clergy for his acts of civil disobedience and by charges that he was an extremist, King could have, perhaps understandably, erupted with the verbal equivalent of a volcano. But he knew that he had to counter his image as an outside agitator, rabble-rouser, and perhaps even a criminal and establish himself as someone who has listened carefully to his critics and understood their position even though he doesn't agree with it.

> My Dear Fellow Clergymen:
>
> While confined here in the Birmingham city jail, I came across your recent statement calling my present activities "unwise and untimely." Seldom do I pause to answer criticism of my work and ideas. If I sought to answer all the criticisms that cross my desk, my secretaries would have little time for anything other than such correspondence in the course of the day, and I would have no time for constructive work. But since I feel that you are men of genuine good will and that your criticisms are sincerely set forth, I want to try to answer your statement in what I hope will be patient and reasonable terms.
>
> —*Why We Can't Wait* (New York: HarperCollins, 1963, 1964), p. 77.

King goes on to respond to his critics' questions and charges about his "unwise and untimely" activities in such a respectful manner that he was almost assured his readers (both the eight Alabama clergymen and the larger public audience that he also had in mind) would consider the validity of his viewpoint and the justice of his actions. History indicates that he succeeded.

DEFINITION
▼

Meaning is created and agreement is negotiated through words. Thus, writers must make sure that readers understand the concepts they are presenting and the words they are using to articulate those concepts.

We should define a word we use when we believe that readers are not familiar with it or that they understand it differently.

Sometimes a concept or the word the writer uses to refer to the concept is basic to the understanding of a text. For instance, in his essay that explains the art of dubbing, Anthony Burgess provides these essential definitions early on:

> A whole collection of terms is applied to the artifice whereby synchronic sound and action are achieved by diachronic means, and the common term is *dubbing*.
>
> Strictly, *dubbing* implies not just the addition of sound to film shot silently. It presupposes an original sound track to be modified either partially or totally. In fact *dub* can be given three definitions: (a) to make a new recording out of an original tape or record or track in order to accommodate changes, cuts or additions; (b) to insert a totally new sound track, often a synchronized translation of the original dialogue; (c) to insert sound into a film or tape.
>
> —"Dubbing," in *The State of the Language*, ed. Leonard Michaels and Christopher Ricks (Berkeley: University of California Press, 1980), p. 297.

These definitions enable readers to grasp the whole concept of dubbing as Burgess will discuss it.

We cannot discuss controversial issues constructively unless we and our readers agree on definition. In the following passage, Margaret Atwood, a Canadian essayist, poet, and novelist, attempts to be very clear about what she means by pornography. She knows that if her readers have a different meaning for the concept of pornography, they will probably not agree with her opinion that it is a serious cultural and social problem.

> When I was in Finland a few years ago for an international writers' conference, I had occasion to say a few paragraphs in public on the subject of pornography. The context was a discussion of political repression, and I was suggesting the possibility of a link between the two. The immediate result was that a male journalist took several large bites out of me. Prudery and pornography are two halves of the same coin, said he, and I was clearly a prude. What could you expect from an Anglo-Canadian? Afterward, a couple of pleasant Scandinavian men

asked me what I had been so worked up about. All "pornography" means, they said, is graphic depictions of whores, and what was the harm in that?

Not until then did it strike me that the male journalist and I had two entirely different things in mind. By "pornography," he meant naked bodies and sex. I, on the other hand, had recently been doing the research for my novel *Bodily Harm*, and was still in a state of shock from some of the material I had seen, including the Ontario Board of Film Censors' "outtakes." By "pornography," I meant women getting their nipples snipped off with garden shears, having meat hooks stuck into their vaginas, being disemboweled; little girls being raped; men (yes, there are some men) being smashed to a pulp and forcibly sodomized. The cutting edge of pornography, as far as I could see, was no longer simple old copulation, hanging from the chandelier or otherwise: it was death, messy, explicit and highly sadistic. I explained this to the nice Scandinavian men. "Oh, but that's just the United States," they said. "Everyone knows they're sick." In their country, they said, violent "pornography" of that kind was not permitted on television or in movies; indeed, excessive violence of any kind was not permitted. They had drawn a clear line between erotica, which earlier studies had shown did not incite men to more aggressive behavior toward women, and violence, which later studies indicated did.

—"Pornography," *Chatelaine Magazine*
(September 1983): 61, 118.

Since Atwood is aware that the word *pornography* means different things to different people, she knows that it is crucial to define the term so that there will be no misunderstanding. Readers for whom pornography means the explicit portrayal of nudity and sex will not understand Atwood's viewpoint. She offers examples of violent pornography, which is far different from the "harmless" entertainment of nudity and sex.

What a word means is partly dependent upon how a reader understands it, and you or the reader may have a meaning for a word that the other is not aware of. You cannot be expected to know all the meanings and private associations readers may attach to the words you use, but understanding that words and concepts have multiple meanings will make it easier for you to determine whether you should define your words and the concepts they stand for.

Using Definition Effectively

Here are three suggestions about definitions to help you as you write.

▶ Determine whether it is the word, the concept, or both that must be defined. You can avoid too much defining by using simple and familiar words. Often readers are familiar with a concept but do not understand the word or words used to refer to the concept. For many, the term *recidivism* is unfamiliar, even though they are familiar with the concept— the tendency of many ex-convicts to return to their former criminal behavior. If it is important to introduce an unfamiliar word to readers, define it the first time you use it.

▶ Rely on short, concise definitions when possible. Unless definition is the whole purpose of a paper, a definition will be somewhat of an interruption to the discussion. So keep definitions as brief and inconspicuous as possible. Several methods are available—formal definition, synonyms, **exemplification**, and etymology.

EXEMPLIFICATION, PAGE 574

One of the most common methods of definition is to provide a formal, logical, three-part definition: the word to be defined, the class to which the word belongs, and the characteristics that differentiate the word from other members of the class. Dictionary definitions are commonly given this way, as this definition of *barometer* from *The American Heritage Dictionary* illustrates:

| | | differentiating |
| word | class | characteristics |

A **barometer** is an **instrument** for **measuring atmospheric pressure, used in weather forecasting and in determining elevation.**

Definitions may be given, as in this sentence, in which a geographical region of the United States is specified parenthetically:

> Until 1975 the Frostbelt (the Northeast and Midwest) contained more than half the nation's population.

Another way is to provide a synonym, such as in this sentence, in which both *anemia* and *hemoglobin* are defined parenthetically:

> Another common cause of nonspecific fatigue is anemia (a term applied to any condition in which the concentration of

hemoglobin—the red oxygen-carrying pigment—in the blood is below level).

A third common way to define a word is to provide examples (exemplification) to show what you mean by the word. Just make sure that readers are likely to be familiar with the examples and that the examples are typical of the concept being defined:

Felines are animals belonging to the family Felidae, which includes lions, tigers, jaguars, pumas, and other wild and domestic cats.

A fourth common method of definition is to explain the etymology or derivation of a word. For instance, if you were discussing the relationship between heat and mechanical action, you would probably use the word *thermodynamics*, which is a combination of the Greek words *heat* and *power*. Providing the etymology helps readers understand the word better. Most standard desk dictionaries include the etymology of a word as part of its definition. There are also several etymological dictionaries available, including *The Oxford English Dictionary*, if you want to trace the history of a word's meaning.

▶ **If the concept is intricate, relatively abstract, or controversial, provide a more extended definition.** For example, you can use not only such strategies as formal definition, synonyms, exemplification, and etymology, but also **analogy, cause and effect, classification, comparison and contrast, description**, and **narration**. Norman Cousins, who has written about the value of patients maintaining a positive attitude when faced with serious illness, defines *placebo* in the following passage. Cousins's definition makes it clear that a placebo is more than just a useless substance given to humor a patient. In many patients, a placebo triggers the body's own healing powers. The first paragraph provides the etymological definition of *placebo;* the second and third paragraphs contrast the negative and positive aspects of placebos; the fourth speculates on the process by which placebos affect the human body.

ANALOGY, PAGE 517

CAUSE AND EFFECT, PAGE 522

CLASSIFICATION, PAGE 527

COMPARISON AND CONTRAST, PAGE 542

DESCRIPTION, PAGE 565

NARRATION, PAGE 618

The word placebo comes from the Latin verb meaning "I shall please." A placebo in the classical sense, then, is an imitation medicine—generally an innocuous milk-sugar tablet dressed up like an authentic pill—given more for the purpose of placating a patient than for meeting a clearly diagnosed organic need. The placebo's most frequent use in recent years, however, has been in the testing of new drugs. Effects achieved by the preparation being tested are measured against those that follow the administration of a "dummy drug," or placebo.

For a long time, placebos were in general disrepute with a large part of the medical profession. The term, for many doctors, had connotations of quack remedies or "pseudomedicaments." There was also a feeling that placebos were largely a shortcut for some practitioners who were unable to take the time and trouble to get at the real source of a patient's malaise.

Today, however, the once lowly placebo is receiving serious attention from medical scholars. Medical investigators such as Dr. Arthur K. Shapiro, the late Dr. Henry K. Beecher, Dr. Stewart Wolf, and Dr. Louis Lasagna have found substantial evidence that the placebo not only can be made to look like a powerful medication but can actually act like a medication. They regard it not just as a physician's psychological prop in the treatment of certain patients but as an authentic therapeutic agent for altering body chemistry and for helping to mobilize the body's defenses in combating disorder or disease.

While the way the placebo works inside the body is still not completely understood, some placebo researchers theorize that it activates the cerebral cortex, which in turn switches on the endocrine system in general and the adrenal glands in particular. Whatever the precise pathways through the mind and body, enough evidence already exists to indicate that placebos can be as potent as—and sometimes more potent than—the active drugs they replace.

—"The Mysterious Placebo," in *Anatomy of an Illness* (Toronto: Bantam, 1981) pp. 50–51.

DESCRIPTION

▼

Whenever writers need to provide more than the most general or abstract statement, they usually add sensory details that enable readers to experience or imagine what they have experienced or imagined. For example, a *Time* magazine correspondent uses specific visual images to portray the grimness of an abandoned apartment building where a homeless Muscovite has found shelter:

Yuri Pronin sleeps on a rough plank door liberated from a neighboring apartment and balanced atop heavy rusting water

pipes in the tiny Moscow abode that he has called home since
last December. The room has no electricity and no running
water. A dented tin bread box and several empty jars serve as
his kitchen, while a cardboard box doubles as chair and closet.
The decor is Dickensian: bare paint-chipped walls, splintering
floorboards, and windows caked with dirt. Apartments in the
old Soviet Union were none too luxurious, but this is a big
step down.

—Ann M. Simmons, "Brother, Can You Spare a
Ruble?" *Time* (July 13, 1992): 58.

The visual details of the first four sentences let readers see at once the
grimness of Pronin's shelter. The statement "The decor is Dickensian"
and the last sentence are comments on the overall impression of the
scene.

Descriptive writing requires keen observation and the ability to
select the details that reveal not only how something, someplace, or
somebody looks, but also how things sound, smell, taste, and feel.
While sight is often the essence of good description, John Steinbeck,
one of America's Nobel Prize winners, relies primarily on details of
sound to recreate the atmosphere of a night in the Gulf of California:

Nights at anchor in the Gulf are quiet and strange. The
water is smooth, almost solid, and the dew is so heavy that the
decks are soaked. The little waves rasp on the shell beaches
with a hissing sound, and all about in the darkness the fishes
jump and splash. Sometimes a great ray leaps clear and falls
back on the water with a sharp report. And again, a school of
tiny fishes whisper along the surface, each one, as it breaks
clear, making the tiniest whisking sound. And there is no feeling, no smell, no vibration of people in the Gulf. Whatever it is
that makes one aware that men are about is not here. Thus, in
spite of the noises of waves and fishes, one has a feeling of
deadness and of quietness. At anchor, with the motor stopped,
it is not easy to sleep, and every little sound starts one awake.
If a dog barks on shore or a cow bellows, we are reassured.
But in many places of anchorage there were utterly no sounds
associated with man.

—*The Log of the Sea of Cortez* (New York:
Viking, 1951), pp. 89–90.

The passage opens with Steinbeck's feelings about the experience, followed by sentences that recreate what he perceived through the senses, primarily the sounds. The success of the description is due largely to the care with which Steinbeck uses verbs such as *rasp, splash, whisper;* refers to auditory images such as "a hissing sound," "a sharp report," and "the tiniest whisking sound;" and notes the absence of the familiar sounds associated with humanity and domesticated animals. In recreating these sounds, he evokes the eeriness of the nighttime anchorage in an isolated place and enables readers to experience vicariously the sensations, impressions, and emotions that affected him.

The following description of the old part of the Moroccan city of Fez appeals equally to our senses of sight, sound, and smell to convey the essential characteristic of a part of the city that has changed very little since the fourteenth century:

> We came out on a plaza at the center of the medina, the old city. It was crowded with people—little girls carrying wooden trays of oven-bound bread dough on their heads, veiled women doing their family wash at an exquisitely tiled public fountain, a bearded old man selling caged birds, old Berber ladies with tattooed chins squatting on curbs with their hands held out in supplication, ragged porters lashing slow-moving donkeys loaded down with ice and sheepskin and Pepsi-Cola cases.
>
> "No cars here, not even motorcycles," Abdellatif said. "The donkey is the taxi of the medina."
>
> The night air was clangorous with the rhythmic hammerings of the ironworkers at work on their kettles, coppersmiths beating a syncopated tap-da-tap-tap-da-tap on their ornate trays, the rasping voices of the street vendors, the tinselly laughter of schoolgirls in their crisp pastel smocks, and, above all, the raucous crying of the roosters, which seem to crow all night from the rooftops as if announcing some perpetual dawn of the spirit.
>
> Adding to the sensory assault were the thousand tingling aromas of spices and newly cut cedarwood, of singed oxhorn (used for combs) and sizzling hot cooking oil, of freshly baked bread and ugly-smelling animal hides—all simmering together, as it were, in the warm night air.
>
> —Harvey Arden, "Morocco's Ancient City of Fez," *National Geographic* 169 (March 1986): 341.

Such details are at the heart of good descriptive writing. They convey unfamiliar scenes and experiences by capturing sight, sound, and smell (and touch and taste), and readers gain a strong sense of reality that is no longer outside their range of knowledge.

Using Description Effectively

Three suggestions will help you write description.

▶ Descriptions must be ordered in some way, or readers run the risk of getting lost in the details. There are several techniques of ordering. You can provide an overview of what is being described followed by a description of its parts. Or, you can describe its most prominent features first and then turn your attention to smaller details. The latter is the method used by William Least Heat-Moon in *PrairyErth* to describe buildings that the Santa Fe Railroad built in the 1920s but that are now abandoned in the 1990s:

> In the narrow river vales of the county, the fields lie in squares and rectangles of row crops, fence lines darkly outlining them with small trees; from above, in autumn, the pattern is of strips of plaid cloth showing through long rents in the burlap of the prairie. Beside one of these tears, which is the South Fork Valley, and up on its western terrace high enough to give a view down on the vale road and the cropped grids, sits a low stone building, gray and grim like a barracks. It has eight rooms, ten doors, five chimneys, and is built like a double-footed L on its side, ⌐‾‾⌐, and between the two longer end rooms is a roofed porch, and in front of it, a covered well. The stone blocks are, in fact, concrete cast to look like hewn rock. . . . No one has lived here in some years, but once five Hispanic families did, and now the ceilings are shucking off their plaster down to their thin lath ribs, dropping pieces onto a miscellany of piled junk; window lights are missing, doors tied shut with twists of wire, and dirt lies so caked to the floor that the cold wind stirs no grit as it haunts through and gives the place an occasional voice—a slapped gutter, a shaken door, a rattled pane.

> —"En las Casitas," in *PrairyErth* (Boston: Houghton Mifflin, 1991), p. 230.

▶ In addition to being organized, descriptive details need to be concrete and specific. To describe what we see, hear, smell, and taste in order to enable readers to experience the sensations is difficult. Many inexperienced writers tend to use a lot of general terms and to rely heavily on adjectives and adverbs to make their descriptions more vivid. Of course, modifiers are sometimes important. But the key to achieving vividness is to use nouns and verbs that appeal directly to the senses.

General and not very descriptive	More specific but relatively vague	Specific and descriptive
thick vegetation	underbrush	kudzu and wild grape vines
journeyed with difficulty	walked slowly	slogged

The more concrete and specific the nouns and verbs, the more vivid and evocative the image. Instead of writing "Cyril journeyed with difficulty through the thick vegetation," write "Cyril slogged through the kudzu and wild grape vines."

▶ Much descriptive writing involves orienting readers to unfamiliar or unknown things. Familiar comparisons, especially analogies, are effective ways to assist readers in connecting the known to the unknown. In the following passage, the author uses the **analogy** of the human hand to describe the topography of the rectangular Chase County, Kansas:

ANALOGY, PAGE 517

> Let this book page, appropriate as it is in shape and proportion, be Chase County. Lay your right hand across the page from right edge to left; tuck middle finger under palm and splay your other fingers wide so that your thumb points down, your little finger nearly upward. You have a configuration of the county watercourses, a manual topography of the place. Everything here has been and continues to be shaped by those four drainages: the South Fork of the Cottonwood River (thumb), the Cottonwood (index finger), Middle Creek (ring), Diamond Creek (little finger). Many more streams and brooks are here, but these four control the county. . . .
>
> —*PrairyErth*, p. 13.

E ►

EMPHASIS

▼

There are always words and ideas that a writer wants to emphasize. Fortunately, writers have a half dozen or more ways to make important words and ideas conspicuous. Three such ways are used in the following sentence to emphasize what the writer identifies as Albert Einstein's chief personal trait:

> He was one of the greatest scientists the world has ever known, yet if I were to convey the essence of Albert Einstein in a single word, I would choose *simplicity.*

> —Banesh Hoffman, "Unforgettable Albert Einstein," *Reader's Digest* 92 (January 1968): 107.

The writer gives weight and importance to Einstein's simplicity these ways:

1. Making a direct statement about the importance of the word ("if I were to convey the essence of Albert Einstein in a single word, I would choose *simplicity.*"). Other explicit statements that emphasize the importance of an idea are "The important point is that," "The most alarming situation," "More importantly," "Above all," and so forth.

2. Placing the key word at the end of the sentence. One of the most effective ways to achieve emphasis is to position the idea at the beginning or the end of a passage (a phrase, a sentence, a paragraph, or a major section of text). Placing it at the beginning gives it primacy; placing it at the end increases suspense. Ideas that are positioned in the middle are not regarded to be as important as ideas at the beginning or the end.

3. Italicizing the word to make it stand out from the rest of the text. Other typographical devices that are used most commonly for emphasis are <u>underlining</u>, **boldface type**, and ALL CAPITAL LETTERS.

These three techniques are easy to use. But they should be used infrequently. The more they are used, the less emphatic they become. Following are three other ways of achieving emphasis, and they, too, should be used sparingly, for if they are overused, they lose their impact.

4. Repeating a word or an idea several times. An idea that is mentioned in the title of the text and is repeated several times throughout the text will catch most readers' attention. In the following paragraph, Stephen Jay Gould emphasizes the topic of an essay titled "Shields of Expectations—and Actuality" by repeating the main subject in the forms of nouns, prounouns, and synonyms and by making the terms the subjects of sentences—perhaps the most prominent slot in sentences (the subject and its repeated forms are circled).

The most beautiful specimens in my office, which I happily share with about 50,000 fossil arthropods, rest in the last cabinet of the farthest corner. They are the head shields of *Eurypterus fischeri,* a large extinct fresh water arthropod related to horsehoe crabs. These exquisite fossils are preserved as brown films of chitin, set off like old rotogravure against a surrounding sediment so fine in grain that the background becomes a uniform sheet of gray. They were collected in Estonia by William Patten, a professor of biology at Dartmouth.

—*Eight Little Piggies: Reflections in Natural History* (New York: Norton, 1993), p. 409.

Another form of repetition—alliteration—the repetition of sounds, can give a statement a marked emphasis and make it memorable.

5. Deviating from normal word order (which is subject-verb-direct object for assertions) in a sentence. Putting the verb before the subject makes the subject more emphatic:

normal word order:	Geraldine aced the test.
inverted word order:	Acing the test was Geraldine.
	It was Geraldine who aced the test.

Placing the modifier of the verb before the subject makes the modifier emphatic:

normal word order:	The price of crude oil tripled in the early months of 1984.
inverted word order:	In the early months of 1984 the price of crude oil tripled.

Setting off "In the early months of 1984" with a comma creates a pause that makes the short phrase even more emphatic:

In the early months of 1984, the price of crude oil tripled.

Words that modify a noun are made emphatic by being placed after the noun they modify:

normal word order:	The poorly lighted and cramped library carrel is a terrible place to try to study.
inverted word order:	The library carrel, poorly lighted and cramped, is a terrible place to try to study.

Words and phrases that are out of their normal order are usually separated from the rest of the sentence by commas. Setting off "poorly lighted and cramped" by dashes instead of commas makes the phrase even more emphatic:

> The library carrel—poorly lighted and cramped—is a terrible place to try to study.

FORECASTING STATEMENTS, PAGE 580

HEADINGS, PAGE 603

6. Using **forecasting statements**, such as displayed lists and **headings**, and numbers to enumerate several facts, ideas, or questions, gives increased visibility to major ideas and the way they are organized. Here, for example, is a passage that discusses exercise programs for pregnant women as it might appear with very little attempt to emphasize the main ideas:

> As might be expected, these concerns make advice about exercising during pregnancy somewhat controversial. There is no reason to tell healthy pregnant women not to exercise. In fact they should be encouraged to do so within limits. Women who have been previously sedentary are not advised to start a strenuous exercise program after becoming pregnant. They are better advised to initiate a conservative program such as daily walking. Women who are already training strenuously and become pregnant are best advised to gradually reduce the intensity during the course of pregnancy. In either case, women should avoid training that requires heart rates in excess of 160 bpm, extends over long periods (e.g., distance running), is likely to produce dehydration or hyperthermia or both, or is likely to increase the risk of abdominal trauma. Informed caution should be the guide during this time.

The passage contains three major points about pregnant women engaging in exercise programs. But most readers will have to read very carefully, perhaps even reread, to pick them out. The reason, of course, is that the words that state the major points look like all the other words in the passage and, thus, are given no particular emphasis.

Two ways to give emphasis to the main points are to provide a statement that lets the reader anticipate that significant information is coming and to number the major points. Here is a version of the passage with slight emphasis added by a new sentence inserted after the third sentence to serve as a lead into the three major points to be made; by numbers to set the major points in sequence; and by lower case letters to identify the subitems of the third major point:

> As might be expected, these concerns make advice about exercising during pregnancy somewhat controversial. There is no reason to tell healthy pregnant women not to exercise. In fact, they should be encouraged to do so within limits. The following plan represents a prudent approach that can help maintain a reasonable fitness level while protecting both the mother and the developing child. 1. Women who have been previously sedentary are advised not to start a strenuous exercise program after becoming pregnant. They are better advised to initiate a conservative program such as daily walking. 2. Women who are already training strenuously and become pregnant are best advised to gradually reduce the intensity during the course of pregnancy. 3. In either case, women should avoid training that a) requires heart rates in excess of 160 bpm, b) extends over long periods (e.g., distance running), c) is likely to produce dehydration or hyperthermia or both, or d) is likely to increase the risk of abdominal trauma. Informed caution should be the guide during this time.

Following is the version as it was actually written. Notice the several devices that emphasize the major ideas and the structure of the passage, especially the change in format so that the three major points and the four subpoints of item 3 are shown in a vertical list. The passage is longer than the other two, primarily because the three items listed are set off on separate lines. But the important thing is that this version is quicker to read and easier to understand. Readers do not have to expend enormous amounts of energy to identify the major points and how they are organized.

> As might be expected, these concerns make advice about exercising during pregnancy somewhat controversial. There is no reason to tell healthy pregnant women not to exercise. In fact, they should be encouraged to do so within limits. The following plan represents a prudent approach that can help maintain a reasonable fitness level while protecting both the mother and the developing child.
>
> > 1. Women who have been previously sedentary are advised not to start a strenuous exercise program after becoming pregnant. They are better advised to initiate a conservative program such as daily walking.

2. Women who are already training strenuously and become pregnant are best advised to gradually reduce the intensity during the course of pregnancy.

3. In either case, women should avoid training that

    a. requires heart rates in excess of 160 bpm

    b. extends over long periods (e.g., distance running)

    c. is likely to produce dehydration or hyperthermia or both

    d. is likely to increase the risk of abdominal trauma

Informed caution should be the guide during this time.

> —David K. Miller and T. Earl Allen, *Fitness: A Lifetime Commitment*, 4th ed. (New York: Macmillan, 1990), p. 71.

As you compare these three passages, you can see in the second and third versions the main ideas emerge with greater and greater clarity, like pictures in a tray of developer. Certainly not all passages would benefit from this kind of formatting. There is such a thing as overkill. But in a passage where you want to be sure that readers can easily identify the major points, this kind of strongly visual **format** is helpful.

FORMAT, PAGE 582

EXEMPLIFICATION (ILLUSTRATION)

▼

When good writers think that readers need more information to understand a term or an idea, they usually provide examples. An example can be as short as a word or two or as long as a few phrases, as in the following statements. In the first statement, the term *lower vertebrates* is defined by examples:

> Few species of the lower vertebrates, that is, the fishes, amphibia, and reptiles, build nests of any kind. . . .

> —Karl von Frisch, *Animal Architecture*, trans. Lisabeth Gombrich (New York: Harcourt Brace Jovanovich, 1974), p. 152.

The specific examples ("the fishes, amphibia, and reptiles") make clear what "the lower vertebrates" refers to.

In the second statement, the aspects that never change are illustrated by five examples:

Some aspects of China never change—the rice planters bent double, the weeder on his stool, the boy pedaling his 2000-year-old irrigation pump, the buffalo man, the duck-herd.

> —Paul Theroux, *Riding the Iron Rooster:*
> *By Train Through China* (New York:
> Ivy Books, 1988), p. 267.

An example might be stated in a sentence, or a series of examples might extend through several sentences or even paragraphs. The following passage, written by the noted science essayist Lewis Thomas, consists of a general statement that is followed by a barrage of specific examples:

Almost anything that an animal can employ to make a sound is put to use. Drumming, created by beating the feet, is used by prairie hens, rabbits, and mice; the head is banged by woodpeckers and certain other birds; the males of death-watch beetles make a rapid ticking sound by percussion of a protuberance on the abdomen against the ground; a faint but audible ticking is made by the tiny beetle *Lepinotus inguellinus*, which is less than two millimeters in length. Fish make sounds by clicking their teeth, blowing air, and drumming with special muscles against tuned inflated air bladders. Solid structures are set to vibrating by toothed bows in crustaceans and insects. The proboscis of the death's head hawk moth is used as a kind of reed instrument, blown through to make high-pitched, reedy notes.

Gorillas beat their chests for certain kinds of discourse. Animals with loose skeletons rattle them, or, like rattlesnakes, get sounds from externally placed structures. Turtles, alligators, crocodiles, and even snakes make various more or less vocal sounds. Leeches have been heard to tap rhythmically on leaves, engaging the attention of other leeches, which tap back, in synchrony. Even earthworms make sounds, faint staccato notes in regular clusters. Toads sing to each other, and their friends sing back in antiphony.

> —"The Music of *This* Sphere," in *The Lives of a*
> *Cell: Notes of a Biology Watcher* (New York:
> Viking, 1974), pp. 21–22.

The passage is more interesting and credible with the examples than if Thomas had remained general and abstract. The number and variety of examples are, in themselves, interesting and informative. Most readers will recognize at least some of the noise-making methods, and all readers will have a better understanding about the great number of signals that are transmitted in nature.

The use of specific examples, typical instances, sample cases, and illustrated anecdotes to clarify a concept or support a point is called *exemplification*. Its most important effect is to link the writer's ideas to concrete and familiar experiences and things that give readers something specific to relate to. Often the link is signaled by such expressions as "for example," "to illustrate," or "for instance," as it is in the following paragraph that explains a problem in certain kinds of federal income transfer programs:

> A third problem with the categorical nature of the transfer system in the United States is that payments sometimes go to nonneedy recipients. As an example, the complex agricultural subsidy programs have ballooned to total spending levels approaching $25 billion in the 1980s and primarily reward affluent corporate farm owners, ironically, in a country that values work, for work they do not perform. Created during the Great Depression, these programs have long outlived their usefulness, encourage overproduction, and have not saved the family farm (which, probably should not be saved at public expense, any more than any declining industry should be saved). If categorical aid were abandoned, and transfer payments were based strictly on poverty and income-based needs, most recipients of agricultural subsidies would not (and should not) be eligible.
>
> —Marcia Lynn Whicker and Raymond A. Moore,
> *Making America Competitive: Policies for a*
> *Global Future* (New York: Praeger, 1988), p. 125.

Writers draw factual examples from their own experiences and those of others. They create hypothetical examples by generalizing from many experiences.

Factual examples have high credibility because they describe real instances or experiences. Being both factual and specific, they are quite effective, because they are as close as writing can get to real experience. In the following passage, a problem is stated in the first paragraph and is followed by a brief anecdote from the writer's personal experience that illustrates the problem:

> . . . I am willing to admit that there are some real and useful things to learn from men. Not from all men—in fact, we may have the most to learn from some of the men we like the least. This realization does not mean that my feminist principles have gone soft with age: what I think women could learn from men is how to get *tough*. After more than a decade of consciousness-raising, assertiveness training, and hand-to-hand combat in the battle of the sexes, we're still too ladylike. Let me try that again—we're just too damn ladylike.
>
> Here is an example from my own experience, a story that I blush to recount. A few years ago, at an international conference held in an exotic and luxurious setting, a prestigious professor invited me to his room for what he said would be an intellectual discussion on matters of theoretical importance. So far, so good. I showed up promptly. But only minutes into the conversation—held in all-too-adjacent chairs—it emerged that he was interested in something more substantial than a meeting of minds. I was disgusted, but not enough to overcome 30-odd years of programming in ladylikeness. Every time his comments took a lecherous turn, I chattered distractingly; every time his hand found its way to my knee, I returned it as if it were something he had misplaced. This went on for an unconscionable period (as much as 20 minutes); then there was a minor scuffle, a dash for the door, and I was out—with nothing violated but my self-esteem. I, a full-grown feminist, conversant with such matters as rape crisis counseling and sexual harassment at the workplace, had behaved like a ninny—or, as I now understand it, like a lady.
>
> —Barbara Ehrenreich, "What I've Learned
> from Men: Lessons for a Full-Grown Feminist,"
> *Ms.* 14, no. 2 (August 1985): 24.

Factual and hypothetical examples are often drawn from research, as illustrated in the passage on the next page by Arlene Skolnick, a research psychologist at the Institute of Human Development, University of California at Berkeley, in which she describes the lack of privacy for families in earlier times.

Perhaps what distinguishes the modern family most from its colonial counterpart is its newfound privacy. Throughout the 17th and 18th centuries, well over 90 percent of the American population lived in small rural communities. Unusual behavior rarely went unnoticed, and neighbors often intervened directly in a family's affairs, to help or to chastise.

The most dramatic example was the rural "charivari," prevalent in both Europe and the United States until the early 19th century. The purpose of these noisy gatherings was to censure community members for familial transgressions—unusual sexual behavior, marriages between persons of grossly discrepant ages, or "household disorder," to name but a few. As historian Edward Shorter describes it in *The Making of the Modern Family*:

> Sometimes the demonstration would consist of masked individuals circling somebody's house at night, screaming, beating on pans, and blowing cow horns . . . on other occasions, the offender would be seized and marched through the streets, seated perhaps backwards on a donkey or forced to wear a placard describing his sins.

The state itself had no qualms about intruding into a family's affairs by statute, if necessary. Consider 17th-century New England's "stubborn child" laws that, though never actually enforced, sanctioned the death penalty for chronic disobedience to one's parents.

> —"The Paradox of Perfection," *Wilson Quarterly* 4, no. 3 (Summer 1980): 116.

Hypothetical examples refer to or describe imaginary things or experiences. They are used when a concrete example is needed to illustrate an idea and no actual example is available, or a hypothetical example would be simpler for the reader to understand. In most cases, a hypothetical example is as good a factual example. Consider the following one that explains how value-added taxation works:

> Value-added taxes are widely used abroad because they raise large amounts of money while simultaneously creating incentives to consume less and save more. Instead of being taxed upon what one puts into society (the income from work and savings) one is taxed on the consumption one takes out of society. With a 15 percent valued-added tax, a person who buys a $10,000 car must pay an extra $1,500 in value-

added taxes when he buys the car but can completely avoid those taxes if he instead saves the $10,000. As a result, the incentive effects of value-added taxes work in favor of what society wants, less consumption, rather than against what society wants, more savings and work, as in the case with higher personal income taxes. As a result value-added taxes are an integral part of any program seeking to encourage more private savings and to transform government from a dis-saver into a saver.

—Daniel Bell, *The Deficits: How Big? How Long? How Dangerous?* (New York: New York University Press, 1985), pp. 110–11.

Using Exemplification Effectively

To be effective, examples must be chosen carefully. Here are three things to consider when selecting examples.

▶ Factual examples, of course, must be factually correct. All examples must be relevant to and representative of the general idea or point being discussed.

▶ Examples must be developed in sufficient detail when readers are not familiar with either the general idea or the example. For instance, when Skolnick uses the example of the shivaree ("charivari") to illustrate community pressure on misbehaving families during the seventeenth and eighteenth centuries, she explains its purpose and occasions and quotes an historian to cite several of its forms.

▶ There is the question of how many examples are sufficient to support a generalization or illustrate a concept. That is a difficult question to answer. The number depends in large part on how well informed the readers are and whether the point being made conflicts with the readers' beliefs. Some concepts and arguments are supported adequately by a single extended example, but most are supported by several, for one example does not always seem to be sufficient. Two or three examples often seem just right. More than three or four seem to belabor the point, unless the writer's argument conflicts with long-held beliefs of the readers, or the writer's generalizations would be insufficiently supported without several more examples.

FORECASTING STATEMENTS

All texts contain information arranged in a specific order. Readers can make their way through a text fairly easily if they can predict (1) the topics that will be discussed, (2) the order of their presentation, and (3) the places where a text will undergo significant changes in topic.

Once they get the big picture, they can read optimally. They can anticipate the way the thesis will be developed, even during the first reading of the text. They can retrieve specific information or parts of the text efficiently when reviewing or rereading the text.

It is the writer's responsibility to orient readers to content and organization. However, because writers are so familiar with what they have written and know what will happen next in their texts, they are not always sensitive to the readers' needs. They forget or are unaware that readers do not know in advance the organization and have to figure it out as they read.

To guide readers through your text, you can provide forecasting statements that announce the topics and preview the way they are organized. There are two kinds of forecasting statements: explicit and implied. The opening paragraph of an essay by Bertrand Russell on the necessity of achieving wisdom illustrates an explicit forecasting statement in the last sentence:

> Most people would agree that, although our age far surpasses all previous ages in knowledge, there has been no correlative increase in wisdom. But agreement ceases as soon as we attempt to define "wisdom" and consider means of promoting it. I want to ask first what wisdom is, and then what can be done to teach it.
>
> —"Knowledge and Wisdom,"
> in *Portraits from Memory* (New York:
> Simon & Schuster, 1956), p. 173.

The last sentence, which introduces the two topics to be discussed, enables readers to form their expectations about what Russell will discuss and in what order. Their view of a text is continuously adjusting to cues that make explicit what will subsequently be presented in more detail.

Implicit forecasting statements provide an overview of text organization without referring so baldly to the writer's intentions. The opening paragraph in a passage that discusses the conflicting theories of the labor market states the subject and then identifies the four conflicting theories that the writer will discuss:

> Just as archaeologists have two sources of information on ancient civilizations—artifacts and writings—so an observer of economic activity has two sources of information on the labor market: he can examine the observed distribution of wages and employment, or he can turn to the economic literature for a view of how wages and employment are determined. There are problems of a striking mismatch between observed data and theory, but within the theoretical literature is another peculiar phenomenon. At least four different theories of the labor market present themselves. Equilibrium price-auction economics, Keynesian macro-economics, monetarists' macro-economics, and labor economics all have different theories to explain what occurs. The theories are mutually inconsistent, but each has its advocates and economic practitioners.
>
> —Lester C. Thurow, *Dangerous Currents:*
> *The State of Economics* (New York:
> Random House, 1983), p. 181.

As readers would expect, Thurow divides his discussion into explanations and contrasts of these four theories, taking them up in the order in which they are listed in the next-to-last sentence of the paragraph. Here are the topic sentences that begin the discussion of each theory:

> In the standard price-auction model, the labor market is treated as if it were like any other market in which price (wage) is the short-run market-clearing mechanism. (p. 181)

> In the economic models of Keynesian macro-economics, the demand for labor depends upon total output, not upon the wage rate. (p. 182)

> Monetarist macro-economics similarly depends upon assumptions of rigidity in the labor market. (p. 182)

> In institutional labor economics, inter-skill or inter-industry wage differentials become the focus of analysis. (p. 183)

After discussing the four theories, the writer cues the reader that the text is shifting into a more generalized discussion of the conflicting theories with this sentence:

> Unfortunately, these four theoretical perspectives are often mutually inconsistent. (p. 183)

TITLES, PAGE 667

HEADINGS, PAGE 603

TRANSITIONS, PAGE 676

Other features you can use to increase readers' ability to predict topics and organization are informative **titles**, a table of contents (for lengthy texts), **headings**, and **transitions**.

FORMAT

▼

Format in writing refers to the physical appearance of the text—the typeface, the white space, the placement of text on the page, the size of the page itself. A text that is professional in appearance, easy and inviting to read, and free of format errors is more likely to be read. Although neatness and attractiveness help create respect and confidence, they are not the most important aspects of format. We assume you know that the kind of sloppy work associated with incorrect spelling, faint type due to a wornout typewriter or printer ribbon, or tattered or smeared paper is unacceptable.

We discuss format here as a way to help readers read what we write. Many texts, like short essays and fiction, make only minimal use of conventions of format. The standard printed page is a rectangular block of text surrounded by white margins. Consistent margins, paragraph indentations, capitalization, punctuation, and spaces between words and after punctuation are the most noticeable visual features of such texts, as the following passage illustrates:

> *Roseanne* the sitcom, which was inspired by Barr the stand-up comic, is a radical departure simply for featuring blue-collar Americans—and for depicting them as something other than half-witted greasers and low-life louts. The working class does not usually get much of a role in the American entertainment spectacle. In the seventies, muscular blue-collar males (*Rocky, The Deer Hunter, Saturday Night Fever*) enjoyed a brief modishness on the screen, while

Archie Bunker, the consummate blue-collar bigot, raved away
on the tube. . . .

—Barbara Ehrenreich, "The Wretched of the
Earth," *The New Republic Magazine* 202,
no. 14 (April 2, 1990): 28.

The format conventions in this paragraph are so familiar, you are probably unaware of them. You probably have learned unconsciously these conventions, which have become customary in our language and culture. However, anything that affects the arrangement and appearance of the text is format. Even these relatively few format conventions provide helpful clues about how to read the text. If paragraph indentation, justified left margin, uppercase and lowercase letters, spacing, and punctuation had not been invented as writing developed, our texts would look like an unbroken string of letters of the same size (or of no particularly consistent size) with no space between them and with no punctuation, much like this:

ROSANNETHESITCOMWHICHWASINSPIREDBY
RAPEDLACIDARASICIMOCPUDNATSEHTRRAB
TURESIMPLYFORFEATURINGBLUECOLLARAM
HTEMOSSAMEHTGNITCIPEDROFDNASNACIRE
INGOTHERTHANHALFWITTEDGREASERSANDL

These few lines are enough to give you an idea of how writing without format (except for the conventions of letters such as *R, S, E,* and so on facing a particular direction and of the lines running horizontally) looked in early manuscripts. You can see the difficulty in trying to read more than a few words of it. Without the stream of letters divided into words, it is difficult to tell where one word ends and another begins. With some lines reading from right to left, the passage looks like it is written in a strange language. So even minimal format conventions, especially those that are so familiar that both writers and readers are unaware of them, are essential for reading ease.

Although easily distinguishable from prose, the format of much poetry shares the generally conservative aspects of this most elemental level of format. The opening two stanzas of "The Demon Lover" illustrate a definite format that is easily recognized because of its neat arrangement—the consistent repetition of line lengths, placement of rhyming words, indentation of alternating lines, and the unjustified right margin. These are signs of certain kinds of poetry in print format.

"O where have you been, my long, long love,
  This long seven years and more?"
"O I'm come to seek my former vows
  Ye granted me before."

"O hold your tongue of your former vows,
  For they will breed sad strife;
O hold your tongue of your former vows
  For I have become a wife."

—Anonymous, "The Demon Lover"

These elements, whether in prose or poetry, are relatively simple matters. But since they establish the basis for a good general appearance on the page, you should give them careful attention even as you begin the first draft.

Other texts, such as letters, brochures, manuals, advertisements, and formal reports, also rely on most of the format elements just mentioned. But longer and more complex texts depend more heavily on visual information. Effective use of white space, variation in typeface, graphics, numbers, bullets, and lists prominently display the structure and logical relationships in the text. At this more advanced level, there are format decisions to make about headings, lists, graphics, and special displays for quotations and equations.

Headings

Headings serve two major purposes: (1) they break up the mass of text to indicate the organization and scope of the material, thus helping browsers who are curious about what information the text contains, and (2) they serve as a kind of outline of the subject matter and as guideposts to readers who seek specific information in a particular part of the text. Headings are distinguished from the regular text by their position and the surrounding white space, and sometimes they are given additional emphasis by their typeface (underlined, bold, italicized, etc.). They are most helpful when they are informative. (See **headings**.)

HEADINGS, PAGE 603

Lists

A list is an itemized series, often arranged in a particular order. It may be part of the running text or in outline form. Lists in outline form should be used sparingly and only when you want to emphasize the items in a series. For example, consider the following list, which is part of the running text:

> The main criteria for selecting a computer monitor should be that the display 1) supports a full assortment of characters, numbers, and punctuation marks, 2) is easy to read, 3) is comfortable to view so as not to cause operator fatigue, 4) has operator controls for brightness and contrast, and 5) minimizes light reflection.

Compare that passage with the following outline list:

> The main criteria for selecting a computer monitor should be that the display
>
> 1. supports a full assortment of characters, numbers, and punctuation marks,
> 2. is easy to read,
> 3. is comfortable to view so as not to cause operator fatigue,
> 4. has operator controls for brightness and contrast, and
> 5. minimizes light reflection.

Allow your eyes to linger on each version a moment, and you will discover that the list has spatial action. The outline form is powerful because it pulls the attention of readers and directs their eyes toward the items in the list, heightening the list by breaking it away from surrounding text, which is normally seen as a solid block. Each item is seen completely and not buried within the passage, enabling readers to distinguish each item in the series. The items of information in the outline list are clearly more noticeable than the ones in the running text, which have only numbers and commas separating them. Numbering the items in a list suggests that the order is important and that the list is complete. If the sequence of the list is unimportant or if the entries in the list represent only some of the possible items, then use bullets (•) or dashes (—) instead of numbers as eye guides.

Format is often an important rhetorical consideration. Because the heightening created by the outline form of lists directs immediate attention to the information it contains, you need to consider your readers' feelings when deciding which list format to use. If you are conveying unwelcome news—perhaps explaining why you cannot grant the reader or readers their request, or perhaps detailing the reasons why you do not share their opinion—politeness and common sense demand that such information be softened by being visually embed-ded on the page and made part of the running text. That way, the list is less accessible, and readers will encounter the items sequentially rather than being directed to them at first glance.

Graphics

GRAPHICS, PAGE 596 **Graphics** (tables and figures) may be incorporated on the page with regular text or may be on separate pages. Unless a graphic is large, it is usually not good practice to place it on a separate page by itself. The advantages of placing graphics on a page with text are that it reduces the number of pages necessary for the composition, and it places the graphic close to the related text, making it less likely that the readers will have to flip pages to look at the graphic and to read the text per-taining to it. In preparing graphics, be sure that the final size of the graphic fits along with other text within the margins of the page with-out being too crowded and that the graphic is placed near its reference in the text.

Quotations

If your composition contains material quoted directly from other sources, there are three conventions of format to observe.

▶ Short direct quotations (normally of four or fewer typed lines) are usually embedded into the text and enclosed in quotation marks:

> The effect of the American Revolution on the nature of gov-ernment in the society of Europe was felt and recognized from the moment it became a fact. After the American rebellion began, "an extraordinary alternation took place in the mind of a great part of the people of Holland," homeland of St. Eustatius, recalled Sir James Harris, Earl of Malmesbury, who was British Ambassador at The Hague in the years immediately following the triumph of the American Revolution. "Doubts arose," he wrote in his memoirs, "about the authority of the Stadtholder" (Sovereign of the Netherlands and Prince of Orange).
>
> —Barbara W. Tuchman, *The First Salute*
> (New York: Knopf, 1988), pp. 5–6.

Embedding short quoted phrases enables you to make a point by quoting credible sources and then to move on in your own voice.

▶ Long direct quotations (normally of five or more typed lines) are typically set off from the running text by indenting the quoted material ten or so spaces to the right and without adding quotation marks. These kinds of quotations are called *displayed* quotations. In the passage below, both short quotations and a longer, displayed quotation are used:

> Freud, on the other hand, remained profoundly concerned throughout his career to overcome the paradox. He was still struggling to do so in the last article he wrote, which he had to leave unfinished. In this article, Freud postulated that the ego of a person in analysis must, when young, "have behaved in a remarkable manner" under the influence of "a powerful trauma." The child must have been tormented both by the desire to satisfy a strong instinct and by fear of the dangers that might ensue through doing so. The response is a split whereby the child both satisfies the instinct symbolically and rejects any knowledge concerning the matter:
>
> > The two contrary reactions to the conflict persist as the center-point of a split in the ego. The whole process seems so strange to us because we take for granted the synthetic nature of the workings of the ego. But we are clearly at fault in this. The synthetic function of the ego, though it is of such extraordinary importance, is subject to particular conditions and is liable to a whole series of disturbances.
>
> —Sissela Bok, "Secrecy and Self-Deception," in *Secrets: On the Ethics of Concealments and Revelation* (New York: Pantheon, 1982), p. 63.

▶ Short direct quotations, especially poetry, are given emphasis by being formatted the same way as long direct quotations:

> In the great chain of being, each organism forms a definite link in a single sequence leading from the lowest amoeba in a drop of water to ever more complex beings, culminating in, you guessed it, our own exalted selves.
> > Mark how it mounts to man's imperial race,
> > from the green myriads in the people grass.
> wrote Alexander Pope in his expostulations in heroic couplets from the *Essay on Man*.
>
> —Stephen Jay Gould, *The Flamingo's Smile* (New York: Norton, 1985), p. 282.

Since they stand out from the regular text, it is important that short quotations be worthy of the attention given them.

Equations and Formulas

Equations and formulas are specialized forms that represent mathematical relationships and chemical or physical processes, and they should be used only if readers can understand them or if they are thoroughly defined. When you use equations or formulas, you will need to give them special attention in making format decisions. Simple equations and formulas sometimes run in the line of text, like this:

> Arithmetic and algebra are also founded on experience. The expressions $2 + 2 = 3 + 1 = 4$ are psychological generalizations. Algebra is simply a more abstract extension of such generalizations.

> —Morris Kline, *Mathematics and the Search for Knowledge* (New York: Oxford, 1985), p. 19.

More often, an equation or formula is *displayed*, placed on a line by itself. No punctuation follows the displayed equation or formula except when it ends a sentence, as in this example:

> The cosmic rays demonstrate the existence of a physical world in which the energy of the particles is many times that of their mass when at rest. The velocities are therefore almost c because

$$p = \frac{mv}{\sqrt{(I-v^2/c^2)}}\, , \quad E = \frac{mc^2}{\sqrt{(I-v^2/c^2)}}$$

> This means that the v are not suitable physical parameters; so much can happen in a minute range of v, which contains an enormous range of p and E values. I interpret this in the sense that p and E cannot be reduced to, or measured by, v, but have an independent significance. There are other indications in support of this, but we cannot go into this here. [Nuclei with v of the order $c/5$ to $c/10$ (for protons or neutrons) are an intermediate stage]. The problem is to extend classical mechanics so as to include this hypothesis. I use the fact that the canonical

transformations are symmetrical in x and p; e.g., if they are defined through the Poisson brackets:

$$(u, v) = \sum_k \left(\frac{\partial u}{\partial x_k} \frac{\partial v}{\partial p_k} - \frac{\partial u}{\partial p_k} \frac{\partial v}{\partial x_k} \right)$$

then the transformation $(x,p) \to (X,P)$ is canonical when

$$(X_{k3} X_l) = 0_3 \quad (P_{k3} P_l) = 0_3 \quad (X_{k3} P_l) = \delta_{kl}$$

—Letter from Max Born to Albert Einstein,
April 11, 1938, from *The Born-Einstein Letters*,
New York: Walker, 1971), p. 132.

A sequence of important equations or formulas is set off from the text (displayed), and if they are referred to elsewhere in the text, they are numbered in parentheses flush with the right margin for easy reference.

He [Galileo] discovered that if air resistance is neglected, all bodies falling to the surface of the Earth have the same constant acceleration a: that is, they gain velocity at the same rate, 32 feet per second each second. In symbols:

$$a = 32 \tag{1}$$

If the body is dropped—that is, merely allowed to fall from the hand—it will start with zero velocity. Hence, at the end of 1 second its velocity is 32 feet per second; at the end of 2 seconds its velocity is 32 times 2 or 64 feet per second; and so forth. At the end of t seconds its velocity v is $32t$ feet per second; in symbols:

$$v = 32t \tag{2}$$

This formula tells us exactly how the velocity of a falling body increases with time. It says, too, that a body that falls for a longer time will have a greater velocity. This is a familiar fact, for most people have observed that bodies dropped from high altitudes hit the ground at higher speeds than bodies dropped from low altitudes.

We cannot multiply the velocity by the time to find the distance that a dropped body falls in a given amount of time. This would give the correct distance only if the velocity were constant. Galileo proved, however, that the correct formula for the distance d the body falls in t seconds is

$$d = 16t^2 \qquad\qquad (3)$$

where d is the number of feet the body falls in t seconds. For example, in 3 seconds, the body falls 16 x 3^2 or 144 feet.

By dividing both sides of formula (3) by 16 and then taking the square root of both sides, we find that the time required for an object to fall a given distance d is given by the formula $t = \sqrt{d/16}$. Notice that the mass of the falling body does not appear in this formula. We can thus see that all bodies take the same time to fall a given distance. This is the lesson Galileo is supposed to have learned by dropping objects from the tower of Pisa. People still find it difficult to believe, nevertheless, that a piece of lead and a feather when dropped from a height in a vacuum reach the ground in the same time.

—Morris Kline, *Mathematics and the Search
for Knowledge* (New York: Oxford, 1985),
pp. 104–106.

For more information on specific methods of expressing equations and formulas, see a standard style guide, such as *The Chicago Manual of Style* or *Mathematics into Type.*

Unorthodox Formats

In addition to the conventional format elements described above, there is yet another style of format that is unorthodox and sometimes violates conventional format designs. This type of format is most often found in poetry and experimental prose. One of the notable writers who departs from conventional format is the poet E. E. Cummings, the author of the following sentence:

> high
> the &   for me is SELF ('the individual or indivisible')
> low

—quoted in Milton A. Cohen, *Poet and
Painter: The Aesthetics of E. E. Cummings'
Early Work* (Detroit: Wayne State
University Press, 1987), p. 79.

The unorthodox placement of *high* above the line of type and *low* beneath the line of type is more than just a stunt or joke. In conjunction with *SELF* spelled in all capital letters, it shows how format is related to the idea expressed by the writer: the sanctity of self.

Many writers have manipulated format—sometimes playfully, as in Lewis Carroll's *Alice in Wonderland*, in which the tale the mouse tells Alice visually resembles a long tail trailing down the page, and sometimes more seriously, as in the emblematic poems of the seventeenth-century English poets Robert Herrick and George Herbert. Much modern poetry departs from conventional format, as does the following poem. At first the poem may appear to be formless, but the unusual typographic features are significant to its aesthetic value and content:

> l(a
>
> le
>
> af
>
> fa
>
> ll
>
> s)
>
> one
>
> l
>
> iness

—E. E. Cummings, *95 Poems* (New York: Harcourt Brace Jovanovich, 1958), p. 1.

To understand the poem, readers are forced to look at it as a physical fact. The vertical arrangement of the poem captures the image of a falling leaf. Upon closer examination, we can rearrange the letters horizontally to read *L (a leaf falls) oneliness*. Then we see that if we move the *L* in front of *oneliness*, we get *loneliness*. The image of a single falling leaf is a traditional symbol of absence or loneliness or death, and the vertical arrangement of the letters down the page is an example of how format matches the action or concept or feeling described. The separation of the *L* from the rest of the word *oneliness* and the separation of letters from each other by lines that are only one to five letters long illustrate visually both the separation that is the primary cause of loneliness and the identification of *loneliness* with *oneliness*.

As E. E. Cummings's innovative uses of capitalization, punctuation, and space in patterns that support meaning illustrate, there are format designs that more appropriately and imaginatively communicate the subject matter than do some conventional formats. Paying attention to format does not mean that you are abandoning well-chosen words or ignoring well-written sentences. Words and sentences continue to be our native media. But you must begin paying more attention to the format. It is always there. Good writers know how to control it for their own purposes.

At the most elemental level there are several format decisions to make concerning paper quality (good-quality bond for important letters and papers), sheet size ($8\frac{1}{2} \times 11$ inches is generally preferred when another size is not specified), binding (paper clipped or stapled once in the upper left corner, etc.), page design (for example, text on one side of the page only, 1-inch margins all around, double-spaced with indented beginnings of paragraphs for regular text, ragged right margins, and page numbers in the upper right corner directly above the end of the type line or at the bottom of the page in the center), and typography (serif type of a size and style that is easy to read, but not too large).

Always check to see if your text should conform to particular format specifications required or preferred by your teacher, editor, coauthor, publisher, or audience. If not, you will have to decide for yourself what format seems best for the situation. Even if there are changes in format later, your initial choice of format will give you a stable target to work toward. The same text formatted different ways is illustrated in Figures 4.1, 4.2, and 4.3.

Figure 4.1 shows the text single-spaced with the long important quotation run in to the text and with the right margin justified. Unless your printer prints proportionally (that is, creates equal spaces between each word in a line), justified right margins create unequal spaces between words as the printer attempts to make all lines the same length. In the first line of text in Figure 4.1, there are wider-than-normal spaces between *Temple* and *Bar* and between *which* and *attempted*. This format is crowded and looks uninviting and difficult to read. It is the poorest format of all.

The text in Figure 4.2 (p. 594) is double-spaced, and the long important quotation is displayed, although not very well. The right-justified margin again creates uneven spacing between words in a line.

The text in Figure 4.3 (p. 595) is double-spaced, and the long important quotation is displayed. The right margin is not justified (that is, the lines have a common starting point on the left margin—except for the indentation at the beginning of paragraphs and the displayed quotation—but the lines do not end at the same space on the right margin). Unjustified right margins allow your printer to create equal spaces between words in the same line. This format is the best of the three.

of <u>Temple Bar</u>, and which attempted to counter
Matthew Arnold's disparagement of Lord Macaulay.
According to the anonymous author of the <u>Temple
Bar</u> article, Arnold is guilty of extreme ingratitude: To be a great civiliser is surely no small
title to gratitude, if not to fame. To leave men
and things better, if by ever so little, than one
found them--he who had done this much, if he had
done no more, may surely go down well content into
his grave. ("A Plea for an Old Friend" 86) As
this writer continued, it was Macaulay who "stimulated and prepared us to receive the higher culture which Mr. Arnold has preached so untiringly,
so elegantly." He has "revived in us the taste
for what our fathers . . . were wont to speak of
as polite learning. . . ." (86-87). This notion
that Macaulay was largely responsible for the
growth of the number of middle-class readers during the generation immediately preceding Arnold's
period of literary criticism provides the kind of
assessment of Macaulay that will allow the last
third of the twentieth century to understand his
place as a literary critic. Macaulay's practice
as a critic, although it was perhaps more energetic and declamatory than Arnold's, was also
serious and responsible. Although his voice was
at times loud and strident, it helped prepare the
way for the quieter, calmer voice of Arnold.

If Macaulay's general goals of criticism were
similar to Arnold's, his approach was not. To
develop taste in his readers and establish critical guidelines for other literary and social critics, Macaulay believed that the literary critic
had to become occupied by what would appear to
Arnold like "practical considerations." What made
this seem so different from Arnold was not his
attitude toward literature but his practice as a
critic. E. K. Brown, in a study of Arnold's
performance as a critic, distinguished between the
disposition and the strategy of Arnold as a "dis-
interested" critic: "In one meaning of the word
Arnold is recommending . . . a critical strategy,
a quality in one's mode of presenting one's ideas
which is essential if these ideas are to become
widely operative. For a Victorian critic's ideas

Figure 4.1 Single-spaced text with justified right margin. Notice the crowded appearance and the uneven spaces between words in the same line. The long important quotation is not displayed.

of _Temple Bar_, and which attempted to counter
Matthew Arnold's disparagement of Lord Macaulay.
According to the anonymous author of the _Temple
Bar_ article, Arnold is guilty of extreme ingrati-
tude:

> To be a great civiliser is surely no small
> title to gratitude, if not to fame. To leave
> men and things better, if by ever so little,
> than one found them--he who had done this
> much, if he had done no more may surely go
> down well content into his grave. ("A Plea
> for an Old Friend" 86)

As this writer continued, it was Macaulay who
"stimulated and prepared us to receive the higher
culture which Mr. Arnold has preached so untiringly, so elegantly." He has "revived in us the
taste for what our fathers . . . were wont to
speak of as polite learning. . . ." (86-87). This
notion that Macaulay was largely responsible for
the growth of the number of middle-class readers
during the generation immediately preceding
Arnold's period of literary criticism provides the
kind of assessment of Macaulay that will allow the

Figure 4.2 Double-spaced text with justified right margin. Notice the uneven spaces between words in the same line. The long important quotation (lines 6 through 12) is displayed, but not displayed well.

of <u>Temple Bar</u>, and which attempted to counter
Matthew Arnold's disparagement of Lord Macaulay.
According to the anonymous author of the <u>Temple Bar</u>
article, Arnold is guilty of extreme ingratitude:

> To be a great civiliser is surely
> no small title to gratitude, if not
> to fame. To leave men and things
> better, if by ever so little, than
> one found them--he who had done this
> much, if he had done no more, may
> surely go down well content into his
> grave. ("A Plea for an Old Friend" 86)

As this writer continued, it was Macaulay who
"stimulated and prepared us to receive the higher
culture which Mr. Arnold has preached so untiringly, so elegantly." He has "revived in us the
taste for what our fathers . . . were wont to speak
of as polite learning. . . ." (86-87). This notion
that Macaulay was largely responsible for the
growth of the number of middle-class readers during
the generation immediately preceding Arnold's period
of literary criticism provides the kind of assessment of Macaulay that will allow the last

Figure 4.3 Double-spaced text with unjustified right margin. Notice that shortening the lines of the displayed quotation (lines 5 through 12) gives the quotation more emphasis.

G

GRAPHICS

▼

Graphics, widely used in business, technical, and scientific writing, can help writers make certain kinds of information readily understandable in other kinds of texts. Pictures, tables, flow diagrams, and charts can convey concepts and data so that objects and scenes are easy to visualize, processes are easy to follow, comparisons are easy to make, and trends and other relationships are easy to spot. Fortunately, you do not have to be an artist or commercial illustrator to create the kinds of graphics that you will most likely use. If you have the opportunity, familiarize yourself with a computer graphics program; one may be available with your word processing program. However, until you learn how to use a computer graphics program, you can create acceptable graphics with a ruler (for measuring and drawing straight lines), a drafting compass (for drawing circles and arcs), and a protractor (for laying down angles).

Photographs and Drawings

DESCRIPTION, PAGE 565 Photographs and drawings are particularly useful in supporting **description**. Photographs are nearly ideal for giving the actual appearance of physical things. Their high degree of reality can show vividly and explicitly the effects of a forest devastated by acid rain, the details of a floral arrangement, or the physique of Arnold Schwarzenegger. Their two major drawbacks are that they show only the external appearance of an object and they may include realistic clutter that can distract from what is being illustrated. Photographs should center on the object of interest and should include as little irrelevant background material as possible. They should be black and white (unless color is important) and be focused to bring out significant details.

While less realistic than photographs, drawings are often more useful because they allow for greater selectivity of details. Figure 4.4 is a line drawing that illustrates four arrangements of nozzles on field equipment for spraying insecticides and herbicides. Unlike a photograph, it shows only the details that need to be shown.

Tables

Almost any kind of data can be presented in tables, one of the easiest forms of presenting information from the standpoint of both writers and readers. Figure 4.5 (p. 598) is a table that reports information about

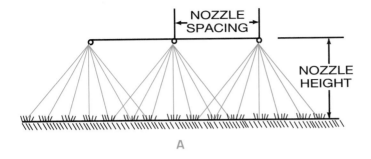

A

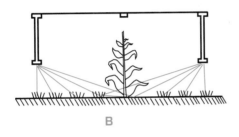

B

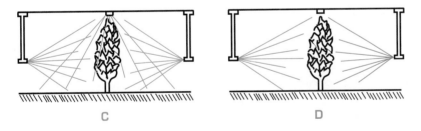

A. Complete overtop coverage for weeds or insects and
between narrow rows for weed control.

B. Between rows for weed control.

C. Over and between rows for insect control.

D. Between rows for insect control.

Figure 4.4 Line drawing illustrating nozzle arrangements for spraying insecticides
and pesticides. Line drawings allow for greater selectivity of details than photographs do, showing only the important details. (William Mayfield, *Field Sprayer
Equipment and Calibration*, Circular R-11.)

No. 440. Congressional Bills Vetoed: 1961 to 1993

(See also *Historical Statistics, Colonial Times to 1970*, Series Y 199–203)

PERIOD	PRESIDENT	Total vetoes	Regular vetoes	Pocket vetoes	Vetoes sustained	Bills passed over veto
1961–1963	Kennedy	21	12	9	21	—
1963–1969	Johnson	30	16	14	30	—
1969–1974	Nixon	42	24	18	36	6
1974–1977	Ford	72	53	19	60	12
1977–1981	Carter	31	13	18	29	2
1981–1989	Reagan	78	39	39	69	9
1989–1993	Bush	35	22	13	34	1

Figure 4.5 A table is a compact display of information in columns and rows. (U.S. Bureau of the Census, *Statistical Abstract of the United States, 1993*, 113th ed., Washington, D.C.: U.S. Government Printing Office, 1993, p. 275.)

presidential vetoes of congressional bills from 1961 to 1993 in such a way that readers can compare the data and draw conclusions quickly and accurately. The table presents the information in a concise and orderly manner in a compact space that allows for easy side-by-side **comparison/contrast** and eliminates the extraneous words that would be necessary if you presented the information in traditional sentence form.

COMPARISON/CONTRAST, PAGE 542

Flow Diagrams

Flow diagrams are especially useful for showing processes and procedures. They trace action through a series of steps, providing good overviews of **narration**. In a block diagram, the simplest kind of flow diagram to make and to read, each step is represented by a "block" (usually a rectangle or square), with the name of the activity appearing in the box. The blocks are connected by lines with arrow heads to indicate the direction of movement in the process. Figure 4.6 is a block diagram that lists the major activities required to build a house. The diagram identifies the four major stages and breaks down the work involved in each stage.

NARRATION, PAGE 618

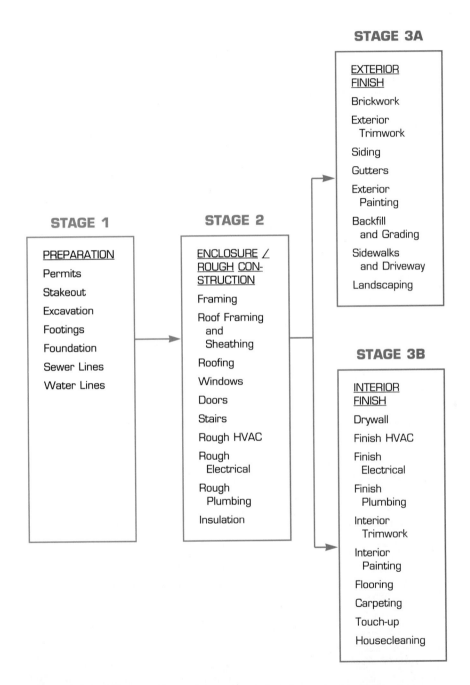

STAGE 3A

EXTERIOR
FINISH

Brickwork

Exterior
 Trimwork

Siding

Gutters

Exterior
 Painting

Backfill
 and Grading

Sidewalks
 and Driveway

Landscaping

STAGE 1

PREPARATION

Permits

Stakeout

Excavation

Footings

Foundation

Sewer Lines

Water Lines

STAGE 2

ENCLOSURE /
ROUGH CON-
STRUCTION

Framing

Roof Framing
 and
 Sheathing

Roofing

Windows

Doors

Stairs

Rough HVAC

Rough
 Electrical

Rough
 Plumbing

Insulation

STAGE 3B

INTERIOR
FINISH

Drywall

Finish HVAC

Finish
 Electrical

Finish
 Plumbing

Interior
 Trimwork

Interior
 Painting

Flooring

Carpeting

Touch-up

Housecleaning

Figure 4.6 Box diagram listing major stages of work required to build a house.
Stage 1 must be completed before Stage 2 can begin; Stage 2 must be completed
before Stages 3A and 3B can begin; Stages 3A and 3B can occur at the same time.

Line Charts

Line charts are useful for showing trends over a definite period of time and for making comparisons of data easy. They are constructed by plotting data on a grid and connecting the data by lines. Figure 4.7 shows data concerning the number of sales and the median sales prices of single-family houses from 1970 to 1992. The data for the number of existing houses and new private houses sold are distinguished by captions; the data on the median sales prices of existing houses and new private houses are distinguished by broken lines for existing houses and solid lines for new private houses as well as clear captioning of each line.

Bar Charts

Bar charts are useful for comparing different items at the same time. The length of the bar corresponds to an item's value or amount. Figure 4.8 shows the number of paying passengers enplaned at the ten busiest airports (the different items) in the United States during 1988 (the same time).

A multiple bar chart is one that compares several items at different times. The multiple bar chart in Figure 4.9 focuses on the comparison

Figure 4.7 Line charts show trends over a period of time. As long as the lines are distinct and clearly labeled, several items can be plotted in a single chart. (U.S. Bureau of the Census, *Statistical Abstract of the United States, 1993*, 113th ed. Washington, D.C.: U.S. Government Printing Office, 1993, p. 710.)

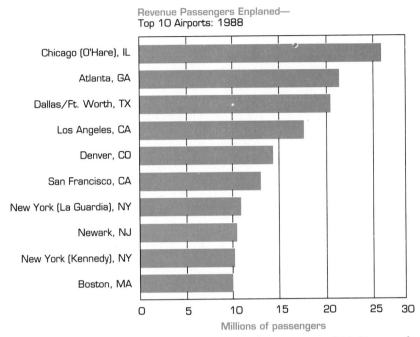

Figure 4.8 Bar charts compare different items at the same time. (U.S. Bureau of Census, *Statistical Abstract of the United States 1990*, 110th ed. Washington, D.C.: U.S. Government Printing Office, 1990, p. 618.)

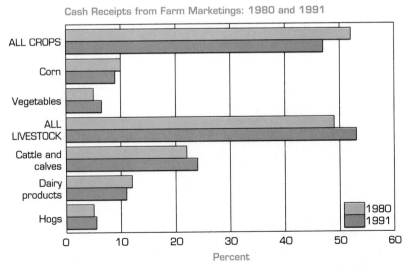

Figure 4.9 Bar charts with multiple bars grouped together compare different items at any given time and also show trends over a longer period of time. (U.S. Bureau of the Census, *Statistical Abstract of the United States, 1993*, 113th ed. Washington, D.C.: U.S. Government Printing Office, 1993, p. 648.)

of cash receipts for crops and livestock. The bars for each item touch each other to emphasize groupings and are shaded to distinguish 1980 and 1991 receipts.

Pie Charts

Pie charts (see Figure 4.10) are useful for showing how parts of a whole (percentages that total 100 percent) are distributed. They compare the portions with one another and with the total at the same time. A pie chart (the analogy is made to the top of a pie) consists of a circle (representing the whole pie) divided into segments (representing the slices of the pie). Five or six segments are about the maximum that can be shown effectively. More than that and the segments become so small that they may be difficult to label.

Using Graphics Effectively

Whether you create graphics by hand or from a computerized graphics program, keep these four principles in mind when using them.

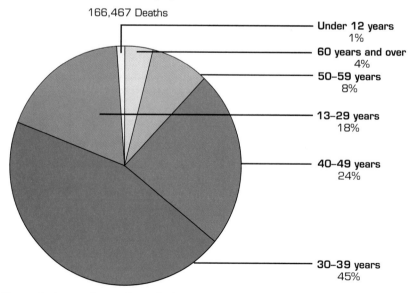

Distribution of AIDS Deaths, by Age: 1982–1992

166,467 Deaths

- Under 12 years 1%
- 60 years and over 4%
- 50–59 years 8%
- 13–29 years 18%
- 40–49 years 24%
- 30–39 years 45%

Figure 4.10 Pie charts, also called circle charts, show how parts of a whole are distributed. Each segment of the circle represents a percent of the whole. (U.S. Bureau of Census, *Statistical Abstract of the United States, 1993*, 113th ed. Washington, D.C.: U.S. Government Printing Office, 1993, p. 70.)

▶ Graphics must be relevant. Use only graphics that can help explain the point or points you want to make. It is tempting to borrow existing graphics from other sources, much as you would quote information from other sources. But graphics in other sources were created for specific purposes and specific audiences that might not be identical or even similar to your purpose and audience. Any graphic you create should make a point and should not contain extraneous details. A photograph of a glistening SST Concorde in flight in an azure sky may make a beautiful picture, but it is of little use to readers who need to know the location of the fuel tanks.

▶ Graphics must be clearly legible with sharp detail and good contrast. If a photograph or a photocopy of a photograph or other graphic is too dark, too light, or too blurry, the resolution of detail will be inadequate. The labels and symbols should be large enough to be read easily. Poorly reproduced graphics test the patience of even the most gentle readers.

▶ Graphics must be easy to understand. Do not try to pack too much data into a table, chart, or diagram. Photographs that are cluttered with lots of extraneous details obscure the main point. Line charts that resemble tangled spaghetti and diagrams that look like global weather patterns make comprehension difficult. A series of graphics is preferable to one that has too much information crammed into it.

▶ Graphics should be conveniently placed—for the readers. If possible, place a graphic close to the discussion of it. It is tempting to place a graphic at the end of the written text regardless of where it is discussed in the text. But a discussion on page 2 of a chart on page 6 that contains the results of a table on page 5 tests the patience of readers as much as a poorly reproduced graphic. Remember that it is the reader's convenience—not the writer's—that should determine where a graphic is placed. Do not force readers to flip back and forth between a graphic and the discussion of the graphic.

HEADINGS
▼

Headings are words or phrases that divide a text into sections and sometimes into subsections. Short texts are usually not divided into formal sections and subsections, but longer texts, especially those that serve pragmatic purposes, generally are. Such evident divisions are frequently helpful in long or complex texts because readers can absorb new information faster if the organization of the text is easily recognizable.

Headings show the organization and scope of the material, thus helping browsers who are curious about what information the text contains and assisting readers who seek specific information in a particular part of the text. Like headings, **forecasting statements**, **format**, **transitions**, and **topic sentences** also help readers use and understand texts and grasp their hierarchical structure.

To see how well-written headings (and subheadings) tell readers what is coming in a text, look at the following excerpt from a student paper by Toni Gagnon that proposes that her university's Small Business Development Center provide accounting advice to its clientele. The excerpt is from a section that discusses possible ways that the Small Business Development Center can offer the service.

FORECASTING STATEMENTS, PAGE 580

FORMAT, PAGE 582

TRANSITIONS, PAGE 676

TOPIC SENTENCES, PAGE 672

PROPOSED SOLUTIONS

Five possible solutions seem worthy of the Small Business Development Center's consideration: 1) requesting additional funds to hire an accounting major to perform the consulting, 2) allowing accounting majors to participate in an SBDC internship for accounting credit, 3) recruiting volunteers to provide the service, 4) taking accounting problems brought to the SBDC by its clientele to accounting classes as course projects, and 5) awarding elective accounting credit to students in exchange for their consulting work.

Hiring an Accounting Major

The most apparent and perhaps most advantageous solution for SBDC clients is for the Center to request an increase in its budget so that it can hire an accounting major to provide the support services. If such employment were offered to students, the position would likely be highly competitive and attract well-qualified students. Because there is a large pool of qualified accounting students available, I would recommend that the search be restricted to accounting students. However, according to Harriett Friedman, Administrative Assistant to the Dean of the College of Business, approval of additional positions does not appear to be available in the near future.

Internships for Accounting Course Credit

The Small Business Development Center could offer internships to senior accounting majors. These internships would allow students the opportunity to work as consultants to those local businesses that are clients of the Center, while receiving academic credit for an accounting course. Although this practice is common in other business disciplines, the School of Accountancy, as a matter of policy, has disallowed AC 400 Student Internship Programs for accounting majors. Therefore, this recommendation does not comply with school policy.

Student Volunteers

The Small Business Development Center should consider requesting accounting students to volunteer to staff the Center. Although the experience would be valuable to students, the lack of either pay or academic credit presents serious disadvantages. Other concerns include various inefficiencies often associated with volunteer programs, such as difficulties in training volunteers, problems in consistent scheduling, and lack of continuity in service to clients. . . .

The opening paragraph provides an overview of the recommendations contained in this section. The headings are derived from the overview list in the opening paragraph.

Using Headings Effectively

A heading should be an integral part of your writing, not something that is tacked on. Following are four suggestions for incorporating headings into your texts.

▶ **Distinguish a heading from regular text** by placing it on a line by itself, and give it additional emphasis by its typeface (<u>underlined</u>, **bold**, *italics*, etc.). Because of the way they are formatted, headings and subheadings provide additional white space and convenient breaks from the normal text so that readers, if they choose, can pause to reflect on what they have just read—to let the ideas sink in—before going to the next section.

▶ **Format headings and subheadings so that they reflect the hierarchical structure of the text.** Centering a main heading on a line by itself and placing subheadings flush left clearly indicate the relationship between major and subordinate topics.

▶ **Use informative headings.** Informative headings identify topics, provide anchors for additional information, and reflect how parts of a text relate. Compare the headings below. The headings on the left are specific enough to give readers a good idea of what is contained in each section. The headings on the right are so abstract that they convey very little of the contents of each section.

<u>Informative headings</u>	<u>Noninformative headings</u>
I. Cycling Your Way to Better Health	Part I
II. Practical Tips for Bicycling Safety	Part II
III. Fitting Your Bicycle to You	Part III
Appendix A: Cycling Terms	Appendix A
Appendix B: Cycling Organizations	Appendix B
Appendix C: Cycling Magazines	Appendix C

Headings should be concise, but precise enough to indicate the content that follows. Single-word headings are usually too vague or weak.

▶ Leave at least two lines of text below the last heading or subheading on a page, or else reposition the heading or subheading to the top of the next page. Do not leave a heading without text at the bottom of a page.

INTRODUCTIONS
▼

Introductions (and **titles**) focus readers' attention and convince them it is worth their time to continue reading. A traditional introduction tells readers what to expect by announcing the subject, providing necessary background information, stating the problem or purpose related to the occasion for writing, and providing an overview of the central points. But if the writer does these things perfunctorily or ploddingly, the introduction can be toxic to readers. Those who are not part of a captive audience most likely will lose interest and stop reading. Even readers who might feel obliged to read a text will read only a few sentences before deciding whether the writer is well-informed and has something interesting to say.

TITLES, PAGE 667

One of the most effective ways to increase the chances that readers will keep reading is to start with an introduction that intrigues them, that catches their interest, gets them excited and emotionally involved with the topic, and plunges them right into the text. Even when it is necessary to provide background information, a short introductory paragraph that arouses the reader's curiosity about the center of interest in the text is crucial.

David Quammen, a columnist for *Outdoor* magazine and a novelist, is exceptionally good at writing such short, admirably vigorous introductions. Here are a few opening paragraphs from some of his articles that have been reprinted in a collection titled *Natural Acts: A Sidelong View of Science and Nature*, which was published in 1985.

> What the world needs is a good vicious sixty-foot-long Amazon snake. ("Rumors of a Snake")

> There are extinctions, and then again there are Extinctions. ("The Big Goodbye")

> In the fifth chapter of Matthew's Gospel, Christ is quoted as saying that the meek shall inherit the earth, but other opinion lately suggests that, no, more likely it will go to the cockroaches. ("A Republic of Cockroaches")

Here's a cheerful thought. Some knowledgeable people believe that black widow spiders, like locusts and jack rabbits, come in plagues. ("The Widow Knows")

As you can see, these introductions are a little different from the traditional textbook introductions. Quammen gets at once into his articles—focusing on a specific detail or sometimes flooding the reader with several details and building an article around them; providing a hypothesis to be explored; or making a general observation and tying it to his subject. They pack a quick punch and have the imagery, density, quickness, and freshness that are associated with poetry. Most of today's readers love this kind of introduction.

Here are three more short opening paragraphs by other writers. Like Quammen's introductory paragraphs, each of these creates a certain expectation about what will follow, introduces the voice of the writer, and provides the crucial incentive to continue reading.

A revolution in chemistry is taking place in a small room in a converted mining building in Tucson, Ariz., where a woman wearing a solid smock and a face mask is painstakingly scraping soot off a metal container.

> —Edward Edelson, "Buckyball: The Magic
> Molecule," *Popular Science* 239, no. 2
> (August 1991): 52.

Suppose an operator asked a machine whether it was intelligent and the machine answered "yes." How would the operator prove it was lying?

> —O. B. Hardison, Jr., "Syntax and Semantics,"
> *Disappearing Through the Skylight: Culture and
> Technology in the Twentieth Century*
> (New York: Viking, 1989), p. 317.

Human beings are the only animals that experience the same sex drive at times when we can—and cannot—conceive.

> —Gloria Steinem, "Erotica and Pornography: A
> Clear and Present Difference," *Ms.* 7, no. 5
> (November 1978): 53.

These introductions are boldly brief and, with only one exception, involve readers in the subject in fewer than twenty-five words.

However, it is not just brevity that makes these opening statements effective. It is also the element of surprise, the directness, the tone, and the focus on something specific that indicates the substance of the information that follows. When well done, such introductions help readers narrow their focus at the beginning and give them a little shove into the text. Introductions, of course, are often longer than a sentence or two, but even longer ones should entice readers to continue reading.

Another way to develop an introduction is to use various methods of development, such as **description**, **comparison/constrast**, **cause and effect**, and the use of specific details and questions. Notice how the writer of the following introduction uses several of these strategies to emphasize *change* and to pique the readers' interest:

DESCRIPTION, PAGE 565

COMPARISON/CONTRAST, PAGE 542

CAUSE AND EFFECT, PAGE 522

> My kitchen has changed. Although never a model of domestic organization, I have always managed to hold complete chaos at bay by refusing to let a sink full of dirty dishes sit around overnight, by tossing out any leftovers I can't identify by basic food group and original date of presentation, and by taking out garbage and trash regularly. (Especially discarded raw chicken innards ever since I made the tragic mistake of tossing some casually in with the garbage one hot summer night and woke up the next morning to find my entire house in the grip of an evil smell I won't even try to describe, but which I promised myself I would never encounter again if I could possibly help it.)
>
> But now everything has changed. The corner by the back door is crowded with bags of aluminum cans, boxes of glass containers and stacks of days-old newspapers. In order to use this door for entrances and exits—or even to crack it just a little to let the breeze blow in between the burglar bars—one must bear the consequences that are the result of any movement of the intricately arranged piles. And to what is this new kitchen complexity attributable? I am, with the zeal of the recently converted, *recycling.*
>
> —Pearl Cleage, "Recycling Blues," *Deals with the Devil* (New York: Ballantine, 1993), pp. 99–100.

The center of interest in this piece is the change that has occurred in the writer's life as a result of her commitment to recycling. Her introduction makes that idea obvious and states it strongly.

NARRATION, PAGE 618   **Narration** is also an effective strategy for introducing a text, especially a narrative that illustrates the main point or creates a little suspense.
In the following introduction, the writer withholds the identity of what
he is experiencing until the end of the second paragraph:

> It happened early on a Sunday morning while I was walking
> in the wooded Luberon hills of southern France. From some-
> where nearby there rose a strange, powerful, indeterminate
> noise, like a thundering waterfall or the roar of a furnace—the
> kind of noise you might expect to hear if a dam had broken
> and it was all coming your way.
>
> Then the pine trees around me began to dance and bend,
> the dust from the track at my feet rose up in boisterous swirls,
> and my jacket took on a life of its own, leaping and flapping
> about me. The whole world seemed suddenly, crazily to be
> misbehaving, and I realized I was experiencing my first mistral.
>
> —Bill Bryson, "Essence of Provence,"
> *National Geographic* 188, no. 3
> (September 1995): 58.

This strategy is similar to that of the ancient and universal puzzle question—the riddle—and readers find it hard not to read on to learn what
"it" is.

A third fruitful strategy for writing an introduction is to begin with
a contrast that appears to contradict or at least challenge conventional
wisdom or to offer a surprising viewpoint. This strategy captures readers'
attention and makes them sit up and blink hard a few times to clear
the intellectual cobwebs and at least consider the possibility of reversing
a cherished opinion. In the following introduction, the writer begins by
denying conventional wisdom and challenging the idea that everyone
thinks it is great to be big.

> We live in a society that is convinced of the benefits of taller
> stature. Conventional wisdom has it that taller, larger people are
> more powerful, effective, and intelligent. Men, especially, are
> often obsessed with height, hoping to reach the magical six-
> foot mark. This social preference for tallness follows our evolu-
> tionary progress; generation by generation, we are getting
> taller. But it prevents us from looking at size objectively. In
> actuality, the widespread conceptions about the benefits of
> taller stature do not stand the test of scientific investigation. If

we want to enhance our survival, we need to start grappling
with the question of our own increasing size.

—Thomas T. Samaras, "Let's Get Small,"
Harper's Magazine (January 1995): 32.

With some exceptions, introductions like these do not come easily, especially early in the writing process, and we often need to write them late, if not last. Early on, we probably have not thought enough about our topic and thesis to nail down an engaging opening. If you cannot come up with a satisfactory introduction, don't just sit there making false start after false start. There is no law that says you must write the introduction first. In fact, it is probably not best to start writing by attempting to draft an introduction, especially if it leads to using trite expressions or straining for profound thoughts profoundly expressed. Go on and draft some other part of your text. You can always come back to the introduction later. It is sometimes difficult, at the beginning, to formulate a strong **thesis** that makes it possible for you to come to the point quickly. So if you have a few false starts, refocus your energy and thinking onto other parts of your text.

THESIS, PAGE 663

Your text grows and develops the entire time that you are thinking and writing. As you get some of your ideas down on paper or on a computer screen, you will begin turning your thoughts over in your mind, exploring the scope of your topic and fleshing out your thinking. When your ideas start taking shape in your mind and you look over what you have written and then rewrite, those changing ideas are fed back into your writing, and you will be able to determine which are the dominant and major ones. As they become clearer, you will be able to sharpen your thesis. Working in this way often achieves the kind of focus that will help you when you go back to your introduction.

In revising your text, don't lose sight of the impact of the first important impression that your introduction makes. So even if you were satisfied with an earlier version of your introduction, be open and flexible to different ways of reworking your opening so that it arouses readers' interest and draws them into your subject. By the time you have worked through your text a few times, you will probably know what your introduction should focus on. Your revision can make the difference between a superb text and just a good one. Always keep in mind that whether readers are skimming your introduction or settling down to a slow, intensive reading of your text, they want—and need—to know what you are writing about, what the main issues are, what the center of interest is, and why they should be interested in what you have to say.

There are no guaranteed ways to write effective introductions. However, here are some suggestions to consider when constructing an introduction.

▶ Since you will already be excited and emotionally involved with your topic, start by using an anecdote, interesting fact, quotation, or dramatically bold statement that gets right to the center of interest in your paper—the thing that made you decide to write about the topic in the first place. Whatever you use, it should illustrate or humanize your topic, get to the point quickly, and provide a general framework for reading the text that follows. This sounds daunting, but your earliest atttempts do not have to produce the world's greatest introduction. You just need something to get started. When you can come up with an introduction early—even a shaky one, you usually gain momentum in writing your text. Your early draft can always be left open for revising until the time for writing expires.

CAUSE AND EFFECT, PAGE 522

CLASSIFICATION, PAGE 527

COMPARISON/CONTRAST, PAGE 542

DESCRIPTION, PAGE 565

EXEMPLIFICATION, PAGE 594

NARRATION, PAGE 618

▶ Use one of the methods of development discussed earlier (**cause and effect**, **classification**, **comparison/contrast**, **description**, **exemplification**, and **narration**). These basic methods are essential in all writing, and they can be used to advantage in introductions.

▶ Begin with a surprising viewpoint, one that questions or perhaps even contradicts conventional thinking. Probably more important than any other thing you could do to connect with readers is to offer them a fresh way of looking at a topic, issue, or problem. Bored readers are unhappy readers. Shake up their world a bit by offering them something new.

▶ Since every paper you write will have a main idea—a thesis, what your paper as a whole says or implies—be straightforward and begin with your thesis statement, something like this:

In baseball, the pitcher holds a distinct advantage over the batter.

or:

Pollution is good for us.

or:

The United States should not deploy armed forces to X-land for two reasons: our national security is not threatened by the fighting in X-land, and we should not intervene on either side of a domestic political dispute.

Beginning with your thesis ensures that your introduction actually introduces the argument or main idea you are making and that your readers will have a clear idea of what your text will be about.

INVENTION (PREWRITING)
▼

Anything you do before you write that helps you when you write can be considered *invention*. Although thinking—constructing a text in your mind—may be the most powerful form of invention, it is not the only form. Invention is often thought of as prewriting, but it is not limited to the thinking you do before you write. Invention encompasses not only writing but also reading, listening, and talking. The reading and research you do, the conversations you have, the scribbling, listing, note taking, and outlining you engage in are all methods of invention—ways of learning about a subject and preparing to write on that subject. Supposedly, a poet named Saint-Pol-Roux even considered sleep a form of invention. When he was asleep, he hung a sign outside his door that read "The poet is working" (Annie Dillard, *The Writing Life*, [New York: HarperPerennial, 1989], p. 14).

Most experienced writers usually depend on an established pattern of invention—a certain routine they go through to prepare for a writing task. For example, according to a recent interview, P. D. James, a well-known British mystery writer, has established the following pattern:

> . . . she prefers to write her novels at the kitchen table, in her dressing gown, before breakfast. But the actual writing takes less time than the planning and plotting, which she does on long solitary walks beside the sea, before making meticulous notes of timetables, room layouts, and so on. Extraordinarily, she writes her big set-piece scenes first, and then wraps the bread-and-butter stuff around them, "rather like knitting."
>
> —Lynn Barber, "The Cautious Heart of P. D. James," *Vanity Fair* (March 1993): 84.

James's combination of writing and thinking, thinking and writing, is typical of most writers' invention processes. Whatever else writers do to prepare to write, they nearly always devote some time to writing and thinking about their subject.

You may think of invention as prewriting and thus relegate it to the first of the writing process, assuming that it occurs and then is over once we begin to write. It is true that invention is usually the focus when writers first assume a writing task, just as revision is usually the focus as writers complete a writing task. But invention does not end once writing begins. At any point in the process, a writer may discover additional information and take new directions. In fact, once writing begins, invention and revision often become one: in revision writers discover new insights and change the direction and shape of a text.

In the real world of writing, where writers assume or acquire writing tasks for real reasons, invention is always an integral part of the task. However, in the composition classroom you may write for no real reason other than to fulfill an assignment or to improve your writing. Under these circumstances, different types of invention strategies are needed. These strategies will help you discover a topic and what you want to say about it.

A number of different invention strategies are described as part of the writing assignments at the end of Chapters 2 through 8. These include primarily listing, outlining, brainstorming, freewriting, and keeping a journal, the most useful forms of invention and the ones that experienced writers use most often. Here are some additional strategies that might be useful to you if you are having difficulty deciding on a subject or discovering something to write about your subject.

Asking the Reporter's Questions

The six questions that every journalist is taught to ask are Who? What? Where? When? Why? How? Answering these questions can generate a great deal of useful information and may even help you discover something interesting about your subject that could be developed into a thesis. Write as much as you can in answer to each question, forcing yourself to be not only complete but specific.

Assuming Different Perspectives

Looking at a subject from more than one perspective is a good way to generate information and to ensure that your view of your subject is not too one-sided. You can assume different physical perspectives, describing a subject from a variety of viewpoints—front, back, and side; above and below; left and right; close and distant. For example, if you are writing about what goes on in a certain class, you can view the class from different places (front of the room, back of the room, by the door, etc.) or from the teacher's perspective behind the desk or lectern at the front of the room. You can also try out different psychological perspectives, writing about your subject from the viewpoint of one who is objective and then biased or from first a positive and then a negative viewpoint. Finally, you can assume different people's perspectives on a subject. How does a teacher's view of a class differ from a student's? How does an administrator's view differ from both the teacher's and student's? This exercise will result not only in your generating a lot of new ideas and perspectives but will help you view your subject more intelligently and fairly.

Mapping

Some writers are more visual than others and, therefore, need to draw a picture of what they are thinking. Such writers often benefit from mapping—drawing a visual representation of the text they plan to write. A map is essentially an informal outline. (See Figure 4.11.) Instead of

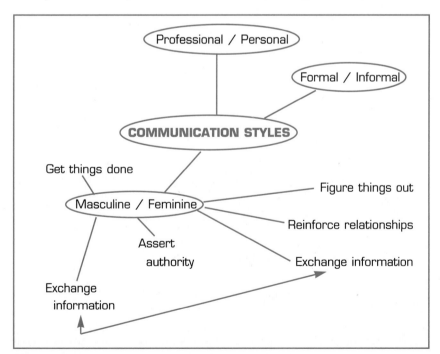

Figure 4.11 Mapping shows possible relationships of key terms and phrases of a topic.

constructing a linear, sequential list of numbered items, however, you begin mapping by writing a key word or phrase in the center of a blank page. You then branch out from the central idea, adding other ideas as they occur. The result is a kind of map of your thinking that makes explicit the connections between ideas, the relative importance of different ideas (what supports what), and the order in which these ideas should unfold. Drawing a map, or picture, of your text may not only help you discover what you want to say but also how you want to say it.

For example, this map shown in Figure 4.11 begins with the phrase "Communication Styles." As associated or related concepts are identified, they are graphically linked.

Brainstorming

Brainstorming consists of generating lots of examples, ideas, and questions to help you explore or expand an idea or topic. Often used as an invention or exploratory strategy by groups, it can also be used by individuals. It is important to try to generate quickly as many ideas as possible, without concern for evaluating the results of your brainstorming.

If you have not done much brainstorming, you might find it awkward at first. But the goal is to produce a lot of information from which you can focus on a topic. You can evaluate the information later.

Whether you are brainstorming as part of a small group or by yourself, success will depend upon your doing these things:

▶ Start with an open mind. List as much information as you can think of about a topic, recording words, phrases, questions, sentences, whatever you think of.

▶ Brainstorm quickly. Let your mind associate freely. If you are brainstorming about the parking problem on your campus, let your mind freely go from shuttle buses to parking decks to limited parking permits to whatever you can think of.

▶ Postpone evaluating things you come up with during brainstorming. It is the generation of ideas that is important early on.

After you have finished a round of brainstorming, you will have lots of topics and ideas but little focus or structure. To begin making sense out of the information you have gathered, try grouping related ideas together by clustering. At any time after initial brainstorming, you should feel free to select a potential topic and go through another round of brainstorming on just that topic. This second round of brainstorming will have a tighter focus, but the results should be similar to the first round—a list of ideas, topics, and questions about the restricted topic. Try to connect related ideas by clustering.

Clustering

This invention strategy is an extension of brainstorming. Once you have generated a brainstorming list, the longer the better, cluster (or connect) those items on the list that are related. For example, if your subject is health care in your community, you might have a long brainstorming list that includes names of individual doctors and health care facilities as well as items such as "expensive," "overburdened," "tied to insurance," "lots of choice," "long waits," and "unavailable to many." Rather than working with this long list of disparate items, you can cluster, or connect, those that seem related. For example, you could cluster the doctors into different specialties, cluster the hospitals and clinics into public and private, and connect items such as "overburdened" and "long waits." By clustering related items from your list, you may discover patterns or connections that will lead you to a thesis.

Looping

Just as clustering is an extension of brainstorming, looping is an extension of freewriting. When you loop, you freewrite for a brief period, then read what you have written, select from your freewriting one sentence or idea that seems true (or important, interesting, essential, or productive), and use it to begin a new freewriting. This spiraling pattern of writing, reading, focusing, and writing again can continue as long as it is productive. The primary benefit of this type of invention strategy is that it can help you narrow a general topic to a more specific, focused subject for writing.

Using Classical Invention Strategies

The methods of development that we emphasize throughout this textbook—**comparison/contrast**, **cause and effect**, **classification**, **description**, **narration**, and **definition**—can also be used as invention strategies. In fact, they were originally used, in Classical Greece and Rome, primarily for the purpose of invention—generating or creating ideas for a text. Rather than using just one of these approaches, you can apply several of them to your subject if your purpose is to generate new ideas and perspectives on your subject. Thus, if your subject is

COMPARISON/CONTRAST, PAGE 542

CAUSE AND EFFECT, PAGE 522

CLASSIFICATION, PAGE 527

DESCRIPTION, PAGE 568

NARRATION, PAGE 618

DEFINITION, PAGE 560

MTV, you could compare and contrast MTV to other types of television programming. You could discuss its causes (why did it come into existence?) and effects (on young people, on television programming, on advertising, on music, on politics, and so forth); classify it (entertainment or advertising, art or business, music or drama); analyze it (why is it successful? what are its main features? how is it structured? which types of music have been adapted to its format?); describe it (irreverent, innovative, visual, etc.); or tell a story about it (how the genre was developed or how a certain song was translated into the MTV format). You can readily see what a wealth of information such an exercise might generate. This strategy will help you develop your topic as well as discover what you want to write about it.

For additional information about invention, see the writing assignments in Chapters 2 through 8 and the entries on comparison/contrast, cause and effect, classification, definition, description, exemplification, and narration.

NARRATION

We are surrounded by narration, the relating of a sequence of events or actions, the telling of stories. There is a great deal of narration—arranged largely in chronological order so that readers see events as they happened—in newspaper and magazine articles, letters, short stories, novels, biographies and autobiographies, and histories and case studies.

Although narration is probably the simplest method of organizing information, it has a wide range of functions, ranging from recounting events that have happened or imaginary events that could have happened or will happen to telling what is taking place currently. A frequent use of narration is to report an event or to set the record straight about exactly what happened in the past. The following account describes one of several incidents in which the United States military failed to recognize the imminent Japanese attack on Pearl Harbor.

> At almost this same moment another warning was being reported to the Army—and also discounted—from the Opana outpost at Kahuku Point on the northern tip of Oahu. Private George Elliott, Jr., of the 515th Signal Aircraft Warning Service, a recent transfer from the Air Corps, had seen a large blip on his radar unit at 7:06 A.M. He called over Private Joseph Lockhart, who had much more experience. It was the largest

group Lockhart had ever seen on the oscilloscope and looked like two main pulses. He figured something had gone wrong with the machine, but after a check agreed with Elliott that it was really a large flight of planes.

By now Elliott had located the blip on the plotting board: 137 miles to the north, 3 degrees east. He was so excited that he suggested they call the Information Center at Fort Shafter. At first Lockhart was reluctant but finally let his assistant make the call. The switchboard operator at the Information Center could find no one on duty except a pilot named Kermit Tyler. When told that the blips were getting bigger and that the planes were now only ninety miles from Oahu, Tyler said, "Don't worry about it," and hung up—the blips must represent the flight of Flying Fortresses coming in from the mainland or planes from a carrier.

> —John Toland, *The Rising Sun: The Decline and Fall of the Japanese Empire 1936–1945*, vol. 1 (New York: Random House, 1970), p. 261.

This brief passage is a good example of narration.

The passage presents the sequence of events in the order in which they occurred. The order is made clear by the use of expressions that show time relationships: "At almost the same moment," "at 7:06 a.m.," "but after a check," "By now," "At first," "but finally when told that," and "the planes were now only ninety miles from Oahu."

The passage is packed with specific details. The details show the action in terms of specific locations and of specific persons and their relationships with others, making the narration vivid and believable and helping readers get involved in the story: What is happening? Where and when are things happening? To whom are these things happening?

The narration has a purpose. This narration supports the thesis that the U.S. military ignored several warnings that a Japanese aerial attack might be imminent. It recounts one of the worst mistakes—assuming the blips on the radar screen represented a flight of friendly aircraft.

Another major use of narration is to describe action, especially how equipment works or how natural or synthetic processes occur. In this example, the writer's purpose is to explain how laser printers work:

> The laser printer is the most significant development in output technology of the past 20 years. Unlike line, daisy-wheel, and dot-matrix printers, which print a line at a time, laser printers store a full page of characters (or dots in an image) before the

printing begins. To create a page, the computer sends signals to the printer, which shines a laser at a mirror system that scans across a charged drum. Whenever the beam strikes the drum, it removes the charge. The drum then rotates through a toner chamber filled with thermoplastic particles. The toner particles stick to the negatively charged areas of the drum in the pattern of characters, lines, or other elements the computer has transmitted and the laser beam mapped.

Once the drum is coated with toner in the appropriate locations, a piece of paper is pulled across a so-called transfer corona wire, which imports a positive electrical charge. The paper then passes across the toner-coated drum. The positive charge on the paper attracts the toner in the same position it occupied on the drum. The final phase of the process involves fusing the toner to the paper with a set of high-temperature rollers.

—Richard Golub and Eric Brus, eds.
The Almanac of Science and Technology
(New York: Harcourt Brace Jovanovich, 1990), p. 226.

The difference between this passage and the earlier one is not in the order or the details, but in the purpose. Here, the purpose is to explain what something does or how it works. Describing a process well makes it seem as if readers had witnessed a demonstration of the process.

Using Narration Effectively

Narration adds substantively to our understanding of the world; therefore, you should put considerable effort into writing it. Here are a few things to keep in mind when writing narration:

▶ **Have a clear purpose for the narration.** Narratives are not simply records of observing an event or a series of events. They deal with contexts, actors, action, sequences, conflicts, consequences, and purposes. Most are efforts to not only get the facts straight, but also to interpret what they mean. Many attempt to solve a problem or seek an answer. Think of why you are narrating the event or series of events. Is it to portray a character? To build a conflict? To explain how something happened or how something works? To move a bigger story along?

▶ **Choose an appropriate point of view.** One of the most common yet difficult points of view to use in narration is an objective one in which you attempt to create the illusion for readers that they are eyewitnesses to the events you are narrating. Both the passage by Toland and the one by Golub and Brus use this point of view. A more personal, subjective point of view effectively creates immediacy and sympathy that are presented in personal experience narrations, poems, and short stories. If you are one of the participants in your own narration, you are using a first-person point of view, and your narration is likely to be more subjective.

▶ Break the actions or series of events into major steps or phases. Use paragraphing to reflect the major divisions. If the narration is lengthy or complicated, consider using **forecasting statements**, **headings**, and **transitions** to display the organization of the narration and help readers follow the narration.

FORECASTING STATEMENTS, PAGE 580

HEADINGS, PAGE 603

TRANSITIONS, PAGE 676

▶ Use **graphics** (pictures and flowcharts) when possible. Pictorials (images that realistically look like what they represent—photographs and drawings) are especially effective in portraying things realistically and concretely. Arbitrary graphics (such as icons) are flat silhouettes or stylized images of events and objects that still convey recognizable concepts, such as the image of a spark or a bolt of lightning to represent the concept of electricity or electric shock.

GRAPHICS, PAGE 596

PACE
▼

Pace refers to the speed or tempo at which information is presented to the reader. A well-paced text feeds information slowly enough for the reader to be able to understand it easily but quickly enough to hold the reader's interest, and it presents important ideas when the reader is ready for them.

A page is filled with words—one after another—arranged left to right in lines across the page and with lines arranged from top to bottom down the page. The fact that the words and lines seem fixed on the page might suggest that writing is static and that it cannot be paced. However, an experienced writer controls the speed at which the reader's eyes and mind travel into, through, and around the writing.

Reading is a relatively unconscious activity, and readers are usually unaware of pace unless it is faulty. The normal silent reading speed for most readers of conventional nonfiction prose is about four words per second on an 8½ × 11-inch page of double-spaced typewritten text in little over a minute. (G.W. McConkie, *Eye Movements and Perception*

During Reading [Technical Report No. 229], Champaign, IL: University of Illinois Center for the Study of Reading, 1982.) Several factors influence how much faster or slower a reader moves through a particular text. Obviously, inept writing can pose problems for readers. Unfamiliar or vague words, unclear pronoun references, and poor sentence structure can unintentionally slow the reading to a crawl or bring it to a standstill. The reader who is forced to slow the pace for such reasons is likely to lose interest and become less receptive. Densely packed passages can present too much information too fast for the reader to assimilate easily. The reader is likely to miss something important or to become exasperated with having to reread a passage in an attempt to pick out the main and supporting ideas. But the writer also can purposely slow the pace when important and complex concepts are being presented or can intentionally quicken the pace when it seems appropriate to do so, as when familiar information is being given straightforwardly or when description or narrative should move rapidly. The proper pace is one that enables readers to grasp new information quickly and work it into their minds, efficiently relating it to what they already know or have already read.

The pace becomes tortuously slow if the passage inches along in a series of short sentences that present information in bits and pieces:

> Alice is my aunt. She is retired. But her day is full. She goes to exercise class every morning. She also is a volunteer in a hospital gift shop for two hours every morning. She walks two miles outdoors every afternoon. She walks outdoors whether it is rainy or sunny.

Choppy, choppy, choppy. This passage has too many stop-and-go points and too many little unnecessary words between significant information. If this snail's pace were to continue much longer, the reader would soon tire. Consolidating the seven sentences into three links the significant information more closely, and getting rid of several unnecessary words shortens and streamlines the passage, as does this version that says the same thing in ten fewer words (a 20 percent reduction):

> Although my Aunt Alice is retired, her day is full. Every morning she goes to exercise class and works as a volunteer for two hours in a hospital gift shop. Every afternoon in rain or sun she walks two miles outdoors.

The significant information and details are necessary, and they are still there. It is all those little unnecessary words and periods that drag the pace to a crawl that have been removed.

A series of very short sentences is not always bad. But the series must be kept short, must play off an established sequence of longer sentences, and must be used sparingly. Such sentences can be used effectively to change the pace from the established normal reading or speaking speed for a rhetorical effect, such as asserting emphatic statements. Note how Lewis Thomas, a noted physician, medical researcher, and best-selling author, alters the pace of the following passage with three very short sentences near the end. The effect may be subtle, but it is definitely there. It is not elusive; it can be sensed and felt. To get the full effect of the change of pace, read the paragraph aloud.

> The argument rests, of course, on certain assumptions about the core of human beings, and is necessarily speculative. You have to agree in advance that man is fundamentally a bad lot, out for himself alone, displaying such graces as affection and compassion only as learned habits. If you take this view, the story of the Iks can be used to confirm it. These people seem to be living together, clustered in small, dense villages, but they are really solitary, unrelated individuals with no evident use for each other. They talk, but only to make ill-tempered demands and cold refusals. They share nothing. They never sing. They turn the children out to forage as soon as they can walk, and desert the elders to starve whenever they can, and the foraging children snatch food from the mouths of the helpless elders. It is a mean society.

> —"The Iks," *The Lives of a Cell:*
> *Notes of a Biology Watcher*
> (New York: Viking, 1974), pp. 107–108.

The change of pace is especially noticeable when we examine the length of the sentences in the paragraph. The paragraph has nine sentences totaling 148 words—an average of 16.5 words per sentence. The average, by the way, means little, as you will see, for only two sentences (the first sentence with 18 words, and the third sentence with 16 words) are close to the average. The other sentences range from 3 words to 35. The number of words per sentence is 18, 28, 16, 26, 11, 3, 3, 35, and 5, and it is in the three short sentences at the end of the paragraph where Thomas slows the pace to drive home those major points about the nature of the Iks: "They share nothing. They never sing." "It is a mean society." Such simple sentences are powerful in summing up major points.

Your writing should move along fairly quickly. But that does not mean that you have to cram everything into one sentence. A pace that is too rapid can be as bad as a pace that is too slow. The pace is too rapid if the reader is presented with too much information within a short passage to grasp on a first reading:

> The candidate, although she does not represent the majority party, is not without a strong opponent, and is not unconcerned that popular opinion might turn against her and cause her to lose votes in Cedar Township, opposes the new school bill.

This information is presented in a form that is grammatically correct but hard to understand, mainly because the density of information is too high for many readers. To sort out and digest the meaningful information, the reader must understand five ideas and their relationships, must hold in mind the subject of the sentence while reading or hearing thirty-four subsequent words until the verb is reached, and must transform two double negatives ("is not without" and "is not unconcerned") into positives. When you think about it, this effort is more than a minor nuisance or strain. It involves lots of bridging and translation work and is usually too much for easy reading. Most readers have good memories and can figure out the sentences, but they are likely to feel the burden is too heavy as they move from the subject at the beginning of the sentence to the verb near the end.

Of course, if your readers *have* to read something and take self-interested action, they will likely make a significant effort to decode even difficult texts. If you need to encourage your readers to read, you must make the text easily assimilable.

There are two ways to make overcrowded sentences easier to read. Perhaps the simplest and most effective way is to minimize the distance between the subject and the verb. Use what linguists call *right-branching sentences*—that is, sentences that branch into modifiers or completing elements *after* the verb:

> The candidate opposes the new school bill, although she does not represent the majority party, has a strong opponent, and is concerned that popular opinion might turn against her and cause her to lose votes in Cedar Township.

Beginning the sentence with the subject, followed by the verb, followed by the modifiers keeps the subject and verb close together and allows the elaboration to follow the main idea. Such sentence structure seems natural and is easy to read. In addition, although most readers tolerate an occasional double negative ("is not without," "is not unconcerned,"), it takes them less time to grasp positive statements ("is with," "is concerned"). So use positive statements unless there is some rhetorical gain in using a harder-to-understand double negative.

Left-branching sentences (those that place modifiers and complements *before* the verb) can be effective used occasionally to delay the main idea until the end of the sentence:

> Although she does not represent the majority party, has a strong opponent, and is concerned that popular opinion might turn against her and cause her to lose votes in Cedar Township, the candidate opposes the new school bill.

This structure forces the reader to hold in suspension the first part of the sentence—approximately 80 percent—before reaching the subject and the verb. This suspension organizes the sentence into a distinctly climactic order, drawing the audience along through the words, withholding an essential piece of information, building toward a sense of revelation or completion, and finally delivering the main idea. Such a sentence can break up the monotony of many standard right-branching sentences and can thus add variety to the text. But because these structures deviate from the right-branching pattern of most sentences, they may appear artificial and slightly stilted. When a lot of modifiers and complements precede the subject and verb, they can overload the audience's ability to retain them until the end of the sentence is reached.

However, you should use left-branching sentences, for when you do them well they are quite effective in changing the pace:

> Having made a little money in cattle in certain years and lost some of it back in others, having worried over an uneconomic small herd through droughts and bad winters with an intensity that would have been more wisely saved for life's main problems, having been kicked, butted, stomped, and run up corral fences countless times by Number Thirty-nine and others of like temperament, having pounded large quantities of time down a rat hole over the years in the maintenance of this grudging place for bovine use, and having liked just about all of it at least in retrospect, I am still fond of cows and of tending them and am sometimes puzzled, along with other devotees, to find that everyone everywhere doesn't feel the same way.
>
> —John Graves, "Nineteen Cows," in *From a Limestone Ledge* (New York: Knopf, 1980), p. 92.

Just use left-branching sentences sparingly, cautiously, and deliberately.

Pace can be an important factor in stretches of text longer than a sentence. For example, a series of brief paragraphs, each briefly enumerating a separate point, are sometimes used to keep the text moving rapidly. In the passage that follows, Richard Shenkman, after introducing his thesis that much of the violence associated with the American frontier is myth, uses five short paragraphs to present five different examples to back up his position before going on to a more sustained and extended treatment of his thesis. The effect is similar to that of a quick list of facts.

> The popular image of the frontier as a place of violence is only partly due to the fact that the place often was violent. Most of it is due to hype, particularly Hollywood hype. The truth is many more people have died in Hollywood westerns than ever died on the real frontier (Indian wars considered apart). In the real Dodge City, for instance, there were just five killings in 1878, the most homicidal year in the little town's frontier history—scarcely enough to sustain a typical two-hour movie. In the most violent year in Deadwood, South Dakota, only four people were killed. The only reason the OK Corral shoot-out even became famous was that town boosters deliberately overplayed the drama to attract new settlers. "They eventually cashed in on the tourist boom," historian W. Eugene Hollon says, "by inventing a myth about a town too tough to die."
>
> The most notorious cow towns in Kansas—Abilene, Dodge City, Ellsworth, Wichita, and Caldwell—did see comparatively more violence than similar size small towns elsewhere but probably not as much violence as is believed. Records indicate that between 1870 and 1885 just forty-five murders occurred in the towns.
>
> Most surprisingly, there is no evidence anyone was ever killed in a frontier shoot-out at high noon.
>
> In fact, few of those who are famous for shooting people shot as many people as commonly thought. Billy the Kid was a "psychopathic murderer," but he hadn't killed twenty-one people by the time he was twenty-one. Hollon says authorities "can only account for three men he killed for sure, and there were probably no more than three or four more."
>
> Bat Masterson is another overrated killer. He's been credited, says Hollon, with killing between twenty and thirty men; "the actual number was only three."

Wild Bill Hickok, the Abilene marshal, claimed to have killed six Kansas outlaws and secessionists in the incident that first made him famous. He lied. He killed just three—all unarmed. And he never killed anybody for violating the ordinance against firing guns within the town limits.

—"The Frontier," *Legends, Lies, and Cherished Myths of American History* (New York: Morrow, 1988), pp. 112–13.

The opening paragraph—which has 7 sentences—is followed by paragraphs that are 2, 1, 3, 2, and 4 sentences long. The paragraphs that immediately follow this passage are 7, 8, 6, and 8 sentences long.

No absolute rules dictate how many short, staccato paragraphs can be run in succession, but here are some guidelines to help you decide when a series of short paragraphs might be effective:

❖ When a short paragraph has not been used for several paragraphs and the pages are filling up with long paragraphs.

❖ When it is desirable to establish a series, pattern, or trend by accumulating specific events, facts, and examples—almost as in a quick list—before moving on to more extended accounts.

❖ When a point can be supported by reference to several familiar examples that do not require thorough explanation.

Five or six very short paragraphs in succession are probably enough. More than that may belabor the point being made or may arouse suspicion that the writer has not thought sufficiently about the subjects of the paragraphs to organize them into a single, coherent paragraph. It is best to end a string of very short paragraphs before readers quit reading.

Using Pace Effectively

Pace is closely related to the readers' attention span and memory capacity. Because of individual differences of experience and interest among readers, no set rules can determine whether a particular passage is so densely packed with information that it is difficult to understand; the pace for one reader may not always be the proper pace for others. In addition, a writer's sense of pace is likely to be much different from the reader's. A writer's response to his or her own writing is immediate, subjective, and almost instinctive. Having already thought and rethought the contents through perhaps several revisions, a writer will understand what is stated regardless of the pace.

However, pace is not an elusive aspect of writing. No specialized knowledge is necessary to develop a sense of pace for most situations. In checking for pace, watch for the kinds of problems just discussed—a series of short, choppy sentences that seem to jolt along a cobblestone road and densely packed passages that overload the reader's attention span and memory. As you read over your text, allow your eyes to catch the length of phrases, clauses, sentences, and paragraphs. If you do not have at least one paragraph break on each 8½ × 11 sheet of paper, your paragraphs are probably too long. Avoid writing sentences or paragraphs that are all the same length. Such monotony distracts readers and makes them less receptive. See if the information is coming at an acceptable pace to someone who is not as familiar with the topic as you are.

Here are seven important tactics to help create the normal reading pace of four words per second:

▶ Read your text aloud to check its pace. The pace of reading aloud is slightly slower than reading silently. But when you speak your words and sentences at a normal speaking pace, you *hear* the pace of your reading, which may help you detect problems with pace that you might otherwise overlook if you only see your words and sentences.

▶ Without cutting details (and hence substance) from sentences, combine short sentences. The rewording and restructuring will (1) avoid choppiness, (2) help create the necessary coordination and subordination of ideas, and (3) result in frequent modification that will bring modifiers and what is modified closer together.

▶ Generally, use right-branching sentences that present the focal point of the sentence—the subject and the verb—before elaborating. Subject-verb-object/complement is the easiest structure to follow.

▶ For the same reason, place topic sentences at or near the beginning of paragraphs. The repetition of opinion or assertion followed by factual support establishes an easily recognized and easily followed pattern, moving from the abstract or general to the concrete and specific.

▶ Vary the length of sentences and paragraphs to avoid monotony. Monotony will induce boredom and, perhaps, heavy eyelids.

GRAPHICS, PAGE 596   ▶ Occasionally relieve long stretches of verbal text by using **graphics** (photographs, line drawings, tables, or charts of various kinds). These visual changes will break up the heavy look of the page as well as break up the density of information.

▶ Use informative **headings** to reveal the topic or main idea of major sections of the text. The headings (1) forecast the focal point of the section, much as a topic sentences do for paragraphs, (2) display how information is organized, and (3) help break up long stretches of text similar to the way graphics do.

HEADINGS, PAGE 603

PARAGRAPHS

▼

In Stephen Jay Gould's *Hen's Teeth and Horse's Toes*, a chapter is entitled "What, If Anything, Is a Zebra?" We might ask a similar question: What, if anything, is a paragraph?

The concept of a paragraph has changed much over the past several centuries, and no consensus exists about how to define a paragraph today. Centuries ago, in Greek manuscripts, a paragraph was a line drawn in the margin to call attention to a particular part of a text (the root word for *paragraph* is the Greek word *paragraphos*; *para* = "beside," *graph* = "to write"). Later, the paragraph mark became the familiar symbol ¶ to designate a change in the subject being discussed in the text. By the seventeenth and eighteenth centuries, the symbol ¶ had fallen into disuse (retained today only as an editing mark, except in certain specialized reference works), and the paragraph had evolved into a section of text set off at the beginning by indentation of the first line and at the end simply by the last line ending with the final word of the last sentence, even when it fell short of the right margin. By the twentieth century, the paragraph was no longer thought of so much as a format device that set off parts of text; rather, it was broadly conceived as the text that lay between the indentations.

Because the characteristics and boundaries of paragraphs shift from time to time and the concept of a paragraph has moved away from a format mark toward a rhetorical unit of text, we might receive several answers to our question about what, if anything, is a paragraph:

1. A paragraph is like an expanded sentence. It contains a **topic sentence** that is developed and modified by other sentences much the same way that the main clause of a sentence is developed and modified by other phrases and clauses.

TOPIC SENTENCE, PAGE 672

2. A paragraph is a miniature essay. It is a self-contained unit that develops a limited idea similar to the way a larger text develops a more comprehensive subject.

3. A paragraph is a subdivision of a longer stretch of text. Instead of being isolated and self-contained, several paragraphs may be connected closely in thought, with each paragraph focusing on a specific aspect yet contributing to the progress of thought from one paragraph to the next.

4. A paragraph is any text that is placed between two indented lines. (In a similar manner, word processors define a paragraph as any text set between two "return" commands.)

Another answer might be that a paragraph is all of the above. Certainly none of the answers just listed are incorrect. Although the definitions overlap, they indicate both the breadth and specificity of perspectives.

The concept of a paragraph undergoes a significant change of emphasis depending upon which definition we consider. In this section we categorize paragraphs as (1) topic paragraphs (related directly to definitions 1 and 2 and partly to definitions 3 and 4), (2) paragraphs in a series (related directly to definition 3 and partly to the other definitions), and (3) short functional paragraphs (directly related to definition 4 and partly to the other definitions).

Topic Paragraphs

Any text longer than a page is usually divided into several paragraphs. While there may be short introductory, transitional, and concluding paragraphs, most of the paragraphs will be topic paragraphs. A topic paragraph is a block of sentences that presents a statement about a fact, an opinion, or an experience, or in some other way treats a topic that is an important part of the subject of the entire text. It is the primary means by which writers organize information into meaningful blocks of text and focus and develop major ideas.

TOPIC SENTENCE, PAGE 672 The meaning of each topic paragraph is usually tied to a **topic sentence** supported by detailed data and examples that furnish clarification, proof, and evidence. Ordinarily, a bare statement unsupported by details is not convincing. Thus, if an idea is important enough to be set off as a separate paragraph, it probably requires several sentences to develop it. For instance, if the statement is "The institution. of the Church stood an extraordinary physical presence in my world," a natural way of supporting this statement is to cite specific examples of the physical presence of the church:

> The institution of the Church stood an extraordinarily physical presence in my world. One block from the house was

Sacred Heart Church. In the opposite direction, another block away, was Sacred Heart Grammar School, run by the Sisters of Mercy. And from our backyard, I could see Mercy Hospital, Sacramento's only Catholic hospital. All day I would hear the sirens of death. Well before I was a student myself, I would watch the Catholic school kids walk by the front of the house, dressed in gray and red uniforms. From the front lawn I could see people on the steps of the church, coming out, dressed in black after funerals, or standing, the ladies in bright-colored dresses in front of the church after a wedding. When I first went to stores on errands for my mother, I could be seen by the golden-red statue of Christ, where it hovered over the main door of the church.

—Richard Rodriguez, *Hunger of Memory*
(Boston: Godine, 1982), p. 81.

Since a topic paragraph can develop one topic or a subtopic of a larger subject, it may be nearly complete in itself or it may be only one of a group of closely related topic paragraphs. Here we discuss the topic paragraph that is nearly complete in itself. In the "Paragraphs in a Series" section, we discuss it as a part of a larger passage.

Few concepts of writing have enjoyed more widespread acceptance in the past century than the topic paragraph. While having multiple purposes, diverse organizational patterns, and varying lengths, it possesses two central features: 1) a main idea usually expressed in a topic sentence and 2) a coherent sequence of information that supports, clarifies, or amplifies the topic sentence (see **amplification**).

AMPLIFICATION, PAGE 508

The topic sentence expresses the main idea or in some way summarizes the contents of a paragraph. It is frequently the first sentence, but it can appear anyplace in the paragraph. Since its primary function is to bring into focus the main point of the paragraph, it is placed where the writer wants the reader to encounter it. One advantage of placing it at the beginning is that it helps establish the important given information that is crucial to understanding new information. Occasionally, for special effects, the topic sentence is placed at the beginning and restated at the end. What follow here are illustrations of the placement of topic sentences and examples of a few typical organizational patterns in topic paragraphs.

First, a topic sentence at or near the beginning of the paragraph—such as the one in the paragraph from Richard Rodriguez's *Hunger for Memory*—makes it more likely that the writer will stick to the subject and that the reader will discover instantly the central idea and will know what to expect in the paragraph.

Second, a topic sentence at the end of the paragraph, such as the following one from James Gleick's *Chaos: Making a New Science*, allows the writer to provide several examples and then comment on their significance or meaning:

> Ravenous fish and tasty plankton. Rain forests dripping with nameless reptiles, birds gliding under canopies of leaves, insects buzzing like electrons in an accelerator. Frost belts where voles and lemmings flourish and diminish with tidy four-year periodicity in the face of nature's bloody combat. The world makes a messy laboratory for ecologists, a cauldron of five million interesting species. Or is it fifty million? Ecologists do not actually know.
>
> —(New York: Penguin, 1987), p. 59.

The topic sentence placed at the end can create climax or vary the structure of paragraphs by holding off the principle idea that unifies the paragraph until the end.

Third, occasionally as a transition from one paragraph to another, the topic sentence of a paragraph is the last sentence of the preceding paragraph, as in this passage (topic sentence is italicized):

> Under the Kennedy and Johnson administration, federal efforts to reduce unemployment through employment and training programs were greatly increased. The 1961 Area Redevelopment Act that introduced federally financed skill training for unemployed workers in distressed areas was short-lived. The 1962 Manpower Development and Training Act and the 1964 Economic Opportunity Act expanded the concepts of direct federal employment and training for the unemployed. A major operating division of the Office of Economic Opportunity was the Job Corps, conceived by OEO director Sargent Shriver, to be not merely a vocational training program, but an educational venture. Up to 100,000 trainees between the ages of 16 and 21 entered the program, and many disadvantaged young men and women graduated to secure steady jobs. Problems of mismanagement plagued the program, which soon fell into disfavor with Congress and then faded away under the Nixon administration. *However, the largest federal employment programs occurred during the 1970s.*
>
> In 1971, the Emergency Employment Act authorized the first large-scale direct federal employment initiative since the 1930s and cost $2.25 billion over two years. In 1973, the Comprehensive

Employment and Training Act (CETA) was passed with bipartisan support. Its purpose was to consolidate more than the dozen separate employment and training programs that had developed in the 1960s into one, and to turn administrative control over to elected state and local officials.

—Marcia Lynn Whicker and Raymond A. Moore,
*Making America Competitive: Policies for a
Global Future* (New York: Praeger, 1988), p. 153.

Fourth, a topic sentence placed at the beginning and restated or paraphrased at the end gives special emphasis to the main idea of the paragraph, rounds out the discussion, and achieves a sense of completeness (topic sentences italicized):

Between 1890 and 1925, dating—in practice and in name— had gradually, almost imperceptibly, become a universal custom in America. By the 1930s it had transcended its origins: Middle America associated dating with neither upper-class rebellion nor the urban lower classes. The rise of dating was usually explained, quite simply, by the invention of the automobile. Cars had given youth mobility and privacy, and so had brought about the system. This explanation—perhaps not consciously but definitely not coincidentally—revised history. The automobile certainly contributed to the rise of dating as a national practice, especially in rural and suburban areas, but it was simply accelerating and extending a process already well under way. *Once its origins were located firmly in Middle America, however, and not in the extremes of urban upper- and lower-middle class life, dating had become an American institution.*

—Beth L. Bailey, *From Front Porch to Back Seat:
Courtship in Twentieth-Century America* (Baltimore:
The Johns Hopkins University Press, 1988), p. 19.

The placement of the topic sentence influences the organization and coherence of the paragraph to some extent. But more important are various organizational patterns—such as **narration**, **description**, **exemplification**, and **comparison/contrast**—that establish the sequence of information. The number of patterns is almost endless. Writers employ whatever patterns enable them to unfold successive ideas intelligibly. Following are only a few examples of the many patterns. For more detailed information on achieving coherence, see **coherence**, especially pages 530–536.

NARRATION, PAGE 618

DESCRIPTION, PAGE 565

EXEMPLIFICATION, PAGE 574

COMPARISON/CONTRAST, PAGE 542

COHERENCE, PAGE 530

▶ Narration. Narration can be used several ways in paragraphs. For example, Richard Rodriguez describes the physical pleasure of working at a summer construction job that he had as an undergraduate at Stanford University by summarizing a typical workday:

> I labored with excitement that first morning—and all the days after. The work was harder than I could have expected. But it was never as tedious as my friends had warned me it would be. There was too much physical pleasure in the labor. Especially early in the day, I would be most alert to the sensations of movement and straining. Beginning around seven each morning (when the air was still damp but the scent of weeds and dry earth anticipated the heat of the sun), I would feel my body resist the first thrusts of the shovel. My arms, tightened by sleep, would gradually loosen; after only several minutes, sweat would gather in beads on my forehead and then—a short while later—I would feel my chest silky with sweat in the breeze. I would return to my work. A nervous spark of pain would fly up my arm and settle to burn like an ember in the thick of my shoulder. An hour, two passed. Three. My whole body would assume regular, even movements. Even later in the day, my enthusiasm for primitive sensation would survive the heat and the dust and the insects pricking my back. I would strain wildly for sensation as the day came to a close. At three-thirty, quitting time, I would stand upright and slowly let my head fall back, luxuriating in the feeling of tightness relieved.
>
> —*Hunger of Memory*, pp. 131–32.

Another type of narration is the anecdote, a brief account of an incident to support or clarify a major point or to illustrate a striking characteristic of a person or group. For instance, Tom Wolfe, a notable writer of so-called literary nonfiction, reports the following anecdote to illustrate the snobbish influence of New York City nannies on the upper-middle-class children in their care. The anecdote comprises the first paragraph.

> Lord, the nannies are absolutely dictatorial about what you have to buy. Charlotte remembers that first day, when she went into the playground by herself, there was this poor little girl, about six, who came in with her nurse. The nurse was a colored girl. Neither of them knew a thing, poor dears. The little girl saw these other little girls her age, and, oh, she wanted to play with them. Her little eyes lit up like birthday

candles in her little buttery face and her little legs started churning, and there she was, the original *tabula rasa* of joy and friendship. Did they let *her* have it! Rather! The first girl she came up to, Carey K———'s little girl, a real budding little bitch named Jennifer, if you wanted Charlotte's frank opinion, just stared at her, no smile at all, and said, "My shoes are Indian Walk T-strap." Then another little girl came up and said the same thing, "My shoes are Indian Walk T-strap." Then Jennifer says it again, "My shoes are Indian Walk T-strap," and then they both start whining this at the poor little thing, "My-shoes-are-Indian-Walk-T-Strap!" And the little girl—all she had done was come into the playground, to try to make friends, with the wrong shoes on—she's about to cry, and she says, "Mine are, too," and little Jennifer starts saying in that awful sarcastic sing-song kids pick up as one of their early instruments of torture: "Oh-no-they're-not—your shoes are *gar*bage!" So the other little girl starts saying it, and they start chanting again, and the little girl is bawling, and the colored girl can't figure out what's going on—and the other nannies, Jennifer's nanny, all of them, they're just *beau*tiful, as Charlotte remembers.

"They just sat there through the whole performance with these masks on, until their little terrors had absolutely annihilated this poor kid, and *then* they were so concerned.

"'Now, Jennifer, you mustn't tease, you know. Mustn't tease'." The whole time, of course, she was just delighted over how well Jennifer had learned her lessons."

—"The Nanny Mafia," in *The Kandy-Kolored Tangerine-Flake Streamline Baby* (New York: Farrar, Straus and Giroux, 1965), pp. 269–70.

A third use of narration is to describe a process, as Lewis Thomas, a physician, medical researcher, and gifted essayist, does in the following paragraph that speculates on the collaborative work of termites:

Termites are even more extraordinary in the way they seem to accumulate intelligence as they gather together. Two or three termites in a chamber will begin to pick up pellets and move them from place to place, but nothing comes of it; nothing is built. As more join in, they seem to reach a critical mass, a quorum, and the thinking begins. They place pellets atop pellets, then throw up columns and beautiful, curving, symmetrical arches, and the crystalline architecture of vaulted chambers is created. It is not known how they communicate with each other, how the chains of termites building one column know when to turn toward the crew on the adjacent column, or how, when the time comes, they manage the flawless joining of the arches. The stimuli that set them off at the outset, building collectively instead of shifting things about, may be pheromones released when they reach committee size. They react as if alarmed. They become agitated, excited, and then they begin working, like artists.

—"Societies as Organisms," in *The Lives of a Cell: Notes of a Biology Watcher* (New York: Viking, 1974), p. 13.

▶ Description. The aim of description is to create sensory details—of sight, sound, touch, taste, and smell—that vividly create images and understanding. Descriptive paragraphs present verbal pictures, as illustrated in the following paragraph by Alfred Kazin, which describes the kitchen of his childhood home in a tenement section of New York City:

The kitchen held our lives together. My mother worked in it all day long, we ate in it almost all meals except the Passover *seder*, I did my homework and first writing at the kitchen table, and in winter I often had a bed made up for me on three kitchen chairs near the stove. On the wall just over the table hung a long horizontal mirror that sloped to a ship's prow at each end and was lined with cherry wood. It took up the whole wall, and drew every object in the kitchen to itself. The walls were a fiercely stippled whitewash, so often rewhitened by my father in slack seasons that the paint looked as if it had been squeezed and cracked into the walls. A large electric bulb hung down the center of the kitchen at the end of a chain that had been hooked into the ceiling; the old gas ring and key still jutted out of the wall like antlers. In the corner next to the toilet was the sink at which we washed, and the square tub in which my mother did our clothes. Above it, tacked to the shelf on which was pleasantly ranged square, blue bordered white sugar and spice jars, hung calendars from the Public National Bank on Pitkin Avenue and the Minsker Progressive Branch of the Workmen's Circle; receipts for the payment of insurance premiums, and household bills on a spindle; two little boxes engraved with Hebrew letters.

—*A Walker in the City* (New York: Harcourt Brace Jovanovich, 1951), pp. 65–66.

▶ Exemplification. One of the most frequently used methods of developing a topic sentence is exemplification—giving a specific example or several examples that show how an idea or concept applies to actual things or in specific instances.

> Good families prize their rituals. Nothing welds a family more than these. Rituals are vital especially for clans without histories, because they evoke a past, imply a future, and hint at continuity. No line in the Seder service at Passover reassures more than the last: "Next year in Jerusalem!" A clan becomes more of a clan each time it gathers to observe a fixed ritual (Christmas, birthdays, Thanksgiving, and so on), grieve at a funeral (anyone may come to most funerals, those who do declare their tribalness), and devises a new rite of its own. Equinox breakfasts and all-white dinners can be at least as welding as Memorial Day parades. Several of us in the old *Life* magazine years used to meet for lunch every Pearl Harbor Day, preferably to eat some politically neutral fare like smorgasbord, to "forgive" our only ancestrally Japanese colleague Irene Kubota Neves. For that and other reasons we became, and remain, a sort of family.
>
> —Jane Howard, *Families* (New York: Simon & Schuster, 1978), pp. 242–43.

▶ Comparison/Contrast. Comparison/contrast shows similarities and differences between two or more things. The contrast between Monte Carlo and Las Vegas in the following paragraph makes a point about the values and atmosphere of Las Vegas:

> Las Vegas has become, just as Bugsy Siegel dreamed, the American Monte Carlo—without any of the inevitable upper-class baggage of the Riviera casinos. At Monte Carlo there is still the plush mustiness of the 19th century noble lions—of Baron Bleichroden, a big winner at roulette who always said, "My dear friends, it is so easy on Black." Of Lord Jersey, who won seventeen maximum bets in a row—on black, as a matter of fact—nodded to the croupier, and said, "Much obliged, old sport, old sport," took his winnings to England, retired to the country and never gambled again in his life. Or of the old Duc de Dinc who said he could win only in the high-toned Club Privé, and who won very heavily one night, saw two Englishmen gaping at his good fortune, threw them every mille-franc note he had in his hands and said, "Here, Englishmen without

money are altogether odious." Thousands of Europeans from the lower orders now have the money to go to the Riviera, but they remain under the century-old status pall of the aristocracy. At Monte Carol there are still Wrong Forks, Deficient Accents, Poor Tailoring, Gauche Displays, Nouveau Richness, Cultural Aridity—concepts unknown in Las Vegas. For the grand debut of Monte Carlo as a resort in 1879 the architect Charles Garnier designed an opera house for the Place du Casino; and Sarah Bernhardt read a symbolic poem. For the debut of Las Vegas as a resort in 1946 Bugsy Siegel hired Abbott and Costello, and there, in a way, you have it all.

—Tom Wolfe, "Las Vegas," in *The Kandy-Kolored Tangerine-Flake Streamline Baby*, p. 16.

Paragraphs in a Series

Many times a topic paragraph is only one of several paragraphs that form a longer stretch of closely related text. Usually the series opens with a statement that makes clear the subject for the entire stretch of text, and the individual paragraphs connect by means of their own opening statements, which are both transitional and topic sentences.

The following passage is an excerpt from Phyllis Rose's *Parallel Lives*, a study of the marriages of five major British literary figures and their spouses during the nineteenth century. The three paragraphs are part of Rose's discussion of the disintegrating marriage of John Ruskin, a late-nineteenth-century art, literary, and social critic, and Effie Gray. Rose contrasts the opinions of the parents of the couple in the first two paragraphs (presenting the Ruskins' viewpoint in the first and the Grays' in the second). The final paragraph offers Rose's interpretation of the two positions and makes clear her own feelings about the matter.

Something had clearly gone wrong with the marriage, and both "sides"—the elder Grays and Ruskins as well as the married pair—attempted to fix the blame. Neither set of parents knew the marriage was unconsummated, but they found plenty of other problems to discuss. From Mr. Ruskin's point of view, Effie was an undutiful wife, unsupportive of her husband's work. She had unaccountably withdrawn from them and gone to Perth, where she knew John would not follow. She seemed unsympathetic to his stay in Europe, perversely wanting him home. Didn't she realize that going home would mean giving up the "Haunts where his Genius finds food and occupation"? Ordinary people might find John's business in the Alps incomprehensible, but didn't Effie realize that only by such labor could he do the work he'd been put on earth to do? Mr. Ruskin recommended (to her father) that she sacrifice all other feelings to duty and attempt to find pleasure in causing her husband no anxiety.

But Mr. Gray saw it differently. He knew that his daughter was not jealous of her husband's work. That was a false issue. There was only one problem in the young people's marriage: the elder Ruskins. If he might offer a word of advice, it was that Mr. and Mrs. Ruskin should leave John and Effie to themselves as much as possible. "Married people," he ventured to say, "are rather restive under the control and supervision of Parents tho' proceeding from the kindest and most affectionate motives."

How one warms to Mr. Gray! How right he seems! While Mr. Ruskin with his notions of duty and submissiveness sounds archaic, Mr. Gray expresses the wisdom a contemporary upper-middle-class American would offer in response to the same situation. Freedom. Independence. Not for nothing did we cut the ties with the Mother Country. But Ruskin, in the opening paragraph of his autobiography, proclaims that he was, like his father before him, a Tory of the old school, of the school of Homer and Sir Walter Scott, men who believed in kings, in some people being better fit to rule than others, in such people exercising power for the good of their followers without the right to expect anything in return except deference. But deference they could expect. This political model applies to the family as well as the state, and one should see that the battle between John and Effie, between the Ruskins and the Grays, was to some extent an ideological battle, a clash of two sets of assumptions about power and authority.

—*Parallel Lives: Five Victorian Marriages*
(New York: Vintage, 1984), pp. 67–68.

A fairly broad lesson about paragraphing can be learned from this passage. It is not always possible to predict where paragraph breaks will occur, although it is fairly easy to identify the points of potential paragraph breaks. A century ago, these three paragraphs might have been written as one paragraph. But today, writers make paragraph breaks more often to avoid the formidable appearance of large blocks of text that offer no place to rest the eye. Once a paragraph becomes longer than it is wide, writers tend to look for places to indent and start a new paragraph. In a series of closely related paragraphs, such as this one, there are certain points where the writer changes the line of thought or shifts to another aspect of the subject. It is at those junctures that writers often make paragraph breaks. Usually the new paragraph begins with a transition and a topic sentence that cue readers to the change.

Short Functional Paragraphs

Defining a paragraph as the text between indented lines raises the question of how long a paragraph can be. The length is sometimes determined by the size of the topic, but not always. It might be that a fairly large and complex topic requires a long paragraph, a relatively minor point a short one. But unity of thought is not always a clear reason for paragraphing. A paragraph break might be related to eye ease, attention span, or emphasis. Although some paragraphs are extremely long, most paragraphs today seldom exceed 200 to 250 words. But it was different a century ago. Paragraphs in William Henry Herndon's biography of Abraham Lincoln, *Herndon's Lincoln* (1884), for example, average several hundred words each. Some are as long as whole essays are these days. Many of the paragraphs in the essays of John Henry Cardinal Newman, Matthew Arnold, Ralph Waldo Emerson, and Henry David Thoreau run over 300 and 400 words.

But paragraphs can also be short.

Many people believe a paragraph develops a thought thoroughly and thus must have a certain heft. While these attributes may be generally appropriate for what we call topic paragraphs, paragraphs today do not always develop a single idea—if they ever did—and seldom reach the marathon lengths of those of a century ago. In fact, sometimes very short paragraphs are desirable. Set off from subsequent paragraphs or surrounding paragraphs, a short paragraph encourages readers to notice it. The shorter the paragraph is in relation to its neighbors, the more emphatic it is. Short paragraphs should be used sparingly for emphasis, for they quickly stop having the desired effect.

A short paragraph—especially a one- or two-sentence one—can make an emphatic and vigorous statement that gets the text (and the readers) off to a quick start (see **introductions**). It can also provide a brief but strong transition between longer paragraphs or sections of text, place significance on a particularly important example or concept, or end a text or a section of text with a brief but emphatic conclusion.

INTRODUCTIONS, PAGE 607

After getting the text off to a striking start, single brief paragraphs are also sometimes needed to carry readers from one long paragraph to another or from one section of the text to another. Readers must feel as if they are moving along; if they bog down, the writer is in trouble (see **pace**). Short transitional paragraphs in the right places keep readers moving through the text. Following is a seven-paragraph passage in which Gloria Steinem, cofounder of *Ms.* magazine and author of numerous articles and books, distinguishes between erotica and pornography. She begins by defining the terms and then illustrates them by examples and analysis. The emphatic two-sentence transition in the second paragraph guides the reader from the long paragraph that discusses the origins of the two words to the paragraphs that provide examples and analysis. It does so by summarizing the preceding paragraph in the first short sentence and by anticipating the contents of the succeeding paragraphs in the second short sentence. Finally, the one-sentence paragraph at the end of the passage restates strongly the contrast between erotica and pornography.

PACE, PAGE 621

> . . . Sex as communication can send messages as different as life and death; even the origins of "erotica" and "pornography" reflect that fact. After all, "erotica" is rooted in *eros* or passionate love, and thus in the idea of positive choice, free will, the yearning for a particular person. (Interestingly, the definition of erotica leaves open the question of gender.) "Pornography" begins with a root meaning "prostitution" or "female captives," thus letting us know that the subject is not mutual love, or love at all, but domination and violence against women. (Though, of course, homosexual pornography may imitate this violence by putting a man in the "feminine" role of victim.) It ends with a root meaning "writing about" or "description of" which puts still more distance between subject and object, and replaces a spontaneous yearning for closeness with objectification and a voyeur.
>
> The difference is clear in words. It becomes even more so by example.
>
> Look at any photo or film of people making love; really making love. The images may be diverse, but there is usually a sensuality and touch and warmth, an acceptance of bodies and nerve endings. There is always a spontaneous sense of people who are there because they *want* to be, out of shared pleasure.
>
> Now look at any depiction of sex in which there is clear force, or an unequal power that spells coercion. It may be very blatant, with weapons or torture or bondage, wounds and bruises, some clear humiliation, or an adult's sexual power being used over a child. It may be much more subtle: a physical attitude of conqueror and victim, the use of race

or class difference to imply the same thing, perhaps a very unequal nudity, with one person exposed and vulnerable while the other is clothed. In either case, there is no sense of equal choice or equal power.

The first is erotic: a mutually pleasurable, sexual expression between people who have enough power to be there by positive choice. It may or may not strike a sense-memory in the viewer, or be creative enough to make the unknown seem real; but it doesn't require us to identify with a conqueror or a victim. It is truly sensuous, and may give us a contagion of pleasure.

The second is pornographic: its message is violence, dominance, and conquest. It is sex being used to reinforce some inequality, or to create one, or to tell us the lie that pain and humiliation (ours or someone else's) are really the same as pleasure. If we are to feel anything, we must identify with conqueror or victim. That means we can only experience pleasure through the adoption of some degree of sadism or masochism. It also means that we may feel diminished by the role of conqueror, or enraged, humiliated, and vengeful by sharing identity with the victim.

Perhaps one could simply say that erotica is about sexuality, but pornography is about power and sex-as-weapon—in the same way we have come to understand that rape is about violence, and not really about sexuality at all.

> —"Erotica and Pornography: A Clear and
> Present Difference," *Ms.* 7, no. 2
> (November 1978): 53.

One of the axioms of writing is that the most important idea, image, or concept should go either at the beginning or the end. Placed in the middle, it gets buried. The section on **introductions** illustrates how brief paragraphs can be used to begin a text. We've also just seen how Gloria Steinem concludes a series of paragraphs emphatically with a brief paragraph. The end of a text often requires paragraphs longer than a sentence or two. Sometimes an entire section of related paragraphs is needed to recapitulate the main line of reason, summarize the main ideas, or re-state a position or problem and call for action.

INTRODUCTIONS, PAGE 607

However, a short paragraph can bring a text or section of a text to an effective end, as illustrated in the following passage that comes from Robert Pirsig's best-selling *Zen and the Art of Motorcycle Maintenance*. Set off by itself, the concluding statement produces the appropriate final feeling, image, or idea in readers in a bold, memorable, and emphatic manner.

The real University . . . has no specific location. It owns no property, pays no salaries and receives no material dues. The real University is a state of mind. It is that great heritage of rational thought that has been brought down to us through the centuries and which does not exist at any specific location. It's a state of mind which is regenerated throughout the centuries by a body of people who traditionally carry the title of professor, but even that title is not part of the real University. The real University is nothing less than the continuing body of reason itself.

In addition to this state of mind, "reason," there's a legal entity which is unfortunately called by the same name but which is quite another thing. This is a nonprofit corporation, a branch of the state with a specific address. It owns property, is capable of paying salaries, of receiving money and of responding to legislative pressures in the process.

But this second University, the legal corporation, cannot teach, does not generate new knowledge or evaluate ideas. It is not the real University at all. It is just a church building, the setting, the location at which conditions have been made favorable for the real church to exist.

Confusion continually occurs in people who fail to see this difference . . . and think that control of the church buildings implies control of the church. They see professors as employees of the second University who should abandon reason when told to and take orders with no backtalk, the same way employees do in other corporations.

They see the second University, but fail to see the first.

—(New York: Bantam, 1974), pp. 143–44.

In eleven words, Pirsig ends by summarizing the principal point of the passage.

PROOFREADING

▼

Writers are responsible for getting the final version of their text in as perfect shape as possible before turning it over to their readers. Even if somebody else has helped them type it or key it into a computer, they must make sure that their text conforms to standard English, is in an acceptable format, and is accurate in everything from spelling to the most minute fact. When their text is in final form, writers proofread it. That is, they check it closely word for word—sometimes character by character—to ensure that all editing changes have been made and that there are no remaining typographic, spelling, punctuation, or usage errors and no stylistic inconsistencies. Only after the text has been "proofed" is it distributed to readers.

However, many writers do this task inadequately. For one thing, they probably work on a text so much—revising it several times, looking at essentially the same ideas again and again—and become so familiar with it that they are unable to see the errors. Their minds, not their eyes, tell them what they think is on the page. For another, all writers occasionally suffer the myopia of assuming that all is finally well and the text does not require a final check. Third, they tire mentally, perhaps even physically, from working on the text for long periods of time and are unable to absorb themselves in what they consider a tedious and boring last step. Fourth, they assume that running their text through a computer spell- or style-checking program has caught the typographical errors, misspelled words, and major grammatical problems. Finally, they sometimes are confronted by a fast-approaching deadline and don't have sufficient time to do more than give the text a quick glance before turning it in.

Here are a few suggestions to overcome some of the more common rationalizations for not doing a thorough job of proofreading.

If you believe . . .	**then . . .**
that you are so familiar with the text that you can no longer see the errors . . .	allow enough time to pass so that you can gain some distance from your own work.
that you have revised the text and that all is well . . .	never assume that all is well. Don't be too satisfied too soon with the condition of your text.
that you are up against a deadline that allows no time for proofreading . . .	ask for a brief extension of the deadline *once*. After that, schedule your work so that you will have sufficient time to let the text sit for a couple of days before you proofread it and make the final necessary changes.

that your spell- or style-checking program has caught the typos, misspellings, and grammatical errors . . .

assume that these computer programs are helpful, but that they cannot substitute for your own proofreading, since no computer program will catch typos or misspellings that are themselves words (for instance, *saw* for *was, pursue* for *peruse, bead* for *bread,* and *argue* for *agree*).

It is essential that you proofread the completed text to make sure that everything is as you want it. Usually you proofread what you believe is the final printed text. You may be allowed to make a neat and legible correction or two per page on the final draft. Or you may be required to correct the errors and print a new copy of your text, which in turn should be proofread to make sure the errors were corrected and that no new errors were introduced in making the corrections. To do these things, you have the great advantage of word processing. Only a few years ago, writers faced the task of retyping entire manuscripts just to make a few corrections. And, of course, occasionally new errors were made in retyping, which meant that those errors had to be corrected. Here is one writer's lament:

> Oh I am so tired of correcting my own writing—these 8 articles—I have however learnt I think to dash: not to finick. I mean the writing is free enough: it's the repulsiveness of correcting that nauseates me. . . .

> I finished my re-typing of *The Waves*. Not that it is finished—oh dear no. For then I must correct this re-re-typing. . . .

> O to seek relief from this incessant correction.

> > —Virginia Woolf, *A Writer's Diary,*
> > ed. Leonard Woolf (New York:
> > Harcourt Brace, 1954), pp. 166, 167.

Proofreading Effectively

Here are some practices that we recommend to help you proofread your text.

▶ Let the text "cool off" before proofreading it. You need to be at least temporarily detached from your text so that you can return to it with a rested mind and fresh eyes.

▶ Use standard proofreading marks. Standard proofreading marks give you a widely recognized system to indicate corrections or changes.

Marks for Insertions

❖ To insert material in your text, place a caret (∧) just below the line where the material should go, and write the material above it:

```
                            any
There does not seem to be ∧doubt about the danger of
                          e
storing nuclar waste.
            ∧
```

If you have omitted an entire line of text or a couple of sentences, it is best to retype that part of the text and print a new page.

❖ To insert a space, place a # just above the line where the space should go:

```
                                        #
The conversation quickly changed into an∧argument.
```

❖ To insert punctuation, use the following proofreading marks:

—To add a comma, insert it where you want it and make a caret (∧) over it:

```
However∧ it was already six o'clock when we arrived.
       ⌣
```

—To add an apostrophe or quotation marks, use an inverted caret (∨), and place the punctuation above it:

```
                      '
We arrived at six o∨clock.
```

```
In "Beauty and Pain: Notes on the Art of Richard
                  "
Selzer,∨David Morris investigates Selzer's sense
of aesthetics.
```

objectivity. Some checks can become automatic through experience and practice, allowing you to pay attention to more and more things in one pass.

▶ **Remember that the rigors of proofreading are justified.** Providing a text that is error-free helps you achieve your purposes in writing. Don't give readers a reason to be dissatisfied with any aspect of your writing.

Although the following contains more errors than usual for such a short text, we use it to show what a text that has been proofread might look like:

> The missfortunes of the north in the first months
> of the Civil War affected Thoreau so profoundly that
> he is known to have said that he could never recover
> while the war lasted and he told his friends that he
> was "sick for his Country (Whicher 70). But he was also
> disastified with his Country, and the base of his
> dissatisfaction was his conviction that humans, and
> hence their countries, are perfectible.

After you have incorporated the changes in your text, print out a hard copy, and try yet a third round to see if there is still that proverbial error somewhere that everybody can see but you:

> The misfortunes of the North in the first months of
> the Civil War affected Thoreau so profoundly that he is
> known to have said that he could never recover while
> the war lasted, and he told his friends that he was
> "sick for his country" (Whicher 74). But he was also
> dissatisfied with his country, and the base of his dis-
> satisfaction was his conviction that humans, and hence
> their countries, are perfectible.

REVISING AND EDITING

Writers often revise their thoughts as they put them on paper or on a computer screen. Even when they are writing briskly, they sometimes revise their thinking even before they formulate an idea completely enough to write it down. The early stages of creating a text consist of false starts, blind alleys, wrong turns, changes of direction, and starting overs.

Don't be too frustrated or discouraged by what seems like a messy and stumbling process that might even appear to be directionless. Things are not necessarily going badly; they are probably proceeding normally. Initial drafting seldom goes smoothly but is never a waste of time. These tentative draftings are part of the normal writing process by which writers capture enough of a newborn idea to get a glimpse of what they think or know or believe and what they want to say about something. There is no clear line of demarcation dividing initial drafting from revising. Just keep writing until you have created a text that is substantial enough to revise—a draft that is variously called an initial draft, a "zero" draft, or a discovery draft. Write as many paragraphs or pages as you can. In general, a text should consist of at least several paragraphs before you attempt to revise it. You must have something to revise.

Revising Content and Meaning

After you have created a text, even if it is fragmentary and messy (and it undoubtedly will be), you have something you can read and work on. You can then begin to revise extensively and repeatedly—adding, deleting, compressing, restructuring, and rewording sentences, paragraphs, and longer stretches of text. You can rewrite, review, and re-think again and again, perhaps occasionally mumbling to yourself as you try to get an idea fixed in your mind or as you try to make one item consistent with another. With this kind of extensive revision, content is likely to be changed substantially as you condense a passage that is too

AMPLIFICATION, PAGE 508 wordy or too detailed, expand a passage that needs **amplification**, come up with better examples to shore up an argument that is on shaky grounds, or discover a better way of expressing an idea. Organization and structure are likely to be altered significantly as you attempt a new way to develop an idea or a different arrangement to strengthen a line of argument or as you emphasize the transition from one topic to another to improve the coherence of a passage.

As you work over a part of your text, you make changes that will probably require modifications elsewhere in the text. This kind of extensive revision should not include the cosmetic changes that you will make later when you edit and proofread the final drafts of your text, although it will be difficult to ignore an obvious misspelling, punctuation error, or usage error. Go ahead and correct such errors if you must, especially if it can be done as you revise. However, it is better to delay looking for these kinds of errors until you have finished revising, because you might spend time tinkering with a statement or polishing a sentence that will be deleted or changed drastically later.

When you revise you are not correcting surface errors, you are exploring your subject and shaping your thoughts. You are bringing discipline to your thinking, which in turn helps bring discipline to your writing. Writing helps you discover what you think, even—actually, especially—when you write something that seems to be different from what you intended to write. Reading what you have written helps clarify your thinking, which, in turn, gets fed back into your writing. This reading, writing, reflecting, and writing again moves you along. Do not regard your text as final until you are satisfied with your revision or you run out of time and must begin editing and **proofreading**.

PROOFREADING, PAGE 643

As experienced writers know, one of the great myths about writing is that good writers can create clean, graceful, and correct texts in an initial draft, beginning with the first sentence and working straight through to the end, pausing only occasionally to think of what comes next. But experienced writers know they are not poor writers because they revise. They know better:

> When you're younger, you think you do a draft or two and then anything after that would be compromising your vision. Well, that's just not the case. Nobody writes first drafts from God, except Mozart.
>
> —David Koepp, "The Talk of the Town,"
> *New Yorker* 21 (March 1994): 57.

Good writers revise, just as good actors rehearse and rehearse, good fishermen practice casting over and over again, and good cross-country runners run and run and run. Revising is essential to discovering what you want to say and to deciding how to say it.

Since the initial draft is sure to be rough, it is sure to need major revisions. But at least at this stage you have text that can be worked on. Since revision requires full attention and alertness, you need to come at it fresh and rested. It is probably a good idea, if time permits, to set the text aside for awhile—at least overnight—so that when you return to it you can see it with fresh eyes. It is now time to begin seriously to revise. Following are several suggestions to keep in mind as you revise.

▶ In the early stages of revision you should concern yourself with content, purpose, and the organization of the entire text. Start by reading it from beginning to end. Check to see that you have covered the topics that you wanted to cover. Does the text make the points you want to make? Look at the organization. Is there some kind of logical structure that can be followed easily? Is there a clear **thesis statement**? Are **paragraphs** arranged in a noticeable order? Are there **topic sentences** that state the main ideas of paragraphs or blocks of paragraphs? Does the text hold together? Do **forecasting statements** and **transitions** help establish **coherence**? Are the lines of development easy to follow? Are there good transitions from idea to idea?

As you read and reread parts of the text, look at the **amplification** of major ideas. Find what you regard as the strongest part of the text, and see if you can develop its main point further. Are there additional examples or details that could strengthen the main point? Will readers understand your **allusions**? Can you substitute another example or detail that would be better than what you already have? Are there gaps in research or presentation? Are there passages that can be deleted? Look for the connections and developments that may unexpectedly pop up and suggest other things to say. Are there other passages that need further development? How is the **pace**? Are ideas presented at a rate that is easy to grasp?

Revising for Style

▶ When you are satisfied with amplification, review your style and voice to determine that they are appropriate. Does the writing sound like your normal way of writing? If you have created a distinct style, is it appropriate for your purpose and audience? Is the level of language appropriate for the readers' backgrounds and familiarity with the subject? Is your way of handling capitalization, plural and singular forms, and punctuation consistent?

▶ Check the accuracy and consistency of the content, especially references to numbers, dates, places, names, and terms. If you have stated that you will discuss five items, make sure that there are five. Consistency and accuracy help keep readers' attention. Recheck your sources to make sure there are no misstatements in quoted material. Review for accuracy any data and statistics that are presented in tables and graphs. Scrutinize formulas and equations. Double-check any math.

▶ If you are working with a word processor, try to make revisions directly on screen. If you are working with printed text, you must make the revisions by hand, and the text will start getting messy. In any event, you will probably need to print a revised text so that you can continue working on it without the interference of your previous revisions. Once you have a clean, revised text, look at the organization again to see if any condensing, deleting, adding, or moving of text has created gaps or inconsistencies between forecasting statements and transitions and the current text. One of the most necessary tasks in revising—especially on a computer—is to check to make sure that the revised text reads logically and smoothly, that the order and logic have not become confused as a result of the changes that have been made. A word processor takes the pick-and-shovel work out of revising, especially since there won't be any large-scale retyping. But since a word processor enables you to make changes quickly, you should check to make sure the text contains no gaps, redundancies, or inconsistencies brought about by revisions.

▶ Now that you have a clean text, examine its **format**. Is each paragraph properly indented? Should some paragraphs be combined? Should others be divided? Are headings and subheadings properly formatted? Are there places where a series should be numbered and broken out into a list? Are equations and long quotations displayed properly? Have you used the appropriate documentation system?

FORMAT, PAGE 582

Editing

Revising focuses on overall organization, content, and meaning; editing concentrates on expression. After revising, you are ready to edit—to make changes at the most local level, the phrase and word level. Work at achieving **conciseness**. Are there words that can be cut or phrases that can be replaced with single words? Make sure that your diction is appropriate, avoiding unnecessary slang and abstract language, and that there are no gross errors such as wrong words or gender-biased language.

CONCISENESS, PAGE 545

When you have finished editing at the word or phrase level, you have completed a substantive revision. However, your text is not ready for proofreading. Not yet. For now, you should have a revised and edited text that is much stronger than the initial one; the focus should be sharper, the meaning clearer, the organization tighter and more obvious, and the evidence stronger. You should be getting a better sense of where your ideas are headed and how well you are doing at getting there. It is now time to cool off from the intensive revision. Allow for a long-enough gestation period to be able to reread and revise and edit again with fresh eyes and an alert mind.

STYLE AND VOICE

Teachers of writing love to talk about style and voice, but in truth, these abstract terms probably don't have a very clear meaning for most students of writing. Even when teachers of writing or experienced writers speak of style or voice, they may not be talking about the same things. Although precise definitions are not possible, you can understand these terms generally and learn to distinguish between them.

Style

Style is most often thought of as a conscious variation in the way a person writes. A writer's decision to adopt a certain style is usually determined by his or her purpose and audience. The most simple variation in style, for example, is level of formality. If the intended reader is someone the writer does not know well or who holds a position of authority, the writer will probably use a rather formal style. If, in contrast, the reader is a close friend, the writer will usually adopt an informal style. Some additional stylistic options include the following:

- terse versus verbose

- businesslike versus chatty

- direct versus indirect

- plain versus ornate

- outspoken versus diplomatic and polite

Such options are available to you as a writer each time you construct a text. Depending upon your purpose and audience, you can choose to be one or the other or anything in between. Rather than absolute choices, these options should be viewed as opposite ends of a continuum. You can opt to be mildly formal in one document and somewhat informal in another, totally outspoken in one document and less so in another. These are qualities over which you have considerable control. As you become a more experienced writer, you will be aware of even more options, and your control over them will increase.

Voice

Whereas variations in style result from deliberate choices, your writing voice is personal and unique. Like your speaking voice, it is characteristic of you—a personal quality that reflects you as a person. Although experienced writers of poetry, fiction, and drama can usually vary their voice, or tone, to represent different characters, most of us have just one writing voice that is reflected in everything we write. In other words, most writers have a variety of styles at their disposal but only one writing voice.

Although you may not be able to change your writing voice as freely and consciously as you do your writing style, it may very well change over the years (or even a quarter or semester) as you become more comfortable and experienced as a writer. Your reading experiences also affect your writing voice. As you read different authors and different types of texts, your own voice will develop and change. But, in general, your writing voice is not something you can change at will.

What Determines Style and Voice

What makes one style or one voice different from another? It is easier to explain what determines style and voice than to define the concepts. Writers work with words. With the exception of a few kinds of **graphics**, words are all they have with which to construct their texts, and all they have with which to vary their writing styles and develop their writing voice. As a writer, you work with words in two ways:

GRAPHICS, PAGE 596

1. You choose which words to use.

2. You arrange these words in different ways.

Word choice (diction) and the arrangement of words into sentences (syntax) determine both style and voice. For example, read the following pair of sentences:

❖ The little boy looked through the window at the cows.

❖ The lad peered through the pane at the cattle.

Both of these sentences say the same thing. But the word choice in the two sentences varies. The second sentence uses less common words and thus has a different style and voice. Your choice of words determines more than the sense of what you say; it determines your style and voice.

Now compare the following sentences:

- The girl mounted the high-strung, impatient horse with speed and grace.

- With speed and grace, the girl mounted the high-strung, impatient horse.

The words are exactly the same in these two sentences, but the arrangement of the words is different. As a result, the style and tone of the sentences differ. The second sentence emphasizes the "speed and grace" rather than the woman or the act of mounting. Notice what happens if we change the syntax in other ways:

- Speedily and gracefully, the girl mounted the high-strung, impatient horse.

- The girl mounted the horse, which was impatient and high strung, speedily and gracefully.

- The impatient, high-strung horse was mounted by the girl with speed and grace.

- The girl mounted the horse, which was impatient and high strung, with speed and grace.

- The horse, high-strung and impatient, was mounted by the girl with speed and grace.

Each of these different ways of arranging the same words results in a slightly different sentence. Although the meaning is the same, the style and voice change subtly but clearly in each.

Now look at still another variation on this same sentence. This time we are changing the word choices:

- The gal hopped on the jittery, nervous bronco quickly and lightly.

You can see how completely the style and voice of this sentence changes with each manipulation of diction and syntax. As a writer, you have these same options in determining your own style and voice.

SUMMARIES

▼

Since nobody has the time to read everything, readers are usually interested in determining quickly whether a piece of writing covers a topic that is of interest to them, what the writer's main ideas are, and what line of argument the writer takes. A summary is a condensed statement of a longer text that gives readers these kinds of information.

There are two basic kinds of summaries:

1. One is a brief summary of another person's text. This kind of summary is valuable in note taking and in commenting on source material in your own writing. Your major objective in writing this kind of summary is to show that you understand the source material and to establish the basis for your own interpretation of the text to which you are referring.

2. The other is a capsule version of the main ideas in your own text—sometimes called an abstract or synopsis. Many reports and articles begin with a clearly labeled abstract that helps readers get the central meaning of the text quickly. Whether it appears in front of your text or as a separate entry in an information data base, its primary function is to preview your text so readers can decide whether they want to read your entire text.

Summarizing Other Writers' Texts

A brief summary of another writer's text might consist of only a few words that indicate the main topic or idea:

> In *The Bell Curve*, Herrnstein and Murray assert that IQ tests measure actual intelligence and are not culturally biased.

This one-sentence summary identifies the source and what the summarizer thinks is its main idea or at least the major idea on which he or she wants to focus. Most experienced writers identify the author's background or role as authority as well:

> Herrnstein, a psychologist at Harvard University until his death last year, and Murray, author of *Losing Ground: American Social Policy 1950–1988* (1986), assert . . .

A longer, more informative summary elaborates briefly on the main ideas of the text, sometimes contextualizing the text by indicating its importance and the general line of thinking or research that it represents:

> Herrnstein and Murray's *The Bell Curve* created a controversy in educational- and social-policy debates in 1994–1995 by reviving the old argument that black Americans categorically score much lower on IQ tests than do whites. The main line of their argument is that there are genetically determined differences in intelligence. They assert that IQ tests measure actual intelligence and are not culturally biased, and consequently, that organized efforts to raise IQ scores, such as the Head Start Program, have failed and will continue to fail.

You should not comment on—certainly not take issue with—another writer's ideas unless readers know in general what the text to which you are referring says.

Such summaries, whether brief or long, perform several important functions:

▶ They help clarify for yourself the main points of the longer piece.

▶ They help readers get the gist of longer texts to which you refer, whether they may or may not wish to read them. Although summaries contain little actual information about the details, examples, and data, those readers who wish to learn more can read the full text, and they can start with the overview that your summary provides. Those readers who decide not to read the full text have the key points.

▶ They demonstrate to readers your familiarity with texts that you cite. This demonstration is an important way to display your open-mindedness and fairness in working with the ideas of others. If readers are familiar with the text you are summarizing, they can compare their own interpretation of the main ideas of the source with yours. If readers are unfamiliar with the source, they can read it if they wish.

▶ They help integrate material from other sources into your own writing. They do this by creating a framework for your own response to the major ideas of another writer's text, whether you are referring to it only as a point of information, challenging it, or agreeing with it.

Summarizing Your Own Text

The main purpose of summarizing your own text is similar to that of summarizing another writer's text—to help readers get the central meaning quickly. Just as you like to know where you are going before the plane leaves the ground, readers like to have a clear idea of exactly where you are taking them in your text. An abstract or summarizing statement at the beginning helps focus readers' attention on the main points of your text. Here is an abstract of a student's research paper that was written for a modern world history course. The student's main purpose in the paper is to examine the challenges democratic governments face in a period of radical change in the world—not just a crisis in a single country or in one region, but crises in many countries around the world.

> Political events are challenging the assumptions that totalitarian systems are strong and durable and that free governments are inherently weak and vulnerable. However, the difficulties that former totalitarian regimes are having in moving toward more democratic government indicate that the trend toward freer governments and more open societies is not inevitable. There is a need for democratic governments to help former totalitarian countries achieve more environmentally friendly industries, cultural toleration, and civil liberty. The world's leading democracies seem to be poorly prepared to assist these emerging nations, primarily because they find it difficult to shift from a policy of containment of totalitarian regimes to a policy of support for new democracies. Most large democratic nations are experiencing their own cultural and economic problems.

This kind of summary focuses the readers' attention on the thesis and main ideas and provides them with an overview that will make it easier for them to grasp the significant supporting points, important facts, and conclusions of the whole text. Once readers have the big picture, they find it much easier to assimilate the facts and minor ideas that develop or flesh out the larger view.

Writing Effective Summaries

A summary is not difficult to write (especially if the longer text is organized well). However, there are two complicating factors when we attempt to write summaries of other writers' texts. One is our tendency to read carefully only that part of the original text that we are interested in and to remember only those ideas with which we agree. The other is our difficulty in distinguishing main ideas from minor ideas and supporting details.

The solution is to read the piece to be summarized carefully more than once (even if it is your own text you are summarizing) to get the whole picture, the main ideas, and the main points that support those ideas.

▶ **Begin by scanning the piece.** Read quickly but attentively through the material, noticing the author and title, and read the opening and closing paragraphs to identify the **thesis**, major topics, and organization. In addition, note the use of **headings**, **transitions**, and other cues about organization. This information will prepare you to read the piece more closely. (See also Reading and Evaluating Sources, pages 435–444.)

THESIS, PAGE 663
HEADINGS, PAGE 603
TRANSITIONS, PAGE 676

▶ Now reread the material more carefully, annotating the text (or jotting notes on a separate sheet of paper or notecard if you do not want to mark up the text). Note how the writer develops each main idea and the relationship of these ideas to the main point of the text.

▶ A productive way to draft a version of a summary is to begin with a sentence that identifies the source, the topic, and the main ideas. You may also explain the writer's purpose in the first sentence, but do not hesitate to go to a second sentence if the first sentence gets too long or overpacked. Then, for each major section of the text, identify in a sentence or two its main points.

▶ Once you have drafted a provisional summary, check it against the longer text to assure that you have reflected its main ideas, scope, and organization. Above all, check to see that you have presented the writer's major ideas fairly and that you have not changed the meaning of the original text.

▶ **Finally, check the length of your summary.** Summaries and abstracts are usually around 200 to 250 words long, although a lot depends upon the length of the text being abstracted. Longer texts—say ten or more pages, probably require more than a couple of hundred words. We cannot tell you what the length of a summary or abstract should be for longer texts. But since a summary or abstract should be a quick overview of the text, we suggest that yours not take more than a minute or two to read.

THESIS AND THESIS STATEMENT

The thesis is the central or dominant idea that controls and unifies the text. Whether it is stated explicitly (hence, the "thesis statement"), or implied, the thesis is the center of interest in a text—it is the point you want to make and the idea, attitude, or opinion that you hope your readers will accept as true and carry away with them after they finish reading. All texts have a thesis, but not all texts contain a thesis statement.

However, when you take a stand on a debatable issue, you don't want to fool around. Most of the time you will want to express your thesis explicitly in a thesis statement both to highlight your main point and to minimize ambiguity. Any text is open to different interpretations—whether the reader is carelessly inattentive or is attentive but influenced by beliefs, knowledge, or expectations that would allow for an interpretation different from what you intend. Thus it is important that you state your thesis as clearly as you can make words express it and in language that your readers understand easily. Express your opinion early (usually in the first or second paragraph) and clearly (either as a declarative sentence or a question), and then support the thesis statement with evidence or answer the question. Such is the nature of most of your texts that have an argumentative edge: They indicate to readers that you are going to argue for a certain proposition, get them involved early, and entice them to want to read the whole text. Here are four thesis statements that do just that.

The first one is the first sentence of an article by a natural science columnist for *Outsider* magazine:

> In the fifth chapter of Matthew's gospel, Christ is quoted as saying that the meek shall inherit the earth, but other opinion lately suggests that, no, more likely it will go to the cockroaches.
>
> —David Quammen, "A Republic of
Cockroaches," Natural Acts: A Sidelong View
of Science and Nature (New York:
Nick Lyon's Books, 1985), p. 53.

The second example is the very first sentence in E. D. Hirsch, Jr.'s, 1987 national best-selling book. It states the essence of his argument that cultural literacy (the background information that an audience needs to understand what is said in books, newspapers, magazines, television programs, and so forth) is essential to being a successful citizen or worker in our society:

> To be culturally literate is to possess the basic information needed to thrive in the modern world.
>
> —*Cultural Literacy: What Every American Needs to Know* (Boston: Houghton Mifflin, 1987), p. xiii.

At times, you may want to lead into your thesis statement by providing brief background or context, as in the third and fourth examples. The third is a strong assertion at the end of the opening paragraph that will be defended by information that follows:

> Each child has a dream. I had two. One was to be a marine and the other was to be a policeman. I tried other endeavors but I was just not cut out for it. I am a policeman. It is one of the most gratifying jobs in the world.
>
> —Studs Terkel, "Vincent Maher," in *Working* (New York: Avon, 1974), p. 183.

The fourth example comes at the end of the second paragraph of one of the most famous articles published in *Ms.* magazine. It states the main idea of the piece, followed by a question that helps focus the issue and propel the reader to read on to find the answers:

> I belong to that classification of people known as wives. I am a wife. And, not altogether incidentally, I am a mother.
> Not long ago a male friend of mine appeared on the scene fresh from a recent divorce. He had one child, who is, of course, with his ex-wife. He is looking for another wife. As I thought about him while I was ironing one evening, it suddenly occurred to me that I, too, would like to have a wife. Why do I want a wife?
>
> —Judy Syfers, "I Want a Wife," *Ms.* (April 1972), p. 56.

In addition to stating the main idea, a thesis statement can also be constructed so it has predictive power. For instance, it can be stated so that it signals a particular method of development for a piece of writing. Here is a statement that suggests a cause-and-effect method of development: "The eighteen percent reduction in employee absenteeism at the Fillmore Plant appears to be the direct result of the new employee incentives programs introduced last year." A thesis statement can also be designed so that it both suggests the method of development and indicates the organization of the contents in a piece of writing. Here is a statement that suggests a comparison method of development and forecasts that three criteria (cost, ease of use, and availability of software) will be discussed in the order listed: "The Azcar 1588b is the best buy because it is the least expensive system in its class, it appears to be the easiest to learn to use, and it has the most available software." Once such an anticipatory summary has been made, it must be fulfilled in the ensuing text (also see **forecasting statements**).

FORECASTING STATEMENTS, PAGE 580

Most of the time, as these sample thesis statements illustrate, the traditional strategy in persuasive writing is to state the thesis first (sometimes also predicting the plan of organization) and then present the reasons, facts, and evidence that will lead the reader to accept your opinion. In their most basic form, such tightly organized arguments look like the one that follows, in an interpretation of Ernest Hemingway's "The Snows of Kilimanjaro."

The opening paragraph ends with this statement of the issue and the author's proposition.

. . . Ernest Hemingway's use of death symbols in "The Snows of Kilimanjaro" has been pointed out many times. Nevertheless, Caroline Gordon and Allen Tate object to Hemingway's use of snow-covered Kilimanjaro as a symbol of death (*The House of Fiction*). They claim that the symbol "does not operate as a controlling image" of the story and that it "seems something the writer has tacked on, rather than an integral part of the story" (p. 421). Yet the snow-covered western summit does serve as symbol; it is the whiteness of Kilimanjaro's snow, the unusual whiteness attending Harry's fatal infection, and the weird aura of whiteness in Harry's reveries which officiate over his death.

<table>
<tr><td>The second paragraph begins with this statement that supports the thesis. The rest of the paragraph consists of factual support for this opinion.</td><td>Hemingway uses whiteness in connection with the death of his central characters . . .</td></tr>
<tr><td>The third paragraph begins with this statement of support for the thesis. The rest of the paragraph consists of factual support of this opinion.</td><td>In "The Snows of Kilimanjaro" whiteness again attends death. . . .</td></tr>
<tr><td>The fourth paragraph begins with these statements that support the thesis. The rest of the paragraph consists of factual support for this opinion.</td><td>As Harry passes through a series of feverish reveries toward death, whiteness appears with increasing recurrence and persistence. The more vacuous Harry becomes, the more obvious the aura of whiteness. . . .</td></tr>
<tr><td>After the three areas of support are each presented in a paragraph, the last paragraph states what the author hopes is the inevitable conclusion.</td><td>The many instances in which Hemingway associates whiteness with the death of his central characters, and particularly the frequent and persistent appearance of whiteness that accompanies Harry's trip to death, make it clear that Hemingway was fully conscious and in control of his symbolic use of the white snows of Kilimanjaro.</td></tr>
</table>

This extract shows the essence of the argument. The most important conclusion and the biggest idea is the thesis: that the snow-covered western summit of Mount Kilimanjaro is an integral symbol in the story. The tight organization of the argument conveys a strong sense of a beginning, middle, and end. The five paragraphs contain the thesis statement, three main statements of support to affirm the thesis, and then the conclusion. This form, easy to master, is one of the most common of all forms in writing, keeping the argument focused by clearly stating the point under dispute and displaying the line of reasoning briskly and efficiently. It satisfies readers' desire to know what the writer wants to tell them and also what to expect in the rest of the text. It is equally well suited to analyzing relatively minor questions and to arguing the complexities of large and difficult subjects.

However, not all texts must have such tightly structured arguments. There are other options. For instance, in more informal, relaxed personal writing, the thesis may appear anywhere, including in the middle of the piece. Russell Baker's chapter about his Uncle Harold in his autobiography *Growing Up* illustrates the variation. The chapter begins: "Uncle Harold was famous for lying." But that sentence, while it starts the chapter with a bang, does not state the main idea. Baker comes to recognize that Uncle Harold was not really a liar but was a romantic who wanted life to be more interesting than it was. Here's the way Baker writes it (in the fifty-sixth paragraph!).

> My first awe of him had softened as I gradually realized his information was not really intended to be information. Gradually I came to see that Uncle Harold was not a liar but a teller of stories and a romantic, and it was Uncle Harold the teller of tales who fascinated me.
>
> —(New York: Congdon & Weed, 1982), p. 143.

Baker's decision to hold back the thesis statement until nearly two-thirds through the chapter is effective in helping us decide whether his opinion of Uncle Harold is accurate. To have begun the chapter with this main point would have robbed Baker (and us) of the opportunity to share the experiences that eventually led him to understand Uncle Harold's true nature. Baker's delaying the main point until late in the chapter reflects his gradual discovery of the truth about Uncle Harold.

TITLES
▼

Positioned as it is at the beginning, the title influences how a reader responds to the text because it is generally the first clue as to what is at the heart of the text—the writer's intention and the topic, subject matter, or theme.

Titles that Indicate the Main Topic

A good title performs several functions, one of the most important of which is to indicate the topic of the text. The following untitled passage illustrates how important a title or the lack of a title is in giving an indication of topic:

> Rocky slowly got up from the mat, planning his escape. He hesitated a moment and thought. Things were not going well. What bothered him most was being held, especially since the charge against him had been weak. He considered his present situation. The lock that held him was strong but he thought he could break it. He knew, however, that his timing would have to be perfect. Rocky was aware that it was because of his early roughness that he had been penalized so severely—much too severely from his point of view. The situation was becoming frustrating; the pressure had been grinding on him too long. He was being ridden unmercifully. Rocky was getting angry now. He felt he was ready to make his move. He knew that his success or failure would depend on what he did in the next few seconds.
>
> —Quoted in Lester Faigley, "The Problem of Topic in Texts," in *The Territory of Language: Linguistics, Stylistics, and the Teaching of Composition,* ed. Donald A. McQuade (Carbondale: Southern Illinois University Press, 1986), p. 134.

Do you know what this passage is about? Your answer depends upon the assumptions you make about the topic. Without a title to inform readers about the topic, the passage is ambiguous, as was demonstrated when researchers read the passage to selected college students. Physical education majors believed the passage was about wrestling; other students thought it was about a prison escape. (Richard C. Anderson, Ralph E. Reynolds, Dianne L. Schallert, and Ernest T. Goetz, *Framework for Comprehending Discourse,* Technical Report No. 12 [Urbana, IL: Center for the Study of Reading, 1976], ERIC Document Reproduction Service No. ED 134 935.) The reader's reactions will inevitably be in terms of his or her own temperament, interests, and background. Thus, physical education majors, wrestlers, former wrestlers, and fans of wrestling are likely to share the same assumptions and come to similar interpretations about the topic.

Because readers' responses are shaped by what they know, are interested in, and think important, the possible meanings in a text are provisional and can shift from one reader to the next and vary from one moment to the next. Key words in a title can help stabilize meaning by establishing a general framework of meaning. They also offer a strong clue to what the topic is by providing information that is not given in the text itself. Lacking such information about an untitled text, readers—like the students in the experiment just cited—must concentrate on building an hypothesis about the topic as they read. This effort to deduce or recognize the topic can be profoundly influenced by these three things: (1) the readers' familiarity with what they assume is the unstated topic (prior knowledge can make a dramatic difference, as illustrated in the preceding passage), (2) the readers' sophistication in reading (the awareness that other interpretations of the topic are possible), and (3) the readers' needs for certain kinds of information (the readers are likely to see what they are interested in).

The meaning of a text is created by these variable subjective perceptions, which leave a text open to a range of different understandings and interpretations. But guided by a title such as "Wrestling" or "The Prisoner," the reader is able to limit possible interpretations of topic and, without much effort, will have particular expectations about the topic and can focus and shape meaning that is more in line with the author's intention. With such an informative title, the readers of the passage would have been able to identify the topic not so much from what the text said as from what the title said. A specific title almost guarantees that the topic will be recognized.

A more ambiguous title, such as "The Escape," would have kept the text open to various interpretations, which is often a desirable feature of literary writing. Thus, a title can destabilize the meaning of a text as well as stabilize it. In choosing a title for your text, you must consider whether you want the title to indicate the topic directly and clearly. If your purpose is primarily informative, a title that clearly states the topic is probably best, since you do not personally accompany your text to make your intention known to readers. If your purpose is primarily literary, a title that is not immediately clear and perhaps even playfully ironic, but which nevertheless becomes clear and appropriate as the reader reads, can be very effective. Titles such as "A Rose for Emily," *To Kill a Mockingbird, Catcher in the Rye, The Color Purple, The Joy Luck Club*, "The Short Happy Life of Francis Macomber," and *Love in the Time of Cholera* are titles of literary works that are symbolic, evocative, ironic, or in some other fashion suggestively rich.

Titles that Indicate Purpose and Scope

A second function of an effective title, especially for pragmatic texts, is to define the writer's purpose and the scope of the text. Titles such as "How to Reduce Stress During Final Examinations," "A Guide to the Ready-Reference Section of the University Library," and "Proposal for an Analysis of Water Imagery in Hemingway's Fiction" are fairly long but allow the reader to identify the writer's purpose in precise terms. Exact and specific titles work well for professional audiences and others who are engaged in the serious reading of informative texts. An example is "Coherent Vortical Features in a Turbulent Two-Dimensional Flow and the Great Red Spot of Jupiter" (Phillip S. Marcus, paper presented at the 110th Meeting of the Acoustical Society of America, Nashville, Tennessee, November 5, 1985).

While most readers no longer expect the title to cover the entire subject, they do expect a title to indicate the main focus. A title such as *Resisting Earthquakes* is too broad if the topic is the design of earthquake-resistant features in tall buildings in Los Angeles. However, a long title does not guarantee a precise title. Here are some examples of deadwood that shows up more often than is desirable in academic and professional writing: *An Analysis of . . ., An Investigation of . . ., A Report on . . ., A Study of . . . .* These words state the obvious and therefore contribute nothing to the meaning of the title. Since they are the first words in titles, they occupy a strong position that should be given to words that contribute more substantively to the title. *An Investigation of the Use of Phase Transitions in Artificial Intelligence Systems* is twice as long as need be: *Phase Transitions in Artificial Intelligence Systems.*

Titles that Capture Attention

A third function of a title is to capture attention and entice the reader to begin reading the text. The amount of luring required depends largely on the audience. For readers of scientific, professional, and academic writing, titles should usually announce the topic, purpose, and scope. The readers' needs for specific kinds of information and the reputation of the publication or publisher are generally sufficient for motivated readers. For readers who are reading primarily for entertainment or to satisfy personal interests, titles need to be more intriguing. There are several ways to do this. Titles such as "Shipwrecked on the Shores of Switzerland," "What You Don't Know About the Selection of the Homecoming Queen," "What They Don't Teach You at the Harvard Business School," and "Pollution Is Good for You" arouse interest and curiosity. Titles that ask questions carry the implied promise that the reader will learn the answer if he or she reads the text. Inquisitive titles such as "Can South Africa Be Saved?" or "Should You Fight a Library Fine?" or "How Long Is the Coast of Britain?" not only express the topic of the text but serve, as well, as hooks if the question interests the reader.

Choosing Effective Titles

Coming up with a good title takes some time, and it is worth thinking about early in your writing. It's probably not quite as important as naming your first-born child, but the effort can help guide you in focusing on your central idea. Here are three suggestions about creating titles.

▶ Choose a title that in some way fits the text. Do not try to fool a reader or yourself with a catchy, humorous, or bizarre title that is not appropriate. Ellen Coughlin, the book review editor for the *Chronicle of Higher Education*, observed that the subtitle of W. V. Quine's book *Quiddities: An Intermittently Philosophical Dictionary* was inappropriate: "This is not a dictionary and it is not terribly philosophical" (October 21, 1987, p. A9).

▶ Do not accept uncritically the first title that pops into your mind. Many well-known books would not be recognized by their original titles: Leo Tolstoy's *All's Well That Ends Well* became *War and Peace,* and Thomas Wolfe's *O Lost* was published as *Look Homeward, Angel*. One of the all-time best sellers in America, Margaret Mitchell's *Gone with the Wind*, at first had the working title *Another Day,* and Mitchell also considered *Milestones, Jettison, Ba! Ba! Blacksheep, Not in Our Day*, and *Bugles Sang True*. It is not necessarily true that a rose by any other name would smell as sweet. Keep plugging away at the title until you have one that can stand for the central idea or symbolize the meaning of your text.

▶ If a good title eludes you early on, keep on writing. It is really not necessary to think up a title before you can write. But sometime during writing and revising, study closely the beginning and ending of your text, looking specifically for cues that might lead to a title. You will probably find a phrase or sentence containing key words that state your purpose and intent or that capture the idea of the thesis. If you are indecisive about a title, draft two or three possible titles, and ask the opinion of a classmate who is providing a critique of your writing. One of the alternative titles might be stronger than the others, or portions of two or more of the alternative titles might be selected in reconstructing a new title. Perhaps even a totally new title will emerge. There will, of course, be some blind alleys, but there will also be a few promising avenues to explore. Sooner or later, you will come up with a title that attracts readers and predisposes them to focus on certain topics as they begin reading your text.

There are two basic positions for a title. The title can be put on a separate sheet of paper, appropriately called a title page, at the front of the text, or it can be centered at the top of the first page of the text. Punctuation and capitalization of titles vary. Do not place the titles of your own texts in quotation marks. Do not place a period at the end, although a question mark or exclamation mark may be used when one is appropriate. Generally, the first word and every important word in the title are capitalized, and articles, conjunctions, and prepositions (*a, the, and, yet, of, with,* etc.) are left in lowercase unless one is the first word of the title: *The Formation of Professions.* Since most titles are short, the title may also be typed in all capitals or underlined for emphasis:

> The Formation of Professions
> THE FORMATION OF PROFESSIONS
> THE FORMATION OF PROFESSIONS

TOPIC SENTENCE

THESIS, PAGE 663   Just as a **thesis statement** is the controlling idea of an essay, a topic sentence is the controlling idea of a paragraph or section of an essay. A topic sentence is like a minithesis: It expresses the main idea of one segment or distinct subdivision of a text, instead of the main idea of an entire text. Sometimes the segment or subdivision is a series of para-

PARAGRAPH, PAGE 629   graphs. More often it is a **paragraph**.

A number of important parallels can be drawn between a thesis statement and a topic sentence. Both, of course, embody a major idea that may be stated or implied. The first sentence of the following paragraph explicitly states the main idea that the ensuing sentences develop:

> One of the cruel aspects of the bombing campaigns of the Second World War was the far worse suffering of the poorer-paid manual worker, whether of Dortmund and Essen, London or Coventry. The poorer people lived close together and close to their places of work, which in turn were prime targets of the

bombers. The rich got out, the middle class were more scattered and often distant from targets. London exemplified this injustice. The Germans were not bombing indiscriminately in 1940, either in London or Coventry. In London the first target in the early days was dockland, where the dockers and their families of the East End lived next door to their work—the people of Bermondsey, Whitechapel, the Isle of Dogs and Stepney. Their agony during the autumn and winter of 1940–41 was appalling and on a different scale from anything experienced in west, north and south London, where life at first was uncomfortable and noisy but nothing like as dangerous as the east of the city.

> —Richard Hough, *Edwina: Countess Mountbatten of Burma* (New York: Morrow, 1983), p. 150.

Sometimes the controlling idea is not explicitly stated but only implied. In such instances, if the segment is well written, all the sentences and paragraphs imply an idea about which a topic sentence *could* be written. However, in most informative and persuasive writing, it is usually desirable to make topic sentences explicit. The value of an explicit topic sentence is that it identifies the topic of the paragraph and focuses the reader's attention on the main point of the passage, to which he or she can relate the more specific details of the passage. Everything falls more easily into place for the reader who at the beginning knows what the passage is about.

In addition to expressing the central idea, a topic sentence shares three other characteristics with a thesis statement: its form, its position, and its need to be substantiated.

Both a thesis statement and a topic sentence are usually expressed as a single declarative statement or question. It may appear anywhere in a passage, but as a matter of emphasis it usually—though not always—appears at the beginning of the segment that it controls. From the following passage, which is taken from a letter written by Albert Einstein, we can see that the topic sentence (italicized) is valuable even in texts that are not essays:

> *Scientific life has almost ceased to exist here.* No journals are being published, neither are there opportunities to have anything printed. A minimum of scientific work is being done; anyone wanting to do it would soon starve. Furthermore, for the last three years we have not received any foreign journals. Therefore,

I have very little idea of what is currently being thought about in scientific circles.

—Letter to Max Born, 18 August 1920,
The Born-Einstein Letters (New York:
Walker, 1971), p. 47.

This topic sentence works just like a topic sentence in an essay: It states a generalization that is developed or substantiated by particular data, concrete examples, and specific facts. Beginning a passage with a topic sentence has the effect of summarizing what is to come and thus offers several advantages to both the writer and to readers: It helps the writer stay on the topic; it enables readers to know at once what the passage is about so they can adjust their thinking to the main focus of the passage; and it provides a framework for holding the many details in the ensuing sentences. Thus, it does not hurt to make the topic sentence—wherever it appears—as obvious and as strong as the thesis sentence statement. That way, especially in longer segments or subdivisions, readers will be sufficiently aware of the main point.

The topic sentence has another equally important function. While it expresses an idea that controls a segment or subdivision of the text, it is subordinate to a larger idea—the thesis statement. A text generally has several topic sentences that relate to the thesis. Each topic sentence, in turn, is at the center of a series of sentences or paragraphs that relate to the topic sentence. Indeed, a text can be regarded as including or as consisting of a series of topic sentences, each with its own lesser series of sentences or paragraphs. Everything is related in a well-structured piece of writing, and topic sentences are a major contributor to the organization and **coherence**.

COHERENCE, PAGE 530

Because of its intermediate position between the thesis and the more specific details, examples, and facts that support the thesis, the topic sentence is a key element in the most basic pattern of composition: introduction containing the thesis statement followed by several paragraphs that support the thesis.

Here are four paragraphs that develop the idea that westerners are succinct in their speech. Note how the topic sentences (which are italicized) start the paragraphs with a little bump and give unmistakable direction to their content.

The solitude in which westerners live makes them quiet. They telegraph thoughts and feelings by the way they tilt their heads and listen; pulling their Stetsons into a steep dive over their eyes, or pigeon-toeing one boot over the other, they lean against a fence with a fat wedge of snoose beneath their lower lips and take the whole scene in. These detached looks of quiet amusement are sometimes cynical, but they can also come from a dry-eyed humility as lucid as the air is clear.

Conversation goes on in what sounds like a private code: a few phrases imply a complex of meanings. Asking directions, you get a curious list of details. While trailing sheep, I was told to "ride up to the kinda upturned rock, follow the pink wash, turn left at the dump, and you'll see the waterhole." One friend told his wife on roundup to "turn at the salt lick and the dead cow," which turned out to be a scattering of bones and no salt lick at all.

Sentence structure is shortened to the skin and bones of a thought. Descriptive words are dropped, even verbs; a cowboy looking over a corral full of horses will say to a wrangler, "Which one needs rode?" People hold back their thoughts in what seems to be a dumbfounded silence, then erupt with an excoriating perceptive remark. Language, so compressed, becomes metaphorical. A rancher ended a relationship with one remark: "You're a bad check," meaning bouncing in and out was intolerable, and even coming back would be no good.

What's behind this laconic style is shyness. There is no vocabulary for the subject of feelings. It's not a hangdog shyness, or anything coy—always there's a robust spirit in evidence behind the restraint, as if the earthdredging wind that pulls across Wyoming had carried its people's voices away but everything else in them had shouldered confidently into the breeze.

—Gretel Ehrlich, "Wyoming," in
The Solace of Open Spaces (New York:
Viking Penguin, 1985), pp. 6–7.

The importance of topic sentences in writing in which clarity is important should be fairly clear from this passage. Each topic sentence and the accumulated past topic sentences make the focus of the text apparent, giving it more solidity and strength. Each topic sentence expresses an idea that relates to an aspect of the thesis. In turn, each embodies the core of meaning and controls the development of its segment of the text. Like **thesis statements**, **paragraphs**, and **transitions**, the topic sentence is an invaluable tool for thinking, writing, and reading.

THESIS, PAGE 663

PARAGRAPHS, PAGE 629

TRANSITIONS, PAGE 676

TRANSITIONS

▼

A transition is both a *process* of moving from one place to another and a *device* that enables the movement to go smoothly.

As readers move from one idea to the next in a piece of writing, they try to understand the relationships among those ideas. In texts in which order, continuity, and logical development are important, writers try to help readers get from place to place by designing a sequence that reveals and reinforces the relationships among ideas and information. Writers can also help readers become aware of those relationships by using transitional words, phrases, or passages and by using certain format devices, such as headings and the placement of text on the page.

To illustrate how simple transitional words can strengthen logic and can smooth style, compare the following passages. In the first, three successive thoughts are not joined by transitions:

> The price of crude oil rose rapidly from 1973 to 1981. It fell in 1982. Petroleum producers did not pump as much crude oil in 1983 as they had done before.

Note how insecurely these thoughts stand together and how bumpily the passage reads. Even though the sentences are successive and closely related in thought, their relationship is not evident. They read jerkily, like a series of separate statements merely strung together. By providing only two transitional words, *but* and *therefore*, we join the thoughts and sentences solidly together and make clear their relationship:

> The price of crude oil rose rapidly from 1973 to 1981. *But* it fell in 1982. Petroleum producers, *therefore*, did not pump as much crude in 1983 as they had before.

Two transitional words in a passage of thirty-one words. That is probably the right ratio in ordinary passages. Transitions comprise a very small percentage of writing, but they serve the crucial tasks of holding a text together, relating ideas, displaying organization, underscoring logic, predicting the direction of ensuing sentences, and generally smoothing out style.

Whenever you are writing a draft, don't worry too much too early about providing a transition from one topic or paragraph to the next. If a transition presents itself naturally while you are writing, fine. Take it. It will probably help you clarify your thinking and strengthen your logic. But sometime during revision look specifically for those places where you need to show the relationship of your successive thoughts, for if you do not take care to show it, your writing may not appear connected even though you have arranged your ideas in an orderly manner. If transitions are not used well, the text will have a disconnected feel to it, appearing to be a random or accidental sequence of statements rather than a connected entity.

Several kinds of transitions and connective devices can be helpful. Some occur rather naturally as you write sentences and paragraphs. Others do not. But all require your careful attention when revising.

Among the most natural transitional and connective devices are variations or substitutions of earlier key words in the form of personal pronouns (*he, she, it, they, I*, etc.) and demonstrative pronouns and adjectives (*this, that, these, those*, etc.). When the word to which the pronoun or adjective refers (its antecedent) is in the preceding sentence, the pronoun or adjective helps readers link the thought of the two sentences. Here is an example of an antecedent-pronoun link:

> *Over one hundred fans* were outside the stadium two hours before game time. *They* wanted to be there to greet the team when it arrived by bus.

The phrase *over one hundred fans* and the word *they* refer to the same entities, thus providing continuity.

Here is a passage that contains an antecedent-demonstrative adjective link:

> In Britain *James Watt* and *Richard Arkwright* embodied the spirit of the industrial revolution. *These two men* were associated with the development of the steam engine and the burst of inventions in the textiles industry.

These two men points back to the previously mentioned men.

Here is a passage that contains antecedent-pronoun-demonstrative adjective links:

> *Tubular tires* are the kind used by track- and road-racing cyclists. *They* come standard on most expensive European bicycles and on a few high-grade American racing bicycles. *These tires* come in a variety of weights. . . .

They and *these tires* refer back to *tubular tires.*

Although each of the sentences in the preceding examples begins with a connective device, not every sentence has to start with a transition of some kind. But when you need a transition to give your text coherence and logic, you need to know where to place it. Because a transition works as a kind of signal or bridge, it should be placed early enough to be effective.

Transitions to indicate logical relationships can usually be achieved by merely adding a word or two where the relationship needs to be made explicit. Such transitions are slightly more formal than the repetition of nouns, pronouns, and demonstrative adjectives. Here is a list of the most important ones that you will likely use.

To add, coordinate, or show sequence	*first, second, the third . . . moreover, also, and, in addition, next, then, last*
To show simultaneity	*meanwhile, at the same time*
To introduce an example	*for example, for instance, in particular, namely*
To show result, cause, or consequence	*consequently, as a result, thus, therefore, for, because, since*
To restate	*in other words, that is*
To conclude or summarize	*in conclusion, to sum up, on the whole*
To contrast, oppose, or show alternatives	*but, yet, on the other hand, nevertheless, on the contrary, in contrast, however, or*
To compare	*similarly, likewise, in like manner*

The following paragraph illustrates how two or three formal transitions like these, wisely placed, reveal logical relationships:

Since the study of extraterrestrial life lacks any proven subject, opinions about the form and frequency of nonearthly beings record the hopes and fears of speculating scientists more than the constraints of evidence. Alfred Russel Wallace, *for example,* Darwin's partner in the discovery of natural selection, and the first great scientist to consider exobiology in any detail, held firmly that man must be alone in the entire cosmos—*for* he could not bear the thought that human intelligence had not been the uniquely special gift of God, conferred upon an ideally suited planet. He wrote in 1903 that the existence of abundant and brainy extraterrestrials "would imply that man is an animal and nothing more, is of no importance in the universe, needed no great preparations for his advent, only, perhaps, a second-rate demon, and a third- or fourth-rate earth."

> —Stephen Jay Gould, "SETI and the Wisdom of Casey Stengel," in *The Flamingo's Smile: Reflections in Natural History* (New York: Norton, 1985), p. 403.

When the text is fairly long or difficult, "megatransitions" (transitional clauses or sentences) help the reader get from one major idea to another, as in the following two examples:

> *We have attempted to explain* the spirit which moderated, and the strength which supported, the power of Hadrian and the Antonines. *We shall now endeavor, with clearness and preciseness, to describe* the provinces once unified under their sway, but, at present, divided into so many independent and hostile states.

> —Edward Gibbon, *The History of the Decline and Fall of the Roman Empire*, vol. I, ed. J. B. Bury (London: Metheun, 1896–1898), pp. 18–19.

The second example is from an even earlier writer, the poet Geoffrey Chaucer, writing in the last part of the fourteenth century:

> *Now that I've told you shortly, in a clause,*
> The rank, the dress, the number, and the cause
> Why these were all assembled at the inn
> Called Tabard—near the Bell—*I must begin*
> *And tell you whast we did that selfsame night,*
> *And later of the pilgrimage I'll write. . . .*

> —"Prologue," in *The Canterbury Tales*, trans. R. M. Stauffer (Baltimore: Penguin, 1958).

Writers can use explicit **forecasting statements** to anticipate what follows without referring so baldly to themselves, as Gibbon and Chaucer did, as in the example that follows.

FORECASTING STATEMENTS, PAGE 580

> The flavor of this book can best be conveyed by showing the motifs which recur most frequently throughout the book: namely, W-Hollow as "place," the cycle of the seasons, home town as joy and agony, death, and the centrality of his father to Stuart's life.
>
> —Ruel Foster, "Introduction" to Jesse Stuart, *The Year of My Rebirth* (Ashland, KY: The Jesse Stuart Foundation, 1991), p. xiii.

The sentence forecasts for the reader that the five major motifs are discussed in the rest of the introduction. By noting the sentences that open the discussion of each of these motifs, we can see how explicitly they cue readers to the organization:

> At first he can only walk to the window and look out on the hills and hollows of W-Hollow and watch the ever changing weather. But he feels the importance of this as "place" to him. (p. xiii)
>
> Interwoven with the W-Hollow motif is Stuart's fascination with the seasons. (p. xv)
>
> Stuart often thought during this year of his recuperation of his strange mixed-up relations with Greenup, his home town. (p. xvi)
>
> One of the major motifs in the journal is death. Conscious as he is of how close he has come to dying, Stuart's mind broods over all his other escapes with death. (p. xviii)
>
> Aside from Stuart himself, the man who dominates *The Year of My Rebirth* is Stuart's father. (p. xix)

Forecasting statements and transitions are also important within a paragraph, as in the following one in which the anticipating and connecting devices are italicized. The italicized sentence forecasts the two subtopics to be developed in the paragraph: ordering from mail order houses and buying from garden centers.

> One never runs out of dahlia stock but does get bored with the endless multiplication of the same cultivars. *There are two ways to buy new ones: mail order or off the shelf at a garden*

*center, and oddly enough I have done better with the latter.
Many mail order houses* send out a single tuber coated with
wax and charge $2.50 and up for it. At best, these produce
a skimpy plant and often they come to nothing. *At garden
centers* you can often find unwaxed clumps from Holland,
packed in peat moss and costing a modest $1.98. A color
photograph is clipped to the packet, and it is accurate. What
you see is what you get, complete with instructions for plant-
ing. These, to my mind, are the best dahlias on the market and
an amazing bargain.

—Eleanor Perenyi, *Green Thoughts: A Writer
in the Garden* (New York: Vintage, 1983),
pp. 52–53.

Sometime during the second sentence, both the writer as she
writes and the reader as he or she reads begin to gain a clear sense of
the direction of the paragraph. By the third sentence, the reader knows
that "mail-order houses" and "garden centers" are at the heart of the
paragraph.

As we describe these simple and megatransitions, you may be
struck by their sheer number. You may wonder at this point whether
such overt statements about organization and logical relationships are
really necessary in writing that is well organized. After all, you might
think, is not good writing brief and to the point? Doesn't inserting these
expressions take up a lot of space? Would the use of such direct statements insult the intelligence of readers by pointing out the obvious?

These are fair questions to ask.

We agree that good writing is not *overloaded* with such expressions.
We also agree that good writing saves space. But we know that good
writing, in which order, unity, and logical development are important,
saves time—the reader's time. There is, of course, another possibility.
There is the option to produce other kinds of writing—extremely informal but energetic, pronouncedly elliptical and disjointed writing—in
which logical relationships are not clarified and connections, if any, are
unmarked. Such ambiguous, disconnected writing is sometimes appropriate in mirroring a confusing, discontinuous, and fragmented world,
especially in fiction and poetry.

But we believe that explicit transitions and connectors such as we
have been describing are necessary in most writing when you are trying to convey information efficiently, for they foster clear thinking in
both the writer and the reader. Simple and megatransitions point back
to what has just been said and point forward to what is going to be

said, thus making the passage hang together. Not providing adequate signals to the logic and organization of the text causes a major problem. The problem lies not in whether the writer has organized his or her material well, but in whether the reader can perceive the logic and organization easily. The writer's view of a text is different from that of the reader. Even when transitional and connective devices are not in a passage, the writer knows the relationships—after all, he or she has internalized them after thinking about them so much. And because he or she sees the unity and logic, the writer assumes that readers also see them.

Unfortunately, such an assumption encourages many writers to omit explicit statements that help guide readers as they move through sentences, between sentences within a paragraph, and between larger units of text. These omissions will inevitably slow readers down and make them work harder to follow the discussion—if they have the interest or patience to do so. Just because writing can be reread and studied does not mean that readers will be willing to do it. Used well, a transition can signal that an example is an example. It can show that an upcoming idea is or is not a change in the subject. It can tell readers that point 4 is point 4. There is no better way to get readers from beginning to end than by marking the route clearly.

PART FIVE

HANDBOOK

▶ INTRODUCTION

Correctness in diction, usage, punctuation, and mechanics—like most principles of writing—is ultimately a matter of audience. You want to follow those rules that readers will expect you to know and observe. If you do not, your credibility will be lessened. Your readers will remember only that you used the wrong word or that your subjects and verbs did not agree rather than being convinced that your arguments were sound or your solution plausible.

In addition, errors may confuse your readers or even cause them a great deal of trouble or expense. At the least, the omission of a comma, the misplacement of a modifier, or an ambiguous word may result in readers having a significantly different understanding than the one you intended.

Part Five focuses on those rules and conventions that will make you a more credible writer. Rather than attempting to be comprehensive, we include only what we think college students need to know.

The Handbook consists of four main sections: diction, usage, punctuation, and mechanics. Each of these is subdivided into different entries, which are arranged alphabetically. Some entries include references to related entries in the Handbook or in Part Four (Strategies for Writing and Reading).

D. DICTION ◀

D.1 CLICHÉS

During the Persian Gulf War, Saddam Hussein's belligerent statement that the United States and its allies would experience "the mother of all battles" struck most Americans as unusual, perhaps even original. Partly in mockery but also partly in imitation of an original saying, Americans within weeks were using phrases like "the mother of all defeats" and "the mother of all parades." Homeowners were referring to "the mother of all telephone bills," and students were fretting over "the mother of all final exams." Quickly "the mother of all" became a cliché. It will be interesting to see how long the expression stays around. Now, nearly five years after the phrase seemed so neat, we hardly hear it any more.

Clichés are tired, trite expressions that when first coined seemed clever and original ways of saying something. The first poet to compare his love to a red rose or old age to autumn made the reader or listener think about the improbable comparison. But because the newly coined expressions were so effective, they became familiar, then overused. Through overuse they quickly lost their sharpness, vividness, and impact and became dull old sayings.

Our language is full of old, stale expressions. Expressions such as "green with envy," "law of the jungle," and "a sea of faces" were once vivid but have long since lost their brightness. Once-famous literary quotations such as "ignorance is bliss," "Eat, drink, and be merry," and "better late than never" have become threadbare. Once sparkling alliterative analogies such as "good as gold," "clear as crystal," and "busy as a bee (or beaver)" are now as flat as a three-day-old cola. How zippy does Bart Simpson's "Man, don't have a cow" or Hussein's "the mother of all battles" sound these days?

The freshness of an original expression usually lasts only a few weeks or months. But while it may no longer ring with compact energy, its half-life may continue for years, tempting us to use it when we are searching for a descriptive figure of speech, because it is ready-made and familiar. However, by the time you have heard or seen a vogue expression a few times, it is no longer fresh and lively, because your readers also have probably heard or seen it several times, too. Its fading freshness will make your ideas and thinking seem stale. In the minds of many readers, clichés of expression indicate clichés of thought—that nothing new is being said.

Clichés are in everybody's vocabulary. For almost all of us, "implications" are "far-reaching," "glances" are "furtive," and "truth" is "somewhere between the two extremes." But even if you believe that expressions like "ignorance is bliss," "better late than never," "don't count your chickens before they are hatched," and "the grass is always greener on the other side of the fence" convey the wisdom of the ages, it is best not to use them. They actually convey little information and take up plenty of space. About their only effect is that they mark those who use them as unimaginative and amateurish.

D.2 CONNOTATIONS

Accuracy in diction is achieved by choosing words that say exactly what is intended. Connotation is one more aspect of diction to be considered.

Several words may refer to the same thing in general, but each has shades of meaning and associations that the others do not. The reason is that in addition to their denotative meanings (meanings found in dictionaries), most words also have connotations—the thoughts and emotions aroused in the reader by the word. For instance, the terms *lactating female* and *nursing mother* denote the same thing, but *nursing mother* is much richer in connotation and will probably evoke an emotional response from a reader or listener. And because such psychological associations as these abound, it is important that writers make sure that their words carry the intended connotations.

Some connotations are fairly easy to predict. These are what we call "loaded words"—words that carry significant emotional baggage. Words like *home, mother,* and *honor* are supercharged with favorable connotations. Other words are equally supercharged with unfavorable connotations. But the connotations of some words are difficult to predict, because what a person associates with a word depends largely on the person's personality and background. The word *Texas*, for example, connotes something very different to a native Texan than it does to somebody who has never visited the state and whose knowledge of the state has been gained only by reading about it. To a career public official, a bureaucrat is an unelected public official who administers government policy and serves the public. To others, a bureaucrat is a person who insists on rigid adherence to arbitrary rules, regulations, forms, and procedures. Alben Barkley, Vice President of the United States under Harry Truman (1949–1952), once defined a bureaucrat as "a Democrat who holds a public office that some Republican wants."

Some words have fewer connotations and are regarded as "neutral" words. Other words have negative or unfavorable connotations, and still others have positive or favorable connotations. Of the three words *horse*, *nag*, and *steed*, for example, the first is the most neutral, the second negative, and the third positive. (Notice how each word creates a different image in your mind.) Think of different degrees of neutrality, approval, or disapproval in words such as *underweight* (neutral), *slim* or *thin* (approval), or *skinny* (disapproval). Oliver Cromwell, the Puritan religious, military, and political leader who served as dictator of England from 1653 to 1658, had more power than most English kings. But since his followers detested the word *king*, he called himself "Lord Protector of the Commonwealth." At the time, *Protector* had no political association and had generally positive connotations.

D.3 EUPHEMISMS

Euphemisms are part of the wide range of choices that our language offers us. A euphemism is a mild word or pleasant-sounding expression that is used in the place of a supposedly harsh or objectional word or disagreeable expression. Its major function is to cushion or disguise an unpleasant or disagreeable fact or idea. H. L. Mencken, an American journalist, editor, and critic during the first half of the twentieth century, called euphemisms "scented words." We use euphemisms when we refer to "perspiration" instead of "sweat"; or call "sexual intercourse" (itself a euphemism) "conjugal relations" or "intimate relations"; or say "Gosh-darn" instead of "Goddamn." The point in using euphemisms is to substitute a socially or politically acceptable expression for one that is considered unacceptable in a particular situation.

Probably more euphemisms are employed in softening the harsh reality of death than with almost any other concept. We can all imagine occasions upon which it would be inappropriate or bad manners, perhaps even thoughtless or cruel, to refer to death in a bald, direct way. The most commonly used euphemisms for the verb *to die* are "to pass away" or "to pass on." Flyers in the U.S. Air Force refer to their comrades who are killed as having "bought the farm." Humorous (and clichéd) euphemisms exist: "launched into eternity," "cashed in his (or her) chips," "kicked the bucket," or "stoking Lucifer's fires (or furnaces)"—referring to some one, we assume, who has apparently led a sinful life. Other, more reverent euphemisms include "was claimed," "went to a better world," "glory bound," or "went to meet his (or her) maker." Less known euphemisms for dying are "returned to dust," "going West," and "his (or her) clock stopped." Some abstract, pseudoscientific euphemisms disguise death in accounts of scientific experiments. The statement "The biota experienced 100% mortality" apparently means that all the specimens died. In military jargon, "collateral casualties" refer to civilians killed during war.

Euphemistic terms abound in our vocabulary. Just as a stairway and an elevator shaft in a new addition of a library can be transformed verbally into an impressive sounding "vertical access area," so can a room furnished with a photocopy machine, a large wastebasket, and a cabinet for storing paper become a "copy center." "Vertical access area" and "copy center" sound more impressive than stairs and elevators and a room with a photocopy machine in it. It's conceivable that a vertical access area might cost considerably more than stairs and an elevator, and it is probably true that it is more fun to work in a copy center than in a room with a photocopier. Such verbal metamorphoses are numerous: Salespersons are now account executives; night watchmen are now private security officers; janitors and custodians (originally euphemisms themselves) now are labeled facility or building services specialists. Unemployment offices are now job centers; economically depressed areas are now known as economic development districts; and underdeveloped countries progress into developing countries and then become Third World nations. *MahiMahi* is now the preferred name of dolphinfish when it appears on menus, primarily because the general public has confused dolphinfish with dolphins and cannot tolerate the thought of eating Flipper or one of his friends.

Certainly not all euphemisms are bad, because many are necessary for polite behavior and are useful for softening harsh reality. But once we start using euphemisms, some problems occur. One problem is that a euphemism usually loses its pleasant sound or scent and becomes as identified with the supposedly distasteful or unpleasant thing as the words it replaced. When this happens, new euphemisms have to be coined. In an attempt to avoid terms that refer to some noticeable physical incapacity, the handicapped (originally a euphemism) became the disabled, and they are now sometimes referred to as the "physically challenged" or the "differently abled." The status and dignity of Indians have been enhanced anew by the recent terms "Amerindian" and "native American." In time, new euphemisms will be needed to replace them. The number of euphemisms that have been used to soften the reality of death indicates how quickly the euphemism loses its dignity and must be replaced.

Another problem with euphemisms is that many are sort of silly, because they exaggerate or aggrandize the normal and the routine (referring to stairwells and elevators as "vertical access areas").

Most readers can see through this kind of pretense. However, some do not. Some euphemisms—the really dangerous ones—are insidious and destructive, because they obfuscate certain truths that discomfort the prudish, genteel, or hypocritical and mask undesirable and possibly heinous acts of politicians and dictators who must retain the loyalty of their followers or subjects. Remember the Nazis' "final solution" (*endgültige Lösung*) for European Jews? the "New-Life Hamlets" of South Viet Nam? the "United Nations Police Action" in Korea from 1950 to 1953? These examples of euphemisms—commonly referred to as "Doubletalk"—are used to mask a truth that some faction, usually political, wants covered up. Among the more memorable examples of Doubletalk in 1991 were the Department of Defense's use of "armed situation" to refer to what news networks called the war in the Persian Gulf and "force packages" to denote bombing attacks against Iraq by warplanes. In a similar manner, Iraqi buildings were called "hard targets"; Iraqi personnel were called "soft targets." More recently, attempts have been made to sanitize the horrors of cultural and racial murders and forced displacement of persons from their homes in Bosnia-Herzegovina and Rwanda as "ethnic cleansing."

You need to be able to identify euphemisms and use them responsibly.

D.4 FOREIGN WORDS

Most native speakers of English are not aware that English has borrowed extensively from other languages and are not informed about the multiplicity of roots from which our language has sprung. Hardly anybody—from Hoboken to Hattiesburg to Hilo—thinks of the Italian word *piano*, the Spanish word *machismo* (from which *macho* is derived), or the Swedish word *sauna* as foreign words. Even fewer regard the German words *pretzel* and *stone* or the Amerindian word *skunk* as foreign. Still fewer think of originally Latin and Greek terms such as *democracy, oral, senate, stadium,* or *stellar* as foreign words. These and countless other words like them have been used so long that they have become part of the language, no longer needing to be italicized to indicate their foreign status. They have become established as good English, and we use them freely without thought to their having been foreign words. Similarly, American English words like *baseball, hotdog,* and *weekend,* and many native English words of Britain, Canada, Australia, and New Zealand have become part of other languages.

As a living language, English changes and evolves. Current words will change meaning, and some will become obsolete. New words will be coined or be borrowed from other languages. The concern about using foreign words in our writing pertains to those words that have not yet become part of the general English vocabulary. If we use an obviously foreign word or phrase, it should be italicized or underlined to indicate that it has not yet been adopted into English.

We should take advantage of the many languages that are available to us through the continuing cultural integration of immigrants to our country. But whether to use foreign words and phrases in a specific piece of writing depends upon purpose and audience. Most of us are acquainted with somebody who sprinkles his or her writing with foreign expressions, such as *c'est la vie, moi, touché, gonif, ciao,* and so forth. Since the vast majority of us are not much given to using consciously foreign expressions, we tend to believe that those who do are overcompensating for doubts about their intellectual attainments. Unless we sense that the words are being used humorously, we tend to suspect the person of parading his or her scant knowledge of foreign languages.

There are, of course, special contexts in which foreign words and expressions are used extensively and acceptably: in law (*bona fide* and many other Latin terms), in politics (*coup d'etat* and especially other French expressions), in logic (*a priori* and other Latin phrases), in music (*fortissimo* and other Italian words), and in literary and philosophical studies (*denouement, Zeitgeist, ethos* and other French, German, and Greek terms). These words and expressions are clear and convenient for readers and listeners who are familiar with legal, political, musical, and literary and philosophical language. But to others, such expressions are not clear without explanation and may appear to be bookish, if not downright pretentious.

With the exception of the special contexts mentioned above, it is probably best not to use foreign expressions when there are perfectly good equivalent expressions in English. We should always consider whether to substitute an easier and much more frequently occurring word or phrase. However, we should not remain rigidly ethnocentric. Braj Kachru, a linguist on the faculty of the University of Illinois, estimated the number of English speakers in 1991 to be from 800 million to 2 billion. (Deane Allen, "Seeing English in a New Light: As World Language," *The Council Chronicle* [National Council of Teachers of English] 1.1 [September 1991]: 1.) As English becomes the dominant language in the world, extending beyond the original native-speaking English cultures, it will in turn continue to borrow words and expressions from native languages of Africa, Asia, Europe, and South American cultures. The globalization of English has helped develop a literature written in English by such writers as Raja Rao (India) and Chinua Achebe (Africa) and will inevitably bring new words into the language that will be regarded at first as foreign expressions. There is nothing inherently wrong with using them if they are the best words to use in a given situation.

D.5   GENDER-NEUTRAL LANGUAGE

Many students of English have noted a gender bias in some words and usages of language that helps perpetuate social and cultural inequality between males and females. Three common signs of this bias are these conventions:

1. Using the masculine third-person singular pronoun (*he, him, his*) as the generic pronoun, when a male or female may be the referent, in a statement like "Each student is to provide his own disk."

2. Using the word *man* or the suffix *-man* to refer to both males and females (*mankind, chairman, policeman, freshman, mailman*).

3. Assuming that a base word is primarily masculine and that a female form is required (poet/poetess, prince/princess, aviator/aviatrix). Where pairs of masculine and feminine terms exist, the feminine often suggests a less important status, as in *governor, governess* and *major, majorette;* or the female version has become pejorative but the male term has not (*master, mistress*).

Some writers are surprised that the use of words like *man, foreman,* and *manhours* instead of more gender-neutral words like *humans, supervisor,* and *employee hours,* etc. offends large groups of readers. However, most people are beginning to understand that how the writer feels is not so important as how readers feel. Readers who object to gender-biased words and expressions point out that the use of such words as *he* and *foreman* creates images of males in the minds of most people and, as a result, presents women in inferior roles or excludes them altogether from the general frame of reference.

The solution to this problem is to use language that treats both sexes in the same way. The following guidelines for avoiding prejudicial gender-role typing and gender-biased language are from the *Prentice Hall Author's Guide*, 5th ed. (Upper Saddle River, NJ: 1978), pp. 19–20:

> In your writing, be certain to treat men and women impersonally in regard to occupation, marital status, physical abilities, attitudes, interests, and so on. Depending on the requirements of your subject, avoid attributing particular characteristics to either sex; instead let your writing convey that one's abilities and achievements are not limited by gender. Your text should support the fact that both sexes play equally important roles in all facets of life and that activities on all levels are open to both women and men alike.
>
> Men and women should be portrayed as people rather than as male or female. Be careful to avoid sexist language that excludes men or women from any activity or that implies that either sex is superior or dominant in a particular role. Where possible, in referring to people use words that have no sexual connotations; for example, human being, salesperson, supervisor, student, and the like. Try to avoid the use of *he* or *man* in the generic sense.

Another source that offers sensible suggestions for creating gender-neutral language is an essay titled "Avoiding Sexist Language" in the Random House *Webster's College Dictionary*.

Here are five ways to achieve gender-neutral language.

▶ If you refer to a man by his last name, refer to a woman by her last name, too. Keep references to people's sex and marital status as equal as possible. No longer is it acceptable to refer to William Jones and Miss Perkins or to Jones and Betty.

▶ Use true generic nouns in the place of *man* or *mankind*. *Humans, human beings, humanity, women and men, people,* and *society* are alternatives, depending upon the context.

▶ Use professional and occupational titles that include both men and women. A helpful authoritative guide is the *U.S. Government Dictionary of Occupational Titles*, which suggests these kinds of substitutes for biased expressions: instead of *manpower*, use *work force*; instead of *policeman* use *police, police officer, officer*. If you refer to a man who is a high-ranking diplomatic official as an *ambassador*, refer to a woman who holds the same rank exactly in the same way: *ambassador*. If gender needs to be distinguished—and more often than not, it does not—using *ambassador* and the person's name (Ambassador Martin, Ambassador Ann Martin) works.

▶ Avoid unnecessarily using third-person singular pronouns. For example, when referring to a hypothetical person or people in general, do not write

> Ideally, a full-time student should spend approximately thirty hours a week studying for his classes.

Instead, write it one of these ways:

❖ Omit the unnecessary pronoun *his*:

> Ideally, a full-time student should spend approximately thirty hours a week studying for classes.

❖ Recast into plural noun and omit the pronoun, or use the plural pronoun *their*:

> Ideally, full-time *students* should spend approximately thirty hours a week studying for classes (or for *their* classes).

❖ Include the third-person feminine pronoun:

> Ideally, a full-time student should spend approximately thirty hours a week studying for *his or her* classes.

❖ Shift person, if appropriate:

> Ideally, you should spend approximately thirty hours a week studying for classes (or your classes).

▶ Avoid using stereotypical expressions such as *housewife, employees and their wives, girls* or any diminutive to refer to adult women, and *man-sized jobs*. Such expressions tend to depict women in thoughtless or derogatory ways. Instead, use expressions such as *homemaker, employees and their spouses, women* (not *ladies*), and *huge jobs* or *challenging jobs*.

D.6 GENERAL AND SPECIFIC WORDS

There are degrees of precision, and it is the writer's responsibility to use the appropriate level. If we state "She entered the room," we have indicated the fact in a very general way. The word *entered* does not tell whether she came into the room on a pair of roller blades, the shoulders of her brother, or a pair of three-inch heels. If we wish others to visualize precisely how she came into the room, we should be more definite and use a word like *glide, burst, slip, totter, strut, stumble, saunter, slink,* or *bustle,* or some expression that describes the specific manner of entry. There are times, though, when a general word like *enter* is appropriate, as in this statement:

> If you enter the building through the walkway from the parking garage, take the left corridor to the elevators and ride the elevator to the fifth floor.

Enter, take, and *ride* are appropriately general words, because it is not necessary in these instructions to specify the manner in which one enters the building or takes the corridor or rides the elevator. In choosing words, use the most specific word required for the idea to be expressed.

The problem is not so much with using general and abstract words themselves, but in using highly general words when the idea is really specific. For instance, the statement "Above a piece of furniture is a picture of a building" conveys only a vague meaning at best, because the words are far removed from the objects themselves. "Above my desk is a watercolor of Cincinnati's old Union Station" is much clearer and more vivid, because the words create a much clearer idea of the objects themselves. A statement such as "Something that the person told us made us feel uneasy" places most of the work on the reader or listener to interpret how we felt, what was told, and who told it. A more specific statement like "The police officer's description of the accident scene sickened us" is much clearer. The more we use concrete words, the closer we move toward reality.

The closer we move toward reality, the clearer our meanings become. "Something," "told," and "made us feel uneasy" are general and relatively vague words and expressions, and readers tend to believe that vague words reflect vague thinking, evasive intentions, or inability to express clearly what is meant. Try to remember that instead of writing something like "The length of the lines during registration was *affected*," write "The length of the lines during registration was *reduced*" or "The lines became shorter during registration" (or however the lines were affected). Instead of remaining on an abstract level, mention the specifics that you are really referring to or the specifics that lead you to use the abstract word. Write about japonica and pyracantha, not a flowering shrub.

Abstract words can sound pretentious. Unnecessarily abstract language can become an obstacle not only to easy understanding but also to clear thinking. Creating a text, at least for most persons, is an act of discovery. Details present themselves, sometimes almost mysteriously, and in the course of writing or speaking these details often lead to further details, concepts, and generalizations. Often it is a cluster or pattern of specific details that leads to insights and new knowledge. But if the level of language remains abstract, the meaning implicit in the text is only dimly discerned by the writer, if at all. Too much general or abstract language presents the same difficulty for readers. Inevitably, if they stay with the text for any length, they will be forced to overinterpret the meager details they are given.

D.7 SLANG

Slang is that special part of the American English vocabulary that names the ocean "the big pond," a dog a "mutt" or "pooch," or refers to a class period that is canceled because of the teacher's absence as "a walk." When sailors call candy "geedunk" and a torpedo a "tinfish," they are using slang. Referring to money as "bread," "dough," "do-re-mi," "lettuce," "bucks," "sawbucks," "George," "shekels," "simoleons," "wad," or "paper" is using slang.

Slang is related to jargon, **technical terms**, and dialect in that it helps foster a sense of community among its users. And it appears in similar ways. Many slang words are formed from other words (*bigwig*, *egghead*, or *snafu*) or extend the meanings of existing words (*bad*, *chill out*, *fierce*, *weird*). Others are coined or invented (*teenybopper*, *rookydoo*, *payola*, *snarf*, *tizzy*, *jazz*). But the fact that this kind of language has its own label—*slang*—indicates that it is different from the larger vocabulary shared among most users of American English.

TECHNICAL TERMS, PAGE 698

Whether to use slang is an important question that is not easily answered. Slang is a mixture of the colorful, trendy, and often humorous on the one hand and of the undignified, flippant, and irreverent on the other. Which it is, of course, is determined by the perceiver.

Many people categorically oppose the use of slang, claiming that it is too restricted in a social and geographical sense, is closely associated with the rejection of prevailing social values, is part of the general debasing of the language, or worse. Opposition to slang has almost always been there, with some people regarding any use of slang as corrupting the language. In the eighteenth century, Jonathan Swift and Richard Steele, who spent much of their considerable literary energy trying to stabilize and purify the English language, railed against the slang word *mob*, which at the time was considered a vulgar abbreviation of the Latin phrase *mobile vulgus*. Of course, today no one questions the use of *mob* as acceptable English.

Many slang expressions do not wear well and are short-lived. *Bought the farm*, which originated as a slang term among military fighter pilots for dying in a plane crash and was popularized by Tom Wolfe in *The Right Stuff*, is now a cliché; *hepcat*, a term used during the 1940s to refer to a performer or devotee of swing or jazz music, has become a verbal fossil. Sometimes, though, slang expressions satisfy a real need and become established in the language. Often they remain unsanctioned as standard English or good usage in serious or formal writing, but they persist just outside the realm of formal acceptability for decades. Sometimes a slang word or expression becomes part of the language and is accepted as standard usage.

Writers may find slang an appropriate language resource at times. However, slang can trigger several negative reactions for the unwary writer, and there are at least these four main reasons for using it carefully and sparingly.

▶ Slang is not always understandable to audiences, as you can see from a quick look at some recent slang used by college students. Here are ten slang words used on college campuses during the mid-1980s. See how many you recognize today. If you do not recognize some of them, you will understand why slang should not be overused—it changes from one place to another:

dweeb	Kraeusened
dork	lurking
generic	nosh
grimbo	'rents
hardcore	'shmen

(For an interesting discussion of these terms and other college slang, see William Safire, "Back to Tool," *New York Times Magazine*, September 22, 1985, p. 14.)

▶ Slang, like overly abstract words, may not convey precisely the meaning intended. Beginning writers are too often satisfied with general or abstract terms, slogans, and catchwords, and they fail to search for precise words to express ideas precisely. For example, stating that an idea was "shot down" or "ixnayed" does not convey whether the idea was rejected completely, only discouraged, or delayed for reconsideration. Slang often impedes the precision and exactness that are necessary for clear thought and communication.

▶ Much slang is generated in the spirit of innocent fun. But some slang comprises a vocabulary of insult and prejudice that is based on fear, distrust, and dislike of one group of people or another. The many words used to deliver ethnic and gender slurs, like *greaser, camel jockey, stud, bitch,* and endless others, are intended to dehumanize and demean persons different from the writer. If you realize that you are using slang to cover discriminatory or derogatory feelings, you need to rethink the entire matter and start revising your thinking as well as your diction.

▶ Most slang is generated to enliven language. There is a lot of word play and creativity in expressions like "wannabe Casanova," "jaw-jacking," and "studmuffin," and these expressions at first seem to be quite expressive. Ironically, most slang quickly loses its linguistic vitality and becomes trite within weeks or months. Few things are more noticeable than last year's fads in clothing, hairstyle, and language. Readers may understand words like *jerk* or *flick* and expressions like "This is where it's at" and "I can work with that," but they will not reward such language for freshness, vividness, or originality.

D.8 STANDARD AND NONSTANDARD WORDS AND EXPRESSIONS

Standard usage is partly in the eye or ear of the message receiver, but most teachers (and many other audiences) expect writers to use language that can be found in a college dictionary and that carries no usage labels (**slang**, archaic, nonstandard, etc.).

SLANG, PAGE 695

Although clarity is of the utmost importance, social approval (especially in terms of the relationship of writers to readers and speakers to listeners) is usually why standard words and expressions should be used. For instance, in the statement "The group is enthused about the new schedule," the word *enthused* is not well established as good usage. Too many persons still prefer *enthusiastic* as the preferred word. Whether *enthused* or *enthusiastic* is used does not affect the meaning of the statement or others' understanding of the statement. But which word is used can affect significantly the reader's or listener's reaction to the one who uses it, for the pressure toward conformity is strong. If one writes "The meeting produced more heat than light as the lawyers argufied over technicalities of procedure" (as opposed to "argued over technicalities of procedure"), it had better be for humorous purposes or to recreate the language of a character or person being quoted. Otherwise, the writer is likely to lose some authority, because the reader will infer that the writer has little acquaintance with the words *argue, argued, argument,* and *arguing* from reading or listening and is relatively uneducated and unsophisticated. In short, the writer should have known better than to use *argufied.*

It is the users of a language—English, German, Chinese, Swahili, or Hopi—that decide whether a word or expression changes, lives, or dies or is deemed standard or nonstandard. It is common sense to use words and expressions that have become standard in our language and to use them in situations where they are expected. The conventions of usage allow many ways to state things differently—but competently—for different audiences, regardless of the efforts of those who attempt to take an authoritative approach and would presume to regulate the language.

D.9   TECHNICAL TERMS

Every occupational, professional, or interest group has its own specialized vocabulary, sometimes referred to as jargon. Actors, airplane pilots, archaeologists, cattle breeders, dental hygienists, dog trainers, financial consultants, lawyers, literary critics, nuclear physicists, parachutists, physicians, sailors, soldiers, violinists, wine drinkers, baseball players, bull fight aficionados, golfers, stamp collectors, scuba divers, tobogganists, and volleyball players all have their own jargon that is not shared commonly by all users of a language. The most obvious difference between the technical terms that make up these specialized vocabularies and the words that are in our general vocabulary is that the technical terms are difficult, if not incomprehensible, for persons who do not have the special knowledge needed to understand them.

Many technical terms are unfamiliar, such as the nautical terms *halyard, capstan, gunnel, bilge, marlin spike,* and *flukes*. Other technical terms are familiar words that have acquired special meanings, such as *boom, watch, fantail, running lights, poop deck,* and *yardarm*. These unfamiliar words and familiar words with unfamiliar meanings are the private languages for those who belong to the group. Some nautical terms, such as *deck, port,* and *starboard*, have become so familiar to persons outside the group that they are now regarded as ordinary language. Other nautical terms, such as *aft, bulkhead, quarterdeck,* and *granny knot*, are on their way to becoming more widely known.

The use of technical terms is appropriate or inappropriate depending on the circumstances, audience, and purpose. One specialist might appropriately use technical terms with another specialist that would be out of place with nonspecialists. Anyone who has had a lawyer draw up a will or contract knows that while the legal language may be strictly accurate and enforceable in a legal sense, it is not very clear to the general reader. But laws and regulations pertaining to clear language aside, most contracts are not written for general readers but for other lawyers and judges to interpret.

Technical terminology has three important uses: (1) it usually conveys exact and precise facts and ideas (the word *ampere* means the same thing to all electricians, electronic technicians, and electrical engineers); (2) it usually presents information economically (the word *bargeboard* is much more concise and economical for carpenters and architects than "the finished board or strip of material covering the exposed edge of a gable roof"); and (3) it serves as a not-so-subtle demonstration of special capability (the ability to state knowingly that "the landing gear seems to be off a Cessna 6061 because it has a lug welded on it, and those off the 2024 don't weld well" displays knowledge and language that indicate the speaker is worthy of belonging to the group that shares that knowledge).

We usually understand when such technical terminology is appropriate. But we also need to remind ourselves that inappropriate use of technical terms is regarded by many writers and readers as pretentious, dull, and perhaps even intentionally obscure. The problem, of course, is that technical terms that puzzle uninformed readers sound normal to those who use them frequently. They hardly know they are using them.

Here are four guidelines for using technical terminology:

▶ **Make sure that you use technical terms accurately.** Use of a **wrong word** in this instance is an especially serious error.

WRONG WORDS, PAGE 700

▶ Be sure that your readers know the meaning of a technical term, or else define it clearly for them. If your readers do not understand the technical terms, you might as well be writing in a foreign language. They are likely to dismiss you as an egghead, propeller head, or some other kind of head.

▶ Be sure that the occasion calls for the precision and brevity of technical terminology or for the demonstration of specialized knowledge. Otherwise, your readers are likely to suspect that you are using gobbledygook or bafflegab to impress or obfuscate rather than to inform.

▶ Do not hesitate to use technical terms when they are appropriate for the occasion.

D.10   WRONG WORDS (MALAPROPS)

Language experts have a technical term for the use of a wrong word for a context: *catachresis* (pronounced "kat-a-KREE-sis"). One kind of wrong word use, called *malapropism*, can have great comedic effect. *Malapropisms* are named after Mrs. Malaprop, a character in Richard Sheridan's eighteenth-century British comedy *The Rivals*, who was absurdly inaccurate in the use of words. Her name has come to be used to describe a ridiculous and comical confusion of words, as in her comment, "She's as obstinate as an allegory on the banks of the Nile." You may have seen performer Norm Crosby, whose comedy routines rely on malapropisms. Usually, however, wrong word choices are not funny. For example, it is a major error to confuse words such as *cellulose* and *celluloid* in informative writing. Writers who confuse the denotative meanings of words (the common definitions as recorded in a dictionary) lose **credibility** with many readers and listeners, who regard such mistakes as signs of ignorance, stupidity, or superficial knowledge.

CREDIBILITY, PAGE 552

A common error is to confuse homonyms, words that sound alike but differ in spelling and meaning: *profit, prophet*; *rain, rein, reign*; *chord, cord*; *gorilla, guerrilla*. Almost as frequent an error is to confuse near homonyms: *lose, loose*; *liable, libel*; *absorb, adsorb*; *fraction, faction*). The spellcheckers on word processing programs are of no help here. Familiarity with the written form of the word is the only prevention for this kind of confusion.

Other words used erroneously are logically related to the right and *descend* or *infer* and *imply*; or words that have distantly related meanings, such as *curtail* and *cease* or *capacity* and *capability*).

Writers also confuse words because they do not have a sufficient grasp of the denotative meanings. Our language is rich in synonyms— words that have the same general meaning: *bait, enticement, incentive, lure; big, gigantic, gargantuan; positive, affirmative, favorable; soldier, warrior; student, scholar.* But these words are only generally interchangeable, for no two words mean exactly the same thing. The terms *farmer, rancher, sharecropper,* and *agriculturalist* all denote a person who makes a living from the soil. But while these terms convey the same general idea, they have different particular meanings.

The words *elderly* and *senior* are appropriate adjectives to describe humans. *Antique* might appropriately describe an object such as a chair or a trunk. *Archaic* or *obsolete* might appropriately describe an outdated word or process. *Old, aged,* and *ancient* might appropriately describe animate or inanimate objects. Careful writers can read, use dictionaries, and ask questions to make sure that their word choices have the right denotation.

▶ U. USAGE

U.1 FRAGMENTS

A complete sentence makes an assertion or asks a question. An incomplete sentence, one that does not make an assertion or ask a question, is known as a fragment. A fragment may or may not have a subject and verb but is often lacking one or the other.

Examples

Fragment:	The student being unfamiliar with the library's new computerized retrieval system. (This fragment has no verb; *being* is not a verb, because it describes the student rather than making a statement about the student.)
Correction:	The student *was* unfamiliar with the library's new computerized retrieval system.
Fragment:	Because the student had always used the card catalog in the past. (This fragment has both a subject and verb [student/had used] but does not make an assertion or ask a question. It is a dependent, or subordinate, clause and should be attached to another sentence.)
Correction:	Because the student had always used the card catalog, she didn't like the new computerized system at first.
Fragment:	A marvelous example of how computer technology can make our lives easier. (This fragment includes a subject and verb [technology/can make], but does not make an assertion or ask a question.)
Correction:	The new system, a marvelous example of how computer technology can make our lives easier, was not difficult to use.

The following suggestions should help you avoid fragments:

1. Be sure each sentence you write has a subject and verb.

2. If a group of words includes a subject and verb, remember that it with a subordinating conjunction such as *because, when, if, as, unless,* etc.).

3. Remember that if a verb ends in *ing,* it cannot serve as the main verb of a sentence unless it is part of a verb phrase (e.g., *was going, is singing, to be leaving*).

4. Test a sentence you suspect of being a fragment by adding a "tag question" to it. For example, to the sentence "The driver was signaling when he turned," you can logically add the tag question "Wasn't he?" But to the fragments "The driver signaling when he turned" and "If the driver signals when he turns," you cannot logically add a tag question. If a sentence is complete, you can always add a tag question to the end of it.

U.2   MISPLACED MODIFIERS

Modifiers should be placed as close as possible to the words they modify. Confusion often occurs when a modifier seems to modify something other than what it was intended to modify. In an attempt to interpret such statements, the reader is forced to rethink and rearrange the order of the parts to untangle the meaning.

Examples

Misplaced: Aunt Georgina stood beside the horse wearing a new green riding outfit.

In this example, the confusion is due to the placement of the phrase *wearing a new green riding outfit* at the end of the sentence where it seems to modify the horse when it actually modifies *Aunt Georgina.* Readers almost automatically assume that modifiers relate to the nearest unit. Placing the phrase next to the word it modifies improves coherence and avoids the ludicrous image of the horse attired in the new green riding outfit:

Correct: Aunt Georgina, wearing a new green riding outfit, stood beside the horse.

or: Wearing a new green riding outfit, Aunt Georgina stood beside the horse.

Misplaced: At age fourteen, my family moved to Denver.

In this sentence, the confusion is caused by the fact that the phrase *At age fourteen* is placed next to *my family,* words that it cannot logically modify. The word modified by the phrase (the person who was fourteen) is not expressed in the sentence. Rephrasing the statement so that there is an element that the phrase logically relates to improves coherence.

> Correct: When I was fourteen, my family moved to Denver.
>
> or: My family moved to Denver when I was fourteen.

No writer intentionally creates a confusing sentence. But because the connections between your thoughts are so clear to you, you may forget that your readers don't know your thinking as well as you do, and you may fail to realize how ambiguous a misplaced modifier can be. There is a difference between understanding something in your own head and explaining it to someone else. *You* know what you mean when you write or say something like this:

> First draft: She discovered what a good role model her mother was later in life.

The possible confusion in this sentence is due to the placement of the phrase *later in life,* which seems to indicate when her mother became a good role model. If that is the intended meaning, then the statement can be improved by restating as follows: "She discovered what a good role model her mother became later in life." However, if the writer meant to state that it was not until later in life that she became aware that her mother had been such a good role model, then she should place the phrase *later in life* next to *she discovered.*

> Revision: She discovered later in life what a good role model her mother had been.
>
> or: Later in life, she discovered what a good role model her mother had been.
>
> Misplaced: As the truck sped along, we noticed the break in the pavement, just as it rounded the curve.

When first reading or hearing this statement, most persons will hesitate between possible meanings—including the possibilities that the break in the pavement rather than the truck came speeding around the curve or that the writer was not in the truck at all but was observing from a distance. You do not want your readers confused, even momentarily. Avoid making readers backtrack to the beginning of the sentence in an attempt to figure out what it meant. To eliminate even momentary confusion, you could write the sentence as follows:

Correct: Just as we sped around the curve in the truck, we noticed the break in the pavement.

Probably the most misplaced words in the English language are one-word modifiers such as *only*, *even*, and *almost*. You should take special care where you place them in a sentence, because their position can drastically change the meaning. To realize the changes in meaning which the position of the word *only* causes, place it in the blanks in this sentence:

_____ Professor Werner _____ teaches _____ Intermediate German.

Only Professor Werner teaches Intermediate German.
(Professor Werner is the only one who teaches Intermediate German.)

Professor Werner *only* teaches Intermediate German.
(Professor Werner has only one responsibility: to teach Intermediate German. She does not do research or serve on committees.)

Professor Werner teaches *only* Intermediate German.
(Intermediate German is the only course that Professor Werner teaches.)

The following suggestions should help you avoid misplaced modifiers:

1. Be sure that each modifying word or phrase modifies a word or group of words that is stated in the sentence.

2. Place modifying words and phrases as close as possible to the word or group of words they modify.

3. Be especially careful to place modifiers like *only*, *even*, and *almost* directly *before* the word or phrase they modify.

U.3   PRONOUN-ANTECEDENT AGREEMENT

U.3

A pronoun should agree with its antecedent (the noun or pronoun to which it refers) in number, person, and gender. Thus, you should use a singular pronoun if the word to which it refers is singular and a plural pronoun if the word to which it refers is plural.

Example

Maria wore a red hat on *her* birthday because *she* wanted to be noticed.

Of course, you should also use pronouns that agree with their antecedents in gender. For example, you would not write that "Maria wore a red hat on *her* birthday because *he* wanted to be noticed." Native speakers of English practically never have problems with gender, and even nonnative speakers find gender one of the more sensible aspects of the English language. In some languages gender is rather arbitrarily assigned to nouns, but in English gender is determined naturally; that is, all nouns are considered neuter if they do not refer to people or animals that are actually male or female.

Similarly, using a pronoun that agrees in person with its antecedent is seldom a problem. You would logically and naturally say "I like myself" or "You should wear your coat," not "I like himself" or "You should wear my coat" (unless you really intend to give your coat to the person to whom you are speaking). The problem that most often occurs in pronoun-antecedent agreement is with number—using a singular pronoun to refer to a plural antecedent or vice versa. The following are some examples of typical errors that occur when subjects and verbs do not agree in number:

I want *each* of my guests to enjoy *themselves*.

Stress affects *everyone* at some time in *their* lives.

A good *dog* is obedient and behaves *themselves*.

Once a *student* has left home, *they* have to make *their* own way in the world.

These errors can be corrected as follows:

I want *all* of my guests to enjoy *themselves*.

Stress affects *everyone* at some time in *his or her* life.

A good *dog* is obedient and behaves *itself*.

Once *students* have left home, *they* have to make *their* own way in the world.

As you can see, most pronoun-antecedent agreement errors involve pronouns that refer to antecedents that are indefinite pronouns. Because indefinite pronouns are responsible for many subject-verb and pronoun-antecedent agreement errors, we include below a chart that indicates which indefinite pronouns are singular and which are plural. Note that, unlike personal pronouns, indefinite pronouns are always third person and have only one form.

<u>**Singular Indefinite Pronouns**</u>

everybody	one
everyone	someone
each	somebody
anyone	nobody
anybody	everything
neither	nothing
none (may also be plural)	

<u>**Plural Indefinite Pronouns**</u>

all	any
some	few
both	several
none (may also be singular)	

Note: See entry on **gender-neutral language** in the Handbook for a discussion of nonsexist use of indefinite and personal pronouns.

GENDER-NEUTRAL LANGUAGE, PAGE 691

The following suggestions should help you avoid errors in pronoun-antecedent agreement:

1. If a sentence includes an indefinite pronoun, be sure that any other pronoun in the sentence that refers to it agrees with it in number.

2. If possible, use plural rather than singular indefinite pronouns when referring to more than one person or thing. For example, write "All of the students will need their books" instead of "Everyone will need their books."

U.4 PRONOUN REFERENCE

Ambiguous references to personal pronouns often cause confusion for readers. The antecedent of every pronoun should be unmistakable, for if readers have to guess at an antecedent, they are likely to guess incorrectly. Examine the following sentences, which are unclear because of problems with pronoun reference.

> Unclear: Mario asked his father if he could help him.

The writer knows what the words *he* and *him* refer to and assumes that a reader would too. But readers cannot create a coherent interpretation of this sentence, because they are unable to decide which of the two possible antecedents (*Mario* and *father*) is correct. The general rule is that a pronoun refers to the nearest preceding noun that agrees with it in number and gender. But here it is impossible to tell whether Mario asked his father to help him or whether he volunteered to help his father. Depending upon the intended meaning, the sentence could be stated in several ways. Substituting nouns for the pronouns would resolve the ambiguity of the references but would result in clumsy, unnecessary repetition:

> Awkward revisions: Mario asked his father if he (his father) could help him.
>
> Mario asked his father if he could help Mario.

Other revisions would be equally clear and would get rid of the clumsy repetition:

> Better revisions: Mario asked his father, "Could you help me?"
>
> Mario asked his father to help him.
>
> Mario asked his father, "Can I help you?"
>
> Mario volunteered to help his father.

However, there are constructions where repeating the noun is probably the best solution:

> Unclear: Learning that Barnes maintained close ties with Garcia, who used to live in Cuba, the Illinois Bureau of Investigation has begun an exhaustive investigation into his background.

The ambiguity in this sentence is caused by two or more possible antecedents. Does *his* refer to Barnes or to Garcia? Readers may automatically assume that *his* refers to the nearest agreeing noun, which in this case is *Garcia*. But there is no way to decide for certain whether Barnes or Garcia is the antecedent. Depending upon the intended meaning, the sentence should end either "into Barnes's background" or "into Garcia's background."

The following suggestions should help you avoid pronoun-reference errors:

1. Be sure that each pronoun you use refers clearly to a stated, unambiguous antecedent.

2. If necessary, repeat a noun rather than using a pronoun that does not have a clear, unambiguous antecedent.

U.5 RUN-ON SENTENCES AND COMMA SPLICE ERRORS

A run-on sentence or comma splice error results when a writer combines two or more sentences incorrectly. In a run-on sentence, the two sentences (or independent clauses) are simply run together. A comma splice error occurs when a comma is placed between the two incorrectly joined sentences (or independent clauses).

Examples

Comma splice:	Amy loved comic books, she had a whole room full of old copies of *Superman*, *Wonder Woman*, and *Archie*.
Comma splice:	She loved them all, however *Batman* was her favorite.
Run-on:	She would spend hours sorting the comics then she would spend even more hours arranging them in neat stacks.

Such errors can usually be eliminated by merely correcting the punctuation. Two sentences, or independent clauses, can be correctly joined or separated in the following ways:

1. By using a period

Example:	Amy loved comic books. She had a whole room full of old copies of *Superman*, *Wonder Woman*, and *Archie*.

2. By using a semicolon and a conjunctive adverb

Example: She loved them all; however, *Batman* was her favorite.

Example: She would spend hours sorting the comics; then she would spend even more hours arranging them in neat stacks.

3. By using just a semicolon

Example: Amy loved comic books; she had a whole room full of them.

4. By using a comma and a coordinating conjunction (*and, or, but, for, yet,* and *so*)

Example: She loved them all, but *Batman* was her favorite.

The following suggestions should help you avoid run-on sentences and comma splice errors:

1. If you have difficulty identifying run-on sentences, check carefully when you use a personal pronoun (such as *I, he, we, they,* etc.), because personal pronouns often function as the subject of a sentence. (Example: It was my turn next. I stepped up to the plate.)

2. Beware the little word *then,* which is often used to begin another sentence. (Example: She turned to go. Then she paused.)

3. Remember that length is not a factor. Run-on sentences may be very short or very long.

U.6   SHIFTS IN POINT OF VIEW

Because readers expect consistency in point of view, take care not to shift needlessly and unintentionally from first person (*I* or *we*) to second person (*you*) or third person (*he, she,* or *it*).

Knowing which point of view to use can be confusing if you have been instructed to avoid first and second person point of view—that is, not to use *I* or *you.* However, it is perfectly all right to use *I* or *you* in many instances. If you are writing about yourself, you should, of course, use *I.* If you want to address your reader directly—for example, when you are writing instructions or advice—you should use *you*.

In fact, avoiding the use of first and second person often results in awkward, hard-to-read prose. For example, the indefinite pronoun *one* can be substituted for *I* or *you*, but the result is stiff and awkward.

> Example: *You* can find the answer in a dictionary.
>
> *One* can find the answer in a dictionary.

You should feel free to use *I* or *you* when you are referring to yourself or your reader. However, you should avoid shifting from one point of view to another for no good reason.

> Example: *I* like walking as a form of exercise because *you* can set *your* own pace.

In the example above there is no reason to shift from first person *I* to second person *you*. To avoid this shift, you can simply use first person.

> Example: *I* like walking as a form of exercise because *I* can set *my* own pace.

Passive Voice

Even more detrimental to effective, clear writing is the use of passive voice to avoid using *I* or *you*.

> Example: I *found* the answer in a dictionary.
> (active)
>
> The answer *was found* in a dictionary.
> (passive)

Passive voice is often less direct, less clear, and less responsible than active voice. In passive voice, the subject of the sentence (*answer*) does not perform the action/being implicit in the verb (*was found*). Rather, the subject is being acted upon (i.e., the answer is not doing the finding but is the object of the finding). It is nearly always better to use a subject that functions as the agent (the doer) in the sentence. Although in the past certain disciplines and professions (especially science, government, and law) seemed to prefer passive voice, this is no longer the case. Everyone now agrees that writers should avoid passive voice when it is possible to do so.

The following suggestions should help you avoid shifts in point of view:

1. Use *I* or *you* if you are referring to yourself or your audience, but be consistent (i.e., don't shift needlessly from one to another).

2. Do not use passive voice as a way of avoiding *I* or *you*.

U.7   SHIFTS IN VERB TENSE

Careful writers do not shift needlessly from one tense to another. If you begin a text using one tense, your reader will expect you to continue in that tense unless there is a logical reason for you to change to another. That is, if you begin in the present tense, you should continue in that tense unless there is an obvious reason to shift to past or future. Illogical, careless shifts in tense are confusing to a reader.

> Example: The concert *began* at 8:00 p.m., *lasts* for two hours, and *will be* over by midnight.

This sentence begins with a past tense verb (*began*), shifts to present tense (*lasts*), and then shifts again to future (*will be*). Notice how much clearer the sentence below is with its consistent use of present tense verbs:

> Example: The concert *begins* at 8:00 p.m., *lasts* for two hours, and *is* over by midnight.

Most shifts in tense occur not within single sentences but within longer texts. It is easy to shift unintentionally from one tense to another several times in writing a text of several pages. Especially common is a shift to conditional verbs (*would go, would think,* etc.).

> Example: The man *drove* like a maniac. He *sped* out of his drive-way in reverse, barely pausing to see if cars were coming. Then he *shifted* into forward and accelerated rapidly down the quiet, tree-lined street on which he lived. He *would sail* through intersections without glancing to the left or right and *would stop* at red lights only if other cars were stopped in front of him.

Unintentional shifts in tense such as these should be eliminated when you edit your text. Remember, however, that some shifts in tense are logical and necessary.

Example: When I *entered* high school, I *weighed* only 102 pounds; today I *weigh* 167 pounds.

It is just the unintentional, illogical shifts that you want to eliminate.

The following suggestions should help you avoid shifts in verb tense:

1. Shift from one tense to another only when a shift is appropriate to your meaning.

2. Avoid using the conditional (*would* or *will*) unless you are indicating condition or probability. (Example: I would go with you if I could./ I will be there if I can.)

U.8 SUBJECT-VERB AGREEMENT

U.8

Subjects and verbs should agree in number (singular or plural) and person. If a subject is singular, then its verb must be singular, and if a subject is first person, then the verb must be first person.

The concept of person is best explained by focusing on pronouns, since it is only pronouns that clearly distinguish person. The following chart will give you an overview of what is meant grammatically by person:

	Singular	*Plural*
First person:	I	we
Second person:	you	you
Third person:	he, she, it	they

First person is used when the writer or speaker refers to herself or himself.

Example: *I* ate my lunch.

Second person is used when the writer or speaker refers to the person being addressed.

Example: *You* ate my lunch.

And third person is used when the writer or speaker refers to someone or something other than himself or herself or the person being
addressed.

> Example: The dog (or *it*) ate my lunch.

Notice in the examples above that the verb (ate) remains the
same because it is a past tense verb. Fortunately, future tense and past
tense verbs (except for the verb *to be*) do not change in form to indicate person, so you can all but forget about agreement problems if you
are writing or speaking in either of these tenses. Unfortunately, present
tense verbs do change to indicate tense, at least in one instance—third
person singular. Notice what happens to our series of examples if we
change to present tense.

> I eat my lunch. (first person singular)
>
> You eat my lunch. (second person singular)
>
> The dog *eats* my lunch. (third person singular)

In the present tense, all third person singular verbs end in an *s*. Thus,
you simply add an *s* (or *es*) to the first person present tense form of
regular verbs (those that add *ed* to form the past tense) to form verbs
such as *jumps, walks,* and *reaches*. Some irregular verbs also require
only an *s* or *es* (e.g., *eats, teaches,* and *does*). However, two irregular
verbs (*to be* and *to have*) change more drastically. The verb *to have*
changes to *has* in the third person singular (note that it still ends in *s*)
but otherwise is like other irregular verbs. However, the verb *to be* is
highly irregular, as the following chart illustrates:

Present tense

	Singular	*Plural*
First person:	I *am*	we *are*
Second person:	you *are*	you *are*
Third person:	he, she, it *is*	they *are*

Past tense

	Singular	*Plural*
First person:	I *was*	we *were*
Second person:	you *were*	you *were*
Third person:	he, she, it *was*	they *were*

Even though the verb *to be* presents some special problems, subject-verb agreement is seldom a problem if the subject is a noun or personal pronoun and/or is located close to the verb.

Example: She *was* an excellent student.

However, if the subject is an indefinite pronoun (such as *each, everyone,* or *anybody*) and is not adjacent to the verb, the agreement between the two is not as obvious.

Example: Everyone in my math and history classes *was* an excellent student.

Example: Each of us *was* an excellent student.

Example: Anybody who takes calculus and economics *is* an excellent student.

The following suggestions should help you avoid errors in subject-verb agreement:

1. Anytime you are in doubt about subject-verb agreement, identify the subject and verb, and be sure they are both singular or both plural.

2. When you are using third person singular present tense verbs, be sure your verb ends in an *s.*

3. When your subject is a singular indefinite pronoun such as *everyone, anybody,* or *each,* check to see if your verb is also singular.

▶ P. PUNCTUATION

P.1   APOSTROPHE

The apostrophe has five main uses.

a. Forming the Possessive of Nouns

To form the possessive of singular nouns and plural nouns not ending in *s*, add *'s*:

Alan Ross's car	the family's trip
the boy's shoes	women's rights
the children's playground	

To form the possessive of plural nouns already ending in *s*, add only an apostrophe:

the Rosses' car	the actors' rehearsal
the boys' shoes	the teachers' salaries
the farmers' trucks	

b. Forming the Possessive of Indefinite Pronouns

Possessive personal pronouns, such as *its, ours, his, hers, yours, theirs,* and *whose,* are written without apostrophes. However, possessive indefinite pronouns such as *each, everybody, everyone, nobody, anybody, anyone,* and *someone* require an apostrophe and *s.*

everybody's shoes

c. Replacing Letters and Numerals

To form a contraction, place an apostrophe where the omitted letter(s) or numeral(s) would be:

I'm sure you're early.

The flight doesn't leave until four o'clock.

Many social critics refer to the '80s as the Decade of Greed.

d. Forming Plurals of Letters, Symbols, and Numerals

Use the apostrophe and *s* to form the plural of letters and symbols:

Accommodate is spelled with two *c*'s and two *m*'s.

How many +'s are in that equation?

You may also use the apostrophe plus *s* to form the plural of numerals, but frequently the *s* is used alone:

In the 1990's (*or* 1990s) biologists began to notice a sharp decrease in frog populations.

e. Indicating a Quotation Within a Quotation

Use single quotation marks around a quotation within a quotation (except in a displayed quotation). Since most typewriters and computer keyboards do not have such a key, writers use the apostrophe:

John Clive discusses what he calls Macaulay's "propulsive imagination," which Clive describes as the "instinctive ability to propel inert facts into motion." Clive, using the analogy of photographic film development, writes: "Macaulay's travels to the scenes of events he was describing helped him collect, as he wrote after his trip to Ireland in 1849, 'a large store of images and thoughts,'—images which his photographic memory retained, so to speak, as negative film to be developed into positives when he came to write" ("Macaulay's Historical Imagination," 22).

P.2 BRACKETS

P.2

Like parentheses, brackets always come in pairs, one at the beginning and one at the end of the enclosed materials. So check to see that both are there. In handwriting, make sure that your brackets look like brackets [ ] not parentheses ( ). Brackets are used as substitutes for parentheses in two situations:

a. Enclosing Text Already Enclosed in Parentheses

incorrect: In all animals certain patterns of motor activities are innate (for example, the way in which mammals and birds scratch themselves ((Figure 3)).

correct: In all animals certain patterns of motor activities are innate (for example, the way in which mammals and birds scratch themselves [Figure 3]).

correct: In all animals certain patterns of motor activities are innate: for example, the way in which mammals and birds scratch themselves (Figure 3).

b. Inserting Text in Another's Writing

Use brackets to enclose text that you wish to insert in quoted material to make the author's meaning clear:

One recent critic has declared that "Bunyan's masterpiece [*Pilgrim's Progress*] is out of harmony with the spirit of the age [the Restoration]."

P.3 COLON

The colon, which focuses attention on the information that follows it, has three main uses:

a. Introducing Lists

There are three types of secondary memory used in microcomputers: cassette tapes, floppy disks, and hard disks.

Isaac Asimov formulated three laws for robots:

1. A robot may not injure a human being or through inaction allow a human being to come to harm.

2. A robot must obey the orders given it by human beings except when such orders would conflict with the First Law.

3. A robot must protect its own existence as long as such protection does not conflict with the First or Second Law.

Do not place a colon between a verb or a preposition and its object(s).

incorrect: For dinner we had: tossed salad, baked ham, mashed potatoes and gravy, and iced tea.

correct: For dinner we had tossed salad, baked ham, mashed potatoes and gravy, and iced tea.

incorrect: The candidates will speak in the southern district at: Berryville, McLeansboro, Jackson's Gap, and Mount Tremaine.

correct: The candidates will speak in the southern district at Berryville, McLeansboro, Jackson's Gap, and Mount Tremaine.

b. Introducing Quotations

W. E. B. DuBois was determined to be a social scientist: "I was going to study the facts, any and all facts, concerning the American Negro and his plight." (*Dusk at Dawn*, 591)

Churchill challenged Chamberlain, the prime minister, to stop the transfer of huge sums of money from Czechoslovakia to Nazi Germany:

Here we are going about urging our people to enlist, urging them to accept new forms of military compulsion; here we are paying taxes on a gigantic scale to protect ourselves. . . . (Hansard's *Parliamentary Debates* 5/26/39)

Notice that indented (displayed) quotations are not enclosed in quotation marks.

c. Introducing Important Words and Phrases

The newspaper headlined the team's pledge: "We will leave Atlanta as champions."

Other Uses of the Colon

To follow the formal salutation in a letter:

Dear Mr. McHenry:

To separate the subtitle from the title of a book or article or to separate the verse from the chapter in Bible references:

Roxana's Children: The Biography of a Nineteenth-Century Vermont Family

Hebrews 13:8

To separate hours from minutes in stating the time of day:

3:15 P.M.

To express a ratio:

10:5:1

Capitalization after a Colon

Usual practice is to start an independent clause (a grammatically complete sentence) following a colon with a capital letter, and a subordinate clause, phrase, or list with a lowercase letter:

The sign provided a clear warning: "Trespassers will be Prosecuted."

We purchased the following items for the camping trip: mosquito netting, dehydrated meals, extra pairs of socks, and a first aid kit.

P.4 COMMA

The comma is the most frequently used mark of punctuation. Because it has so many uses, most of us tend to be unsure of when to use it. But the comma is not all that difficult to use correctly. Here are eight of its most important uses.

a. Separating Items in a Series

The long, hot, dusty ride lasted nearly three hours.

The portfolio must contain an essay, a report, a short story, and a poem.

It is remarkable how well we remember people, places, tunes, words, ideas, stories, events, and a host of other things without much conscious effort.

In separating items in a series, the comma may be used these ways: *first, second, and third* or *first, second and third. First, second, and third* is preferred, because it is never ambiguous. Be consistent in your practice, whichever you choose.

b. Separating Clauses of a Compound Sentence

Use a comma to separate the independent clauses of a compound sentence joined by a coordinating conjunction (*and, but, or, nor, yet, for*):

> Yesterday was hot, but today is cooler.

> The work is not yet completed, for we were interrupted several times.

> Professor Frobish spoke twenty minutes over her allotted time, and when she finished we all sighed a big sigh of relief.

c. Setting Off Introductory Matter

> However, this practice is open to debate.

> Ultimately, David Bleich places primary emphasis on the reader's response.

> As you know, a person's appetite diminishes after strenuous exercise.

> In the midst of writing the paper, Anita realized that she needed to rethink the thesis.

d. Setting Off Appositives

> Carlos, the project engineer, will be flying to the site Thursday.

> Her Aunt, a Zeta, is hoping that Cindy pledges the sorority.

> I saw Grethel, who is my brother's former wife, driving the tractor.

e. Setting Off Nouns of Address

> Sit over there, Frank, next to the window.

> Marita, where are you going?

f. Setting Off Interrupting Matter

> This practice, however, is open to debate.

Anita, realizing that she needed to rethink the thesis, started over again.

Nicole, who is taking freshman composition this semester, spends a lot of time in the library.

g. Separating a Quotation from Other Parts of a Sentence

"Vote early," she said, "and often."

"Everybody writes books here," McLuhan told his mother, "not many of them worth reading, either."

h. Preventing Possible Ambiguity

ambiguous	*clear*
Above the limbs swayed gently in the breeze.	Above, the limbs swayed gently in the breeze.
The question is is it worth the investment?	The question is, is it worth the investment?
When the casket passed the crowd was silent.	When the casket passed, the crowd was silent.
A few days after I saw Kelly driving her new convertible.	A few days after, I saw Kelly driving her new convertible.

Other Uses of the Comma

* To end the informal salutation in a letter—

Dear Jonathan,

* To punctuate the complimentary close in a letter—

Sincerely,

* To separate names and titles or degrees—

Elaine Grissom, DVM, has been named as an interim board member.

* To separate elements in a date—

July 25, 1975, is my birthdate.

(Note that *I was born on 25 July 1975* is also acceptable, as is *I was born in July 1975*.)

* To separate a city from a state and the state from the word that follows it—

This year's convention in Lincoln, Nebraska, attracted 204 delegates.

❖ To indicate thousands in figures of five or more digits—

5200 or *5,200*, but *43,276* and *16,527,089.* (Certain numbers, however, omit commas: *Engine No. 843D629115A* and *pages 2360–2362; 12970 Boulevard East.*)

Using the Comma with Other Marks of Punctuation

When a sentence element that is normally set off by a comma is followed by a parenthetical expression, place the comma *after* the closing parenthesis:

Dr. McKelly, tweedy, bearded, and young (like so many male assistant professors of philosophy), likes to expound on Jacques Derrida's influential books.

When a sentence element that is normally set off by a comma ends with a quotation mark, place the comma *inside* the closing quotation mark:

"Now *that's* a dog," Sara said, patting the big mongrel on the head.

One form of the "peg-word," which is a method taught by many memory experts, relies on memorizing words that rhyme with the concept you want to learn.

P.5 DASH

The dash, employed intelligently and sparingly, does the same things that commas and colons do. But the dash does them with pronounced emphasis.

To form a handwritten dash, make a line about twice as long as a hyphen. If your typewriter or computer keyboard does not have a dash key, strike the hyphen key twice, with no space between strikes or on either side of the dash. It should look like this:

This new concept--that space is a continuum--is difficult to grasp.

Some of the dash's most important uses are setting off interpolated material; introducing a list or emphasizing items in a list; indicating an interruption or change in thought; and introducing the author or source line of a direct quotation.

a. Setting Off Interpolated Material

Mount Saint Helens is a typical volcano along the "Ring of Fire"--the Pacific coasts of North and South America, Japan, the Philippines, Indonesia, and New Zealand--the site of over 60 percent of the world's active volcanoes.

The plan--unprecedented in principle and vast in scope--is being studied by a committee.

As these examples illustrate, interrupting material must be set off by *paired* dashes, one at the opening and one at the closing.

b. Introducing a List or Emphasizing Items in a List

In the first generation of American leaders five men stood out--George Washington, Benjamin Franklin, Thomas Jefferson, Alexander Hamilton, and John Marshall.

Little more than a drop, a cubic millimeter of blood contains

--5,000,000 erythrocytes (red blood cells)

--5,000 to 10,000 leukocytes (white blood cells)

--200,000 to 300,000 platelets (cell fragments that initiate coagulation or clotting).

c. Indicating an Interruption or Change in Thought

He was ambitious and aggressive--but not at the expense of others.

I'm not so sure that we should--oh, what the hell, let's do it.

d. Introducing the Author and/or Source Line of a Direct Quotation

All truths wait in all things.

--Leaves of Grass

I am captivated more by dreams of the future than by the history of the past.

--Thomas Jefferson

P.6 ELLIPSIS POINTS

Ellipsis points are spaced periods that indicate the omission of part of a quoted passage. When deleting material from a direct quotation, take care not to change the meaning of the original passage.

A three-period ellipsis (. . .) indicates that what is omitted occurs *within* a sentence:

original passage: To write the Life of him who excelled all mankind in writing the lives of others, and who, whether we consider his extraordinary endowments, or his various works, has been equalled by few in any age, is an arduous, and may be reckoned in me a presumptuous task.

—James Boswell, *Life of Johnson*

passage as quoted: Boswell states at the beginning of his *Life of Johnson* that "to write the Life of him who excelled all mankind in writing the lives of others . . . may be reckoned . . . a presumptuous task."

A four-period ellipsis (. . . .) shows that what is omitted contained end punctuation. The extra period is usually either the period of the preceding sentence or of the one from which the omission is taken.

original passage: For a structure to him meant a habit, and a habit implied not only an internal need but outer forces to which, for good or evil, the organism had to become habituated. The orchid's flower was a device by which the plant took advantage of the habits of insects, and it was only by inquiring into this use of its various parts—which he called adaptation—that he was able to put time into natural history, and order in taxonomy. In one sense, therefore, he might well have called his book *The Origin of Habits* rather than *The Origin of Species.* Like many others, he was never quite certain just what a species was.

—F. Huxley, "Charles Darwin: Life and Habit," *American Scholar* 28 (1959): 496.

passage as quoted: Francis Huxley has summarized Darwin's attitude as follows:

> A structure to him meant a habit, and a habit implied not only an internal need but outer forces to which, for good or evil, the organism had to become habituated. . . . In one sense, therefore, he might well have called his book *The Origin of Habits* rather than *The Origin of Species.* Like many others, he was never quite sure what a species was.

P.7 EXCLAMATION POINT

Because the effect of the exclamation point relies on its infrequent use, it should be used sparingly and only after an expression of strong feeling—surprise, pleasure, anger, determination. It is used after an exclamatory expression or a short exclamatory sentence.

Wow! That lightning strike was close!

Fire!

"Let's stop it!" yelled Janis from the other boat.

When an exclamation point and a quotation mark fall together (as in the last example), place the exclamation point according to the sense of the statement. If the exclamation is part of the quotation, the exclamation point goes inside the quotation mark:

One of the archeologists shouted, "The riddle is solved!"

If the entire sentence is an exclamation, the exclamation point goes outside the quotation mark:

One of the archeologists just announced, "The riddle is solved"!

P.8   HYPHEN

Generally the hyphen has two basic uses: to form compound words and to divide words.

a. Forming Compound Words

Compound words consist of two or more words that function as one word. Some are written as separate words; some are written as one word with no space between them; and some are hyphenated. Since there is little logic to guide writers about how to write compounds, you should check a college-level dictionary for words that you are not sure of. However, certain practices have been established through usage, and we present them here.

▶ Compound Nouns. Use a hyphen to form the following types of compound nouns.

❖ Spelled-out cardinal and ordinal numbers from twenty-one to ninety-nine:

forty-eight   fifty-fifth

twenty-five   eighty-eighth

Numbers lower than twenty-one are single words and are not hyphenated:

thirteen   sixteenth

❖ Words that indicate certain family relationships:

great-grandfather   mother-in-law

great-aunt   great-great-grandmother

But many such words are single words with no hyphen:

grandson, grandmother, stepdaughter.

❖ Words that indicate dual roles or joint functions:

player-manager   radio-cassette player

Mercedes-Benz

❖ Compound words formed by capital letters and numerals or compounds of capital letters followed by a noun:

DC-10   A-frame   H-bomb

❖ Compounds that begin with the prefix *ex-*, *self-*, and *all-*:

ex-husband   self-starter   all-important

❖ Compounds that consist of a prefix and a proper noun:

anti-Semiticism   all-American   pre-Columbian

❖ Compounds that end with *-elect* or *-designate*:

senator-elect   ambassador-designate

❖ Compounds in which the absence of a hyphen forms a word of a different meaning:

re-form, reform   re-cover, recover   re-create, recreate

❖ Most compounds in which the prefix ends with the same vowel that the base word begins with:

semi-independent   co-owner   non-native

▶ Compound Adjectives. Use a hyphen when two or more adjectives function as a unit to modify the noun that follows:

foreign-born professionals   English-speaking people

When a compound adjective follows the word or words it modifies, the elements are written as separate words with no hyphens:

before the word	*after the word*
the door-to-door canvass	the canvass was door to door
a full-time job	the position is full time
paper-thin coating	the coating was paper thin

Two or more compound adjectives that modify the same element are hyphenated as follows:

a two- or four-door car (not *two or four-door car*)

sixth-, seventh-, and eighth-grade students
(not *sixth, seventh, and eighth-grade students*)

b. Dividing Words

Thanks to the word-wrap feature of most word processing programs, the practice of dividing a word at the end of a line and carrying the last part of the word to the next line is fast disappearing. However, if you must divide a word at the end of a line (in handwriting or type-writing), observe these four practices:

- Divide the word at a syllable break as in feu•dal•ism. If you are unsure of where the syllable breaks are in a word, look them up in a college-level dictionary.

- Divide hyphenated compounds at the hyphen (or one of the hyphens if there are two or more).

- Do not divide a word that consists of one syllable or is pronounced as one syllable: *seer, proved, clutched.*

- Do not divide a word if the division will result in one letter standing alone: *a-while, cit-y.*

Additional Uses of the Hyphen

- To indicate spelling:

  Can "gauge" be spelled g-a-g-e?

- To separate segments of numbers:

  (608)491-3826   (telephone numbers)

  000-00-0000   (social security numbers)

- To indicate a range of values or span of time, etc.

  $100-150   106-100 B.C.   1:00-2:30 P.M.

- To represent dialect:

  I'm a-coming . . . .

P.9 PARENTHESES

P.9

Parentheses are used for two purposes:

a. Enclosing Additional Information

Snowflake crystals generally have a sixfold symmetry, but each is unique (Figure 4).

For me, the experience meant that in a crisis (despite comfort and sympathy from others), I can feel completely alone.

Henry James (writing of old English country houses) refers to "accumulation of expressions" as the historical associations that convey meaning to the sensitive observer (*The Complete Notebooks of Henry James*, p. 224).

When the parenthetical matter is a short sentence inserted within another sentence, omit a period that ends the enclosed sentence, but include a question mark or an exclamation point:

Although the U.S. Army Corps of Engineers has always had its critics (Justice William O. Douglas labeled it "public enemy number one"), the corps faced increasing public hostility during the 1970s.

Leaving her mother and sisters behind (how painful!), she escaped to Vienna and eventually made her way to Canada.

When a parenthetical sentence stands alone (is not included in another sentence), place the end punctuation *inside* the closing parenthesis:

In recent years, the direction of most Artificial Intelligence research has been to make computers capable of dealing with real-world objects. (But many of the processes involved, though easy for a human being, turn out to be extremely difficult to simulate on a computer.)

b. Enclosing Letters or Numbers in a List

Parentheses may be used to enclose the letters or numbers of items a list:

The engine consists of four functional systems: (1) the fuel system, (2) the ignition system, (3) the lubrication system, and (4) the cooling system.

BRACKETS, PAGE 717

Note: Parentheses should not be used to enclose text that is part of a statement already enclosed in parentheses (see **brackets**).

P.10   PERIOD

The period has five main uses: to provide a stop for declarative and imperative sentences; to indicate abbreviations; to indicate initials; to serve as leaders in tables and in tables of contents; and to set off side headings.

a. Providing an End Stop for Declarative and Imperative Sentences

> She is working on a book about Truman Capote.

> Select the color you want from the charts on the next few pages.

If a declarative or imperative sentence ends with an abbreviation that ends in a period itself, a second period is not used:

> The Beaux Arts Trio will perform Friday night in the Clapham Ballroom at 8 P.M.

b. Indicating Abbreviations

> Mr. James Ryder
>
> Louise Caudill, M.D.
>
> Gen. Colin Powell
>
> etc.
>
> 8-in. drain pipe

Certain abbreviations are written without periods:

> HMO (Health Maintenance Organization)

For more information about particular abbreviations, consult a college-level dictionary.

c. Indicating Initials

> Maria C. Tomas
>
> Kenneth R. Crockmeier

d. Serving as Leaders

Leaders are a series of periods that lead the eye. They are often used in tables and tables of contents:

Table of Contents

e. Setting Off Run-in Side Headings

Headings that are followed by text on the same line are usually set off
by a period:

> *Fruit Limb Support.* Fruit trees occasionally have more fruit than they
> can hold. As a result, limbs drop under the increasing weight until
> they snap. The entire tree may split down the middle if major branches
> on opposite sides of the trunk are heavy. . . .

f. Using the Period
with Other Marks of Punctuation

❖ If a question ends with an abbreviation that requires a period,
include both the period and the question mark:

What is the meaning of *etc.?*

❖ Use a period *within* parenthetical expressions only if the expression forms a complete sentence and is not enclosed in another
sentence, as in the second example:

Gloria Anzaldua writes in *Borderlands/LaFrontera*: "I grew up in two
cultures, the Mexican (with a heavy Indian influence) and the Anglo
(as a member of a colonized people in our own territory).

Almost every three or four years, the normal pattern of ocean temper-
atures in the tropical Pacific Ocean is disrupted by a phenomenon
known as El Niño. (The event is called El Niño, which is Spanish for
"the Christ Child," because the appearance of warm ocean waters off
the western South American coast often occurs around Christmas.)
During El Niño, the surface waters become unusually warm in the
region and extend from the South American coast westward to the
International Date Line.

❖ Always put the period inside the closing quotation mark:

> In Hemingway's "The Lack of Passion," the young matador's performance in the bullring is the result not of cowardice, but of an overwhelming apathy: "I'd have killed him. Or let them take him away alive. I don't care. Let them take them all out alive."

> An athlete who performs far above his normal level is referred to as being in a "zone."

See also the entry for **ellipsis points.**   ELLIPSIS POINTS, PAGE 725

P.11   QUESTION MARK   P.11

The question mark has three main uses:

a. Using Question Marks for Direct Questions

The question mark indicates the end of a direct question:

> When will Wolfgang and Karen arrive?

> Have you ever been to Wall, South Dakota?

Do not use a question mark after an indirect question. *Why are you late?* is a direct question, and it properly ends with a question mark. But look at the following example:

> She asked why you were late.

This sentence is not a direct question. It is a statement that contains an indirect question, and it should not end with a question mark.

b. Punctuating Polite Requests

Polite requests may be punctuated with a question mark or a period:

> May I see you at one o'clock.

> May I see you at one o'clock?

c. Using Question Marks for a Series of Questions

When asking a series of questions in the same sentence, you may place a question mark at the end of the sentence or after each question, depending on how you want to emphasize the questions:

> How many people are in the car? Six or seven?

> How many people are in the car? Six? Seven?

Using Question Marks with Other Marks of Punctuation

- ❖ Place the question mark inside a closing quotation mark only when it is part of the quoted word(s). Place it outside if the entire sentence containing the quoted word(s) is a question:

  The captain asked, "Why was the ship mothballed?"

  What does it mean for a ship to be "mothballed"?

- ❖ Place the question mark inside a closing parenthesis only if it is part of the parenthetical matter:

  Hemingway was probably exaggerating the severity of his war wounds (with the new biographical data available, who can think otherwise?).

- ❖ Place the quotation mark outside the parenthesis if the entire sentence is a question:

  Did Hemingway exaggerate his war wounds (as the new biographical data available suggests)?

P.12 QUOTATION MARKS

Quotation marks are used in pairs in the three following ways:

a. Enclosing Direct Quotations

When you include another person's exact words in your writing, enclose them in quotation marks:

"Since about 1930," wrote George Orwell in 1945, "the world has given no reason for optimism whatever" (82).

By 1870 "over one-half of Idaho's miners and nearly one-third of the territory's population were Chinese" (Peterson 60).

Polyani (1969) has stated that "it is customary today to represent the process of scientific inquiry as the setting up of a hypothesis followed by its subsequent testing. I cannot accept these terms. All true scientific research starts with hitting on a deep and promising problem. . . ." (118)

An exception is the displayed direct quotation—one that is set off from the words that introduce and follow it and is indented. Because the setting off serves to signal that the words are being quoted, a displayed quotation uses no quotation marks unless there are quotation marks in the original source:

> Of course, constant vigilance by adults was impossible, and the
> romance of Mary Todd's friends Cassius Clay and Mary Jane
> Warfield was an example. Unable to meet Mary Jane privately
> in her own house because her parents and brothers always
> took up stations in the parlor, Cassius was delighted when
> "graceful" Mary Jane
>> said quietly she was going on a certain day hickory picking
>> with a few girls—In the woods Mary Jane came to me
>> when the others were farthest off, and picking up the nuts,
>> empties her handkerchief in a pile. I said "Come and help
>> me." She replied, with some tremor in her voice, "I have
>> no seat." Putting my feet closer together as they were
>> stretched out on the ground, I said, "You may sit down
>> here, if you will be mine." She hesitated a moment and
>> then down she came. . . . She just touched me with the
>> skirts of her dress, and said "I am yours." Then she hur-
>> ried off to mingle with her companions again.[64]
> But not for long, for these two married in 1832, with Elizabeth
> Todd Edwards as one of their attendants.
>
> —Jean H. Baker, *Mary Todd Lincoln: A
> Biography* (New York: Norton, 1987): p. 50.

MLA documentation style calls for setting off prose quotations more than four lines long, and poetry quotations of more than three lines. APA documentation style calls for setting off quotations of forty or more words.

Paraphrases should not be set off in quotation marks:

> In 1945 George Orwell observed that nothing had occurred during the previous fifteen years to give much reason for optimism (82).

Since these words are not Orwell's exact words, quotation marks would be misleading.

b. Enclosing Words Referred to as Words

You may use either quotation marks or italics (or underlining to indicate italics) to set off words referred to as words; underlining (italics) is preferred. Whichever format you use, use it consistently in a given piece of writing.

> "Bleed" means the printing of an image so that it extends completely across the page, leaving no margin.

> *Bleed* means the printing of an image so that it extends completely across the page, leaving no margin.

c. Enclosing Titles of Published Works

Place in quotation marks the titles of articles, essays, short stories, poems, songs, and subordinate parts of long works. (Titles of magazines, books, plays, and motion pictures should be italicized or underlined.)

> My favorite song from K. T. Oslin's *'80s Ladies* is "Do Ya."

> "Big Two-Hearted River" is the longest short story in *In Our Time*.

> A young girl's eavesdropping teaches her a lot about life in the short story "Fulfillment," which is the first story in the "Earth" section of Ferrol Sams's *The Widow's Mite and Other Stories*.

> The best writing of Oscar Wilde, outside his plays, is to be found in such essays as "The Truth of Masks," "The Critic as Artist," and "The Decay of Lying."

However, do *not* place the title of your own essay in quotation marks.

Using the Quotation Mark with Other Punctuation

> ❖ When a comma or a period and a closing quotation mark occur together, place the comma or period *inside* the quotation mark, even when it does not seem logical.

Bennett did not regard his next novel, *A Great Man*, as having a serious theme. In a letter to J. B. Pinker, he called it "purely humorous," and remarked, "Personally I don't see how anyone can read the book without laughing."

❖ Since ellipsis points indicate an omission in quoted text, place them *inside* the quotation marks.

Jung (1959) used the term *archetype* for habitual patterns and thought they were built up by collective repetition: "There are as many archetypes as there are typical situations in life. Endless repetition has engraved these experiences into our psychic constitutions. . . ."

Although Bennett complained that writing *Clayhanger* drove him "nearly . . . mad," he enjoyed the composition of *A Great Man* (Hepburn 185).

❖ When a question mark or an exclamation point is part of the quotation, place it *inside* the quotation mark.

Looking up from the flowchart, she asked, "Is that the way coal is processed?"

Judy Carne used to get big laughs by yelling, "Sock it to me!"

❖ When a question mark or an exclamation point is part of the entire sentence, place it *outside* the quotation mark.

"Deadline" is such an awful term. Why not use "delivery date"?

Did you see that sign? It read "Falling Rock Zone"!

❖ Place a semicolon or colon *outside* the quotation marks.

The professor keeps referring to "atavism"; I'm not sure what it means.

Professor Tung provides this definition of "atavism": "It is the reappearance of characteristics of more or less remote ancestors." He also calls it "reversion" and "a throw-back characteristic."

P.13 SEMICOLON

P.13

The semicolon has two main uses: to separate independent clauses in a compound sentence; and to separate items in a series when some of the items already have commas.

a. Separating Independent Clauses in a Compound Sentence

❖ Use a semicolon between independent clauses of a compound sentence when they are not connected by a coordinating conjunction (*and, but, for, or, nor, so, yet*).

We might as well decide now; we will have to soon.

Of course, this sentence can be punctuated two other ways as well.

We might as well decide now. We will have to soon.

We might as well decide now, for we will have to soon.

The period creates a more pronounced break between the two statements, by dividing them into two separate sentences. The comma and conjunction *for* create a much closer tie. The semicolon creates a close tie somewhere between the period and the comma and conjunction.

❖ Use a semicolon between independent clauses when they are joined by conjunctive adverbs (*however, therefore, moreover, consequently, nevertheless*).

good: A company's image gets a definite boost when it advertises in what the average reader considers to be a national, prestigious magazine; little does the reader know that the company has only purchased a limited geographical circulation of the magazine.

good: A company's image gets a definite boost when it advertises in what the average reader considers to be a national, prestigious magazine; however, little does the reader know that the company has only purchased a limited geographical circulation of the magazine.

poor: A company's image gets a definite boost when it advertises in what the average reader considers to be a national, prestigious magazine, however, little does the reader know that the company has only purchased a limited geographical circulation of the magazine.

The lack of a semicolon before *however* in the last example causes confusion because the readers cannot tell for sure to which clause the *however* belongs.

b. Separating Items in a Series When Some of the Items Already Have Commas

An uncomplicated series of items needs nothing more than commas: *The steering committee consists of Debra Johnston, Yoshiaki Shinoda, and Ben Alexander.* But if the statement is *The steering committee consists of Debra Johnson, the senior engineer, Yoshiaki Shinoda, the contract accountant, and Ben Alexander, the security supervisor,* it needs semicolons to separate the items. Otherwise, the series could be understood to list up to five or six people, three of whom are named.

> The steering committee consists of Debra Johnston, the senior engineer; Yoshiaki Shinoda, the contract accountant; and Ben Alexander, the security supervisor.

Another example:

> Three kinds of engines are produced in the plant: military jet engines, in the government products division; nonmilitary jet engines, in the commercial products division; and nonmilitary gasoline engines, in the special products division.

Using the Semicolon with Other Punctuation

Place the semicolon *outside* quotation marks and parentheses.

> Those who contend that the extinction of dinosaurs occurred over a period of thousands of years are called "gradualists"; those who believe that a sudden event was responsible are called "catastrophists."

> If the climate of North America warms, a great change will occur in the boreal forests in the upper Midwest (which consists primarily of fir, pine, and spruce); they will retreat slowly into Canada and gradually be replaced by northern hardwood forests (consisting primarily of beech, maple, and yellow birch).

P.14   SLASH

P.14

The slash, sometimes called a slant sign, a diagonal, a solidus, or a virgule, is used to separate elements. With the exception of its use with poetry, there is no space between it and the text on either side of it.

Here are three main uses of the slash:

a. Separating the Numerator from the Denominator in Mathematical Equations and in Fractions

$$PV/T = P_1V_1/T_1$$

1/2, 3/5, 33 1/3

b. Separating Elements in an Address

The address is Major Elizabeth Chai/APO 8425/New York, NY 10009.

c. Separating Lines in Short Passages of Quoted Poetry

Use this format only to quote directly a short passage of poetry that is run into your own sentence. When quoting longer excerpts, separate the poetry completely from your own sentences, and present the lines as the poet expressed them.

Labor unrest in Ireland and England was a theme in some Victorian poetry. For example, Sybil Baker's "Belfast is a famous Northern town / Ships and linen its occupation / And the workers have a riot on / The slightest provocation" is only one of many references to labor strikes in Belfast, Londonderry, Birmingham, Manchester, Liverpool, and London.

M. MECHANICS

M.1 ABBREVIATIONS

Abbreviations are shortened forms of words or a group of words. They are used primarily to save space (*mpg* as opposed to *miles per gallon*; *MASH* instead of *Mobil Army Surgical Hospital*), although some abbreviations are also used because they are more familiar and pronounceable than the spelled-out words (*DNA* instead of *deoxyribonucleic acid*; *TNT* instead of *trinitrotoluene*).

Abbreviations are usually formed two ways: using the first letter or first few letters of a word (*m=meter*, *IBM=International Business Machines*, *Wed.=Wednesday*) or dropping the middle of the word and using only the first and last letters (*Dr.=Doctor*, *Mr.=Mister*, *St.=Saint*).

Some abbreviations are followed by a period; others are not. It is a more conservative practice to use a period after an abbreviation, although sometimes a period is necessary to clarify that an abbreviation is not another word, as in *in.* for *inch* or *inches*. Consult a college-level dictionary or style guide on whether a period is appropriate.

Here are guidelines to help you use abbreviations effectively:

▶ Do not begin a sentence with an abbreviation.

▶ Use abbreviations sparingly in your text, although abbreviations may be used with discretion in lists, tables, and charts where space may be limited. Abbreviations should be used primarily to enhance the readability of the text for the writer and readers.

▶ Use standard abbreviations that are sanctioned by professional organizations or college-level dictionaries. Usually a list of standard abbreviations is included in style manuals.

▶ Do not capitalize abbreviations unless the word abbreviated is a proper noun:

Btu	British thermal unit
F	Fahrenheit
CST	Central Standard Time

▶ If you are uncertain that your reader will understand the abbreviation, spell out the full expression the first time you use it, and follow with the abbreviation in parentheses, or vice versa. The abbreviation may be used alone in subsequent references:

> During the 1960s huge corporations bought smaller companies, leading to the need to develop large centralized computer systems known as Management Information Systems (MIS) networks. However, few of these conglomerates made significant gains in centralization using MIS.

> The standard reference source for finding out the history of meanings for a word is the *Oxford English Dictionary*. In addition to the typical information about a word's pronunciation, etymology, and current meanings, the *OED* provides a history of the changing meaning of the word throughout the period in which it has been used, with examples of these uses.

▶ Be consistent. Once you abbreviate, use the same abbreviation throughout the text.

▶ Use the same abbreviation for both singular and plural: *in.* for *inch* or *inches*, *ft.* for *foot* or *feet*. However, an exception is *lb.* for *pound* and *lbs.* for *pounds*. Use customary abbreviations.

❖ Titles before names

Dr. Peggy Porter

Mr. Pierre Donique

Sgt. Sharon Little

❖ Designations after names

Hadley K. Franklin, Jr.

Sen. Robert Dole (R-Kansas)

Sir William Sloyd, M.P.

❖ Academic degrees

A.A., A.B., M.S., M.D., Ph.D., Ed.D., LL.D.

❖ Common units of measure

mph, rpm, C, cm, sq. ft.

❖ Long Names of Organizations and Countries

NAACP
National Association for the Advancement of Colored People (Either
NAACP or N.A.A.C.P. is acceptable.)

NCAA
National Collegiate Athletic Association

USDA
United States Department of Agriculture

USA
United States of America

❖ Abbreviations in bibliographic notations

ch.	chapter
sec.	section
n.d.	not dated

❖ Common Latin terms used instead of their English equivalents:

etc. (and so forth)

e.g. (for example)

i.e. (that is)

❖ U.S. Postal Service two-letter abbreviations for states and outlying
regions

Alabama	AL	Georgia	GA
Alaska	AK	Guam	GU
Arizona	AZ	Hawaii	HI
Arkansas	AR	Idaho	ID
California	CA	Illinois	IL
Colorado	CO	Indiana	IN
Connecticut	CT	Iowa	IA
Delaware	DE	Kansas	KS
District of Columbia	DC	Kentucky	KY
Florida	FL	Louisiana	LA

Maine	ME	Oklahoma	OK
Maryland	MD	Oregon	OR
Massachusetts	MA	Pennsylvania	PA
Michigan	MI	Puerto Rico	PR
Minnesota	MN	Rhode Island	RI
Mississippi	MS	South Carolina	SC
Missouri	MO	South Dakota	SD
Montana	MT	Tennessee	TN
Nebraska	NE	Texas	TX
Nevada	NV	Utah	UT
New Hampshire	NH	Vermont	VT
New Jersey	NJ	Virginia	VA
New Mexico	NM	Virgin Islands	VI
New York	NY	Washington	WA
North Carolina	NC	West Virginia	WV
North Dakota	ND	Wisconsin	WI
Ohio	OH	Wyoming	WY

M.2   CAPITAL LETTERS

All letters were once written only as capitals. By the fourteenth century, both capital letters (uppercase letters) and lowercase letters were used. Printers used capital letters only for the first letters of words that they felt were particularly important. That practice is still in use today, although the tendency is toward capitalizing fewer and fewer words. For instance, one of the most widely recognized style manuals, *The Chicago Manual of Style*, 14th edition (1994), is less prescriptive than in its previous editions on the issue of capitalization. It identifies an "*up* style" (a tendency to use uppercase, i.e., capital letters) and a "*down* style" (a tendency to use lowercase). The choice is yours, but be consistent.

In general, the following rules govern the use of capitals:

▶ Capitalize the first word of a sentence and of a quotation that is formally introduced.

A long rainy season in the fall makes deciduous trees look drab.

What does this mean?

My mother asked the stranger: "Are you looking for work?"

▶ Capitalize proper nouns.

Julian Bond, a civil rights activist and politician, was born January 14, 1940, in Nashville, Tennessee.

Julian Bond, January, and *Nashville, Tennessee* are proper nouns, because they are particular names of an individual person and a specific month, city, and state. The words *civil rights activist* and *politician* are common nouns, because they are words that refer to general classes consisting of hundreds, perhaps thousands, of people.

Proper nouns and their derivatives include the following:

❖ Names of people

William Shakespeare, Shakespearean sonnet

Charles Darwin, Darwinism

Woodrow Wilson, Wilsonian diplomacy

William Fulbright, Fulbright scholar

Practice is divided on capitalizing words derived from proper nouns. Many style manuals sanction *homeric* instead of *Homeric, arabic* numerals instead of *Arabic* numerals (from *Arab*). You must decide which to follow, the "up" style or the "down" style, and be consistent.

❖ Days of the week, months of the year, holidays, holy days, and days and weeks of special significance

Monday	Mother's Day
April	Yom Kippur
Ramadan	National Dairy Month
Thanksgiving Day	

Do not capitalize the names of the seasons: *winter, spring, summer,* and *fall* or *autumn.*

❖ Names of geographic and popular places and names of buildings and structures

Columbia River	St. Louis County
Rocky Mountains	Greece
the Everglades	the Bay Area (San Francisco)
the Orient	Walden Pond
Pacific Ocean	the Eiffel Tower
North Pole	the Golden Gate Bridge
the Alfred P. Murrah Federal Building	

Do not capitalize points of the compass—north, south, east, west—unless they designate a specific geographic region:

(*uppercase*) The railroads played a crucial role in opening the American West.

(*lowercase*) Weatherly is a little over an hour's drive west of Oklahoma City.

(*uppercase*) The Northwest Passage was first navigated in 1903–1905.

(*lowercase*) Macomb is northwest of Springfield.

❖ Historical events, eras, and documents

the War of the Roses	the Holocaust
the Renaissance	the Johnstown Flood
the Chia-Ching Period	the Declaration of Independence
the Great Depression	the Versailles Treaty

❖ Political parties and religious sects

Republicans	Judaism
Whigs	Muslim
Southern Baptist	Branch Davidians
Catholic	Quakers

❖ Organizations, institutions, and complexes

Better Business Bureau	Rock Bridge High School
Pemex Corporation	St. Clair Medical Center

First Christian Church   the Mid-South Coliseum

University of South Dakota   the Internet

❖ Government bodies and organizations

Fifty-third Congress

President's Council of Economic Advisors

U.S. Government Printing Office

Department of Justice

the Supreme Court

California National Guard

Maricopa County Sheriff's Office

House of Lords

the Diet

❖ Titles, degrees, decorations, and honors

Vice President Gore

Governor Wilson

General Shalikashvili

Rabbi Keyfetz

Betty Boothroyd, Speaker of the British Commons

Queen Elizabeth

Ambassador Lumb

Elroy Crenshaw, recipient of the Congressional Medal of Honor and
the Order of the Purple Heart

Deborah Hunter-Shemwell, Ph.D.

Nobel Peace Prize

Pulitzer Prize

❖ Kinship names

Aunt Sarah

Are you going to visit Mother?

I know that Grandfather Perkins's middle name is Leonard.

However, it is customary to lowercase kinship names when they are preceded by modifiers:

Sarah is my aunt.

My mother expects you for lunch.

Her grandfather's middle name is John.

❖ Trade names

Coca-Cola	Polaroid
Kleenex	Pyrex
Sanka	

❖ Languages and ethnic groups

Chicano	Indian
Russian	Korean-American
Yiddish	

❖ Sporting events

the Final Four	the Kentucky Derby
the World Series	the Olympic Games
the Rose Bowl Parade	the Super Bowl
the World Cup	

▶ **Capitalize letters used to describe objects by their shapes.**

A-frame	T-square
C-clamp	U-turn
O-ring	

▶ **Capitalize the first word in a line of conventional poetry.**

On either side the river lie
Long fields of barley and of rye,
That clothe the wold and meet the sky;
And thro' the field the road runs by
    To many towered Camelot;

—Alfred, Lord Tennyson, "Lady of Shallot"

▶ According to many documentation forms, capitalize the first words and the other important words in the title of a book, article, poem, picture, song, or other work of art.

Garcia Marquez's *Love in the Time of Cholera*

Katherine Mansfield's short story "The Fly"

Anne Sexton's poem "Her Kind"

Hieronymus Bosch's *The Garden of Delights*

Gershwin's *Rhapsody in Blue*

Articles, conjunctions, and prepositions are not capitalized unless they are the first word in the title.

M.3   ITALICS

Roman type is the standard typeface used today, probably because it is the most readable. These words, like most of the words in this book, are set in Roman type. Italics is another of the principal classifications of typeface, but it is used very sparingly for emphasis. It slants to the right and looks like this: *Atlantic Monthly*. When you type or handwrite, you indicate italics by underlining, like this: <u>Atlantic Monthly</u>.

Italics are used in five principal ways:

a. Indicating Titles

James Gleick's *Chaos: Making a New Science* was published in 1987.

The Wall Street Journal is the nation's leading financial newspaper.

The 1855 edition of Walt Whitman's *Leaves of Grass* sold only a few hundred copies.

The editors of *Time* magazine received considerable criticism for using a retouched photograph of O. J. Simpson on its cover.

b. Indicating Foreign Words and Phrases

Cogito, ergo sum is attributed to René Descartes, but several philosophers had used the phrase before Descartes was born.

The Spanish name for Texas is *Tejas*.

1819 was an *annus mirablis*, being the birthyear of James Russell Lowell, Herman Melville, and Walt Whitman.

Do not italicize foreign words and expressions that have become so common in English that they are considered part of the language: milieu, samurai, alma mater, bombardier, and so on.

c. Indicating Names of Ships, Aircraft, and Spacecraft

The sinking of the Cunard liner the *Lusitania* on May 7, 1915, off the coast of Ireland was a contributing factor to the United States entry into World War I.

The atomic bomb was dropped from a B-29 named *Enola Gay*, named after the pilot's mother.

The *Voyager* satellite gave us our first good look at the Great Red Spot on Jupiter.

d. Designating Words, Letters, and Numbers as Words

The overuse of *very* and *great* lessen their impact as intensifiers.

Writers who misspell *similar* usually add a third *i*, ending the word with *-iar* (similiar), apparently modeling the spelling on the word *familiar*.

Bookkeeping is one of the few words in English that have three double letters in a row: *oo-kk-ee*.

My basketball jersey was *14*, which was also more points than I ever scored in a game.

Europeans use *7* to distinguish *7* clearly from *1*.

e. Placing Extra Emphasis on a Word or Phrase

Studies show that almost 50 percent of *fatal* automobile accidents involve a driver who was driving under the influence of alcohol or drugs or both.

George Orwell claims that it is the *privateness* of the British that causes their addiction to hobbies.

Applicants are required to have their packets postmarked *no later than April 15*.

M.4 NUMBERS

Numbers can be expressed as words (*seventeen*) or figures (*17*). The following general and specific guidelines will help you decide which form to use.

General Guidelines

❖ Use Arabic numerals (*5*) instead of Roman numerals (*V*), except when you want to use Roman numerals in section or chapter headings and in numbering tables.

❖ Do not state numbers twice, once in words and again as a figure. The restatement adds nothing to accuracy or clarity.

not: The ledger contained entries on thirty (30) transactions.

but: The ledger contained entries on 30 transactions.

Specific Guidelines

Many style and usage books suggest spelling out numbers under ten and using figures for everything else except numbers that are more than two or three words long.

not: Sixteen hundred and fifty-two

but: 1652 or 1,652

However, there are so many exceptions to this rule that it is not always reliable. Here are some guidelines you can depend on when deciding whether to express a number as a word or a figure.

▶ Numbers in Figure Form. Writing a number as a figure is almost always done in the following instances.

Addresses: 1603 Vandiver Drive, Apartment 812, St. Paul, MN 55111

Dates: December 21, 1996 or 21 December 1996
(But not *December 21 1996*)

Decimals: 5.2 liter engine

0.025 grams

16.5 kilometers

Exact sums of money with *$* or *¢*:	$4.88 47¢
Identifying numbers:	Station No. 7
	Engine Number HD-27598-32-G
	Account #394
Percentages:	30 percent 4.5%
References to pages, figures, etc.:	page 6
	Figure 2-10
	Note 25
Time:	4:55 A.M. (But also *12 noon*; otherwise, *eight o'clock*)
Units of measure:	180 miles 66 kilometers
	500 cc 200 lbs.

▶ Numbers in word form. The general trend is to use figures more often than words. Most style and usage manuals state that numbers smaller than ten should be spelled out and that those ten and above should be represented as figures: *six whales, 30 whales; nine entries, 100 entries*. However, there are at least four important exceptions to this rule:

❖ When a series of numbers contains a number greater than 10, each number is expressed as a figure:

The class enrolled 3 sophomores, 14 juniors, 1 senior, and 1 graduate student.

❖ Large numbers that are rounded off are usually formed by a figure and a word:

The estate is expected to exceed $65 million.

The estate is expected to exceed 65 million dollars.
    (But usually not *The estate is expected to exceed sixty-five million dollars*, *The estate is expected to exceed 65,000,000 dollars*, or *The estate is expected to exceed $65,000,000*.)

❖ Normally, spell out numbers at the beginning of a sentence, or rewrite so that the number appears later in the sentence.

not: 10,000 bags of peanuts were shipped by mistake.

but: Ten thousand bags of peanuts were shipped by mistake.

or: They shipped 10,000 bags of peanuts by mistake.

❖ Small fractions are usually spelled out:

A third of the workers were transferred.

Two-thirds of the workers remained at the old facility.

❖ When there are adjoining numbers, spell out one of them:

ten 5-minute laps

10 five-minute laps

8 twelve-volt batteries

eight 12-volt batteries

M.5 SYMBOLS

A symbol is a letter (or letters) or other mark that stands for a word or words. When you read *Fe*, the chemical symbol for iron, or Ω, the Greek letter symbol for *ohm* or *omega* (ending), the symbol is pronounced as if it were a spelled-out word. A chemical formula, such as $2Na + Cl^2 \rightarrow 2NaCl$ (which is the formula for common table salt), is read something like this: "When two atoms of sodium are reacted with one molecule of chlorine, two molecules of sodium chloride are formed."

Symbols are used widely in tables and technical material to save space. They are used less often in regular text. Symbols are one of the most abstract forms of language, and most readers are familiar with only a few standard symbols. Be sure that your reader will understand the meaning of a symbol you use, or explain it in parentheses or an explanatory note the first time it appears (as you would explain an unfamiliar abbreviation).

The first letter of a chemical symbol is always capitalized (*H, hydrogen; O, oxygen; H_2O, water*). When the symbol for a chemical consists of two letters, the second is always lowercase, *Au, gold*).

CREDITS

INDEX

761